Contents

Cambridge Essential English Dictionary

Managing Editor
Kate Woodford

Senior Commissioning Editor
Elizabeth Walter

Senior Systems Developer
Dominic Glennon

Corpus Development
Ann Fiddes
Diane Nicholls

Typesetting
Morton Word Processing Ltd., Scarborough

Design and Production
Samantha Dumiak
Clive Rumble
Sue Tuck

Illustrators
Corinne Burrows
Ray Burrows
David Shenton

How to use this dictionary

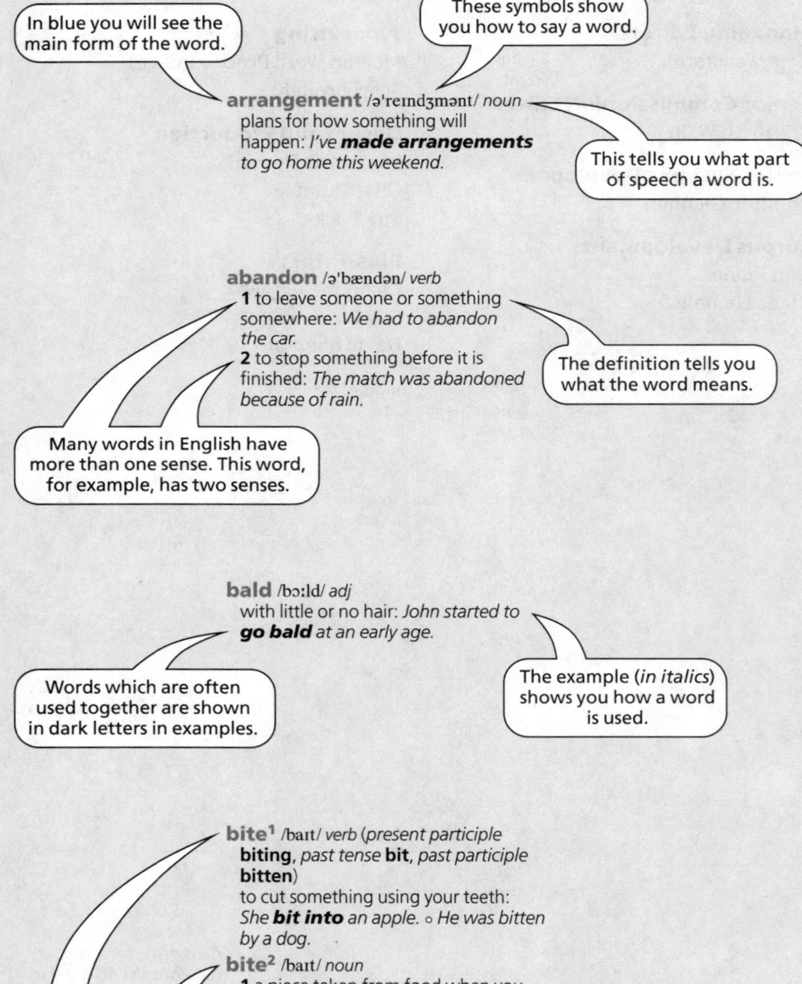

bite[1] /baɪt/ *verb* (*present participle* **biting**, *past tense* **bit**, *past participle* **bitten**)
to cut something using your teeth: *She **bit into** an apple.* ○ *He was bitten by a dog.*

bite[2] /baɪt/ *noun*
1 a piece taken from food when you bite it: *She **took a bite** from her pizza.*
2 an injury cause when an animal or insect bites you: *mosquito bites*

bite[1] and **bite**[2] have the same spelling but are separate because **bite**[1] is a verb and **bite**[2] is a noun.

Bromley

BROMLEY LIBRARIES
3 0128 6000 67428

CAMBRIDGE UNIVERSITY PRESS
Cambridge, New York, Melbourne, Madrid, Cape Town, Singapore, São Paulo

Cambridge University Press
The Edinburgh Building, Cambridge CB2 2RU, UK

www.cambridge.org
Information on this title: www.cambridge.org/9780521005371

First published 2004
4th printing 2006

Printed in Italy by Legoprint S.p.A.

A catalogue record for this publication is available from the British Library

ISBN-13 978-0-521-00537-1 paperback
ISBN-10 0-521-00537-X paperback

ISBN-13 978-0-521-69901-3 Skills for life edition
ISBN-10 0-521-69901-0 Skills for life edition

This shows you that sense 3 of *centre* is a phrase (= a group of words which are often used together).

centre[1] *UK (US* **center***)* /ˈsentə^{r}/ *noun*
1 the middle point or part of something: *Cars are not allowed in the town centre.*
2 a building used for a particular activity: *a health centre*
3 to be the centre of attention to get more attention than anyone else

Past tenses which are not regular are shown.

burn[1] /bɜːn/ *verb* (*present participle* **burning**, *past* **burnt**)
1 to destroy something with fire, or to be destroyed by fire: *I burnt all his letters.* ○ *The factory burned to the ground.*

Comparatives and superlatives which are not regular are shown.

baggy /ˈbægi/ *adj* (**baggier**, **baggiest**) baggy clothes are big and loose

brass /brɑːs/ *noun* [**no plural**] a shiny yellow metal: *a door with a brass handle*

[**no plural**] shows you that you cannot add 's' to this noun to make a plural.

child /tʃaɪld/ *noun* (*plural* **children**)
1 a young person who is not yet an adult
2 a son or daughter, also when they are adults

Plurals which are not regular are shown.

Opposites are shown at the end of an entry.

certain /ˈsɜːt^{ə}n/ *adj*
1 definite: *I feel certain that you're doing the right thing.* ○ *It now looks certain that she will resign.* ➲ Opposite **uncertain**

chemist's /ˈkemɪsts/ *UK (US* **drugstore***) noun* a shop where you can buy drugs, soap, beauty products, etc

UK only used in British English
US only used in American English
This entry shows you that *chemist's* is used in British English and *drugstore* is used in American English.

slob /slɒb/ *noun informal* a lazy or dirty person

informal tells you that this word is not usually used in serious writing.

Aa

A, a /eɪ/
the first letter of the alphabet

a (*also* **an**) *strong form* /eɪ/ *weak form* /ə/ *determiner*
1 used before a noun to mean one thing or person: *I need a car.*
2 every or each: *Take one tablet three times a day.*

abandon /ə'bændən/ *verb*
1 to leave someone or something somewhere: *We had to abandon the car.*
2 to stop something before it is finished: *The match was abandoned because of rain.*

abbreviate /ə'briːvieɪt/ *verb* (*present participle* **abbreviating,** *past* **abbreviated)**
to make a word or phrase shorter: *The word 'street' is often* ***abbreviated to*** *'St'.*

abbreviation /əˌbriːvi'eɪʃ^{ə}n/ *noun*
a shorter form of a word or phrase, especially used in writing

abdomen /'æbdəmən/ *noun formal*
the front, lower part of your body that has your stomach and other parts in it

ability /ə'bɪləti/ *noun* (*plural* **abilities)**
the skill or qualities that you need to do something: *He had the* ***ability to*** *explain things clearly.*

able /'eɪbl/ *adj*
If you are able to do something, you can do it: *He'll* ***be able to*** *help you.*
➲Opposite **unable**

abnormal /æb'nɔːm^{ə}l/ *adj*
not normal: *abnormal behaviour*

aboard /ə'bɔːd/ *adv, preposition*
on or onto an aeroplane, ship, bus, or train: *Welcome aboard flight BA109 to Paris.*

abolish /ə'bɒlɪʃ/ *verb*
to end a law or system: *National Service was abolished in Britain in 1962.*

abolition /ˌæbə'lɪʃ^{ə}n/ *noun* **[no plural]**
when a law or system is ended: *the abolition of slavery*

about[1] /ə'baʊt/ *preposition*
1 relating to a particular subject: *What was she talking about?*
2 *UK* to different parts of a place: *We heard someone moving about outside.*
3 what/how about ...?
used to suggest something: *How about some food?*

about[2] /ə'baʊt/ *adv*
1 close to a particular number or time, although not exactly that number or time: *It happened about two months ago.*
2 *UK* to or in different parts of a place: *She just leaves her clothes lying about.*
3 about to do something going to do something very soon: *I'm about to leave.*

above /ə'bʌv/ *adv, preposition*
1 in a higher position than something else: *It's on the shelf above your head.*
2 more than an amount or level: *The toys are for children aged four and above.*
3 above all most important of everything: *Above all, I'd like to thank my family.*

abroad /ə'brɔːd/ *adv*
in or to a different country: *Are you* ***going abroad*** *this summer?*

abrupt /ə'brʌpt/ *adj*
sudden: *The conversation came to an abrupt end.*

absence /'æbs^{ə}ns/ *noun*
1 a time when you are not in a place: *His absence was noticed.*
2 [no plural] when something does not exist: *the absence of proof*
➲Opposite **presence**

absent /'æbs^{ə}nt/ *adj*
not in a place, especially school or work: *He has been* ***absent from*** *school all week.*

absent-minded /ˌæbs^{ə}nt'maɪndɪd/ *adj*
often forgetting things

absolute /'æbsəluːt/ *adj*
complete: *The trip to Paris was an* ***absolute disaster****.*

absolutely /ˌæbsə'luːtli/ *adv*
1 completely: *The food was absolutely delicious.*
2 used to strongly agree with someone: *"Do you agree?" "Absolutely."*

absorb /əb'zɔːb/ *verb*
1 to take a liquid in through a

a b c d e f g h i j k l m n o p q r s t u v w x y z

a b c d e f g h i j k l m n o p q r s t u v w x y z

surface: *The fabric absorbs all the moisture.*
2 to understand and remember something: *It's hard to absorb so much information.*

absorbent /əb'zɔːbənt/ *adj*
able to take in liquids: *an absorbent fabric*

absorbing /əb'zɔːbɪŋ/ *adj*
very interesting: *an absorbing book*

abuse[1] /ə'bjuːs/ *noun*
1 when something is used for the wrong purpose in a way that is bad: *alcohol abuse*
2 **[no plural]** when someone is violent or cruel to another person: *child abuse*
3 **[no plural]** rude words said to someone: *The crowds were shouting abuse at him.*

abuse[2] /ə'bjuːz/ *verb* (*present participle* **abusing**, *past* **abused**)
1 to be cruel and violent with someone
2 to use something for the wrong purpose in a way that is bad: *He abused alcohol all his life.*
3 to say rude words to someone: *The crowd started abusing him.*

abusive /ə'bjuːsɪv/ *adj*
saying rude words to someone: *an abusive phone call*

academic /ˌækə'demɪk/ *adj*
related to education, schools, universities, etc: *academic standards*

accent /'æksᵊnt/ *noun*
the way in which someone speaks, showing where they come from: *an American accent* ○ *a French accent*

accept /ək'sept/ *verb*
1 to take something that someone offers you: *He accepted the job.* ○ *He won't accept advice from anyone.*
2 to say that something is true, often something bad: *He refuses to* ***accept that*** *he's made a mistake.*

acceptable /ək'septəbl/ *adj*
good enough: *Is her work of an acceptable standard?*

acceptance /ək'septəns/ *noun* **[no plural]**
when you take something that someone offers you: *her acceptance of the job*

access[1] /'ækses/ *noun* **[no plural]**
1 when you can use or see something: *Do you have* ***access to*** *a computer?* ○ *Internet access*
2 the way in which you go into a place: *The only* ***access to*** *the village is by boat.*

access[2] /'ækses/ *verb*
to find information, especially using a computer: *You can access the files over the Internet.*

accident /'æksɪdᵊnt/ *noun*
1 something bad which happens by chance, and hurts someone or damages something: *a car accident* ○ *She* ***had an accident*** *in the kitchen.*
2 **by accident** without wanting to: *I deleted the wrong file by accident.*

accidental /ˌæksɪ'dentᵊl/ *adj*
by chance: *accidental damage*

accidentally /ˌæksɪ'dentlɪ/ *adv*
If you do something bad accidentally, you do it without wanting to: *I accidentally knocked over a bottle of water.*

accommodation /əˌkɒmə'deɪʃᵊn/ *noun* **[no plural]**
a place where you live or stay: *rented accommodation*

accompany /ə'kʌmpəni/ *verb* (*present participle* **accompanying**, *past* **accompanied**)
1 (*formal*) to go to a place with someone: *All children must be accompanied by an adult.*
2 to happen or exist at the same time as something else: *The teachers' book is accompanied by a video cassette.*
3 to play a musical instrument with someone else who is playing or singing

accord /ə'kɔːd/ *noun* **[no plural]**
of your own accord because you decide to, and not because someone tells you to: *She left of her own accord.*

according to /ə'kɔːdɪŋtuː/ *preposition*
as said by someone or as shown by something: *According to Susie, he was alone.*

account[1] /ə'kaʊnt/ *noun*
1 a description of something that happened: *They* ***gave*** *different* ***accounts*** *of the event.*
2 an arrangement with a bank to keep your money there: *I paid the money into my account.*

3 take something into account to think about something when judging a situation: *They took his age into account when judging his performance.*
4 by all accounts as said by a lot of people: *The party was, by all accounts, a great success.*
5 on no account *UK* not for any reason: *On no account must these records be changed.*

account[2] /ə'kaʊnt/ *phrasal verb*
account for something
to explain something: *Could she account for the missing money?*

accountant /ə'kaʊntənt/ *noun*
someone whose job is keeping records of all the money that people or companies spend and get

accounts /ə'kaʊnts/ *plural noun*
an official record of all the money a company spends and gets

accurate /'ækjərət/ *adj*
correct or exact: *accurate information*
➲Opposite **inaccurate**

accusation /ˌækjʊ'zeɪʃ^{ə}n/ *noun*
when you say that someone has done something bad: *She **made** a number of **accusations** against him.*

accuse /ə'kjuːz/ *verb* (*present participle* **accusing**, *past* **accused**)
to say that someone has done something bad: *She **accused** him **of** stealing from her.*

accustomed /ə'kʌstəmd/ *adj*
be accustomed to something to have done or had something so often that it is normal for you: *She wasn't accustomed to all the attention.*

ache[1] /eɪk/ *noun*
pain which continues for a long time: *I've got stomach ache.*

ache[2] /eɪk/ *verb* (*present participle* **aching**, *past* **ached**)
to hurt continuously: *My legs are aching after all that exercise.*

achieve /ə'tʃiːv/ *verb* (*present participle* **achieving**, *past* **achieved**)
to succeed in doing something difficult: *If I finish this essay I'll feel I've achieved something.*

achievement /ə'tʃiːvmənt/ *noun*
something good that you have done that was difficult: *This film is his greatest achievement to date.*

acid /'æsɪd/ *noun*
a liquid which burns or dissolves things: *hydrochloric acid*

acknowledge /ək'nɒlɪdʒ/ *verb* (*present participle* **acknowledging**, *past* **acknowledged**)
1 to accept that something is true or exists: *He **acknowledged that** there was a problem.*
2 to tell someone in a letter that you have got what they sent you: *Did they acknowledge your letter?*

acne /'ækni/ *noun* **[no plural]**
a skin problem that causes a lot of red spots on the face

acorn /'eɪkɔːn/ *noun*
a nut which grows on oak trees

acorn

acquaintance /ə'kweɪnt^{ə}ns/ *noun*
someone who you know slightly: *a business acquaintance*

acquire /ə'kwaɪə^{r}/ *verb* (*present participle* **acquiring**, *past* **acquired**)
to get something: *I've acquired a few skills in this job.*

acre /'eɪkə^{r}/ *noun*
a unit for measuring area, equal to 4,047 square metres

acrobat /'ækrəbæt/ *noun*
someone who entertains people by doing difficult things with their body, such as walking on a wire high above the ground

acrobat

across /ə'krɒs/ *adv, preposition*
1 from one side to the other: *I was walking across the road.*
2 on the opposite side of: *There's a library just across the street.*

act[1] /ækt/ *verb*
1 to behave in a particular way, usually a bad way: *Stop **acting like** a child!*
2 to do something to stop a problem: *We have to act now to stop the spread of this disease.*
3 to perform in a play or film
act as something *phrasal verb*
to do a job for a short time: *He acted as an adviser on the project.*

act[2] /ækt/ *noun*
1 something that someone does: *an*

a b c d e f g h i j k l m n o p q r s t u v w x y z

act of kindness
2 a law made by a government: *an act of Parliament*
3 one of the parts in a play
4 when someone pretends to be or feel something: *She's not really upset – it's just an act.*

acting /'æktɪŋ/ *noun* **[no plural]**
the job of performing in plays and films

action /'ækʃᵊn/ *noun*
1 something that you do: *We must* ***take action*** *before the problem gets worse.*
2 **[no plural]** exciting or important things which are happening: *He likes films with a lot of action.*
3 **out of action** damaged or hurt and not able to operate or move: *My car's out of action.*

active /'æktɪv/ *adj*
1 busy doing a lot of things: *Even at 87 she's still very active.*
2 In an active verb or sentence, the subject of the verb is the person or thing doing the action. For example, 'Andy drove the car.' is an active sentence.

activity /æk'tɪvəti/ *noun*
1 (*plural* **activities**) something that you do for enjoyment: *Activities on offer include cycling, swimming, and tennis.*
2 **[no plural]** when a lot of people are moving around: *There was a lot of activity at the back of the hall.*

actor /'æktəʳ/ *noun*
someone, especially a man, who performs in plays and films

actress /'æktrəs/ *noun* (*plural* **actresses**)
a woman who performs in plays and films

actual /'æktʃuəl/ *adj*
real, not guessed or imagined: *We were expecting about fifty people, though the actual number was a lot higher.*

actually /'æktʃuəli/ *adv*
1 used when you are saying what is true in a situation: *He didn't actually say anything important.* ○ *So what actually happened?*
2 *UK* used when you are disagreeing with someone or saying no to them: *"You never told me." "Actually, I did."* ○ *"Do you mind if I smoke?" "Actually, I'd rather you didn't."*

acute /ə'kjuːt/ *adj*
An acute problem is very bad: *There's an acute shortage of medical staff.*

AD /ˌeɪ'diː/
used to show that a particular year came after the birth of Christ: *1066 AD*

ad /æd/ *noun*
an advertisement

adapt /ə'dæpt/ *verb*
1 to change for a new situation: *It takes time to* ***adapt to*** *a new country.*
2 to change something for a different use: *Courses are* ***adapted for*** *different markets.*

adaptable /ə'dæptəbl/ *adj*
able to change for a different situation or use: *Children are more adaptable than you think.*

add /æd/ *verb*
1 to put something with something else: ***Add*** *the eggs* ***to*** *the cream.*
2 to say another thing: *She said she liked him but* ***added that*** *he was difficult to work with.*
3 to put two or more numbers together to get a total: *Have you added the figures together?*
add (something) up *phrasal verb*
to put two or more numbers together to get a total: *Could you add up those figures?*

adder /'ædəʳ/ *noun*
a small, poisonous snake

addict /'ædɪkt/ *noun*
someone who cannot stop taking a drug: *a drug addict*

addicted /ə'dɪktɪd/ *adj*
not able to stop taking a drug

addition /ə'dɪʃᵊn/ *noun*
1 **in addition (to something)** added to what already exists: *In addition to teaching, she works as a nurse in the holidays.*
2 **[no plural]** adding numbers together in order to get a total
3 a new or extra thing which is added to something: *Baby Eva is the latest* ***addition to*** *the family.*

address[1] /ə'dres/ *noun* (*plural* **addresses**)
1 the number of a building and the name of the street, city, etc where it is
2 a group of letters and signs used

to send email to someone or to find information on the Internet: *an email/web address*

address[2] /ə'dres/ *verb*
1 to write a name or address on an envelope or parcel: *A parcel arrived* ***addressed to*** *Emma.*
2 to do something in order to stop a problem: *We have to address the problem now.*

adequate /'ædɪkwət/ *adj*
enough: *I didn't have adequate time to prepare.*

adjective /'ædʒɪktɪv/ *noun*
a word that describes a noun or pronoun. The words 'big', 'boring' and 'blue' are all adjectives.

adjust /ə'dʒʌst/ *verb*
to change something slightly to improve it: *You can adjust the heat using this switch here.*

administration /əd,mɪnɪ'streɪʃən/ *noun* **[no plural]**
the things that you have to do in order to manage the work of an organization

admiration /,ædmə'reɪʃən/ *noun* **[no plural]**
the feeling of liking or respecting someone or something because they are good or clever: *My* ***admiration for*** *him grows daily.*

admire /əd'maɪəʳ/ *verb* (*present participle* **admiring,** *past* **admired)**
1 to like or respect someone or something because they are good or clever: *I* ***admire*** *him* ***for*** *being so determined.*
2 to look at something or someone, thinking they are attractive: *I was just admiring your shirt.*

admission /əd'mɪʃən/ *noun*
1 [no plural] the money that you pay to enter a place: *Art exhibition – admission free.*
2 when you agree that you did something bad: *Her departure was seen by many as an* ***admission of*** *guilt.*

admit /əd'mɪt/ *verb* (*present participle* **admitting,** *past* **admitted)**
1 to agree that you did something bad, or that something bad is true: *Both men admitted taking illegal drugs.* ○ *I was wrong – I admit it.*
2 to allow someone to enter somewhere: *It says on the ticket 'admits 2'.*

adolescence /,ædəl'esəns/ *noun* **[no plural]**
the period of time in someone's life between being a child and an adult

adolescent /,ædəl'esənt/ *noun*
a young person who is between being a child and an adult

adopt /ə'dɒpt/ *verb*
1 to take someone else's child into your family and become the parent of that child: *He was adopted as a small child.*
2 to start doing or using something new: *I've adopted a different method.*

adore /ə'dɔːʳ/ *verb* (*present participle* **adoring,** *past* **adored)**
to love someone or something: *Sarah adored her father.*

adult[1] /'ædʌlt, ə'dʌlt/ *noun*
a person or animal that has finished growing and is not now a child

adult[2] /'ædʌlt/ *adj*
1 having finished growing: *an adult male rat*
2 for adults or relating to adults: *adult education*

advance[1] /əd'vɑːns/ *noun*
1 in advance before a particular time: *We booked our tickets in advance.*
2 new discoveries and inventions: *scientific advances*

advance[2] /əd'vɑːns/ *verb* (*present participle* **advancing,** *past* **advanced)**
1 to develop or progress, or to make something develop or progress: *Research has advanced our understanding of the virus.*
2 to move forward, especially while fighting

advanced /əd'vɑːnst/ *adj*
1 having developed to a late stage: *advanced technology*
2 at a higher, more difficult level: *an advanced English course*

advantage /əd'vɑːntɪdʒ/ *noun*
1 something good that helps you: *One* ***advantage of*** *living in town is having the shops so near.*
2 take advantage of something to use the good things in a situation: *Take advantage of the sports facilities while you're here.*

adventure /əd'ventʃəʳ/ *noun*
an exciting and sometimes

a b c d e f g h i j k l m n o p q r s t u v w x y z

dangerous experience: *They had quite a few adventures on their travels.*

adventurous /ədˈventʃərəs/ *adj* liking to try new or difficult things: *I'm going to be more adventurous with my cooking.*

adverb /ˈædvɜːb/ *noun* a word that gives more information about a verb, adjective, phrase, or other adverb. In the sentence 'He ate quickly.' 'quickly' is an adverb.

advert /ˈædvɜːt/ *noun UK* an advertisement

advertise /ˈædvətaɪz/ *verb* (*present participle* **advertising**, *past* **advertised**) to tell people about something, on television or in newspapers, etc, so that people will buy it: *Companies are not allowed to advertise cigarettes on television.*

advertisement /ədˈvɜːtɪsmənt/ *noun* a picture, short film, song, etc which tries to persuade people to buy something: *a newspaper/television advertisement*

advice /ədˈvaɪs/ *noun* **[no plural]** suggestions about what you think someone should do: *There's a book* ***giving advice on*** *how to set up your own club.* ○ *I* ***took*** *your* ***advice*** *and went home early.*

advise /ədˈvaɪz/ *verb* (*present participle* **advising**, *past* **advised**) to tell someone they should do something: *I would* ***advise*** *him* ***to*** *see a doctor*

aerial /ˈeəriəl/ *noun UK* a piece of metal that is used for receiving television or radio signals

aerial

aerobics /eəˈrəʊbɪks/ *noun* **[no plural]** physical exercises that you do to music, especially in a class

aeroplane *UK*, airplane *US*

aeroplane /ˈeərəpleɪn/ *UK* (*US* **airplane**) *noun* a vehicle that flies and has an engine and wings

aerosol /ˈeərəsɒl/ *noun* a metal container that forces liquid out in small drops when you press a button

aerosol

affair /əˈfeər/ *noun*
1 a situation, especially a bad one: *The government's handling of the affair has been widely criticized.*
2 a sexual relationship between two people when one or both of them is married to someone else: *He* ***had an affair*** *with a woman at work.*

affairs /əˈfeəz/ *plural noun* situations or subjects that involve you: *He refused to discuss his financial affairs.*

affect /əˈfekt/ *verb* to make problems for someone or something or change them: *The disease affects many older people.*

affection /əˈfekʃən/ *noun* **[no plural]** a feeling of liking or loving someone

affectionate /əˈfekʃənət/ *adj* often showing that you like or love someone: *an affectionate little girl*

afford /əˈfɔːd/ *verb* to have enough money to buy something or enough time to do something: *We* ***can't afford*** *a new car.*

afraid /əˈfreɪd/ *adj*
1 I'm afraid used to politely tell someone something bad or to politely disagree with someone: *We haven't got any tickets left, I'm afraid.*
2 frightened or worried: *She's* ***afraid of*** *water.*

after[1] /ˈɑːftər/ *preposition*
1 when something has happened: *We went swimming after lunch.*
2 following in order: *H comes after G in the alphabet.*
3 *US* used to say how many minutes past the hour it is: *It's five after three.*
4 following someone or something: *We ran after him.*
5 be after something to be trying to get something: *What type of job are you after?*

after² /ˈɑːftəʳ/ *conjunction*
at a later time than something else happens: *We arrived after the game had started.*

afternoon /ˌɑːftəˈnuːn/ *noun*
the time between the middle of the day, and the evening: *I played tennis on Saturday afternoon.*

afterwards /ˈɑːftəwədz/ *adv*
at a later time, after something else has happened: *I did my homework and went swimming afterwards.*

again /əˈgen/ *adv*
1 once more: *Ask her again.*
2 as before: *Get some rest and you'll soon be well again.*
3 all over again repeated from the beginning: *We had to start all over again.*

against /əˈgenst/ *preposition*
1 disagreeing with a plan or activity: *Andrew wants to change offices but I'm against it.*
2 competing with someone or something: *Liverpool are playing against AC Milan.*
3 touching something: *Push the bed against the wall.*
4 against the law/the rules not allowed by a law or rule: *It's against the law to leave young children alone in the house.*

age /eɪdʒ/ *noun*
1 the number of years that someone has lived, or that something has existed: *People of all ages were there.* ○ *She left India **at the age of** 12.*
2 a period of history: *the Ice Age*
3 [no plural] when someone or something is old: *Some wines improve **with age**.*
4 under age too young to do something legally

aged /eɪdʒd/ *adj*
having a particular age: *They have one daughter, aged three.*

agency /ˈeɪdʒᵊnsi/ *noun* (*plural* **agencies)**
a business that provides a service: *an advertising agency*

ages /ˈeɪdʒɪz/ *noun informal*
a very long time: *I've been waiting here **for ages**.*

aggression /əˈgreʃᵊn/ *noun* **[no plural]**
angry or violent behaviour

aggressive /əˈgresɪv/ *adj*
angry and violent towards another person: *aggressive behaviour*

ago /əˈgəʊ/ *adv*
in the past: *It happened a long time ago.*

agony /ˈægəni/ *noun* **[no plural]**
very bad pain: *She lay on the bed **in agony**.*

agree /əˈgriː/ *verb* (*present participle* **agreeing,** *past* **agreed)**
1 to have the same opinion as someone: *I **agree with** you.* ○ *We all **agreed that** mistakes had been made.*
➲Opposite **disagree**
2 to say you will do something that someone asks you to do: *She **agreed to** help him.*
3 to decide something with someone: *They **agreed to** meet on Sunday.*

agree with something *phrasal verb*
to think that something is right: *I don't agree with hunting.*

agreement /əˈgriːmənt/ *noun*
1 a promise or decision made between two or more people: *an international agreement*
2 [no plural] when people have the same opinion as each other: *Not everyone was **in agreement**.*

agriculture /ˈægrɪkʌltʃəʳ/ *noun* **[no plural]**
the work of growing plants and looking after animals which are then used for food
• **agricultural** /ˌægrɪˈkʌltʃᵊrᵊl/ *adj agricultural machinery*

ahead /əˈhed/ *adj, adv*
1 in front: *She walked on **ahead of** us.*
2 in the future: *He has a difficult time **ahead of** him.*
3 with more points than someone else in a competition: *Barcelona was ahead after ten minutes.*
4 go ahead *informal* said to allow someone to do something: *"Can I use your phone?" "Sure, go ahead."*

aid /eɪd/ *noun*
1 help, or something such as food or equipment that gives help: *Emergency aid was sent to the flood victims.* ○ *teaching aids*
2 in aid of someone/something *UK* in order to get money for a group of people who need it: *There's a concert in aid of famine relief.*

AIDS, aids /eɪdz/ *noun* **[no plural]**
a serious illness that stops the body from fighting other illnesses

aim[1] /eɪm/ *noun*
the purpose of doing something: *The* ***aim of*** *the film was to make people laugh.*

aim[2] /eɪm/ *verb*
1 to try to do something: *We're* ***aiming for*** *a 10% increase in sales.*
2 to point a weapon towards someone or something: *He* ***aimed*** *the gun* ***at*** *the lion.*

air[1] /eəʳ/ *noun*
1 [no plural] the mixture of gases around the Earth which we breathe: *air pollution*
2 the air the space above and around things: *He fired his gun into the air.*
3 [no plural] travel in an aeroplane: *air travel*

air[2] /eəʳ/ *verb*
air your opinions/views, etc to say your opinions: *The meeting will give everyone a chance to air their views.*

air conditioning /ˈeəʳ kənˌdɪʃᵊnɪŋ/ *noun* **[no plural]**
a system that keeps the air cool in a building or car

aircraft /ˈeəkrɑːft/ *noun*
a vehicle that can fly

air force /ˈeəʳ ˌfɔːs/ *noun*
the part of a country's military organization that uses aeroplanes to fight wars

airline /ˈeəlaɪn/ *noun*
a company that takes people and things to places in aeroplanes

airmail /ˈeəmeɪl/ *noun* **[no plural]**
the sending of letters or parcels by aeroplane

airplane /ˈeəpleɪn/ *US* (*UK* **aeroplane**) *noun*
a vehicle that flies and has an engine and wings

airport /ˈeəpɔːt/ *noun*
a place where aeroplanes take off and land

aisle /aɪl/ *noun*
a passage between the lines of seats or goods in an aeroplane, church, or supermarket

aisle

alarm[1] /əˈlɑːm/ *noun*
1 a loud noise that tells you there is danger: *a fire alarm*
2 [no plural] a sudden feeling of fear that something bad might happen: *There's no need for alarm – it is completely safe.*

alarm[2] /əˈlɑːm/ *verb*
to worry someone: *I didn't want to alarm him by saying she was ill.*

alarm clock /əˈlɑːm ˌklɒk/ *noun*
a clock that makes a noise to wake you

alarm clock

album /ˈælbəm/ *noun*
1 many songs or pieces of music on a CD, disk, etc
2 a book in which you keep photographs, stamps, etc

alcohol /ˈælkəhɒl/ *noun* **[no plural]**
drinks such as wine and beer that can make you drunk

alcoholic /ˌælkəˈhɒlɪk/ *adj*
containing alcohol: *alcoholic drinks*

alert /əˈlɜːt/ *adj*
quick to notice things around you

A level /ˈeɪ ˌlevᵊl/ *noun*
in England and Wales, an exam taken at the age of eighteen, or the qualification itself

algebra /ˈældʒɪbrə/ *noun* **[no plural]**
a type of mathematics in which numbers are shown by letters and symbols

alien /ˈeɪliən/ *noun*
a creature from another planet

alike /əˈlaɪk/ *adj, adv*
similar, or in a similar way: *The children look so alike.* ○ *We think alike.*

alive /ə'laɪv/ *adj*
living, not dead: *Are your grandparents still alive?*

all[1] /ɔːl/ *pronoun, determiner*
1 every person or thing in a group: *We were all dancing.*
2 the whole amount of something: *He spends **all of** his money on clothes.*
3 the only thing: *All I remember is waking up in hospital.*
4 at all in any way: *He hasn't changed at all.*

all[2] /ɔːl/ *adv*
completely or very: *You're all wet!*

allergic /ə'lɜːdʒɪk/ *adj*
having an allergy: *I'm **allergic to** eggs.*

allergy /'ælədʒi/ *noun* (*plural* **allergies**)
a medical problem in which you get ill if you eat, breathe, or touch something: *He has an **allergy to** cat fur.*

alley /'æli/ *noun*
a narrow road between buildings

alligator /'ælɪgeɪtə^{r}/ *noun*
a long animal with a long mouth and sharp teeth, that lives in hot areas with water

alligator

allow /ə'laʊ/ *verb*
to say that someone can do something: *Smoking is not allowed in the restaurant.*

allowance /ə'laʊəns/ *noun*
money that you are given regularly to pay for a particular thing: *a clothes allowance*

all right[1] (*also* **alright**) /ˌɔːl'raɪt/ *adj, adv*
1 good enough, although not excellent: *The hotel wasn't brilliant but it was all right.*
2 safe or well: *You look pale – are you all right?*
3 That's all right. used as an answer when someone thanks you: *"Thanks for cleaning the kitchen." "That's all right."*

all right[2] (*also* **alright**) /ɔːlraɪt/ *exclamation*
used to say yes to a suggestion or request: *"How about going out for dinner?" "All right."*

ally /'ælaɪ/ *noun* (*plural* **allies**)
a person or country that helps you when you are arguing or fighting

almond /'ɑːmənd/ *noun*
a flat, oval nut, often used in cooking

almost /'ɔːlməʊst/ *adv*
nearly: *I almost missed the bus.*

alone /ə'ləʊn/ *adj, adv*
1 without other people: *She lives alone.*
2 only: *Last year alone the company made a million dollars.*
3 leave someone alone to stop talking to someone or annoying them: *Leave him alone, he's tired.*
4 leave something alone to stop touching something: *Leave your hair alone!*

along[1] /ə'lɒŋ/ *preposition*
1 from one part of a road, river, etc to another: *a walk along the beach*
2 in a line next to something long: *There is a row of new houses along the river.*

along[2] /ə'lɒŋ/ *adv*
1 forward: *We were just walking along, talking.*
2 come along to arrive somewhere: *Three buses came along at once.*
3 bring/take someone along to take someone with you to a place: *Can I bring some friends along to the party?*

alongside /əˌlɒŋ'saɪd/ *adv, preposition*
next to someone or something: *A car pulled up alongside ours.*

aloud /ə'laʊd/ *adv*
in a way that other people can hear: *I laughed aloud.*

alphabet /'ælfəbet/ *noun*
a set of letters used for writing a language: *The English alphabet starts at A and ends at Z.*

alphabetical /ˌælfə'betɪk^{ə}l/ *adj*
in the same order as the letters of the alphabet: *Put the names **in alphabetical order**.*
• **alphabetically** *adv*

already /ɔːl'redi/ *adv*
1 before now, or before a time in the past: *I've already told him.*
2 used to say that something has happened earlier than you expected: *I can't believe you've already finished!*

alright /ɔːl'raɪt/ *adj, adv, exclamation*
another spelling of all right

also /ˈɔːlsəʊ/ *adv*
in addition: *She speaks French and also a little Spanish.*

alter /ˈɔːltəʳ/ *verb*
to change, or to make someone or something change: *Your life alters completely when you have children.*

alteration /ˌɔːltᵊrˈeɪʃᵊn/ *noun*
a change: *We've **made** a few **alterations to** the kitchen.*

alternate[1] /ɔːlˈtɜːnət/ *adj*
1 one out of every two days, weeks, years, etc: *I work alternate Saturdays.*
2 with first one thing, then another thing, and then the first thing again, etc: *a dessert with alternate layers of chocolate and cream*
3 *US* different: *an alternate plan*
• **alternately** *adv*

alternate[2] /ˈɔːltəneɪt/ *verb* (*present participle* **alternating**, *past* **alternated**)
If two things alternate, one thing happens, then the other thing happens, then the first thing happens again, etc: *She **alternates between** happiness and deep despair.*

alternative[1] /ɔːlˈtɜːnətɪv/ *noun*
one of two or more things that you can choose between: *It's a healthy **alternative to** butter.*

alternative[2] /ɔːlˈtɜːnətɪv/ *adj*
different: *We can make alternative arrangements if necessary.*

alternatively /ɔːlˈtɜːnətɪvli/ *adv*
used to give a second possibility: *We could go there by train or, alternatively, I could drive.*

although /ɔːlˈðəʊ/ *conjunction*
1 despite the fact that: *She walked home by herself, although she knew it was dangerous.*
2 but: *He's coming tomorrow, although I don't know what time.*

altogether /ˌɔːltəˈgeðəʳ/ *adv*
1 completely: *The train slowed down and then stopped altogether.*
2 in total: *There were twenty people there altogether.*

aluminium /ˌæljəˈmɪniəm/ *UK* (*US* **aluminum** /əˈluːmɪnəm/) *noun* **[no plural]**
a light, silver-coloured metal

always /ˈɔːlweɪz/ *adv*
1 every time, or at all times: *I always walk to work.*
2 at all times in the past: *We've always lived here.*
3 forever: *I will always remember you.*

a.m. /ˌeɪˈem/
in the morning: *We're open from 9 a.m. to 5 p.m. daily.* ➲Compare **p.m.**

am *strong form* /æm/ *weak forms* /əm, m/
present simple of be, used with 'I'

amateur /ˈæmətəʳ/ *adj*
doing something as a hobby: ➲Opposite **professional** *an amateur photographer*
• **amateur** *noun*
someone who does something as a hobby ➲Opposite **professional**

amaze /əˈmeɪz/ *verb* (*present participle* **amazing**, *past* **amazed**)
to make someone very surprised: *It amazes me how much energy you have.*

amazed /əˈmeɪzd/ *adj*
very surprised: *I was **amazed at** the price.*

amazement /əˈmeɪzmənt/ *noun* **[no plural]**
when you are very surprised: *I watched **in amazement**.*

amazing /əˈmeɪzɪŋ/ *adj*
very surprising: *It's amazing how many people can't read.*
• **amazingly** *adv*: *She looked amazingly well.*

ambassador /æmˈbæsədəʳ/ *noun*
an important person who officially represents their country in a different country: *the French **ambassador to** Britain*

ambition /æmˈbɪʃᵊn/ *noun*
1 something that you want to do in your life: *My ambition is to retire at forty.*
2 **[no plural]** a strong feeling that you want to be successful or powerful

ambitious /æmˈbɪʃəs/ *adj*
wanting to be successful or powerful: *an ambitious young lawyer*

ambulance /ˈæmbjələns/ *noun*
a vehicle that takes people to hospital when they are ill or hurt

ambulance

ammunition /ˌæmjəˈnɪʃᵊn/ *noun* **[no plural]**

bullets and bombs to be fired from guns

among /əˈmʌŋ/ (*also* **amongst** /əˈmʌŋst/) *preposition*
1 in the middle of something: *He disappeared among the crowd.*
2 in a particular group: *The decision will not be popular among students.*
3 to each one in a group: *She divided the cake among the children.*

amount /əˈmaʊnt/ *noun*
how much there is of something: *He ate a huge* ***amount of*** *food.*

amp /æmp/ *noun*
a unit for measuring the strength of an electric current

amplifier /ˈæmplɪfaɪəʳ/ *noun*
a piece of electronic equipment that makes sounds louder

amuse /əˈmjuːz/ *verb* (*present participle* **amusing**, *past* **amused**)
1 to make someone smile or laugh: *I thought this article might amuse you.*
2 to keep someone interested and help them to enjoy themselves: *I bought a magazine to amuse myself on the train.*

amusement /əˈmjuːzmənt/ *noun* **[no plural]**
the feeling that you have when something makes you smile or laugh: *I watched the performance* ***with*** *great* ***amusement****.*

amusing /əˈmjuːzɪŋ/ *adj*
funny: *an amusing letter*

an *strong form* /æn/ *weak form* /ᵊn/ *determiner*
used instead of 'a' when the next word starts with a vowel sound: *an apple* ○ *an hour*

anaesthetic *UK* (*US* **anesthetic**) /ˌænəsˈθetɪk/ *noun*
a drug that stops you from feeling pain during an operation: *The operation is done* ***under anaesthetic*** (= using anaesthetic).

analyse /ˈænᵊlaɪz/ *verb* (*present participle* **analysing**, *past* **analysed**)
to look at and think about something carefully, in order to understand it: *to analyse information*

analysis /əˈnæləsɪs/ *noun* (*plural* **analyses** /əˈnæləsiːz/)
the process of analysing something: *A sample of soil was sent for analysis.*

ancestor /ˈænsestəʳ/ *noun*
a person in your family who lived a long time ago: *My ancestors came from Ireland.*

anchor

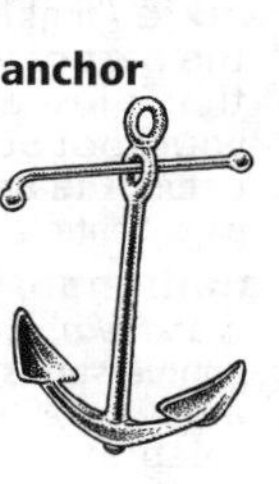

anchor /ˈæŋkəʳ/ *noun*
a heavy, metal object that is dropped into water to stop a boat from moving

ancient /ˈeɪnʃᵊnt/ *adj*
from a long time ago: *ancient Greece*

and *strong form* /ænd/ *weak forms* /ənd, ən/ *conjunction*
used to join two words or two parts of a sentence: *tea and coffee* ○ *We were tired and hungry.*

anesthetic /ˌænəsˈθetɪk/ *noun US spelling of* anaesthetic

angel /ˈeɪndʒᵊl/ *noun*
a creature like a human with wings, who some people believe lives with God in heaven

angel

anger /ˈæŋgəʳ/ *noun* **[no plural]**
the feeling that you want to shout at someone or hurt them because they have done something bad

angle

angle /ˈæŋgl/ *noun*
a space between two lines or surfaces that meet at one point, which you measure in degrees: *an angle of 90 degrees*

angry /ˈæŋgri/ *adj*
feeling that you want to shout at someone or hurt them because they have done something bad: *He's really* ***angry with*** *me for upsetting Sophie.*
• **angrily** *adv*: *He said it angrily.*

animal /ˈænɪmᵊl/ *noun*
1 something that lives and moves but is not a person, bird, fish, or insect: *a wild animal*
2 anything that lives and moves, including people, birds, etc: *Are*

humans the only animals to use *language?*

ankle /ˈæŋkl/ *noun*
the part of your leg that is just above your foot ➲See colour picture **The Body** on page Centre 2

ankle

anniversary /ˌænɪˈvɜːsᵊri/ *noun (plural* **anniversaries)**
a day on which you remember or celebrate something that happened on that day in the past: *a wedding anniversary ○ the 40th anniversary of Kennedy's death*

announce /əˈnaʊns/ *verb (present participle* **announcing,** *past* **announced)**
to tell people new information, especially officially: *The company has announced plans to open six new stores.*

announcement /əˈnaʊnsmənt/ *noun*
something that someone says officially, giving new information about something: *The Prime Minister **made** an unexpected **announcement** this morning.*

announcer /əˈnaʊnsəʳ/ *noun*
someone who speaks between programmes on the radio or television

annoy /əˈnɔɪ/ *verb*
to make someone angry: *He's always late and it's starting to annoy me.*
• **annoyance** *noun* **[no plural]**
the feeling of being annoyed

annoyed /əˈnɔɪd/ *adj*
angry: *I was **annoyed with** Charlotte for being late.*

annoying /əˈnɔɪɪŋ/ *adj*
making you feel angry: *an annoying habit*

annual /ˈænjuəl/ *adj*
1 happening or made once a year: *an annual meeting*
2 measured over a period of one year: *annual income*
• **annually** *adv*

anonymous /əˈnɒnɪməs/ *adj*
not saying or writing a name: *an anonymous phone call*

another /əˈnʌðəʳ/ *pronoun, determiner*
1 one more person or thing: *Would you like another drink?*
2 a different person or thing: *I'm going to look for another job.*

answer¹ /ˈɑːnsəʳ/ *verb*
1 to speak or write back to someone who has asked you a question: *I asked when she was leaving but she didn't answer. ○ I must answer his letter.*
2 to open the door to someone who has arrived: *I knocked several times but no one answered.*
3 to say hello to someone who has telephoned you: *Could someone answer the phone?*
4 to write or say something as a reply to a question in a test

answer² /ˈɑːnsəʳ/ *noun*
1 something that you say or write back to someone who has asked you a question: *I asked him if he was going but I didn't hear his answer.*
2 when someone answers the telephone or the door: *I rang the bell but there was no answer.*
3 a way of stopping a problem: *It's a big problem and I don't know what the answer is.*
4 the correct information given as a reply to a question in a test: *Did you get the answer to Question 6?*

answerphone /ˈɑːnsəfəʊn/ *UK (US* **answering machine)** *noun*
a machine that records your message if you telephone someone and they do not answer: *I left a message **on** her **answerphone**.*

ant /ænt/ *noun*
a small insect that lives in groups on the ground

antelope /ˈæntɪləʊp/ *noun*
an animal like a large deer with long horns

antibiotic /ˌæntɪbaɪˈɒtɪk/ *noun*
a medicine which cures infections by destroying bad bacteria: *He is taking antibiotics for an ear infection.*

anticipate /ænˈtɪsɪpeɪt/ *verb (present participle* **anticipating,** *past* **anticipated)**
to expect something: *We **anticipate that** prices will fall next year.*

anticipation /ænˌtɪsɪˈpeɪʃᵊn/ *noun* **[no plural]**
when you are waiting for something to happen, usually with excitement

anti-clockwise /ˌæntɪˈklɒkwaɪz/ *UK (US* **counterclockwise)** *adj, adv*
in the opposite direction to the way the hands of a clock move: *Turn the knob anti-clockwise.*

antique /æn'tiːk/ *noun*
an object that is old, and rare or beautiful

anxiety /æŋ'zaɪəti/ *noun* **[no plural]**
the feeling of being very worried

anxious /'æŋkʃəs/ *adj*
1 worried and nervous: *She's very **anxious about** her exams.*
2 wanting something to happen soon: *He's **anxious to** get home.*
● **anxiously** *adv*: *We waited anxiously by the phone.*

any[1] *strong form* /'eni/ *weak form* /əni/ *pronoun, determiner*
1 used in questions and negatives to mean 'some': *Is there any cake left?* ○ *I haven't seen any of his films.*
2 used to mean 'one' when it is not important which one: *Any of those shirts would be fine.*

any[2] *strong form* /'eni/ *weak form* /əni/ *adv*
used in questions and negatives before a comparative adjective or adverb to make the sentence stronger: *Do you feel any better?* ○ *I can't walk any faster.*

anybody /'eniˌbɒdi/ *pronoun*, *another word for*
anyone

anyhow /'enihaʊ/ *adv*, *another word for*
anyway

any more (*also* **anymore**) /ˌeni 'mɔːʳ/ *adv*
now: *This coat doesn't fit me any more.*

anyone /'eniwʌn/ *pronoun*
1 used in questions and negatives to mean 'a person or people': *I didn't know anyone at the party.*
2 any person or any people: *Anyone could do that – it's easy.*

anyplace /'enipleɪs/ *adv US*
anywhere

anything /'eniθɪŋ/ *pronoun*
1 used in questions and negatives to mean 'something': *I haven't got anything to wear.* ○ *Was there **anything else** you wanted to say?*
2 any object, event, or situation: *Tom will eat anything.*

anyway /'eniweɪ/ *adv*
1 used to give a more important reason for something that you are saying: *I don't need a car and I can't afford one anyway.*
2 despite that: *I hate carrots but I ate them anyway.*
3 used when you are returning to an earlier subject: *Anyway, as I said, I'll be away next week.*

anywhere /'eniweəʳ/ *adv*
1 in or to any place: *Just sit anywhere.* ○ *I couldn't find a post office anywhere.*
2 used in questions and negatives to mean 'a place': *He doesn't have anywhere to stay.* ○ *Is there **anywhere else** you'd like to visit while you're here?*

apart /ə'pɑːt/ *adv*
1 separated by a space or period of time: *Stand with your feet wide apart.* ○ *Our children were born eighteen months apart.*
2 into separate, smaller pieces: *My jacket is so old, it's coming apart.*
3 apart from except for: *Apart from Jodie, who hurt her leg, all the children were fine.*

apartment /ə'pɑːtmənt/ *noun*
a set of rooms for someone to live in on one level of a building or house

ape /eɪp/ *noun*
a hairy animal like a monkey but with no tail and long arms

apologize /ə'pɒlədʒaɪz/ *verb* (*present participle* **apologizing**, *past* **apologized**)
to say sorry for something bad you have done: *He **apologized for** being rude.* ○ *I **apologized to** her.*

apology /ə'pɒlədʒi/ *noun* (*plural* **apologies**)
something you say or write to say sorry for something bad you have done: *a letter of apology*

apostrophe /ə'pɒstrəfi/ *noun*
1 a mark (') used to show that letters or numbers are not there: *I'm* (= I am) *hungry.* ○ *I graduated in '98* (= 1998).
2 a punctuation mark (') used before the letter 's' to show that something belongs to someone or something: *I drove my brother's car.*

appalling /ə'pɔːlɪŋ/ *adj*
very bad: *appalling behaviour*

apparent /ə'pærᵊnt/ *adj*

easy to notice: *It soon became **apparent that** she had lost interest.*

apparently /ə'pærəntli/ *adv*
used to say that you have read or been told something: *Apparently it's going to rain today.*

appeal[1] /ə'piːl/ *noun*
1 when a lot of people are asked to give money, information, or help: *The appeal raised over £2 million for AIDS research.*
2 **[no plural]** the quality that makes you like someone or something: *I've never understood the appeal of skiing.*

appeal[2] /ə'piːl/ *verb*
1 to ask people to give money, information or help: *The police have **appealed for** more information.*
2 to attract or interest someone: *Cycling has never **appealed to** me.*

appear /ə'pɪəʳ/ *verb*
1 to seem: *He appeared calm and relaxed.*
2 to start to be seen: *He suddenly appeared in the doorway.* ➲Opposite **disappear**

appearance /ə'pɪərᵊns/ *noun*
1 an occasion when someone is seen in public: *a public appearance*
2 the way a person or thing looks: *She's very concerned with her appearance.*

appetite /'æpɪtaɪt/ *noun*
the feeling that makes you want to eat: *All that walking has given me an appetite.*

applaud /ə'plɔːd/ *verb*
to hit your hands together to show that you have enjoyed a performance, talk, etc: *The audience applauded loudly.*

applause /ə'plɔːz/ *noun* **[no plural]**
when people hit their hands together to show they have enjoyed something: *There was loud applause at the end of her speech.*

apple /'æpl/ *noun*
a hard, round fruit with a green or red skin ➲See colour picture **Fruit and Vegetables** on page Centre 8

apple

appliance /ə'plaɪəns/ *noun*
a piece of electrical equipment with a particular purpose in the home: *They sell fridges, radios, and other electrical appliances.*

application /ˌæplɪ'keɪʃᵊn/ *noun*
1 an official request for something, usually in writing: *an application for a bank loan*
2 a computer program with a particular purpose

application form /æplɪ'kaɪʃᵊn 'fɔːm/ *noun*
a form that you use to officially ask for something, for example a job

apply /ə'plaɪ/ *verb* (*present participle* **applying,** *past* **applied)**
1 to ask officially for something: *I've **applied for** a job.*
2 to affect a particular person or situation: *This law only **applies to** married people.*
3 to spread something on a surface: *Apply the cream daily until the symptoms disappear.*

appoint /ə'pɔɪnt/ *verb*
to officially choose someone for a job: *He was **appointed as** company director last year.*

appointment /ə'pɔɪntmənt/ *noun*
1 a time you have arranged to see someone: *I've **made** an **appointment** with the dentist.*
2 a job

appreciate /ə'priːʃieɪt/ *verb* (*present participle* **appreciating,** *past* **appreciated)**
1 to understand how good something or someone is: *He wouldn't appreciate an expensive wine.*
2 to feel grateful for something: *I really appreciate all your help.*
3 to understand that a situation is difficult: *I **appreciate that** this is a difficult decision for you.*

appreciation /əˌpriːʃi'eɪʃᵊn/ *noun* **[no plural]**
1 when you understand how good something or someone is: *His **appreciation of** art increased as he grew older.*
2 when you feel grateful for something: *To show our appreciation, we've bought you a little present.*

approach[1] /ə'prəʊtʃ/ *noun*
a way of doing something: *Liam has a different **approach to** the problem.*

approach[2] /ə'prəʊtʃ/ *verb*
to come close in distance or time:

The train approaching platform 2 is for London, Kings Cross. ○ *Christmas is fast approaching.*

appropriate /ə'prəupriət/ *adj*
right for a particular situation or person: *Is this film* ***appropriate for*** *young children?* ➲Opposite **inappropriate**
● **appropriately** *adv*: *She was appropriately dressed.*

approval /ə'pruːvəl/ *noun* **[no plural]**
when you think that something or someone is good or right ➲Opposite **disapproval**

approve /ə'pruːv/ *verb* (*present participle* **approving,** *past* **approved)**
1 to allow something: *The council has approved plans for a new shopping centre.*
2 to think that something is good or right: *I don't* ***approve of*** *smoking.* ➲Opposite **disapprove**

approximate /ə'prɒksɪmət/ *adj*
not completely accurate but close: *Do you have an approximate idea of when he's arriving?*

approximately /ə'prɒksɪmətli/ *adv*
close to a particular number or time, although not exactly that number or time: *The college has approximately 700 students.*

apricot /'eɪprɪkɒt/ *noun*
a small, soft, orange fruit

April /'eɪprəl/ *noun*
the fourth month of the year

apron /'eɪprən/ *noun*
a piece of clothing that keeps your clothes clean when you cook

apron

arch /ɑːtʃ/ *noun* (*plural* **arches)**
a curved structure that usually supports something, for example a bridge or wall

archaeologist /ˌɑːki'ɒlədʒɪst/ *noun*
someone who studies archaeology

archaeology /ˌɑːki'ɒlədʒi/ *noun* **[no plural]**
the study of people from long ago by looking at things such as their buildings and tools

architect /'ɑːkɪtekt/ *noun*
someone who designs buildings

architecture /'ɑːkɪtektʃər/ *noun* **[no plural]**
the design and style of buildings: *modern architecture*

are *strong form* /ɑːr/ *weak form* /ər/
present simple of be, *used with 'you', 'we' and 'they'*

area /'eəriə/ *noun*
1 a part of a country or city: *a poor area*
2 a part of a building or piece of land used for a particular purpose: *a picnic area*
3 the size of a flat surface

arch

arena /ə'riːnə/ *noun*
a flat area with seats around where you can watch sports and performances: *an Olympic arena*

aren't /ɑːnt/
1 *short for* are not: *We aren't going to the party.*
2 aren't I? *short for* am I not?: *I am invited, aren't I?*

argue /'ɑːgjuː/ *verb* (*present participle* **arguing,** *past* **argued)**
to speak angrily to someone, telling them that you disagree with them: *My parents are always* ***arguing about*** *money.*

argument /'ɑːgjəmənt/ *noun*
when you tell someone that you disagree with them and are angry with them: *They* ***had*** *an* ***argument*** *about who should do the cleaning.*

arise /ə'raɪz/ *verb* (*present participle* **arising,** *past tense* **arose,** *past participle* **arisen)**
If a problem arises, it starts to happen: *The whole problem* ***arose from*** *a lack of communication.*

aristocracy /ˌærɪ'stɒkrəsi/ *noun* **[no plural]**
the highest social class

arithmetic /ə'rɪθmətɪk/ *noun* **[no plural]**
when you calculate numbers, for example by multiplying or adding

a b c d e f g h i j k l m n o p q r s t u v w x y z

arm /ɑːm/ *noun*
the long part at each side of the human body, ending in a hand: *She held the tiny baby in her arms.*

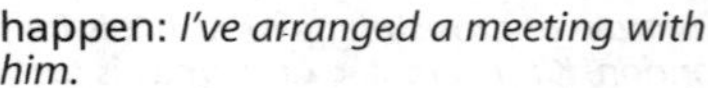
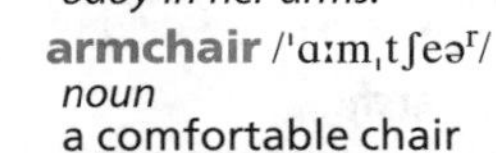

armchair /ˈɑːmˌtʃeəʳ/ *noun*
a comfortable chair with sides that support your arms

armed /ɑːmd/ *adj*
carrying or using weapons: *armed police*

the armed forces /ˌɑːmd ˈfɔːsɪz/ *noun*
a country's military forces, for example the army and the navy

armour *UK* (*US* **armor**) /ˈɑːməʳ/ *noun* **[no plural]**
metal clothes which soldiers wore in the past when fighting: *a suit of armour*

armpit /ˈɑːmpɪt/ *noun*
the part of your body under your arm, where your arm meets your body

arms /ɑːmz/ *plural noun*
weapons: *the sale of arms*

army /ˈɑːmi/ *noun* (*plural* **armies**)
a military force that fights wars on the ground: *the British Army*

arose /əˈrəʊz/
past tense of arise

around /əˈraʊnd/ *adv, preposition*
1 on all sides of something: *They sat around the table.*
2 to the opposite direction: *He turned around and looked at her.*
3 in a circular movement: *This lever turns the wheels around.*
4 to different parts of a place: *I spent a year travelling around Australia.*
5 here, or near this place: *Is there a cafe around here?*
6 used before a number or amount to mean 'close to, although not exactly': *around four o'clock*

arrange /əˈreɪndʒ/ *verb* (*present participle* **arranging**, *past* **arranged**)
1 to make plans for something to happen: *I've arranged a meeting with him.*
2 to put objects in a particular order or position: *Arrange the books alphabetically by author.*

arrangement /əˈreɪndʒmənt/ *noun*
plans for how something will happen: *I've **made arrangements** to go home this weekend.*

arrest¹ /əˈrest/ *verb*
if the police arrest someone, they take them away to ask them about a crime which they might have done: *He **was arrested for** possession of illegal drugs.*

arrest² /əˈrest/ *noun*
when the police arrest someone: *Police **made** 20 **arrests** at yesterday's demonstration.*

arrival /əˈraɪvəl/ *noun* **[no plural]**
when someone or something arrives somewhere: *There was a car waiting for him **on arrival**.* ➲Opposite **departure**

arrive /əˈraɪv/ *verb* (*present participle* **arriving**, *past* **arrived**)
to get to a place: *We **arrived in** Paris at midday.* ○ *I was the last to **arrive at** the station.* ➲Opposite **leave**

arrogant /ˈærəgənt/ *adj*
believing that you are better than other people
• **arrogance** /ˈærəgəns/ *noun* **[no plural]**

arrow /ˈærəʊ/ *noun*
1 this symbol ➔, used on signs to show a direction
2 a long stick with a sharp point at one end which is fired from a bow (= curved piece of wood)

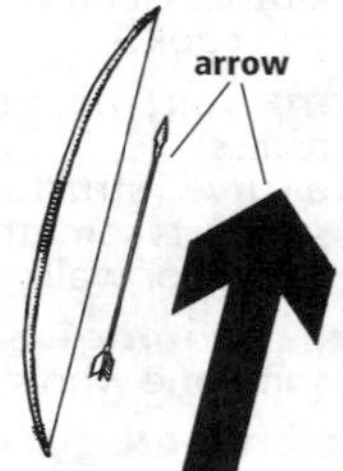

art /ɑːt/ *noun*
1 [no plural] the making of paintings, drawings, etc or the things made: *modern art* ○ *an art gallery*
2 a skill: *the art of conversation*

artery /ˈɑːtəri/ *noun* (*plural* **arteries**)

a b c d e f g h i j k l m n o p q r s t u v w x y z

a tube in your body that carries blood from your heart

arthritis /ɑː'θraɪtɪs/ *noun* **[no plural]**
an illness which causes pain in the parts of the body where bones meet
• **arthritic** /ɑː'θrɪtɪk/ *adj*: *an arthritic hip*

article /'ɑːtɪkl/ *noun*
1 a piece of writing in a magazine or newspaper: *I read an* ***article on*** *astrology.*
2 an object: *articles of clothing*
3 in grammar, used to mean the words 'the', 'a', or 'an'

artificial /ˌɑːtɪ'fɪʃəl/ *adj*
not natural, but made by people: *artificial flowers*

artist /'ɑːtɪst/ *noun*
someone who makes art, especially paintings and drawings

artistic /ɑː'tɪstɪk/ *adj*
1 good at making things such as paintings and drawings
2 relating to art: *the artistic director of the theatre*

arts /ɑːts/ *noun*
1 subjects of study which are not science, such as history and languages: *an arts degree*
2 the arts activities such as painting, music, film, dance, and writing

as *strong form* /æz/ *weak form* /əz/ *preposition, conjunction*
1 as .... as used to compare two things, people, amounts, etc: *He's not as tall as his brother.* ○ *She earns three times as much as I do.*
2 while: *I saw James as I was leaving.*
3 used to describe something's purpose or someone's job: *She* ***works as*** *a waitress.*
4 because: *You can go first as you're the oldest.*
5 as if/as though used to describe how a situation seems to be: *It looks as if it might rain.*

ash /æʃ/ *noun* **[no plural]**
the soft, grey powder which remains when something has burnt: *cigarette ash*

ashamed /ə'ʃeɪmd/ *adj*
feeling bad because you have done something wrong: *I felt so* ***ashamed of*** *my behaviour.*

ashtray /'æʃˌtreɪ/ *noun*
a small, open container used to put cigarette ash in

aside /ə'saɪd/ *adv*
in a direction to one side: *I gave her some food but she pushed it aside.*

ask /ɑːsk/ *verb*
1 to say something to someone as a question: *I* ***asked*** *him* ***about*** *his hobbies.* ○ *I* ***asked why*** *the plane was so late.*
2 to say to someone that you would like something from them: *He's* ***asked for*** *a bike for his birthday.*
3 to invite someone to do something: *She* ***asked*** *him* ***out*** *to lunch.*
4 to say something to someone because you want to know if you can do something: *I* ***asked if*** *I could go.*

asleep /ə'sliːp/ *adj*
sleeping: *The children are asleep.* ○ *He* ***fell asleep*** *in front of the TV.*

asparagus /ə'spærəgəs/ *noun* **[no plural]**
a long, green vegetable with a pointed end

aspect /'æspekt/ *noun*
one part of a situation, problem, or subject: *His illness affects every aspect of his life.*

aspirin /'æspərɪn/ *noun*
a common drug used to stop pain and fever

assassinate /ə'sæsɪneɪt/ *verb* (*present participle* **assassinating,** *past* **assassinated)**
to kill someone important or famous
• **assassination** /əˌsæsɪ'neɪʃən/ *noun*

assault /ə'sɔːlt/ *noun*
an attack: *There was an* ***assault on*** *a police officer.*
• **assault** *verb*
to attack someone

assembly /ə'sembli/ *noun* (*plural* **assemblies)**
a meeting of a large group of people

assess /ə'ses/ *verb*
to decide how good, important, or serious something is: *The tests are designed to assess a child's reading skills.*
• **assessment** *noun*

assist /ə'sɪst/ *verb formal*
to help: *The army arrived to* ***assist in*** *the search*

assistance /ə'sɪstᵊns/ *noun* **[no plural]** *formal*
help: *financial assistance*

assistant /ə'sɪstᵊnt/ *noun*
1 someone whose job is to help a person who has a more important job: *assistant manager*
2 a sales/shop assistant *UK* someone who works in a shop

associate /ə'səʊʃieɪt/ *verb* (*present participle* **associating,** *past* **associated)**
to relate two things or people in your mind: *Most people **associate** this brand **with** good quality.*

be associated with something *phrasal verb*
to be caused by something: *There are many health problems associated with smoking.*

association /əˌsəʊʃi'eɪʃᵊn/ *noun*
an organization of people with the same interests or purpose: *the Football Association*

assume /ə'sjuːm/ *verb* (*present participle* **assuming,** *past* **assumed)**
to think that something is true, although you have no proof: *You weren't here so I assumed you were at home.*

assumption /ə'sʌmʃᵊn/ *noun*
something that you think is true without having any proof: *We tend to **make assumptions about** people who are fat.*

assure /ə'ʃɔːʳ/ *verb* (*present participle* **assuring,** *past* **assured)**
to stop someone worrying by telling them that something is certain: *She **assured** me **that** she would be safe.*

asterisk /'æstᵊrɪsk/ *noun*
the symbol (*)

asthma /'æsmə/ *noun* **[no plural]**
an illness which makes it difficult to breathe: *an asthma attack*

astonished /ə'stɒnɪʃt/ *adj*
very surprised: *I was astonished at the news.*

astonishing /ə'stɒnɪʃɪŋ/ *adj*
very surprising: *What an astonishing thing to say!*

astonishment /ə'stɒnɪʃmənt/ *noun* **[no plural]**
a feeling of great surprise: *I tried to hide my astonishment.*

astrology /ə'strɒlədʒi/ *noun* **[no plural]**
the study of the positions and movements of stars and planets and how people think they change people's lives
• **astrologer** *noun*
someone who studies astrology

astronaut

astronaut /'æstrənɔːt/ *noun*
someone who travels into space

astronomy /ə'strɒnəmi/ *noun* **[no plural]**
the scientific study of stars and planets
• **astronomer** *noun*
a scientist who studies astronomy

at *strong form* /æt/ *weak form* /ət/ *preposition*
1 in a particular place or position: *We met at the station.* ○ *She was sitting at the table.*
2 used to show the time something happens: *The meeting starts at three.*
3 towards: *She threw the ball at him.*
4 used after an adjective to show a person's ability to do something: *He's good at making friends.*
5 used to show the cause of something, especially a feeling: *We were surprised at the news.*
6 used to show the price, speed, or level of something: *He was driving at 120 miles per hour.*
7 the @ symbol, used in email addresses to separate the name of a person from the name of the organization

ate /eɪt, et/
past tense of eat

athlete /'æθliːt/ *noun*
someone who is good at sports such as running, jumping, or throwing things

athletic /æθ'letɪk/ *adj*
1 strong, healthy, and good at sports
2 relating to athletes or to the sport of athletics

athletics /æθ'letɪks/ *UK* (*US* **track and field)** *noun* **[no plural]**
the sports which include running, jumping, and throwing

atlas /'ætləs/ *noun* (*plural* **atlases)**
a book of maps: *a road atlas*

ATM /ˌeɪtiːˈem/ *noun US*
a machine that you get money from using a plastic card

atmosphere /ˈætməsfɪəʳ/ *noun*
1 [no plural] the feeling which exists in a place or situation: *The atmosphere in the office is very relaxed.*
2 the atmosphere the gases around the Earth

atom /ˈætəm/ *noun*
the smallest unit that an element can be divided into

atomic /əˈtɒmɪk/ *adj*
1 relating to atoms
2 using the energy created when an atom is divided: *atomic power/ weapons*

attach /əˈtætʃ/ *verb*
to join one thing to another: *She* ***attached*** *a photograph* ***to*** *her letter.*

attached /əˈtætʃt/ *adj*
be attached to someone/something to like someone or something very much: *I'm rather attached to my old car.*

attachment /əˈtætʃmənt/ *noun*
1 a feeling of love or liking for someone or something
2 a computer file which is sent together with an email message: *Have you* ***opened*** *the* ***attachment****?*

attack¹ /əˈtæk/ *noun*
1 a violent act which is done to hurt or damage someone or something: *There was a terrorist* ***attack on*** *the capital.*
2 a sudden, short illness: *He had a nasty* ***attack of*** *flu.*

attack² /əˈtæk/ *verb*
1 to use violence to hurt or damage someone or something: *He was attacked by a gang of youths.*
2 to say that someone or something is bad: *She has attacked the government's new education policy.*

attacker /əˈtækəʳ/ *noun*
a person who tries to hurt someone

attempt¹ /əˈtempt/ *noun*
when you try to do something: *This is his second* ***attempt at*** *the exam.*

attempt² /əˈtempt/ *verb*
to try to do something: *He* ***attempted to*** *escape through a window.*

attend /əˈtend/ *verb formal*
to go to an event: *He attended the meeting.*

attendance /əˈtendəns/ *noun*
1 the number of people who go to an event: *We have seen falling* ***attendances at*** *football grounds.*
2 [no plural] when you often go somewhere, such as a school or church: *His* ***attendance at*** *school is very poor.*

attendant /əˈtendənt/ *noun*
someone whose job is to help the public in a particular place: *a parking attendant*

attention /əˈtenʃən/ *noun* **[no plural]**
1 when you watch or listen to something carefully: *Ladies and gentlemen, could I have your attention, please* (= please listen to me)*?* ○ *I wasn't* ***paying attention*** (= listening) *to what she was saying.*
2 attract someone's attention to make someone notice you: *I waved at him to attract his attention.*

attic /ˈætɪk/ *noun*
a room at the top of a house under the roof

attitude /ˈætɪtjuːd/ *noun*
how you think or feel about something: *He has a very bad* ***attitude towards*** *work.*

attract /əˈtrækt/ *verb*
1 to make people come to a place or do a particular thing: *The castle attracts more than 300,000 visitors a year.*
2 to cause someone to be interested: *So what* ***attracted*** *you* ***to*** *Joe in the first place?*

attraction /əˈtrækʃən/ *noun*
1 something that makes people come to a place: *a tourist attraction*
2 [no plural] when you like someone because of the way they look or behave: *physical attraction*

attractive /əˈtræktɪv/ *adj*
beautiful or pleasant to look at: *an attractive woman*

aubergine /ˈəʊbəʒiːn/ *UK* (*US* **eggplant**) *noun*
an oval, purple vegetable that is white inside

auction /ˈɔːkʃən/ *noun*
a sale in which things are sold to the person who offers the most money
• **auction** *verb*
to sell something at an auction

audience /ˈɔːdiəns/ *noun*

a b c d e f g h i j k l m n o p q r s t u v w x y z

a b c d e f g h i j k l m n o p q r s t u v w x y z

the people who sit and watch a performance at a theatre, cinema, etc

August /ˈɔːgəst/ *noun*
the eighth month of the year

aunt /ɑːnt/ *noun*
the sister of your mother or father, or the wife of your uncle

au pair /ˌəʊˈpeəʳ/ *noun*
a young person who stays with a family in another country and looks after their children

authentic /ɔːˈθentɪk/ *adj*
real and not false: *authentic Italian food*

author /ˈɔːθəʳ/ *noun*
someone who writes a book, article, etc: *a popular author of children's fiction*

authority /ɔːˈθɒrəti/ *noun*
1 **[no plural]** the official power to make decisions or control people
2 an official group with the power to control a particular public service: *a health authority*

autobiography /ˌɔːtəʊbaɪˈɒgrəfi/ *noun* (*plural* **autobiographies**)
a book that someone has written about their own life

autograph /ˈɔːtəgrɑːf/ *noun*
a famous person's name, written by that person

automatic /ˌɔːtəˈmætɪk/ *adj*
An automatic machine works by itself or with little human control: *automatic doors*

autumn /ˈɔːtəm/ (*also US* **fall**) *noun*
the season of the year between summer and winter, when leaves fall from the trees: *I'm starting a new job **in the autumn**.*

available /əˈveɪləbl/ *adj*
If something is available, you can use it or get it: *This information is available free on the Internet.*

avalanche /ˈævəlɑːnʃ/ *noun*
when a large amount of snow falls down the side of a mountain

avenue /ˈævənjuː/ *noun*
a wide road in a town or city

average¹ /ˈævərɪdʒ/ *adj*
1 usual and like the most common type: *an average day*
2 An average amount is calculated by adding some amounts together and then dividing by the number of amounts: *The average age of the students is 18.*
3 not excellent, although not bad: *The food was pretty average.*

average² /ˈævərɪdʒ/ *noun*
an amount calculated by adding some amounts together and then dividing by the number of amounts:*They work an average of 30.5 hours per week.*

avocado /ˌævəˈkɑːdəʊ/ *noun*
a dark green, oval fruit which is pale green inside and is not sweet

avoid /əˈvɔɪd/ *verb*
1 to stay away from a person or place: *Try to avoid the city centre.*
2 to not do something because you do not want to: *She managed to avoid answering my question.*

await /əˈweɪt/ *verb formal*
to wait for something: *We are awaiting the results of the tests.*

awake /əˈweɪk/ *adj*
not sleeping: *I was awake half the night.*

award¹ /əˈwɔːd/ *noun*
a prize given to someone for something good they have done: *the award for best actress*

award² /əˈwɔːd/ *verb*
to officially give someone something such as a prize or an amount of money: *He was awarded the Nobel Prize for Physics.*

aware /əˈweəʳ/ *adj*
knowing about something: *Were you **aware of** the problem?* ➲Opposite **unaware**

away /əˈweɪ/ *adv*
1 to a different place: *Go away and leave me alone.* ○ *We moved **away from** the town centre.*
2 at a particular distance from a place: *The nearest town is ten miles away.*
3 not at the place where someone usually lives or works: *Sophie is feeding the cat while we're away.*
4 at a particular time in the future: *My exam's only a week away now.*

awful /ˈɔːfəl/ *adj*
very bad: *an awful place* ○ *The film was absolutely awful.*

awkward /ˈɔːkwəd/ *adj*
1 difficult or causing problems: *an awkward question*
2 embarrassing and not relaxed: *an awkward silence*
3 moving in a way that is not attractive: *His movements were slow and awkward.*

axe /æks/ *noun*
a tool with a sharp piece of metal at one end, used for cutting trees or wood

a b c d e f g h i j k l m n o p q r s t u v w x y z

Bb

B, b /biː/
the second letter of the alphabet

baby

baby /ˈbeɪbi/ *noun* (*plural* **babies**)
a very young child: *a baby girl*

babysit /ˈbeɪbɪsɪt/ *verb* (*present participle* **babysitting**, *past* **babysat**)
to look after children while their parents are not at home
● **babysitter** *noun*
someone who looks after children while their parents are not at home

bachelor /ˈbætʃ^{ə}lə^{r}/ *noun*
a man who has never married

back[1] /bæk/ *adv*
1 where someone or something was before: *When do you go back to college?* ○ *I put it back in the cupboard.*
2 in a direction behind you: *She stepped back.*
3 as a reply or reaction to something: *Can I call you back later?*
4 to the state something or someone was in before: *Try to go back to sleep.*
5 to an earlier time: *Looking back, I think we did the right thing.*

back[2] /bæk/ *noun*
1 the part of something that is away from the front: *I was sitting in the back of the car.*
2 the part of your body from your shoulders to your bottom: *He was lying on his back.*
3 back to front *UK* with the back part of something where the front should be: *You've got your trousers on back to front.*
4 in back of *US* behind: *They sat in back of us on the plane.*

back[3] /bæk/ *verb*
1 to give support to a person or plan: *He backed Clark in the recent election.*
2 to move or drive backwards: *It's best to back into a parking space.*
back something up *phrasal verb*
1 to prove that something is true: *His theory is backed up by recent evidence.*
2 to make an extra copy of computer information

back[4] /bæk/ *adj*
at the back of something: *the back garden*

backbone

backbone /ˈbækbəʊn/ *noun*
the line of bones along the centre of your back

background /ˈbækgraʊnd/ *noun*
1 the things at the back of a picture or view: *He had a photo of Paul with his children* ***in the background***.
2 a person's education and family: *He was* ***from*** *a poor* ***background***.

backpack

backpack /ˈbækpæk/ *noun*
a bag that you carry on your back

backstroke /ˈbækstrəʊk/ *noun* **[no plural]**
a style of swimming on your back

backup /ˈbækʌp/ *noun*
an extra copy of computer information: *Have you* ***made*** *a* ***backup*** *of that document?*

backward /ˈbækwəd/ *adj*
in the direction behind you: *a backward glance*

backwards /ˈbækwədz/ (*also* **backward**) *adv*
1 towards the direction behind you: *She took a couple of steps backwards.*
2 in the opposite order to what is usual: *'Erehwon' is 'nowhere' spelled backwards.*
3 with the part that is usually at the front at the back: *You've got your skirt on backwards.*
4 backwards and forwards *UK* in one direction then the opposite way, many times: *I drive backwards and forwards between Oxford and London every day.*

backyard /ˌbækˈjɑːd/ *noun US*
the area behind a house

bacon /ˈbeɪk^{ə}n/ *noun* **[no plural]**

meat from a pig cut into long, thin slices

bacteria /bæk'tɪəriə/ *plural noun*
very small living things that can cause disease

bad /bæd/ *adj*
1 not good or pleasant: *bad weather* ○ *bad news*
2 serious: *a bad injury* ○ *bad flooding*
3 not bad quite good: *"What's his work like?" "Not bad."*
4 be bad for someone to be harmful for someone: *Too much fat is bad for you.*
5 feel bad to feel guilty: *I felt bad about leaving her on her own.*
6 A bad heart, leg, or other body part hurts or does not work well.
7 evil: *She's not a bad person.*
8 Food that is bad is not fresh.

badge /bædʒ/ *noun*
a small thing with a picture or words on it that you put on your clothes

badger /'bædʒəʳ/ *noun*
a wild animal with black and white fur that lives under the ground

badger

badly /'bædli/ *adv*
1 very much: *He was badly hurt in the accident.*
2 not well: *He behaved very badly.* ○ *They played badly in the first half.*

badminton /'bædmɪntən/ *noun* **[no plural]**
a sport in which two or four people hit a light object with feathers over a net

bag /bæg/ *noun*
a container used for carrying things: *a paper bag* ○ *I was carrying three bags of shopping.*

bagel /'beɪgəl/ *noun*
a small piece of bread in the shape of a ring.

bagel

baggage /'bægɪdʒ/ *noun* **[no plural]**
all the cases and bags that you take with you when you travel

baggy /'bægi/ *adj* **(baggier, baggiest)**
Baggy clothes are big and loose.

bait /beɪt/ *noun* **[no plural]**
food that is used to attract and catch animals or fish

bake /beɪk/ *verb* (*present participle* **baking**, *past* **baked)**
to cook something such as bread or a cake in an oven

baker /'beɪkəʳ/ *noun*
someone who makes and sells bread, cakes, etc

bakery /'beɪkəri/ *noun* (*plural* **bakeries)**
a shop where you can buy bread, cakes, etc

balance¹ /'bæləns/ *noun* **[no plural]**
when weight is spread in such a way that something does not fall over: *I **lost my balance** and fell off the bike.*

balance² /'bæləns/ *verb* (*present participle* **balancing**, *past* **balanced)**
1 to be in a position where you will not fall to either side, or to put something in this position: *She was trying to balance a book on her head.*
2 to give the same amount of attention to each thing: *I try to balance work and family commitments.*

balcony /'bælkəni/ *noun* (*plural* **balconies)**
a small area on the outside wall of a high building where you can stand or sit

bald /bɔːld/ *adj*
with little or no hair: *John started to **go bald** at an early age.*

bald

ball /bɔːl/ *noun*
1 a round object that you throw, kick, or hit in a game, or something with this shape: *a tennis ball* ○ *a ball of string*
2 a formal occasion where a lot of people dance

ballet /'bæleɪ/ *noun* **[no plural]**
a type of dancing that is done in a theatre and tells a story, usually with music

ballet

balloon /bə'luːn/ *noun*

a round rubber thing filled with air or gas that floats in the air

ballot /ˈbælət/ *noun*
a secret written vote

ballpoint pen /ˌbɔːlpɔɪntˈpen/ *noun*
a pen with a small ball in the end that rolls ink onto the paper

bamboo /bæmˈbuː/ *noun* **[no plural]**
a tall plant with hard, hollow stems, often used for making furniture

bamboo

ban¹ /bæn/ *verb* (*present participle* **banning**, *past* **banned**)
to officially stop a person or many people from doing something: *She thinks boxing should be banned.*

ban² /bæn/ *noun*
an official rule that people must not do or use something: *There is a* ***ban on*** *developing land around the city.*

banana /bəˈnɑːnə/ *noun*
a long, white fruit with a yellow skin

band /bænd/ *noun*
1 a group of musicians who play modern music together: *a jazz band*
2 a line of a different colour or design
3 a piece of material put around something: *an elastic band*

band

bandage¹ /ˈbændɪdʒ/ *noun*
a long piece of cloth that you tie around a part of the body that is hurt

bandage² /ˈbændɪdʒ/ *verb* (*present participle* **bandaging**, *past* **bandaged**)
to put a bandage around a part of the body

Band-Aid /ˈbændeɪd/ *US trademark* (*UK* **plaster**) *noun*
a small piece of sticky material that you put on a cut on your body

bang¹ /bæŋ/ *noun*
1 a sudden, loud noise: *The door shut with a bang.*
2 when you hit part of your body on something hard: *She had a nasty bang on her head.*

bang² /bæŋ/ *verb*
1 to make a loud noise by hitting something against something hard: *We heard the door bang.*
2 to hit part of your body against something hard: *Ted fell and banged his head.*

bangs /bæŋz/ *plural noun US* (*UK* **fringe**)
hair that is cut short and straight at the top of someone's face

banish /ˈbænɪʃ/ *verb*
to send someone away from a place as a punishment

banister /ˈbænɪstəʳ/ *noun*
a long piece of wood that you hold as you go up or down stairs

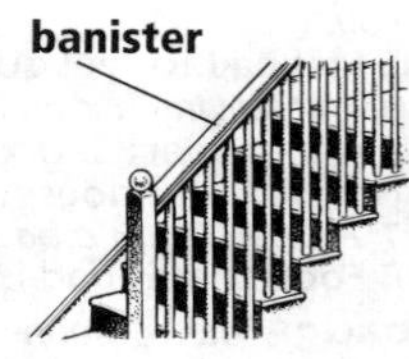

bank¹ /bæŋk/ *noun*
1 an organization or place where you can save and borrow money: *I must remember to go to the bank on my way home.*
2 the land along the side of a river

bank² /bæŋk/ *verb*
to put or keep money in a bank: *Who do you* ***bank with****?*

bank on someone/something *phrasal verb*
to depend on someone doing something or something happening: *Chrissie might arrive on time, but I wouldn't bank on it.*

bank account /ˈbæŋk əˌkaʊnt/ *noun*
an arrangement with a bank to keep your money there and take it out when you need it

banker /ˈbæŋkəʳ/ *noun*
someone who has an important job in a bank

bank holiday /ˌbæŋk ˈhɒlədeɪ/ *noun UK*
an official holiday when all banks and most shops and offices are closed: *Spring bank holiday*

banking /ˈbæŋkɪŋ/ *noun* **[no plural]**
the business of operating a bank

banknote /ˈbæŋknəʊt/ *UK* (*US* **bill**) *noun*
a piece of paper money

bankrupt /ˈbæŋkrʌpt/ *adj*
not able to continue in business because you owe too much money:

*He **went bankrupt** after only a year in business.*

banner /ˈbænəʳ/ *noun*
a long piece of cloth, often stretched between poles, with words or a sign written on it

baptism /ˈbæptɪzᵊm/ *noun*
a Christian ceremony in which water is put on someone to show that they are a member of the Church

baptize/bæpˈtaɪz/ *verb* (*present participle* **baptizing**, *past* **baptized**)
to do a baptism ceremony for someone

bar[1] /bɑːʳ/ *noun*
1 a place where alcoholic drinks are sold and drunk: *I met him in a bar in Soho.*
2 a small block of something solid: *a chocolate bar*
3 a long, thin piece of metal or wood: *There were bars on the windows.*

bar[2] /bɑːʳ/ *verb* (*present participle* **barring**, *past* **barred**)
to officially stop someone doing something or going somewhere: *The court **barred** him **from** contacting his children.*

barbecue /ˈbɑːbɪkjuː/ *noun*
1 a party at which you cook food over a fire outdoors
2 a metal frame for cooking food over a fire outdoors

barbecue

barbed wire /ˌbɑːbdˈwaɪəʳ/ *noun* **[no plural]**
strong wire with short, sharp points on it to keep people out of a place: *a barbed wire fence*

barbed wire

barber /ˈbɑːbəʳ/ *noun*
someone whose job is to cut men's hair
• **barber's** *noun*
a shop where men have their hair cut

bar code /ˈbɑːʳ ˌkəʊd/ *noun*
a row of black lines on something you buy, that a computer reads to find the price

bare /beəʳ/ *adj*
1 not covered by clothes: *bare legs*
2 empty: *a bare room* ○ *The cupboard was bare.*

barefoot /beəˈfʊt/ *adj, adv*
not wearing any shoes or socks: *They ran barefoot along the beach.*

barely /ˈbeəli/ *adv*
only just: *He was barely alive when they found him.*

bargain[1] /ˈbɑːgɪn/ *noun*
something that is sold for less than its usual price: *At $8.95, it's a bargain.*

bargain[2] /ˈbɑːgɪn/ *verb*
to try to agree how much you will pay for something: *We **bargained over** the price.*

barge /bɑːdʒ/ *noun*
a long, narrow boat with a flat bottom that is used to carry things

bark[1] /bɑːk/ *noun*
1 **[no plural]** the hard surface of a tree
2 the sound that a dog makes

bark[2] /bɑːk/ *verb*
If a dog barks, it makes loud, short sounds.

barley /ˈbɑːli/ *noun* **[no plural]**
a type of grain used for making food and alcoholic drinks

barmaid /ˈbɑːmeɪd/ *noun UK*
a woman who serves drinks in a bar

barman /ˈbɑːmən/ *noun UK*
a man who serves drinks in a bar

barn /bɑːn/ *noun*
a large building on a farm where crops or animals are kept

barrel /ˈbærᵊl/ *noun*
1 a large, round container for storing liquids such as oil or wine
2 the tube in a gun that the bullet shoots out of

barrel

barrier /ˈbæriəʳ/ *noun*
a wall that stops people from going into an area: *Police erected barriers to hold back the crowd.*

base[1] /beɪs/ *noun*
1 the bottom part of something: *I felt a sharp pain at the base of my back.*
2 the main place where a person lives or works, or from where they do things: *Keswick is an excellent base*

for exploring the Lake District.

base[2] /beɪs/ *verb* (*present participle* **basing**, *past* **based**)

be based at/in If you are based at or in somewhere, that is where you live or work: *The company is based in Geneva.*

base something on something *phrasal verb*
If you base something on facts or ideas, you use those facts or ideas to develop it: *Her latest book is based on a true story.*

baseball /ˈbeɪsbɔːl/ *noun* **[no plural]**
a game in which two teams try to win points by hitting a ball and running around four fixed points

basement /ˈbeɪsmənt/ *noun*
part of a building that is under the level of the ground

bases[1] /ˈbeɪsɪz/
plural of base

bases[2] /ˈbeɪsiːz/
plural of basis

basic /ˈbeɪsɪk/ *adj*
1 being the main or most important part of something: *These are basic needs, such as food and water.*
2 very simple, with nothing special added: *The software is very basic.*

basically /ˈbeɪsɪkᵊli/ *adv*
1 in the most important ways: *The two PCs are basically the same.*
2 used before you explain something simply: *Basically, there aren't enough people.*

basil /ˈbæzᵊl/ *noun* **[no plural]**
a plant whose leaves are used to add flavour to food

basin /ˈbeɪsᵊn/ *noun UK*
1 the bowl that is fixed to the wall in a bathroom, where you can wash your hands
2 a big bowl

basis /ˈbeɪsɪs/ *noun* (*plural* **bases** /ˈbeɪsiːz/)
1 on a daily/monthly/regular basis how often something is done: *Meetings are held on a weekly basis.*
2 a situation or idea from which something can develop: *Dani's essay can serve as **a basis for** our discussion.*

basket /ˈbɑːskɪt/ *noun*
a container for carrying things, made of thin pieces of plastic, metal, or wood: *a shopping basket*

basketball /ˈbɑːskɪtbɔːl/ *noun* **[no plural]**
a game in which two teams try to win points by throwing a ball through a high net

bat[1] /bæt/ *noun*
1 a piece of wood used to hit the ball in some sports
2 a small animal like a mouse with wings that flies at night

bat[2] /bæt/ *verb* (*present participle* **batting**, *past* **batted**)
to try to hit a ball with a bat

batch /bætʃ/ *noun* (*plural* **batches**)
a group of things or people that are dealt with at the same time: *I've looked through the first **batch of** application forms.*

bath[1] /bɑːθ/ *noun*
1 *UK* the container that you fill with water and sit in to wash your body
2 when you wash your body in a bath: *I'll just **have a** quick **bath**.*

bath[2] /bɑːθ/ *verb UK*
to wash yourself or someone else in a bath: *I was just bathing the baby.*

bathe /beɪð/ *verb* (*present participle* **bathing**, *past* **bathed**)
1 to wash yourself in a bath
2 to swim

bathing suit /ˈbeɪðɪŋ ˌsuːt/ *noun*
a piece of clothing that you wear for swimming

bathroom /ˈbɑːθruːm/ *noun*
1 a room with a bath, sink (= bowl for washing), and often a toilet
2 go to the bathroom *US* to use the toilet

bathtub /ˈbɑːθtʌb/ *noun US*
the container that you fill with water and sit in to wash your body

batter /ˈbætəʳ/ *verb*

a b c d e f g h i j k l m n o p q r s t u v w x y z

to hit someone or something hard, many times

battery /ˈbætᵊri/ *noun* (*plural* **batteries**)
an object that provides electricity for things such as radios, toys, or cars

battery

battle[1] /ˈbætl/ *noun*
a fight between two armies in a war: *the Battle of Waterloo*

battle[2] /ˈbætl/ *verb* (*present participle* **battling**, *past* **battled**)
to try very hard to do something difficult: *Both teams* ***are battling for*** *a place in the final.*

bay /beɪ/ *noun*
an area of coast where the land curves in: *a sandy bay*

BC /biːˈsiː/
used to show that a particular year came before the birth of Christ: *331 BC*

be[1] *strong form* /biː/ *weak forms* /bi, bɪ/ *verb* (*present participle* **being**, *past tense* **was**, *past participle* **been**)
1 used to describe someone or something: *I'm Maria* (= I am Maria). ○ *I'm sixteen.* ○ *He's German* (= He is German). ○ *They were ill.* ○ *Be quiet!*
2 there is/there are used to show that someone or something exists: *There are three of us.* ○ *Is there a bank near here?*
3 used to show where someone or something is: *She's in the kitchen.*
4 it is/it was, etc used to give a fact or your opinion about something: *It's a good idea.* ○ *It's a big problem.*

be[2] *strong form* /biː/ *weak forms* /bi, bɪ/ *verb*
1 used with the -ing form of other verbs to describe actions that are still happening: *Are you leaving?* ○ *He was talking to Andrea.*
2 used with other verbs to describe actions that will happen in the future: *I'm going to France next week.* ○ *I'll be coming back on Tuesday.*
3 used with the past participle of other verbs to show that something happens to someone or something: *He was injured in a car crash.* ○ *The results will be announced next week.*

beach /biːtʃ/ *noun* (*plural* **beaches**)
an area of sand or rocks next to the sea

beach

bead /biːd/ *noun*
a small, round ball of glass, plastic, or wood that is used for making jewellery

beads

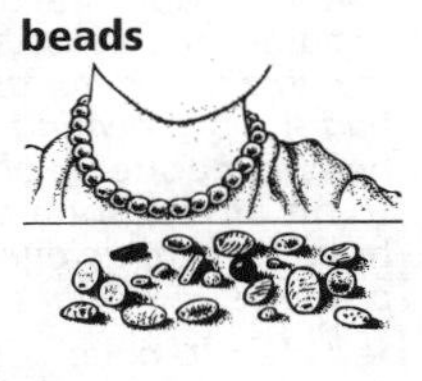

beak /biːk/ *noun*
the hard part of a bird's mouth

beam[1] /biːm/ *noun*
1 a line of light shining from something: *a laser beam*
2 a long, thick piece of wood that supports a building

beam[2] /biːm/ *verb*
to smile very happily: *The baby* ***beamed at*** *me.*

bean /biːn/ *noun*
1 a seed or seed case of some climbing plants, that is used as food: *soya beans*
2 a plant seed used to make coffee and chocolate: *coffee beans*

bear[1] /beəʳ/ *verb* (*present participle* **bearing**, *past tense* **bore**, *past participle* **borne**)
1 to accept someone or something bad: *I* ***can't bear*** *her* (= I dislike her very much). ○ *The pain was too much to bear.*
2 to support something: *I don't think that chair will bear his weight.*
bear with someone *phrasal verb*
to wait while someone does something: *If you'll bear with me a moment, I'll just find your details.*

bear[2] /beəʳ/ *noun*
a large, strong, wild animal with thick fur

bear

beard /bɪəd/ *noun*
the hair that grows on a man's chin (= the bottom of his face)

beast /biːst/ *noun*
formal

a b c d e f g h i j k l m n o p q r s t u v w x y z

an animal, especially a large or wild one

beat[1] /biːt/ *verb* (*present participle* **beating**, *past tense* **beat**, *past participle* **beaten**)
1 to defeat someone in a competition: *Our team beat Germany 3-1.*
2 to hit against something hard, making a regular sound: *Rain beat against the windows.*
3 When your heart beats, it makes regular movements and sounds: *By the time the doctor arrived, his heart had stopped beating.*
beat someone up *phrasal verb*
to hit or kick someone until they are hurt: *He beat up one of the other prisoners.*

beat[2] /biːt/ *noun*
1 a regular sound that is made by your heart or by something hitting a surface: *a heart beat* ○ *the beat of a drum*
2 the main rhythm of a piece of music: *I like music with a strong beat.*

beautiful /ˈbjuːtɪfəl/ *adj*
1 very attractive: *a beautiful woman* ○ *beautiful scenery*
2 very pleasant: *beautiful music* ○ *It's a beautiful day* (= the sun is shining).
• **beautifully** *adv She sings beautifully.*

beauty /ˈbjuːti/ *noun* **[no plural]**
the quality of being beautiful: *The area is famous for its natural beauty.*

became /bɪˈkeɪm/
past tense of become

because /bɪˈkɒz/ *conjunction*
used to give a reason for something: *I'm calling because I need to ask you something.*

because of /bɪˈkɒzəv/ *preposition*
as a result of someone or something: *I'm only here because of you.*

become /bɪˈkʌm/ *verb* (*present participle* **becoming**, *past tense* **became**, *past participle* **become**)
1 to begin to be something: *They became great friends.*
2 what became of? something you say when you want to know what has happened to someone: *What became of your friend Harry?*

bed /bed/ *noun*
1 a piece of furniture that you sleep on: *What time did you* ***go to bed*** *last night?* ○ *She's still* ***in bed.*** ○ *Have you* ***made the bed*** (= tidied the bed after you have slept in it)*?*
2 the ground at the bottom of the sea or a river: *the sea bed*

bed and breakfast /ˌbed ænd ˈbrekfəst/ *noun*
a house where you pay for a room to sleep in for the night and a meal in the morning

bedclothes /ˈbedkləʊðz/ *plural noun*
bedding

bedding /ˈbedɪŋ/ *noun* **[no plural]**
the sheets and other pieces of cloth that cover you and keep you warm in bed

bedroom /ˈbedruːm/ *noun*
a room used for sleeping in

bedspread /ˈbedspred/ *noun*
a cloth cover that is put over a bed

bedtime /ˈbedtaɪm/ *noun*
the time that you usually go to bed

bee /biː/ *noun*
a yellow and black insect that makes honey (= sweet, sticky food)

beef /biːf/ *noun* **[no plural]**
the meat of a cow: *roast beef*

beefburger /ˈbiːfˌbɜːgəʳ/ *noun UK*
meat in a round, flat shape, that you eat between bread

beehive /ˈbiːhaɪv/ *noun*
a special container where people keep bees

been /biːn, bɪn/ *verb*
1 *past participle of* be: *It's been so hot today.*
2 have been to to have gone to a place and come back: *Have you ever been to Thailand?*

beep /biːp/ *verb*
If a machine beeps, it makes a short, high noise
• **beep** *noun*

beer /bɪəʳ/ *noun* **[no plural]**
an alcoholic drink made from grain: *a pint of beer*

beetle /ˈbiːtl/ *noun*
an insect with a hard, usually black, shiny body

beetroot /ˈbiːtruːt/ *UK* (*US* **beet**) *noun*
a round, dark red vegetable, that is usually cooked and eaten cold

before[1] /bɪˈfɔːʳ/ *preposition*

1 earlier than something or someone: *a week before Christmas* ○ *She arrived before me.*
2 in a position in front of someone or something: *I've never performed this before an audience.*

before² /bɪ'fɔːʳ/ *conjunction*
earlier than the time when something happens: *He was a teacher before he became famous.*

before³ /bɪ'fɔːʳ/ *adv*
at an earlier time: *I've never seen her before.*

beforehand /bɪ'fɔːhænd/ *adv*
before a particular time or event: *Did you know beforehand what would happen?*

beg /beg/ *verb* (*present participle* **begging,** *past* **begged)**
1 to ask someone for food or money, because you do not have any: *Young children were begging on the streets.*
2 to ask for something in a strong and emotional way: *I* ***begged*** *him not* ***to*** *leave.*

began /bɪ'gæn/
past tense of begin

beggar /'begəʳ/ *noun*
a poor person who asks other people for money and food

begin /bɪ'gɪn/ *verb* (*present participle* **beginning,** *past tense* **began,** *past participle* **begun)**
1 to start to do something: *She* ***began to*** *cry.*
2 to start to happen: *What time does the film begin?*
3 **begin with something** to have something at the start: *Local phone numbers begin with 018.*
4 **to begin with** at the start of a situation: *To begin with, I was very nervous.*

beginner /bɪ'gɪnəʳ/ *noun*
someone who is learning or doing something for the first time: *a Spanish class for beginners*

beginning /bɪ'gɪnɪŋ/ *noun*
the start of something: *We met at the* ***beginning of*** *1998.*

begun /bɪ'gʌn/
past participle of begin

behalf /bɪ'hɑːf/ *noun*
on behalf of someone for someone or instead of someone: *Will you accept the prize on my behalf?*

behave /bɪ'heɪv/ *verb* (*present participle* **behaving,** *past* **behaved)**
1 to do or say things in a particular way: *He behaved very badly.* ○ *You're behaving like a child!*
2 **behave yourself** to be polite and not make a situation difficult: *Did the children behave themselves?*

behaviour /bɪ'heɪvjəʳ/ *noun* **[no plural]**
the way that you behave: *good/bad behaviour*

behind¹ /bɪ'haɪnd/ *preposition*
1 at or to the back of someone or something: *Close the door behind you.* ○ *There's a hotel behind the train station.*
2 slower or less successful than someone or something: *Our team is 3 points behind the winners.*
3 giving your help or support to someone: *The group is 100 percent behind her.*

behind² /bɪ'haɪnd/ *adv*
1 at or to the back of someone or something: *Somebody pulled me from behind.*
2 in the place where someone or something was before: *When we got to the restaurant, I realized that I had* ***left*** *my purse* ***behind.***

beige /beɪʒ/ *noun* **[no plural]**
a pale brown colour
● **beige** *adj*

being¹ /'biːɪŋ/ *noun*
a living person or imaginary creature: *human beings*

being² /'biːɪŋ/
present participle of be

belief /bɪ'liːf/ *noun*
1 an idea that you are certain is true: *political beliefs*
2 **[no plural]** when you believe that something is true or real: *my belief in God*

believable /bɪ'liːvəbl/ *adj*
If something is believable, you can believe that it could be true or real.
➲Opposite **unbelievable**

believe /bɪ'liːv/ *verb* (*present participle* **believing,** *past* **believed)**
1 to think that something is true, or that what someone says is true: *She says she's only thirty but I don't believe it.* ○ *Do you believe him?*

2 to think something, although you are not completely sure: *The murderer is believed to be in his thirties.*
3 believe it or not used to say that something surprising is true: *He even remembered my birthday, believe it or not.*

believe in something *phrasal verb*
to be certain that something exists: *Do you believe in life after death?*

bell /bel/ *noun*
1 a hollow, metal object, shaped like a cup, that makes a ringing sound: *church bells*
2 an electrical object that makes a ringing sound when you press a switch: *Please ring the bell for attention.*

belong /bɪ'lɒŋ/ *verb*
to be in the right place: *That chair belongs in the dining room.*

belong to someone *phrasal verb*
If something belongs to you, you own it: *This necklace belonged to my grandmother.*

belong to something *phrasal verb*
to be a member of an organization: *We belong to the same health club.*

belongings /bɪ'lɒŋɪŋz/ *plural noun*
the things that you own: *I took a few* ***personal belongings*** *with me.*

below /bɪ'ləʊ/ *adv, preposition*
1 in a lower position than someone or something else: *He could hear people shouting below his window.*
2 less than an amount or level: *The temperature there rarely drops below 22°C.*

belt /belt/ *noun*
a thin piece of leather or plastic that you wear around the middle of your body

belt

bench /benʃ/ *noun* (*plural* **benches**)
a long seat for two or more people, usually made of wood: *a park bench*

bend[1] /bend/ *verb* (*present participle* **bending**, *past* **bent**)
1 to move your body or part of your body so that it is not straight: *Bend your knees when lifting heavy objects.*
2 to become curved, or to make something become curved: *The road bent to the left.*

bend[2] /bend/ *noun*
a curved part of something: *a bend in the road/river*

beneath /bɪ'niːθ/ *adv, prep*
under something, or in a lower position than something: *He hid the letter beneath a pile of papers.*

benefit[1] /'benɪfɪt/ *noun*
1 something good that helps you: *I've had* ***the benefit of*** *a happy childhood.*
2 for someone's benefit in order to help someone: *We bought the piano for the children's benefit.*

benefit[2] /'benɪfɪt/ *verb*
to help someone: *These changes will benefit all staff.*

bent[1] /bent/ *adj*
curved and not now straight or flat: *The metal bars were bent and twisted.*

bent[2] /bent/
past of bend

berry /'beri/ *noun* (*plural* **berries**)
a small, round fruit on some plants and trees

beside /bɪ'saɪd/ *preposition*
next to someone or something: *She lay down beside him.*

besides[1] /bɪ'saɪdz/ *preposition*
in addition to: *Do you play any other sports besides football?*

besides[2] /bɪ'saɪdz/ *adv*
1 used to give another reason for something: *She won't mind if you're late – besides, it's not your fault.*
2 in addition to: *Besides looking after the children, she also runs a successful business.*

best[1] /best/ *adj (superlative of* **good***)*
better than any other: *She's one of our best students.* ○ *Susie's my best friend.*

best[2] /best/ *adv (superlative of* **well***)*
1 most, or more than any other: *Which of the songs did you like best?*
2 in the most suitable or satisfactory way: *I sleep best with the windows open.*

best[3] /best/ *noun*
1 the best someone or something that is better than any other: *He's the best of the new players.*
2 do your best to try very hard to do something

best man /ˌbest 'mæn/ *noun*
a man who is chosen to help another man on his wedding day

bet[1] /bet/ *verb* (*present participle*

betting, *past* **bet)**
1 to risk money on the result of a game or competition: *I* ***bet*** *him a dollar* ***that*** *I was right.*
2 I bet *informal* something you say to show that you are certain something is true or will happen: *I bet he's late.*

bet² /bet/ *noun*
when you risk money on the result of a game or competition: *She won her bet.*

betray /bɪˈtreɪ/ *verb*
to behave in a dishonest way to someone who trusts you

better¹ /ˈbetəʳ/ *adj*
1 *(comparative of* **good***)* of a higher quality or more enjoyable than someone or something else: *He got a better job in the States.* ○ *Her English is* ***getting better*** (= improving).
2 less ill than before: *I feel much better.* ○ *I hope you* ***get better*** *soon.*

better² /ˈbetəʳ/ *adv*
1 *(comparative of* **well***)* more, or in a more successful way: *I'd like to get to know him better.* ○ *Helen did much* ***better than*** *me in the exam.*
2 you had better do something used in order to say what someone should do: *You'd better hurry or you'll miss the train.*

between /bɪˈtwiːn/ *preposition*
1 in the space that separates two places, people, or things: *The town lies halfway between Florence and Rome.*
2 in the period of time that separates two events or times: *The shop is closed for lunch between 12.30 and 1.30.*
3 involving two or more groups of people: *Tonight's game is between the New Orleans Saints and the Los Angeles Rams.*
4 connecting two or more places or things: *the train service between Glasgow and Edinburgh*
5 used when comparing two people or things: *What's the* ***difference between*** *these two cameras?*
6 shared by a particular number of people: *We shared the cake between the four of us.*
7 If something is between two amounts, it is larger than the first amount but smaller than the second: *The temperature will be between 20 and 25 degrees today.*
8 If you choose between two things, you choose one thing or the other.

beware /bɪˈweəʳ/ *verb*
used in order to warn someone to be careful: ***Beware of*** *the dog.*

beyond /biˈɒnd/ *preposition*
1 on the other side of something: *Our house is just beyond the bridge.*
2 If something is beyond you, you cannot understand it: *It's beyond me why anyone would want to buy that house.*

bible /ˈbaɪbl/ *noun*
the Bible the holy book of the Christian and Jewish religions

bicycle /ˈbaɪsɪkl/ *noun*
a vehicle with two wheels that you sit on and move by turning the two pedals (= parts you press with your feet) ➲See colour picture **Sports 2** on page Centre 16

bicycle

bid¹ /bɪd/ *noun*
1 an attempt to do something good: *a successful* ***bid for*** *re-election*
2 an offer to pay a particular amount of money for something: *I made a* ***bid*** *of $150* ***for*** *the painting.*

bid² /bɪd/ *verb (present participle* **bidding,** *past* **bid)**
to offer to pay an amount of money for something: *They* ***bid*** *$500 million* ***for*** *the company.*

big /bɪg/ *adj*
1 large in size or amount: *I come from a big family.* ○ *We're looking for a bigger house.* ➲Opposite **small** *or* **little**
2 important or serious: *Buying that car was a big mistake.*
3 your big brother/sister *informal* your older brother/sister

bike /baɪk/ *noun*
informal short for bicycle

bikini /bɪˈkiːni/ *noun*
a piece of clothing with two parts that women wear for swimming ➲See colour picture **Clothes** on page Centre 5

bikini

a b c d e f g h i j k l m n o p q r s t u v w x y z

bilingual /baɪˈlɪŋgwəl/ *adj*
using or able to speak two languages: *a bilingual dictionary* ○ *She's bilingual.*

bill /bɪl/ *noun*
1 a piece of paper that tells you how much you must pay for something: *Have you* ***paid the*** *electricity* ***bill****?*
2 *US* (*UK* **note**) a piece of paper money: *a five dollar bill*

billfold /ˈbɪlfəʊld/ *US* (*UK* **wallet**) *noun*
a small, flat container for carrying paper money and credit cards (= plastic cards used for paying with)

billion /ˈbɪliən/
the number 1,000,000,000

bin /bɪn/ *noun UK*
a container that is used to put waste in: *I threw it in the bin.* ➲See colour picture **The Office** on page Centre 12

bind /baɪnd/ *verb* (*present participle* **binding,** *past* **bound)**
to tie something together with string, rope, etc: *His hands were bound behind his back.*

binoculars /bɪˈnɒkjələz/ *plural noun*
a piece of equipment for looking at things that are far away, made from two tubes with glass at the ends

binoculars

biography /baɪˈɒgrəfi/ *noun* (*plural* **biographies)**
the story of a person's life written by another person
• **biographical** /ˌbaɪəʊˈgræfɪkəl/ *adj*
about someone's life: *biographical information*

biology /baɪˈɒlədʒi/ *noun* **[no plural]**
the study of living things
• **biologist** *noun*
a scientist who studies biology

bird /bɜːd/ *noun*
an animal that has wings and feathers and is usually able to fly

bird

Biro /ˈbaɪərəʊ/ *noun UK trademark*
a pen with a small ball in the end that rolls ink onto the paper

birth /bɜːθ/ *noun*
1 give birth to produce a baby from your body: *She gave birth to twins.*
2 the time when a baby is born: *a difficult birth* ○ *What's your* ***date of birth*** (= the date when you were born)?

birthday /ˈbɜːθdeɪ/ *noun*
the day of the year on which someone was born: *Her birthday is on March the eighteenth.* ○ *Happy Birthday!*

biscuit /ˈbɪskɪt/ *noun*
UK a thin, flat cake that is dry and usually sweet ➲See colour picture **Food** on page Centre 7

biscuit

bishop /ˈbɪʃəp/ *noun*
an important priest in some Christian churches: *the Bishop of Oxford*

bit[1] /bɪt/ *noun*
1 a small amount or piece of something: *I wrote it down on a bit of paper.* ○ *There's a little bit more pasta left.*
2 a bit slightly: *It was a bit too expensive.*
3 quite a bit *informal* a lot: *He does quite a bit of travelling.*
4 bit by bit gradually: *She saved up the money, bit by bit.*
5 a unit of information in a computer

bit[2] /bɪt/
past tense of bite

bite[1] /baɪt/ *verb* (*present participle* **biting,** *past tense* **bit,** *past participle* **bitten)**
to cut something using your teeth: *She* ***bit into*** *an apple.* ○ *He was bitten by a dog.*

bite[2] /baɪt/ *noun*
1 a piece taken from food when you bite it: *She* ***took a bite*** *from her pizza.*
2 an injury caused when an animal or insect bites you: *mosquito bites*

bitten /ˈbɪtən/
past participle of bite

bitter /ˈbɪtəʳ/ *adj*
1 angry and upset: *She is still very* ***bitter about*** *the way she was treated.*
2 having a strong, sour taste
3 very cold
• **bitterness** *noun* **[no plural]**

bizarre /bɪˈzɑːʳ/ *adj*
very strange and surprising: *bizarre behaviour*
• **bizarrely** *adv*

black[1] /blæk/ *adj*

1 being the colour of the sky on a dark night: *a black jacket* ➲See colour picture **Colours** on page Centre 6
2 Someone who is black has the dark skin typical of people from Africa: *black Americans*
3 funny about unpleasant or frightening subjects: *black comedy*
• **blackness** *noun* **[no plural]**

black² /blæk/ *noun*
1 the colour of the sky on a dark night: *She always dresses* ***in black***. ➲See colour picture **Colours** on page Centre 6
2 a black person

blackberry /ˈblækbᵊri/ *noun* (*plural* **blackberries**)
a small, soft, purple fruit with seeds

blackbird /ˈblækbɜːd/ *noun*
a bird with black feathers and a yellow beak

blackboard /ˈblækbɔːd/ *noun*
a large black or green board that teachers write on with chalk (= soft, white, rock)

blackcurrant /ˌblækˈkʌrᵊnt/ *noun UK*
a small, round, dark purple fruit

blackmail /ˈblækmeɪl/ *noun* **[no plural]**
when someone makes you do something by saying they will tell another person something secret if you do not
• **blackmail** *verb*

blade /bleɪd/ *noun*
1 the flat, sharp, metal part of a knife, tool, or weapon
2 a long, thin leaf of grass: *a blade of grass*

blame¹ /bleɪm/ *verb* (*present participle* **blaming**, *past* **blamed**)
to say that someone or something has done something bad: *She still* ***blames*** *him* ***for*** *Tony's death.*

blame² /bleɪm/ *noun* **[no plural]**
take the blame to be the person that everyone thinks has done something bad: *When a team loses it's always the manager who takes the blame.*

bland /blænd/ *adj*
1 boring and without excitement
2 If food is bland, it has no taste.

blank /blæŋk/ *adj*
1 with no writing, pictures, or sound: *a blank page* ○ *a blank tape*
2 go blank If your mind goes blank, you suddenly cannot remember or think of something.

blanket /ˈblæŋkɪt/ *noun*
1 a thick, warm cover that you sleep under
2 a thick layer of something: *a blanket of snow*

blast /blɑːst/ *noun*
1 an explosion: *a bomb blast*
2 a sudden, strong movement of air: *a blast of cold air*
3 full blast at the loudest or strongest level: *The heating was on full blast.*

blast-off /ˈblɑːstɒf/ *noun* **[no plural]**
when a spacecraft leaves the ground

blaze¹ /bleɪz/ *verb* (*present participle* **blazing**, *past* **blazed**)
to burn or shine very brightly or strongly: *the blazing sun*

blaze² /bleɪz/ *noun*
1 a large fire: *The blaze started in the hall.*
2 a blaze of colour a lot of bright colours: *The flowers were a blaze of colour outside her window.*

blazer /ˈbleɪzəʳ/ *noun*
a type of jacket, often worn as part of a school uniform

bleak /bliːk/ *adj*
1 sad and without hope: *a bleak film*
2 If a place is bleak, it is cold and empty: *a bleak landscape*
• **bleakness** *noun* **[no plural]**

bleat /bliːt/ *verb*
to make the noise of a sheep or goat
• **bleat** *noun*

bled /bled/
past of bleed

bleed *verb* (*present participle* **bleeding**, *past* **bled**)
to have blood coming out from a cut in your body

blend¹ /blend/ *verb*
1 to mix two or more things together completely: *Blend the sugar and butter till smooth.*
2 to look, sound, or taste good together: *The flavours blend very nicely.*

blend² /blend/ *noun*
two or more things that are put together: *Their music is a blend of jazz and African rhythms.*

bless /bles/ *verb*
1 to ask God to help or protect

a b c d e f g h i j k l m n o p q r s t u v w x y z

someone or something: *The priest blessed their marriage.*
2 Bless you! something you say when someone sneezes

blew /bluː/
past tense of blow

blind[1] /blaɪnd/ *adj*
not able to see: *She **went blind** after an accident.*
• **blindness** *noun* **[no plural]**

blind[2] /blaɪnd/ *noun*
a cover that you pull down over a window

blindfold /ˈblaɪndfəʊld/ *noun*
a piece of cloth that you put over someone's eyes so they cannot see
• **blindfold** *verb*
to put a blindfold on someone

blink /blɪŋk/ *verb*
to quickly close and open your eyes
• **blink** *noun*

blister /ˈblɪstəʳ/ *noun*
a raised area of skin which hurts, caused by rubbing or burning

blizzard /ˈblɪzəd/ *noun*
a storm with strong winds and snow

blob /blɒb/ *noun*
a small amount of a thick liquid: *a blob of cream* ➲See colour picture **Quantities** on page Centre 14

block[1] /blɒk/ *noun*
1 a solid piece of something, in the shape of a square: *a block of wood*
2 a group of buildings between streets: *They only live two blocks away from the school.*
3 a large building containing many apartments or offices: *a block of flats*

block[2] /blɒk/ *verb*
to stop anyone or anything from passing through a place: *A fallen tree blocked the road.*

blonde (*also* **blond**) /blɒnd/ *adj*
Blonde hair is yellow. ➲See colour picture **Hair** on page Centre 9

blood /blʌd/ *noun* **[no plural]**
the red liquid that flows around your body

bloom /bluːm/ *verb*
If a plant blooms, its flowers open.

blossom /ˈblɒsᵊm/ *noun*
a small flower, or the small flowers on a tree or plant: *cherry blossom*

blouse/blaʊz/ *noun*
a shirt that women wear

blow[1] /bləʊ/ *verb* (*present participle* **blowing**, *past tense* **blew**, *past participle* **blown**)
1 If the wind blows, it moves and makes currents of air: *A cool sea breeze was blowing.*
2 to force air out through your mouth: *I blew on my coffee to cool it.*
3 If the wind blows something somewhere, it makes it move in that direction: *The storm blew trees across the road.*
4 to make shapes out of something by blowing it: *to blow bubbles*
5 blow your nose to clear your nose by forcing air through it into a piece of paper
blow something out *phrasal verb*
to stop a flame burning by blowing on it: *Emma blew out the candle.*
blow something up *phrasal verb*
1 to destroy something with a bomb
2 to fill something with air: *Terrorists blew up an office building in the city.*

blow[2] /bləʊ/ *noun*
1 a shock or disappointment: *Losing his job was a terrible **blow to** him.*
2 a hard hit with a hand or heavy object
3 come to blows to fight or argue

blown /ˈbləʊn/
past participle of blow

blue[1] /bluː/ *adj*
being the same colour as the sky when there are no clouds: *a dark blue jacket* ➲See colour picture **Colours** on page Centre 6

blue[2] /bluː/ *noun*
1 the colour of the sky when there are no clouds ➲See colour picture **Colours** on page Centre 6
2 out of the blue If something happens out of the blue, you did not expect it.

blunt /blʌnt/ *adj*
1 not sharp: *a blunt knife*
2 saying exactly what you think without caring if you upset people
• **bluntness** *noun* **[no plural]**

blush /blʌʃ/ *verb*
If you blush, your face becomes red because you are embarrassed: *He **blushed with** shame.*
• **blush** *noun*

board[1] /bɔːd/ *noun*
1 a long, thin, flat piece of wood: *He*

a b c d e f g h i j k l m n o p q r s t u v w x y z

put some boards across the broken window.
2 a flat object or surface used for a particular purpose: *an ironing board* ○ *a chopping board* ○ *There's a notice on the board.* ○ *a chess board*
3 a group of people who control a company: *The board approved the sales plan.*
4 on board on a boat, train or aeroplane

board² /bɔːd/ *verb*
1 to get on a bus, boat, or aeroplane
2 If an aeroplane or train is boarding, passengers are getting onto it: *The plane is now boarding at gate 26.*

boast /bəʊst/ *verb*
to talk too proudly about something good that you have done or that you own: *I wish she would stop* ***boasting about*** *her exam results.*

boat /bəʊt/ *noun*
a vehicle for travelling on water: *a fishing/sailing boat*

bob /bɒb/ *verb* (*present participle* **bobbing,** *past* **bobbed)**
to move up and down quickly and gently: *boats bobbing in the harbour*

body /ˈbɒdi/ *noun* (*plural* **bodies)**
1 all of a person or animal: *the human body* ➲See colour picture **The Body** on page Centre 2
2 a dead person: *Police found the body in a field.*
3 the main part of a person or animal's body, not the head, arms, or legs: *a dog with a thin body and short legs*

boil /bɔɪl/ *verb*
1 If a liquid boils, or if you boil it, it reaches the temperature where bubbles rise up in it and it produces steam: *I'll boil some water for a cup of tea.* ○ *boiling water*
2 to cook food in water that is boiling: *Boil the pasta for 10 minutes.*

bold /bəʊld/ *adj*
1 brave: *It was a bold decision to go and live abroad.*
2 strong in colour or shape: *a bold design*
• **boldly** *adv*

bolt¹ /bəʊlt/ *noun*
1 a metal bar that you push across a door or window to lock it
2 a piece of metal that is used to fix things together by going through a nut (= piece of metal with a hole in it)

bolt² /bəʊlt/ *verb*
1 to lock a door or window with a bolt: *I bolted the door before going to bed.*
2 to suddenly run away: *The cat bolted out of the door when it saw the dog.*

bomb¹ /bɒm/ *noun*
a weapon that explodes and causes damage: *The* ***bomb went off*** (= exploded)*, destroying the building.*

bomb² /bɒm/ *verb*
to attack a place using bombs: *Factories were bombed during the war.*

bone /bəʊn/ *noun*
one of the hard, white pieces inside the body of a person or animal: *He broke a bone in his hand.*

bone

bonnet /ˈbɒnɪt/ *noun*
UK (*US* **hood)**
the metal cover of a car's engine ➲See colour picture **Car** on page Centre 3

book¹ /bʊk/ *noun*
1 a set of pages with writing on them fastened together in a cover: *I've just read a really good book.*
2 a set of pages fastened together in a cover and used for writing on: *an address book*

book² /bʊk/ *verb*
to arrange to use or do something at a time in the future: *I've booked a hotel room.* ○ *We've booked a trip to Spain for next month.*

bookcase /ˈbʊkkeɪs/ *noun*
a piece of furniture with shelves for putting books on ➲See colour picture **The Living Room** on page Centre 11

bookshop /ˈbʊkʃɒp/ *UK* (*US* **bookstore** /ˈbʊkstɔːʳ/) *noun*
a shop that sells books

boost /buːst/ *verb*
to increase or improve something: *Getting the job has boosted his confidence.*

boot /buːt/ *noun*
1 a shoe that covers your foot and part of your leg: *a pair of boots* ➲See colour picture **Clothes** on page Centre 5
2 *UK* (*US* **trunk)** a closed space at the

back of a car for storing things in ➲See colour picture **Car** on page Centre 3

border /ˈbɔːdəʳ/ *noun*
1 the line that separates two countries or states: *the border between France and Spain*
2 a line around the edge of something: *white plates with a blue border*

bore[1] /bɔːʳ/ *verb* (*present participle* **boring**, *past* **bored**)
to make someone feel bored

bore[2] /bɔːʳ/ *noun*
a situation that annoys you by causing difficulties: *It's a real bore not having a car.*

bore[3] /bɔːʳ/
past tense of bear

bored /bɔːd/ *adj*
tired and unhappy because something is not interesting or because you are doing nothing: *I'm **bored with** doing homework.*
• **boredom** /ˈbɔːdəm/ *noun* **[no plural]**
when you are bored

boring /ˈbɔːrɪŋ/ *adj*
not interesting or exciting: *a boring job* ○ *The film was so boring, I fell asleep.*

born /bɔːn/ *verb* **be born**
When a person or animal is born, they come out of their mother's body and start to exist: *She was born in London in 1973.*

borne /bɔːn/
past participle of bear

borrow /ˈbɒrəʊ/ *verb*
1 to use something that belongs to someone else: *Can I borrow a pen please?*
2 to take money from a bank and pay it back over a period of time

boss[1] /bɒs/ *noun* (*plural* **bosses**)
someone who is responsible for employees and tells them what to do

boss[2] /bɒs/ (*also* **boss around**) *verb*
to tell someone what they should do all the time: *She's always bossing her little brother around.*

bossy /ˈbɒsi/ *adj* **(bossier, bossiest)**
always telling other people what to do

both /bəʊθ/ *pronoun,determiner, quantifier*
used to talk about two people or things: *Both her parents are dead.* ○ ***Both of** my sisters are teachers.*

bother[1] /ˈbɒðəʳ/ *verb*
1 to annoy someone by talking to them when they are busy: *Don't bother your father when he's working.*
2 to worry or upset someone: *I'm used to living on my own – it doesn't bother me.*
3 to make the effort to do something: *He didn't even **bother to** call.*
4 can't be bothered *informal* If you can't be bothered to do something, you are too lazy or tired to do it: *I can't be bothered to iron my clothes.*

bother[2] /ˈbɒðəʳ/ *noun* **[no plural]**
trouble or problems: *"I'll drive you there – it's no bother!"*

bottle /ˈbɒtl/ *noun*
a container for liquids, usually made of glass or plastic, with a narrow top: *a bottle of wine*

bottom /ˈbɒtəm/ *noun*
1 the lowest part of something: *Click on the icon **at the bottom of** the page.*
2 the flat surface on the lowest side of something: *There was a price tag on **the bottom of** the box.*
3 the lowest position in a group or organization: *His team are **at the bottom of** the first division.*
4 the part of an area that is furthest from where you are: *the bottom of the garden*
5 the part of your body that you sit on

bought /bɔːt/
past of buy

bounce /baʊns/ *verb* (*present participle* **bouncing**, *past* **bounced**)
1 to hit a surface and then move quickly away, or to make something do this: *The ball bounced high into the air.*
2 to jump up and down many times on a soft surface: *The children love bouncing on the bed.*

bound[1] /baʊnd/ *adj*
bound to do something certain to do something, or certain to happen: *You're bound to feel nervous before a test.*

bound[2] /baʊnd/ *past of* **bind**

boundary /ˈbaʊndəri/ *noun* (*plural* **boundaries**)

a line that divides two areas or forms an edge around an area: *The mountains mark the* ***boundary between*** *the two countries.*

bouquet /bʊ'keɪ/ *noun*
flowers that are tied together in an attractive way

bow[1] /baʊ/ *verb*
to bend your head or body forward in order to show respect or to thank an audience: *The actors all bowed after the performance.*

bow[2] /baʊ/ *noun*
when you bow: *The actors came back on stage and* ***took a bow****.*

bow[3] /bəʊ/ *noun*
1 a knot with two circles that is used to tie shoes or as decoration
2 a long, thin piece of wood with hair stretched between the ends, used to play some musical instruments
3 a piece of curved wood with string fixed to both ends, used for shooting arrows

bowl /bəʊl/ *noun*
a round, deep dish used for holding soup and other food

box /bɒks/ *noun* (*plural* **boxes**)
a square or rectangular container: *a cardboard box* ○ *a* ***box of*** *chocolates*

boxer /'bɒksə^r/ *noun*
someone who does the sport of boxing

boxing

boxing /'bɒksɪŋ/ *noun* **[no plural]**
a sport in which two people hit each other while wearing big, leather gloves (= pieces of clothing for your hands) ➲See colour picture **Sports 1** on page Centre 15

Boxing Day /'bɒksiŋ ˌdeɪ/ *noun*
26 December, a public holiday in Britain and Canada

box office /'bɒks ˌɒfɪs/ *noun*
the place in a theatre or cinema where you buy tickets

boy /bɔɪ/ *noun*
a male child or young man: *We've got three children – a boy and two girls.*

boyfriend /'bɔɪfrend/ *noun*
a man or boy who someone is having a romantic relationship with

bra /brɑː/ *noun*
a piece of woman's underwear that supports the breasts ➲See colour picture **Clothes** on page Centre 5

brace /breɪs/ *noun*
a wire object that some children wear to make their teeth straight

bracelet /'breɪslət/ *noun*
a piece of jewellery that you wear around your wrist

brackets /'brækɪts/ *noun UK*
two curved lines ( ) used around information that is separate from the main part

brag /bræg/ *verb* (*present participle* **bragging,** *past* **bragged)**
to talk too much about the good things you have done or what you own: *He's always* ***bragging about*** *how much money he earns.*

braid /breɪd/ *noun US*
a single piece of hair made by twisting three thinner pieces over and under each other ➲See colour picture **Hair** on page Centre 9

brain

brain /breɪn/ *noun*
the part inside your head that controls your thoughts, feelings, and movements: *brain damage*

brake[1] /breɪk/ *noun*
the part of a vehicle that makes it stop or go more slowly

brake[2] /breɪk/ *verb* (*present participle* **braking,** *past* **braked)**
to make a car stop by using its brake

branch

branch /brɑːnʃ/ *noun* (*plural* **branches)**

a b c d e f g h i j k l m n o p q r s t u v w x y z

a b c d e f g h i j k l m n o p q r s t u v w x y z

1 one of the many parts of a tree that grows out from its trunk (= main, vertical part)
2 one of many shops or offices that are part of a company: *a bank with branches all over the country*

brand /brænd/ *noun*
a product that is made by a particular company: *Which brand of toothpaste do you use?*

brand new /ˌbrænd ˈnjuː/ *adj*
completely new: *a brand new sports car*

brandy /ˈbrændi/ *noun* **[no plural]**
a strong alcoholic drink made from wine

brass /brɑːs/ *noun* **[no plural]**
a shiny yellow metal: *a door with a brass handle*

brave /breɪv/ *adj* **(braver, bravest)**
not afraid of dangerous or difficult situations: *He died after a brave fight against cancer.*
• **bravely** *adv*

bravery /ˈbreɪvəri/ *noun* **[no plural]**
when someone is brave

bread

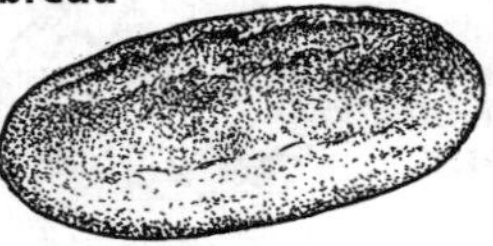
loaf of bread

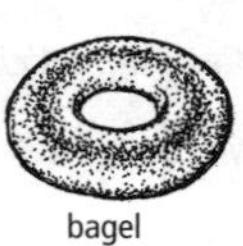
bagel

roll

bread /bred/ *noun* **[no plural]**
a basic food made by mixing and baking flour and water: *a slice of bread* ○ *a loaf of white bread*

break[1] /breɪk/ *verb* (*present participle* **breaking,** *past tense* **broke,** *past participle* **broken)**
1 to separate into two or more pieces, or to make something separate into two or more pieces: *They had to break a window to get in.*
2 to damage a bone in your body: *She broke her leg in the accident.*
3 to stop working or to make

break

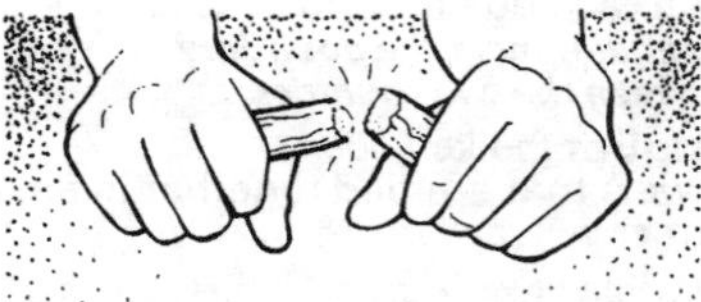

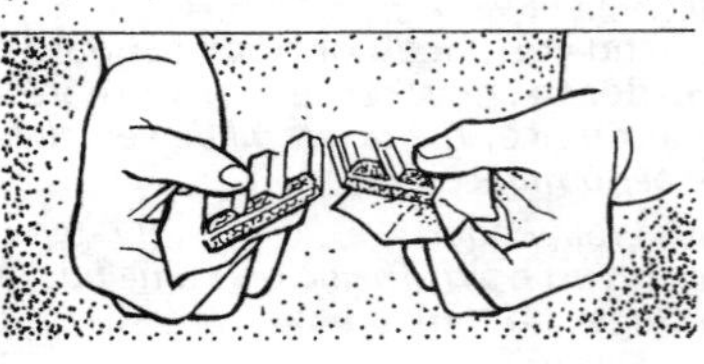

something stop working: *Who broke the video?*
4 to not do something that you should do: *I don't like to* ***break promises.***
5 break the law to do something that the law says you must not do
6 to stop an activity and have a short rest: *Let's* ***break for*** *five minutes and have a drink.*
7 When a boy's voice breaks, it starts to sound like a man's voice.

break down *phrasal verb*
If a car or machine breaks down, it stops working: *My car broke down on the way to work.*

break into something *phrasal verb*
to get into a building or car using force, usually to steal something: *Someone broke into the office and stole some computers.*

break up *phrasal verb*
1 to stop having a relationship: *He's just* ***broken up with*** *his girlfriend.*
2 *UK* When schools or colleges break up, the classes end and the holidays begin.

break[2] /breɪk/ *noun*
1 when you stop an activity for a short time, usually to rest: *a coffee break*
2 a holiday or period of time away from work or school: *a weekend break to Paris*

breakdown /ˈbreɪkdaʊn/ *noun*
1 a short period of mental illness
2 when a problem causes people to stop speaking: *a* ***breakdown in*** *the peace talks*
3 when a car stops working

breakfast /ˈbrekfəst/ *noun* **[no plural]**

the food you eat in the morning after you wake up

breast /brest/ *noun*
one of the two soft, round parts on a woman's chest

breaststroke /ˈbreststrəʊk/ *noun* **[no plural]**
a way of swimming in which you push your arms forward and then to the side, while kicking your legs

breath /breθ/ *noun*
1 [no plural] the air that comes out of your lungs: *His breath smells of garlic.*
2 when air goes into or out of your lungs: *She* ***took a deep breath*** *before she started.*
3 be out of breath to be breathing quickly because you have been running
4 hold your breath to keep air in your lungs and not let it out: *How long can you hold your breath under water?*

breathe /briːð/ *verb* (*present participle* **breathing,** *past* **breathed)**
to take air into and out of your lungs: *breathe in/out* ○ *breathe deeply*

bred /bred/
past of breed

breed[1] /briːd/ *noun*
a type of dog, sheep, pig, etc: *a rare breed of cattle*

breed[2] /briːd/ *verb* (*present participle* **breeding,** *past* **bred)**
1 If animals breed, they produce babies.
2 to keep animals in order to produce baby animals

breeze /briːz/ *noun*
a gentle wind: *a cool breeze*

bribe /braɪb/ *noun*
money or a present that you give to someone so that they will do something for you: *The politician was accused of accepting bribes from businessmen.*
• **bribe** *verb* (*present participle* **bribing,** *past* **bribed)**

brick /brɪk/ *noun*
a hard, rectangular block used for building walls: *a brick wall*

brick

bride /braɪd/ *noun*
a woman who is getting married

bridegroom /ˈbraɪdgruːm/ *noun*
a man who is getting married

bridesmaid /ˈbraɪdzmeɪd/ *noun*
a woman or girl who helps the bride on her wedding day

bridge /brɪdʒ/ *noun*
a structure that is built over a river or road so that people can go across it: *Brooklyn Bridge*

brief /briːf/ *adj*
1 lasting only for a short time: *a brief visit*
2 using only a few words: *a brief description*
• **briefly** *adv*: *They discussed the matter briefly.*

bridge

briefcase /ˈbriːfkeɪs/ *noun*
a flat, rectangular case with a handle for carrying documents or books

bright /braɪt/ *adj*
1 having a strong, light colour: *bright yellow/blue*
2 full of light or shining strongly: *bright sunshine*
3 intelligent: *He's a bright boy.*
• **brightness** *noun* **[no plural]**

brighten /ˈbraɪtᵊn/ *verb*
to become lighter or more colourful, or to make something become lighter or more colourful: *A picture or two would brighten up the room.*

brilliant /ˈbrɪliənt/ *adj*
1 *UK* very good: *We saw a brilliant film.*
2 very clever: *a brilliant scholar*
3 full of light or colour: *The sky was a brilliant blue.*

brim /brɪm/ *noun*
1 the flat part around the bottom of a hat
2 the top edge of a container: *He* ***filled*** *my glass* ***to the brim.***

bring /brɪŋ/ *verb* (*present participle*

a b c d e f g h i j k l m n o p q r s t u v w x y z

bringing, *past* **brought)**
to take someone or something with you when you go somewhere: *Did you bring an umbrella with you? ○ He brought me some flowers.*
bring someone up *phrasal verb*
to look after a child until he or she becomes an adult: *Her grandparents brought her up.*

brittle /ˈbrɪtl/ *adj*
hard but able to be broken easily: *brittle bones*

broad /brɔːd/ *adj*
1 wide: *broad shoulders*
2 including many different things: *a broad range of subjects*

broadcast¹ /ˈbrɔːdkɑːst/ *noun*
a television or radio programme: *a news broadcast*

broadcast² /ˈbrɔːdkɑːst/ *verb* (*present participle* **broadcasting,** *past* **broadcast)**
to send out a programme on television or radio: *The concert will be broadcast live next week.*

broke /brəʊk/
past tense of break

broken¹ /ˈbrəʊkən/ *adj*
1 damaged and separated into pieces: *broken glass*
2 with a damaged bone: *a broken leg*
3 not working: *The video's broken.*

broken² /ˈbrəʊkən/
past participle of break

bronze /brɒnz/ *noun* **[no plural]**
a shiny orange-brown metal

brooch /brəʊtʃ/ *noun* (*plural* **brooches)**
a piece of jewellery for women which is fixed onto clothes with a pin

broom /bruːm/ *noun*
a brush with a long handle used for cleaning the floor

brother /ˈbrʌðəʳ/ *noun*
a boy or man who has the same parents as you: *an older brother*

brother-in-law /ˈbrʌðərɪnlɔː/ *noun* (*plural* **brothers-in-law)**
the man married to your sister, or the brother of your husband or wife

brought /brɔːt/
past of bring

brown /braʊn/ *adj*
being the same colour as chocolate: *dark brown hair* ➲See colour picture **Colours** on page Centre 6
● **brown** *noun*
the colour brown

browser /ˈbraʊzəʳ/ *noun*
a computer program which allows you to look at pages on the Internet

bruise /bruːz/ *noun*
a dark area on your skin where you have been hurt: *He suffered cuts and bruises after falling off his bike.*
● **bruise** *verb* (*present participle* **bruising,** *past* **bruised)**
to make someone have a bruise: *He was badly bruised in the accident.*

brush¹ /brʌʃ/ *noun* (*plural* **brushes)**
an object made of short, thin pieces of plastic, wire, etc fixed to a handle and used to tidy hair, to clean, or to paint: *a stiff wire brush*

brush

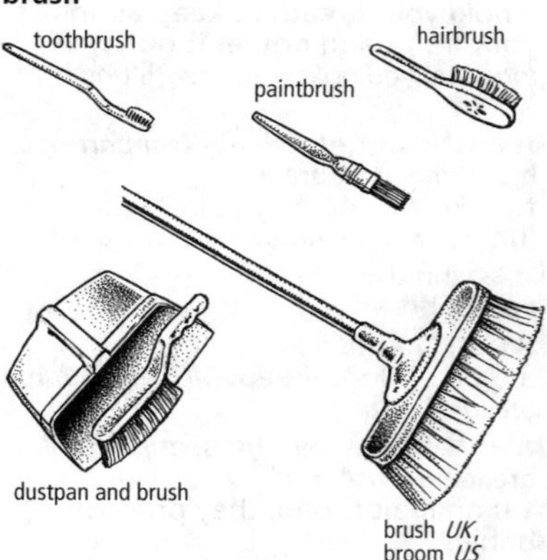

brush² /brʌʃ/ *verb*
to use a brush to clean or tidy something: *to brush your hair/teeth*

brutal /ˈbruːtᵊl/ *adj*
very violent or cruel: *a brutal murder*
● **brutally** *adv brutally murdered*

bubble /ˈbʌbl/ *noun*
a ball of air or gas with liquid around it: *an air bubble*

bubble

bucket /ˈbʌkɪt/ *noun*
a round, open container with a handle used for carrying liquids: *a bucket of water*

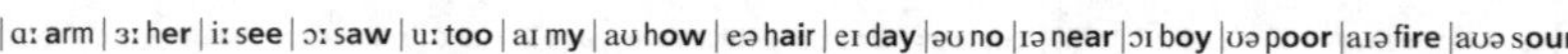

buckle /ˈbʌkl/ *noun*
a metal object used to fasten the ends of a belt or strap: *a silver buckle* ➲See colour picture **Clothes** on page Centre 5

bud /bʌd/ *noun*
1 a part of a plant that develops into a leaf or a flower: *In spring the trees are covered in buds.*
2 nip something in the bud to stop a small problem from getting worse by stopping it soon after it starts

Buddhism /ˈbʊdɪzᵊm/ *noun* **[no plural]**
a religion based on the teachings of Buddha

Buddhist /ˈbʊdɪst/ *noun*
someone who believes in Buddhism
• **Buddhist** *adj a Buddhist temple*

budget¹ /ˈbʌdʒɪt/ *noun*
a plan that shows how much money you have and how you will spend it

budget² /ˈbʌdʒɪt/ *verb*
to plan how much money you will spend

budgie /ˈbʌdʒi/ *noun UK*
a small, brightly coloured bird often kept as a pet

bug /bʌg/ *noun*
1 a bacteria or virus, or the illness that it causes: *a stomach bug*
2 a mistake in a computer program
3 a small insect

build /bɪld/ *verb* (*present participle* **building**, *past* **built**)
to make something by putting materials and parts together: *He built his own house.*
build up *phrasal verb*
to increase: *Traffic builds up in the late afternoon.*

builder /ˈbɪldəʳ/ *noun*
someone who makes or repairs buildings as a job

building /ˈbɪldɪŋ/ *noun*
1 a structure with walls and a roof, such as a house or school: *an office building*
2 [no plural] the activity of putting together materials and parts to make structures

built /bɪlt/
past of build

bulb /bʌlb/ *noun*
a glass object containing a wire which makes light from electricity: *an electric light bulb*

bulge /bʌldʒ/ *verb* (*present participle* **bulging**, *past* **bulged**)
to look larger and rounder or fuller than normal: *Her bags were* ***bulging with*** *shopping.*

bulk /bʌlk/ *noun*
in bulk in large amounts: *She buys in bulk.*

bulky /ˈbʌlki/ *adj* **(bulkier, bulkiest)**
too big and taking up too much space

bull /bʊl/ *noun*
a male cow

bulldog /ˈbʊldɒg/ *noun*
a short, strong dog with a large head and neck

bullet /ˈbʊlɪt/ *noun*
a small, metal object that is fired from a gun

bully¹ /ˈbʊli/ *verb* (*present participle* **bullying**, *past* **bullied**)
to try to frighten someone who is smaller or weaker than you: *He was bullied at school by some older boys.*
• **bullying** *noun* **[no plural]** *Bullying is a problem in many schools.*

bully² /ˈbʊli/ *noun* (*plural* **bullies**)
someone who frightens a person who is smaller or weaker than them

bump¹ /bʌmp/ *verb*
to hurt part of your body by hitting it against something hard: *I bumped my head on the door.*
bump into someone *phrasal verb*
to meet someone you know without planning it: *I bumped into an old school friend in town today.*

bump² /bʌmp/ *noun*
1 a round, raised area on a surface: *My bike hit a bump in the road.*
2 a raised area on your body where it has been hurt: *a nasty bump on the head*

bumper /ˈbʌmpəʳ/ *noun*
a bar fixed along the front or back of a car to protect it in an accident

bumpy /ˈbʌmpi/ *adj* **(bumpier, bumpiest)**
A bumpy road or surface is not smooth.

bun /bʌn/ *noun*
1 *UK* a small, round cake: *an iced bun*
2 a small, round piece of bread: *a*

hamburger bun

bunch /bʌnʃ/ *noun* (*plural* **bunches**)
1 a number of things of the same type which are joined together: *a* ***bunch of*** *flowers* ➲See colour picture **Quantities** on page Centre 14
2 *informal* a group of people: *His friends are a nice bunch.*

bundle /ˈbʌndl/ *noun*
a number of things that are tied together: *a bundle of letters/clothes*

bungalow /ˈbʌŋɡəlәʊ/ *noun*
a house that has all its rooms on the ground floor

buoy /bɔɪ/ *noun*
a floating object used in water to mark dangerous areas for boats

burger /ˈbɜːɡəʳ/ *noun*
meat in a round, flat shape, that you eat between bread

burglar /ˈbɜːɡləʳ/ *noun*
someone who gets into buildings illegally and steals things

burglarize /ˈbɜːɡləraɪz/ *verb* (*present participle* **burglarizing**, *past* **burglarized**) *US*
burgle

burglary /ˈbɜːɡlәri/ *noun* (*plural* **burglaries**)
when someone gets into a building illegally and steals things

burgle /ˈbɜːɡl/ *UK verb* (*present participle* **burgling**, *past* **burgled**)
to get into a building illegally and steal things: *They've been burgled twice recently.*

burial /ˈberiəl/ *noun*
when a dead body is put into the ground

burn¹ /bɜːn/ *verb* (*present participle* **burning**, *past* **burnt**)
1 to destroy something with fire, or to be destroyed by fire: *I burnt all his letters.* ○ *The factory burned to the ground.*
2 to produce flames: *The fire's burning well.*
3 to be hurt by fire or heat: *He burned his hand on the iron.*
4 to copy music, information or images onto a CD: *He's burnt all his favourite records onto a CD.*
5 to use fuel to produce heat or energy: *to burn fuel*

burn down *phrasal verb*
to be destroyed by fire: *Their house burnt down while they were away on holiday.*

burn² /bɜːn/ *noun*
a place where fire or heat has damaged or hurt something: *She has a nasty burn on her arm.*

burnt¹ /bɜːnt/ *adj*
destroyed or made black by fire or heat: *burnt toast*

burnt² /bɜːnt/
past of burn

burp /bɜːp/ *verb*
to let air from your stomach come out of your mouth in a noisy way
• **burp** *noun*

burrow /ˈbʌrəʊ/ *noun*
a hole or passage in the ground dug by an animal to live in

burst /bɜːst/ *verb* (*present participle* **bursting**, *past* **burst**)
1 If a container bursts, or if you burst it, it breaks suddenly, so that what is inside it comes out: *A water pipe burst and flooded the cellar.* ○ *He burst all the balloons.*
2 burst into flames to suddenly start burning
3 burst into tears to suddenly start crying: *She burst into tears and ran away.*
4 burst out laughing to suddenly start laughing

bury /ˈberi/ *verb* (*present participle* **burying**, *past* **buried**)
1 to put a dead body into the ground: *He was buried next to his wife.*
2 to hide something in the ground or under something: *buried treasure*

bus /bʌs/ *noun* (*plural* **buses**)
a large vehicle that carries passengers by road, usually along a fixed route: *a school bus*

bush /bʊʃ/ *noun* (*plural* **bushes**)
a short, thick plant with a lot of branches: *a rose bush*

busily /ˈbɪzɪli/ *adv*
in a busy, active way: *He was busily writing notes.*

business /ˈbɪznɪs/ *noun*
1 [**no plural**] the buying and selling of goods or services: *We* ***do*** *a lot of* ***business with*** *China.*
2 (*plural* **businesses**) an organization that sells goods or services: *He* ***runs a*** *small decorating* ***business.***
3 be none of someone's business to

a b c d e f g h i j k l m n o p q r s t u v w x y z

be something private that another person should not be interested in
4 mind your own business used to rudely tell someone that a subject is private and they should not ask you about it

businessman, businesswoman /ˈbɪznɪsmən, ˈbɪznɪsˌwʊmən/ *noun*
someone who works in business, usually having an important job in a company

busy /ˈbɪzi/ *adj*
1 working hard, or giving your attention to a particular activity: *Mum was busy in the kitchen.* ○ *I've got plenty of jobs to* ***keep*** *you* ***busy****.*
2 full of activity or people: *a busy restaurant*

but[1] *strong form* /bʌt/ *weak form* /bət/ *conjunction*
used to introduce something new that you say, especially something which is different from what you have just said: *I'd drive you there, but I haven't got my car.* ○ *The food was nice but very expensive.*

but[2] *strong form* /bʌt/ *weak form* /bət/ *preposition*
except: *Everyone but Andrew knows.*

butcher /ˈbʊtʃəʳ/ *noun*
someone who prepares and sells meat

butter /ˈbʌtəʳ/ *noun* **[no plural]**
a soft, yellow food made from cream that you put on bread ➲See colour picture **Food** on page Centre 7

butterfly /ˈbʌtəflaɪ/ *noun* (*plural* **butterflies**)
1 an insect with large, coloured wings
2 have butterflies (in your stomach) to feel very nervous about something: *She had butterflies in her stomach as she walked out onto the stage.*

buttock /ˈbʌtək/ *noun*
one of the two sides of your bottom

button /ˈbʌtᵊn/ *noun*
1 a small, round object that you push through a hole to fasten clothes: *You haven't done your buttons up on your shirt.*
2 a switch that you press to control a piece of equipment: *Press the play button to listen to your recording.*

buy /baɪ/ *verb* (*present participle* **buying,** *past* **bought)**
to get something by giving money for it: *I went to the shop to buy some milk.*

buzz /bʌz/ *verb*
to make a continuous sound like a bee: *I can hear something buzzing.*

by[1] *strong form* /baɪ/ *weak forms* /bɪ, bə/ *preposition*
1 used to show the person or thing that does something: *a painting by Van Gogh* ○ *The building had been destroyed by fire.*
2 through doing or using something: *I sent it by email.* ○ *We'll get there by car.*
3 near or next to: *I'll meet you by the post office.*
4 before a particular time or date: *Applications have to be in by the 31st.*
5 past: *He sped by me on a motorcycle.*
6 used to show measurements or amounts: *twelve by ten metres of floor space* ○ *I'm paid by the hour.*

by[2] /baɪ/ *adv*
past: *I sat there, watching people walk by.*

bye /baɪ/ (*also* **bye-bye)** *exclamation*
goodbye: *Bye, see you tomorrow.*

byte /baɪt/ *noun*
a unit for measuring the amount of information a computer can store

a b c d e f g h i j k l m n o p q r s t u v w x y z

a b c d e f g h i j k l m n o p q r s t u v w x y z

Cc

C, c /siː/
the third letter of the alphabet

C *written abbreviation for*
Celsius or centigrade: measurements of temperature: *30°C*

cab /kæb/ *noun informal*
a taxi (= car that you pay to travel in): *We* ***took a cab*** *to the theatre.*

cabbage /ˈkæbɪdʒ/ *noun*
a large, round vegetable with a lot of green or white leaves

cabin /ˈkæbɪn/ *noun*
1 a small house made of wood: *a log cabin*
2 the area where most people sit on an aeroplane

cabinet /ˈkæbɪnət/ *noun*
1 a group of people in a government who advise the leader: *a Cabinet minister*
2 a cupboard with shelves or drawers: *a bathroom cabinet*

cable /ˈkeɪbl/ *noun*
1 a wire that carries electricity or telephone signals
2 a metal rope
3 [no plural] the system of sending television programmes or telephone signals along wires in the ground: *cable TV*

cactus /ˈkæktəs/ *noun* (*plural* **cacti** /ˈkæktaɪ/ or **cactuses**)
a plant with thick leaves and sharp points that grows in hot, dry places

cactus

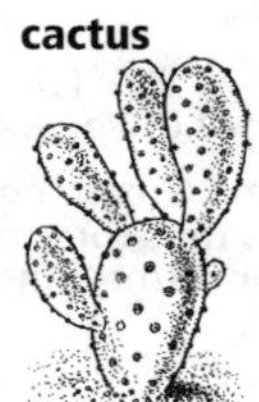

cafe (*also* **café**)/ˈkæfeɪ/ *noun*
a small restaurant where you buy drinks and small meals

cage

cage /keɪdʒ/ *noun*
a container made of wire or metal bars, used for keeping birds or animals in: *a bird cage*

cake /keɪk/ *noun*
a sweet food made from flour, butter, sugar, and eggs mixed together and cooked: *a chocolate cake* ➲See colour picture **Food** on page Centre 7

cake

calculate /ˈkælkjəleɪt/ *verb* (*present participle* **calculating,** *past* **calculated)**
to discover an amount or number using mathematics: *I'm trying to calculate the cost.*

calculation /ˌkælkjəˈleɪʃᵊn/ *noun*
when you use mathematics to discover a number or amount

calculator /ˈkælkjəleɪtəʳ/ *noun*
a small machine that you use to do mathematics

calendar /ˈkæləndəʳ/ *noun*
something that shows all the days, weeks, and months of the year

calf /kɑːf/ *noun* (*plural* **calves)**
1 a young cow
2 the back of your leg below your knee ➲See colour picture **The Body** on page Centre 2

call[1] /kɔːl/ *verb*
1 to give someone a name: *They called their first son Joshua.*
2 to describe someone or something in a particular way: *Are you calling me a liar?*
3 to ask someone to come somewhere: *She called me into her office.*
4 to shout: *I heard someone call my name.*
5 to telephone someone: *Call the police.*
6 *UK* to visit someone for a short time: *Pete called in to see you.*

call someone back *phrasal verb*
to telephone someone a second time, or to telephone someone who telephoned you earlier

call something off *phrasal verb*
to decide that something that is planned will not happen: *The game was called off because of bad weather.*

call[2] /kɔːl/ *noun*
1 when you use the telephone: ***Give me a call*** *at the weekend.* ○ *I* ***got a call*** *from Sue this morning.*
2 when someone shouts something
3 a sound made by a bird or other animal

calm[1] /kɑːm/ *adj*
1 relaxed and not worried or frightened: *a calm voice*
2 If the weather or the sea is calm, it is quiet and peaceful.
• **calmly** *adv*
in a relaxed way: *He spoke slowly and calmly.*

calm[2] /kɑːm/ *verb*
calm down *phrasal verb*
to stop feeling angry or excited: *Calm down and tell me what's wrong.*

calves /kɑːvz/
plural of calf

camcorder /ˈkæmˌkɔːdəʳ/ *noun*
a camera that you hold in your hand and that takes moving pictures

came /keɪm/
past tense of come

camel /ˈkæməl/ *noun*
a large animal that lives in hot, dry places and has one or two humps (= raised parts on its back)

camel

camera /ˈkæmərə/ *noun*
a piece of equipment used to take photographs

camp[1] /kæmp/ *noun*
an area where people stay in tents for a short time

camp[2] /kæmp/ *verb*
to stay in a tent: *We camped on the beach for two nights.*

campaign[1] /kæmˈpeɪn/ *noun*
1 a group of activities which are planned to get a result: *an election campaign*
2 a lot of military attacks: *a bombing campaign*

campaign[2] /kæmˈpeɪn/ *verb*
to organize a group of activities to try to make something happen

camping /ˈkæmpɪŋ/ *noun* **[no plural]**
when you stay in a tent for a holiday

campsite /ˈkæmpsaɪt/ *noun*
an area where people stay in tents for a holiday

campus /ˈkæmpəs/ *noun*
the land and buildings belonging to a college or university

can[1] *strong form* /kæn/ *weak form* /kən/ *verb*
1 to be able to do something: *Can you drive? ○ I can't swim.*
2 to be allowed to do something: *You can't park here. ○ Can I go now?*

can[2] /kæn/ *noun*
a metal container for food or liquids: *a can of soup*

canal /kəˈnæl/ *noun*
a river made by people

canary /kəˈneəri/ *noun* (*plural* **canaries**)
a small, yellow bird that sings

cancel /ˈkænsəl/ *verb* (*present participle* **cancelling**, *past* **cancelled**)
to say that an organized event will not happen: *The meeting has been cancelled.*

cancellation /ˌkænsəlˈleɪʃən/ *noun*
when someone decides that an event will not happen

cancer /ˈkænsəʳ/ *noun*
a serious disease that is caused when cells in the body grow too much: *lung cancer*

candidate /ˈkændɪdət/ *noun*
1 a person who takes part in an election or tries to get a job
2 *UK* someone who is taking an exam

candle /ˈkændl/ *noun*
a stick of wax with string inside it that you burn to make light ➲See colour picture **The Living Room** on page Centre 11

candle

candy /ˈkændi/ *noun*
US (*plural* **candies**)
a small piece of sweet food: *a candy bar*

cane /keɪn/ *noun*
a stick taken from a plant, sometimes used to make furniture

cannon /ˈkænən/ *noun*
a very large gun

cannot /ˈkænɒt/ *verb*
the negative form of 'can': *I cannot say what will happen.*

canoe /kəˈnuː/ *noun*
a small, thin boat with pointed ends for one or two people

canoe

can't /kɑːnt/ *verb*

a b c d e f g h i j k l m n o p q r s t u v w x y z

short for cannot: *I can't drive.*

canteen /kæn'tiːn/ *noun*
a restaurant in an office, factory, or school

canvas /'kænvəs/ *noun* **[no plural]**
a strong cloth

cap /kæp/ *noun*
1 a hat with a flat part at the front: *a baseball cap* ➲See colour picture **Clothes** on page Centre 5
2 the top part of a bottle or tube that you take off

capable /'keɪpəbl/ *adj*
1 able to do things well: *She's a very capable young woman.*
2 capable of able to do something: *I know the quality of work she is capable of.* ➲Opposite **incapable**

capacity /kə'pæsəti/ *noun*
1 the largest amount that a container or building can hold: *The restaurant has* ***a capacity of*** *about 200.*
2 the ability to do or feel something: *She has a great* ***capacity for*** *love.*

capital /'kæpɪtᵊl/ *noun*
1 the most important city in a country or state: *Paris is the capital of France.*
2 [no plural] money used in business
3 (*also* ˌ**capital** '**letter**) a large letter of the alphabet used at the beginning of sentences

capital punishment /ˌkæpɪtᵊl 'pʌnɪʃmənt/ *noun* **[no plural]**
when someone is killed by the state for doing a crime

captain /'kæptɪn/ *noun*
1 the person in control of a ship or aeroplane
2 the leader of a team
3 an officer in the army, navy, or air force

captive /'kæptɪv/ *noun*
a prisoner

captivity /kæp'tɪvəti/ *noun* **[no plural]**
when a person or animal is kept somewhere and not allowed to leave: *lion cubs born* ***in captivity***

capture /'kæptʃəʳ/ *verb* (*present participle* **capturing**, *past* **captured**)
to catch someone and make them your prisoner: *Two soldiers were captured by the enemy.*

car /kɑːʳ/ *noun*
a vehicle with an engine, four wheels, and seats for a few people ➲See colour picture **Car** on page Centre 3

caravan /'kærəvæn/ *noun UK*
a vehicle which people stay in on holiday and which is pulled by a car

card /kɑːd/ *noun*
1 a piece of folded paper with a picture on the front and some writing inside: *a birthday card*
2 a piece of hard paper or plastic with information on it: *a library card*
3 (*also* **playing card**) a piece of hard paper with numbers and pictures used for playing games: *We spent the evening* ***playing cards*** (= playing games using cards).
4 [no plural] *UK* thick paper

cardboard /'kɑːdbɔːd/ *noun* **[no plural]**
thick, hard paper that is used for making boxes

cardigan /'kɑːdɪgən/ *noun*
a piece of clothing, often wool, that covers the top part of your body and fastens at the front ➲See colour picture **Clothes** on page Centre 5

cardigan

care¹ /keəʳ/ *verb* (*present participle* **caring**, *past* **cared**)
1 to feel interested in something or worried about it: *I don't* ***care what*** *she thinks.*
2 to love someone: *I only worry about him because I* ***care about*** *him.*
care for someone *phrasal verb*
to look after someone who is young, old, or ill: *The children are being cared for by a relative.*

care² /keəʳ/ *noun*
1 [no plural] when you look after someone or something, especially someone who is young, old, or ill: *A small baby requires constant care.*
2 take care to give a lot of attention to what you are doing, especially something dangerous: *The roads are very icy so take care when you drive home.*
3 Take care! *informal* used when saying goodbye to someone: *See you soon, Bob – take care!*

4 take care of to look after someone or something: *My parents take care of the house while we're away.*

career /kəˈrɪəʳ/ *noun*
a job that you do for a lot of your life, especially one for which you are trained: *a successful career in marketing*

careful /ˈkeəfᵊl/ *adj*
giving a lot of attention to what you are doing so that you do not have an accident or make a mistake: ***Be careful**, Michael – that knife's sharp.*
• **carefully** *adv*: *He carefully lifted the baby.*

careless /ˈkeələs/ *adj*
not giving enough attention to what you are doing: *He was fined £250 for careless driving.*
• **carelessly** *adv*

cargo /ˈkɑːgəʊ/ *noun* (*plural* **cargoes**)
things that are carried in a vehicle: *a cargo of oil*

carnival /ˈkɑːnɪvᵊl/ *noun*
a public occasion where people wear special clothes and dance in the streets

car park /ˈkɑː ˌpɑːk/ *noun*
a place where you can leave your car for a short time

carpet /ˈkɑːpɪt/ *noun*
thick material for covering floors, often made of wool

carriage /ˈkærɪdʒ/ *noun UK*
one of the separate parts of a train where people sit

carrier bag /ˈkærɪə ˌbæg/ *noun UK*
a large paper or plastic bag that you are given in a shop to carry the things you have bought

carrot

carrot /ˈkærət/ *noun*
a long, thin, orange vegetable that grows in the ground ➲See colour picture **Fruit and Vegetables** on page Centre 8

carry /ˈkæri/ *verb* (*present participle* **carrying**, *past* **carried**)
1 to hold something or someone with your hands or on your back and take them somewhere: *He was carrying my bags.*
2 to move someone or something from one place to another: *The plane was carrying 30 passengers.*
carry on *phrasal verb*
to continue doing something: ***Carry on with** your work while I'm gone.*

cart /kɑːt/ *noun US*
a metal structure on wheels that is used for carrying things

carton /ˈkɑːtᵊn/ *noun*
a container for food and drink that is made from strong paper or plastic: *a carton of milk/fruit juice*

cartoon /kɑːˈtuːn/ *noun*
1 a film made using characters that are drawn and not real: *Mickey Mouse and other famous cartoon characters*
2 a funny drawing, especially in a newspaper or magazine

carve /kɑːv/ *verb* (*present participle* **carving**, *past* **carved**)
1 to make an object or shape by cutting wood or stone: *The statue was **carved out of** stone.*
2 to cut a piece of cooked meat into thin pieces

case /keɪs/ *noun*
1 a particular situation or example of something: *We usually ask for references, but in your case it will not be necessary.*
2 something that is decided in a court of law: *a divorce case*
3 a container for storing or protecting something: *a pencil case*
4 a large bag with a handle which you use for carrying clothes in when you are travelling
5 in case because something might happen: *I don't think it will rain, but I'll bring an umbrella just in case.*
6 in that case because that is the situation: *"Peter will be there." "Oh, in that case, I'll come too."*

cash¹ /kæʃ/ *noun* **[no plural]**
money in the form of coins or notes (= paper money): *I'm taking £50 **in cash**.*

cash² /kæʃ/ *verb*
cash a cheque to get money in return for a cheque (= piece of paper printed by a bank and used to pay for things): *I need to cash a traveller's cheque.*

cash desk /ˈkæʃ ˌdesk/ *noun UK*

the place in a shop where you pay for things

cashier /kæʃ'ɪə^r/ *noun*
someone whose job is to take and pay out money in a shop or bank

cashpoint

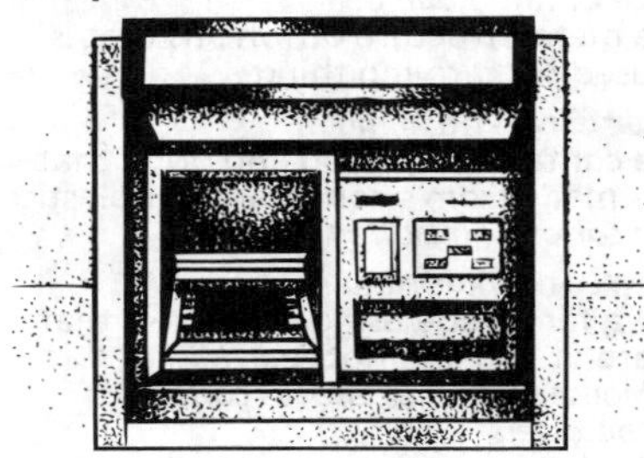

cashpoint /'kæʃpɔɪnt/ *noun UK*
a machine in a wall that you get money from using a plastic card

cassette /kə'set/ *noun*
a flat, plastic case containing a long piece of magnetic material that is used to record and play sound or pictures: *a video cassette*

cast /kɑːst/ *verb* (*present participle* **casting**, *past* **cast**)
cast a spell on someone to use magic to make something happen to someone: *The witch cast a spell on him and turned him into a frog.*

castle /'kɑːsl/ *noun*
a large, strong building that was built in the past to protect the people inside from being attacked

castle

casual /'kæʒjuəl/ *adj*
1 not planned: *a casual remark*
2 relaxed and not seeming very interested in someone or something: *a casual manner*
3 Casual clothes are comfortable and not formal.

cat /kæt/ *noun*
an animal with fur that is kept as a pet

catalogue (*also US* **catalog**) /'kæt^{ə}lɒg/ *noun*
a book with a list of all the things that you can buy from a shop: *a clothing catalogue*

catch /kætʃ/ *verb* (*present participle* **catching**, *past* **caught**)
1 to stop someone or something that is moving through the air by getting them in your hands: *Try to catch the ball.*
2 to find and stop a person or animal who is trying to escape: *He ran after his attacker but couldn't catch him.*
3 to get an illness or disease: *I think I've caught a cold.*
4 to get on a bus, train, etc: *I caught the last train home.*
5 to stick somewhere, or to make something stick somewhere: *My dress caught on the door handle as I was leaving.*
6 catch fire to start burning

catch (someone/something) up *phrasal verb*
to reach someone or something that is in front of you by moving faster: *We soon* ***caught up with*** *the car in front.*

category /'kætəg^{ə}ri/ *noun* (*plural* **categories**)
a group of people or things of a similar type: *Our customers fall into two main categories.*

caterpillar /'kætəpɪlə^r/ *noun*
a small, long animal with many legs that eats leaves

caterpillar

cathedral /kə'θiːdr^{ə}l/ *noun*
the largest and most important church in an area

Catholic /'kæθ^{ə}lɪk/ *adj*
belonging to the part of the Christian religion whose leader is the Pope: *a Catholic priest*
• **Catholic** *noun*

cattle /'kætl/ *plural noun*
cows kept on a farm for their milk and meat

caught /kɔːt/
past of catch

cauliflower /'kɒlɪˌflaʊə^r/ *noun*
a round, white vegetable with green leaves around the outside
➲See colour picture **Fruit and Vegetables** on page Centre 8

cause[1] /kɔːz/ *verb* (*present participle* **causing**, *past* **caused**)

a b c d e f g h i j k l m n o p q r s t u v w x y z

to make something happen, especially something bad: *What caused the fire?*

cause² /kɔːz/ *noun*
1 someone or something that makes something happen: *They still don't know the* ***cause of*** *the accident.*
2 [no plural] a reason to feel something: *There is no* ***cause for*** *alarm.*
3 a reason for doing something, especially one that involves helping other people: *The money will go to the local hospital – it's a good cause.*

caution /ˈkɔːʃᵊn/ *noun* **[no plural]**
great care to avoid danger or bad situations: *Caution! Wet surface.*

cautious /ˈkɔːʃəs/ *adj*
taking care to avoid danger or bad situations: *a cautious driver*
• **cautiously** *adv*

cave /keɪv/ *noun*
a large hole in the ground or in the side of a mountain

CD /ˌsiːˈdiː/ *noun*
a small disc on which music or information is recorded ➲See colour picture **The Office** on page Centre 12

CD player /ˌsiːˈdiː ˈpleɪəʳ/ *noun*
a machine that is used for playing CDs

cease /siːs/ *verb* (*present participle* **ceasing,** *past* **ceased)** *formal*
to stop: *He ordered his men to cease firing.*

ceiling /ˈsiːlɪŋ/ *noun*
the top surface of a room

celebrate /ˈseləbreɪt/ *verb* (*present participle* **celebrating,** *past* **celebrated)**
to have a party or a nice meal because it is a special day or something good has happened: *We went out to celebrate Richard's promotion.*

celebration /ˌseləˈbreɪʃᵊn/ *noun*
when you celebrate: *You've passed your test? This calls for a celebration.*

cell /sel/ *noun*
1 the smallest living part of an animal or a plant: *brain cells*
2 a small room where a prisoner is kept

cellar /ˈseləʳ/ *noun*
a room under the floor of a building

cello /ˈtʃeləʊ/ *noun*
a large, wooden musical instrument that you hold between your knees to play

Celsius /ˈselsiəs/ (*written abbreviation* **C)** *noun* **[no plural]**
a measurement of temperature

cement /sɪˈment/ *noun* **[no plural]**
a powder used in building which is mixed with water to make a hard substance

cent /sent/ *noun*
a coin with a low value in some countries

centigrade /ˈsentɪgreɪd/ (*written abbreviation* **C)** *noun* **[no plural]**
a measurement of temperature

centimetre *UK* (*US* **centimeter)** (*written abbreviation* **cm)** /ˈsentɪˌmiːtəʳ/ *noun*
a unit for measuring length, equal to 0.01 metres

central /ˈsentrᵊl/ *adj*
in or near the centre of a place or thing: *central America*
• **centrally** *adv*

centre *UK* (*US* **center)** /ˈsentəʳ/ *noun*
1 the middle point or part of something: *Cars are not allowed in the town centre.*
2 a building used for a particular activity: *a health centre*
3 be the centre of attention to get more attention than anyone else

century /ˈsenʃᵊri/ *noun* (*plural* **centuries)**
a period of 100 years: *the twentieth century*

cereal /ˈsɪəriəl/ *noun*
1 a plant that is grown to produce grain for food
2 a food that is made from grain and eaten with milk, especially in the morning: *breakfast cereals* ➲See colour picture **Food** on page Centre 7

ceremony /ˈserɪməni/ *noun*
1 (*plural* **ceremonies)** a formal event that is performed on important social or religious occasions: *a wedding ceremony*
2 [no plural] formal words and actions that are part of a ceremony

certain /ˈsɜːtᵊn/ *adj*
1 definite: *I feel certain that you're doing the right thing.* ○ *It now looks certain that she will resign.* ➲Opposite **uncertain**

2 some: *The museum is only open at certain times of the day.*

certainly /ˈsɜːtənli/ *adv*
1 definitely: *They certainly deserved to win.* ○ *"Do you regret what you said?" "**Certainly not**!"*
2 used to politely agree to do something: *"Could you pass the salt, please?" "Certainly."*

certificate /səˈtɪfɪkət/ *noun*
an official document that gives details to show that something is true: *a marriage certificate*

chain

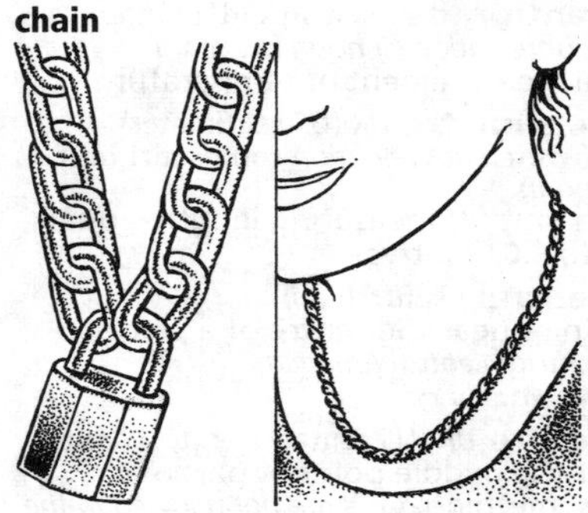

chain[1] /tʃeɪn/ *noun*
a line of metal rings connected together: *She wore a gold chain around her neck.*

chain[2] /tʃeɪn/ *verb*
to tie someone or something using a chain: *I **chained** my bike **to** a lamppost.*

chair /tʃeəʳ/ *noun*
a seat for one person, with a back and usually four legs ➲See colour picture **The Office** on page Centre 12

chairman, chairwoman /ˈtʃeəmən, ˈtʃeəˌwʊmən/ *noun*
a man/woman who controls a meeting or company

chalk /tʃɔːk/ *noun*
1 **[no plural]** a soft, white rock
2 a small stick of chalk used for writing ➲See colour picture **Classroom** on page Centre 4

challenge[1] /ˈtʃælɪndʒ/ *noun*
1 something difficult that tests your ability: *Managing a large team is quite a challenge.*
2 when someone asks you to compete in a game or a fight

challenge[2] /ˈtʃælɪndʒ/ *verb* (*present participle* **challenging**, *past* **challenged**)
1 to tell someone you do not accept their rules or you think they are wrong: *The election results are being challenged.*
2 to ask someone to compete in a game or fight: *He's **challenged** me **to** a game of tennis.*

challenging /ˈtʃæləndʒɪŋ/ *adj*
difficult, in a way that tests your ability: *This has been a challenging time for us all.*

champagne /ʃæmˈpeɪn/ *noun* **[no plural]**
French white wine with a lot of bubbles in it

champagne

champion /ˈtʃæmpiən/ *noun*
a person or animal that wins a competition

championship /ˈtʃæmpiənʃɪp/ *noun*
a competition to find the best team or player in a game or sport

chance /tʃɑːns/ *noun*
1 the possibility that something will happen: *There's a **chance that** she'll still be there.* ○ *She has little **chance of** passing the exam.*
2 the opportunity to do something: *I didn't **get a chance** to speak to you at the party.*
3 **[no plural]** when something happens because of luck, or without being planned: *I saw her **by chance** in the shop.*
4 **stand a chance** to have a chance of success or of doing something good: *He stands a good chance of winning the election.*
5 **chances are** it is likely: *Chances are that he'll say no.*
6 **No chance!** used to say that there is no possibility of something happening: *"Are you going to lend her any money?" "No chance!"*

change[1] /tʃeɪndʒ/ *verb* (*present participle* **changing**, *past* **changed**)
1 to become different, or to make someone or something become different: *She's changed a lot in the last few years.* ○ *The course changed my life.*
2 to stop having one thing, and start having another: *I've changed my doctor.*
3 to take off your clothes and put on

different ones: *Is there somewhere I can **get changed**?*
4 to get off one bus, plane, etc and get on a different one: *I have to change trains at Bristol.*
5 to get one type of money in exchange for a different type: *Where can I change my dollars?*
change something around/round *phrasal verb*
to move things such as furniture into different positions: *The room looks very different since you've changed the furniture around.*
change over *phrasal verb UK*
to stop using or having one thing and start using or having something else: *We've just **changed over from** gas central heating **to** electric.*

change[2] /tʃeɪndʒ/ *noun*
1 when something becomes different: *We need to **make** a few **changes to** the design.*
2 when you stop having one thing and start having another: *a **change of** government*
3 a different experience: *Let's have white wine **for a change***
4 **[no plural]** the money that you get back when you pay more for something than it costs: *There's your receipt and £3 change.*
5 **[no plural]** coins, not paper money: *Have you got any change for the parking meter?*

channel /ˈtʃænᵊl/ *noun*
1 a number on a television that you choose in order to watch a programme
2 a long passage for water or other liquids to move along

chaos /ˈkeɪɒs/ *noun* **[no plural]**
a situation where there is no order: *The country is at war and everything is **in chaos***

chapter /ˈtʃæptəʳ/ *noun*
one of the parts that a book is divided into

character /ˈkærəktəʳ/ *noun*
1 the qualities that make one person or thing different from another: *The whole character of the village changed when the road was built.*
2 a person in a book, film, etc: *a cartoon character*

characteristic /ˌkærəktəˈrɪstɪk/ *noun*
a quality that someone or something has

charge[1] /tʃɑːdʒ/ *noun*
1 the price of something, especially a service: *bank charges*
2 **be in charge** to be responsible for something: *She's in charge of the team.*
3 something written by the police saying that someone has done a crime

charge[2] /tʃɑːdʒ/ *verb (present participle* **charging**, *past* **charged)**
1 to ask for money for something: *How much do you **charge for** delivery?*
2 to officially say that someone has done a crime: *He has been **charged with** three counts of murder.*
3 to run: *The children charged around the house.*

charity /ˈtʃærɪti/ *noun*
1 (*plural* **charities**) an official organization that gives money, food, or help to people who need it: *We're raising money **for charity**.*
2 **[no plural]** money, food, or other help that is given to people

charm /tʃɑːm/ *noun*
1 a quality that makes you like someone or something: *I know why women like him – he has a certain charm.*
2 something that brings you good luck: *a lucky charm*

charming /ˈtʃɑːmɪŋ/ *adj*
nice and attractive: *a charming smile*

chart /tʃɑːt/ *noun*
a drawing which shows information in a simple way: *a sales chart*

chase

chase /tʃeɪs/ *verb (present participle* **chasing**, *past* **chased)**
to run after someone or something in order to catch them: *The dog was chasing a rabbit.*

chat¹ /tʃæt/ *verb* (*present participle* **chatting,** *past* **chatted)**
to talk with someone in a friendly way

chat² /tʃæt/ *noun*
when you talk with someone in a friendly way: *We were* ***having a chat****.*

cheap /tʃiːp/ *adj*
not expensive, or costing less than usual: *a cheap flight* ➲Opposite **expensive**

cheat /tʃiːt/ *verb*
to do something that is not honest, in order to get something: *He* ***cheats at*** *cards.*

check¹ /tʃek/ *verb*
1 to look at something to make sure that it is right or safe: *Check that you've locked the door.*
2 to find out information about something: *I'll check whether Peter knows about the party.*
3 *US* to put a mark (✓) by an answer to show that it is correct
check in *phrasal verb*
1 to show your ticket at an airport so they can tell you your seat number
2 to go to the desk at a hotel in order to say that you have arrived
check out *phrasal verb*
to leave a hotel after paying

check² /tʃek/ *noun*
1 when you look at something to make sure it is right or safe: *We do safety* ***checks on*** *all our equipment.*
2 *US* a piece of paper printed by a bank that you use to pay for things
3 *US* a mark (✓) that shows that an answer is correct
4 a pattern of squares of different colours

checkbook /ˈtʃekbʊk/ *noun US*
a book of papers printed by a bank that you use to pay for things

checkout /ˈtʃekaʊt/ *noun*
a place in a large shop where you pay for things: *a supermarket checkout*

cheek /tʃiːk/ *noun*
1 one of the two soft parts of your face below your eyes: *Tears ran down his cheeks.* ➲See colour picture **The Body** on page Centre 2
2 *UK* rude behaviour that shows you do not respect someone: *She* ***had the cheek to*** *ask me to pay for her!*

cheeky /ˈtʃiːki/ **(cheekier, cheekiest)** *adj UK*
rude, often in a funny way: *a cheeky little boy*
● **cheekily** *adv*

cheer¹ /tʃɪəʳ/ *verb*
to shout loudly at someone that you like or want to encourage: *The crowd were cheering as he ran into the stadium.*
cheer up *phrasal verb*
to stop feeling sad: *Cheer up. It's not the end of the world!*

cheer² /tʃɪəʳ/ *noun*
a shout that shows you like someone or want to encourage them

cheerful /ˈtʃɪəfᵊl/ *adj*
happy: *She seemed fairly cheerful.*

cheers! /tʃɪəz/ *exclamation*
something friendly that you say before you start to drink alcohol with someone

cheese /tʃiːz/ *noun*
a yellow or white solid food made from milk ➲See colour picture **Food** on page Centre 7

chef /ʃef/ *noun*
someone who cooks food in a restaurant

chemical¹ /ˈkemɪkᵊl/ *adj*
relating to chemistry or chemicals

chemical² /ˈkemɪkᵊl/ *noun*
a substance that is used in chemistry or produced by chemistry

chemist /ˈkemɪst/ *noun*
1 *UK* (*US* **pharmacist)** someone who prepares and sells drugs in a shop
2 a scientist who does work that involves chemistry

chemistry /ˈkemɪstri/ *noun* **[no plural]**
the scientific study of substances and how they change when they combine

chemist's /ˈkemɪsts/ *UK* (*US* **drugstore)** *noun*
a shop where you can buy drugs, soap, etc

cheque /tʃek/ *noun UK*
a piece of paper printed by a bank that you use to pay for things: *Are you* ***paying by cheque****?*

chequebook /ˈtʃekbʊk/ *noun UK*
a book of cheques

cherry /ˈtʃeri/ *noun* (*plural* **cherries)**

a small, round red or black fruit with a large seed inside

chess /tʃes/ *noun* **[no plural]**
a game that two people play by moving different shaped pieces around a board of black and white squares

chest /tʃest/ *noun*
1 the front of your body between your neck and your stomach ➲See colour picture **The Body** on page Centre 2
2 a big wooden box for keeping things in

chest of drawers /ˌtʃest əv ˈdrɔːz/ *UK* (*US* **bureau**) *noun*
a piece of furniture with drawers for keeping clothes in

chew /tʃuː/ *verb*
to break food between your teeth as a part of eating

chewing gum /ˈtʃuːɪŋ ɡʌm/ *noun* **[no plural]**
a sweet that you chew but do not eat

chick /tʃɪk/ *noun*
a baby bird, especially a baby chicken

chicken /ˈtʃɪkɪn/ *noun*
1 a bird kept on a farm for its meat and eggs
2 [no plural] the meat of a chicken

chief[1] /tʃiːf/ *adj*
most important: *The weather was our chief reason for coming here.*

chief[2] /tʃiːf/ *noun*
the leader of a group

child /tʃaɪld/ *noun*
1 a young person who is not yet an adult
2 a son or daughter, also when they are adults

childhood /ˈtʃaɪldhʊd/ *noun*
the part of your life when you are a child: *She* ***had*** *an unhappy* ***childhood****.*

childish /ˈtʃaɪldɪʃ/ *adj*
silly, like the behaviour of a child: *Don't be so childish!*
• **childishly** *adv*

children *noun*
the plural of 'child'

chilly /ˈtʃɪli/ *adj*
too cold: *It's chilly outside.*

chimney /ˈtʃɪmni/ *noun*
a pipe that takes smoke from a fire out through a roof

chimney

chimpanzee /ˌtʃɪmpənˈziː/ *noun*
an African animal like a large monkey with no tail

chin /tʃɪn/ *noun*
the bottom part of your face, below your mouth ➲See colour picture **The Body** on page Centre 2

chip[1] /tʃɪp/ *noun*
1 (*US* **french fry**) a long, thin piece of potato that is cooked in oil: *fish and chips* ➲See colour picture **Food** on page Centre 7
2 *US* (*UK* **crisp**) a thin, dry slice of fried potato ➲See colour picture **Food** on page Centre 7
3 a microchip (= very small part of a computer that stores information)

chip[2] /tʃɪp/ *verb* (*present participle* **chipping**, *past* **chipped**)
to break a small piece off something that is hard: *a chipped plate*

chocolate /ˈtʃɒkələt/ *noun*
1 [no plural] a sweet, brown food that is usually sold in a block: *a bar of chocolate ○ milk chocolate*
2 a small piece of sweet food covered in chocolate: *a box of chocolates*

choice /tʃɔɪs/ *noun*
1 when you can choose between two or more things: *If I had a choice, I'd stop working.*
2 the decision to choose one thing or person and not someone or something else: *In the past women had to* ***make a choice between*** *a career or marriage.*
3 the things or people you can choose from: *The dress is available in a* ***choice of*** *colours.*
4 the person or thing that someone has chosen: *Harvard was not his* ***first choice****.*

choir /kwaɪər/ *noun*
a group of people who sing together: *a church choir*

choke /tʃəʊk/ *verb* (*present participle* **choking**, *past* **choked**)
to stop breathing because

a b c d e f g h i j k l m n o p q r s t u v w x y z

something is in your throat: *Children can **choke on** peanuts.*

choose /tʃuːz/ *verb* (*present participle* **choosing,** *past tense* **chose,** *past participle* **chosen)**
1 to decide which thing you want: *Have you chosen a name for the baby?* ○ *There were lots of books to **choose from**.*
2 choose to do something to decide to do something: *Manuela chose to take a job in Paris.*

chop

chop¹ /tʃɒp/ *verb* (*present participle* **chopping,** *past* **chopped)**
1 to cut something into small pieces: *Chop the onion and pepper.*

chop² /tʃɒp/ *noun*
a flat piece of meat with a bone in it: *a lamb chop*

chord /kɔːd/ *noun*
two or more musical notes that are played at the same time

chorus /ˈkɔːrəs/ *noun* (*plural* **choruses)**
the part of a song that is repeated many times

chose /tʃəʊz/
past tense of choose

chosen /ˈtʃəʊzən/
past participle of choose

christen /ˈkrɪs^{ə}n/ *verb*
to give a baby a name at a Christian ceremony and make them a member of the Christian Church

christening /ˈkrɪs^{ə}nɪŋ/ *noun*
a ceremony where someone is christened

Christian /ˈkrɪstʃən/ *noun*
someone who believes in Christianity

Christianity /ˌkrɪstiˈænəti/ *noun* **[no plural]**
a religion based on belief in God and the life and teachings of Jesus Christ

Christmas /ˈkrɪsməs/ *noun*
the Christian period of celebration around 25 December, when Christians celebrate the birth of Jesus Christ and people give each other presents: *Merry Christmas!*

chubby /ˈtʃʌbi/ *adj* **(chubbier, chubbiest)**
fat in a way that is attractive: *the baby's chubby legs*

chunk /tʃʌŋk/ *noun*
a large piece of something: *a chunk of cheese* ➲See colour picture **Quantities** on p. Centre 14

church /tʃɜːtʃ/ *noun*
a building where Christians go to pray: *We used to go to church every Sunday morning.*

cigar /sɪˈɡɑː^r/ *noun*
a thick tube made from rolled tobacco leaves, that people smoke

cigarette /ˌsɪɡ^{ə}rˈet/ *noun*
a thin tube of paper filled with tobacco, that people smoke

cinema /ˈsɪnəmə/ *noun UK*
a building where you go to watch films

circle /ˈsɜːkl/ *noun*
a round, flat shape like the letter O: *We all sat on the floor in a circle.*

circular /ˈsɜːkjələ^r/ *adj*
shaped like a circle

circulate /ˈsɜːkjəleɪt/ *verb* (*present participle* **circulating,** *past* **circulated)**
to move around: *Hot water circulates through the pipes.*

circulation /ˌsɜːkjəˈleɪʃ^{ə}n/ *noun*
[no plural] the movement of blood around the body

circumstances /ˈsɜːkəmstænsɪz/ *plural noun*
1 the facts or events of a situation: *I think they coped very well **under the circumstances*** (= in that difficult situation).
2 under no circumstances used to say that something must never happen: *Under no circumstances should you approach the man.*

circus /ˈsɜːkəs/ *noun* (*plural* **circuses)**

a show in which a group of people and animals perform in a large tent

citizen /ˈsɪtɪzᵊn/ *noun*
someone who lives in a particular town or city: *the citizens of Berlin*

city /ˈsɪti/ *noun* (*plural* **cities**)
a large town

civilian /sɪˈvɪliən/ *noun*
someone who is not a member of a military organization or the police

civilization /ˌsɪvᵊlaɪˈzeɪʃᵊn/ *noun*
the way that people live together, with laws to control their behaviour, education and a government: *Nuclear war could mean the end of civilization.*

civilized /ˈsɪvəlaɪzd/ *adj*
A civilized society is advanced and has laws/education and a government

civil war /ˌsɪvəl ˈwɔːʳ/ *noun*
a war between groups of people who live in the same country

claim[1] /kleɪm/ *verb*
1 to say that something is true: *She* ***claimed that*** *the dog attacked her.*
2 to ask for something because it belongs to you or you have the right to have it: *She claimed $2,500 in travel expenses.*

claim[2] /kleɪm/ *noun*
1 when someone says that something is true: *There were* ***claims that*** *he had lied.*
2 an official demand for something you think you have a right to: *a claim for compensation*

clap /klæp/ *verb* (*present participle* **clapping**, *past* **clapped**)
to hit your hands together to show that you have enjoyed a performance, talk, etc: *The crowd clapped and cheered for more.*

clap

clash[1] /klæʃ/ *verb*
1 to fight or argue: *Government troops* ***clashed with*** *rebel soldiers.*
2 If colours clash, they do not look good together.
3 *UK* If two events clash, they happen at the same time so that you cannot go to them both: *Emma's party* ***clashes with*** *my brother's wedding.*

clash[2] /klæʃ/ *noun* (*plural* **clashes**)
1 a fight or argument
2 a loud sound that is made when metal objects hit each other: *the clash of pans in the sink*

clasp /klɑːsp/ *verb*
to hold something or someone tightly: *He clasped his daughter in his arms.*

class /klɑːs/ *noun* (*plural* **classes**)
1 a group of students who have lessons together: *We were in the same class at school.*
2 a period of time in which students are taught something: *My first class starts at 8.30.*
3 one of the groups in a society with the same social and economic position
4 a group of similar or related things, especially plants and animals

classic[1] /ˈklæsɪk/ *adj*
1 A classic book, film, etc is one that has been popular for a long time and is very good: *the classic film 'Gone with the Wind'*
2 typical: *He's a classic example of a child who's clever but lazy.*

classic[2] /ˈklæsɪk/ *noun*
a classic book, film, etc

classical /ˈklæsɪkᵊl/ *adj*
classical music serious music by people like Mozart and Stravinsky

classroom /ˈklɑːsruːm/ *noun*
a room in a school where students have lessons ➲See colour picture **Classroom** on page Centre 4

clatter /ˈklætəʳ/ *verb*
to make a lot of noise: *I could hear Sophie clattering about in the kitchen.*
• **clatter** *noun*: *He dropped his spoon with a clatter.*

clause /klɔːz/ *noun*
a group of words containing a subject and a verb, that is usually only part of a sentence

a b **c** d e f g h i j k l m n o p q r s t u v w x y z

a b **c** d e f g h i j k l m n o p q r s t u v w x y z

claw

claw /klɔː/ *noun*
one of the sharp, curved nails on the feet of some animals and birds

clay /kleɪ/ *noun* **[no plural]**
a heavy soil that is hard when it is dry, used for making bricks and containers

clean[1] /kliːn/ *adj*
not dirty: *clean hands*

clean[2] /kliːn/ *verb*
to remove the dirt from something: *I spent the morning cleaning the house.*

cleaner /ˈkliːnəʳ/ *noun*
someone whose job is to clean houses, offices, and other places

clear[1] /klɪəʳ/ *adj*
1 easy to understand: *clear instructions*
2 easy to hear, read, or see: *These photos are very clear.*
3 obvious and not possible to doubt: *It was* ***clear that*** *she didn't like him.*
4 not covered or blocked by anything: *a clear road* ○ *a clear sky*
5 easy to see through: *clear glass*

clear[2] /klɪəʳ/ *verb*
1 to take away all the things or people from a place: *I've completely cleared the room.*
2 If the sky or weather clears, the clouds and rain disappear.
clear up *phrasal verb*
1 *UK* to make a place tidy: *Dad was clearing up in the kitchen.*
2 to improve: *If the weather clears up we'll go out.*

clearly /ˈklɪəli/ *adv*
1 in a way that is easy to see, hear, or understand: *He spoke very clearly.*
2 in a way that you cannot doubt: *He's clearly not interested.*

clerk /klɑːk/ *noun*
someone who works in an office but does not have an important job: *a bank clerk*

clever /ˈklevəʳ/ *adj*
1 good at learning and understanding things: *a clever student*
2 showing intelligence: *a clever idea*
● **cleverly** *adv*

click[1] /klɪk/ *verb*
1 to make a short, sharp sound: *The door clicked shut behind him.*
2 to push part of a computer mouse (= small computer control) to make the computer do something: *To start the program,* ***click on*** *its icon.*

click[2] /klɪk/ *noun*
a short, sharp sound: *the click of a switch*

client /klaɪənt/ *noun*
someone who pays for services or advice

cliff /klɪf/ *noun*
an area of high rocks next to the sea

cliff

climate /ˈklaɪmət/ *noun*
the weather conditions of an area: *a hot, dry climate*

climax /ˈklaɪmæks/ *noun* (*plural* **climaxes**)
the most exciting or important time: *The* ***climax of*** *her career was winning a gold medal.*

climb /klaɪm/ *verb*
to go up something: *Slowly we climbed the hill.*
● **climb** *noun*: *a long climb*

cling /klɪŋ/ *verb* (*present participle* **clinging**, *past* **clung**)
to hold someone or something tightly: *I* ***clung to*** *his hand in the dark.*

clinic /ˈklɪnɪk/ *noun*
a place where people go for medical treatment or advice: *an eye clinic*

clip[1] /klɪp/ *noun*
1 a small metal object used for holding things together: *a paper clip*
2 a short part of a film: *They showed clips from his new movie.*

clip[2] /klɪp/ *verb* (*present participle*

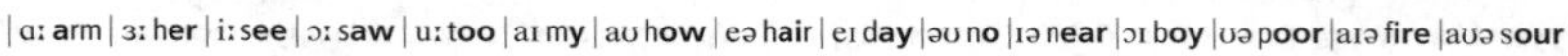

clipping, *past* **clipped)**
1 to fix things together with a clip: ***Clip*** *the microphone* ***to*** *the collar of your jacket.*
2 to cut small pieces from something

cloak /kləʊk/ *noun*
a loose coat with no parts for the arms

cloakroom /'kləʊkruːm/ *noun*
a room where you leave your coat at a theatre, school, etc

clock /klɒk/ *noun*
a large piece of equipment that shows you what time it is: *There was a clock on the wall.* ➲See colour picture **The Living Room** on page Centre 11

clockwise

clockwise | anti-clockwise *UK*, counterclockwise *US*

clockwise /'klɒkwaɪz/ *adj, adv*
in the same direction as the hands (= parts that point to the numbers) on a clock move ➲Opposite **anti-clockwise** *UK*, **counterclockwise** *US*

close[1] /kləʊz/ *verb* (*present participle* **closing,** *past* **closed)**
1 If something closes, it moves so that it is not open, and if you close something, you move it so that it is not open: *Jane closed the window.* ○ *Suddenly the door closed.*
2 If a shop or restaurant, etc closes, people cannot go in it: *The supermarket closes at 8 p.m.*
3 If a business closes, it stops operating forever.
close down *phrasal verb*
If a business closes down, it stops operating: *So many shops are closing down.*

close[2] /kləʊs/ *adj*
1 near in distance: *His house is* ***close to*** *the sea.*
2 near in time: *It was* ***close to*** *lunchtime when we arrived.*
3 If people are close, they know each other well and like each other: *close friends*
4 A close competition is one in which people's scores are very similar.
5 looking at or listening to someone or something very carefully: ***Keep a close watch on*** *the children* (= watch them carefully).

closed /kləʊzd/ *adj*
1 not open for business: *We went to the library but it was closed.*
2 not open: *Her eyes were closed.*

closely /'kləʊsli/ *adv*
1 If you look at something closely, you look at it carefully.
2 If two things are closely related, they are very similar: *The two languages are closely related.*

cloth /klɒθ/ *noun*
1 [no plural] material made from cotton, wool, etc, and used, for example, to make clothes or curtains
2 a piece of material used for cleaning or drying things

clothes /kləʊðz/ *plural noun*
things such as shirts and trousers that you wear on your body: *She was* ***wearing*** *her sister's* ***clothes.*** ➲See colour picture **Clothes** on page Centre 5

clothing /'kləʊðɪŋ/ *noun* **[no plural]**
clothes, especially of a particular type: *outdoor clothing*

cloud /klaʊd/ *noun*
one of the white or grey things in the sky that are made of small water drops: *rain clouds*

cloud

cloudy /'klaʊdi/ *adj* **(cloudier, cloudiest)**
with many clouds in the sky: *a cloudy day*

clown /klaʊn/ *noun*
someone with funny clothes and a painted face, who makes people laugh by being silly

clown

club[1] /klʌb/ *noun*

a b c d e f g h i j k l m n o p q r s t u v w x y z

1 a group of people who do a sport or other activity together: *a health club*
2 a long, thin stick used to hit the ball in golf ➲See colour picture **Sports 2** on page Centre 16
3 a place where people dance late at night

club[2] /klʌb/ *verb* (*present participle* **clubbing,** *past* **clubbed)**
go clubbing *UK* to go to clubs where there is music and dancing

clue /kluː/ *noun*
1 something that helps you to solve a problem or answer a question: *Police are searching the area for* ***clues to*** *the murder.*
2 not have a clue *informal* to know nothing about something: *I haven't a clue what you're talking about.*

clumsy /ˈklʌmzi/ *adj* **(clumsier, clumsiest)**
Clumsy people move in a way that is not controlled or careful, and often knock or damage things.

clung /klʌŋ/
past of cling

clutch[1] /klʌtʃ/ *verb*
to hold something tightly: *She clutched a coin in her hand.*

clutch[2] /klʌtʃ/ *noun* (*plural* **clutches)**
the part of a car that you press with your foot when you change gear (= the part that controls how fast the wheels turn) ➲See colour picture **Car** on page Centre 3

cm *written abbreviation for*
centimetre (= a unit for measuring length)

coach[1] /kəʊtʃ/ *noun* (*plural* **coaches)**
1 *UK* a comfortable bus used to take groups of people on long journeys: *a coach trip*
2 someone who gives lessons, especially in a sport: *a tennis coach*

coach[2] /kəʊtʃ/ *verb*
to give someone lessons, especially in a sport or school subject
• **coaching** *noun* **[no plural]**

coal /kəʊl/ *noun* **[no plural]**
a hard, black substance that is found in the ground and burnt as fuel: *a lump of coal*

coarse /kɔːs/ *adj*
rough or made of large pieces: *coarse cloth*

coast /kəʊst/ *noun*
the land next to the sea: *They live* ***on the*** *east* ***coast*** *of Scotland.*

coat /kəʊt/ *noun*
1 a piece of clothing that you wear over your other clothes when you are outside: *a winter coat* ➲See colour picture **Clothes** on page Centre 5
2 the fur that covers an animal's body
3 a layer of a liquid over a surface: *a coat of paint*

coat hanger /ˈkəʊt ˌhæŋəʳ/ *noun*
a wire, wooden, or plastic thing for hanging clothes on

cobweb /ˈkɒbweb/ *noun*
a structure of thin threads made by a spider (= creature with eight legs) to catch insects

cobweb

Coca Cola /ˌkəʊkəˈkəʊlə/ *noun* **[no plural]** *trademark*
a sweet, brown drink with bubbles

cock[1] /kɒk/ *noun UK*
an adult male chicken

cock[2] /kɒk/ *verb*
cock something up *phrasal verb, UK informal*
to do something wrong or badly: *I really cocked up my exams.*

cocoa /ˈkəʊkəʊ/ *noun* **[no plural]**
1 the dark brown powder used to make chocolate
2 a drink made by mixing cocoa powder with hot milk

coconut /ˈkəʊkənʌt/ *noun*
a large nut with a hard, hairy shell, a white part that you eat, and liquid in the centre

cod /kɒd/ *noun*
a large sea fish which is eaten as food

code /kəʊd/ *noun*
1 a set of letters, numbers, or signs that are used instead of ordinary words to keep a message secret: *It was written* ***in code.***
2 *UK* a set of numbers used at the beginning of a telephone number for a particular area

coffee /ˈkɒfi/ *noun*
1 a hot drink made from dark beans which are made into a powder, or a

cup of this drink: *Do you want a cup of coffee?*
2 [no plural] the beans from which coffee is made, or the powder made from these beans: *instant coffee*

coffin /ˈkɒfɪn/ *noun*
a box in which a dead body is buried

coin /kɔɪn/ *noun*
a flat, round piece of metal used as money: *a pound coin*

coincidence /kəʊˈɪnsɪdᵊns/ *noun*
when two very similar things happen at the same time but there is no reason for it: *It was just coincidence that we were travelling on the same train.*
● **coincidental** /kəʊˌɪnsɪˈdentᵊl/ *adj*
happening by coincidence: *The similarities are coincidental.*

Coke /kəʊk/ *noun trademark*
short for Coca Cola (= a sweet, brown drink with bubbles)

cold[1] /kəʊld/ *adj*
having a low temperature: *cold water/weather*

cold[2] /kəʊld/ *noun*
1 a common illness which makes your nose produce liquid: *I've got a cold.*
2 the cold cold weather: *Don't go out in the cold!*

collapse /kəˈlæps/ *verb* (*present participle* **collapsing**, *past* **collapsed**)
to fall down, sometimes breaking into pieces: *The roof collapsed under the weight of the snow.* ○ *He collapsed and died of a heart attack.*

collar /ˈkɒləʳ/ *noun*
1 the part of a shirt or coat that goes round your neck
2 a thin piece of leather that goes round the neck of dog or cat

colleague /ˈkɒliːg/ *noun*
someone that you work with

collect /kəˈlekt/ *verb*
1 to get things from different places and bring them together: *Police collected a lot of information during the investigation.* ○ *She collects dolls as a hobby.*
2 *UK* to go to a place and bring someone or something away from it: *She **collects** Anna **from** school at three o'clock.*
3 to ask people for money for something, for example a charity (= organization that helps people): *I'm collecting on behalf of Oxfam.*

collection /kəˈlekʃᵊn/ *noun*
1 a group of objects of the same type that have been brought together: *a private art collection*
2 [no plural] when something is taken away from a place: *rubbish collection*

college /ˈkɒlɪdʒ/ *noun UK*
a place where students are educated after they have stopped going to school: *a teacher-training college*

collision /kəˈlɪʒᵊn/ *noun*
an accident in which vehicles hit each other

colon /ˈkəʊlɒn/ *noun*
a mark (:) used before a list, an example, an explanation, etc

colony /ˈkɒləni/ *noun* (*plural* **colonies**)
a country or area controlled by a more powerful country

colour *UK* (*US* **color**) /ˈkʌləʳ/ *noun*
1 red, blue, green, yellow, etc: *What colour shall I paint the kitchen?* ➲See colour picture **Colours** on page Centre 6
2 [no plural] the colour of a person's skin, which shows their race

colourful *UK* (*US* **colorful**) /ˈkʌləfᵊl/ *adj*
having bright colours

column /ˈkɒləm/ *noun*
1 a tall, stone post which supports a roof
2 a long, vertical line of something

comb[1] /kəʊm/ *noun*
a flat piece of metal or plastic with a line of long, narrow parts along one side, that you use to tidy your hair

comb

comb[2] /kəʊm/ *verb*
to tidy your hair using a comb

combination /ˌkɒmbɪˈneɪʃᵊn/ *noun*
a mixture of different people or things: *Strawberries and cream – a perfect combination!*

combine /kəmˈbaɪn/ *verb* (*present participle* **combining**, *past* **combined**)
to become mixed or joined, or to mix or join things together: *Combine the sugar and the butter.*

come /kʌm/ *verb* (*present participle* **coming**, *past tense* **came**, *past participle* **come**)

1 to move or travel towards a person who is speaking: *Come here.* ○ *Can you* ***come to*** *my party?* ○ ***Here comes*** *Adam* (= Adam is coming).
2 to arrive somewhere: *I've come to see Mr Curtis.* ○ *Has the paper come yet?*
3 to go somewhere with the person who is speaking: ***Come with*** *us later.*
4 to have a particular position in a competition or list: *Our team came third.*
5 **come apart/off** to become separated or removed from something: *The book* ***came apart*** *in my hands.* ○ *The handle* ***came off.***
6 to happen: *Spring has come early.*
come back *phrasal verb*
to return to a place: *I've just come back from the dentist's.*
come from something *phrasal verb*
to be born, got from, or made somewhere: *She comes from Poland.* ○ *Milk comes from cows.*
come in *phrasal verb*
to enter a room or building: *Come in and have a cup of coffee.*
Come on! *phrasal verb, informal*
used to tell someone to hurry: *Come on, we're going to be late!*
come round *UK phrasal verb*
to visit someone at their house: *You must come round for dinner some time.*

comedy /ˈkɒmədi/ *noun* (*plural* **comedies**)
a funny film or play: *The film is described as a romantic comedy.*

comfort¹ /ˈkʌmfət/ *noun* **[no plural]**
a nice feeling of being relaxed and without pain: *Now you can watch the latest films* ***in the comfort of*** *your sitting room.*

comfort² /ˈkʌmfət/ *verb*
to make someone feel better when they are sad: *The family of the dead are being comforted by friends.*

comfortable /ˈkʌmftəbl/ *adj*
1 making you feel relaxed and free from pain: *comfortable shoes* ○ *a comfortable bed*
2 relaxed and without pain: ***Make yourself comfortable*** *while I fetch you a drink.* ➲Opposite **uncomfortable**
• **comfortably** *adv*

comic /ˈkɒmɪk/ *noun*
a magazine with stories told in pictures

comma /ˈkɒmə/ *noun*
a mark (,) used to separate parts of a sentence, or to separate the items in a list

command¹ /kəˈmɑːnd/ *noun*
1 an instruction to a computer
2 **[no plural]** control over someone or something and responsibility for them: *Jones was* ***in command*** (= the leader).
3 an order to do something

command² /kəˈmɑːnd/ *verb formal*
to order someone to do something: *The officer commanded his men to shoot.*

comment¹ /ˈkɒment/ *noun*
something that you say or write that shows your opinion: *He read my essay and* ***made*** *a few* ***comments.***

comment² /ˈkɒment/ *verb*
to make a comment: *My mum always* ***comments on*** *what I'm wearing.*

commentary /ˈkɒməntᵊri/ *noun* (*plural* **commentaries**)
a spoken description of an event while the event is happening: *the football commentary*

commerce /ˈkɒmɜːs/ *noun* **[no plural]**
the activities involved in buying and selling things

commercial¹ /kəˈmɜːʃᵊl/ *adj*
1 relating to buying and selling things
2 done in order to make a profit: *commercial television*

commercial² /kəˈmɜːʃᵊl/ *noun*
an advertisement on the radio or television

commit /kəˈmɪt/ *verb* (*present participle* **committing,** *past* **committed)**
1 to do something bad or illegal: *He went to prison for a crime he didn't commit.*
2 to make a definite decision to do something: *I've said I might be interested in the job but I haven't* ***committed myself*** *yet.*

commitment /kəˈmɪtmənt/ *noun*
1 a promise to do something: *Players must* ***make a commitment to*** *daily training.*
2 **[no plural]** when you give a lot of your time and energy to something

committed /kəˈmɪtɪd/ *adj*
giving a lot of your time and energy to something: *She's* ***committed to*** *the job.*

committee /kəˈmɪti/ *noun*
a group of people who represent a larger organization and make decisions for it

common[1] /ˈkɒmən/ *adj*
1 happening often or existing in large numbers: *Injuries are common in sports such as hockey.*
2 belonging to two or more people or things: *We don't have any common interests.*

common[2] /ˈkɒmən/ *noun*
have something in common to have the same interests, experiences, or qualities as someone or something else: *Sue and I don't have much in common.*

communicate /kəˈmjuːnɪkeɪt/ *verb* (*present participle* **communicating,** *past* **communicated)**
to talk or write to someone in order to share information with them: *I usually* ***communicate with*** *him by email.*

communication /kəˌmjuːnɪˈkeɪʃᵊn/ *noun* **[no plural]**
the act of communicating with other people: *The school is improving* ***communication between*** *teachers and parents.*

communications /kəˌmjuːnɪˈkeɪʃᵊnz/ *plural noun*
the different ways of sending information between people and places, such as post, telephones, computers, and radio: *the communications industry*

community /kəˈmjuːnəti/ *noun* (*plural* **communities)**
1 the people living in a particular area: *the local community*
2 a group of people with the same interests, religion, or nationality: *the Chinese community in London*

commute /kəˈmjuːt/ *verb*
to often travel between work and home
• **commmuter** *noun*

companion /kəmˈpænjən/ *noun*
someone who you spend a lot of time with or go somewhere with: *a travelling companion*

company /ˈkʌmpəni/ *noun*
1 (*plural* **companies)** an organization which sells things or services: *a software company*
2 [no plural] when you have a person or people with you: *I enjoy his company.*

comparable /ˈkɒmpᵊrəbl/ *adj*
similar in size, amount, or quality to something else: *Our prices are* ***comparable to*** *those in other shops.* ◦ *The two experiences are not comparable.*

comparative /kəmˈpærətɪv/ *noun*
the form of an adjective or adverb that is used to show that someone or something has more of a particular quality than someone or something else. For example 'better' is the comparative of 'good' and 'smaller' is the comparative of 'small'.

compare /kəmˈpeəʳ/ *verb* (*present participle* **comparing,** *past* **compared)**
1 to examine the ways in which two people or things are different or similar: *The teachers are always* ***comparing me with*** *my sister.*
2 compared to/with used when saying how one person or thing is different from another: *This room is very tidy compared to mine.*

comparison /kəmˈpærɪsᵊn/ *noun*
1 when you compare two or more people or things: *She's so tall that he looks tiny* ***by/in comparison****.*
2 There's no comparison. used to say that someone or something is much better than someone or something else

compartment /kəmˈpɑːtmənt/ *noun*
1 one of the separate areas inside a train
2 a separate part of a container, bag, etc: *a fridge with a small freezer compartment*

compass /ˈkʌmpəs/ *noun* (*plural* **compasses)**
a piece of equipment which shows you which direction you are going in

compass

compatible /kəmˈpætɪbl/ *adj*
happy or successful when together or combined: *This keyboard is* ***compatible with*** *all of our computers.*

compensation /ˌkɒmpənˈseɪʃᵊn/ *noun* **[no plural]**

a b c d e f g h i j k l m n o p q r s t u v w x y z

money that you give someone because you have hurt them or damaged something that they own

compete /kəm'piːt/ *verb* (*present participle* **competing,** *past* **competed)** to try to win a competition *She's **competing for** a place in next year's Olympics.*

competition /ˌkɒmpə'tɪʃən/ *noun* an event in which people try to win something by being the best, fastest, etc

competitive /kəm'petɪtɪv/ *adj* wanting to win or be better than other people: *She's very competitive.*

competitor /kəm'petɪtər/ *noun* someone who is trying to win a competition

complain /kəm'pleɪn/ *verb* to say that something is wrong or that you are angry about something: *Lots of people have **complained about** the noise.* ○ *She **complained** that no one listened to her.*

complaint /kəm'pleɪnt/ *noun* when someone says that something is wrong or not good enough: *I wish to **make a complaint**.*

complete[1] /kəm'pliːt/ *adj*
1 with all parts: *the complete works of Oscar Wilde*
2 used to make what you are saying stronger: *The meeting was a complete waste of time.*

complete[2] /kəm'pliːt/ *verb* (*present participle* **completing,** *past* **completed)**
1 to finish doing or making something: *The palace took 15 years to complete.*
2 to provide the last part needed to make something whole: *Complete the sentence with one of the adjectives provided.*

completely /kəm'pliːtli/ *adv* in every way or as much as possible: *I completely forgot that you were coming.* ○ *The two sisters are completely different.*

complicated /'kɒmplɪkeɪtɪd/ *adj* with many different parts and difficult to understand: *The instructions were so complicated.*

complication /ˌkɒmplɪ'keɪʃən/ *noun* something which makes a situation more difficult

compliment /'kɒmplɪmənt/ *noun* something good that you say about someone, showing that you admire them

compose /kəm'pəʊz/ *verb*
1 be composed of If something is composed of other things, it has those things in it: *The committee is composed of three men and six women.*
2 to write a piece of music

composer /kəm'pəʊzər/ *noun* someone who writes music

comprehensive school /ˌkɒmprɪ'hensɪv ˌskuːl/ *noun* a school in Britain for students aged 11 to 18 of all levels of ability

compulsory /kəm'pʌlsəri/ *adj* If something is compulsory, you must do it because a law or rule says you must: *The wearing of seat belts in cars is compulsory.*

computer /kəm'pjuːtər/ *noun* an electronic machine that can store and organize large amounts of information: *We put all our records **on computer**.*

conceal /kən'siːl/ *verb* to hide something: *I couldn't conceal my anger.*

concentrate /'kɒnsəntreɪt/ *verb* (*present participle* **concentrating,** *past* **concentrated)** to think very hard about the thing you are doing and nothing else: *Be quiet – I'm trying to concentrate.* ○ *I can't **concentrate on** my work. It's too noisy.*

concentration /ˌkɒnsən'treɪʃən/ *noun* **[no plural]** the ability to think only about something you are doing

concern[1] /kən'sɜːn/ *verb*
1 to be important to someone: *Environmental issues concern us all.*
2 to worry or upset someone: *What concerns me is her lack of experience.*
3 If a story, film, etc concerns a particular subject, it is about that subject.

concern[2] /kən'sɜːn/ *noun*
1 a feeling of worry about something: *I have **concerns about** his health.*
2 something that involves you or is important to you: *Our primary concern is safety.*

concerned /kən'sɜːnd/ *adj*

1 worried: *I'm a bit **concerned about** her health.*
2 as far as someone is concerned used to show what someone thinks about something: *He can do what he wants as far as I'm concerned.*

concerning /kən'sɜːnɪŋ/ *preposition* about something: *I've had a letter concerning my tax payments.*

concert /'kɒnsət/ *noun* a performance of music and singing: *a pop concert*

conclude /kən'kluːd/ *verb* (*present participle* **concluding**, *past* **concluded**)
1 *formal* to end something: *I would like to **conclude by** thanking you all for attending.*
2 to decide something after studying all the information about it: *The report **concluded that** the drug was safe.*

conclusion /kən'kluːʒᵊn/ *noun* your opinion after considering all the information about something: *I've **come to the conclusion that** we'll have to sell the car.*

concrete /'kɒŋkriːt/ *noun* **[no plural]** a wet mixture that is used in building and that becomes hard when it dries: *concrete blocks*

condemn /kən'dem/ *verb* to say very strongly that you think something is very bad: *The Prime Minister was quick to condemn the terrorists.*

condition /kən'dɪʃᵊn/ *noun*
1 the state that something or someone is in: *My bike's a few years old but it's **in** really **good condition**.*
2 something that must happen or be agreed before something else can happen: *One of the conditions of the contract is that we can't keep pets.*
3 an illness: *a heart condition*

conduct[1] /'kɒndʌkt/ *noun* **[no plural]** the way someone behaves

conduct[2] /kən'dʌkt/ *verb*
1 to organize or do something: *We are conducting a survey.*
2 to stand in front of a group of musicians and control how they play

conductor /kən'dʌktəʳ/ *noun* someone who stands in front of a group of musicians and controls how they play

cone /kəʊn/ *noun* a solid shape with a round bottom and a pointed top

conference /'kɒnfᵊrᵊns/ *noun* a large meeting, often lasting a few days, where people talk about a subject: *the annual sales conference*

confess /kən'fes/ *verb* to say that you have done something wrong: *He finally **confessed to** the murder.*

confession /kən'feʃᵊn/ *noun* when you say that you have done something wrong: *Sutcliffe has **made** a full **confession** to the police.*

confidence /'kɒnfɪdᵊns/ *noun* **[no plural]** when you are certain of your ability to do things well: *He's a good student, but he **lacks confidence**.*

confident /'kɒnfɪdᵊnt/ *adj*
1 certain about your ability to do things well
2 certain that something will happen: *I am **confident that** we can win this.*

confirm /kən'fɜːm/ *verb* to say or show that something is true: *His wife **confirmed that** he'd left the house at 8.00*

confirmation /ˌkɒnfə'meɪʃᵊn/ *noun* **[no plural]** when someone says or writes that something is true or certain

conflict[1] /'kɒnflɪkt/ *noun* disagreement or fighting: *The **conflict between** the two sides lasted for years.*

conflict[2] /kən'flɪkt/ *verb* to be different: *Her views on raising children **conflict with** mine.*

confuse /kən'fjuːz/ *verb* (*present participle* **confusing**, *past* **confused**)
1 to stop someone from understanding something: *My explanation just confused her.*
2 to think that one person or thing is another person or thing: *People often **confuse** me **with** my brother.*

confused /kən'fjuːzd/ *adj*
1 not able to think clearly or to understand something: *Sorry, I'm completely confused. ○ The politicians themselves are **confused about** what to do.*
2 not clear: *The witnesses gave confused accounts of what happened.*

confusion /kən'fjuːʒᵊn/ *noun* **[no plural]**
when people do not understand what is happening or what they should do: *The new system has caused a lot of confusion.*

congratulate /kən'grætʃʊleɪt/ *verb* (*present participle* **congratulating**, *past* **congratulated)**
to tell someone that you are happy about something good that they have done: *I **congratulated** Lulu **on** passing her exam.*

congratulations! /kənˌgrætʃʊ'leɪʃᵊnz/ *exclamation*
something that you say when you want to congratulate someone: *I hear you're getting married. Congratulations!*

conjunction /kən'dʒʌŋkʃᵊn/ *noun*
a word that is used to connect phrases or parts of a sentence. For example the words 'and' and 'because' are conjunctions.

connect /kə'nekt/ *verb*
to join two things or places together: *A small bridge connects the two parts of the building.*

connection /kə'nekʃᵊn/ *noun*
1 a relationship between people or things: *The **connection between** smoking and heart disease is well known.*
2 something that joins things together: *Many companies now offer free connection to the Internet.*

conquer /'kɒŋkəʳ/ *verb*
to take control of a country or to defeat people by war: *Peru was conquered by the Spanish in 1532.*

conquest /'kɒŋkwest/ *noun*
when someone takes control of a country, area, or situation: *the Roman conquest of Britain*

conscience /'kɒnʃᵊns/ *noun*
the part of you that makes you feel bad when you have done something wrong: *a guilty conscience*

conscious /'kɒnʃəs/ *adj*
awake and able to think and notice things: *He's still conscious but he's very badly injured.* ➲Opposite **unconscious**

consent[1] /kən'sent/ *noun* **[no plural]**
when you are allowed to do something: *You can't come without your parents' consent.*

consent[2] /kən'sent/ *verb*
to agree to do something: *They eventually **consented to** let us enter.*

consequence /'kɒnsɪkwəns/ *noun*
the result of an action, especially a bad result: *If you make him angry, you'll have to **suffer the consequences**.*

consequently /'kɒnsɪkwəntli/ *adv*
as a result: *I had car trouble and was consequently late.*

conservation /ˌkɒnsə'veɪʃᵊn/ *noun* **[no plural]**
the protection of nature: *wildlife conservation*

conservative /kən'sɜːvətɪv/ *adj*
not liking sudden changes or new ideas: *Older people tend to be more conservative.*

consider /kən'sɪdəʳ/ *verb*
to think carefully about something: *We're considering buying a new car.*

consideration /kənˌsɪdᵊr'eɪʃᵊn/ *noun*
1 something that you have to think about when you make decisions: *Safety is our main consideration.*
2 [no plural] when you are kind to people and try not to upset them: *They always treated me with consideration.*

consist /kən'sɪst/ *verb*
consist of something *phrasal verb*
to be made from two or more things: *The dessert consisted of fruit and cream.*

consonant /'kɒnsᵊnənt/ *noun*
a letter of the alphabet that is not a vowel. (The vowels are a,e,i,o and u.)

constant /'kɒnstənt/ *adj*
happening a lot or all the time: *She's in constant pain.*

construct /kən'strʌkt/ *verb*
to build something from many parts: *The building was constructed in 1930.*

construction /kən'strʌkʃᵊn/ *noun* **[no plural]**
the work of building houses, offices, bridges, etc: *railway construction*

consul /'kɒnsᵊl/ *noun*
someone whose job is to work in a foreign country and help people from their own country who go there

consult /kən'sʌlt/ *verb*

1 to go to a person or book to get information or advice: *For more information, consult your travel agent.*
2 to talk with someone before you decide something: *Why didn't you consult me about this?*

consume /kən'sjuːm/ *verb* (*present participle* **consuming**, *past* **consumed)**
to use something: *These lights consume a lot of electricity.*

consumer /kən'sjuːməʳ/ *noun*
someone who buys or uses goods or services: *These price cuts are good news for consumers.*

consumption /kən'sʌmʃᵊn/ *noun* **[no plural]**
the amount of something that someone uses, eats, or drinks: *China's total energy consumption*

contact¹ /'kɒntækt/ *noun*
1 **[no plural]** when you talk or write to someone: *We* ***keep in*** *close* ***contact*** *with our grandparents.*
2 **[no plural]** when two people or things are touching each other: *Wash your hands if they* ***come into contact with*** *chemicals.*
3 someone you know who can help you because of their job: *business contacts*

contact² /'kɒntækt/ *verb*
to telephone someone or write to them: *I've been trying to contact you for days.*

contact lens /'kɒntækt ˌlenz/ *noun* (*plural* **contact lenses)**
a small piece of plastic that you put on your eye to make you see more clearly

contain /kən'teɪn/ *verb*
If one thing contains another, it has it inside it: *a box containing a diamond ring*

container /kən'teɪnəʳ/ *noun*
an object such as a box or a bottle that is used for holding something

content /kən'tent/ *adj*
happy: *I was* ***content to*** *stay home and read.*

contented /kən'tentɪd/ *adj*
happy: *a contented smile*

contents /'kɒntents/ *plural noun*
all of the things that are contained inside something: *Please empty out the contents of your pockets.*

container

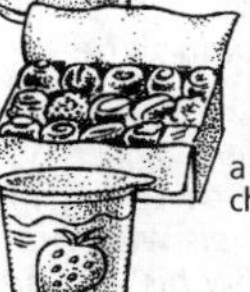

contest /'kɒntest/ *noun*
a competition

continent /'kɒntɪnənt/ *noun*
one of the seven main areas of land on the Earth, such as Asia, Africa, or Europe

continental /ˌkɒntɪ'nentᵊl/ *adj*
relating to a continent

continual /kən'tɪnjuəl/ *adj*
happening again and again over a long period of time: *I can't work with these continual interruptions.*
• **continually** *adv*: *Dad continually complains about money.*

continue /kən'tɪnjuː/ *verb* (*present participle* **continuing**, *past* **continued)**
1 to keep happening or doing something: *It* ***continued to*** *snow for three days.* ○ *Ava continued working until June.*
2 to start doing or saying something again, after stopping: *We'll have to continue this discussion tomorrow.*
3 to go further in a particular direction: *Continue down the road until you reach Elm Street.*

continuous /kən'tɪnjuəs/ *adj*
not stopping: *continuous pain*
• **continuously** *adv*: *Their baby cried*

continuously all afternoon.

contract /ˈkɒntrækt/ *noun*
a legal agreement between two people or organizations

contrary[1] /ˈkɒntrᵊri/ *noun*
to the contrary saying or showing the opposite: *She claimed she was innocent, despite evidence to the contrary.*

contrary[2] /ˈkɒntrᵊri/ *adj* **contrary to something**
opposite to what someone said or thought: *Contrary to popular belief, he is not a stupid man.*

contrast[1] /ˈkɒntrɑːst/ *noun*
an obvious difference between two people or things: *The* ***contrast between*** *their lifestyles couldn't be greater.*

contrast[2] /kənˈtrɑːst/ *verb*
to compare two people or things: *If you* ***contrast*** *his early novels* ***with*** *his later work, you can see how his writing has developed.*

contribute /kənˈtrɪbjuːt/ *verb* (*present participle* **contributing**, *past* **contributed**)
to give something, especially money: *I* ***contributed*** *$20* ***towards*** *Andrea's present.*

contribution /ˌkɒntrɪˈbjuːʃᵊn/ *noun*
an amount of money that is given to help pay for something: *a generous* ***contribution to*** *charity*

control[1] /kənˈtrəʊl/ *noun*
1 [no plural] the power to make a person or thing do what you want: *The new teacher has no* ***control over*** *the class.* ○ *He* ***lost control of*** *the car.*
2 under control If a situation is under control, things are happening in the way that you want them to: *Don't worry – everything's under control.*
3 out of control behaving very badly and not stopped by anyone: *The children were out of control.*

control[2] /kənˈtrəʊl/ *verb* (*present participle* **controlling**, *past* **controlled**)
to make a person or thing do what you want: *Can't you control your dogs?* ○ *This switch controls the temperature.*

control freak /kənˈtrəʊl friːk/ *noun informal*
someone who wants to do all of an activity and will not let anyone else be involved: *He's a real control freak in the kitchen.*

convenience /kənˈviːniəns/ *noun*
1 [no plural] when something is easy to use and suitable for what you want to do: *the convenience of credit cards* ➲Opposite **inconvenience**
2 something that makes life easier: *Fortunately, the house has every modern convenience.*

convenient /kənˈviːniənt/ *adj*
1 easy and helpful: *When would be a convenient time to meet?*
2 near or easy to get to: *The new supermarket is very convenient for me.* ➲Opposite **inconvenient**
• **conveniently** *adv*

convent /ˈkɒnvənt/ *noun*
a building where nuns (= religious women) live together

conversation /ˌkɒnvəˈseɪʃᵊn/ *noun*
when two or more people talk together: *a telephone conversation* ○ *We* ***had a conversation*** *about football.*

convert /kənˈvɜːt/ *verb*
to change something into something else: *The old factory was* ***converted into*** *offices.*

convict /kənˈvɪkt/ *verb*
to decide officially in a court of law that someone has done a crime: *He was* ***convicted of*** *murder.*

convince /kənˈvɪns/ *verb* (*present participle* **convincing**, *past* **convinced**)
to make someone believe that something is true: *He tried to* ***convince*** *me* ***that*** *I needed a new car.*

convinced /kənˈvɪnst/ *adj*
completely certain about something: *I'm* ***convinced that*** *he's wrong.*

cook[1] /kʊk/ *verb*
to make food ready to eat: *Who's cooking this evening?* ○ *She cooked the meat in oil and spices.*
• **cooked** *adj*
not raw

cook[2] /kʊk/ *noun*
someone who prepares food for people to eat

cooker /ˈkʊkəʳ/ *UK* (*US* **stove**) *noun*
a piece of equipment used to cook food: *an electric cooker*

cookery /ˈkʊkᵊri/ *noun* **[no plural]** *UK*
preparing food for people to eat

cook

cookie /ˈkʊki/ *noun US*
a thin, flat cake that is sweet and dry ➲See colour picture **Food** on page Centre 7

cooking /ˈkʊkɪŋ/ *noun* **[no plural]**
preparing food for people to eat: *I **do** the **cooking**.*

cool[1] /kuːl/ *adj*
1 slightly cold: *a cool drink*
2 *informal* good or fashionable: *Cool hat, Maria!*
3 calm and not worried: *She seemed very cool before her exam.*
• **coolness** *noun* **[no plural]**

cool[2] /kuːl/ *verb*
to become less hot, or make something become less hot: *Allow the bread to cool.*
cool down *phrasal verb*
to become less hot: *We went for a swim to cool down.*

cool[3] /kuːl/ *exclamation informal*
used when you like something or agree to something: *"I'll see you at 6.00, then?" "Cool!"*

cooperate /kəʊˈɒpəreɪt/ *verb* (*present participle* **cooperating**, *past* **cooperated**)
1 to work together with someone: *Witnesses are **cooperating with** detectives.*
2 to do what someone asks you to do: *We will get there on time as long as the children cooperate.*

cooperation /kəʊˌɒpəˈreɪʃən/ *noun* **[no plural]**
when you work together with someone or do what they ask you: *international cooperation*

cooperative /kəʊˈɒpərətɪv/ *adj*
willing to help or do what people ask: *If I need any help she is usually very cooperative.*

cope kəʊp/ *verb* (*present participle* **coping**, *past* **coped**)
to do something well in a difficult situation: *She has a lot of work but somehow she copes.*

copper /ˈkɒpəʳ/ *noun* **[no plural]**
a soft, red-brown metal

copy[1] /ˈkɒpi/ *noun* (*plural* **copies**)
1 something that is made to look exactly like something else: *Always **make copies of** important documents.*
2 a single book, newspaper, etc of which many have been made: *a copy of the New York Times*

copy[2] /ˈkɒpi/ *verb* (*present participle* **copying**, *past* **copied**)
1 to make something that is the same as something else: *Copy the file onto a disk.*
2 to behave like someone else: *He likes to copy his older brother.*
3 to cheat by using someone else's work: *She copied his answers.*

cord /kɔːd/ *noun*
1 thick string, or a piece of this
2 a piece of wire covered in plastic, used to connect electrical equipment to a power supply: *a telephone cord*

core /kɔːʳ/ *noun*
1 the most important part of something: *Lack of money is **at the core of** the problem.*
2 the hard, central part of fruits such as apples, which contains the seeds

cork /kɔːk/ *noun*
1 [no plural] a light material that comes from the outside of a particular tree
2 a small piece of this material put in the top of a wine bottle to close it

corn /kɔːn/ *noun* **[no plural]** *UK*
a crop of grain, or the seed from this crop used to make flour: *fields of corn*

corner /ˈkɔːnəʳ/ *noun*
the point or area where two lines, walls, or roads meet: *the corner of the table ○ There was a television **in the corner** of the room. ○ The pub is **at the corner** of Ross Street and Mill Road.*

corporation /ˌkɔːpərˈeɪʃən/ *noun*
a large company or group of companies

a b c d e f g h i j k l m n o p q r s t u v w x y z

a b c d e f g h i j k l m n o p q r s t u v w x y z

corpse /kɔːps/ *noun*
a dead person's body

correct /kəˈrekt/ *adj*
accurate, or having no mistakes: *Check that you have the correct information.* ○ *Was that the correct answer?*
• **correctly** *adv*

correction /kəˈrekʃən/ *noun*
a change to make something right or better: *She* ***made*** *some* ***corrections*** *before giving the essay to her teacher.*

correspond /ˌkɒrɪˈspɒnd/ *verb*
to be the same or very similar: *The newspaper story does not* ***correspond with*** *what really happened.*

correspondence /ˌkɒrɪˈspɒndəns/ *noun* **[no plural]**
letters from one person to another: *business correspondence*

corridor /ˈkɒrɪdɔːʳ/ *noun*
a passage in a building or train with rooms on one or both sides

cosmetics /kɒzˈmetɪks/ *plural noun*
substances that you put on your face or body to make you look better

cost[1] /kɒst/ *noun*
1 the amount of money that you need to buy or do something: *The* ***cost of*** *rail travel is terrible.*
2 at all costs If something must be done at all costs, it is very important that it is done: *We have to succeed at all costs.*

cost[2] /kɒst/ *verb* (*present participle* **costing**, *past* **cost**)
If something costs a particular amount of money, you have to pay that in order to buy or do it: *How much do these shoes cost?* ○ ***It costs*** *$5 to send the package by airmail.*

costume /ˈkɒstjuːm/ *noun*
all the clothes that you wear at the same time, usually special clothes

cosy /ˈkəʊzi/ *adj* **(cosier, cosiest)** *UK*
comfortable and warm: *It's nice and cosy in this room.*

cot /kɒt/ *UK* (*US* **crib**) *noun*
a bed with high sides for a baby

cottage /ˈkɒtɪdʒ/ *noun*
a small house, usually in the countryside

cotton /ˈkɒtən/ *noun* **[no plural]**
1 cloth or thread that is made from the cotton plant: *a cotton shirt*
2 a plant that produces a soft, white substance used for making thread and cloth

cotton wool /ˌkɒtən ˈwʊl/ *noun* **[no plural]** *UK*
a soft mass of cotton, usually used for cleaning your skin ➲See colour picture **The Bathroom** on page Centre 1

couch /kaʊtʃ/ *noun*
a long, comfortable piece of furniture that two or more people can sit on

cough[1] /kɒf/ *verb*
to make air come out of your throat with a short sound: *Paul has been coughing and sneezing all day.*

cough[2] /kɒf/ *noun*
when you make air come out of your throat with a short sound

could *strong form* /kʊd/ *weak form* /kəd/ *verb*
1 used as the past form of 'can' to talk about what someone or something was able or allowed to do: *I couldn't see him.* ○ *But you said I could go!*
2 used to talk about what is possible or might happen: *She could arrive any time now.*
3 used for asking politely for something: *Could I have another drink?* ○ *Could I speak to Mr Davis, please?*

couldn't /ˈkʊdənt/ *short for*
could not: *I couldn't understand what he was saying.*

could've /ˈkʊdəv/ *short for*
could have: *It could've been much worse.*

council, Council /ˈkaʊnsəl/ *noun*
a group of people who are chosen to control a town, city, or area: *Edinburgh City Council*

councillor /ˈkaʊnsələʳ/ *noun UK*
a member of a council

count[1] /kaʊnt/ *verb*
1 to see how many people or things there are: *I counted the money on the table.*
2 to say numbers in their correct order: *Can you count to twenty in French?*
3 to be important: *Doesn't my opinion* ***count for*** *anything?*
count on someone *phrasal verb*
to be certain that you can depend on someone: *I can always count on my*

parents to help me.
count up someone/something *phrasal verb*
to add together all the people or things in a group
count² /kaʊnt/ *noun* **[no plural]**
1 when you count something, or the total number you get after counting: ***At the last count*** *there were 410 club members.*
2 lose count to forget how many of something there is: *I've lost count of the number of times she's arrived late.*
counter /ˈkaʊntəʳ/ *noun*
the place in a shop, bank, etc, where people are served: *The woman* ***behind the counter*** *took his money.*
countless /ˈkaʊntləs/ *adj*
very many: *She has had countless jobs.*
country /ˈkʌntri/ *noun*
1 (*plural* **countries**) an area of land that has its own government, army, etc: *European countries*
2 the country the areas that are away from towns and cities
countryside /ˈkʌntrɪsaɪd/ *noun* **[no plural]**
land that is not in towns or cities and has farms, fields, etc
county /ˈkaʊnti/ *noun* (*plural* **counties**)
an area of Britain, Ireland, or the US
couple /ˈkʌpl/ *noun*
1 two or a few: *I went to New York with* ***a couple of*** *friends.*
2 two people who are married or having a romantic relationship: *a married couple*
coupon /ˈkuːpɒn/ *noun*
a piece of paper that you can use to buy something at a cheaper price
courage /ˈkʌrɪdʒ/ *noun* **[no plural]**
the quality that makes you able to do dangerous or difficult things: *The soldiers fought with great courage.* ○ *She didn't* ***have the courage*** *to tell him the truth.*
courageous /kəˈreɪdʒəs/ *adj*
brave: *He was a courageous fighter.*
• **courageously** *adv*
course /kɔːs/ *noun*
1 of course
a used to say 'yes' strongly, often to be polite: *"Can you help me?" "Of course!"*
b used to show that what you are saying is obvious: *Of course, the Olympics are not just about money.*
2 of course not used to say 'no' strongly: *"Do you mind if I borrow your pen?" "Of course not."*
3 a set of lessons about a particular subject: *She did a ten-week computer course.*
4 a part of a meal: *a three-course dinner*
5 an area used for horse races or playing golf: *a golf course*
6 the direction in which a ship, aeroplane, etc is moving: *During the storm, the boat was blown* ***off course*** (= in the wrong direction).
7 the way something develops, usually over a long time: *Nuclear weapons have changed* ***the course of*** *modern history.*
court /kɔːt/ *noun*
1 the place where a judge decides if someone has done a crime: *The suspect appeared* ***in court*** *charged with robbery.*
2 an area for playing a sport: *a tennis court*
3 the home of a king or queen and the people who live with them
courteous /ˈkɜːtiəs/ *adj*
polite and showing respect
courtesy /ˈkɜːtəsi/ *noun* **[no plural]**
behaviour that is polite and shows respect
cousin /ˈkʌzᵊn/ *noun*
the child of your aunt or uncle
cover¹ /ˈkʌvəʳ/ *verb*
1 to put something over something else: *They covered him with a blanket.* ○ *He covered his face with his hands.*
2 to form a layer on the surface of something: *Snow covered the trees.*
3 to include or deal with a subject or piece of information: *The book covers European history from 1789-1914.*
cover something up *phrasal verb*
to put something over something else, in order to hide it: *We used a picture to cover up a hole in the wall.*
cover² /ˈkʌvəʳ/ *noun*
1 the outer part of a book, magazine, etc, that protects the pages: *Her picture was on the cover of 'Vogue' magazine.*
2 something you put over something else, usually to protect it: *an ironing board cover*
cow /kaʊ/ *noun*

a large female farm animal kept for milk or meat

coward /kaʊəd/ *noun*
someone who is not brave and does not do dangerous things

cowboy /ˈkaʊbɔɪ/ *noun*
a man whose job is to look after cows in the US, and who rides a horse

crab /kræb/ *noun*
a sea animal with ten legs and a shell

crack[1] /kræk/ *verb*
1 to break something so that thin lines appear on its surface, or to become broken in this way: *Linda cracked her tooth when she fell.* ○ *The glass cracked in my hand.*
2 to make a sudden, short noise

crack[2] /kræk/ *noun*
1 a line on the surface of something that is damaged: *Several cups had cracks in them.*
2 a narrow space between two parts of something or between two things: *I could see sunlight through a crack in the curtains.*
3 a sudden, short noise: *a crack of thunder*

cradle /ˈkreɪdl/ *noun*
a baby's bed, especially one that moves from side to side

craft /krɑːft/ *noun*
1 an activity in which you make something using a lot of skill, especially with your hands: *traditional crafts such as weaving*
2 (*plural* **craft**) a boat

crafty /ˈkrɑːfti/ *adj* **(craftier, craftiest)**
clever at getting what you want, especially by deceiving people

cram /kræm/ *verb* (*present participle* **cramming,** *past* **crammed)**
to force too many things into a small space: *The refugees were crammed into the truck.*

crane /kreɪn/ *noun*
a large machine used for lifting and moving heavy things

crash[1] /kræʃ/ *noun* (*plural* **crashes)**
1 an accident in which a vehicle hits something: *a car/plane crash*
2 a sudden, loud noise made when something falls or breaks: *I heard a crash and hurried into the kitchen.*

crash[2] /kræʃ/ *verb*
1 If a vehicle crashes, it hits something by accident: *The van skidded and* ***crashed into*** *a tree.*
2 If a computer crashes, it suddenly stops working.
3 to hit something and make a loud noise: *The waves crashed against the rocks.*

crash helmet /ˈkræʃ ˌhelmɪt/ *noun*
a hard hat that protects your head when you ride a motorcycle

crate /kreɪt/ *noun*
a large box used for carrying or storing things

crawl /krɔːl/ *verb*
to move on your hands and knees: *I crawled under the desk to plug the lamp in.*

crawl

crayon /ˈkreɪɒn/ *noun*
a stick of coloured wax used for drawing

crazy /ˈkreɪzi/ *adj* **(crazier, craziest)**
1 stupid or strange: *a crazy idea*
2 annoyed or angry: *Dad* ***went crazy*** *when I told him what had happened.*
3 be crazy about someone/something to love someone very much, or to be very interested in something: *Mia's crazy about baseball.*

creak /kriːk/ *verb*
If something such as a door or a piece of wood creaks, it makes a long noise when it moves: *creaking floorboards*

cream[1] /kriːm/ *noun*
1 [no plural] a thick, white liquid that is taken from milk
2 a soft substance that you put on your skin: *hand cream*

cream[2] /kriːm/ *adj*
being a yellow-white colour

create /kriˈeɪt/ *verb* (*present participle* **creating,** *past* **created)**
to make something happen or exist: *The project will create more than 500 jobs.* ○ *The snow created further problems.*

creation /kriˈeɪʃᵊn/ *noun*
1 [no plural] when someone makes something happen or exist: *the creation of a new political party*
2 something that someone has

made: *The museum contains some of his best creations.*

creative /kri'eɪtɪv/ *adj*
good at thinking of new ideas and making interesting things: *Her book is full of creative ways to decorate your home.*

creature /'kriːtʃə^r/ *noun*
anything that lives but is not a plant: *Dolphins are intelligent creatures.*

credit[1] /'kredɪt/ *noun*
1 [no plural] a way of buying something in which you pay for it at a later time: *He bought most of the furniture* ***on credit****.*
2 [no plural] praise that is given to someone for something they have done: *I did most of the work but Dan* ***got*** *all* ***the credit****!*
3 in credit having money in your bank account

credit[2] /'kredɪt/ *verb*
to add money to someone's bank account

credit card /'kredɪt ˌkɑːd/ *noun*
a small plastic card that allows you to buy something and pay for it later: *He paid* ***by credit card****.*

creep /kriːp/ *verb* (*present participle* **creeping**, *past* **crept**)
to move very quietly and carefully: *I crept out of the room.*

creepy /'kriːpi/ *adj* **(creepier, creepiest)** *informal*
strange and frightening: *a creepy story*

crept /krept/
past of creep

crest /krest/ *noun*
the highest part of a hill or wave

crew /kruː/ *noun*
the people who work together on a ship, aeroplane or train: *a crew member*

cricket /'krɪkɪt/ *noun*
1 [no plural] a game in which two teams of eleven people score points by hitting a ball and running between two sets of sticks ➲See colour picture **Sports 2** on page Centre 16
2 an insect that jumps and makes a noise by rubbing its wings together

crime /kraɪm/ *noun*
1 [no plural] illegal activities: *violent crime*
2 something someone does that is illegal: *He* ***committed*** *a serious* ***crime****.*

criminal /'krɪmɪnᵊl/ *noun*
someone who has done a crime

crisis /'kraɪsɪs/ *noun* (*plural* **crises** /'kraɪsiːz/)
a situation or time that is very dangerous or difficult: *an economic crisis* ○ *The country's leadership is* ***in crisis****.*

crisp[1] /krɪsp/ *adj*
Crisp food is hard and pleasant: *a crisp apple*

crisp[2] /krɪsp/ *UK* (*US* **chip**) *noun*
a very thin slice of potato that has been cooked in oil and is eaten cold: *a packet of crisps* ➲See colour picture **Food** on page Centre 7

critic /'krɪtɪk/ *noun*
1 someone who says that they do not approve of someone or something: *a critic of the government*
2 someone whose job is to give their opinion of a book, play, film, etc: *a film critic*

critical /'krɪtɪkᵊl/ *adj*
1 saying that someone or something is bad or wrong: *He is very* ***critical of*** *the way I work.*
2 very important for the way things will happen in the future: *a critical decision*
3 very serious or dangerous: *The doctors said her condition was critical.*

criticism /'krɪtɪsɪzᵊm/ *noun*
when you say that something or someone is bad

criticize /'krɪtɪsaɪz/ *verb* (*present participle* **criticizing**, *past* **criticized**)
to say that something or someone is bad: *The film was criticized for being too violent.*

crocodile /'krɒkədaɪl/ *noun*
a big reptile with a long mouth and sharp teeth, that lives in lakes and rivers

crooked /'krʊkɪd/ *adj*
not straight: *crooked teeth*

crop /krɒp/ *noun*
a plant such as a grain, fruit, or vegetable that is grown in large amounts by farmers

cross[1] /krɒs/ *verb*
1 to go from one side of something to the other side: *It's not a good place to cross the road.*
2 If two lines, roads, etc cross, they

go over or across each other.
3 cross your arms/fingers/legs to put one of your arms, fingers, or legs over the top of the other

cross² /krɒs/ *noun*
1 an object in the shape of a cross (†), used as a symbol of the Christian religion
2 a written mark (x), used for showing that something is wrong

cross³ /krɒs/ *adj*
angry: *Don't be* ***cross with*** *me!*

crossing /ˈkrɒsɪŋ/ *noun*
a place where people can go across a road, river, etc

crossword /ˈkrɒswɜːd/ (*also* **ˈcrossword ˌpuzzle**) *noun*
a game in which you write words which are the answers to questions in a pattern of black and white squares

crouch /kraʊtʃ/ *verb*
to move your body close to the ground by bending your knees: *I crouched behind the chair to avoid being seen.*

crow /krəʊ/ *noun*
a large black bird that makes a loud noise

crowd¹ /kraʊd/ *noun*
a large group of people who are together in one place: *A large crowd had gathered to wait for the princess.*

crowd² /kraʊd/ *verb*
crowd around (someone/something) *phrasal verb*
to stand in a group around someone or something: *Everyone crowded around my desk.*

crowded /ˈkraʊdɪd/ *adj*
very full of people: *a crowded train*

crown /kraʊn/ *noun*
a round object made of gold and jewels (= valuable stones) that a king or queen wears on their head

crown

crude /kruːd/ *adj*
1 simple and made without skill: *It's a fairly crude device.*
2 rude: *a crude remark*

crude oil /ˌkruːd ˈɔɪl/ *noun* **[no plural]**
oil in its natural state

cruel /ˈkruːəl/ *adj*
very unkind, or causing people or animals to suffer: *a cruel joke* ○ *Many people think hunting is* ***cruel to*** *animals.*

cruelty /ˈkruːəlti/ *noun* **[no plural]**
cruel behaviour or a cruel action: *laws against cruelty to animals*

cruise¹ /kruːz/ *noun*
a holiday on a ship, sailing from place to place

cruise² /kruːz/ *verb* (*present participle* **cruising**, *past* **cruised**)
to move in a vehicle at a speed that does not change: *The plane is cruising at 500 miles per hour.*

crumb /krʌm/ *noun*
a very small piece of bread, cake, etc
➲See colour picture **Quantities** on page Centre 14

crumble /ˈkrʌmbl/ *verb* (*present participle* **crumbling**, *past* **crumbled**)
to break into small pieces, or to make something break into small pieces: *Buildings crumbled as the earthquake struck.*

crumple /ˈkrʌmpl/ *verb* (*present participle* **crumpling**, *past* **crumpled**)
to press paper or cloth so that it is not smooth: *a crumpled shirt*

crunch /krʌnʃ/ *verb*
1 to make a noise by chewing hard food: *She was* ***crunching on*** *an apple.*
2 to make a sound as if something is being crushed: *The gravel crunched under our feet.*

crush /krʌʃ/ *verb*
to press something so hard that it is made flat or broken into pieces: *Her car was crushed by a falling tree.*

crust /krʌst/ *noun*
the hard part on the outside of bread or other baked foods

crutch /krʌtʃ/ *noun* (*plural* **crutches**)
a stick that you put under your arm to help you walk if your leg is hurt: *Charles was* ***on crutches*** (= walking with crutches) *for six weeks.*

cry¹ /kraɪ/ *verb* (*present participle* **crying**, *past* **cried**)
1 to produce tears from your eyes because you are sad: *My baby brother cries all the time.*
2 to speak or say something loudly: *"Look at this!" cried Raj.*

cry

cry[2] /kraɪ/ *noun* (*plural* **cries**)
a shout: *I could hear the cries of children playing in the street.*

cub /kʌb/ *noun*
a young bear, fox, lion, etc

cube /kjuːb/ *noun*
a solid object with six square sides of the same size

cuckoo /ˈkʊkuː/ *noun*
a small bird that makes a sound like its name

cucumber /ˈkjuːkʌmbəʳ/ *noun*
a long, green vegetable that you eat in salads ➲See colour picture **Fruit and Vegetables** on page Centre 8

cuddle /ˈkʌdl/ *verb* (*present participle* **cuddling**, *past* **cuddled**)
to put your arms around someone to show them that you love them: *Her mother cuddled her until she stopped crying.*
• **cuddle** *noun*

cuff /kʌf/ *noun*
the bottom part of a sleeve that goes around your wrist

cultivate /ˈkʌltɪveɪt/ *verb* (*present participle* **cultivating**, *past* **cultivated**)
to prepare land and grow crops on it
• **cultivation** /ˌkʌltɪˈveɪʃᵊn/ *noun* **[no plural]**

culture /ˈkʌltʃəʳ/ *noun*
1 the habits, traditions, and beliefs of a country or group of people: *American/Japanese culture*
2 **[no plural]** music, art, theatre, literature, etc: *popular culture*

cunning /ˈkʌnɪŋ/ *adj*
clever at getting what you want, especially by tricking people

cup

cup /kʌp/ *noun*
1 a small, round container with a handle on the side, used to drink from: *a cup of tea*
2 a prize given to the winner of a competition

cupboard /ˈkʌbəd/ *noun*
a piece of furniture with a door on the front and shelves inside, used for keeping things ➲See colour picture **Kitchen** on page Centre 10

cure[1] /kjʊəʳ/ *noun*
something that makes someone with an illness healthy again: *They are trying to find* ***a cure for*** *cancer.*

cure[2] /kjʊəʳ/ *verb* (*present participle* **curing**, *past* **cured**)
to make someone with an illness healthy again

curiosity /ˌkjʊəriˈɒsəti/ *noun*
[no plural] the feeling of wanting to know or learn about something: *Just* ***out of curiosity****, how did you get my address?*

curious /ˈkjʊəriəs/ *adj*
wanting to know or learn about something: *I was* ***curious about*** *his life in India.*

curl[1] /kɜːl/ *noun*
something with a small, curved shape, especially a piece of hair: *a child with blonde curls*

curl[2] /kɜːl/ *verb*
to make something into the shape of a curl, or to be this shape: *The cat curled its tail around its body.*
curl up *phrasal verb*
to sit or lie in a position with your arms and legs close to your body: *She curled up and went to sleep.*

curly /ˈkɜːli/ *adj* **(curlier, curliest)**
with many curls: *curly hair* ➲See colour picture **Hair** on page Centre 9

currant /ˈkʌrᵊnt/ *noun*
a small, black dried fruit used in cooking

currency /ˈkʌrᵊnsi/ *noun* (*plural* **currencies**)
the units of money used in a particular country: *foreign currency*

current[1] /ˈkʌrᵊnt/ *adj*
happening or existing now: *What is your current address?*
• **currently** *adv The factory currently* (= now) *employs 750 people.*

current[2] /ˈkʌrᵊnt/ *noun*
1 the natural flow of air or water in one direction: *a current of air*
2 the flow of electricity through a

a b c d e f g h i j k l m n o p q r s t u v w x y z

wire: *an electrical current*

curry /ˈkʌri/ *noun* (*plural* **curries**)
a type of food from India, made of vegetables or meat cooked with hot spices

curse[1] /kɜːs/ *noun*
magic words which are intended to bring bad luck to someone: *The witch* ***put a curse on*** *him.*

curse[2] /kɜːs/ *verb* (*present participle* **cursing**, *past* **cursed**)
to use rude words because you are angry: *He cursed angrily under his breath.*

cursor /ˈkɜːsəʳ/ *noun*
a symbol on a computer screen which shows the place where you are working

curtain /ˈkɜːtᵊn/ *noun*
a piece of material which hangs down to cover a window, stage, etc ➲See colour picture **The Living Room** on page Centre 11

curve[1] /kɜːv/ *noun*
a line which bends round like part of a circle: *a road with gentle curves*

curve[2] /kɜːv/ *verb* (*present participle* **curving**, *past* **curved**)
to move in a curve or form a curve: *The road curves to the left.*

cushion /ˈkʊʃᵊn/ *noun*
a cloth bag filled with something soft which you put on a chair ➲See colour picture **The Living Room** on page Centre 11

custom /ˈkʌstəm/ *noun*
a habit or tradition

customer /ˈkʌstəməʳ/ *noun*
a person or organization that buys things or services from a shop or business

customs /ˈkʌstəmz/ *noun* **[no plural]**
the place where your bags are examined when you are going into a country

cut[1] /kʌt/ *verb* (*present participle* **cutting**, *past* **cut**)
1 to use a knife or other sharp tool to divide something or make a hole in something: *Cut the meat into small pieces.* ○ *He cut the piece of wood in half.* ○ *I had my hair cut last week.*
2 to reduce the size or amount of something: *Prices have been cut by 25%.*
3 to hurt yourself on a sharp object

cut

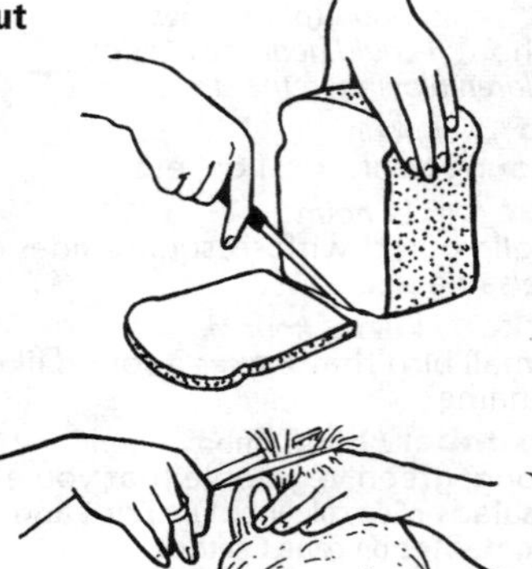

which makes you bleed: *She cut her finger on a broken glass.*

cut back (something) *phrasal verb*
to reduce the amount of money being spent on something: *We have had to* ***cut back on*** *training this year.*

cut something down *phrasal verb*
to make a tree or other plant fall to the ground by cutting it near the bottom

cut something out *phrasal verb*
to remove something made of paper or cloth: *She cut out his picture from the magazine.*

cut something up *phrasal verb*
to cut something into pieces

cut[2] /kʌt/ *noun*
1 an injury made when the skin is cut with something sharp: *He suffered cuts and bruises in the accident.*
2 an opening made with a sharp tool: *She made a cut in the material.*
3 a reduction in the number or amount of something: *job cuts* ○ *The workers were angry about the* ***cut in*** *pay.*

cutlery /ˈkʌtlᵊri/ *UK* (*US* **silverware**) *noun* **[no plural]**
knives, forks, and spoons

cycle /ˈsaɪkl/ *verb* (*present participle* **cycling**, *past* **cycled**)
to ride a bicycle
• **cycling** *noun* **[no plural]** the activity of riding a bicycle ➲See colour picture **Sports 2** on page Centre 16
• **cyclist** *noun*

someone who rides a bicycle

cylinder /ˈsɪlɪndə^r/ *noun*

a shape with circular ends and long, straight sides

Dd

D, d /diː/
the fourth letter of the alphabet

dad /dæd/ *noun informal*
father: *My dad has curly brown hair.*

daddy /ˈdædi/ *noun*
a word for 'father', used especially by children

daffodil /ˈdæfədɪl/ *noun*
a yellow flower that grows in spring

daffodil

daft /dɑːft/ *adj UK informal*
silly: *That's a daft idea.*

dagger /ˈdægəʳ/ *noun*
a short knife, used as a weapon

daily /ˈdeɪli/ *adj, adv*
happening or made every day or once a day: *a daily newspaper* ○ *He exercises daily.*

dairy /ˈdeəri/ *noun* (*plural* **dairies**)
1 a place where milk products are made
2 a company which sells milk products

daisy /ˈdeɪzi/ *noun* (*plural* **daisies**)
a small flower with white petals and a yellow centre

dam /dæm/ *noun*
a strong wall built across a river to stop the water and make a lake

damage¹ /ˈdæmɪdʒ/ *noun* **[no plural]**
harm or injury: *The strong wind caused serious* ***damage to*** *the roof.*

damage² /ˈdæmɪdʒ/ *verb* (*present participle* **damaging**, *past* **damaged**)
to harm or break something: *Many buildings were damaged in the storm.*
• **damaging** *adj*
harmful: *the damaging effects of pollution*

damp /dæmp/ *adj*
slightly wet, usually in a bad way: *It was cold and damp outside.*

dance¹ /dɑːns/ *verb* (*present participle* **dancing**, *past* **danced**)
to move your feet and body to the rhythm of music: *She's dancing with Steven.*
• **dancer** *noun*: someone who dances

dance² /dɑːns/ *noun*
1 a set of movements that you do to music
2 a social event where people dance to music

dandelion /ˈdændɪlaɪən/ *noun*
a yellow wild flower

dandruff /ˈdændrʌf/ *noun* **[no plural]**
small pieces of dead skin in someone's hair or on their clothes

danger /ˈdeɪndʒəʳ/ *noun*
1 the possibility that someone or something will be harmed or killed: *the dangers of rock climbing* ○ *The soldiers were* ***in*** *serious* ***danger***.
2 something or someone that may hurt you: *Icy roads are a* ***danger to*** *drivers.*

dangerous /ˈdeɪndʒᵊrəs/ *adj*
If someone or something is dangerous, they could hurt you: *It's dangerous to ride a motorcycle without a helmet.*
• **dangerously** *adv*: *She was dangerously close to the edge.*

dare /deəʳ/ *verb* (*present participle* **daring**, *past* **dared**)
1 dare do something to be brave enough to do something: *I didn't dare tell Dad that I'd scratched his car.*
2 dare someone to do something to try to make someone do something dangerous: *She dared her friend to climb onto the roof.*
3 Don't you dare! *informal* used to tell someone angrily not to do something: *Don't you dare hit your sister!*
4 How dare she/you!, etc said when you are very angry about something someone has done: *How dare you talk to me like that!*

dark¹ /dɑːk/ *adj*
1 with no light or not much light: *It doesn't* ***get dark*** *until 9 o'clock in the evening.*
2 nearer to black than white in colour: *dark blue/green*
3 having black or brown hair or brown skin: *A short, dark woman with glasses arrived.* ➲See colour picture **Hair** on page Centre 9

dark² /dɑːk/ *noun*
1 the dark when there is no light

somewhere: *He's scared of the dark.*
2 before/after dark before/after it becomes night: *She doesn't let her children out after dark.*

darkness /ˈdɑːknəs/ *noun* **[no plural]**
when there is little or no light: *He stumbled around in the darkness looking for the light switch.*

darling /ˈdɑːlɪŋ/ *noun*
used when you speak to someone you love: *Would you like a drink, darling?*

dart /dɑːt/ *verb*
to move somewhere quickly and suddenly: *A cat darted across the street.*

darts

darts /dɑːts/ *noun* **[no plural]**
a game played by throwing small arrows at a round board

dash[1] /dæʃ/ *verb*
to go somewhere quickly: *She dashed downstairs when she heard the phone.*

dash[2] /dæʃ/ *noun* (*plural* **dashes**)
1 a mark (–) used to separate parts of sentences
2 when you run somewhere very quickly: *As the rain started, we **made a dash for** shelter.*

dashboard /dæʃbɔːd/ *noun*
the part at the front of a car with equipment to show things such as how fast you are going and how hot it is ↄSee colour picture **Car** on page Centre 3

data /ˈdeɪtə/ *noun* **[no plural]**
information or facts about something: *financial data*

database /ˈdeɪtəbeɪs/ *noun*
information stored in a computer in an organized structure so that it can be searched in different ways: *a national database of missing people*

date /deɪt/ *noun*
1 a particular day of the month or year: *"What's the date today?" "It's the fifth."* ○ *Please give your name, address and **date of birth**.*
2 a romantic meeting when two people go out somewhere: *He's asked her out on a date.*
3 a sticky brown fruit with a long seed inside

daughter /ˈdɔːtəʳ/ *noun*
your female child

daughter-in-law /ˈdɔːtərɪnlɔː/ *noun* (*plural* **daughters-in-law**)
your son's wife

dawn /dɔːn/ *noun* **[no plural]**
the early morning when light first appears in the sky: *We woke **at dawn**.*

day /deɪ/ *noun*
1 a period of 24 hours: *the days of the week* ○ *I saw her the day before yesterday.*
2 the period during the day when there is light from the sun: *a bright, sunny day*
3 the time that you usually spend at work or school: *She's had a very busy day at the office.*
4 the other day a few days ago: *I saw Terry the other day.*
5 day after day every day for a long period of time: *Day after day they marched through the mountains.*
6 one day used to talk about something that happened in the past: *One day, I came home to find my windows smashed.*
7 one day/one of these days used to talk about something you think will happen in the future: *One of these days I'll tell her what really happened.*
8 these days used to talk about the present time: *I don't go out much these days.*

daybreak /ˈdeɪbreɪk/ *noun* **[no plural]**
the time in the morning when light first appears in the sky

daydream /ˈdeɪdriːm/ *verb*
to have good thoughts about something you would like to happen

daylight /ˈdeɪlaɪt/ *noun* **[no plural]**
the natural light from the sun during the day

daytime /ˈdeɪtaɪm/ *noun* **[no plural]**

the period of the day when there is light from the sun, or the period when most people are at work: *a daytime telephone number*

dead /ded/ *adj*
1 not now alive: *She's been dead for 20 years now.* ○ *There were three children among **the dead**.*
2 If a piece of equipment is dead, it is not working: *a dead battery* ○ *The phone suddenly **went dead**.*
3 *informal* If a place is dead, it is too quiet and nothing interesting is happening there.

deadline /'dedlaɪn/ *noun*
a time by which something must be done: *The deadline for entering the competition is tomorrow.*

deadly /'dedli/ *adj*
causing death: *a deadly virus*

deaf /def/ *adj*
not able to hear: *Many deaf people learn to lip read.* ○ *He goes to a school for **the deaf**.*
• **deafness** *noun* **[no plural]**

deal[1] /diːl/ *noun*
1 an arrangement or an agreement, especially in business: *The police refused to **do a deal** with the terrorists.*
2 a good/great deal a lot: *A great deal of time and effort went into arranging this party.*

deal[2] /diːl/ *verb* (*present participle* **dealing,** *past* **dealt)**
to give cards to players in a game: *Whose turn is it to deal?*
deal with something *phrasal verb*
to take action in order to do something: *How do you deal with this problem?*

dealer /'diːləʳ/ *noun*
a person or company that buys and sells things for profit: *a car dealer*

dealt /delt/
past of deal

dear[1] /dɪəʳ/ *adj*
1 used at the beginning of a letter, before the name of the person you are writing to: *Dear Amy* ○ *Dear Sir/ Madam*
2 *UK* expensive: *The hotel was very dear.*

dear[2] /dɪəʳ/ *exclamation*
Oh dear! used to express surprise and disappointment: *Oh dear! I forgot my keys!*

death /deθ/ *noun*
the end of life: *Do you believe in life after death?* ○ *We need to reduce the number of deaths from heart attacks.*

debate[1] /dɪ'beɪt/ *noun*
talk or arguments about a subject: *There has been a lot of public **debate on** the safety of food.*

debate[2] /dɪ'beɪt/ *verb* (*present participle* **debating,** *past* **debated)**
1 to talk about a subject in a formal way: *These issues need to be debated.*
2 to try to make a decision about something: *I'm still debating whether to go out tonight or not.*

debit card /'debɪt ˌkɑːd/ *noun*
a plastic card used to pay for things directly from your bank account

debt /det/ *noun*
1 an amount of money that you owe someone: *She's working in a bar to try to **pay off her debts**.*
2 [no plural] when you owe money to someone: *We don't want to **get into debt**.* ○ *He's **in debt**.*

decade /'dekeɪd/ *noun*
a period of ten years

decay /dɪ'keɪ/ *verb*
to gradually become bad or be destroyed: *Sugar makes your teeth decay.*
• **decay** *noun* **[no plural]** *tooth decay*

deceive /dɪ'siːv/ *verb* (*present participle* **deceiving,** *past* **deceived)**
to make someone believe something that is not true: *The company deceived customers by selling old computers as new ones.*

December /dɪ'sembəʳ/ *noun*
the twelfth month of the year

decent /'diːsᵊnt/ *adj*
1 of a quality or level that is good enough: *a decent meal/salary*
2 honest and good: *He seemed like a very decent man.*

decide /dɪ'saɪd/ *verb* (*present participle* **deciding,** *past* **decided)**
to choose something after thinking about the possibilities: *She's **decided to** take the job.* ○ *Have you decided what to wear?*

decision /dɪ'sɪʒᵊn/ *noun*
a choice that you make about something after thinking about many possibilities: *What was your decision – are you coming or not?* ○ *We*

need to ***make a decision***.

deck /dek/ *noun*
one of the floors of a ship, bus, or aircraft: *The children like to sit on the top deck of the bus.*

deckchair /ˈdektʃeəʳ/ *noun*
a folding chair that you use outside

declaration /ˌdekləˈreɪʃᵊn/ *noun*
something that someone says officially, giving information about something: *a declaration of independence*

decorate /ˈdekᵊreɪt/ *verb (present participle* **decorating,** *past* **decorated)**
1 to make something look more attractive by putting things on it: *They decorated the room with balloons for her party.*
2 to put paint or paper on the walls of a room or building: *The whole house needs decorating.*

decoration /ˌdekᵊˈreɪʃᵊn/ *noun*
when you make something look more attractive by putting things on it, or something that you use to do this: *Christmas decorations* ○ *She hung some pictures around the room for decoration.*

decrease /dɪˈkriːs/ *verb (present participle* **decreasing,** *past* **decreased)**
to become less, or to make something become less: *Prices have decreased.*
● **decrease** /ˈdiːkriːs/ *noun: There has been a* ***decrease in*** *the number of violent crimes.* ➲Opposite **increase**

deed /diːd/ *noun formal*
something that you do: *good deeds*

deep

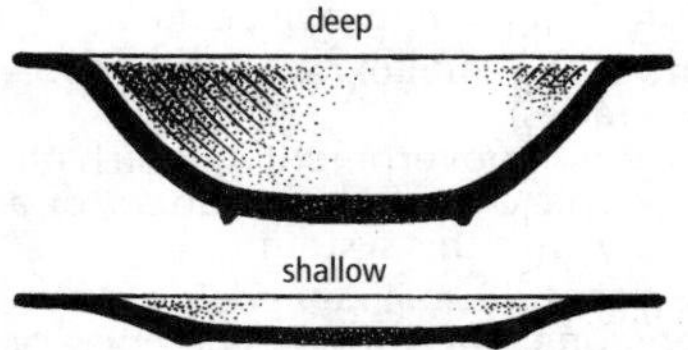

deep /diːp/ *adj*
1 having a long distance from the top to the bottom or the front to the back: *The water is a lot deeper than it seems.*
2 one metre/6ft, etc deep one metre/6 ft, etc from the top to the bottom, or from the front the back: *This end of the pool is two metres deep.*
3 A deep feeling is very strong: *deep affection*
4 a deep sleep when someone is sleeping in a way that makes it difficult to wake them up
5 A deep sound is low: *a deep voice*
6 A deep colour is strong and dark: *deep brown eyes*

deeply /ˈdiːpli/ *adv*
very much: *I have fallen deeply in love with her.*

deer /dɪəʳ/ *noun*
a large, wild animal that has antlers (= long horns) if it is male

deer

defeat /dɪˈfiːt/ *verb*
to win against someone in a fight or competition: *She was defeated by an Australian player in the first round of the tournament.*
● **defeat** *noun*
when someone loses a fight or competition

defence /dɪˈfens/ *noun*
protection, or something that provides protection against attack or criticism: *the body's defences against infection* ○ *She argued strongly* ***in defence of*** *her actions.*

defend /dɪˈfend/ *verb*
to protect someone or something from being attacked or criticized: *She tried to defend herself with a knife.* ○ *The editor defended his decision to publish the photos.*

defiant /dɪˈfaɪənt/ *adj*
refusing to obey someone or something: *a defiant child*
● **defiantly** *adv*

define /dɪˈfaɪn/ *verb (present participle* **defining,** *past* **defined)**
to say exactly what something means: *Your duties are clearly defined in the contract.*

definite /ˈdefɪnət/ *adj*
certain, clear, and not likely to change: *We need a definite answer by tomorrow.*

definite article /ˌdefɪnət ˈɑːtɪkl/ *noun*

in grammar, used to mean the word 'the'

definitely /ˈdefɪnətli/ *adv*
without any doubt: *This book is definitely worth reading.*

definition /ˌdefɪˈnɪʃᵊn/ *noun*
an explanation of the meaning of a word or phrase: *a dictionary definition*

defy /dɪˈfaɪ/ *verb* (*present participle* **defying**, *past* **defied**)
to refuse to obey someone or something

degree /dɪˈgriː/ *noun*
1 a unit for measuring temperatures or angles, shown by the symbol ° written after a number
2 a qualification given for completing a university course: *She has a* ***degree in*** *physics.*

delay[1] /dɪˈleɪ/ *verb*
1 to make something happen at a later time than you planned: *Can you delay your departure until next week?*
2 to make someone or something late: *I was delayed by traffic.*

delay[2] /dɪˈleɪ/ *noun*
when you have to wait longer than expected: *An accident caused long delays on the motorway.*

delete /dɪˈliːt/ *verb* (*present participle* **deleting**, *past* **deleted**)
to remove something, especially on a computer: *I deleted the file by mistake.*

deliberate /dɪˈlɪbᵊrət/ *adj*
If an action is deliberate, you wanted or planned to do it: *This was a deliberate attempt by them to deceive us.*

deliberately /dɪˈlɪbᵊrətli/ *adv*
If you do something deliberately, you wanted or planned to do it: *He deliberately lied to the police.*

delicate /ˈdelɪkət/ *adj*
1 soft, light, or gentle: *a delicate shade of pink*
2 easy to damage or break: *a delicate shell*

delicatessen /ˌdelɪkəˈtesᵊn/ *noun*
a shop which sells cheeses and cooked meats

delicious /dɪˈlɪʃəs/ *adj*
very good to eat or drink: *This soup is absolutely delicious.*

delight[1] /dɪˈlaɪt/ *noun* **[no plural]**
happiness and pleasure: *The children screamed with delight.*

delight[2] /dɪˈlaɪt/ *verb*
to make someone feel very pleased: *The new discovery has delighted scientists everywhere.*

delighted /dɪˈlaɪtɪd/ *adj*
very pleased: *They are* ***delighted with*** *their new car.*

delightful /dɪˈlaɪtfᵊl/ *adj*
very pleasant or attractive: *We had a delightful evening.*

deliver /dɪˈlɪvəʳ/ *verb*
1 to take letters or things to a person or place: *They can deliver the sofa on Wednesday.*
2 deliver a baby to help take a baby out of its mother when it is being born

delivery /dɪˈlɪvᵊri/ *noun* (*plural* **deliveries**)
when someone takes letters or things to a person or place: *Is there a charge for delivery?*

demand[1] /dɪˈmɑːnd/ *noun*
1 a strong request or need for something: *a final* ***demand for*** *payment ○ an increasing demand for cheap products*
2 in demand wanted or needed in large numbers: *Good teachers are always in demand.*

demand[2] /dɪˈmɑːnd/ *verb*
to ask for something in an angry way: *I demanded an explanation.*

demo /ˈdeməʊ/ *noun*
1 an example of a product, given or shown to someone to try to make them buy it: *a software demo*
2 *UK short for* demonstration (= political walk): *a student demo*

democracy /dɪˈmɒkrəsi/ *noun* (*plural* **democracies**)
a system of government in which all the people choose their leaders, or a country with this system

democrat /ˈdeməkræt/ *noun*
1 someone who supports democracy
2 Democrat someone who supports the Democratic Party in the US

democratic /ˌdeməˈkrætɪk/ *adj*
following or supporting the political system of democracy: *a democratic society*

demolish /dɪˈmɒlɪʃ/ *verb*
to destroy something such as a

building: *The factory is dangerous, and will have to be demolished.*

demonstrate /ˈdemənstreɪt/ *verb* (*present participle* **demonstrating**, *past* **demonstrated**)
1 to show someone how to do something: *She demonstrated how to use the new software.*
2 to show that something exists or is true: *The experiment clearly **demonstrates that** there are positive benefits.*
3 to walk or stand with a group of people to show that you have a strong opinion about something: *Thousands of people gathered to **demonstrate against** the new proposals.*

demonstration /ˌdemənˈstreɪʃᵊn/ *noun*
1 when a group of people walk or stand together to show that they have a strong opinion about something: *They're taking part in a **demonstration against** nuclear weapons.*
2 showing how to do something: *We asked the sales assistant to give us a demonstration.*

den /den/ *noun*
the home of some wild animals

denim /ˈdenɪm/ *noun* **[no plural]**
thick, strong, cotton cloth, used to make clothes: *denim jeans*

dense /dens/ *adj*
1 with a lot of people or things close together: *dense forest*
2 thick and difficult to see through: *dense fog*
• **densely** *adv*

dentist /ˈdentɪst/ *noun*
someone who looks at and repairs teeth: *I've got an appointment at **the dentist's** (= where the dentist works) tomorrow.*

dentist

deny /dɪˈnaɪ/ *verb* (*present participle* **denying**, *past* **denied**)
to say that something is not true, or that you have not done something: *She denies any involvement in the attack.*

deodorant /diˈəʊdᵊrᵊnt/ *noun*
something that you put on your body to stop bad smells

depart /dɪˈpɑːt/ *verb formal*
to leave a place: *The train to Lincoln will **depart from** platform 9.*

department /dɪˈpɑːtmənt/ *noun*
a part of an organization which does a particular type of work: *the sales department*

department store /dɪˈpɑːtmənt ˌstɔːʳ/ *noun*
a large shop which sells different types of things

departure /dɪˈpɑːtʃəʳ/ *noun*
when someone or something leaves a place: *the departure of flight BA117*

depend /dɪˈpend/ *verb*
it/that depends used to say that you are not certain about something because other things affect your answer: *"Are you coming out tonight?" "It depends where you're going."*

depend on someone or **something** *phrasal verb*
1 to need the help of someone or something: *Our economy depends on the car industry.*
2 to be affected by someone or something: *The choice of products depends on what you can spend.*

dependant /dɪˈpendənt/ *noun UK*
someone, usually a child, who needs your money to live: *The pension provides for him and all his dependants.*

dependent /dɪˈpendənt/ *adj*
needing the help of someone or something: *She's completely **dependent on** her parents for money.*

deposit[1] /dɪˈpɒzɪt/ *noun*
1 a payment that you make immediately when you decide to buy something: *They've put down a **deposit on** a house.*
2 money that you pay into a bank: *to make a deposit*
3 money that you pay when you rent something, and that is returned to you if you do not damage anything

deposit[2] /dɪˈpɒzɪt/ *verb*
1 to put something down somewhere: *He **deposited** his books **on** the table.*
2 to put money into a bank: *She*

a b c d e f g h i j k l m n o p q r s t u v w x y z

***deposited** $150,000 **in** a Swiss bank account.*

depot /ˈdepəʊ/ *noun*
a place where vehicles or goods are kept

depress /dɪˈpres/ *verb*
to make someone feel very sad: *This place really depresses me.*

depressed /dɪˈprest/ *adj*
very sad, often for a long time: *She 's been very depressed since her marriage broke up.*

depressing /dɪˈpresɪŋ/ *adj*
making you feel sad and without any hope for the future: *The news is very depressing.*

depression /dɪˈpreʃᵊn/ *noun*
when you feel very sad, or a mental illness that makes you feel very sad: *Nearly three million people suffer from depression every year.*

depth /depθ/ *noun*
the distance from the top of something to the bottom: *Dig a hole 10 cm **in depth**.*

deputy /ˈdepjəti/ *noun* (*plural* **deputies**)
someone who has the second most important job in an organization: *the deputy Prime Minister*

descend /dɪˈsend/ *verb formal*
to move down or go down: *We descended four flights of stairs.*

descendant /dɪˈsendənt/ *noun*
someone who is related to someone who lived a long time ago

describe /dɪˈskraɪb/ *verb* (*present participle* **describing,** *past* **described)**
to say what someone or something is like: *I tried to describe what I had seen.*

description /dɪˈskrɪpʃᵊn/ *noun*
words that tell you what someone or something is like: *I **gave** the police a **description of** the stolen jewellery.*

desert /ˈdezət/ *noun*
a large, hot, dry area of land with very few plants: *the Sahara Desert*

deserted /dɪˈzɜːtɪd/ *adj*
A deserted place has no people in it: *a deserted street*

desert island /ˌdezət ˈaɪlənd/ *noun*
a tropical island where no one lives, far from any other places

deserve /dɪˈzɜːv/ *verb* (*present participle* **deserving,** *past* **deserved)**
If you deserve something good or bad, it should happen to you because of the way you have behaved: *He deserves to be locked up for life.*

design[1] /dɪˈzaɪn/ *noun*
1 a drawing which shows how something will be made: *Production engineers are working on the new designs.*
2 a pattern or decoration: *a design of fish and sea shells*

design[2] /dɪˈzaɪn/ *verb*
to draw or plan something before making it: *She designs furniture.*

designer[1] /dɪˈzaɪnəʳ/ *noun*
someone who draws and plans how something will be made: *a fashion designer*

designer[2] /dɪˈzaɪnəʳ/ *adj*
designer jeans/sunglasses, etc expensive clothes or things

desire /dɪˈzaɪəʳ/ *noun*
wanting something very much: *the desire to have children*

desk /desk/ *noun*
a table that you sit at to write or work ➲See colour picture **The Office** on page Centre 12

desk

despair /dɪˈspeəʳ/ *noun* **[no plural]**
a feeling of having no hope: *She shook her head **in despair**.*
• **despair** *verb*

desperate /ˈdespᵊrət/ *adj*
1 feeling that you have no hope and will do anything to change the situation you are in: *He was desperate to get her back.*
2 needing or wanting something very much: *By two o'clock I was **desperate for** something to eat.*
• **desperately** *adv*
• **desperation** /ˌdespᵊˈreɪʃᵊn/ *noun* **[no plural]**

despise /dɪˈspaɪz/ *verb* (*present participle* **despising,** *past* **despised)**
to hate someone or something and have no respect for them: *The two groups despise each other.*

despite /dɪˈspaɪt/ *preposition*
although something happened or is

true: *I'm still pleased with the house despite all the problems we've had.*

dessert

dessert /dɪ'zɜːt/ *noun*
sweet food that is eaten after the main part of a meal

destination /ˌdestɪ'neɪʃᵊn/ *noun*
the place where someone or something is going: *Spain is a very popular holiday destination.*

destroy /dɪ'strɔɪ/ *verb*
to damage something so badly that it cannot be used or does not exist: *Many works of art were destroyed in the fire.*

destruction /dɪ'strʌkʃᵊn/ *noun* **[no plural]**
when something is destroyed: *We are all responsible for the* ***destruction of*** *the forest.*

detach /dɪ'tætʃ/ *verb*
to take a part of something off so that it is separate: *Please complete and detach the form below.*

detail /'diːteɪl/ *noun*
1 a piece of information about something: *Please send me* ***details of*** *your training courses.*
2 in detail including every part of something: *He explained it all in great detail.*

detailed /'diːteɪld/ *adj*
giving a lot of information: *a detailed description*

detect /dɪ'tekt/ *verb*
to discover or notice something: *This special camera can detect bodies by their heat.*

detective /dɪ'tektɪv/ *noun*
someone whose job is to discover information about a crime

detergent /dɪ'tɜːdʒᵊnt/ *noun*
a liquid or powder that is used to clean things

determination /dɪˌtɜːmɪ'neɪʃᵊn/ *noun* **[no plural]**
when someone continues trying to do something, although it is very difficult: *He'll need great determination and skill to win this match.*

determined /dɪ'tɜːmɪnd/ *adj*
wanting so much to do something that you keep trying very hard: *He's* ***determined to*** *win this match.*

detest /dɪ'test/ *verb*
to hate someone or something: *They used to be friends, but now they absolutely detest each other.*

develop /dɪ'veləp/ *verb*
1 to change and become better, or to make someone or something become better: *He's* ***developing into*** *a very good tennis player.*
2 to start to have a problem or feeling: *Shortly after take-off the plane developed engine trouble.*
3 to use special chemicals on a piece of film to make photographs appear

development /dɪ'veləpmənt/ *noun*
1 when someone or something changes and becomes better: *There have been some major developments in technology recently.*
2 something new that happens and changes a situation: *Have there been any more developments since I left?*

device /dɪ'vaɪs/ *noun*
a piece of equipment: *an electronic device for sending messages.*

devil /'devᵊl/ *noun*
1 the Devil the most powerful evil spirit, according to the Christian and Jewish religions
2 an evil spirit

devote /dɪ'vəʊt/ *verb* (*present participle* **devoting**, *past* **devoted)**
to use time or energy for a particular purpose: *She devotes most of her free time to charity work.*

dew /djuː/ *noun* **[no plural]**
drops of water that form on surfaces outside during the night

diagonal /daɪ'ægᵊnᵊl/ *adj*
going from the top corner of a square to the bottom corner on the other side
• **diagonally** *adv*

diagram /'daɪəgræm/ *noun*

a b c **d** e f g h i j k l m n o p q r s t u v w x y z

a simple picture which shows what something looks like or explains how something works

dial[1] /daɪəl/ *noun*
a round part on a clock or piece of equipment that shows you the time or other measurement

dial[2] /daɪəl/ *verb* (*present participle* **dialling,** *past* **dialled)**
to make a telephone call to a particular number: *Dial 0 for the operator.*

dialect /ˈdaɪəlekt/ *noun*
a form of a language that people speak in a particular part of a country

dialogue /ˈdaɪəlɒg/ *noun*
the talking in a book, play, or film

diamond /ˈdaɪəmənd/ *noun*
1 a very hard, transparent stone that is very valuable and is often used in jewellery: *a diamond ring*
2 a shape with four straight sides of equal length that join to form two large angles and two small angles

diamond

diarrhoea /ˌdaɪəˈrɪə/ *noun* **[no plural]**
an illness that makes a person go to the toilet more often

diary /ˈdaɪəri/ *noun* (*plural* **diaries)**
1 a book in which you write things that you must remember to do: *According to my diary, I've got two meetings on Monday.*
2 a book in which you write about what you have done and your thoughts and feelings: *She* ***kept a diary*** *of her trip to Egypt.*

dice /daɪs/ *noun*
a small object with six equal square sides, each with between one and six spots on it, used in games

dice

dictate /dɪkˈteɪt/ *verb* (*present participle* **dictating,** *past* **dictated)**
to say or read something for someone to write down: *Tony was busy* ***dictating*** *letters* ***to*** *his secretary.*
• **dictation** *noun*

dictator /dɪkˈteɪtə^{r}/ *noun*
a leader who has complete power in a country

dictionary /ˈdɪkʃ^{ə}n^{ə}ri/ *noun* (*plural* **dictionaries)**
a book that contains a list of words in alphabetical order with their meanings explained or written in another language: *Use your dictionaries to look up any words you don't understand.*

did /dɪd/
past tense of do

didn't /ˈdɪd^{ə}nt/
short for did not

die /daɪ/ *verb* (*present participle* **dying,** *past* **died)**
1 to stop living: *Many of the refugees* ***died of*** *hunger.*
2 be dying for something; be dying to do something *informal* to very much want to have or do something: *I'm dying for a drink.*

diesel /ˈdiːz^{ə}l/ *noun* **[no plural]**
fuel used in the engines of some vehicles

diet /daɪət/ *noun*
1 the type of food that someone usually eats: *His diet isn't very healthy.*
2 when someone eats a particular type or amount of food because they are ill or want to become thinner: *No cake for me, thanks – I'm* ***on a diet****.*

difference /ˈdɪf^{ə}r^{ə}ns/ *noun*
1 the way in which two people or things are not the same: *What's the* ***difference between*** *an ape and a monkey?*
2 make any difference to have an effect on a situation: *Do what you like, it doesn't make any difference.*

different /ˈdɪf^{ə}r^{ə}nt/ *adj*
1 not the same as someone or something else: *Jo's very* ***different from*** *her sister, isn't she?*
2 used to talk about separate things or people of the same type: *eight different flavours of ice cream*
• **differently** *adv*

difficult /ˈdɪfɪk^{ə}lt/ *adj*
1 not easy to do or understand: *Japanese is a difficult language to learn.*
2 not friendly or easy to deal with: *a difficult teenager*

difficulty /ˈdɪfɪk^{ə}lti/ *noun* (*plural* **difficulties)**

a problem: *I had difficulty finding somewhere to park.*

dig /dɪɡ/ *verb* (*present participle* **digging,** *past* **dug)**
to make a hole in the ground by moving some of the ground or soil away: *They've dug a huge hole in the road.*

dig

digest /daɪˈdʒest/ *verb*
to change food in your stomach into substances that your body can use: *Your stomach contains acid to help you digest your food.*
• **digestion** *noun* **[no plural]**

digital /ˈdɪdʒɪtᵊl/ *adj*
1 using an electronic system that changes sounds or images into numbers before it stores or sends them: *digital television*
2 A digital clock or watch shows the time in the form of numbers.

dignified /ˈdɪɡnɪfaɪd/ *adj*
calm, serious and behaving in a way that makes people respect you: *a quiet, dignified woman*

dilute /daɪˈluːt/ *verb* (*present participle* **diluting,** *past* **diluted)**
to make a liquid thinner by adding another liquid to it: *You need to dilute this before you drink it.*

dinghy /ˈdɪŋi/ *noun* (*plural* **dinghies)**
a small boat

dining room /ˈdaɪnɪŋ ruːm/ *noun*
a room where you eat your meals

dinner /ˈdɪnəʳ/ *noun*
the main meal of the day that people usually eat in the evening

dinosaur

dinosaur /ˈdaɪnəsɔːʳ/ *noun*
a very large animal that lived millions of years ago

dip /dɪp/ *verb* (*present participle* **dipping,** *past* **dipped)**
to put something into a liquid for a short time: *She* ***dipped*** *the brush* ***into*** *the paint.*

diploma /dɪˈpləʊmə/ *noun*
an official document showing that someone has done a course of study: *a diploma in art and design*

direct[1] /dɪˈrekt, daɪˈrekt/ *adj, adv*
1 going straight from one place to another without turning or stopping: *We went by the most direct route.*
2 with no other person or thing involved or between: *direct sunlight*
➲Opposite **indirect**

direct[2] /dɪˈrekt, daɪˈrekt/ *verb*
1 to tell the actors in a film or play what to do: *a film directed by Alfred Hitchcock*
2 to show or tell someone how to get to a place: *Can you* ***direct*** *me* ***to*** *the manager's office please?*

direction /dɪˈrekʃᵊn/ *noun*
the way that someone or something is going or facing: *The car sped away* ***in the direction of*** *the airport.*

directions /dɪˈrekʃᵊnz/ *plural noun*
instructions that tell you how to get to a place, or how to do something: *We stopped to ask for directions.*

directly /dɪˈrektli/ *adv*
with no other person or thing involved or between: *Why don't you speak to him directly?*

director /dɪˈrektəʳ/ *noun*
1 an important manager in an organization or company: *Meet the new sales director.*
2 someone who tells the actors in a film or play what to do

directory /dɪˈrektᵊri/ *noun* (*plural* **directories)**
a book or list of names and numbers: *a telephone directory*

dirt /dɜːt/ *noun* **[no plural]**
an unpleasant substance that makes something not clean: *You've got some dirt on your trousers.*

dirty /ˈdɜːti/ *adj* **(dirtier, dirtiest)**
not clean: *dirty clothes/dishes*

disabled /dɪˈseɪbld/ *adj*
having an illness or condition that

makes it difficult to do the things that other people do: *They are demanding equal rights for* ***the disabled****.*

disadvantage /ˌdɪsədˈvɑːntɪdʒ/ *noun*
something which makes a situation more difficult: *One disadvantage of living in the country is the lack of public transport.*

disagree /ˌdɪsəˈɡriː/ *verb* (*present participle* **disagreeing**, *past* **disagreed)**
to have a different opinion from someone else: *I* ***disagree with*** *most of what he said.* ○ *Experts* ***disagree about*** *the causes of the disease.*

disagreement /ˌdɪsəˈɡriːmᵊnt/ *noun*
when people have a different opinion about something or have an argument: *They* ***had*** *a* ***disagreement*** *about money.*

disappear /ˌdɪsəˈpɪəʳ/ *verb*
to suddenly go somewhere and be impossible to see or find: *She watched him* ***disappear into*** *the crowd.* ○ *Her husband disappeared in 1991.*

disappearance /ˌdɪsəˈpɪərᵊns/ *noun*
when someone or something suddenly goes somewhere and is impossible to see or find: *Police are investigating the girl's disappearance.*

disappoint /ˌdɪsəˈpɔɪnt/ *verb*
to make someone feel sad because someone or something was not as good as they had expected: *We don't want to disappoint the fans.*

disappointed /ˌdɪsəˈpɔɪntɪd/ *adj*
sad because something was not as good as you expected, or because something did not happen: *I was very disappointed that he didn't come.*

disappointing /ˌdɪsəˈpɔɪntɪŋ/ *adj*
making you feel disappointed: *a disappointing performance*

disappointment /ˌdɪsəˈpɔɪntmənt/ *noun*
1 **[no plural]** the feeling of being disappointed
2 someone or something that disappoints you: *I'm sorry I'm such* ***a disappointment to*** *you.*

disapproval /ˌdɪsəˈpruːvᵊl/ *noun* **[no plural]**
when you think that someone or something is bad or wrong

disapprove /ˌdɪsəˈpruːv/ *verb* (*present participle* **disapproving**, *past* **disapproved)**
to think that someone or something is bad or wrong: *Her family* ***disapproved of*** *the marriage.*

disaster /dɪˈzɑːstəʳ/ *noun*
a very bad situation, especially something that causes a lot of harm or damage: *floods and other natural disasters*

disastrous /dɪˈzɑːstrəs/ *adj*
very bad and causing big problems: *a disastrous week*

disc /dɪsk/ *noun*
1 a flat, round shape or object
2 a record or CD

discipline /ˈdɪsəplɪn/ *noun* **[no plural]**
when people's behaviour is controlled using rules and punishments: *There should be better discipline in schools.*
● **discipline** *verb* (*present participle* **disciplining**, *past* **disciplined)**

disc jockey /ˈdɪsk ˌdʒɒki/ (*also* **DJ)** *noun*
someone who plays music on the radio or at discos

disco /ˈdɪskəʊ/ *noun*
a place or event where people dance to pop music

discount /ˈdɪskaʊnt/ *noun*
when a price is made lower: *They offer a 10 percent* ***discount on*** *rail travel for students.*

discourage /dɪˈskʌrɪdʒ/ *verb* (*present participle* **discouraging**, *past* **discouraged)**
to try to persuade someone to stop doing something: *a campaign to discourage people from smoking*

discouraging /dɪˈskʌrɪdʒɪŋ/ *adj*
making you feel less confident about something: *discouraging results*

discover /dɪˈskʌvəʳ/ *verb*
to find something or get information about something for the first time: *The body was discovered in a river.* ○ *She* ***discovered that*** *he had been married three times before.*

discovery /dɪˈskʌvᵊri/ *noun* (*plural* **discoveries)**
finding something or someone for the first time: *Scientists have* ***made*** *some important* ***discoveries*** *about genetics recently.*

discuss /dɪˈskʌs/ *verb*

a b c d e f g h i j k l m n o p q r s t u v w x y z

to talk about something with someone and tell each other your ideas or opinions: *Have you discussed this matter with anyone else?*

discussion /dɪ'skʌʃᵊn/ *noun* when people talk about something and tell each other their ideas or opinions: *They were **having** a **discussion** about football.*

disease /dɪ'ziːz/ *noun* an illness: *heart disease*

disgrace /dɪs'greɪs/ *noun* **[no plural]** when someone does something very bad that makes people stop respecting them: *They were sent home **in disgrace**.*

disgraceful /dɪs'greɪsfᵊl/ *adj* very bad: *disgraceful behaviour*

disguise[1] /dɪs'gaɪz/ *noun* things that you wear to change the way you look so that people cannot recognize you: *She usually goes out **in disguise** to avoid being bothered by the public.*

disguise[2] /dɪs'gaɪz/ *verb* (*present participle* **disguising**, *past* **disguised**) to change the way you look so that people cannot recognize you: *He managed to escape by **disguising** himself **as** a woman.*

disgust /dɪs'gʌst/ *noun* **[no plural]** a very strong feeling of dislike: *She walked out **in disgust**.*
• **disgust** *verb*

disgusted /dɪs'gʌstɪd/ *adj* feeling extreme dislike of something: *I'm totally **disgusted with** your behaviour!*

disgusting /dɪs'gʌstɪŋ/ *adj* extremely unpleasant: *What's that disgusting smell?*

dish /dɪʃ/ *noun* (*plural* **dishes**)
1 a container for food that you eat from and cook food in
2 part of a meal: *She cooked a very nice chicken dish.*

dishcloth /'dɪʃklɒθ/ *noun* a cloth used for washing dirty dishes

dishonest /dɪ'sɒnɪst/ *adj* not honest and likely to lie

dishwasher /'dɪʃˌwɒʃəʳ/ *noun* a machine that washes plates, glasses and other kitchen equipment ↄSee colour picture **Kitchen** on page Centre 10

disinfectant /ˌdɪsɪn'fektənt/ *noun* **[no plural]** a chemical substance that destroys bacteria

disk /dɪsk/ *noun* a piece of computer equipment that records and keeps information: *How much disk space is there ?* ↄSee colour picture **The Office** on page Centre 12

diskette /dɪ'sket/ *noun* a small, flat, plastic object that you put in your computer to record and keep information

dislike /dɪ'slaɪk/ *verb* (*present participle* **disliking**, *past* **disliked**) to not like someone or something: *Why do you dislike her so much?*
• **dislike** *noun*

dismal /'dɪzməl/ *adj* very bad and making you feel sad: *What dismal weather!*

dismay /dɪ'smeɪ/ *noun* **[no plural]** a feeling of sadness and disappointment: ***To our dismay**, it started raining.*
• **dismayed** *adj*

dismiss /dɪ'smɪs/ *verb*
1 to officially make someone leave their job: *Anyone who breaks company rules will be dismissed.*
2 to give someone official permission to leave: *The bell rang and the teacher dismissed the class.*

disobedient /ˌdɪsəʊ'biːdiənt/ *adj* refusing to do what someone in authority tells you to do: *a disobedient child*

disobey /ˌdɪsəʊ'beɪ/ *verb* to not do what you are told to do by someone in authority: *How dare you disobey me!*

disorganized /dɪ'sɔːgənaɪzd/ *adj*
1 not planned or organized well: *The competition was completely disorganized.*
2 not good at planning or organizing things: *She's terribly disorganized.*

display[1] /dɪ'spleɪ/ *noun*
1 a performance or a collection of things for people to look at: *a firework display ○ a display of children's paintings*
2 on display If something is on display, it is there for people to look

at: *Many old aircraft are on display at the museum.*

display² /dɪ'spleɪ/ *verb*
to arrange something somewhere so that people can see it: *There were some family photographs displayed on his desk.*

disposal /dɪ'spəʊzᵊl/ *noun* **[no plural]**
when you get rid of something: *waste disposal*

dispose /dɪ'spəʊz/ *verb* (*present participle* **disposing**, *past* **disposed**)
dispose of something *phrasal verb*
to get rid of something: *How did they dispose of the body?*

dispute /'dɪspjuːt/ *noun*
a disagreement, especially one that lasts a long time: *A man stabbed his neighbour in a* ***dispute over*** *noise.*

dissatisfied /dɪs'sætɪsfaɪd/ *adj*
not happy with something: *Are you* ***dissatisfied with*** *our service?*

dissolve /dɪ'zɒlv/ *verb* (*present participle* **dissolving**, *past* **dissolved**)
If a solid dissolves, it becomes part of a liquid, and if you dissolve it, you make it become part of a liquid: *These tablets dissolve in water.*

distance /'dɪstᵊns/ *noun*
1 the length of the space between two places: *We're only a short* ***distance from*** *my house.*
2 somewhere that is far away: *I could see Mary* ***in the distance****.*

distant /'dɪstᵊnt/ *adj*
far away in space or time: *distant galaxies* ○ *We hope to see you in the not too distant future.*

distinct /dɪ'stɪŋkt/ *adj*
1 different and separate: *This word has three distinct meanings.*
2 clear and easy to see or hear: *The voices gradually became louder and more distinct.*
• **distinctly** *adv*

distinguish /dɪ'stɪŋgwɪʃ/ *verb*
to see or understand the differences between two people, ideas, or things: *Children must learn to* ***distinguish between*** *right and wrong.*

distinguished /dɪ'stɪŋgwɪʃt/ *adj*
famous or admired: *a distinguished writer*

distract /dɪ'strækt/ *verb*
to make someone stop giving their attention to something: *Stop distracting me – I'm trying to finish my essay.*

distress /dɪ'stres/ *noun* **[no plural]**
1 the feeling of being very upset or worried: *The newspaper reports caused her a great deal of distress.*
2 when someone or something is in danger and needs help: *an aircraft* ***in distress***
• **distress** *verb*
to make someone feel upset or worried

distribute /dɪ'strɪbjuːt/ *verb* (*present participle* **distributing**, *past* **distributed**)
to give something to a lot of people or places: *The books will be* ***distributed*** *free* ***to*** *local schools.*
• **distribution** *noun* **[no plural]**

district /'dɪstrɪkt/ *noun*
a part of a city or country: *the fashion district of New York*

disturb /dɪ'stɜːb/ *verb*
1 to stop what someone is doing or make problems for them, often by making a noise: *Georgia is working so try not to disturb her.*
2 to upset someone or worry them: *He was disturbed by the violence in the film.*

disused /dɪ'sjuːzd/ *adj*
not used now: *a disused warehouse*

ditch /dɪtʃ/ *noun* (*plural* **ditches**)
a long, narrow hole in the ground next to a road or field which water moves through

dive

dive /daɪv/ *verb* (*present participle*

diving, *past tense* **dived,** *past participle* **dived)**
1 to jump into water with your head and arms going in first: *He dived off the side of the boat into the sea.*
2 to swim under water, usually with breathing equipment

diver /ˈdaɪvəʳ/ *noun*
someone who swims under water, usually with breathing equipment

divide /dɪˈvaɪd/ *verb* (*present participle* **dividing,** *past* **divided)**
1 to separate into parts or groups, or to make something separate into parts or groups: *We* ***divided up into*** *teams of six.*
2 to calculate how many times a number can go into another number: *12* ***divided by*** *6 equals 2.*

divine /dɪˈvaɪn/ *adj*
relating to or coming from God or a god

diving board /ˈdaɪvɪŋ ˌbɔːd/ *noun*
a raised board next to a swimming pool that you jump from into the water

division /dɪˈvɪʒən/ *noun*
1 [no plural] when something is separated into parts or groups: *the equal division of wealth*
2 one of the groups in an organization: *the sales division*
3 [no plural] when you calculate how many times one number goes into another number

divorce /dɪˈvɔːs/ *noun*
when two people officially stop being married: *My parents are* ***getting a divorce****.*
• **divorce** *verb* (*present participle* **divorcing,** *past* **divorced)** *She's divorcing her husband.*

divorced /dɪˈvɔːst/ *adj*
1 married before but not married now
2 get divorced to officially stop being married: *My parents got divorced when I was seven.*

DIY /ˌdiːaɪˈwaɪ/ *noun* **[no plural]** *UK*
when you do building, decorating, or repairs in your own home

dizzy /ˈdɪzi/ *adj*
feeling like everything is turning round and as if you might fall

DJ /ˈdiːˌdʒeɪ/ *noun*
someone who plays music on the radio or at discos

do[1] *strong form* /duː/ *weak form* /də/ *verb*
1 used with another verb to form questions and negative phrases: *Do you need any help?* ○ *I don't know.*
2 used in a phrase at the end of a sentence to make it into a question: *Sarah lives near here, doesn't she?*
3 used to avoid repeating a verb that has just been used: *"I hate that song." "So do I."*
4 used to make the main verb stronger: *He does like you, he's just shy.*

do[2] /duː/ *verb* (*present participle* **doing,** *past tense* **did,** *past participle* **done)**
1 to perform an action or job: *Go upstairs and do your homework.* ○ *What does she do?* (= What is her job?)
2 to make or prepare something: *Max's Cafe does great sandwiches.*
3 do badly/well to not succeed or to succeed: *Sam did very well in her exams.*
4 do someone good to have a good effect on someone: *A holiday would do you good.*
5 will do will be satisfactory: *You don't have to pay now, next week will do.*

do something up *phrasal verb*
1 *mainly UK* to fasten something: *Do your coat up. It's cold outside.*
2 to repair or decorate a building so that it looks attractive

do with something *phrasal verb*
used to ask where someone put something: *What did you do with my keys?*

do with someone/something *phrasal verb*
could do with someone/something to need or want someone or something: *I could do with a few days off work.*

do without someone/something *phrasal verb*
to do something well without having someone or something: *Jack's the kind of player we can't do without.*

dock /dɒk/ *noun*
the place where ships stop and goods are taken off or put on
• **dock** *verb*
to arrive at a dock

doctor /ˈdɒktəʳ/ *noun*
a person whose job is to treat

people who are ill or hurt

document /ˈdɒkjəmənt/ *noun*
1 a piece of paper with official information on it
2 a piece of text produced on a computer: *How do I create a new document?*

documentary /ˌdɒkjəˈmentəri/ *noun* (*plural* **documentaries**)
a film or television programme that gives facts about a real situation

dodge /dɒdʒ/ *verb* (*present participle* **dodging,** *past* **dodged**)
1 to move quickly to avoid someone or something: *He managed to dodge past the security guard.*
2 to avoid doing something you should do: *The minister dodged questions about his relationship with the actress.*

does *strong form* /dʌz/ *weak form* /dəz/
present simple of do, used with 'he', 'she' and 'it'

doesn't /ˈdʌzənt/
short for does not: *Keith doesn't like mushrooms or garlic.*

dog /dɒg/ *noun*
an animal with fur, four legs and a tail that is kept as a pet

doll /dɒl/ *noun*
a child's toy that looks like a small person

dollar /ˈdɒləʳ/ *noun*
the unit of money used in the US, Canada, and some other countries; $

dolphin /ˈdɒlfɪn/ *noun*
an intelligent sea animal that breathes air and looks like a large, grey fish

dome *noun*
a curved, round roof of a building

domestic /dəˈmestɪk/ *adj*
1 relating to the home and family relationships: *domestic violence*
2 inside one country: *a domestic flight*
3 A domestic animal is kept as a pet.

dominate /ˈdɒmɪneɪt/ *verb* (*present participle* **dominating,** *past* **dominated**)
to control or have power over someone or something: *You often find that one person dominates a meeting.*

domino /ˈdɒmɪnəʊ/ *noun*
a small, rectangular object that has spots on it, used in a game

• **dominoes** *noun* **[no plural]**
a game played using dominoes

donate /dəʊˈneɪt/ *verb* (*present participle* **donating,** *past* **donated**)
to give something, especially money, to a person or organization that needs help: *Four hundred new computers were donated to the college.*

• **donation** *noun*

done[1] /dʌn/ *adj*
finished or completed: *Did you get your essay done in time?*

done[2] /dʌn/
past participle of do

donkey /ˈdɒŋki/ *noun*
an animal that looks like a small horse with long ears

donkey

donor /ˈdəʊnəʳ/ *noun*
someone who gives something to a person or organization that needs help

don't /dəʊnt/
short for do not: *Please don't talk during the exam.*

doodle /ˈduːdl/ *verb* (*present participle* **doodling,** *past* **doodled**)
to draw little pictures or patterns without thinking about it

doodle

door /dɔːʳ/ *noun*
1 the part of a building or room that you open or close to get inside it or out of it: *Please shut the door behind you.*
2 two/three, etc doors away in a place that is two/three, etc houses away: *We live just a few doors away from the Smiths.*

door

doorbell /ˈdɔːbel/ *noun*
a button that you press next to a door that makes a noise to let someone know that you are there

doorknob /ˈdɔːnɒb/ *noun*
a round object on a door that you use to open or close it

doormat /ˈdɔːmæt/ *noun*
a piece of thick material on the floor

by a door used to clean your shoes before entering a building

doorway /ˈdɔːweɪ/ *noun*
an entrance to a building or room through a door

dormitory /ˈdɔːmɪtᵊri/ *noun* (*plural* **dormitories**)
a large bedroom with a lot of beds, especially in a school

dosage /ˈdəʊsɪdʒ/ *noun*
how much medicine you should take and how often you should take it: *the recommended daily dosage*

dose /dəʊs/ *noun*
a measured amount of medicine that is taken at one time or during a period of time: *What is the recommended dose?*

dot /dɒt/ *noun*
1 a small, round mark or spot: *a pattern of blue and green dots*
2 [no plural] *spoken* the spoken form of '.' in an internet address: *dot co dot uk* (= .co.uk)
3 on the dot at that exact time: *We have to leave at 7.30 on the dot.*

double[1] /ˈdʌbl/ *adj*
1 having two parts of the same type or size: *My number is four, two, six, double two, five* (= 426225).
2 twice the amount, number, or size of something: *a double hamburger*
3 made to be used by two people: *a double bed/room*

double[2] /ˈdʌbl/ *verb* (*present participle* **doubling**, *past* **doubled**)
to increase and become twice the size or amount, or to make something do this: *Our house has almost* ***doubled in*** *value.*

double-click /ˌdʌblˈklɪk/ *verb*
to quickly press a button twice on a mouse (= small computer control) to make something happen on a computer screen: *Double-click on the icon to start the program.*

doubt[1] /daʊt/ *noun*
1 when you are not certain about something, or do not trust someone or something: *I have some* ***doubts about*** *his ability to do the job.*
2 be in doubt to not be certain: *The future of the project is in doubt.*
3 no doubt used to say that something is very likely: *No doubt she'll spend the money on new clothes.*

doubt[2] /daʊt/ *verb*
to not feel certain about something or think that something will not happen: *I* ***doubt that*** *I'll get the job.*

doubtful /ˈdaʊtfᵊl/ *adj*
If something is doubtful, it probably will not happen: *It's* ***doubtful whether*** *he'll be able to come.*

doubtless /ˈdaʊtləs/ *adv*
probably: *He will doubtless be criticized by journalists.*

doughnut /ˈdəʊnʌt/ *noun*
a small, round, fried cake

doughnut

dove /dʌv/ *noun*
a white bird, sometimes used as a symbol of peace

down /daʊn/
adv, preposition
1 towards or in a lower place: *I bent down to have a look.*
2 towards or at a lower level or amount: *Can you turn the music down?*
3 moving from above and onto a surface: *Put that box down on the floor.*
4 down the road/river along or further along the road/river: *There's another pub further down the street.*
5 note/write something down to write something on a piece of paper: *Can I just write down your phone number?*

downhill /ˌdaʊnˈhɪl/ *adv*
towards the bottom of a hill or slope: *It's so much easier cycling downhill.*

download /ˌdaʊnˈləʊd/ *verb*
to copy computer programs or information electronically, usually from a large computer to a small one: *You can download this software free from their website.*

downstairs /ˌdaʊnˈsteəz/ *adv*
on or to a lower level of a building: *She went downstairs to see who was at the door.*

doze /dəʊz/ *verb* (*present participle* **dozing**, *past* **dozed**)
to sleep lightly
doze off *phrasal verb*
to gradually start sleeping, usually during the day: *He dozed off during the film.*

a b c d e f g h i j k l m n o p q r s t u v w x y z

dozen /ˈdʌzᵊn/ *noun, determiner*
1 twelve, or a group of twelve: *There were about a dozen people at the party.*
2 **dozens** *informal* a lot: *She's got* ***dozens of*** *friends.*

Dr
written abbreviation for doctor: *Dr Anna Prescott*

drag /dræg/ *verb* (*present participle* **dragging**, *past* **dragged**)
1 to pull something or someone along the ground somewhere, usually with difficulty: *The table was too heavy to lift, so we had to drag it across the room.*
2 to move something somewhere on a computer screen using a mouse (= small computer control)
3 (*also* **drag on**) to continue for too much time in a boring way: *The talks dragged on for months.*

dragon /ˈdrægᵊn/ *noun*
a big, imaginary creature which breathes out fire

dragonfly /ˈdrægᵊnflaɪ/ *noun*
an insect with long wings and a thin, colourful body, often seen flying near water

drain¹ /dreɪn/ *verb*
1 to remove the liquid from something, usually by pouring it away: *Drain the pasta and add the tomatoes.*
2 If something drains, liquid flows away or out of it.

drain² /dreɪn/ *noun*
a pipe or hole that takes away waste liquids or water: *She poured the dirty water down the drain.*

drama /ˈdrɑːmə/ *noun*
1 a play in a theatre or on television or radio: *a historical drama*
2 **[no plural]** plays and acting generally: *modern drama*
3 when something exciting happens: *There was a bit of drama at work today.*

dramatic /drəˈmætɪk/ *adj*
1 very sudden or exciting: *a dramatic change/improvement*
2 relating to plays and acting

drank /dræŋk/
past tense of drink

draught /drɑːft/ *noun UK*
when you can feel cold air coming into a room: *There's a terrible draught coming from under the door.*

draughts /drɑːfts/ *noun* **[no plural]** *UK*
a game that two people play by moving flat, round objects around on a board of black and white squares

draw /drɔː/ *verb* (*present participle* **drawing**, *past tense* **drew**, *past participle* **drawn**)
1 to make a picture with a pen or pencil: *She drew a picture of a tree.*
2 to pull something or someone in a particular direction: *He took her hand and drew her towards him.*
3 to move somewhere, usually in a vehicle: *The train drew into the station.*
4 **draw the curtains** to pull curtains open or closed
5 *UK* to finish a game or competition with each team or player having the same score: *England drew 2-2 against Italy.*
6 **draw near/close** to become nearer in space or time: *Her birthday's drawing nearer every day.*
7 (*also* **draw out**) to take money from your bank account

draw back *phrasal verb*
to move away from someone or something: *She drew back in disgust when she saw the snake.*

draw something up *phrasal verb*
to prepare something by writing it: *He drew up some plans for the new office.*

drawer /drɔːʳ/ *noun*
a container like a box that is part of a piece of furniture and moves in and out

drawing /ˈdrɔːɪŋ/ *noun*
1 a picture made with a pencil or pen: *There were some children's drawings pinned up on the wall.*
2 **[no plural]** the skill or activity of making pictures using a pencil or pen: *Do you want to do some drawing?*

drawing pin /ˈdrɔːɪŋ pɪn/ *noun UK*
a pin with a wide, flat top, used for fastening pieces of paper to a wall

drawn /drɔːn/
past participle of draw

dreadful /ˈdredfᵊl/ *adj*

very bad

dreadfully /ˈdredfəli/ *adv*
1 *UK, formal* very: *I'm dreadfully sorry.*
2 very badly: *The children behaved dreadfully.*

dream[1] /driːm/ *noun*
1 a series of events and images that happen in your mind while you are sleeping: *I **had** a very strange **dream** last night.*
2 something that you want to happen although it is not very likely: *It was his dream to become an actor.*

dream[2] /driːm/ *verb*
1 to have events and images in your mind while you are sleeping: *Last night I dreamed that I was flying.*
2 to imagine something that you would like to happen: *I dream of living on a desert island.*

dreary /ˈdrɪəri/ *adj*
boring and making you feel sad: *a dreary job*

dress[1] /dres/ *verb*
1 to put clothes on yourself or someone else: *I usually **get dressed** before having breakfast.* ➲Opposite **undress**
2 to wear a particular type, style, or colour of clothes: *She was **dressed in** black.*
dress up *phrasal verb*
1 to wear formal clothes for a special occasion: *Weddings are a great opportunity to dress up.*
2 to wear special clothes for a game or party: *He **dressed up as** Superman for the party.*

dress[2] /dres/ *noun*
1 a piece of clothing for women which covers the top of the body and hangs down over the legs ➲See colour picture **Clothes** on page Centre 5
2 [no plural] a particular style of clothes: *casual dress*

dressing /ˈdresɪŋ/ *noun*
1 a sauce, especially a mixture of oil and vinegar for salad
2 a covering that protects an injury

dressing gown /ˈdresiŋ ˌgaʊn/ *noun UK*
a piece of clothing, like a long coat, that you wear at home when you are not dressed

dressing table /ˈdresɪŋ ˌteɪbl/ *noun UK*
a piece of bedroom furniture like a table with a mirror and drawers

drew /druː/
past tense of draw

dried /draɪd/
past of dry

drift /drɪft/ *verb*
to be moved slowly somewhere by wind or water: *The boat drifted towards the beach.*

drill /drɪl/ *noun*
a machine for making holes in a hard substance: *an electric drill*
• **drill** *verb*

drink[1] /drɪŋk/ *verb* (*present participle* **drinking**, *past tense* **drank**, *past participle* **drunk**)
1 to put liquid into your mouth and swallow it: *He was drinking a glass of milk.*
2 to drink alcohol, usually regularly: *She doesn't smoke or drink.*

drink[2] /drɪŋk/ *noun*
a liquid or an amount of liquid that you drink: *a cold drink*

drip /drɪp/ *verb* (*present participle* **dripping**, *past* **dripped**)
1 If a liquid drips, it falls in drops: *There was water **dripping from** the ceiling.*
2 to produce drops of liquid: *The candle's dripping.*

drive[1] /draɪv/ *verb* (*present participle* **driving**, *past tense* **drove**, *past participle* **driven**)
1 to make a car, bus, or train move, and control what it does: *She's learning to drive.*
2 to travel somewhere in a car, or to take someone somewhere in a car: *Annie drove me home last night.*

drive[2] /draɪv/ *noun*
1 a journey in a car: *The drive from Boston to New York took 4 hours.*
2 the area of ground that you drive on to get from your house to the road: *You can park on the drive.*
3 a part of a computer that can keep information: *Save your work on the C: drive.*

driven /ˈdrɪvᵊn/
past participle of drive

driver /ˈdraɪvəʳ/ *noun*
someone who drives a vehicle: *a bus/train driver*

a b c d e f g h i j k l m n o p q r s t u v w x y z

driving licence /ˈdraɪvɪŋ ˌlaɪsᵊns/ *noun UK*
an official document that allows you to drive a car

droop /druːp/ *verb*
to hang down: *He was tired and his eyelids were starting to droop.*

drop

drop[1] /drɒp/ *verb* (*present participle* **dropping**, *past* **dropped**)
1 to fall or let something fall: *She tripped and dropped the vase.*
2 If a level or amount drops, it becomes less: *Unemployment has dropped from 8% to 6% in the last year.*
3 (*also* **drop off**) to take someone or something to a place, usually by car as you travel somewhere else: *I can drop you at the station on my way to work.*
4 If you drop a plan, activity, or idea, you stop doing or planning it: *Plans for a new supermarket have been dropped.*
drop by/in *phrasal verb*
to visit someone for a short time, usually without arranging it before: *I **dropped in on** George on my way home from school.*
drop someone/something off *phrasal verb*
to take someone or something to a place, usually by car
drop out *phrasal verb*
to stop doing something before you have completely finished: *He **dropped out of** school at 14.*

drop[2] /drɒp/ *noun*
1 a small, round shaped amount of liquid: *I felt a few drops of rain.* ➲See colour picture **Quantities** on page Centre 14
2 when the level or amount of something becomes less: *There has been a **drop in** crime recently.*

drought /draʊt/ *noun*
a long period when there is no rain and people do not have enough water: *A severe drought ruined the crops.*

drove /drəʊv/
past tense of drive

drown /draʊn/ *verb*
to die because you are under water and cannot breathe, or to kill someone in this way

drowsy /ˈdraʊzi/ *adj*
feeling tired and wanting to sleep

drug /drʌg/ *noun*
1 an illegal substance that people take to make them feel happy: *a drug dealer*
2 a chemical substance used as a medicine: *Scientists are developing a new drug to treat cancer.*

drug addict /ˈdrʌg ædɪkt/ *noun*
someone who cannot stop taking drugs

drum

drum[1] /drʌm/ *noun*
1 a round, hollow, musical instrument that you hit with your hands or with sticks
2 a large, round container for holding things such as oil or chemicals

drum[2] /drʌm/ *verb* (*present participle* **drumming**, *past* **drummed**)
to hit something many times and make a sound like a drum: *the sound of rain drumming on the roof*

drunk[1] /drʌŋk/ *adj*
not able to behave or speak normally because you have drunk too much alcohol: *He usually **gets drunk** at parties.*

drunk[2] /drʌŋk/
past participle of drink

dry[1] /draɪ/ *adj*
1 without water or liquid on the surface: *dry paint* ○ *Is your hair dry yet?*
2 without rain: *a dry summer*
3 Dry wine is not sweet.

dry[2] /draɪ/ *verb* (*present participle* **drying**, *past* **dried**)
to become dry, or to make something become dry: *He dried his hands on a towel.*

duchess /ˈdʌtʃɪs/ *noun* (*plural* **duchesses**)
a woman of very high social rank in some European countries: *the Duchess of Windsor*

duck

duck[1] /dʌk/ *noun*
a bird with short legs that lives in or near water, or the meat

from this bird

duck[2] /dʌk/ *verb*
to move your body down quickly to avoid being hit or seen: *Billy ducked behind a car when he saw his teacher.*

duckling /ˈdʌklɪŋ/ *noun*
a young duck

due /djuː/ *adj*
1 expected or planned: *When is the baby due* (= expected to be born)? ○ *He was* ***due to*** *fly back this morning.*
2 due to something because of something: *The train was late due to snow.*
3 owed to someone: *The rent is due today.* ○ *He didn't get the praise and recognition that was* ***due to*** *him.*
4 be due for something If you are due for something, it should happen very soon: *She's due for a pay rise.*

duet /djuˈet/ *noun*
a piece of music for two people to perform together

dug /dʌg/
past of dig

duke /djuːk/ *noun*
a man of very high social rank in some parts of Europe: *the Duke of Beaufort*

dull /dʌl/ *adj*
1 not interesting: *a dull place*
2 not bright: *dull colours*
3 A dull sound is not loud or clear: *a dull thud*

dumb /dʌm/ *adj*
not able to talk

dummy /ˈdʌmi/ *noun* (*plural* **dummies**) *UK*
a small, rubber object that a baby sucks to stop it crying

dump[1] /dʌmp/ *verb*
1 to put something somewhere to get rid of it: *The company was fined for illegally dumping toxic chemicals.*
2 to quickly put something somewhere: *He dumped his bag on the table.*

dump[2] /dʌmp/ *noun*
a place where people take things that they do not want

dune /djuːn/ *noun*
a hill of sand in the desert or on the coast

dungarees /ˌdʌŋgəˈriːz/ *plural noun UK*
trousers with a part that covers your chest and straps that go over your shoulders

dungeon /ˈdʌndʒən/ *noun*
a dark, underground prison

during /ˈdjʊərɪŋ/ *preposition*
1 for the whole of a period of time: *Emma's usually at home during the day.*
2 at a particular moment in a period of time: *We'll arrange a meeting some time during the week.*

dusk /dʌsk/ *noun* **[no plural]**
the time in the evening when it starts to become dark

dust[1] /dʌst/ *noun* **[no plural]**
a powder of dirt that you see on a surface or in the air: *The shelves were covered in a thick layer of dust.*

dust[2] /dʌst/ *verb*
to remove dust from something: *I tidied and dusted the shelves.*

dustbin /ˈdʌstbɪn/ *noun UK*
a large container for rubbish kept outside your house

duster /ˈdʌstəʳ/ *noun UK*
a cloth used for removing dust (= powder of dirt) from furniture and other objects

dustman /ˈdʌstmən/ *noun UK*
someone whose job is to remove rubbish from containers outside people's houses

dustpan /ˈdʌstpæn/ *noun*
a flat container with a handle, used with a brush for removing dirt from a floor

dusty /ˈdʌsti/ *adj*
covered with dust (= powder of dirt)

duty /ˈdjuːti/ *noun* (*plural* **duties**)
1 something you must do because the law says you must or because it is right: *Rail companies* ***have a duty*** *to provide safe transport.*
2 on/off duty If a doctor, police officer, etc is on duty, they are working, and if they are off duty, they are not working: *I'm on duty tomorrow night.*

duty-free /ˌdjuːtiˈfriː/ *adj*
Duty-free goods are things that you can buy and bring into a country without paying tax.

duvet /ˈdjuːveɪ/ *noun UK*
a cover filled with feathers or warm material that you sleep under

DVD /ˌdiːviːˈdiː/ *noun*
a small disc for storing music, films and information: *Is this film available **on DVD**?*

dwarf /dwɔːf/ *noun* (*plural* **dwarves**)
an imaginary creature like a little man, in children's stories

dye[1] /daɪ/ *noun*
a substance that is used to change the colour of something

dye[2] /daɪ/ *verb* (*present participle* **dyeing**, *past* **dyed**)
to change the colour of something by using a dye: *I dyed my hair blonde.*

dying /ˈdaɪɪŋ/
present participle of die

dynamite /ˈdaɪnəmaɪt/ *noun* **[no plural]**
a type of explosive: *a stick of dynamite*

a b c d e f g h i j k l m n o p q r s t u v w x y z

Ee

E, e /iː/
the fifth letter of the alphabet

each /iːtʃ/ *pronoun, determiner*
every one in a group: ***Each of*** *the teams has four players.* ○ *The bill comes to £79 so that's about £10 each.*

each other /iːtʃ ˈʌðə^{r}/ *pronoun*
used to show that each person in a group of two or more people does something to the others: *The children are always arguing with each other.*

eager /ˈiːgə^{r}/ *adj*
wanting to do or have something very much: *Sam was* ***eager to*** *go home and play on his computer.*
• **eagerly** *adv*: *The results were eagerly awaited.*
• **eagerness** *noun* **[no plural]**

eagle /ˈiːgl/ *noun*
a large, wild bird with a big, curved beak, that hunts smaller animals

eagle

ear /ɪə^{r}/ *noun*
one of the two things on your head that you hear with: *She whispered something in his ear.*

earache /ˈɪəreɪk/ *noun*
pain in your ear: *I've got earache.*

early /ˈɜːli/ *adj, adv* **(earlier, earliest)**
1 near the beginning of a period of time, process, etc: *the early 1980s*
2 before the usual time or the time that was planned: *The plane arrived ten minutes early.*
3 early on in the first stage or part of something: *I lost interest quite early on in the book.*

earn /ɜːn/ *verb*
1 to get money for doing work: *She earns about £40,000 a year.*
2 earn a living to work to get money for the things you need
3 to get something good because you have done something good: *As a teacher you have to earn the respect of your students.*

earphones /ˈɪəfəʊnz/ *plural noun*
a piece of electronic equipment that you put on your ears so that you can listen to radio, recorded music, etc

earring /ˈɪərɪŋ/ *noun*
a piece of jewellery that you wear on your ear: *silver earrings*

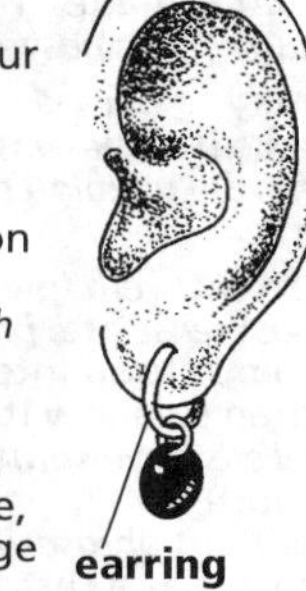
earring

earth /ɜːθ/ *noun*
1 (*also* **the Earth**) the planet that we live on
2 [no plural] soil or ground: *a pile of earth*

earthquake /ˈɜːθkweɪk/ *noun*
a sudden movement of the Earth's surface, often causing damage

ease[1] /iːz/ *noun*
1 [no plural] If you do something with ease, it is very easy for you to do it: *Luca passed his exams* ***with ease****.*
2 at ease feeling relaxed: *I felt completely at ease with him.*

ease[2] /iːz/ *verb* (*present participle* **easing,** *past* **eased)**
to become less bad, or to make something become less bad: *The pain eased after a few minutes.*

easel /ˈiːzəl/ *noun*
something used to support a painting while you paint it

easel

easily /ˈiːzɪli/ *adv*
with no difficulty: *She makes friends very easily.*

east, East /iːst/ *noun* **[no plural]**
the direction that you face to see the sun rise: *Which way's east?*
• **east** *adj*: *New York is east of Chicago.*
• **east** *adv*: *They sailed east.*

Easter /ˈiːstə^{r}/ *noun*
a holiday in March or April when Christians celebrate the return to life of Jesus Christ: *the Easter holidays*

Easter egg /ˈiːstə^{r} eg/ *noun*
a chocolate egg that people eat at Easter

eastern, Eastern /ˈiːstən/ *adj*
in or from the east part of an area: *eastern Europe*

easy[1] /ˈiːzi/ *adj*

a b c d e f g h i j k l m n o p q r s t u v w x y z

1 not difficult: *The exam was easy.* ○ *It's easy to see why he's so popular.* ➲Opposite **hard** or **difficult**.

2 I'm easy *informal* used to say that you will agree with any decision that is made: *"Would you like pizza or curry?" "I'm easy – you choose."*

easy² /ˈiːzi/ *adv*
take it easy to relax and not work hard: *I'm going to take it easy this weekend.*

eat /iːt/ *verb* (*present participle* **eating,** *past tense* **ate,** *past participle* **eaten)**
to put food into your mouth and then swallow it: *Who ate all the cake?* ○ *Let's have **something to eat*** (= some food).

eat out *phrasal verb*
to eat at a restaurant: *Let's eat out tonight.* ➲See colour picture **Phrasal Verbs** on page Centre 13

echo¹ /ˈekəʊ/ *verb*
If a sound echoes you hear it again and again, usually because you are in a large, empty space: *Their voices echoed around the room.*

echo² /ˈekəʊ/ *noun* (*plural* **echoes)**
a sound that you hear more than once because you are in a big, empty space

eclipse /ɪˈklɪps/ *noun*
when the sun is covered by the moon, or the moon is covered by the Earth's shadow (= dark area)

ecological /ˌiːkəˈlɒdʒɪkəl/ *adj*
relating to ecology or to the environment: *an ecological disaster*

ecology /iːˈkɒlədʒi/ *noun*
the relationship between living things and the environment, or the scientific study of this
• **ecologist** *noun*
someone who studies ecology

economic /ˌiːkəˈnɒmɪk, ˌekəˈnɒmɪk/ *adj*
relating to trade, industry, and money: *economic policies*
• **economically** *adv*: *The country would benefit economically.*

economical /ˌiːkəˈnɒmɪkəl/ *adj*
using little money, fuel, etc: *It's a very economical car.*
• **economically** *adv*

economy /ɪˈkɒnəmi/ *noun* (*plural* **economies)**
the system by which a country makes and uses goods and money: *the US economy* ○ *a global economy*

edge /edʒ/ *noun*
1 the part around something that is furthest from the centre: *Rick was sitting on the edge of the bed.* ○ *She ran down to the water's edge.*
2 the part of a knife or tool that cuts

edible /ˈedɪbl/ *adj*
safe to eat: *edible berries*

edition /ɪˈdɪʃən/ *noun*
one of many books or newspapers that are the same and were made at the same time: *a new edition*

editor /ˈedɪtəʳ/ *noun*
someone who is in charge of a newspaper or magazine

educate /ˈedʒʊkeɪt/ *verb* (*present participle* **educating,** *past* **educated)**
1 to teach someone at a school or college: *She was educated at the Perse School.*
2 to give people information about something: *Children are **educated about** the dangers of smoking.*

education /ˌedʒʊˈkeɪʃən/ *noun* **[no plural]**
teaching and learning in a school or college: *More money should be spent on education.*
• **educational** *adj*
providing education: *the educational system*

eel /iːl/ *noun*
a long fish that looks like a snake

effect /ɪˈfekt/ *noun*
a change or result that is caused by something: *The accident **had a** huge **effect** on her life.* ○ *We don't know the long-term **effects of** this drug.*

effective /ɪˈfektɪv/ *adj*
getting the result that you want: *What is the most effective way of teaching grammar?*

effectively /ɪˈfektɪvli/ *adv*
in a way that gets what you want: *Teachers need to be able to communicate ideas effectively.*

efficient /ɪˈfɪʃənt/ *adj*
working well and not wasting time or energy: *Email is a quick and efficient way of contacting people.*
• **efficiently** *adv*

effort /ˈefət/ *noun*
1 an attempt to do something: *He was **making an effort** to be sociable.*

2 [no plural] the energy that you need to do something: *I **put** a lot of **effort into** organizing the party.*

e.g. (*also* **eg**) /ˌiːˈdʒiː/
used to give an example of what you mean: *green vegetables e.g. spinach and cabbage*

egg /eg/ *noun*
1 an oval object made by a female chicken, that you eat as food: *a boiled/fried egg*
2 an oval object with a hard shell that contains a baby bird, insect, or other creature: *The bird **lays** its **eggs** in a nest.*

eggplant /ˈegplɑːnt/ *US* (*UK* **aubergine**) *noun*
an oval, purple vegetable that is white inside

eight /eɪt/
the number 8

eighteen /ˌeɪˈtiːn/
the number 18
• **eighteenth**
18th written as a word

eighth[1] /eɪtθ/
8th written as a word

eighth[2] /eɪtθ/ *noun*
one of eight equal parts of something; ⅛

eighty /ˈeɪti/
the number 80

either[1] /ˈaɪðəʳ, ˈiːðəʳ/ *conjunction*
either... or used when you are giving a choice of two or more things: *Either you or I can go.*

either[2] /ˈaɪðəʳ, ˈiːðəʳ/ *pronoun, determiner*
one of two people or things when it is not important which: *"A hot or a cold drink?" "Oh, either."*

either[3] /ˈaɪðəʳ, ˈiːðəʳ/ *adv*
used in negative sentences to mean that something else is also true: *The food was bad and it wasn't cheap either.*

elaborate /ɪˈlæbərət/ *adj*
complicated or with a lot of details: *an elaborate design*
• **elaborately** *adv*

elastic /ɪˈlæstɪk/ *adj*
Something that is elastic can stretch and return to its original size: *Your skin is more elastic when you are young.*

elastic band /ɪˈlæstɪk bænd/ *noun UK*
a thin circle of rubber used to hold things together

elbow /ˈelbəʊ/ *noun*
the part in the middle of your arm where it bends ➲See colour picture **The Body** on page Centre 2

elderly /ˈeldəli/ *adj*
Elderly people are old: *an elderly man*

eldest /ˈeldɪst/ *adj*
eldest child/daughter/brother, etc the oldest child/daughter/brother, etc: *My eldest brother is a doctor.*

elect /ɪˈlekt/ *verb*
to choose someone for a particular job or position by voting: *He was elected president in 1997.*

election /ɪˈlekʃən/ *noun*
a time when people vote in order to choose someone for a political or official job

electric /ɪˈlektrɪk/ *adj*
using or giving electricity: *an electric heater ○ an electric socket*

electrical /ɪˈlektrɪkəl/ *adj*
using or relating to electricity: *electrical goods ○ an electrical engineer*

electrician /ɪˌlekˈtrɪʃən/ *noun*
someone whose job is to put in or repair electrical equipment

electricity /ɪˌlekˈtrɪsəti/ *noun* **[no plural]**
a type of energy that can produce light and heat, or make machines work: *The electricity has been turned off.*

electronic /ɪˌlekˈtrɒnɪk/ *adj*
Electronic equipment consists of things such as computers, televisions, and radios.
• **electronically** *adv*

electronics /ˌɪlekˈtrɒnɪks/ *noun* **[no plural]**
the science of making electronic equipment: *the electronics industry*

elegant /ˈelɪgənt/ *adj*
stylish and attractive: *an elegant dining room ○ She's a very elegant woman.*

element /ˈelɪmənt/ *noun*
1 a part of something: *This book has all the elements of a good story.*
2 an element of something a small amount of something: *There's an element of truth in what she says.*
3 a simple substance which you cannot reduce to smaller chemical

a b c d e f g h i j k l m n o p q r s t u v w x y z

parts: *Iron is one of the elements of the Earth's crust.*

elementary /ˌelɪˈmentəri/ *adj* relating to the early stages of studying a subject: *students at elementary level*

elephant /ˈelɪfənt/ *noun* a very large, grey animal with big ears and a very long nose

elevator /ˈelɪveɪtəʳ/ *US* (*UK* **lift**) *noun* a machine that carries people up and down in tall buildings

eleven /ɪˈlevən/ the number 11
- **eleventh** 11th written as a word

elf /elf/ *noun* (*plural* **elves**) a small person with pointed ears, in children's stories

else /els/ *adv*
1 in addition to someone or something: *Would you like* ***anything else*** *to eat?* ○ ***What else*** *did he say?*
2 different from someone or something: *I don't like it here. Let's go* ***somewhere else****.*
3 other things or people: *I forgot my toothbrush, but I remembered* ***everything else****.*
4 or else used to say what will happen if another thing does not happen: *We must be there by six, or else we'll miss the beginning.*

elsewhere /ˌelsˈweəʳ/ *adv* in or to another place: *If we can't find it here, we'll have to* ***go elsewhere****.*

elves /elvz/ *plural of* elf

email (*also* **e-mail**) /ˈiːmeɪl/ *noun*
1 [no plural] a way of sending messages, from one computer to another: *What's your* ***email address****?*
2 a message sent to a computer: *I got an email from Danielle yesterday.*
- **email** *verb* to send a message using email

embarrass /ɪmˈbærəs/ *verb* to make someone feel ashamed or shy: *My dad's always embarrassing me in front of my friends.*

embarrassed /ɪmˈbærəst/ *adj* feeling ashamed or shy: *I was too embarrassed to admit that I was scared.*

embarrassing /ɪmˈbærəsɪŋ/ *adj* making you feel embarrassed: *I forgot his name – it was very embarrassing.*

embarrassment /ɪmˈbærəsmənt/ *noun* **[no plural]** when you feel embarrassed: *He blushed with embarrassment.*

embassy /ˈembəsi/ *noun* (*plural* **embassies**) the official group of people who live in a foreign country and represent their government there, or the building where they work

embrace /ɪmˈbreɪs/ *verb* (*present participle* **embracing**, *past* **embraced**) to put your arms around someone: *They embraced and kissed each other.*

embroidery /ɪmˈbrɔɪdəri/ *noun* **[no plural]** decoration on cloth made by sewing small patterns onto it

embryo /ˈembriəʊ/ *noun* a human or an animal that is starting to grow inside its mother

emerald /ˈemərəld/ *noun* a bright green stone used in jewellery

emerge /ɪˈmɜːdʒ/ *verb* (*present participle* **emerging**, *past* **emerged**) to appear from somewhere or come out of somewhere: *A figure* ***emerged from*** *the shadows.*

emergency /ɪˈmɜːdʒənsi/ *noun* (*plural* **emergencies**) a serious or dangerous situation that needs immediate action: *In an emergency, call this number.* ○ *an emergency exit*

emigrant /ˈemɪgrənt/ *noun* someone who leaves their own country to live in a different one

emigrate /ˈemɪgreɪt/ *verb* (*present participle* **emigrating**, *past* **emigrated**) to leave your own country to live in a different one: *He* ***emigrated to*** *New Zealand.*
- **emigration** /ˌemɪˈgreɪʃən/ *noun* **[no plural]**

emotion /ɪˈməʊʃən/ *noun* a strong feeling such as love or anger: *He finds it hard to express his emotions.*

emotional /ɪˈməʊʃᵊnᵊl/ *adj*
1 relating to emotions: *a child's emotional development*
2 showing strong feelings: *an emotional speech*

empathy /ˈempəθi/ *noun* **[no plural]**
the ability to imagine how another person feels in their situation

emphasize /ˈemfəsaɪz/ *verb* (*present participle* **emphasizing,** *past* **emphasized)**
to show that something is important or needs special attention: *He emphasized the importance of learning foreign languages.*

empire /ˈempaɪəʳ/ *noun*
a group of countries that is ruled by one person or government

employ /ɪmˈplɔɪ/ *verb*
to pay someone to work for you: *The company employs 2500 staff.*

employee /ɪmˈplɔɪiː/ *noun*
someone who is paid to work for a person or company: *How many employees does the firm have?*

employer /ɪmˈplɔɪəʳ/ *noun*
a person or company that pays people to work for them

employment /ɪmˈplɔɪmənt/ *noun* **[no plural]**
when someone is paid to work for a person or company: *It is not easy to* ***find employment*** *in the countryside.*

empty¹ /ˈempti/ *adj*
with nothing or no one inside: *an empty house* ○ *empty bottles*
• **emptiness** *noun* **[no plural]**

empty² /ˈempti/ *verb* (*present participle* **emptying,** *past* **emptied)**
(*also* **empty out)** to remove everything that is inside something: *Where can I empty this ashtray?*

enable /ɪˈneɪbl/ *verb* (*present participle* **enabling,** *past* **enabled)**
to make someone able to do something: *This money enabled me to buy a new computer.*

enclose /ɪnˈkləʊz/ *verb* (*present participle* **enclosing,** *past* **enclosed)**
to send something in the same envelope or parcel as something else: *I enclose a map of the area.*

encourage /ɪnˈkʌrɪdʒ/ *verb* (*present participle* **encouraging,** *past* **encouraged)**
to say good things to someone that will make them confident about doing something: *My parents encouraged me to try new things.*

encouragement *noun* **[no plural]**
good things that you say to someone in order to make them more confident: *Children need lots of encouragement from their parents.*

encouraging /ɪnˈkʌrɪdʒɪŋ/ *adj*
making you feel more hope and confidence: *The team's performance was very encouraging.* ➲Opposite **discouraging**

end¹ /end/ *noun*
1 the final part of something: *I'll pay you at the end of next month.*
2 the furthest part: *They live at the other end of the street.*
3 when something stops happening: *They are calling for* ***an end to*** *the violence.*
4 in the end finally: *We thought we might go abroad for Christmas, but in the end we stayed at home.*

end² /end/ *verb*
to stop, or to make something stop: *What time does the concert end?* ○ *These talks do not look likely to end the war.*

end up *phrasal verb*
to finally be in a particular place or situation: *He ended up in prison.*

ending /ˈendɪŋ/ *noun*
the last part of a story: *I hope this film has a happy ending.*

endless /ˈendləs/ *adj*
never seeming to stop: *We used to have endless arguments about politics.*
• **endlessly** *adv*

endure /ɪnˈdjʊəʳ/ *verb* (*present participle* **enduring,** *past* **endured)** *formal*
to suffer something difficult or unpleasant: *She's already had to endure three painful operations on her leg.*

enemy /ˈenəmi/ *noun* (*plural* **enemies)**
a person or country that you are arguing or fighting with: *I try not to* ***make enemies.***

energetic /ˌenəˈdʒetɪk/ *adj*
having or needing a lot of energy: *an energetic young woman*

energy /ˈenədʒi/ *noun* **[no plural]**
1 the ability to be very active without becoming tired: *Looking after children takes up a lot of time and*

a b c d e f g h i j k l m n o p q r s t u v w x y z

energy. ○ *I didn't even have the energy to get out of bed.*
2 the power that comes from electricity, gas, etc: *nuclear energy*

engaged /ɪn'geɪdʒd/ *adj*
1 If two people are engaged, they have agreed to marry each other: *When did they **get engaged**?*
2 *UK* If a telephone line or a toilet is engaged, it is already being used.

engagement /ɪn'geɪdʒmənt/ *noun*
1 an agreement to get married to someone: *an engagement ring*
2 an arrangement to meet someone

engine /'endʒɪn/ *noun*
the part of a vehicle that uses oil, electricity, or steam to make it move

engineer /ˌendʒɪ'nɪəʳ/ *noun*
someone whose job is to design, build, or repair machines, engines, roads, bridges, etc: *a mechanical engineer*

engineering /ˌendʒɪ'nɪərɪŋ/ *noun* **[no plural]**
the work of an engineer, or the study of this work

English /'ɪŋglɪʃ/ *noun*
1 [no plural] the language that is spoken in the UK, the US, and in many other countries
2 the English the people of England

enjoy /ɪn'dʒɔɪ/ *verb*
1 If you enjoy something, you like doing it: *I hope you enjoy your meal.* ○ *I really enjoyed being with him.*
2 enjoy yourself to like something that you are doing: *It was a great party – I really enjoyed myself.*

enjoyable /ɪn'dʒɔɪəbl/ *adj*
If something is enjoyable, you like doing it: *We had a very enjoyable evening.*

enjoyment /ɪn'dʒɔɪmənt/ *noun* **[no plural]**
when you enjoy something: *She gets a lot of enjoyment from music.*

enlarge /ɪn'lɑːdʒ/ *verb* (*present participle* **enlarging**, *past* **enlarged**)
to make something become bigger: *I want to get this photo enlarged.*

enormous /ɪ'nɔːməs/ *adj*
very large: *They have an enormous house.*
● **enormously** *adv*
very or very much: *The show was enormously popular.*

enough¹ /ɪ'nʌf/ *pronoun, quantifier*
as much as you need: *Have you had enough to eat?*

enough² /ɪ'nʌf/ *adv*
as much as you need: *Are you old enough to vote?* ○ *You're not going fast enough.*

enquire *UK* (*US* **inquire**) /ɪn'kwaɪəʳ/ *verb* (*present participle* **enquiring**, *past* **enquired**)
to ask someone for information about something: *I **enquired about** dentists in the area.*

enter /'entəʳ/ *verb*
1 to go into a place: *The police entered by the back door.*
2 to put information into a computer, book, or document: *You have to enter a password to access this information.*
3 to do an exam or competition: *Are you going to enter the photography competition?*

entertain /ˌentə'teɪn/ *verb*
1 to keep someone interested and help them to have an enjoyable time: *We hired a clown to entertain the children.*
2 to invite someone to be your guest and give them food and drink: *We don't entertain as much as we used to.*

entertainer /ˌentə'teɪnəʳ/ *noun*
someone whose job is to make people laugh and enjoy themselves by singing, telling jokes, etc

entertaining /ˌentə'teɪnɪŋ/ *adj*
interesting and helping someone to have an enjoyable time: *an entertaining and informative book*

entertainment /ˌentə'teɪnmənt/ *noun* **[no plural]**
shows, films, television, or other performances or activities that entertain people: *There is live entertainment in the bar every night.*

enthusiasm /ɪn'θjuːziæzᵊm/ *noun* **[no plural]**
when you feel very interested in something and want to do it: *She has always had a lot of **enthusiasm for** her work.*

enthusiastic /ɪnˌθjuːzi'æstɪk/ *adj*
showing enthusiasm: *The teacher was very **enthusiastic about** my project.*

entire /ɪn'taɪəʳ/ *adj*
whole or complete: *She spent her*

a b c d e f g h i j k l m n o p q r s t u v w x y z

entire life caring for other people.

entirely /ɪn'taɪəli/ *adv*
completely: *It was entirely my fault.*

entrance /'entrəns/ *noun*
1 a door or other opening which you use to go in somewhere: *I'll meet you* ***at the*** *main* ***entrance****.*
2 when someone comes into or goes into a place: *Everyone went quiet when he* ***made his entrance*** (= came in).

entry /'entri/ *noun*
1 [no plural] when you come into or go into a place: *Police gained entry by breaking a window.*
2 (*plural* **entries**) a piece of work that you do to try to win a competition: *The first ten correct entries will receive a prize.*

envelope /'envələʊp/ *noun*
a flat paper container for a letter

envious /'enviəs/ *adj*
wanting something that someone else has: *She was* ***envious of*** *his successful career.*

environment /ɪn'vaɪərᵊnmənt/ *noun*
1 the environment the air, land, and water where people, animals, and plants live: *The new road may cause damage to the environment.*
2 the situation that you live or work in, and how it changes how you feel: *We are working in a very competitive environment.*
● **environmental** *adj*: relating to the environment: *environmental issues*

envy¹ /'envi/ *noun* **[no plural]**
the feeling of wanting something that someone else has: *I watched with envy as he climbed into his brand new sports car.*

envy² /'envi/ *verb* (*present participle* **envying**, *past* **envied**)
to want something that someone else has: *I envy her good looks.*

epic /'epɪk/ *noun*
a story or film which is very long and has a lot of action

epidemic /ˌepɪ'demɪk/ *noun*
when a large number of people get the same disease at the same time: *the AIDS epidemic*

equal¹ /'iːkwəl/ *adj*
the same in amount, number, or size: *The sides are of equal length.* ○ *One metre is* ***equal to*** *39.37 inches.*
● **equally** *adv*

equal² /'iːkwəl/ *verb* (*present participle* **equalling**, *past* **equalled**)
to have the same value, size, etc as something else, often shown using a symbol (=): *Two plus two equals four.*

equal³ /'iːkwəl/ *noun*
someone who has the same ability or rights as someone else: *The teacher treats us all as equals.*

equality /ɪ'kwɒləti/ *noun* **[no plural]**
when everyone is equal and has the same rights, etc: *racial/sexual equality*

equator /ɪ'kweɪtəʳ/ *noun* **[no plural]**
the imaginary line around the Earth that divides it into equal north and south parts

equip /ɪ'kwɪp/ *verb* (*present participle* **equipping**, *past* **equipped**)
be equipped with something to include the things that are needed for a particular purpose: *The new trains are equipped with all the latest technology.*

equipment /ɪ'kwɪpmənt/ *noun*
1 [no plural] the things that are used for an activity or purpose: *kitchen/office equipment*
2 a piece of equipment a tool or object used for an activity or purpose

er /ɜːʳ/ *exclamation UK spoken*
something that you say while you are thinking what to say next: *Well, er, I'm not too sure about that.*

erect /ɪ'rekt/ *verb formal*
to build or put up a structure: *When was this building erected?*

erotic /ɪ'rɒtɪk/ *adj*
making you feel strong sexual feelings: *an erotic film*

errand /'erənd/ *noun*
a short journey in order to buy or do something for someone: *I've got to* ***run*** *a few* ***errands*** *this morning.*

error /'erəʳ/ *noun*
a mistake: *a computer error* ○ *to make an error*

erupt /ɪ'rʌpt/ *verb*
If a volcano erupts, it suddenly throws out fire and melted rocks.
● **eruption** /ɪ'rʌpʃᵊn/ *noun*: *a volcanic eruption*

escalator /'eskəleɪtəʳ/ *noun*
moving stairs that take people from one level of a building to another:

We took the escalator down to the basement.

escape[1] /ɪˈskeɪp/ *verb* (*present participle* **escaping**, *past* **escaped**)
to succeed in getting away from a place where you do not want to be: *The two killers* ***escaped from*** *prison last night.*

escape[2] /ɪˈskeɪp/ *noun*
when someone succeeds in getting out of a place or a dangerous or bad situation: *He made his escape while no one was watching.*

escort[1] /ˈeskɔːt/ *noun*
a person or vehicle that goes somewhere with someone to protect them: *She was driven to court* ***under*** *police* ***escort***.

escort[2] /ɪˈskɔːt/ *verb*
to go somewhere with someone, often to protect them: *He offered to escort me home.*

especially /ɪˈspeʃəli/ *adv*
1 more than other things or people: *I liked all the food but I especially liked the dessert.*
2 for one particular person, purpose, or reason: *I cooked this meal* ***especially for*** *you.*

essay /ˈeseɪ/ *noun*
a short piece of writing about a subject, especially one written by a student: *He wrote an* ***essay on*** *modern Japanese literature.*

essential /ɪˈsenʃəl/ *adj*
very important and necessary: *Computers are an essential part of our lives.* ○ *It is absolutely* ***essential that*** *she gets this message.*

establish /ɪˈstæblɪʃ/ *verb*
to start a company or organization that will continue for a long time: *The company was established in 1822.*

estate agent /ɪˈsteɪt ˌeɪdʒənt/ *UK* (*US* **real estate agent**) *noun*
someone who sells buildings and land as their job

estimate /ˈestɪmeɪt/ *verb* (*present participle* **estimating**, *past* **estimated**)
to guess the cost, size or value of something: *They* ***estimate that*** *a hundred people were killed in the accident.*

etc /etˈsetrə/
used after a list of words to show that other, similar words could be added: *This shelf here is for pens, paper, etc.*

eternal /ɪˈtɜːnəl/ *adj*
continuing forever: *eternal youth*

euro /ˈjʊərəʊ/ *noun*
a unit of money that is used in many European countries; €

European /ˌjʊərəˈpiːən/ *adj*
relating or belonging to Europe: *the European Parliament*
• **European** *noun*: *Many Europeans speak English.*

eve /iːv/ *noun*
Christmas Eve/New Year's Eve the day or night before Christmas Day/New Year's Day

even[1] /ˈiːvən/ *adj*
1 flat, level, or smooth: *Find an even surface to work on.* ⊃Opposite **uneven**
2 An even race or competition is one in which both teams or people involved have the same chance of winning.

even[2] /ˈiːvən/ *adv*
1 used to emphasize something that is surprising: *Everyone danced, even Mick.* ○ *I said hello, but he didn't even look at me.*
2 even better/faster/smaller, etc used when comparing things, to emphasize the difference: *Alex will be even taller than his father.*

evening /ˈiːvnɪŋ/ *noun*
the part of the day between the afternoon and the night: *Are you doing anything this evening?*

evenly /ˈiːvənli/ *adv*
into equal amounts: *They divided the prize money evenly between them.*

even number /ˌiːvən ˈnʌmbər/ *noun*
a number which can be exactly divided by two, for example four, six, or eight ⊃Opposite **odd number**

event /ɪˈvent/ *noun*
something that happens, especially something important or strange: *Local people have been shocked by recent events in the town.*

eventually /ɪˈventʃuəli/ *adv*
in the end, especially after a long time: *We all hope that an agreement can be reached eventually.*

ever /ˈevər/ *adv*
1 at any time: *Have you ever been skiing?* ○ *No one ever calls me any more.*
2 ever since always since that time:

We met at school and have been friends ever since.

every /'evri/ *determiner*
each one of a group of people or things: *He knows the name of every child in the school.*

everybody /'evri,bɒdi/ *pronoun*
another word for everyone

everyone /'evriwʌn/ (*also* **everybody**) *pronoun*
every person: *I've received a reply from everyone now.* ○ *Everyone agreed with the decision.*

everything /'evriθɪŋ/ *pronoun*
1 all things or each thing: *They lost everything in the fire.* ○ *What's the matter Nick, is everything all right?*
2 everything else all the other things: *The meat tasted strange, but everything else was okay.*

everywhere /'evriweəʳ/ *adv*
in or to every place: *I've looked everywhere, but I still can't find that letter.*

evidence /'evɪdᵊns/ *noun* **[no plural]**
1 something that makes you believe that something is true or exists: ***evidence of*** *global warming* ○ *There is no scientific evidence that the drug is harmful.*
2 information that is given or things that are shown in a court of law to help to prove if someone has done a crime: *He was arrested despite the lack of evidence against him.*
3 give evidence *UK* to give information and answer questions in a court of law: *She was called to give evidence at his trial.*

evident /'evɪdᵊnt/ *adj formal*
obvious to everyone and easy to see or understand: *It was evident from his voice that he was upset.*

evil /'iːvᵊl/ *adj*
very bad and cruel: *an evil monster*

exact /ɪg'zækt/ *adj*
completely correct: *I don't know the exact price*

exactly /ɪg'zæktli/ *adv*
1 used when you are giving or asking for information that is completely correct: *What exactly is the problem?* ○ *The train got in at exactly ten o'clock.*
2 used to make stronger what you are saying: *I found a dress that's exactly the same colour as my shoes.*
3 something you say when you agree completely with someone: *"Surely they should have told us about this problem sooner?" "Exactly."*

exaggerate /ɪg'zædʒᵊreɪt/ *verb* (*present participle* **exaggerating,** *past* **exaggerated)**
to make something seem larger, better or worse than it really is: *Don't exaggerate – it didn't cost that much!*

exam /ɪg'zæm/ *noun*
an official test of how much you know about something, or how well you can do something: *a maths exam* ○ *to fail/pass an exam*

examination /ɪg,zæmɪ'neɪʃᵊn/ *noun*
1 when someone looks at something very carefully: *a medical examination*
2 *formal* an exam: *a written examination*

examine /ɪg'zæmɪn/ *verb* (*present participle* **examining,** *past* **examined)**
1 to look at someone or something very carefully, especially to try to discover something: *She picked up the knife and examined it closely.*
2 *formal* to test someone to see how much they know or how well they can do something: *You'll be examined in three main areas: speaking, listening, and reading.*

example /ɪg'zɑːmpl/ *noun*
1 something that is typical of the group of things that you are talking about: *This is a good* ***example of*** *the architecture of the period.*
2 for example used to give an example of what you are talking about: *Some people, students for example, can get cheaper tickets.*

exasperated /ɪg'zæspᵊreɪtɪd/ *adj*
extremely annoyed

exceed /ɪk'siːd/ *verb*
to be more than a particular number or amount: *Sales have exceeded $1 million so far this year.*

excellent /'eksᵊlᵊnt/ *adj*
very good, or of a very high quality: *That was an excellent meal.*

except /ɪk'sept/ *preposition, conjunction*
not including a particular fact, thing, or person: *He works every day*

a b c d e f g h i j k l m n o p q r s t u v w x y z

except Sunday. ○ *Everyone passed the exam* ***except for*** *Camilla.* ○ *So nothing changed,* ***except that*** *Anna saw her son less and less.*

exception /ɪk'sepʃᵊn/ *noun*
1 someone or something that is not included in a rule, group, or list: *There are* ***exceptions to*** *every rule.* ○ *I like all kinds of movies,* ***with the exception of*** *horror films.*
2 make an exception to treat someone differently from all other people: *I don't usually accept credit cards, but for you I'll make an exception.*

exceptional /ɪk'sepʃᵊnᵊl/ *adj*
very good and better than most other people or things: *an exceptional student*
• **exceptionally** *adv*: *an exceptionally clever child*

excess /ɪk'ses/ *noun* (*plural* **excesses**)
more of something than is usual or needed: *There's a charge for excess luggage on a plane.*

exchange[1] /ɪks'tʃeɪndʒ/ *noun*
1 when you give something to someone and they give you something else: *an* ***exchange of*** *ideas* ○ *They were given food and shelter* ***in exchange for*** *work.*
2 when students and teachers from one country go to stay with students and teachers in another: *I have happy memories of going on an exchange to France.*

exchange[2] /ɪks'tʃeɪndʒ/ *verb* (*present participle* **exchanging,** *past* **exchanged)**
1 to give something to someone and get something similar from them: *The two teams usually exchange shirts after the game.*
2 to take something back to the shop where you bought it and get something else: *Could I* ***exchange*** *this shirt* ***for*** *a larger size?*

exchange rate /ɪks'tʃeɪndʒ reɪt/ *noun*
how much of a country's money you can buy with a particular amount of another country's money

excited /ɪk'saɪtɪd/ *adj*
feeling very happy and interested: *happy, excited faces* ○ *The children are getting really* ***excited about*** *the party.*

excitement /ɪk'saɪtmənt/ *noun* **[no plural]**
when people feel very happy and interested: *The competition is causing a lot of excitement.*

exciting /ɪk'saɪtɪŋ/ *adj*
making you feel very happy and interested: *an exciting football match* ○ *You're going to Africa? How exciting!*

exclamation /ˌekskləˈmeɪʃᵊn/ *noun*
something that you say loudly and suddenly because you are surprised or angry: *an exclamation of delight*

exclamation mark /ˌekskləˈmeɪʃn ˌmɑːk/ *noun*
a mark (!) used at the end of a sentence to show surprise or excitement

exclude /ɪks'kluːd/ *verb* (*present participle* **excluding,** *past* **excluded)**
1 to not allow someone or something to do an activity or enter a place: *Women are still* ***excluded from*** *the club.*
2 to not include something: *The insurance cover excludes particular medical conditions.*

excluding /ɪks'kluːdɪŋ/ *preposition*
not including: *That's $600 per person for seven days, excluding travel costs.*

excuse[1] /ɪk'skjuːz/ *verb* (*present participle* **excusing,** *past* **excused)**
1 to forgive someone for something that is not serious: *Please excuse my appearance, I've been painting.*
2 to say that someone does not have to do something: *Could I be excused from football training today?*
3 excuse me
a used to politely get someone's attention: *Excuse me, does this bus go to Oxford Street?*
b used to say sorry for something that you have done: *Oh, excuse me, did I take your seat?*

excuse[2] /ɪk'skjuːs/ *noun*
a reason that you give to explain why you did something wrong: *I hope he's got a good* ***excuse for*** *being so late.*

execute /'eksɪkjuːt/ *verb* (*present participle* **executing,** *past* **executed)**
to kill someone as a legal punishment: *He was executed for murder.*

execution /ˌeksɪˈkjuːʃᵊn/ *noun*
when someone is killed as a legal punishment

executive /ɪg'zekjətɪv/ *noun*

someone who has an important job in a business

exercise[1] /ˈeksəsaɪz/ *noun*
1 activity that you do with your body to make your body strong: *Swimming is my favourite form of exercise.*
2 a piece of written work that helps you learn something: *For your homework, please do exercise 3 on page 24.*

exercise[2] /ˈeksəsaɪz/ *verb* (*present participle* **exercising**, *past* **exercised**)
to do activities with your body to make your body strong and healthy: *I try to exercise every day.*

exhausted /ɪgˈzɔːstɪd/ *adj*
very tired: *He looks exhausted.*

exhausting /ɪgˈzɔːstɪŋ/ *adj*
making you feel very tired: *What an exhausting day!*

exhaustion /ɪgˈzɔːstʃən/ *noun* **[no plural]**
when you are very tired: *The tennis star was suffering from exhaustion.*

exhaust pipe /ɪgˈzɔːst ˌpaɪp/ *noun UK*
the pipe that waste gas from a vehicle's engine goes through

exhibition /ˌeksɪˈbɪʃən/ *noun*
when things such as paintings are shown to the public: *There's a new* ***exhibition of*** *sculpture on at the city gallery.*

exile /ˈeksaɪl, ˈegzaɪl/ *noun* **[no plural]**
when someone has to leave their home and live in another country, often for political reasons: *He spent the war years* ***in exile*** *in New York.*

exist /ɪgˈzɪst/ *verb*
to be real or present: *Poverty still exists in this country.*

existence /ɪgˈzɪstəns/ *noun* **[no plural]**
when something or someone exists: *The theatre company that we started is still* ***in existence*** *today.*

exit /ˈeksɪt/ *noun*
the door which you use to leave a public building or place: *a fire exit* ○ *an emergency exit*

expand /ɪkˈspænd/ *verb*
to get larger, or to make something get larger: *The company has expanded in recent years.*

expansion /ɪkˈspænʃən/ *noun* **[no plural]**
when something gets larger: *the rapid expansion of the software industry*

expect /ɪkˈspekt/ *verb*
1 to think that something will happen: *He didn't* ***expect to*** *see me.* ○ *I* ***expect that*** *she'll be very angry about this.*
2 be expecting someone/something to be waiting for someone or something to arrive: *We've been expecting you.*
3 to think that someone should do a particular thing: *You will be* ***expected to*** *work some weekends.*
4 I expect *UK informal* used to show that you think that something is true: *"Will you be coming to the party?" "**I expect so**."*
5 be expecting to be going to have a baby: *I'm expecting my first baby in May.*

expectation /ˌekspekˈteɪʃən/ *noun*
when you think good things will happen in the future

expedition /ˌekspɪˈdɪʃən/ *noun*
an organized journey, especially a long one for a particular purpose: *Peary led the first expedition to the North Pole.*

expel /ɪkˈspel/ *verb* (*present participle* **expelling**, *past* **expelled**)
to make someone leave a school, organization, or country: *He was* ***expelled from*** *school* ***for*** *fighting.*

expense /ɪkˈspens/ *noun*
the money that you spend on something: *You have to pay your own medical expenses.*

expensive /ɪkˈspensɪv/ *adj*
costing a lot of money: *expensive jewellery* ➲Opposite **cheap**
• **expensively** *adv*: *expensively dressed*

experience[1] /ɪkˈspɪəriəns/ *noun*
1 [no plural] knowledge that you get from doing a job, or from doing, seeing, or feeling something: *Do you have any* ***experience of*** *working with children?* ○ *He knows* ***from experience*** *how difficult she can be.*
2 something that happens to you that affects how you feel: *My trip to Australia was an experience I'll never forget.*

experience[2] /ɪkˈspɪəriəns/ *verb*

a b c d e f g h i j k l m n o p q r s t u v w x y z

(*present participle* **experiencing,** *past* **experienced)**
If you experience something, it happens to you, or you feel it: *It was the worst pain I had ever experienced.*

experienced /ɪk'spɪəriənst/ *adj*
having skill and knowledge because you have done something many times: *Karsten's a very experienced ski instructor.* ➲Opposite **inexperienced**

experiment¹ /ɪk'sperɪmənt/ *noun*
a test, especially a scientific one, that you do in order to discover if something is true: *We **do** a lot of **experiments** in class.*

experiment² /ɪk'sperɪment/ *verb*
1 to try something in order to discover what it is like: *Did he ever **experiment with** drugs?*
2 to do an experiment: *He's against **experimenting on** animals.*

expert /'ekspɜːt/ *noun*
someone who has a lot of skill in something or a lot of knowledge about something: *He's **an expert on** Japanese literature.*

explain /ɪk'spleɪn/ *verb*
to make something clear or easy to understand by giving reasons for it: *Can you **explain why** you did this?* ○ *Can you **explain to** me how this phone works?* ○ *He **explained that** he was going to stay with his sister.*

explanation /ˌeksplə'neɪʃᵊn/ *noun*
the details or reasons that someone gives to make something clear or easy to understand: *What's your **explanation for** the team's poor performance?* ○ *Could you give me a quick **explanation of** how it works?*

explode /ɪk'spləʊd/ *verb* (*present participle* **exploding,** *past* **exploded)**
If a bomb explodes, it bursts (= breaks suddenly from inside) with noise and force: *One of the bombs did not explode.*

explore /ɪk'splɔːʳ/ *verb* (*present participle* **exploring,** *past* **explored)**
to go around a place where you have never been in order to find out what is there: *The children love exploring.* ○ *The best way to explore the countryside is on foot.*
● **exploration** /ˌeksplə'reɪʃᵊn/ *noun*: *She's always loved travel and exploration.*

explorer /ɪk'splɔːrəʳ/ *noun*
someone who travels to places where no one has ever been in order to find out what is there

explosion /ɪk'spləʊʒᵊn/ *noun*
when something such as a bomb explodes: *Forty people were killed in the explosion.*

explosive /ɪk'spləʊsɪv/ *adj*
able to cause an explosion: *The explosive device was hidden in a suitcase.*

export¹ /'ekspɔːt/ *noun*
a product that you sell in another country: *Scottish beef exports to Japan* ➲Opposite **import**

export² /ɪk'spɔːt/ *verb*
to send goods to another country in order to sell them there: *Singapore exports large quantities of rubber.*
➲Opposite **import**
● **exporter** *noun*: *Brazil is the world's largest exporter of coffee.*

expose /ɪk'spəʊz/ *verb* (*present participle* **exposing,** *past* **exposed)**
to show something by removing its cover: *He removed the bandage to expose the wound.*

express /ɪk'spres/ *verb*
to show what you think or how you feel using words or actions: *I'm simply expressing my opinion.*

expression /ɪk'spreʃᵊn/ *noun*
1 the look on someone's face showing what they feel or think: *He had a sad expression on his face.*
2 a group of words that has a special meaning: *'A can of worms' is an expression meaning 'a difficult situation'.*

exquisite /ɪk'skwɪzɪt/ *adj*
very beautiful or perfect: *a garden of exquisite flowers*

extend /ɪk'stend/ *verb*
1 to make something bigger or longer: *We're going to extend our kitchen.*
2 to make an activity, agreement, etc last for a longer time: *They have extended the deadline by one week.*

extension /ɪk'stenʃᵊn/ *noun*
a new room or rooms that are added to a building: *You could build an extension onto the back of the house.*

extent /ɪk'stent/ *noun*
the size or importance of something: *They are just beginning to*

realize the full extent of the damage.

exterior /ɪk'stɪəriəʳ/ *noun* the outside part of something or someone: *The exterior of the house was painted white.*
• **exterior** *adj*: *an exterior wall* ➲Opposite **interior**

external /ɪk'stɜːnᵊl/ *adj* relating to the outside part of something: *the external walls of the house* ➲Opposite **internal**
• **externally** *adv*

extinct /ɪk'stɪŋkt/ *adj* If a type of animal is extinct, it does not now exist.

extinguish /ɪk'stɪŋgwɪʃ/ *verb* to stop something burning: *The fire took two hours to extinguish.*

extra /'ekstrə/ *adj* more, or more than usual: *Can I invite a few extra people?*

extraordinary /ɪk'strɔːdᵊnᵊri/ *adj* very special or strange: *She was an extraordinary young woman.*

extravagant /ɪk'strævəgənt/ *adj* spending too much money: *the extravagant lifestyle of a movie star*
• **extravagance** /ɪk'strævəgəns/ *noun* when someone or something is extravagant

extreme /ɪk'striːm/ *adj*
1 the worst or most serious: *extreme weather conditions*
2 very large in amount or degree: *extreme pain*
3 at the furthest point of something: *in the extreme south of the island*

extremely /ɪk'striːmli/ *adv* very: *extremely beautiful* ○ *He works extremely hard.*

eye /aɪ/ *noun*
1 one of the two organs in your face, which you use to see with: *Sara has black hair and brown eyes.* ○ *She closed her eyes and fell asleep.*
2 the small hole at the end of a needle, that you put the thread through
3 keep an eye on someone/something to watch or look after someone or something: *Could you keep an eye on this pan of soup for a moment?*

eye

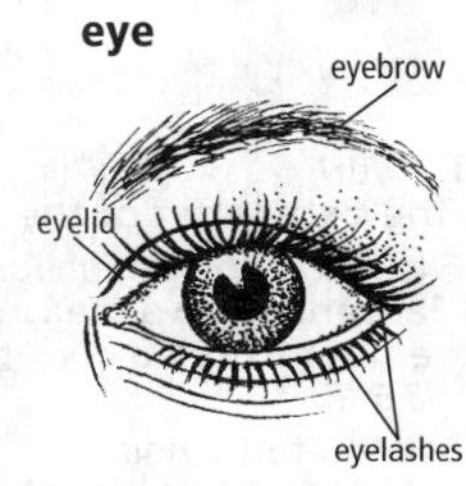

eyebrow /'aɪbraʊ/ *noun* the thin line of hair that is above each eye ➲See colour picture **The Body** on page Centre 2

eyelash /'aɪlæʃ/ (*also* **lash**) *noun* (*plural* **eyelashes**) one of the short hairs that grow from the edge of your eyelids: *false eyelashes*

eyelid /'aɪlɪd/ *noun* the piece of skin that covers your eyes when you close them

eyesight /'aɪsaɪt/ *noun* **[no plural]** the ability to see: *My eyesight is getting worse.*

Ff

F, f /ef/
the sixth letter of the alphabet

F *written abbreviation for*
Fahrenheit (= a measurement of temperature): *a body temperature of 98.6 °F*

fable /ˈfeɪbl/ *noun*
a short story which shows people how to behave

fabric /ˈfæbrɪk/ *noun*
cloth: *a light/woollen fabric*

fabulous /ˈfæbjələs/ *adj*
very good: *They've got a fabulous house.*

face[1] /feɪs/ *noun*
1 the front part of the head where the eyes, nose, and mouth are: *She's got a long, thin face.*
2 the front or surface of something: *the north face of the cliff ○ a clock face*

face

face[2] /feɪs/ *verb* (*present participle* **facing**, *past* **faced**)
1 to be or turn in a particular direction: *The room faces south. ○ She turned to face him.*
2 to have a problem: *Passengers could face long delays.*
3 let's face it something that you say before you say something that is bad but true: *Let's face it, none of us are getting any younger.*

facilities /fəˈsɪlətiz/ *plural noun*
buildings or equipment that are provided for a particular purpose: *sports/washing facilities*

fact /fækt/ *noun*
1 something that you know is true, exists, or has happened: ***The fact is** that we don't have enough money. ○ No decision will be made until we know all the facts.*
2 in fact/in actual fact used to say what is really true: *I was told there were some tickets left, but in actual fact they were sold out.*

factory /ˈfæktəri/ *noun* (*plural* **factories**)
a place where things are made or put together: *a textile factory*

fade /feɪd/ *verb* (*present participle* **fading,** *past* **faded**)
If a colour or sound fades, it becomes less bright or strong: *The music began to fade.*

Fahrenheit /ˈfærənhaɪt/ (*written abbreviation* **F**) *noun* **[no plural]**
a measurement of temperature in which water freezes at 32°and boils at 212°

fail /feɪl/ *verb*
1 to not be successful: *Dad's business failed after just three years.*
2 fail to do something to not do what is expected: *He failed to turn up for football practice yesterday.*
3 to not pass a test or an exam: *I've just failed my driving test.* ➲Opposite **succeed**

failure /ˈfeɪljər/ *noun*
1 [no plural] when someone or something does not succeed: *Their attempt to climb the mountain ended in failure.*
2 someone or something that does not succeed: *All my life I've felt like a failure.* ➲Opposite **success**

faint[1] /feɪnt/ *adj*
1 slight and not easy to notice: *a faint smell of smoke*
2 feel faint to feel very weak and as if you might fall down: *Seeing all the blood made me feel faint.*

faint[2] /feɪnt/ *verb*
to suddenly become unconscious for a short time

fair[1] /feər/ *adj*
1 treating everyone in the same way: *a fair trial*
2 having pale skin or a light colour of hair: *a boy with fair hair*
3 a fair amount/number... quite a large amount: *There's still a fair bit of work to be done on the house.*
4 quite good, although not very good: *He has a fair chance of winning.*
5 sunny and not raining

fair

fair[2] /feər/ *noun*
a place outside where you can ride

on big machines for pleasure and play games

fairly /ˈfeəli/ *adv*
1 more than slightly, but less than very: *a fairly big family*
2 done in a fair way: *treating people fairly*

fair trade /feə^{r} treɪd/ *noun* **[no plural]**
a way of buying and selling things in which the original producer gets enough money: *fair trade coffee*

fairy /ˈfeəri/ *noun* (*plural* **fairies)**
a small, imaginary person with wings who has magic powers

fairy

fairy tale /ˈfeəri teɪl/ *noun*
a story told to children with magic in it and a happy ending

faith /feɪθ/ *noun*
1 [no plural] the belief that someone or something is good and can be trusted: *I have great* ***faith in*** *her ability.*
2 a religion: *the Jewish and Christian faiths*

faithful /ˈfeɪθf^{ə}l/ *adj*
always liking and supporting someone or something: *She's a trusted and faithful friend.*

faithfully /ˈfeɪθf^{ə}li/ *adv*
Yours faithfully used to end a formal letter to someone whose name you do not know

fall[1] /fɔːl/ *verb* (*present participle* **falling**, *past tense* **fell**, *past participle* **fallen)**
1 to move down towards the ground: *Huge drops of rain were* ***falling from*** *the sky.*
2 to suddenly go down and hit the ground: *She* ***fell off*** *her bike.*
3 to become less in number or amount: *House prices have* ***fallen by*** *15% since last year.*
4 fall asleep to start to sleep
fall apart *phrasal verb*
to break into pieces: *These old boots are falling apart.*
fall out *phrasal verb UK*
to argue with someone: *She has* ***fallen out with*** *Sam again.*
fall over *phrasal verb*
to fall to the ground: *She fell over and hurt her knee.*

fall[2] /fɔːl/ *noun*
1 when the number or amount of something becomes smaller: *There's been a sharp* ***fall in*** *prices.*
2 when someone or something moves down to the ground: *a heavy fall of snow*
3 *US* (*UK* **autumn)** the season of the year between summer and winter, when leaves fall from the trees

fallen /ˈfɔːlən/
past participle of fall

false /fɔːls/ *adj*
1 not true or correct: *a false name*
2 not real: *false teeth*

fame /feɪm/ *noun* **[no plural]**
when you are known by many people

familiar /fəˈmɪliə^{r}/ *adj*
1 If something is familiar, you know it well or have seen it before: *This street looks* ***familiar to*** *me.*
2 be familiar with something to know about something or have done or seen it many times before: *Anyone who's familiar with his poetry will find the course easy.*

family /ˈfæm^{ə}li/ *noun* (*plural* **families)**
a group of people who are related to each other, especially parents and children: *I'm from a big family.*

famine /ˈfæmɪn/ *noun*
when people living in an area do not have enough food

famous /ˈfeɪməs/ *adj*
known by many people: *a famous actress*

fan

fan /fæn/ *noun*
1 someone who likes a person or thing very much: *He's a big* ***fan of*** *country music.*
2 something that is used to move the air around so that it feels cooler: *an electric fan*

fancy /ˈfænsi/ *verb* (*present participle* **fancying,** *past* **fancied**)
1 *UK* to want to have or do something: *Do you fancy a drink?*
2 *UK informal* to feel sexually attracted to someone: *I fancied him the first time I saw him.*

fancy dress /fænsi ˈdres/ *noun* **[no plural]** *UK*
special clothes that people wear for a party, which make them look like a different person: *a fancy dress party*

fantastic /fænˈtæstɪk/ *adj informal*
very good: *He looks fantastic in that suit.*

FAQ /ˌefeɪˈkjuː/ *noun*
something that many people ask when they use the Internet or a computer program, or a document containing these questions and their answers

far[1] /fɑːʳ/ *adv* **farther** or **further, farthest** or **furthest**
1 used to talk about how distant something is: ***How far*** *is it to the supermarket?*
2 very much: *Young people are far more independent these days.*
3 as far as I know used to say what you think is true, although you do not know all the facts: *As far as I know, they are coming.*
4 by far used to say that something is very much the biggest, the best, etc: *This is his best film by far.*
5 so far until now: *So far, we haven't made much progress.*

far[2] /fɑːʳ/ *adj*
describing the part of something that is most distant from you: *His office is at the far end of the corridor.*

fare /feəʳ/ *noun*
the price that you pay to travel on an aeroplane, train, bus, etc: *air/train fares*

farm /fɑːm/ *noun*
land and buildings used for growing crops and keeping animals: *a pig farm*

farmer /ˈfɑːməʳ/ *noun*
someone who owns or looks after a farm

farming /fɑːmɪŋ/ *noun* **[no plural]**
the job of working on a farm

farmyard /ˈfɑːmjɑːd/ *noun*
an area of ground with farm

farm

buildings around it

farther /ˈfɑːðəʳ/ *adj, adv (comparative of* **far***)*
more distant: *I couldn't walk any farther.*

farthest /ˈfɑːðɪst/ *adj, adv (superlative of* **far***)*
most distant: *They walked to the farthest edge of the garden.*

fascinated /ˈfæsɪneɪtɪd/ *adj*
very interested: *They were absolutely fascinated by the game.*

fascinating /ˈfæsɪneɪtɪŋ/ *adj*
very interesting: *a fascinating film*

fascination /ˌfæsɪˈneɪʃᵊn/ *noun* **[no plural]**
when you find someone or something very interesting

fashion /ˈfæʃᵊn/ *noun*
the most popular style of clothes or behaviour at a particular time: *Long hair is back* ***in fashion.*** ○ *Fur coats have gone* ***out of fashion.***

fashionable /ˈfæʃᵊnəbl/ *adj*
popular at a particular time: *fashionable clothes* ➲Opposite **unfashionable**

fast[1] /fɑːst/ *adj*
1 quick: *fast cars* ○ *a fast swimmer* ➲Opposite **slow**
2 If a clock or watch is fast, it shows a time that is later than the correct time: *My watch is five minutes fast.*

fast[2] /fɑːst/ *adv*
1 quickly: *We ran as fast as we could.*
2 fast asleep completely asleep (= sleeping)
3 in a firm or tight way: *He tried to get away, but she held him fast.*

fasten /ˈfɑːsᵊn/ *verb*
1 to close or fix something together:

Fasten your seat belts.
2 to fix one thing to another: *He fastened the rope to a tree.*

fast food /ˌfɑːst ˈfuːd/ *noun* **[no plural]**
hot food that is served very quickly in a restaurant because it is already made

fat¹ /fæt/ *adj*
Someone who is fat weighs too much: *She eats all the time but never **gets fat**.* ↄOpposite **thin**

fat² /fæt/ *noun* **[no plural]**
a solid or liquid substance like oil that is taken from plants or animals and used in cooking: *animal/ vegetable fat*

fatal /ˈfeɪtᵊl/ *adj*
A fatal accident or illness makes someone die: *a fatal car crash*

fate /feɪt/ *noun* **[no plural]**
a power that some people believe decides what will happen: *I believe it was fate that caused us to meet again.*

father /ˈfɑːðəʳ/ *noun*
your male parent

Father Christmas /ˌfɑːðəʳ ˈkrɪsməs/ *noun UK*
a kind, fat, old man in red clothes who children believe brings presents at Christmas

fatherhood /ˈfɑːðəhʊd/ *noun* **[no plural]**
being a father

father-in-law /ˈfɑːðərɪnlɔː/ *noun* (*plural* **fathers-in-law**)
the father of your husband or wife

fault /fɔːlt/ *noun*
1 someone's fault If something bad that happened is someone's fault, they made it happen: *She believes it was the doctor's fault that Peter died.*
2 something that is wrong with something or someone's character: *The car has a serious design fault.*

faulty /ˈfɔːlti/ *adj*
not working correctly: *faulty brakes*

favour /ˈfeɪvəʳ/ *noun*
1 something that you do to help someone: *Could you **do me a favour** please?*
2 be in favour of something to agree with a plan or idea: *Most people are in favour of reducing traffic in cities.*

favourite /ˈfeɪvᵊrət/ *adj*
Your favourite person or thing is the one that you like best: *What's your favourite colour?*

fax /fæks/ *noun* (*plural* **faxes**)
1 a document that is sent using a special machine and a telephone line
2 a machine that is used to send and receive faxes
• **fax** *verb*

fear¹ /fɪəʳ/ *noun*
a strong, bad feeling that you get when you think that something bad might happen: *She was trembling with fear.* ○ *There are **fears that** the disease will spread.*

fear² /fɪəʳ/ *verb*
1 to be worried or frightened that something bad might happen or might have happened: *Police **fear that** the couple may have drowned.*
2 to be frightened of something or someone unpleasant: *Most older employees fear unemployment.*

fearless /ˈfɪələs/ *adj*
not frightened of anything

feast /fiːst/ *noun*
a large meal, especially to celebrate something special

feather /ˈfeðəʳ/ *noun*
one of the soft, light things that cover a bird's skin

feature /ˈfiːtʃəʳ/ *noun*
1 an important part of something: *This phone has several new features.*
2 one of the parts of a person's face that you notice when you look at them: *His eyes are his best feature.*

February /ˈfebruᵊri/ *noun*
the second month of the year

fed /fed/
past of feed

fed up /ˌfed ˈʌp/ *adj informal*
bored by something that you have done for too long: *I'm **fed up with** my job.*

fee /fiː/ *noun*
an amount of money that you pay to do or use something: *university fees*

feeble /ˈfiːbl/ *adj*
very weak: *She became too feeble to get out of bed.*

feed /fiːd/ *verb* (*present participle* **feeding**, *past* **fed**) a b c d e **f** g h i j k l m n o p q r s t u v w x y z

to give food to a person or animal: *I fed Simone's cat while she was away.*

feel /fiːl/ *verb* (*present participle* **feeling**, *past* **felt**)
1 to have an emotion or a physical feeling: *You shouldn't feel embarrassed.* ○ *I felt a sharp pain in my side.*
2 to have an opinion about something: *I **feel that** she's the best person for the job.*
3 to touch something in order to examine it: *He felt her ankle to see if it was broken.*
4 feel like something/doing something to want something, or want to do something: *Jane felt like crying.*

feeling /ˈfiːlɪŋ/ *noun*
1 an emotion: *guilty feelings*
2 when you feel something physical: *I had a strange feeling in my fingers.*
3 an opinion or belief: *My feeling is that we should wait until they come back.*

feelings /ˈfiːlɪŋz/ *plural noun*
hurt someone's feelings to upset someone by saying something bad about them

feet /fiːt/
plural of foot

fell /fel/
past tense of fall

fellow /ˈfeləʊ/ *adj*
used to describe people with the same interests or situation: *her fellow students*

felt /felt/
past of feel

felt-tip pen /felt tɪp ˈpen/ *noun*
a pen with a soft point and coloured ink for colouring pictures

female /ˈfiːmeɪl/ *adj*
belonging to the sex that can have babies: *a female butterfly*
● **female** *noun*

feminine /ˈfemɪnɪn/ *adj*
showing qualities that people think are typical of women: *feminine beauty*

fence

fence /fens/ *noun*
a wood or metal structure that goes around an area: *a garden fence*

fern /fɜːn/ *noun*
a green plant with narrow leaves like feathers and no flowers

fern

ferocious /fəˈrəʊʃəs/ *adj*
very angry or violent: *a ferocious dog*

ferry /ˈferi/ *noun* (*plural* **ferries**)
a boat that regularly carries people and vehicles across an area of water: *a car/passenger ferry*

fertile /ˈfɜːtaɪl/ *adj*
1 Fertile land or soil produces a lot of healthy plants.
2 If people or animals are fertile, they are able to have babies.

fertilizer /ˈfɜːtɪlaɪzəʳ/ *noun*
something that you put on land in order to make plants grow well

festival /ˈfestɪvəl/ *noun*
1 a series of special events or performances: *a dance/music festival*
2 a special day or period when people celebrate something, especially a religious event: *the Jewish festival of Hanukkah*

fetch /fetʃ/ *verb*
to go to another place to get something or someone: *Can you fetch my glasses from the bedroom?*

fête /feɪt/ *noun UK*
an event that happens outside and includes competitions, games, and things for sale: *a village fête*

fever /ˈfiːvəʳ/ *noun*
when someone's body temperature goes up because they are ill
● **feverish** *adj*
having a fever

few /fjuː/ *quantifier*
1 a few some, or a small number of: *I'm just here for a few days.* ○ *I've met **a few of** her friends.*
2 quite a few quite a large number of: *Quite a few people have had the same problem.*
3 not many, or only a small number of: ***Very few** people can afford to pay those prices.*

fiancé /fiˈɑːnseɪ/ *noun*
A woman's fiancé is the man that she has promised to marry.

fiancée /fiˈɑːnseɪ/ *noun*

A man's fiancée is the woman that he has promised to marry.

fib /fɪb/ *noun informal*
a small lie that is not important: *Don't* ***tell fibs****!*

fibre /ˈfaɪbəʳ/ *noun UK*
one of the thin threads that cloth is made of: *The fibres are woven into fabric.*

field /ˈfiːld/ *noun*
1 an area of land used for growing crops or keeping animals
2 an area of grass where you can play a sport: *a football field*

fierce /fɪəs/ *adj*
very strong or violent: *fierce storms* ○ *a fierce dog*

fifteen /ˌfɪfˈtiːn/
the number 15
• **fifteenth**
15th written as a word

fifth[1] /fɪfθ/
5th written as a word

fifth[2] /fɪfθ/ *noun*
one of five equal parts of something; ⅕

fifty /ˈfɪfti/
the number 50
• **fiftieth**
50th written as a word

fig /fɪg/ *noun*
a dark, sweet fruit with lots of seeds

fight[1] /faɪt/ *verb* (*present participle* **fighting**, *past* **fought**)
1 to try to hurt or kill someone using your body or weapons: *Two men were arrested for fighting outside a bar.*
2 to argue: *Don't fight in front of the children!*

fight[2] /faɪt/ *noun*
1 when people try to hurt or kill each other using their body or weapons: *He's always getting into fights.*
2 when people try very hard to achieve something or to stop something: *She was very active in the* ***fight against*** *drugs.* ○ *Join us in our* ***fight for*** *freedom!*

figure /ˈfɪgəʳ/ *noun*
1 a symbol for a number: *Write down the amount in words and figures.*
2 a person that you cannot see clearly: *I could see two figures in the distance.*
3 the shape of someone's body, usually an attractive shape: *She's got a good figure for her age.*

file[1] /faɪl/ *noun*
1 a collection of information stored electronically: *Do you want to download all these files?*
2 a box or folded piece of thick paper used to put documents in: *He keeps all his bank statements in a file.*
3 a small tool with a rough edge that is used to make a surface smooth: *a nail file*

file[2] /faɪl/ *verb* (*present participle* **filing**, *past* **filed**)
1 to put documents into an ordered system so that you can easily find them: *She filed all her tax returns under T.*
2 to rub something with a rough tool in order to make it smooth

filing cabinet /ˈfaɪlɪŋ ˌkæbɪnət/ *noun*
a piece of office furniture with deep drawers for storing documents

fill /fɪl/ *verb*
to make a container or space full, or to become full: *He filled the bucket with water.* ○ *I made a drink while the bath was filling.*

fill something in/out *phrasal verb*
to write all the information that is needed on a document: *She filled in the form.*

fill (something) up *phrasal verb*
to become full, or to make something become full: *The restaurant soon filled up with people.*

filling /ˈfɪlɪŋ/ *noun*
a hard substance that is put in a hole in a tooth

film /fɪlm/ *noun*
1 (*also US* **movie**) a story shown at the cinema or on television: *a cowboy film*
2 special thin plastic used for making photographs

film star /ˈfɪlm stɑːʳ/ *noun*
a famous cinema actor or actress

filter /ˈfɪltəʳ/ *noun*
a piece of equipment that you pass liquid through in order to remove particular substances: *a coffee filter*
• **filter** *verb*

filthy /ˈfɪlθi/ *adj*
very dirty: *filthy hands*

fin /fɪn/ *noun*
a thin, triangular part on a fish,

a b c d e f g h i j k l m n o p q r s t u v w x y z

which helps it to swim

final[1] /ˈfaɪnᵊl/ *adj*
last or coming at the end: *the final paragraph* ○ *They scored a goal in the final minute.*

final[2] /ˈfaɪnᵊl/ *noun*
1 the last part of a competition to decide who will win: *the European Cup Final*
2 finals exams that you take at the end of a university course

finally /ˈfaɪnᵊli/ *adv*
1 after a long time: *We finally got home just after midnight.*
2 used before you say the last point or idea: *Finally, I'd like to thank everyone for coming.*

finance[1] /ˈfaɪnæns/ *noun* **[no plural]**
the control of how large amounts of money should be spent

finance[2] /ˈfaɪnæns/ *verb* (*present participle* **financing,** *past* **financed)**
to give the money that is needed to do something: *Who's financing the project?*

financial /faɪˈnænʃᵊl/ *adj*
relating to money or how money is used: *financial advice*

find /faɪnd/ *verb* (*present participle* **finding,** *past* **found)**
1 to discover something or someone that you have been looking for: *I can't find my glasses and I've looked everywhere.*
2 to become aware of something: *I came home to find that the kitchen window had been smashed.*
3 to think or feel a particular way about someone or something: *I still find exams very stressful.*
4 find someone guilty to judge that someone is guilty in a law court: *She was found guilty of murder.*
find (something) out *phrasal verb*
to get information about something: *I must find out the train times.*

fine[1] /faɪn/ *adj*
1 well, healthy, or happy: *"How are you?" "I'm fine thanks. And you?"*
2 good enough: *"Is the soup okay?" "Yes, it's fine."*
3 excellent, or of very good quality: *fine wines*
4 (that's) fine used to agree with a suggestion: *"Shall we meet at 8 o'clock?" "Yes, that's fine by me."*
5 thin: *fine, brown hair*
6 *UK* sunny and not raining

fine[2] /faɪn/ *noun*
an amount of money that you must pay for doing something wrong: *a parking fine*
• **fine** *verb* (*present participle* **fining,** *past* **fined)**
to punish someone by making them pay some money

finger /ˈfɪŋgəʳ/ *noun*
one of the five long parts at the end of your hand

finger
fingernail
fingertip

fingernail /ˈfɪŋgəneɪl/ *noun*
the hard, thin part on the top of the end of your finger

fingerprint /ˈfɪŋgəprɪnt/ *noun*
the mark made on something by the pattern of curved lines on the end of someone's finger: *The police found fingerprints all over the murder weapon.*

fingertip /ˈfɪŋgətɪp/ *noun*
the end of your finger

finish /ˈfɪnɪʃ/ *verb*
1 to complete something: *I've finished my homework.*
2 to end: *The meeting should finish at five o'clock.*
3 (*also* **finish off**) to eat, drink, or use something completely: *They finished their drinks and left the bar.*
finish something off *phrasal verb*
to do the last part of something: *I have to finish off this report by Friday.*

fir /fɜːʳ/ *noun*
a tree with very thin, straight leaves that do not fall in winter

fire

fire[1] /faɪəʳ/ *noun*
1 heat, light, and flames that are made when something burns: *Three people were killed in the fire.*

2 catch fire to start burning: *The car crashed and caught fire.*
3 on fire burning: *That house is on fire.*
4 set fire to something to make something start burning: *Enemy troops set fire to the village.*
5 a pile of wood or coal that is burning to produce heat

fire² /ˈfaɪəʳ/ *verb* (*present participle* **firing**, *past* **fired**)
to shoot a bullet from a gun: *She* ***fired*** *three shots* ***at*** *him.*

fire brigade /ˈfaɪə brɪˌgeɪd/ *noun UK*
an organization of people whose job is to stop fires

fire engine /ˈfaɪər ˌendʒɪn/ *noun*
a vehicle for carrying firemen and equipment for stopping large fires

fire extinguisher /ˈfaɪər ɪkˌstɪŋgwɪʃəʳ/ *noun*
a piece of equipment kept inside buildings which is used to stop small fires

firefighter /ˈfaɪəfaɪtəʳ/ *noun*
someone whose job is to stop fires burning

fireman /ˈfaɪəmən/ *noun* (*plural* **firemen**)
a man whose job is to stop fires burning

fireplace /ˈfaɪəpleɪs/ *noun*
the part of a wall in a room where you can have a fire

fire station /ˈfaɪə ˌsteɪʃn/ *noun*
the building where fire engines are kept, and firemen wait when they are not fighting fires

fireworks

firework /ˈfaɪəwɜːk/ *noun*
a small object that explodes and makes a loud noise and bright colours in the sky: *a firework display*

firm¹ /fɜːm/ *adj*
1 not soft, but not completely hard: *A firm bed is better for your back.*
2 If you are firm you make certain that people do what you want: *You've got to be firm with children.*
• **firmly** *adv*

firm² /fɜːm/ *noun*
a company that sells goods or services: *a law firm*

first¹ /ˈfɜːst/ *adj*
1 coming before all others: *Ken was the first person to arrive.*
2 '1st' written as a word

first² /ˈfɜːst/ *adv*
1 before everything or everyone else: *Jason* ***came first*** *in the 400 metres* (= he won).
2 for the first time: *He first started playing the piano at school.*
3 at first at the beginning of a situation or period of time: *I didn't really like her at first.*
4 first; first of all before doing anything else: *First of all, check you have all the correct ingredients.*

first³ /ˈfɜːst/ *noun, pronoun*
the first the first person or thing: *I enjoyed his second film more than the first.*

first aid /ˌfɜːst ˈeɪd/ *noun* **[no plural]**
basic help that a person who is not a doctor can give give to a person who is hurt or ill: *The policeman* ***gave*** *him* ***first aid*** *before the ambulance arrived.*

first-class /ˌfɜːstˈklɑːs/ *adj*
relating to the best and most expensive service: *a first-class ticket* ○ *a first-class stamp*
• **first class** *adv*: *I want to send this letter first class.*

first floor /ˌfɜːst ˈflɔːʳ/ *noun UK*
the level of a building directly above the ground level

firstly /ˈfɜːstli/ *adv*
used to introduce the first of many ideas: *The aim of this activity is firstly to have fun, and secondly to keep fit.*

first name /ˈfɜːst ˌneɪm/ *noun*
the name that comes before your family name: *Ms Jackson – what's your first name?*

fish¹ /fɪʃ/ *noun* (*plural* **fish** *or* **fishes**)
an animal that lives only in water, swims, and can be eaten as food

fish[2] /fɪʃ/ *verb*
to try to catch fish

fisherman /ˈfɪʃəmən/ *noun* (*plural* **fishermen**)
someone who catches fish as a job or as a hobby

fist /fɪst/ *noun*
a hand closed into a ball with the fingers and thumb curled tightly together: *He banged his fist down angrily on the table.*

fit[1] /fɪt/ *verb* (*present participle* **fitting**, *past* **fitted**)
1 to be the right shape or size for someone or something: *These trousers don't fit any more.*
2 If people or things fit somewhere, that place is big enough for them: *How many people can you fit in your car?*
3 *UK* to put or fix something somewhere: *You ought to fit a smoke alarm in the kitchen.*

fit[2] /fɪt/ *adj*
1 healthy, especially because you exercise a lot: *He's very fit for his age.*
➲Opposite **unfit**
2 good enough for a particular purpose: *Is this water **fit to** drink?*

five /faɪv/
the number 5

fix /fɪks/ *verb*
1 to repair something: *Can you fix my watch?*
2 to decide a date or price: *Let's fix a day to have lunch together.*
3 to fasten something in a particular place: *They fixed the bookcase to the wall.*

fizzy

fizzy /ˈfɪzi/ *adj*
A fizzy drink has lots of bubbles of gas in it.

flag

flag /flæg/ *noun*
a piece of cloth with a special design and colours, that is the symbol of a country or group

flake /fleɪk/ *noun*
a small, flat, thin piece of something: *flakes of skin*

flame /fleɪm/ *noun*
hot, bright, burning gas made by something on fire: *The car crashed and **burst into flames*** (= suddenly started burning).

flap[1] /flæp/ *noun*
something that hangs over an opening and is fixed on one side

flap[2] /flæp/ *verb* (*present participle* **flapping**, *past* **flapped**)
If a bird flaps its wings, it moves them up and down.

flash[1] /flæʃ/ *verb*
1 to shine brightly and suddenly, or to make something shine in this way: *The doctor flashed a light into my eye.*
2 (*also* **flash up**) to appear for a short time, or to make something appear for a short time: *An icon flashed up on the screen.*

flash[2] /flæʃ/ *noun* (*plural* **flashes**)
1 a sudden bright light: *The bomb exploded in a **flash of** yellow light.*
2 a piece of camera equipment that produces a bright light when you take a photograph in a dark place

flask

flask /flɑːsk/ *noun UK*
a special container that keeps drinks hot or cold: *a flask of coffee*

flat[1] /flæt/ *UK* (*US* **apartment**) *noun*
a set of rooms to live in, with all the rooms on one floor: *a large block of flats*

flat[2] /flæt/ *adj*
1 smooth and level with nothing sticking up: *a flat surface ○ The countryside around here is very flat.*
2 If a tyre is flat, it does not contain enough air.

flat[3] /flæt/ *adv*
in a horizontal or level position: *She spread the cloth flat across the kitchen table.*

flatter /ˈflætəʳ/ *verb*
1 to say nice things to someone so that they will feel more attractive or important: *Don't flatter him!*
2 be flattered to feel very pleased and proud: *She was flattered by his attention.*

flattering /ˈflætərɪŋ/ *adj*
making you look more attractive than usual: *a flattering picture*

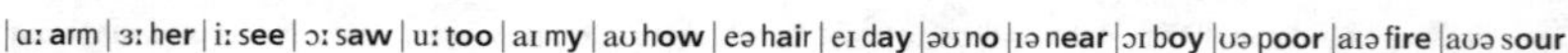

flattery /ˈflætᵊri/ *noun* **[no plural]**
when you say nice things to someone, often because you want something from that person

flavour *UK* (*US* **flavor**) /ˈfleɪvəʳ/ *noun*
the taste of a type of food or drink: *We sell 50 different flavours of ice cream.*

flea /fliː/ *noun*
a small, jumping insect that lives on animals or people and drinks their blood

flee /fliː/ *verb* (*present participle* **fleeing,** *past* **fled)**
to leave a place quickly because you are in danger: *He fled the country.*

fleece /fliːs/ *noun*
1 a warm, soft jacket, or the material used to make it
2 the thick covering of wool on a sheep

fleet /fliːt/ *noun*
a group of ships

flesh /fleʃ/ *noun* **[no plural]**
the soft part of a person's or animal's body under the skin

flew /fluː/
past tense of fly

flex /fleks/ *UK* (*US* **cord)** *noun* (*plural* **flexes)**
a piece of wire covered in plastic, that is used to connect electrical equipment to a power supply

flexible /ˈfleksɪbl/ *adj*
1 able to change or be changed easily according to the situation: *I'd like a job with more flexible working hours.*
2 able to bend easily without breaking

flight /flaɪt/ *noun*
a journey in an aircraft

fling /flɪŋ/ *verb* (*present participle* **flinging,** *past* **flung)**
to suddenly throw something: *She flung her jacket on the sofa.*

flirt /flɜːt/ *verb*
to behave as if you are sexually attracted to someone: *She was* ***flirting with*** *a guy at the bar.*

float /fləʊt/ *verb*
1 to stay on the surface of a liquid and not go under: *I like floating on my back in the pool.*
2 to move gently through the air: *A balloon floated across the sky.*

float

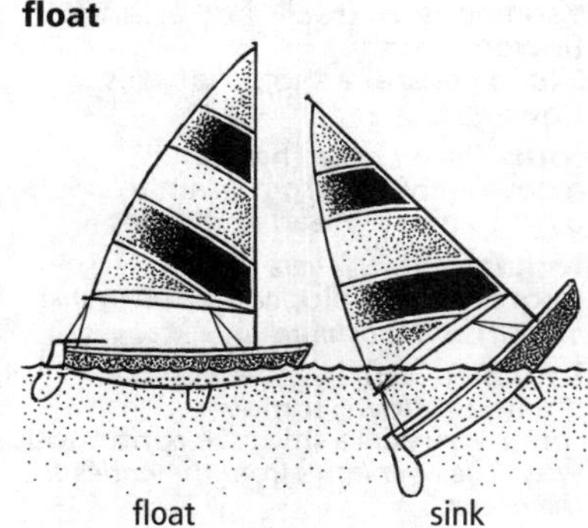

flock /flɒk/ *noun*
a group of birds or sheep: *a flock of geese*

flood

flood¹ /flʌd/ *verb*
to become covered with water: *The town was flooded when the river burst its banks.*

flood² /flʌd/ *noun*
when a lot of water covers an area that is usually dry: *The flood destroyed thousands of homes.*

floodlights /ˈflʌdlaɪts/ *plural noun*
powerful lights used at night to light up sports fields or the outside of buildings

floor /flɔːʳ/ *noun*
1 a surface that you walk on inside a building: *a wooden floor*
2 a particular level of a building: *the second/third floor*

floorboard /ˈflɔːbɔːd/ *noun*
a long, thin wooden board that is part of a floor in a building

florist /ˈflɒrɪst/ *noun*

1 someone who sells and arranges flowers in a shop
2 (*also* **florist's**) a shop that sells flowers

flour /flaʊəʳ/ *noun* **[no plural]**
a powder made from grain that is used to make bread and cakes

flourish /ˈflʌrɪʃ/ *verb*
to grow or develop well: *The tourist industry is flourishing.*

flow /fləʊ/ *verb*
If a liquid flows, it moves somewhere in a smooth, continuous way: *The river flows from the Andes to the ocean.*
•**flow** *noun*
the continuous, smooth movement of something: *the flow of traffic through the town*

flower /flaʊəʳ/ *noun*
the attractive, coloured part of a plant where the seeds grow: *a bunch of flowers*

flown /fləʊn/
past participle of fly

flu /fluː/ *noun* **[no plural]**
an illness like a very bad cold

fluent /ˈfluːənt/ *adj*
able to use a language naturally without stopping or making mistakes: *She is* ***fluent in*** *six languages.*

fluff /flʌf/ *noun* **[no plural]**
small, loose bits of wool or other soft material

fluffy /ˈflʌfi/ *adj*
made or covered with soft fur or cloth: *a fluffy toy*

fluid /ˈfluːɪd/ *noun*
a liquid: *Drink plenty of fluids.*

flush /flʌʃ/ *verb*
1 to clean a toilet by sending water through it: *Remember to flush the toilet after you.*
2 to get a red face because you are embarrassed or angry

flute /fluːt/ *noun*
a musical instrument that you hold out to the side and play by blowing

flutter /ˈflʌtəʳ/ *verb*
to move quickly and gently up in the air: *The flag was fluttering in the breeze.*

fly¹ /flaɪ/ *verb* (*present participle* **flying**, *past tense* **flew**, *past participle* **flown**)
1 to move through the air: *The robin flew up into a tree.*
2 to travel through the air in an aircraft: *I'm flying to Delhi tomorrow.*
3 to move somewhere very quickly: *He grabbed some clothes and flew down the stairs.*

fly² /flaɪ/ *noun* (*plural* **flies**)
1 a small insect with two wings
2 (*also UK* **flies**) the part where trousers open and close at the front: *a button fly*

foal /fəʊl/ *noun*
a young horse

foam /fəʊm/ *noun* **[no plural]**
a lot of small, white bubbles on the surface of a liquid

fog /fɒg/ *noun* **[no plural]**
thick cloud close to the ground or sea that makes it difficult to see
•**foggy** *adj*
with fog: *a foggy day*

foil /fɔɪl/ *noun* **[no plural]**
metal made into very thin sheets like paper, used mainly for covering food: *aluminium foil*

fold¹ /fəʊld/ *verb*
1 to bend something so that one part of it lies flat on top of another part: *Can you help me fold the sheets?*
2 fold your arms to bend your arms across your chest, with one crossing over the other: *He sat with his arms folded.*

fold² /fəʊld/ *noun*
a line made where paper or cloth is folded: *Make a fold across the centre of the card.*

folder /ˈfəʊldəʳ/ *noun*
1 a folded piece of plastic or thick paper used to store loose papers
2 a place on a computer where files (= documents, pictures) are kept

folk /fəʊk/ *plural noun UK informal* (*US* **folks**)
people: *old folk*

follow /ˈfɒləʊ/ *verb*
1 to move behind someone or something and go where they go: *She followed me into the kitchen.*
2 to happen or come after something: *There was a bang,* ***followed by*** *a cloud of smoke.*
3 follow a path/road to travel along a path or road: *Follow the main road down to the traffic lights.*
4 follow instructions/orders to do what instructions or orders say you

should do: *Did you follow the instructions on the packet?*
5 to understand something: *Could you say that again? I didn't quite follow.*

following /ˈfɒləʊɪŋ/ *adj*
the following day/morning, etc the next day, morning, etc

fond /fɒnd/ *adj*
be fond of someone/something to like someone or something: *We're still very fond of each other.*

food /fuːd/ *noun* **[no plural]**
something that people and animals eat to keep them alive: *baby/dog food*

foodie /ˈfuːdi/ *noun informal*
someone who loves food and knows a lot about it

fool[1] /fuːl/ *noun*
1 a stupid person
2 make a fool of yourself to behave in a silly or embarrassing way: *He got drunk and started making a fool of himself.*

fool[2] /fuːl/ *verb*
to trick someone: *He fooled the old man into giving him the money.*
fool around/about *phrasal verb*
to behave in a silly way: *Stop fooling around – this is serious!*

foolish /ˈfuːlɪʃ/ *adj*
silly: *a foolish mistake* ○ *It would be foolish to ignore his advice.*

foot /fʊt/ *noun*
1 (*plural* **feet**) one of the two flat parts on the ends of your legs that you stand on: *bare feet*
2 (*plural* **foot** or **feet**) a unit for measuring length, equal to 0.3048 metres or 12 inches: *Alex is about 6 feet tall.*
3 the foot of something the bottom of something: *He was standing at the foot of the stairs.*
4 on foot walking

football /ˈfʊtbɔːl/ *noun*
1 [no plural] *UK* a game in which two teams of players kick a round ball and try to score goals: *a football match/team*
2 a large ball for kicking
• **footballer** *noun UK*
someone who plays football, especially as their job

footpath /ˈfʊtpɑːθ/ *noun UK*
a path or track for people to walk along, especially in the countryside: *a public footpath*

footprint /ˈfʊtprɪnt/ *noun*
a mark made by a foot or shoe

footstep /ˈfʊtstep/ *noun*
the sound of a foot hitting the ground when someone walks: *I heard footsteps behind me and quickly turned round.*

for *strong form* /fɔːʳ/ *weak form* /fəʳ/ *preposition*
1 to be given to or used by someone or something: *I've bought a few clothes for the new baby.* ○ *We need some curtains for the spare bedroom.*
2 having a particular purpose: *What are those large scissors for?*
3 because of something: *Scotland is famous for its beautiful countryside.*
4 used to show an amount of time or distance: *We walked for miles.* ○ *I lived with my parents for a year.*
5 in order to help someone: *I'll carry those bags for you.*
6 in exchange for something, especially an amount of money: *How much did you pay for your computer?*
7 supporting or agreeing with someone or something: *Who did you vote for?*
8 representing a country or organization: *He plays football for Cambridge United.*
9 towards or in the direction of: *Just follow the signs for the airport.*
10 when compared to a particular fact: *She's quite tall for her age.*
11 meaning or representing something: *What's the German word for 'cucumber'?*

forbid /fəˈbɪd/ *verb* (*present participle* **forbidding**, *past tense* **forbade**, *past participle* **forbidden**)
to tell someone that they must not do something
• **forbidden** *adj*
not allowed by an official rule: *Smoking is forbidden in this area.*

force[1] /fɔːs/ *noun*
1 [no plural] physical power or strength: *The army has seized power **by force**.*
2 a group of people who work together for a particular purpose, for example in military service: *the police force* ○ *the Royal Air Force*

force[2] /fɔːs/ *verb* (*present participle*

forcing, *past* **forced**)
1 to make someone do something that they do not want to do: *You can't* ***force*** *her* ***to*** *eat.*
2 to make an object move by pushing or pulling it hard: *She forced the window open.*

forecast[1] /ˈfɔːkɑːst/ *noun*
something that says what will happen in the future: *the weather forecast*

forecast[2] /ˈfɔːkɑːst/ *verb* (*present participle* **forecasting,** *past* **forecast**)
to say what will happen in the future: *They forecast more snow for this area.*
• **forecaster** *noun*: *a weather forecaster*

forehead /ˈfɔːhed/ *noun*
the part of your face between your eyes and your hair

foreign /ˈfɒrɪn/ *adj*
from a country that is not yours: *a foreign language/student*

foreigner /ˈfɒrɪnəʳ/ *noun*
someone from another country

forename /ˈfɔːneɪm/ *noun UK formal*
your first name, which comes before your family name

foresee /fɔːˈsiː/ *verb* (*present participle* **foreseeing,** *past tense* **foresaw,** *past participle* **foreseen**)
to think that something will happen in the future: *I don't foresee any problems.*

forest /ˈfɒrɪst/ *noun*
a large area of trees growing together: *pine forest*

forest

forever /fəˈrevəʳ/ *adv*
for all time in the future: *I don't think I'll live here forever.*

forgave /fəˈgeɪv/
past tense of forgive

forge /fɔːdʒ/ *verb* (*present participle* **forging,** *past* **forged**)
to make an illegal copy of something in order to deceive people: *a forged passport*

forgery /ˈfɔːdʒəri/ *noun*
1 (*plural* **forgeries**) an illegal copy of something
2 **[no plural]** the crime of making an illegal copy of something: *He was found guilty of forgery.*

forget /fəˈget/ *verb* (*present participle* **forgetting,** *past tense* **forgot,** *past participle* **forgotten**)
1 to not remember something: *I've forgotten his name.* ○ *Don't forget to feed the cat.* ○ *He'd forgotten his passport.*
2 (*also* **forget about**) to stop thinking about someone or something: *Let's try to forget about work.*

forgetful /fəˈgetfəl/ *adj*
often forgetting things: *She's 84 now and a bit forgetful.*

forgive /fəˈgɪv/ *verb* (*present participle* **forgiving,** *past tense* **forgave,** *past participle* **forgiven**)
to decide not to be angry with someone or not to punish them for something bad they have done: *Jane never* ***forgave*** *her mother* ***for*** *lying to her.*

forgot /fəˈgɒt/
past tense of forget

forgotten /fəˈgɒtən/
past participle of forget

fork /fɔːk/ *noun*
a small object with three or four points and a handle, that you use to eat with: *a knife and fork*

form[1] /fɔːm/ *noun*
1 a type of something or way of doing something: *Swimming is the best* ***form of*** *exercise.*
2 a printed document with spaces for you to write information: *Please* ***fill in the form*** *using black ink.*
3 *UK* a school class for students of the same age or ability: *the third form*
4 the body or shape of someone or something

form[2] /fɔːm/ *verb*
1 to begin to exist, or to make something begin to exist: *This plant forms new leaves in the spring.*
2 to make a shape: *Hold hands and form a circle.*
3 to make something by putting different parts together: *In English you form the present participle by adding -ing to the verb.*
4 to start an organization or business: *Brown formed her own*

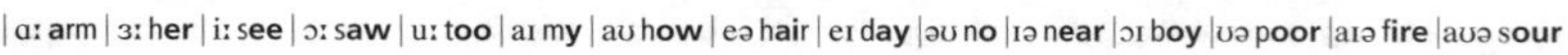

company eleven years ago.

formal /ˈfɔːməl/ *adj*
1 used about clothes, language, and behaviour that are serious and not friendly or relaxed: *a formal dinner party*
2 public or official: *a formal announcement*

former /ˈfɔːməʳ/ *adj*
happening or existing in the past but not now: *the former Soviet Union*
• **formerly** *adv*
in the past: *The European Union was formerly called the European Community.*

formula /ˈfɔːmjələ/ *noun* (*plural* **formulas** *or* **formulae**)
a list of the substances that something is made of: *a secret formula*

fortieth /ˈfɔːtiəθ/
40th written as a word

fortnight /ˈfɔːtnaɪt/ *noun UK*
two weeks: *a fortnight's holiday*

fortunate /ˈfɔːtʃənət/ *adj*
lucky: *It was* ***fortunate that*** *someone was available to take over.* ➲Opposite **unfortunate**

fortunately /ˈfɔːtʃənətli/ *adv*
happening because of good luck: *Fortunately, no one was hurt in the accident.* ➲Opposite **unfortunately**

fortune /ˈfɔːtʃuːn/ *noun*
1 a lot of money: *Nick's new car must have cost a fortune!*
2 the good or bad things that happen to you: *The family's fortunes changed almost overnight.*
3 tell someone's fortune to say what will happen to someone in the future

forty /ˈfɔːti/
the number 40

forward /ˈfɔːwəd/ (*also* **forwards**) *adv*
towards the direction that is in front of you: *She leaned forward to make sure I could hear her.*

fought /fɔːt/
past of fight

foul /faʊl/ *adj*
very dirty or bad: *a foul smell* ○ *The toilets were foul.*

found¹ /faʊnd/ *verb*
to start an organization, especially by giving money: *He founded the charity in 1861.*

found² /faʊnd/
past of find

foundations /faʊnˈdeɪʃən/ *plural noun UK*
the part of a building that is under the ground and supports it: *concrete foundations*

fountain /ˈfaʊntɪn/ *noun*
a structure that forces water up into the air as a decoration

fountain

fountain pen /ˈfaʊntən pen/ *noun*
a pen that you fill with ink

four /fɔːʳ/
the number 4

fourteen /ˌfɔːˈtiːn/
the number 14
• **fourteenth**
14th written as a word

fourth /fɔːθ/
4th written as a word

fox /fɒks/ *noun* (*plural* **foxes**)
a wild animal like a dog with brown fur and a long thick tail

fraction /ˈfrækʃən/ *noun*
a number less than 1, such as ½ or ¾

fracture /ˈfræktʃəʳ/ *verb* (*present participle* **fracturing**, *past* **fractured**)
to break a bone: *She's fractured her ankle.*
• **fracture** *noun*

fragile /ˈfrædʒaɪl/ *adj*
easy to break: *a fragile china cup*

fragment /ˈfrægmənt/ *noun*
a small piece of something: *fragments of pottery*

fragrance /ˈfreɪgrəns/ *noun*
a good smell: *the delicate fragrance of roses*

fragrant /ˈfreɪgrənt/ *adj*
with a good smell: *fragrant flowers*

frail /freɪl/ *adj*
not strong or healthy: *a frail old lady*

frame¹ /freɪm/ *noun*
1 a structure that goes around the edge of something such as a picture or window: *a window frame*
2 the main structure of a building or vehicle that other parts are added onto: *a bicycle frame*

frame

frame² /freɪm/ *verb* (*present participle* **framing**, *past* **framed**)
to put something such as a picture into a frame: *I've framed that photograph.*

frank /fræŋk/ *adj*
honest and saying what you really think: *It was a frank discussion.*

frankly /ˈfræŋkli/ *adv*
in an honest way: ***Quite frankly**, I think you're making a big mistake.*

fraud /frɔːd/ *noun* **[no plural]**
when someone does something illegal in order to get money: *credit card fraud*

fray /freɪ/ *verb*
If material frays, the threads at the edge break and become loose.

freak /friːk/ *noun*
1 *informal* someone who is very interested in something: *My brother is a computer freak.*
2 someone who looks strange or behaves in a strange way: *They made me feel like a freak.*

freckle /ˈfrekl/ *noun*
a light brown spot on a person's skin

free¹ /friː/ *adj*
1 able to do things without being controlled: *People should be **free to** say what they think.*
2 costing no money: *Entry is free for children under 12.*
3 not in prison or in a cage: *He opened the cage and **set** the birds **free**.*
4 not busy doing anything: *Are you free this evening?* ○ *free time*
5 not being used by anyone: *Is this seat free?*

free² /friː/ *adv*
without paying money: *Children under five travel free.*

free³ /friː/ *verb* (*present participle* **freeing**, *past* **freed**)
to allow someone to leave a prison or place where they have been kept: *The last hostages were finally freed yesterday.*

freedom /ˈfriːdəm/ *noun* **[no plural]**
the right to live in the way you want without being controlled by anyone else

freeway /ˈfriːweɪ/ *US* (*UK* **motorway**) *noun*
a long, wide road, usually used by cars travelling fast

freeze /friːz/ *verb* (*present participle* **freezing**, *past tense* **froze**, *past participle* **frozen**)
1 If something freezes, it becomes hard and solid because it is very cold: *The river had frozen overnight.*
2 to make food last a long time by making it very cold and hard: *Freeze any cakes that you have left over.*

freezer /ˈfriːzəʳ/ *noun*
a large container operated by electricity in which food can be frozen and kept ➲See colour picture **Kitchen** on page Centre 10

freezing /ˈfriːzɪŋ/ *adj informal*
very cold: *It's absolutely freezing in here.*

freezing point /ˈfriːziŋ ˌpɔɪnt/ *noun* **[no plural]**
the temperature at which a liquid freezes

french fries /ˈfrentʃ ˌfraɪz/ *US* (*UK* **chips**) *plural noun*
long, thin pieces of potato that have been cooked in hot oil

frequent /ˈfriːkwənt/ *adj*
happening often: *He is a frequent visitor to the US.*

frequently /ˈfriːkwəntli/ *adv formal*
often: *I see him quite frequently.*

fresh /freʃ/ *adj*
1 new or different from what was there before: *fresh ideas*
2 Fresh food has been made or collected recently and has not been frozen or dried: *fresh fruit/vegetables* ○ *fresh bread*
3 smelling clean or feeling cool: *a fresh breeze* ○ *fresh air*

Friday /ˈfraɪdeɪ/ *noun*
the day of the week after Thursday

and before Saturday

fridge /frɪdʒ/ *noun*
a large cupboard that uses electricity to keep food cold

fried /fraɪd/ *adj*
cooked in hot oil or fat: *a fried egg*

friend /frend/ *noun*
1 someone who you know well and like: *Sarah's my best friend* (= the friend I like most).
2 make friends (with someone) to begin to know and like someone: *He's shy and finds it difficult to make friends.*

friendly *adj*
behaving in a pleasant, kind way towards someone: *a friendly face/smile* ⊃Opposite **unfriendly**

friendship /ˈfrendʃɪp/ *noun*
when two people are friends: *a close friendship*

fries /fraɪz/ *US* (*also UK* **chips**) *noun*
long, thin pieces of potato that have been cooked in hot oil

fright /fraɪt/ *noun* **[no plural]**
a sudden feeling of shock and fear: *The dog ran up to her and **gave** her **a fright**.*

frighten /ˈfraɪtᵊn/ *verb*
to make someone afraid or nervous: *It frightens me when he drives so fast.*

frightened /ˈfraɪtᵊnd/ *adj*
afraid or nervous: *I've always been **frightened of** going to the dentist.*

frightening /ˈfraɪtᵊnɪŋ/ *adj*
making you feel afraid or nervous: *a frightening film*

fringe /frɪndʒ/ *noun*
1 *UK* (*US* **bangs**) hair that is cut short and straight at the top of someone's face
2 loose threads that hang along the edge of cloth as a decoration

frog /frɒg/ *noun*
a small, green animal with long back legs for jumping that lives in or near water

from *strong form* /frɒm/ *weak form* /frəm/ *preposition*
1 used to show the place or time that someone or something started at: *Did you walk all the way from Bond Street?*
2 used to say where someone was born, or where someone lives or works: *Steve's father was from Poland.*
3 used to say how far away something is: *The house is about 5 kilometres from the sea.*
4 used to say who gave or sent something to someone: *Who are your flowers from?*
5 If you take something from a person, place, or amount, you take it away: *He took a knife from the drawer.*
6 used to say what something is made of: *juice made from oranges*
7 used to say what causes something: *Deaths from heart disease continue to rise every year.* ○ *He **suffers from** asthma.*

front¹ /frʌnt/ *noun*
1 the front
a the side of something that is most often seen because it faces forward: *Write the address **on the front of** the envelope.*
b the part of something that is furthest forward: *He was standing right **at the front**.*
2 in front further forward than someone or something else: *He was sitting **in front of** me.*
3 in front of something close to the front part of something: *He parked the car in front of the house.*

front² /frʌnt/ *adj*
in or at the front of something: *the front door/garden*

frontier /frʌnˈtɪəʳ/ *noun*
a line or border between two countries

frost /frɒst/ *noun* **[no plural]**
a thin, white layer of ice that forms on very cold surfaces

frosty /ˈfrɒsti/ *adj*
very cold, with a thin layer of white ice covering everything: *a frosty morning*

frown /fraʊn/ *verb*
to look angry or worried because your eyebrows are lower than usual: *She frowned when I mentioned his name.*

froze /frəʊz/
past tense of freeze

frozen¹ /ˈfrəʊzᵊn/ *adj*
1 Frozen food has been made so that it will last a long time by freezing: *frozen peas*

2 turned into ice: *The pond was frozen this morning.*

frozen[2] /ˈfrəʊzᵊn/
past participle of freeze

fruit /fruːt/ *noun* **[no plural]**
things such as apples or oranges that grow on a tree or a bush, contain seeds, and can be eaten as food: *dried/fresh fruit*

fry /fraɪ/ *verb* (*present participle* **frying,** *past* **fried)**
to cook something in hot oil: *Fry the onions in a little butter.*

frying pan /ˈfraɪ.ɪŋ ˌpæn/ *noun*
a flat, metal pan with a long handle that is used for frying food ➲See colour picture **Kitchen** on page Centre 10

ft
written abbreviation for foot (= a unit for measuring length)

fuel /ˈfjuːəl/ *noun*
a substance that is burned to give heat or power

fulfil /fʊlˈfɪl/ *verb* (*present participle* **fulfilling,** *past* **fulfilled)**
to do something that you have promised or planned to do: *I finally fulfilled my ambition.*

full /fʊl/ *adj*
1 If a container or a space is full, it contains as many things or people as possible: *a full bottle of red wine*
2 containing a lot of things or people: *The room was **full of** people.*
3 complete and including every part: *Please give your full name and address.*
4 *informal* (*also UK* **full up**) having eaten enough food: *No more for me, thanks, I'm full.*

full stop /ˌfʊl ˈstɒp/ *noun UK*
a mark (.) used at the end of a sentence, or to show that the letters before it are an abbreviation

full-time /ˌfʊlˈtaɪm/ *adj*
happening or working for the whole of the working week and not only part of it: *a full-time job/course*

fully /ˈfʊli/ *adv*
completely: *The restaurant was fully booked.*

fun /fʌn/ *noun* **[no plural]**
1 enjoyment or pleasure, or something that gives you enjoyment or pleasure: *Did you **have fun** at the party?*
2 make fun of someone/something to make a joke about someone or something in a way that is not kind: *The other children used to make fun of his red hair.*

function /ˈfʌŋkʃᵊn/ *noun*
the purpose of something or someone: *Each button has a different function.*

fund /fʌnd/ *noun*
an amount of money that is collected or given for a purpose: *a pension fund*

funeral /ˈfjuːnᵊrəl/ *noun*
a ceremony for burying or burning the body of a dead person: *The funeral will be held next Friday.*

fungus /ˈfʌŋgəs/ *noun* (*plural* **fungi)**
a type of plant without leaves which gets its food from other living or decaying things: *The mushroom is a fungus.*

funnel /ˈfʌnᵊl/ *noun*
a tube with a wide part at the top that you use to pour liquid into a small opening

funnel
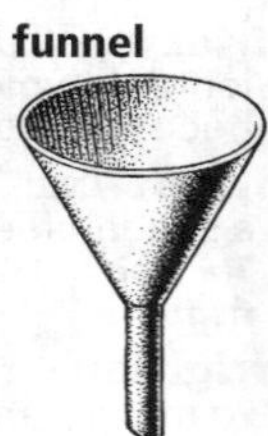

funny /ˈfʌni/ *adj*
1 making you smile or laugh: *a funny story*
2 strange or unusual and not what you expect: *This chicken tastes a bit funny.*

fur /fɜːʳ/ *noun* **[no plural]**
the thick hair that covers the bodies of some animals like cats and rabbits

furious /ˈfjʊəriəs/ *adj*
very angry: *My boss was **furious with** me.*

furnace /ˈfɜːnɪs/ *noun*
a container which is heated until it is very hot and used to melt metals

furnished /ˈfɜːnɪʃt/ *adj*
If a room is furnished, there is furniture in it: *a fully furnished apartment*

furniture /ˈfɜːnɪtʃəʳ/ *noun* **[no plural]**
things such as chairs, tables, and beds that you put into a room or building

furry /ˈfɜːri/ *adj*
covered with fur

further[1] /ˈfɜːðəʳ/ *adv*
1 more: *He refused to discuss the matter further.*

2 *(comparative of* **far***)* at or to a place or time that is a longer distance away: *Let's walk a bit further down the road.*

further[2] /ˈfɜːðəʳ/ *adj*
more or extra: *For further details about the offer, call this number.*

furthest /ˈfɜːðɪst/ *adj, adv (superlative of* **far***)*
most distant: *What is the furthest distance you can run?*

fury /ˈfjʊəri/ *noun* **[no plural]**
very strong anger: *He could hardly control his fury.*

fuse /fjuːz/ *noun*
a small object that stops electrical equipment working if there is too much electricity going through it: *a fuse box*

fuss[1] /fʌs/ *noun* **[no plural]**
1 when people become excited or worried about something which is not important: *What's all the fuss about?*
2 make a fuss to complain about something: *He made such a fuss because I was five minutes late.*
3 make a fuss of someone to give someone a lot of attention and treat them well: *My uncle always makes a big fuss of the children.*

fuss[2] /fʌs/ *verb*
to worry too much or get too excited, especially about things which are not important: *Please don't fuss, Mum. Everything's under control.*

fussy /ˈfʌsi/ *adj* **(fussier, fussiest)**
only liking particular things and very difficult to please: *She's very fussy with her food.*

future[1] /ˈfjuːtʃəʳ/ *noun* **[no plural]**
1 the future
a the time which is to come: *At some point* ***in the future*** *we'll probably move.*
b in grammar, the form of the verb used to talk about something that will happen
2 in future *UK* beginning from now: *In future, I'll be more careful.*

future[2] /ˈfjuːtʃəʳ/ *adj*
happening or existing in the time which is to come: *in future years*

Gg

G, g /dʒiː/
the seventh letter of the alphabet

gadget /ˈgædʒɪt/ *noun*
a small piece of equipment that does a particular job: *a kitchen gadget*

gain /geɪn/ *verb*
1 to get something good: *You'll gain a lot of experience working there.*
2 to increase: *He's gained a lot of weight in the last few months.*

galaxy /ˈgæləksi/ *noun* (*plural* **galaxies**)
a very large group of stars held together in the universe

gale /geɪl/ *noun*
a very strong wind

gallery /ˈgælᵊri/ *noun* (*plural* **galleries**)
a room or building that is used for showing paintings and other art to people: *a museum and art gallery*

gallon /ˈgælən/ *noun*
a unit for measuring liquid, equal to 4.546 litres in the UK and 3.785 litres in the US

gallop /ˈgæləp/ *verb*
If a horse gallops, it runs very fast.

gamble[1] /ˈgæmbl/ *verb* (*present participle* **gambling,** *past* **gambled**)
to try to win money by saying who will win in a game, race, or competition: *He gambled away all of our savings.*
• **gambler** *noun* /ˈgæmbləʳ/
someone who often gambles

gamble[2] /ˈgæmbl/ *noun*
when you do something that you hope will have a good result although you know that this might make something bad happen: *Buying this place was a big gamble, but it seems to have paid off.*

game /geɪm/ *noun*
an activity or sport that people play, usually with rules and needing skill: *a computer game* ○ *Football's such an exciting game.* ○ *Do you want to* ***play*** *a different* ***game****?*

game show /ˈgeɪm ˌʃəʊ/ *noun*
a programme on television in which people play games to try to win prizes

gang /gæŋ/ *noun*
1 a group of young people who spend time together, often fighting with other groups: *one of a gang*
2 a group of criminals who work together: *a gang of armed robbers*
3 *informal* a group of young friends

gangster /ˈgæŋstəʳ/ *noun*
one of a group of violent criminals

gaol /dʒeɪl/ *noun another UK spelling of* jail (= a place where criminals are kept as a punishment)

gap /gæp/ *noun*
1 an empty space or hole in the middle of something, or between two things: *There's a big* ***gap between*** *the door and the floor.* ○ *The sun was shining through a* ***gap in*** *the curtains.*
2 a difference between two groups of people or two situations: *an age gap* ○ *The* ***gap between*** *rich and poor is increasing.*

garage /ˈgærɑːʒ/ *noun*
1 a small building where you put your car
2 a place where cars are repaired or sold and sometimes fuel is sold

garbage /ˈgɑːbɪdʒ/ *US* (*UK* **rubbish**) *noun* **[no plural]**
1 things that you throw away because you do not want them: *Could you take out the garbage?*
2 something that is wrong or very bad: *There's so much garbage on TV.*

garden /ˈgɑːdᵊn/ *noun UK* (*US* **yard**)
an area of ground next to a house, often with grass, flowers, or trees: *the front/back garden* ○ *Dad's outside* ***in the garden****.*
• **garden** *verb*
to work in a garden, growing plants and making it look attractive

gardening /ˈgɑːdᵊnɪŋ/ *noun* **[no plural]**
the work that you do in a garden in order to grow plants and keep it attractive

garlic /ˈgɑːlɪk/ *noun* **[no plural]**
a vegetable like a small onion with a very strong taste and smell: ➲See colour picture **Fruit and Vegetables** on page Centre 8

garment /ˈgɑːmənt/ *noun formal*
a piece of clothing

gas /gæs/ *noun*
1 (*plural* **gases**) a substance in a form which is like air and not solid or liquid: *poisonous gases*
2 [no plural] a substance in a form which is like air and is used for cooking and burning: *a gas cooker*
3 [no plural] (*UK* **petrol**) *US* a liquid fuel used in cars: *a tank of gas*

gasp /gɑːsp/ *verb*
to make a noise by suddenly breathing in because you are shocked or surprised: *She gasped in amazement.*
• **gasp** *noun*: *a gasp of surprise*

gas station /ˈgæs ˌsteɪʃn/ *US* (*UK* **petrol station)** *noun*
a place where you can buy petrol (= fuel for cars)

gate /geɪt/ *noun*
1 a door in a fence or outside wall: *Please shut the gate.*
2 the part of an airport where you get on or off an aeroplane: *The flight to Dublin is now boarding at gate 8.*

gather /ˈgæðəʳ/ *verb*
1 to join other people somewhere to make a group: *Crowds of fans gathered at the stadium for the big match.*
2 to collect a lot of things together, often from different places or people: *She* ***gathered*** *her things* ***together*** *and left.*
3 to think something is true, although you are not completely sure: *I gather they're arriving on Friday.*

gathering /ˈgæðərɪŋ/ *noun*
when many people get together as a group: *a family gathering*

gave /geɪv/
past tense of give

gaze /geɪz/ *verb*
to look at someone or something for a long time: *They gazed into each other's eyes.*

GCSE /ˌdʒiːsiːesˈiː/ *noun*
in the UK, an exam in one subject that students take at the age of sixteen, or the qualification itself: *Katie's got nine GCSEs.*

gear /gɪəʳ/ *noun*
1 the parts in a car or bicycle that control how fast the wheels turn: *a mountain bike with 21 gears* ○ *to change gear* ○ *I* ***got into*** *first* ***gear***.
2 [no plural] the clothes and equipment used for a particular purpose: *sports/swimming gear*

geek /giːk/ *noun informal*
a man who is boring and not fashionable

geese /giːs/
plural of goose

gel /dʒel/ *noun* **[no plural]**
a thick, clear liquid that you use to wash your body or to make you hair stay in the right position: *shower gel* ○ *hair gel*

gem /dʒem/ *noun*
a valuable stone, especially one that is used in jewellery

gender /ˈdʒendəʳ/ *noun*
the state of being male or female

gene /dʒiːn/ *noun*
a part of a cell that is passed on from a parent to a child and that controls particular characteristics: *Red hair is* ***in*** *my* ***genes***.

general[1] /ˈdʒenᵊrᵊl/ *adj*
1 with the most basic or necessary information but no details: *These leaflets contain some general information about the school.*
2 relating to or involving all or most people, things, or places: *There seems to be general agreement on this matter.*
3 in general
a considering the whole of someone or something: *I still have a sore throat, but I feel much better in general.*
b usually, or in most situations: *In general, the weather here is good.*

general[2] /ˈdʒenᵊrᵊl/ *noun*
a very important officer in the army

general election /ˌdʒenᵊrᵊl ɪˈlekʃᵊn/ *noun*
a big election in which the people living in a country vote to decide who will represent them in the government

general knowledge /ˌdʒenᵊrᵊl ˈnɒlɪdʒ/ *noun* **[no plural]**
knowledge of many different subjects

generally /ˈdʒenᵊrᵊli/ *adv*
usually or mostly: *I generally wake up early.* ○ *The children were generally very well-behaved.*

generate /ˈdʒenᵊreɪt/ *verb* (*present participle* **generating,** *past* **generated)**

1 to make something exist: *This film has generated a lot of interest.*
2 to make energy: *We need to generate more electricity.*

generation /ˌdʒenəˈreɪʃᵊn/ *noun*
all the people who are about the same age: *the older/younger generation* ○ *This is the story of three generations of women.*

generator /ˈdʒenᵊreɪtəʳ/ *noun*
a machine that produces electricity

generosity /ˌdʒenᵊˈrɒsəti/ *noun* **[no plural]**
the quality of being generous

generous /ˈdʒenᵊrəs/ *adj*
often giving people money or presents: *It was very generous of you to buy her flowers.*

genetic /dʒəˈnetɪk/ *adj*
relating to genes: *genetic research*

genetics /dʒəˈnetɪks/ *noun* **[no plural]**
the scientific study of genes

genius /ˈdʒiːniəs/ *noun* (*plural* **geniuses**)
someone who is extremely intelligent or extremely good at doing something: *Einstein was a genius.*

gentle /ˈdʒentl/ *adj*
1 kind and careful not to hurt or upset anyone: *My mother was such a gentle, loving person.*
2 not strong or unpleasant: *a gentle breeze*
• **gently** *adv*: *He gently stroked her cheek.*

gentleman /ˈdʒentlmən/ *noun* (*plural* **gentlemen**)
1 a very polite man: *He was a perfect gentleman.*
2 a polite word for 'man': *There's a gentleman here to see you.*

genuine /ˈdʒenjuɪn/ *adj*
real or true: *a genuine antique* ○ *Was her disappointment genuine?*
• **genuinely** *adv*
used to say that something really is true: *I think she was genuinely concerned.*

geography /dʒiˈɒgrəfi/ *noun* **[no plural]**
the study of all the countries of the world, and of the surface of the Earth such as the mountains and seas

geology /dʒiˈɒlədʒi/ *noun* **[no plural]**
the study of rocks and soil and how they were made

geometry /dʒiˈɒmɪtri/ *noun* **[no plural]**
a type of mathematics that deals with points, lines, angles and shapes

germ /dʒɜːm/ *noun*
a very small living thing that causes disease: *Wash your hands before cooking so that you don't spread germs.*

gesture[1] /ˈdʒestʃəʳ/ *noun*
1 a movement you make with your hand, arm, or head to show what you are thinking or feeling: *He made a rude gesture at the crowd.*
2 something you do to show people how you feel about a person or situation: *It would be a nice gesture to invite her to dinner.*

gesture[2] /ˈdʒestʃəʳ/ *verb* (*present participle* **gesturing**, *past* **gestured**)
to point at something or show something using your hand, arm, or head: *He gestured towards the window.*

get /get/ *verb* (*present participle* **getting**, *past tense* **got**, *past participle* **got**)
1 to obtain or buy something: *Where did you get your shoes?* ○ *I got you a ticket.*
2 to go somewhere and bring back someone or something: *Wait here while I get the car.*
3 to receive something: *Did you get anything nice for your birthday?* ○ *Guy still hasn't got my email.*
4 to understand something: *He never gets any of my jokes.*
5 to arrive somewhere: *What time do you get home from work?*
6 **get ill/rich/wet, etc** to become ill/rich/wet, etc: *It's getting late – we should go.*
7 to become ill: *I feel like I'm getting a cold.*

get away with something *phrasal verb*
to do something bad without being punished for it: *If he's rude to you, don't let him get away with it.*

get back *phrasal verb*
to return to a place: *We got back from London last night.*

get off (something) *phrasal verb*
to leave a bus, train, aeroplane, or boat: *We should get off at the next stop.*

get on (something) *phrasal verb*
to go onto a bus, train, aeroplane,

or boat: *I think we got on the wrong bus.* ➲See colour picture **Phrasal Verbs** on page Centre 13

get on *phrasal verb UK*
If two or more people get on, they like each other and are friends: *Karen and Sophie don't get on.*

get out *phrasal verb*
to move out of a car: *I'll get out when you stop at the traffic lights.*

get over something *phrasal verb*
to feel better after being ill or sad: *She's just getting over a cold.*

get (someone) up *phrasal verb*
to wake up and get out of bed, or to make someone do this: *I had to get up at five o'clock this morning.* ➲See colour picture **Phrasal Verbs** on page Centre 13

get up *phrasal verb*
to stand up: *The whole audience got up and started clapping.*

ghetto /ˈgetəʊ/ *noun* (*plural* **ghettoes**)
a poor part of a city

ghost /gəʊst/ *noun*
a dead person's spirit which some people believe can be seen by people who are alive: *Do you believe in ghosts?* ○ *a ghost story*

ghost

giant[1] /ˈdʒaɪənt/ *adj*
very big: *a giant spider*

giant[2] /ˈdʒaɪənt/ *noun*
a very big man in children's stories

gift /gɪft/ *noun*
1 something that you give to someone, usually on a special day: *a birthday/wedding gift*
2 a natural ability: *She* ***has a gift for*** *design.*

gigantic /dʒaɪˈgæntɪk/ *adj*
very big: *a gigantic teddy bear*

giggle /ˈgɪgl/ *verb* (*present participle* **giggling**, *past* **giggled**)
to laugh in a nervous or silly way: *She started giggling and couldn't stop.*
● **giggle** *noun*

gill /gɪl/ *noun*
a part on each side of a fish which it uses for breathing

ginger[1] /ˈdʒɪndʒə^{r}/ *noun* **[no plural]**
a root with a strong taste which is used in cooking

ginger[2] /ˈdʒɪndʒə^{r}/ *adj UK*
Ginger hair is an orange-brown colour.

giraffe /dʒɪˈrɑːf/ *noun*
a large African animal with a very long neck and long, thin legs

giraffe

girl /gɜːl/ *noun*
a female child or young woman: *We have three children – a boy and two girls.*

girlfriend /ˈgɜːlfrend/ *noun*
1 a woman or girl who someone is having a romantic relationship with: *Have you met Steve's new girlfriend?*
2 a female friend, especially of a woman

give /gɪv/ *verb* (*present participle* **giving**, *past tense* **gave**, *past participle* **given**)
1 to provide someone with something: *I gave her a bike for her birthday.* ○ *Do you* ***give*** *money* ***to*** *charity?*
2 to put something in someone's hand so that they can use it or look at it: *Can you give me that pen?*
3 to tell someone something: *Can you give Jo a message?*
4 to do an action: *He gave her a kiss.*
5 give someone a call/ring to telephone someone
6 to perform or speak in public: *Tony gave a great speech.*

give something back *phrasal verb*
to give something to the person who gave it to you: *Has she given you those books back yet?*

give in *phrasal verb*
to finally agree to do something that someone wants: *We will never* ***give in to*** *terrorists' demands.*

give something out *phrasal verb*
to give something to a lot of people: *He gave out copies of the report.*

give up something *phrasal verb*
1 If you give up something bad, such as smoking, you stop doing it or having it: *I gave up smoking two years ago.*
2 to stop doing something because

it is too difficult: *I've given up trying to help her.*
3 to stop doing a regular activity or job: *Are you going to give up work when you have your baby?*

glacier /ˈglæsiəʳ/ *noun*
a very large piece of ice that moves very slowly

glad /glæd/ *adj*
1 happy about something: *I'm very* ***glad that*** *you like your present.*
2 very willing to do something: *I'd be* ***glad to*** *help.*

gladly /ˈglædli/ *adv*
If you would gladly do something, you would like to do it: *I would gladly pay extra for better service.*

glamorous /ˈglæmᵊrəs/ *adj*
attractive in an exciting and special way: *She's very glamorous.*

glamour (*also US* **glamor**) /ˈglæməʳ/ *noun* **[no plural]**
the quality of being attractive, exciting and special: *the glamour of Hollywood*

glance[1] /glɑːns/ *verb* (*present participle* **glancing,** *past* **glanced)**
to look somewhere for a short time: *He* ***glanced at*** *his watch.*

glance[2] /glɑːns/ *noun*
a quick look: *She* ***had*** *a quick* ***glance*** *around the restaurant.*

glare[1] /gleəʳ/ *noun*
a long, angry look

glare[2] /gleəʳ/ *verb* (*present participle* **glaring,** *past* **glared)**
to look at someone in an angry way: *She* ***glared at*** *him.*

glaring /ˈgleərɪŋ/ *adj*
1 A glaring mistake is a very bad one that everyone will notice.
2 glaring light/sun, etc light which is too strong and bright

glass /glɑːs/ *noun*
1 [no plural] a hard, clear substance that objects such as windows and bottles are made of: *broken glass* ○ *glass jars*
2 (*plural* **glasses)** a container made of glass that is used for drinking: *Would you like* ***a glass of*** *water?*

glasses /ˈglɑːsɪz/ *plural noun*
a piece of equipment with two transparent parts that you wear in front of your eyes to help you see better: *a pair of glasses* ○ *She was* ***wearing glasses.***

gleam /gliːm/ *verb*
to shine in a pleasant, soft way: *Her new car gleamed in the sun.*

glee /gliː/ *noun* **[no plural]**
a feeling of great happiness: *Rosa was laughing with glee.*

glide /glaɪd/ *verb* (*present participle* **gliding,** *past* **glided)**
to move somewhere smoothly and quietly: *The train slowly glided out of the station.*

glider /ˈglaɪdəʳ/ *noun*
an aeroplane that has no engine

glimmer /ˈglɪməʳ/ *noun*
1 a glimmer of happiness/hope, etc a small sign of something good
2 when a light shines in a weak way

glimpse /glɪms/ *noun*
when you see something or someone for a very short time: *He* ***caught a glimpse of*** *her as she got into the car.*
• **glimpse** *verb* (*present participle* **glimpsing,** *past* **glimpsed)**
to see something or someone for a very short time: *She glimpsed him out of the corner of her eye.*

glisten /ˈglɪsᵊn/ *verb*
If something glistens, it shines, often because it is wet: *Their faces were* ***glistening with*** *sweat.*

glitter /ˈglɪtəʳ/ *verb*
to shine with small flashes of light: *Snow glittered on the mountains.*

glittering /ˈglɪtᵊrɪŋ/ *adj*
1 shining with small flashes of light: *glittering jewels*
2 successful and exciting: *a glittering career*

global /ˈgləʊbᵊl/ *adj*
relating to the whole world: *global problems*

global warming /ˌgləʊbᵊl ˈwɔːmɪŋ/ *noun* **[no plural]**
when the air around the world becomes warmer because of pollution

globe

globe /gləʊb/ *noun*
1 the globe the world: *This event was watched by 200 million people around the globe.*
2 a model of the world shaped like a

a b c d e f g h i j k l m n o p q r s t u v w x y z

ball with a map of all the countries on it

gloomy /ˈgluːmi/ *adj* **(gloomier, gloomiest)**
1 sad or without hope: *a gloomy face* ○ *gloomy predictions*
2 dark in a bad way: *a small, gloomy room*
• **gloomily** *adv*

glorious /ˈglɔːriəs/ *adj*
1 beautiful or very good: *We had four days of glorious sunshine.* ○ *glorious colours*
2 getting praise and respect: *a glorious career*

glory /ˈglɔːri/ *noun* **[no plural]**
when people praise and respect you for doing something very brave and good

glove /glʌv/ *noun*
a piece of clothing which covers your fingers and hand: *a pair of gloves*

glow[1] /gləʊ/ *noun*
1 a soft, warm light: *the warm glow of the moon*
2 when your face appears warm and healthy: *Sam's face had lost its rosy glow.*

glow[2] /gləʊ/ *verb*
1 to produce a soft, warm light: *toys which glow in the dark*
2 to have a warm and healthy appearance: *She glows with health.*
3 glow with happiness/pride, etc to feel very happy, proud, etc: *Glowing with pride, she showed me her painting.*

glowing /ˈgləʊɪŋ/ *adj*
praising someone a lot: *She got a glowing report from her teacher.*

glue[1] /gluː/ *noun* **[no plural]**
a substance used to stick things together: *Put a bit of glue on both edges and hold them together.*

glue[2] /gluː/ *verb* (*present participle* **glueing**, *past* **glued**)
to stick something to something else with glue: *Do you think you can **glue** this vase back **together**?*

glum /glʌm/ *adj*
sad: *Why are you looking so glum today?*
• **glumly** *adv*

gm
written abbreviation for gram (= a unit for measuring weight)

GM /dʒiːˈem/ *adj abbreviation for* genetically modified: changed by adding genes from another plant or animal: *GM foods*

GMT /ˌdʒiːemˈtiː/ *noun* **[no plural]** *abbreviation for* Greenwich Mean Time: the time at Greenwich in London, which is used as an international measurement for time

gnaw /nɔː/ *verb*
to bite something with a lot of small bites: *He was gnawing on a bone.*

go[1] /gəʊ/ *verb* (*present participle* **going**, *past tense* **went**, *past participle* **gone**)
1 to move or travel somewhere: *I'd love to go to America.* ○ *We went into the house.* ○ *Are you **going by** train?*
2 to move or travel somewhere in order to do something: *Let's **go for** a walk.* ○ *We're going camping tomorrow.*
3 to disappear or no longer exist: *When I turned round, the man had gone.*
4 to work correctly: *I managed to get the car going.*
5 If two things go, they match each other: *Does the jacket **go with** the trousers?*

go off *phrasal verb*
1 to leave a place and go somewhere else: *She went off with Laurie.*
2 If a bomb or gun goes off, it explodes or fires.

go on *phrasal verb*
1 to last for a particular period of time: *The film seemed to go on forever.*
2 to continue doing something: *We can't go on living like this.*
3 to happen: *What's going on?*

go out *phrasal verb*
to leave a place in order to go somewhere else: *Are you going out tonight?*

go through something *phrasal verb*
to have a difficult or bad situation: *She's going through a difficult time with her job.*

go up *phrasal verb*
to become higher in level: *House prices keep going up.*

go[2] /gəʊ/ *noun* (*plural* **goes**)
1 *UK* when someone tries to do something: *I **had a go at** catching a fish.*
2 *UK* the time when you do something in a game: *Throw the dice*

a b c d e f g h i j k l m n o p q r s t u v w x y z

Jane, it's your go.

goal /gəʊl/ *noun*
1 a point scored in sports such as football when a player sends a ball into a particular area, such as between two posts: *He scored two goals in the second half.*
2 in some sports, the area between two posts where players try to send the ball
3 something that you want to do in the future: *Andy's goal is to run in the New York Marathon.*

goalkeeper /ˈgəʊlˌkiːpəʳ/ *noun*
the player in a sport such as football who tries to stop the ball going into the goal

goalkeeper

goat /gəʊt/ *noun*
an animal with horns which is kept for the milk it makes

god /gɒd/ *noun*
1 God in Jewish, Christian, or Muslim belief, the spirit who made the universe and everything in it, and who rules over it
2 a spirit, especially a male one, that people pray to: *the ancient Greek gods and goddesses*

goddess /ˈgɒdes/ *noun* (*plural* **goddesses**)
a female spirit that people pray to: *the ancient goddess of hunting*

goggles /ˈgɒglz/ *plural noun*
special glasses for protecting your eyes: *a pair of goggles*

gold[1] /gəʊld/ *noun* **[no plural]**
a valuable, shiny, yellow metal used to make coins and jewellery

gold[2] /gəʊld/ *adj*
1 made of gold: *gold jewellery*
2 being the shiny yellow colour of gold: *gold paint*

golden /ˈgəʊldᵊn/ *adj*
being a bright yellow colour: *bright golden hair*

golf /gɒlf/ *noun* **[no plural]**
a game on grass where you try to hit a small ball into holes using a long, thin stick
• **golfer** *noun*

golf

gone /gɒn/
past participle of go

good[1] /gʊd/ *adj*
(better, best)
1 enjoyable or nice: *a good book* ○ *Did you have a good time at the party?*
2 of a high quality: *The food at this restaurant is very good.*
3 able to do something well: *Anna is a good cook.*
4 kind or helpful: *She's a good friend.*
5 A good child or animal behaves well.
6 morally right: *a good person*
7 something you say when you are pleased about something: *Oh good, he's arrived at last.*

good[2] /gʊd/ *noun*
1 do someone good to be useful or helpful to someone: *A holiday will do you good.*
2 [no plural] what people think is morally right: *Children don't always understand the difference between good and bad.*
3 for good forever: *When he was 20, he left home for good.*

good afternoon /ˌgʊd ɑːftəˈnuːn/ *exclamation*
something you say to someone when you meet them in the afternoon

goodbye /gʊdˈbaɪ/ *exclamation*
something you say when you leave someone or when they leave you: *Goodbye Vicki! See you next week.*

good evening /ˌgʊd ˈiːvnɪŋ/ *exclamation*
something you say to someone when you meet them in the evening

good-looking /ˌgʊdˈlʊkɪŋ/ *adj*
attractive: *a good-looking woman*

good morning /ˌgʊd ˈmɔːnɪŋ/ *exclamation*
something you say to someone when you meet them in the morning

goodness /ˈgʊdnəs/ *noun*
1 [no plural] the quality in people that makes them behave well and treat other people kindly: *She*

believes in the goodness of human nature.
2 *informal* something you say when you are surprised: *Goodness, he's a big baby isn't he?*

good night /ˌgʊd ˈnaɪt/ *exclamation*
something you say when you leave someone in the evening or when someone is going to bed

goose /guːs/ *noun* (*plural* **geese**)
a large water bird similar to a duck

gorgeous /ˈgɔːdʒəs/ *adj*
very beautiful or pleasant: *You look gorgeous in that dress!*

gorilla /gəˈrɪlə/ *noun*
a big, black, hairy animal, like a large monkey

gossip[1] /ˈgɒsɪp/ *noun* **[no plural]**
talk about other people's private lives that might not be true: *an interesting piece of gossip*

gossip[2] /ˈgɒsɪp/ *verb*
to talk about other people's private lives

got /gɒt/
past of get

gotten /ˈgɒtᵊn/ *US*
past participle of get

govern /ˈgʌvᵊn/ *verb*
to officially control a country: *The country is now governed by the Labour Party.*

government /ˈgʌvᵊnmənt/ *noun*
the group of people who officially control a country: *The Government has cut taxes.*

governor /ˈgʌvᵊnəʳ/ *noun*
someone who controls a region or organization: *the Governor of Texas*

gown /gaʊn/ *noun*
a woman's long dress: *a silk gown*

grab /græb/ *verb* (*present participle* **grabbing**, *past* **grabbed**)
to take hold of something or someone suddenly with your hand: *He grabbed my arm and pulled me away.*

grace /greɪs/ *noun* **[no plural]**
the quality of moving in a smooth and attractive way: *She moved **with** such **grace**.*

graceful /ˈgreɪsfᵊl/ *adj*
moving in a smooth and attractive way: *graceful movements*
• **gracefully** *adv*

gracious /ˈgreɪʃəs/ *adj*
behaving in a pleasant and polite way: *our gracious host*
• **graciously** *adv*

grade[1] /greɪd/ *noun*
1 a number or letter that shows how good your work is: *Carla got a grade A in German.*
2 a level of quality, size, importance, etc: *I applied for a position a grade higher than my current job.*
3 *US* (*UK* **form**) a school class for students of the same age or ability: *My son is in fifth grade.*

grade[2] /greɪd/ *verb* (*present participle* **grading**, *past* **graded**)
to separate people or things into different levels of quality, size, importance, etc: *The fruit is washed and then **graded by** size.*

gradual /ˈgrædʒuəl/ *adj*
happening slowly: *a gradual change*

gradually /ˈgrædʒuəli/ *adv*
slowly over a period of time: *Gradually he got better.*

graduate[1] /ˈgrædʒuət/ *noun UK*
someone who has studied for and got a degree (= qualification) from a university: *a science graduate*

graduate[2] /ˈgrædjueɪt/ *verb* (*present participle* **graduating**, *past* **graduated**)
to complete your education successfully at a university, college, or, in the US, at school: *He **graduated from** Cambridge University in 1997.*

grain /greɪn/ *noun*
1 a seed or seeds from types of grass which are eaten as food: *grains of wheat/rice*
2 a very small piece of something: *a grain of sand/sugar*

gram /græm/ *noun*
a unit for measuring weight, equal to 0.001 kilograms

grammar /ˈgræməʳ/ *noun* **[no plural]**
the way you combine words and change their form and position in a sentence, or the rules of this

grammatical /grəˈmætɪkᵊl/ *adj*
obeying the rules of grammar: *a grammatical sentence*

grand /grænd/ *adj*
very large and special: *a grand hotel*

grandchild /ˈgrændtʃaɪld/ *noun* (*plural* **grandchildren**)
the child of your son or daughter

granddad /ˈgrændæd/ *noun UK informal* grandfather

granddaughter /ˈgrændˌdɔːtəʳ/ *noun* the daughter of your son or daughter

grandfather /ˈgrændˌfɑːðəʳ/ *noun* the father of your mother or father

grandma /ˈgrændmɑː/ *noun informal, another word for* grandmother

grandmother /ˈgrændˌmʌðəʳ/ *noun* the mother of your mother or father

grandparent /ˈgrændˌpeərᵊnt/ *noun* the parent of your mother or father

grandson /ˈgrændsʌn/ *noun* the son of your son or daughter

granny /ˈgræni/ *noun informal* (*plural* **grannies**) *another word for* grandmother

grant¹ /grɑːnt/ *verb*
1 *formal* to give or allow someone something, usually in an official way: *He was granted a visa.*
2 take something/someone for granted to expect something and not understand that you are lucky to have it: *Most of us take our freedom for granted.*

grant² /grɑːnt/ *noun* an amount of money that an organization gives you for a special purpose: *They received a grant for the project.*

grape /greɪp/ *noun* a small, round fruit that grows in large groups and is used to make wine: *a bunch of grapes*

grapefruit /ˈgreɪpfruːt/ *noun* a large, round, yellow fruit with a sour taste

graph /grɑːf/ *noun* a picture that shows different amounts by using a line or many lines

graph

grapple /ˈgræpl/ *verb* (*present participle* **grappling**, *past* **grappled**)
grapple with something *phrasal verb* to try to do or understand something difficult

grasp /grɑːsp/ *verb*
1 to take hold of something firmly with your hand: *He grasped my hand.*
2 to understand something: *I didn't grasp what she was saying.*

grass /grɑːs/ *noun* **[no plural]** a common plant with thin green leaves that grows close to the ground: *We lay on the grass in the sunshine.*

grasshopper /ˈgrɑːsˌhɒpəʳ/ *noun* a green insect which jumps about using its long back legs

grasshopper

grate /greɪt/ *verb* (*present participle* **grating**, *past* **grated**) to break food such as cheese into small, thin pieces by rubbing it against a grater (= kitchen tool with holes): *grated cheese*

grateful /ˈgreɪtfᵊl/ *adj* wanting to say 'thank you' to someone who has done something good for you: *I'm really **grateful to** you **for** all your help.* ➲Opposite **ungrateful**
• **gratefully** *adv*

grater /ˈgreɪtəʳ/ *noun* a kitchen tool with a surface full of holes, used to grate (= break into small pieces) food such as cheese ➲See colour picture **Kitchen** on page Centre 10

gratitude /ˈgrætɪtjuːd/ *noun* **[no plural]** when you want to say 'thank you' to someone who has done something good for you

grave¹ /greɪv/ *noun* a place in the ground where a dead body is buried

grave² /greɪv/ *adj* very serious: *grave doubts* ○ *a grave mistake*

gravel /ˈgrævᵊl/ *noun* **[no plural]** small pieces of stone used to make paths and roads

gravestone /ˈgreɪvstəʊn/ *noun* a stone that shows the name of a dead person who is buried under it

graveyard /ˈgreɪvjɑːd/ *noun* an area of land where dead bodies are buried, usually next to a church

gravity /ˈgrævəti/ *noun* **[no plural]**
1 the force that makes objects fall to

the ground: *the laws of gravity*
2 *formal* when a problem is very serious

gravy /ˈɡreɪvi/ *noun* **[no plural]**
a warm, brown sauce that you put on meat

graze[1] /ɡreɪz/ *verb* (*present participle* **grazing**, *past* **grazed**)
1 to eat grass
2 *UK* to hurt your skin by rubbing it against something rough: *I fell and grazed my knee.*

graze[2] /ɡreɪz/ *noun UK*
an injury on your skin caused by rubbing against something: *She has a nasty* ***graze on*** *her elbow.*

grease /ɡriːs/ *noun* **[no plural]**
a substance such as oil or fat

greasy /ˈɡriːsi/ *adj* **(greasier, greasiest)**
containing or covered with fat or oil: *greasy food*

great /ɡreɪt/ *adj*
1 very good: *We had a great time.*
2 important or famous: *a great actor*
3 large: *a great crowd of people*
4 great big/long, etc very big/long, etc: *They've got a great big house.*

great- /ɡreɪt/ *prefix*
1 great-grandfather/-grandmother the father/mother of your grandfather or grandmother
2 great-aunt/-uncle the aunt/uncle of your mother or father
3 great-grandchild/-granddaughter, etc the child/daughter, etc of your grandson or granddaughter
4 great-niece/-nephew the daughter/son of your niece or nephew

greatly /ˈɡreɪtli/ *adv*
very much: *We will miss her greatly.*

greed /ɡriːd/ *noun* **[no plural]**
when you want a lot more food, money, etc, than you need

greedy /ˈɡriːdi/ *adj* **(greedier, greediest)**
wanting a lot more food, money, etc, than you need: *greedy, selfish people*

green[1] /ɡriːn/ *adj*
1 being the same colour as grass
2 relating to nature and protecting the environment: *green issues*
3 covered with grass or other plants: *green spaces*

green[2] /ɡriːn/ *noun* **[no plural]**
the colour of grass

greenhouse /ˈɡriːnhaʊs/ *noun*
a building made of glass for growing plants in

greet /ɡriːt/ *verb*
to say hello to someone who has arrived in a place: *He greeted me at the door.*

greeting /ˈɡriːtɪŋ/ *noun*
something friendly or polite that you say or do when you see someone

grew /ɡruː/
past tense of grow

grey[1] *UK* (*US* **gray**) /ɡreɪ/ *adj*
being a colour that is a mixture of black and white: *grey clouds* ○ *an old man with grey hair*

grey[2] *UK* (*US* **gray**) /ɡreɪ/ *noun* **[no plural]**
a colour that is a mixture of black and white

grief /ɡriːf/ *noun* **[no plural]**
the great sadness that you feel when someone dies

grieve /ɡriːv/ *verb* (*present participle* **grieving**, *past* **grieved**)
to feel very sad because someone has died: *He is still* ***grieving for*** *his wife.*

grill[1] /ɡrɪl/ *noun* (*also US* **broiler**)
a piece of equipment which cooks food using heat from above

grill[2] /ɡrɪl/ *verb* (*also US* **broil**)
to cook food using direct heat: *Grill the fish for 2 to 3 minutes on each side.*
• **grilled** *adj*
cooked under a grill: *grilled fish*

grim /ɡrɪm/ *adj*
1 worrying and bad: *grim news*
2 sad and serious: *a grim expression*
3 A grim place is ugly and unpleasant.

grin /ɡrɪn/ *verb* (*present participle* **grinning**, *past* **grinned**)
to smile a big smile: *He* ***grinned at*** *me.*
• **grin** *noun*: *She had a big grin on her face.*

grind /ɡraɪnd/ *verb* (*present participle* **grinding**, *past* **ground**)
1 to make something change into powder by rubbing it between two hard things: *to grind coffee*
2 to rub a blade against a hard

surface to make it sharp

grip[1] /grɪp/ *noun*
when you hold something tightly: *She tightened her* ***grip on*** *my arm.*

grip[2] /grɪp/ *verb* (*present participle* **gripping**, *past* **gripped**)
1 to hold something tightly: *She gripped his arm.*
2 to keep someone's attention completely: *This trial has gripped the whole nation.*

gripping /grɪpɪŋ/ *adj*
very interesting and exciting: *a gripping film*

groan /grəʊn/ *verb*
to make a long, low sound because you are sad or in pain: *He collapsed, groaning with pain.*
• **groan** *noun*

groceries /ˈgrəʊsəriz/ *plural noun*
things that you buy to use in the home such as food and cleaning products

groom /gruːm/ *noun* (*also* **bridegroom**)
a man who is getting married

grope /grəʊp/ *verb* (*present participle* **groping**, *past* **groped**)
to try to get hold of something with your hand, usually when you cannot see it: *I* ***groped*** *in my bag* ***for*** *my keys.*

ground[1] /graʊnd/ *noun*
1 the ground the surface of the Earth: *I sat down* ***on the ground****.*
2 [no plural] the soil in an area: *soft ground*
3 an area of land used for a particular activity: *a football ground*

ground[2] /graʊnd/
past of grind

ground floor /ˌgraʊnd ˈflɔːʳ/ *UK* (*US* **first floor**) *noun*
the level of a building which is on the ground

group /gruːp/ *noun*
1 a number of people or things that are together in one place: *She was with a* ***group of*** *friends.*
2 a few musicians or singers who perform together, usually playing popular music: *a pop group*

grow /grəʊ/ *verb* (*present participle* **growing**, *past tense* **grew**, *past participle* **grown**)
1 to become bigger or taller as time passes: *Children grow very quickly.*
2 If a plant grows, or you grow it, it develops from a seed to a full plant: *These plants grow well in sandy soil.*
3 to increase: *The problem grows every year.*
4 to become: *We've grown older.*
5 If your hair or nails grow, or if you grow them, they get longer.

grow up *phrasal verb*
to become older or an adult: *She grew up in Madrid.*

growl /graʊl/ *verb*
If a dog growls, it makes a deep, angry noise.
• **growl** *noun*

grown /grəʊn/
past participle of grow

grown-up[1] /ˈgrəʊnʌp/ *noun*
an adult, used especially when talking to children: *Ask a grown-up to cut the shape out for you.*

grown-up[2] /ˌgrəʊnˈʌp/ *adj*
adult: *Jenny has a grown-up son of 24.*

growth /grəʊθ/ *noun*
1 [no plural] when something grows or increases: *population growth*
2 something that grows on your skin or inside your body, that should not be there

grub /grʌb/ *noun*
a young, developing insect which has a fat, white tube shape

grubby /ˈgrʌbi/ *adj*
dirty: *a grubby little boy*

grudge /grʌdʒ/ *noun*
a bad or angry feeling towards someone because of something they did in the past: *He is not the type of person to* ***bear a grudge*** *against anyone.*

gruesome /ˈgruːsəm/ *adj*
very unpleasant or violent, usually involving injury or death: *a gruesome murder*

grumble /ˈgrʌmbl/ *verb* (*present participle* **grumbling**, *past* **grumbled**)
to keep complaining about something: *She's always* ***grumbling about*** *something.*
• **grumble** *noun*

grumpy /ˈgrʌmpi/ *adj*
easily annoyed and often complaining: *a grumpy old man*

grunt /grʌnt/ *verb*
If a pig grunts, it makes short, low sounds.

guarantee[1] /ˌgærᵊnˈtiː/ *verb* (*present participle* **guaranteeing**, *past* **guaranteed**)
1 to promise that something is true or will happen: *We can't guarantee that it will arrive in time.*
2 If a company guarantees a product, it promises to repair it or give you a new one if it has a fault: *The TV is guaranteed for 12 months.*

guarantee[2] /ˌgærᵊnˈtiː/ *noun*
1 a written promise made by a company to repair one of its products or give you a new one if it has a fault: *a three-year guarantee*
2 a promise that something will be done or will happen: *There's no guarantee that it actually works.*

guard[1] /gɑːd/ *noun*
1 someone whose job is to protect a person or make sure that a person does not escape: *prison guards*
2 be on your guard to be ready to do something if a problem happens: *Companies were warned to be on their guard for suspicious packages.*

guard[2] /gɑːd/ *verb*
1 to protect someone or something so that no one attacks or steals them: *Soldiers guarded the main doors of the embassy.*
2 to watch someone and make certain that they do not escape from a place: *Five prison officers guarded the prisoners.*

guardian /ˈgɑːdiən/ *noun*
someone who is legally responsible for someone else's child

guerrilla /gəˈrɪlə/ *noun*
a soldier who fights to achieve their political beliefs: *guerrilla warfare*

guess[1] /ges/ *verb*
1 to give an answer or opinion about something without knowing all the facts: *Guess how old he is.*
2 to say something that is right without knowing all the facts: *How did you guess I was pregnant?*

guess[2] /ges/ *noun* (*plural* **guesses**)
1 an attempt to give the right answer when you are not certain: *How old do you think John is? Go on, **have a guess**.*
2 an opinion that you have formed by guessing: *My guess is she probably won't come.*

guest /gest/ *noun*
1 someone who comes to visit you: *We've got some guests coming this weekend.*
2 someone who is staying in a hotel: *The hotel has accommodation for 200 guests.*

guidance /ˈgaɪdᵊns/ *noun* **[no plural]**
help or advice: *I need some careers guidance.*

guide[1] /gaɪd/ *noun*
1 someone whose job is to show interesting places to visitors: *a tour guide*
2 a book that gives information about something or tells you how to do something: *a hotel/restaurant guide ○ a user's guide*

guide[2] /gaɪd/ *verb* (*present participle* **guiding**, *past* **guided**)
to help someone or something go somewhere: *He gently guided her back to her chair.*

guidebook /ˈgaɪdbʊk/ *noun*
a book that gives visitors information about a place

guilt /gɪlt/ *noun* **[no plural]**
1 the bad feeling you get when you know you have done something bad, such as upsetting someone: *He suffered a lot of guilt over leaving his children.*
2 the fact that someone has done something illegal: *He was never convinced of her guilt.* ➲Opposite **innocence**

guilty /ˈgɪlti/ *adj*
1 feeling bad because you have done something wrong: *I feel so guilty about not going to see them.*
2 having broken a law: *The jury **found her guilty*** (= decided that she was guilty of a crime). ○ *They found him **guilty of** murder.* ➲Opposite **innocent**

guitar /gɪˈtɑːʳ/ *noun*
a musical instrument with strings that you play by pulling the strings: *an electric guitar*

guitar

gulf /gʌlf/ *noun*
a large area of sea that has land almost all the way around it: *the Arabian Gulf*

gulp /gʌlp/ *verb*
(*also* **gulp down**) to drink or eat

something quickly: *I just had time to gulp down a cup of coffee.*

• **gulp** *noun*
when you swallow something: *He* ***took a gulp of*** *tea.*

gum /gʌm/ *noun*
the hard, pink part inside your mouth that your teeth grow out of

gun /gʌn/ *noun*
a weapon that you fire bullets out of

gush /gʌʃ/ *verb*
If liquid gushes from an opening, a lot of it comes out quickly: *Blood was gushing from the wound.*

gust /gʌst/ *verb*
If winds gust, they blow strongly.

• **gust** *noun*
when the wind suddenly blows strongly: *a gust of air*

guts /gʌts/ *noun informal*
the bravery that you need to do something difficult or frightening: *It takes guts to admit that you were wrong.*

gutter /ˈgʌtəʳ/ *noun*
the edge of a road where water flows away

guy /gaɪ/ *noun informal*
a man: *What a nice guy!*

gym /dʒɪm/ *noun*
1 a building with equipment for doing exercises: *Nick goes to the gym three times a week.*
2 [no plural] exercises done inside, especially as a school subject

gymnast /ˈdʒɪmnæst/ *noun*
someone who does gymnastics: *an Olympic gymnast*

gymnastics

gymnastics /dʒɪmˈnæstɪks/ *noun* **[no plural]**
a sport in which you do physical exercises on the floor and on different pieces of equipment

a b c d e f **g** h i j k l m n o p q r s t u v w x y z

H, h /eɪtʃ/
the eighth letter of the alphabet

habit /ˈhæbɪt/ *noun*
something that you often do, without thinking about it: *I got into the **habit of** having biscuits with my coffee.*

hack /hæk/ *verb*
to use a computer to illegally get into someone else's computer system and read the information that is kept there

had *strong form* /hæd/ *weak forms* /həd, əd/ *verb*
past of have

hadn't /ˈhædᵊnt/
short for had not: *I hadn't seen Megan since college.*

haggle /ˈhægl/ *verb* (*present participle* **haggling**, *past* **haggled**)
to argue, especially about the price of something: *I spent 20 minutes **haggling over** the price of a leather bag.*

hail¹ /heɪl/ *noun* **[no plural]**
small, hard pieces of frozen rain that fall from the sky

hail² /heɪl/ *verb*
If it hails, small, hard pieces of frozen rain fall from the sky.

hair /heəʳ/ *noun* **[no plural]**
the thin, thread-like parts that grow on the head and body of people and animals: *a girl with long, fair hair*

hairbrush /ˈheəbrʌʃ/ *noun* (*plural* **hairbrushes**)
a brush that you use to make your hair look tidy

haircut /ˈheəkʌt/ *noun*
1 when someone cuts your hair: *I really need a haircut.*
2 the style in which your hair has been cut: *I like your new haircut.*

hairdresser /ˈheəˌdresəʳ/ *noun*
1 someone whose job is to cut people's hair
2 hairdresser's the place where you go to have your hair cut, coloured, etc

hairdryer /ˈheəˌdraɪəʳ/ *noun*
a piece of electrical equipment for drying your hair with hot air

hairstyle /ˈheəstaɪl/ *noun*
the style of someone's hair: *Do you like my new hairstyle?*

hairy /ˈheəri/ *adj* (**hairier, hairiest**)
covered in hair: *a hairy chest*

half¹ /hɑːf/ *noun, determiner* (*plural* **halves**)
1 one of two equal parts of something; ½: *Divide the lemons into halves.* ○ *It'll take **half an hour** to get there.* ○ *Jenny lived in Beijing for a year and a half.*
2 half past one/two, etc *UK* 30 minutes past one o'clock/two o'clock, etc: *We got back to our hotel at half past seven.*

half² /hɑːf/ *adv*
partly, but not completely: *The room was half empty.* ○ *Sophia is half Greek and half Spanish* (= she has one Greek parent and one Spanish parent).

half-term /hɑːfˈtɜːm/ *noun UK*
a short holiday in the middle of a school term (= one of the periods the school year is divided into)

half-time /ˌhɑːfˈtaɪm/ *noun* **[no plural]**
a short period of rest between the two halves of a game

halfway /ˌhɑːfˈweɪ/ *adj, adv*
in the middle between two places, or in the middle of a period of time: ***halfway between** London and Oxford* ○ *We were already halfway through the week.*

hall /hɔːl/ *noun*
1 a room which leads to other rooms: *I left my coat and umbrella in the hall.*
2 a large room or building where meetings and concerts, etc. happen: *The Albert Hall* ○ *the school hall*

hallo /həˈləʊ/ *exclamation UK*
1 said when you meet someone or start talking with someone: *Hallo, Chris, how are you?*
2 used when you start speaking on the telephone: *Hallo, this is Alex.*

Halloween /ˌhæləʊˈiːn/ *noun* **[no plural]**
the night of 31 October when children dress in special clothes and people try to frighten each other

halt¹ /hɒlt/ *noun* **[no plural]**
when something stops moving or

a b c d e f g h i j k l m n o p q r s t u v w x y z

happening: *The car* ***came to a halt***.

halt² /hɒlt/ *verb formal*
to stop or make something stop: *Work on the project was halted immediately.*

halve /hɑːv/ *verb* (*present participle* **halving**, *past* **halved**)
to divide something into two equal parts: *Peel and halve the potatoes.*

ham /hæm/ *noun* **[no plural]**
meat from a pig's back or leg: *a ham sandwich*

hamburger /ˈhæmˌbɜːɡəʳ/ *noun*
a round, flat shape of meat which is eaten between round pieces of bread: *a hamburger and fries*

hammer /ˈhæməʳ/ *noun*
a tool with a heavy, metal part at the top that you use to hit nails into something

hammer

hamster /ˈhæmstəʳ/ *noun*
a small animal with soft fur and no tail that is often kept as a pet

hand¹ /hænd/ *noun*
1 the part of your body on the end of your arm that has fingers: *I had my hands in my pockets.*
2 hold hands If two people hold hands, they hold each other's hand.
3 by hand done or made by a person and not a machine: *This sweater has to be washed by hand.*
4 one of the long, thin pieces that point to the numbers on a clock or watch
5 give someone a hand to help someone: *Could you give me a hand with these suitcases?*
6 on the one hand ... on the other hand used when you are comparing two different ideas or opinions: *On the one hand, I'd like more money but on the other hand, I don't want to work more.*

hand² /hænd/ *verb*
1 to give something to someone: *Could you hand me that book, please?*

hand something in *phrasal verb*
to give a piece of writing to a teacher: *Have you handed your history essay in yet?*

hand something out *phrasal verb*
to give something to all the people in a group: *A girl was handing out leaflets at the station.*

handbag /ˈhændbæɡ/ *UK* (*US* **purse**) *noun*
a bag carried by a woman with her money, keys, etc inside

handcuffs /ˈhændkʌfs/ *plural noun*
two metal rings that are joined by a chain and are used for holding a prisoner's hands together

handcuffs

handful /ˈhændfʊl/ *noun*
1 the amount of something that you can hold in one hand
2 a handful of something a small number of people or things: *Only a handful of people came to the meeting.*
3 a handful *informal* someone who is difficult to control, especially a child: *Daisy's only three and she's quite a handful.*

handicap /ˈhændɪkæp/ *noun*
1 something that is wrong with your mind or body permanently: *a mental/physical handicap*
2 something that makes it more difficult for you to do something: *I found not having a car quite a handicap in the countryside.*

handicapped /ˈhændɪkæpt/ *adj*
not able to use part of your body or your mind because it has been damaged: *mentally/physically handicapped*

handkerchief /ˈhæŋkətʃiːf/ *noun*
a small piece of cloth or soft paper that you use to dry your eyes or nose

handle¹ /ˈhændl/ *verb* (*present participle* **handling**, *past* **handled**)
1 to take action to improve a difficult situation: *He handled the situation very well.*
2 to touch, hold, or pick up something: *You must wash your hands before handling food.*

handle² /ˈhændl/ *noun*
the part of something that you use to hold it or open it: *a door handle* ○ *the handle on a suitcase*

handle

handlebars /ˈhændlbɑːz/ *plural noun* the metal bars at the front of a bicycle or motorcycle that you hold onto

handlebars

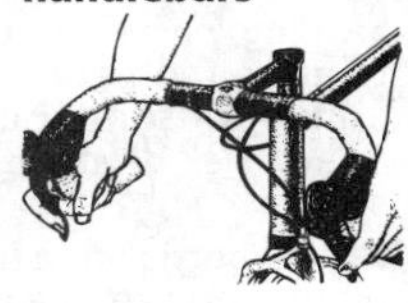

handsome /ˈhændsəm/ *adj* A handsome man is attractive: *He was tall, dark and handsome.*

hands-on /ˌhændzˈɒn/ *adj* doing something and not only studying it or watching someone else do it: *hands-on experience*

handwriting /ˈhændˌraɪtɪŋ/ *noun* **[no plural]** the way that someone makes the letters when they write with a pen or pencil

handy /ˈhændi/ *adj* **(handier, handiest)**
1 useful or easy to use: *a handy container/tool*
2 *UK informal* near to a place: *It's a nice house and it's* ***handy for*** *the station.*

hang /hæŋ/ *verb* (*present participle* **hanging**, *past* **hung**)
1 to fasten something so that the top part is fixed but the lower part is free to move: *He* ***hung*** *his coat* ***on*** *the hook behind the door.*
2 (*past also* **hanged**) to kill someone by putting a rope around their neck and making them drop
hang around *phrasal verb, informal* to spend time somewhere, usually doing little: *Teenagers hang around on street corners.*
hang on *phrasal verb, informal* to wait for a short time: *Hang on – I'm coming.*
hang up *phrasal verb* to finish talking on the telephone
hang something up *phrasal verb* to put something such as a coat somewhere where it can hang: *You can hang up your jacket over there.*

hanger /ˈhæŋəʳ/ (*also* **coat hanger**) *noun* a wire, wooden, or plastic object for hanging clothes on

happen /ˈhæpᵊn/ *verb* If an event or situation happens, it exists or starts to be done: *Accidents can happen to anyone.* ○ *We can't let a mistake like this happen again.* ○ *Did you hear what* ***happened to*** *Jamie last night?*

happily /ˈhæpɪli/ *adv*
1 in a happy way: *They are very happily married.*
2 in a way that is very willing: *I'd happily drive you to the airport.*

happiness /ˈhæpɪnəs/ *noun* **[no plural]** the feeling of being happy

happy /ˈhæpi/ *adj* **(happier, happiest)**
1 pleased and in a good mood, especially because something good has happened: *She looked really happy.* ➲Opposite **unhappy**
2 happy to do something to be willing to do something: *I'd be very happy to help, if you need a hand.*

harbour

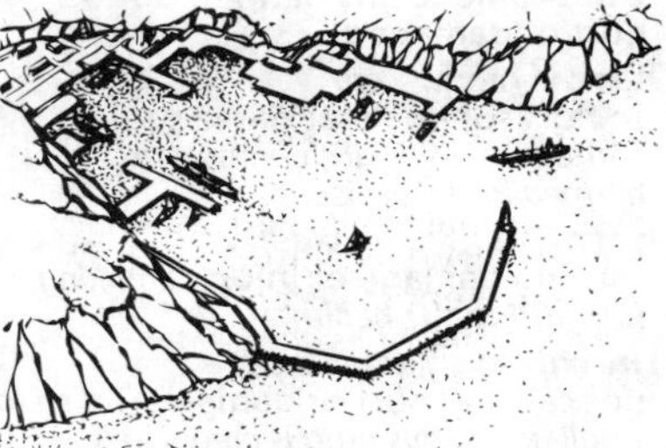

harbour *UK* (*US* **harbor**) /ˈhɑːbəʳ/ *noun* an area of water near the coast where ships are kept

hard¹ /hɑːd/ *adj* **(harder, hardest)**
1 firm and not easy to press or bend: *a hard surface* ○ *The seats were really hard.* ➲Opposite **soft**
2 difficult to do or understand: *It*

must be hard to study with all this noise.
➲Opposite **easy**
3 do/learn something the hard way to do or learn something by having a lot of problems or difficulty

hard² /hɑːd/ *adv* **(harder, hardest)**
1 with a lot of effort: *She tried so hard.* ○ *You must work harder.*
2 with a lot of force: *She kicked the ball hard.*

hard disk /ˌhɑːd ˈdɪsk/ *UK* (*also* **ˈhard ˌdrive**) *noun*
the part inside a computer that keeps very large amounts of information

harden /ˈhɑːdᵊn/ *verb*
to become hard and stiff, or to make something become hard and stiff

hardly /ˈhɑːdli/ *adv*
almost not, or only a very small amount: *I was so tired that I could hardly walk.* ○ *There's* ***hardly any*** *food left in the fridge.*

hardware /ˈhɑːdweəʳ/ *noun* **[no plural]**
the machines or equipment that a computer system is made from, not the programs

hare /heəʳ/ *noun*
an animal like a large rabbit that can run very fast and has long ears

harm¹ /hɑːm/ *noun* **[no plural]**
1 hurt or damage: *Smoking can* ***cause*** *serious* ***harm to*** *the lungs.*
2 not come to any harm to not be hurt or damaged

harm² /hɑːm/ *verb*
to hurt someone or damage something: *Luckily, no one was harmed in the accident.*

harmful /ˈhɑːmfᵊl/ *adj*
causing damage or injury: *Smoking is* ***harmful to*** *the health.*

harmless /ˈhɑːmləs/ *adj*
not causing hurt or damage: *Taken in small doses, this drug is completely harmless.*

harsh /hɑːʃ/ *adj*
1 cruel or unkind: *harsh criticism*
2 too strong, bright, loud, etc: *harsh chemicals* ○ *harsh lighting*
• **harshly** *adv*

harvest¹ /ˈhɑːvɪst/ *noun*
1 when crops are cut and collected from fields
2 the amount of crops that are collected

harvest² /ˈhɑːvɪst/ *verb*
to cut and collect crops when they are ready

has *strong form* /hæz/ *weak forms* /həz, əz/
present simple of have, *used with 'he', 'she', 'it'*

hasn't /ˈhæzᵊnt/
short for has not: *It hasn't rained for three weeks.*

hassle¹ /ˈhæsl/ *noun*
a problem: *It's such a hassle finding a place to park.*

hassle² /ˈhæsl/ *verb* (*present participle* **hassling**, *past* **hassled**)
to annoy someone, especially by asking for something again and again: *He's always* ***hassling*** *me* ***for*** *money.*

haste /heɪst/ *noun* **[no plural]**
when you are in a hurry and do something too quickly: *In their haste to escape, they left behind all their belongings.*

hasty /ˈheɪsti/ *adj* **(hastier, hastiest)**
done very quickly: *I don't want to make a hasty decision.*

hat /hæt/ *noun*
something that you wear to cover your head: *a cowboy hat*

hatch /hætʃ/ *verb*
to come out of an egg: *When will the chicks hatch?*

hate /heɪt/ *verb* (*present participle* **hating**, *past* **hated**)
to dislike someone or something very much: *I hate going to the dentist's.*

hatred /ˈheɪtrɪd/ *noun* **[no plural]**
when you dislike someone or something very much: *He developed an intense* ***hatred of*** *all women.*

haul /hɔːl/ *verb*
to pull something somewhere slowly and with difficulty: *They hauled the piano into the living room.*

haunt /hɔːnt/ *verb*
If a ghost haunts a place, it appears there often: *a haunted house*

have¹ *strong form* /hæv/ *weak forms* /həv, əv/ *verb*
used with the past participle of another verb to make the present and past perfect tenses: *Have you*

seen Roz? ○ *I've* (= I have) *passed my test.* ○ *He hasn't* (= has not) *visited London before.*

have² /hæv/ *verb* **have to do something; have got to do something** to need to do something: *I have to go to Manchester tomorrow.* ○ *Do we have to finish this today?*

have³ *strong form* /hæv/ *weak forms* /həv, əv/ *verb* (*present participle* **having**, *past* **had**)
1 (*also* **have got**) to own something: *I have two horses.* ○ *Laura has got beautiful blue eyes.*
2 used to say that someone is holding something: *He had a pen in his hand.* ○ *She had a baby with her.*
3 (*also* **have got**) If you have a particular illness, you are suffering from it: *Have you ever had the measles?*
4 to eat or drink something: *Can I have a drink of water?*
5 have a bath/sleep/walk, etc used with nouns to say that someone does something: *Can I have a quick shower?*
6 have difficulty/fun/problems, etc used with nouns to say that someone experiences something: *We had a great time in Barcelona.*
7 have a baby to give birth to a baby

hawk /hɔːk/ *noun*
a large bird that kills small animals for food

hay /heɪ/ *noun* **[no plural]**
dried grass for animals to eat

hazard /ˈhæzəd/ *noun*
something that is dangerous: *a fire hazard* ○ *a health hazard*

hazardous /ˈhæzədəs/ *adj*
dangerous: *hazardous chemicals*

haze /heɪz/ *noun* **[no plural]**
smoke or water in the air, making it difficult to see: *There was a haze over the horizon.*

hazy /ˈheɪzi/ *adj* **(hazier, haziest)**
If the air is hazy, it is not clear: *a hazy day*

he *strong form* /hiː/ *weak form* /hi/ *pronoun*
used when talking about a man or male animal who has already been talked about: *"When is Paul coming?" "He should be here soon."*

head /hed/ *noun*
1 the part of your body which contains your brain, eyes, ears, mouth, nose, etc: *He fell and hit his head on the table.*
2 your mind: *All these thoughts were going round in my head.*
3 the person who is in charge of an organization: *Her father is the head of an oil company.*
4 (*also* ˌ**head** ˈ**teacher**) *UK* the person in charge of a school
5 the front or top part of something: *Who is that at the head of the table?*
6 come to a head If a problem comes to a head, it becomes very bad.
7 go over someone's head to be too difficult for someone to understand: *All this talk about philosophy went right over my head.*

headache /ˈhedeɪk/ *noun*
pain inside your head: *I've got a bad headache.*

heading /ˈhedɪŋ/ *noun*
words at the top of a piece of writing that tell you its subject

headlight /ˈhedlaɪt/ *noun*
one of the two large lights on the front of a car

headline /ˈhedlaɪn/ *noun*
the title of a newspaper story that is printed in large letters above it: *a front-page headline*

headmaster /ˌhedˈmɑːstəʳ/ *UK* (*US* **principal**) *noun*
a man who is in charge of a school

headmistress /ˌhedˈmɪstrəs/ *UK* (*US* **principal**) *noun* (*plural* **headmistresses**)
a woman who is in charge of a school

headphones /ˈhedfəunz/ *plural noun*
a piece of equipment that you wear over your ears so that you can listen to music: *a pair of headphones*

headphones

headquarters /ˈhedˌkwɔːtəz/ *plural noun*
the place from where an organization is controlled: *police headquarters*

headteacher /ˌhedˈtiːtʃəʳ/ *UK* (*US*

a b c d e f g **h** i j k l m n o p q r s t u v w x y z

a b c d e f g h i j k l m n o p q r s t u v w x y z

principal) *noun*
the person in charge of a school

heal /hiːl/ (*also* **heal up**) *verb*
If an injury heals, it becomes healthy again, and if something heals it, it makes it healthy again: *The wound on his head had begun to heal.*

health /helθ/ *noun* **[no plural]**
the condition of your body: *Her health is very poor.*

healthy /ˈhelθi/ *adj* **(healthier, healthiest)**
1 not ill: *Maria is a normal healthy child.*
2 good for your health: *a healthy diet*

heap /hiːp/ *noun*
an untidy pile of things: *a heap of rubbish*

hear /hɪəʳ/ *verb* (*present participle* **hearing**, *past* **heard)**
1 to be aware of a sound through your ears: *I could hear his voice in the distance.*
2 to be told some information: *When did you first **hear about** this?* ○ *Have you heard the news?*
hear from someone *phrasal verb*
to get a letter, telephone call, or other message from someone: *Have you heard from Helena recently?*

hearing /ˈhɪərɪŋ/ *noun* **[no plural]**
the ability to hear sounds: *He lost his hearing when he was a child.*

heart

heart /hɑːt/ *noun*
1 the thing inside your chest that sends blood around your body: *My heart was beating fast.*
2 the centre of something: *Her office is **in the heart of** Tokyo.*
3 someone's deepest feelings and true character: *She has a kind heart.*
4 a shape that is used to mean love
5 with all your heart used to say that you feel something very strongly: *I thank you with all my heart.*
6 break someone's heart to make someone very unhappy

heartache /ˈhɑːteɪk/ *noun* **[no plural]**
extreme sadness

heartbeat /ˈhɑːtbiːt/ *noun*
the regular movement of the heart as it moves blood around the body

heartbroken /ˈhɑːtˌbrəʊkᵊn/ *adj*
very sad because someone who you loved has stopped loving you

heartless /ˈhɑːtləs/ *adj*
cruel and not caring about other people

heat¹ /hiːt/ *noun*
1 [no plural] the quality of being hot or warm: *the heat of summer*
2 the heat when it is very hot: *I don't really like the heat.*
3 the temperature of something: *Cook on a low heat.*
4 a competition, especially a race, which decides who will be in the final event

heat² /hiːt/ (*also* **heat up)** *verb*
to make something become hot or warm: *I'll just heat up some soup.*

heater /ˈhiːtəʳ/ *noun*
a machine that heats air or water

heating /ˈhiːtɪŋ/ *UK* (*US* **heat)** *noun* **[no plural]**
the system that keeps a building warm

heaven /ˈhevᵊn/ *noun* **[no plural]**
the place where some people think good people go when they die
➲Compare **hell**

heavy /ˈhevi/ *adj* **(heavier, heaviest)**
1 Heavy objects weigh a lot: *heavy bags* ➲Opposite **light**
2 used to say how much someone or something weighs: *How heavy are you?*
3 large in amount or degree: *heavy traffic*
4 a heavy drinker/smoker someone who drinks/smokes a lot
5 heavy snow/rain when a lot of snow/rain falls

heavy metal /ˌhevi ˈmetl/ *noun* **[no plural]**
a type of very loud, modern music

hectare /ˈhekteəʳ/ *noun*

a unit for measuring area, equal to 10,000 square metres

hectic /ˈhektɪk/ *adj*
very busy and full of activity: *I've had a very hectic day.*

he'd /hiːd/
1 *short for* he had: *We knew he'd taken the money.*
2 *short for* he would: *No one thought he'd get the job.*

hedge /hedʒ/ *noun*
a row of bushes growing close together

hedge

heel /hiːl/ *noun*
1 the back part of your foot
2 the part of a shoe that is under your heel: *high heels*

height /haɪt/ *noun*
1 how tall or high something or someone is: *The tower measures 27.28 metres* ***in height****.*
2 how far above the ground something is: *The aircraft was flying at a height of about 6000 metres.*

heir /eəʳ/ *noun*
a person who will get someone's money and things when that person dies: *He is the* ***heir to*** *a huge fortune.*

held /held/
past of hold

helicopter

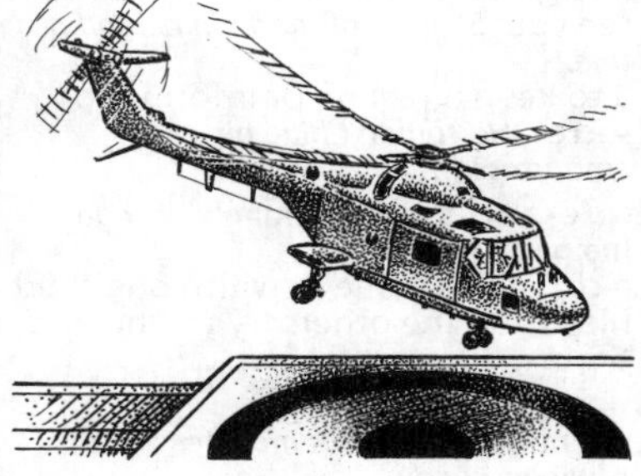

helicopter /ˈhelɪkɒptəʳ/ *noun*
an aeroplane which flies using long, thin parts on top of it that turn round and round very fast

he'll /hiːl/
short for he will: *He'll be home soon.*

hell /hel/ *noun* **[no plural]**
1 the place where some people think bad people go when they die
➲Compare **heaven**
2 *informal* an experience that is very bad: *It's been hell working with him.*
3 from hell *informal* used to say that someone or something is very bad: *We had the holiday from hell.*

hello /helˈəʊ/ *exclamation*
1 said when you meet someone or start talking with someone: *Hello, Christina, how are you?*
2 used when you start speaking on the telephone: *Hello, this is Alex.*

helmet /ˈhelmət/ *noun*
a hard hat that protects your head: *a cycling helmet*

helmet

help¹ /help/ *verb*
1 to do something for someone: *Thank you for helping.* ○ *Dad always* ***helps*** *me* ***with*** *my homework.*
2 can't/couldn't help something to not be able to stop doing something: *I couldn't help laughing.*
3 help yourself to something to take something, especially food or drink, without asking: *Please help yourself to some coffee.*

help² /help/ *noun*
1 [no plural] when someone does something for another person: *Do you want any help?*
2 something or someone that makes things easier for you: *Dave has been a great help to me.*

helpful /ˈhelpfᵊl/ *adj*
1 useful: *helpful advice*
2 willing to help: *The staff here are very helpful.* ➲Opposite **unhelpful**

helping /ˈhelpɪŋ/ *noun*
an amount of food given to one person at one time: *She gave me a very large helping of pasta.*

helpless /ˈhelpləs/ *adj*
not able to do things for yourself or protect yourself: *a helpless animal/child*

hem /hem/ *noun*
the edge of a piece of clothing or cloth that has been folded under and sewn

hen /hen/ *noun*
a female bird, especially a chicken

her¹ *strong form* /hɜːʳ/ *weak forms* /həʳ, əʳ/ *pronoun*
used to mean a woman or girl who you have already talked about: *Where's Kath – have you seen her?*

her² *strong form* /hɜːʳ/ *weak form* /həʳ/ *determiner*
belonging to a woman or girl who you have already talked about: *That's her house on the corner.* ○ *It's not her fault.*

herb /hɜːb/ *noun*
a plant that is used in cooking to add flavour to food

herd¹ /hɜːd/ *noun*
a large group of animals such as cows that live and eat together: *a herd of cattle/deer*

herd² /hɜːd/ *verb*
to move a group of people or animals somewhere: *The passengers were quickly herded onto a bus.*

here /hɪəʳ/ *adv*
1 in the place where you are: *Does Lucy live near here?* ○ *Come here!*
2 Here you are. used when you are giving someone something: *"Have you got the paper?" "Here you are."*
3 used when saying who you are on the telephone: *Hello, it's Tim here.*
4 here and there in many different places: *Tall trees were growing here and there.*

hero /ˈhɪərəʊ/ *noun* (*plural* **heroes**)
1 a very brave man that a lot of people admire: *He became a national hero for his part in the revolution.*
2 the main man in a book or film: *the hero of her new novel*

heroic /hɪˈrəʊɪk/ *adj*
very brave: *a heroic figure*

heroine /ˈherəʊɪn/ *noun*
1 a very brave woman that a lot of people admire
2 the main woman in a book or film: *the heroine of the film 'Alien'*

hers /hɜːz/ *pronoun*
the things that belong to a woman or girl: *That's Sara's coat over there – at least I think it's hers.*

herself /həˈself/ *pronoun*
1 used to show that the woman or girl who does the action is also the person who is affected by it: *She looked at herself in the mirror.*
2 used to show that a particular woman or girl did something: *She decorated the cake herself.*
3 by herself alone or without anyone else's help: *She mended the bike by herself.*

he's /hiːz/
1 *short for* he is: *He's my best friend.*
2 *short for* he has: *Sam must be tired – he's been dancing all night!*

hesitate /ˈhezɪteɪt/ *verb* (*present participle* **hesitating**, *past* **hesitated**)
to stop before you do something, especially because you are not sure: *Richard hesitated before answering.*

hesitation /ˌhezɪˈteɪʃᵊn/ *noun*
when you stop before you do something, especially because you are not sure: *After a moment's hesitation, he unlocked the door.*

hi /haɪ/ *exclamation, informal*
hello: *Hi! How are you?*

hibernate /ˈhaɪbəneɪt/ *verb* (*present participle* **hibernating**, *past* **hibernated**)
If an animal hibernates, it goes to sleep for the winter.

hiccups /ˈhɪkʌps/ *plural noun*
sudden noises you make in your throat when a muscle in your chest moves suddenly: *I **got hiccups** from drinking too quickly.*

hide /haɪd/ *verb* (*present participle* **hiding**, *past tense* **hid**, *past participle* **hidden**)
1 to put something in a place where no one can see it: *I hid the money in a drawer.*
2 to go to a place where no one can see you: *She ran off and hid behind a tree.*
3 to keep a feeling or information secret: *He couldn't hide his embarrassment.*

hide-and-seek /ˌhaɪdənˈsiːk/ *noun* **[no plural]**
a children's game in which one child hides and the others try to find them

hideous /ˈhɪdiəs/ *adj*
very ugly: *a hideous monster*
• **hideously** *adv*

hi-fi /ˈhaɪfaɪ/ *noun*
equipment for playing music, consisting of a CD player, radio, etc

high /haɪ/ *adj*
1 having a large distance from the bottom to the top: *a high building/*

mountain ➲Opposite **low**
2 a large distance above the ground or the level of the sea: *The village was **high up** in the mountains.*
3 used to say how big the distance is from the top of something to the bottom: *How high is it?* ○ *It's ten metres high.*
4 great in amount or level: *a high temperature* ○ *high prices* ➲Opposite **low**
5 A high sound or note is near the top of the set of sounds that people can hear. ➲Opposite **low**

higher education /ˌhaɪər edjʊ-ˈkeɪʃn/ *noun* **[no plural]**
education at a college or university

highly /ˈhaɪli/ *adv*
very: *It is a highly effective treatment.*

Highness /ˈhaɪnəs/ *noun* (*plural* **highnesses**)
Her/His/Your Highness used when you are speaking to or about a royal person: *Thank you, Your Highness.*

high school /ˈhaɪ skuːl/ *noun*
a school in the US which children go to between the ages of 14 and 18

high street /ˈhaɪ striːt/ *noun UK*
the main road in the centre of a town where there are shops

highway /ˈhaɪweɪ/ *noun US*
a main road, especially between two cities

hijack /ˈhaɪdʒæk/ *verb*
to take control of an aeroplane during a journey, especially using violence: *The plane was hijacked by terrorists.*
• **hijacker** /haɪdʒækəʳ/ *noun*

hill /hɪl/ *noun*
a high area of land that is smaller than a mountain: *They climbed up the hill to get a better view.*

him /hɪm/ *pronoun*
used to mean a man or boy who you have already talked about: *I'm looking for Al – Have you seen him?*

himself /hɪmˈself/ *pronoun*
1 used to show that the man or boy who does the action is also the person who is affected by it: *John always cuts himself when he's shaving.*
2 used to show that a particular man or boy did something: *He made the bookcase himself.*
3 by himself alone or without anyone else's help: *My three-year-old son can tie his shoe-laces by himself.*

hinder /ˈhɪndəʳ/ *verb*
to make it difficult to do something: *Our progress was hindered by bad weather.*

Hindu /ˈhɪnduː/ *noun*
someone who believes in Hinduism
• **Hindu** *adj*: *a Hindu temple*

Hinduism /ˈhɪnduːɪzᵊm/ *noun* **[no plural]**
the main religion of India

hinge /ˈhɪndʒ/ *noun*
a metal fastening that joins the edge of a door or window and allows you to open or close it

hint[1] /hɪnt/ *noun*
1 when you say something that suggests what you think or want, but not in a direct way: *He **dropped*** (= made) *several **hints** that he wanted a CD player for his birthday.*
2 a small piece of advice: *The magazine gives lots of useful hints on how to save money.*

hint[2] /hɪnt/ *verb*
to suggest something, but not in a direct way: *He **hinted that** he wanted to leave the company.*

hip /hɪp/ *noun*
one of the two parts of your body above your leg and below your waist ➲See colour picture **The Body** on page Centre 2

hippopotamus /ˌhɪpəˈpɒtəməs/ *noun* (*plural* **hippopotamuses**)
a very large animal with a thick skin that lives near water in parts of Africa

hire[1] /haɪəʳ/ *verb* (*present participle* **hiring**, *past* **hired**) *UK*
to pay money in order to use something for a short time: *They hired a car for a few weeks.*

hire[2] /haɪəʳ/ *noun* **[no plural]** *UK*
when you arrange to use something by paying for it: *Do you have bikes **for hire**?*

his[1] *strong form* /hɪz/ *weak form* /ɪz/ *determiner*
belonging to a man or boy who you have already talked about: *Phillip is sitting over there with his daughter.* ○ *It's not his fault.*

his[2] /hɪz/ *pronoun*
the things that belong to a man or boy: *That's Bruno's coat over there – at*

least I think it's his.

hiss /hɪs/ *verb*
to make a long noise like the letter 's': *The gas hissed through the pipes.*

historian /hɪˈstɔːriən/ *noun*
someone who studies or writes about history

historic /hɪˈstɒrɪk/ *adj*
important in history: *historic buildings* ○ *a historic day*

historical /hɪˈstɒrɪkᵊl/ *adj*
relating to the past: *historical documents*

history /ˈhɪstᵊri/ *noun* **[no plural]**
1 events that happened in the past: *American history*
2 the study of events in the past: *a history book*

hit¹ /hɪt/ *verb* (*present participle* **hitting**, *past* **hit**)
to touch something quickly and with force, usually hurting or damaging something: *She hit him on the head with her tennis racket.* ○ *As she fell, she hit her head on the pavement.*
2 hit it off *informal* If people hit it off, they like each other immediately.

hit² /hɪt/ *noun*
1 a very successful song, film, book, etc: *The film 'Titanic' was a big hit.*
2 when you touch something or when something touches you quickly and with force
3 a request to see a document on the Internet that is then counted to find the number of people looking at the page

hitchhike /ˈhɪtʃhaɪk/ *verb* (*present participle* **hitchhiking**, *past* **hitchhiked**)
to get free rides in other people's cars by waiting next to the road

• **hitchhiker** /ˈhitʃhaɪkəʳ/ *noun*

HIV /ˌeɪtʃaɪˈviː/ *noun* **[no plural]**
a virus which causes AIDS (= a serious disease that destroys the body's ability to fight infection)

hive /haɪv/ *noun* (*also* **beehive**)
a special container where people keep bees

hoard /hɔːd/ *verb*
to collect a lot of something, often secretly: *He hoarded antique books in the attic.*
• **hoard** *noun*
a lot of something that someone keeps secretly: *Police found a* ***hoard of*** *stolen jewellery in the car.*

hoarse /hɔːs/ *adj*
If you are hoarse, your voice sounds rough, often because you are ill: *I was hoarse from shouting.*

hobby /ˈhɒbi/ *noun* (*plural* **hobbies**)
an activity that you like and often do when you are not working: *Do you have any hobbies?*

hockey /ˈhɒki/ *noun* **[no plural]**
a game which two teams play in which a small ball is hit with a long stick

hold¹ /həʊld/ *verb* (*present participle* **holding**, *past* **held**)
1 to have something in your hand or arms: *He was holding a glass of wine.* ○ *She held the baby in her arms.*
2 to keep something in a particular position: *Can you hold the door open please?* ○ *Hold your hand up if you know the answer.*
3 to organize an event: *They are holding an election.*
4 to contain something: *The bucket holds about 10 litres.*
5 Hold it! *informal* used to tell someone to wait: *Hold it! I've forgotten my coat.*
6 hold your breath to stop breathing for a time

hold on *phrasal verb informal*
to wait: *Hold on! I'll just check my diary.*

hold something/someone up *phrasal verb*
to make something or someone slow or late: *Sorry I'm late. I got held up in traffic.*

hold² /həʊld/ *noun*
1 when you have something in your hand: *Keep a tight hold on your tickets.*
2 catch/grab, etc hold of something/someone to start holding something or someone: *He tried to escape, but I grabbed hold of his jacket.*
3 get hold of something/someone to get something: *I got hold of a copy at the local library.*
4 an area on an aeroplane or ship for storing things: *a cargo hold*

hold-up /ˈhəʊldʌp/ *noun UK*
1 something that makes you move slowly or makes you late: *There were several hold-ups on the motorway.*
2 when someone steals money from a bank, shop, or car, etc. using force

hole /həʊl/ *noun*
a hollow space in something, or an opening in something: *There's a* ***hole in*** *the roof.* ○ *We dug a hole to plant the tree.*

holiday /ˈhɒlədeɪ/ *noun UK* (*US* **vacation**)
1 a time when you do not have to go to work or school: *the school holidays*
2 a long visit to a place away from where you live, for pleasure: *a skiing holiday* ○ *Are you* ***going on holiday*** *this year?*

hollow /ˈhɒləʊ/ *adj*
having a hole or empty space inside: *a hollow shell/tube* ⊃Opposite **solid**

holy /ˈhəʊli/ *adj*
1 relating to a religion or a god: *the holy city of Jerusalem*
2 very religious or pure: *a holy man*

home[1] /həʊm/ *noun*
1 the place where you live: *He wasn't* ***at home****.*
2 a place where people who need special care live: *an old people's home*
3 feel at home to feel happy and confident in a place or situation: *After a month she felt at home in her new job.*

home[2] /həʊm/ *adv*
to the place where you live: *He didn't* ***come home*** *until midnight.* ○ *I* ***went home*** *to visit my parents.*

home[3] /həʊm/ *adj*
1 home address/phone number, etc an address/telephone number, etc for the place where someone lives
2 made or used in the place where someone lives: *home cooking* ○ *a home computer*

homeless /ˈhəʊmləs/ *adj*
without a place to live: *10,000 people were made homeless by the floods.*

homemade /ˌhəʊmˈmeɪd/ *adj*
made at home and not bought from a shop: *homemade bread*

homesick /ˈhəʊmsɪk/ *adj*
feeling sad because you are away from your home

homework /ˈhəʊmwɜːk/ *noun* **[no plural]**
work which teachers give students to do at home: *Have you* ***done*** *your* ***homework*** *yet?*

honest /ˈɒnɪst/ *adj*
1 sincere and not lying or stealing: *What is your honest opinion?* ○ *an honest man*
2 to be honest *informal* used to say your real opinion: *To be honest, I didn't really enjoy the party.*

honestly /ˈɒnɪstli/ *adv*
1 used to say that you are telling the truth: *Thanks, but I honestly couldn't eat another piece of cake.*
2 without lying or stealing: *We have always dealt honestly with our customers.*

honesty /ˈɒnɪsti/ *noun* **[no plural]**
the quality of being honest: *I appreciate your honesty.*

honey /ˈhʌni/ *noun*
1 [no plural] a sweet, sticky food that is made by bees
2 a name that you call someone you love or like very much

honeymoon /ˈhʌnimuːn/ *noun*
a holiday for two people who have just got married: *We went to Paris* ***on*** *our* ***honeymoon****.*

honour *UK* (*US* **honor**) /ˈɒnə^r/ *noun*
1 [no plural] qualities such as goodness, honesty and bravery that make people respect you: *a man of honour*
2 in honour of someone/something in order to show great respect for someone or something: *a banquet in honour of the President*
3 something which makes you feel proud and pleased: *I had the great* ***honour of*** *meeting the King.*

hood /hʊd/ *noun*
1 a part of a coat or jacket that covers your head and neck: *a waterproof jacket with a hood*
2 *US* (*UK* **bonnet**) the metal part that covers a car engine

hoof /huːf/ *noun* (*plural* **hooves**)
the hard part on the foot of a horse and some other large animals

hook /hʊk/ *noun*
1 a curved piece of metal or plastic used for hanging something on, or a similar object used for catching fish:

His coat was hanging from a hook on the door.
2 off the hook If a telephone is off the hook, the part you speak into is not in its correct position, so the telephone will not ring.

hooligan /ˈhuːlɪgᵊn/ *noun*
someone who behaves badly or violently and causes damage in a public place

hooray (*also* **hurrah**) /hʊˈreɪ/ *exclamation*
something that you shout when you are happy because of something that has just happened: *He's here – hooray!*

hoot[1] /huːt/ *noun*
a short sound made by an owl (= bird) or by a car horn (= warning equipment)

hoot[2] /huːt/ *verb UK*
to make a short sound with your car's horn (= part you press to make a warning noise): *The van driver hooted his horn.*

Hoover /ˈhuːvəʳ/ *UK trademark* (*UK/US* **vacuum cleaner)** *noun*
an electric machine which cleans floors by taking up dirt
• **hoover** *verb*
to use a Hoover to clean a floor

hooves /huːvz/
plural of hoof

hop[1] /hɒp/ *verb* (*present participle* **hopping**, *past* **hopped)**
1 to jump on one foot
2 If a small animal hops, it moves by jumping on all of its feet at the same time: *Rabbits were hopping across the field.*

hop[2] /hɒp/ *noun*
1 a short jump, especially on one leg
2 a short hop *informal* a short journey: *London to Paris is only a short hop by plane.*

hope[1] /həʊp/ *verb* (*present participle* **hoping**, *past* **hoped)**
1 to want something to happen or be true: *I* ***hope that*** *the bus won't be late.* ○ *We had* ***hoped for*** *better weather than this.* ○ *"Is he coming?" "I hope so."*
2 hope to do something to want to do something: *Dad hopes to retire next year.*

hope[2] /həʊp/ *noun*
1 a good feeling about the future, or something that you want to happen: *a message full of hope* ○ *What are your* ***hopes for*** *the future?*
2 a person or thing that could help you and make you succeed: *Doctors say his only hope is an operation.*
3 in the hope of/that because you want something good to happen: *She went to Paris in the hope of improving her French.*

hopeful /ˈhəʊpfᵊl/ *adj*
feeling good or confident about something in the future: *Many teenagers do not feel* ***hopeful about*** *the future.* ○ *Police are still* ***hopeful that*** *they will find the missing girl.*

hopefully /ˈhəʊpfᵊli/ *adv*
used when you are saying what you would like to happen: *Hopefully it won't rain.*

hopeless /ˈhəʊpləs/ *adj*
1 very bad and probably not going to improve: *a hopeless situation*
2 very bad at a particular activity: *I'm* ***hopeless at*** *sports.*

horizon /həˈraɪzᵊn/ *noun*
the line in the distance where the sky and the land or sea seem to meet

horizontal/vertical

horizontal stripes
vertical stripes

horizontal /ˌhɒrɪˈzɒntᵊl/ *adj*
level and flat, or parallel to the ground: *a horizontal line* ➲Compare **vertical**

hormone /ˈhɔːməʊn/ *noun*
one of many chemicals made in your body that make the body grow and develop

horn /hɔːn/ *noun*
1 one of the two long, hard things on the heads of cows, goats, and some other animals

2 a piece of equipment used to make a loud sound as a warning: *a car horn*
3 a musical instrument that you blow into to make a sound

horrible /ˈhɒrəbl/ *adj*
very unpleasant or bad: *What's that horrible smell?*

horrific /hɒrˈɪfɪk/ *adj*
very bad and shocking: *a horrific crime* ○ *horrific injuries*

horrify /ˈhɒrɪfaɪ/ *verb* (*present participle* **horrifying,** *past* **horrified)**
to make someone feel very shocked: *I was horrified to hear about her accident.*

horror /ˈhɒrəʳ/ *noun* **[no plural]**
a strong feeling of shock or fear: *She watched* ***in horror*** *as the car skidded across the road.*

horse /hɔːs/ *noun*
a large animal with four legs, which people ride or use to pull heavy things

horseback /ˈhɔːsbæk/ *noun*
on horseback riding a horse: *police on horseback*

horse riding /ˈhɔːs ˌraɪdɪŋ/ *UK noun* **[no plural]**
the sport or activity of riding a horse

horseshoe /ˈhɔːsʃuː/ *noun*
a U-shaped piece of metal on a horse's foot

hose /həʊz/ *noun*
a long pipe made of plastic and used for putting water somewhere, usually onto a garden or fire

hospitable /hɒsˈpɪtəbl/ *adj*
A hospitable person or place is friendly and pleasant for people who visit.

hospital /ˈhɒspɪtəl/ *noun*
a place where ill or injured people go to be treated by doctors and nurses: *He was* ***in hospital*** *for two weeks.*

host /həʊst/ *noun*
someone who is having a party

hostage /ˈhɒstɪdʒ/ *noun*
someone who is kept as a prisoner and may be hurt or killed in order to make other people do something

hostel /ˈhɒstəl/ *noun*
a cheap hotel, where you can live when you are away from home: *a student hostel*

hostess /ˈhəʊstɪs/ *noun* (*plural* **hostesses)**
a woman who is having a party

hostile /ˈhɒstaɪl/ *adj*
not friendly and not liking or agreeing with something: *Some politicians were very* ***hostile to*** *the idea.*

hot /hɒt/ *adj* **(hotter, hottest)**
1 very warm: *a hot summer's day* ○ *a hot drink* ○ *I'm too hot in this jacket.* ⊃Opposite **cold**
2 Hot food contains strong spices which cause a burning feeling in your mouth: *The sauce is very hot – be careful!* ⊃Opposite **mild**

hot dog /ˈhɒt ˌdɒg/ *noun*
a cooked sausage (= tube of meat and spices) that you usually eat inside bread

hotel /həʊˈtel/ *noun*
a place where you pay to stay when you are away from home

hour /aʊəʳ/ *noun*
1 a period of time equal to 60 minutes: *It's a six-hour flight.*
2 the period of time when a particular activity happens or when a shop etc is open: *working hours* ○ *Our opening hours are from 8 to 6.*
3 hours *informal* a long time: *I spent hours doing my homework.*
4 the hour the point when a new hour begins: *My watch beeps* ***on the hour***.

hourly /ˈaʊəli/ *adj, adv*
1 happening every hour: *There is an hourly bus service.*
2 for each hour: *an hourly rate/wage*

house /haʊs/ *noun*
a building where people live, usually one family or group: *We went to my aunt's house for dinner.*

household /ˈhaʊshəʊld/ *noun*
a family or group of people who live together in a house

housewife /ˈhaʊswaɪf/ *noun* (*plural* **housewives)**
a woman who stays at home to cook, clean, and take care of her family

housework /ˈhaʊswɜːk/ *noun* **[no plural]**
the work that you do to keep your house clean: *I can't stand* ***doing housework***.

a b c d e f g h i j k l m n o p q r s t u v w x y z

hover /ˈhɒvəʳ/ *verb*
to stay up in the air but without moving anywhere: *A helicopter hovered over us.*

how /haʊ/ *adv*
1 used to ask about the way something happens or is done: *How did he die?* ○ *How do you keep the house so tidy?*
2 used to ask about quantity, size, or age: *How big is the house?* ○ *How old are they?* ○ *How much* (= what price) *was that dress?*
3 How are you? used to ask someone if they are well and happy: *"How are you, Ellie?" – "Oh, not so bad thanks."*
4 How about..? used to make a suggestion: *How about going to the cinema?*

however /haʊˈevəʳ/ *adv*
1 however cold/difficult/slowly, etc used to say that it does not make any difference how cold/difficult/slowly, etc: *We're not going to get there in time, however fast we drive.*
2 but: *This is one solution to the problem. However, there are others.*

howl /haʊl/ *verb*
to make a long, high sound: *He **howled in** pain.*
• **howl** *noun*

huddle /ˈhʌdl/ *verb* (*present participle* **huddling**, *past* **huddled**)
to move closer to other people because you are cold or frightened: *They huddled around the fire to keep warm.*

hug[1] /hʌg/ *verb* (*present participle* **hugging**, *past* **hugged**)
to put your arms around someone and hold them, usually because you love them: *They hugged and kissed each other.*

hug

hug[2] /hʌg/ *noun*
when you put your arms around someone and hold them: *She **gave** me a big **hug** before she left.*

huge /hjuːdʒ/ *adj*
very large: *a huge house*

hugely /ˈhjuːdʒli/ *adv*
very: *The film was hugely successful.*

hullo *UK* (*UK/US* **hello**) /həˈləʊ/ *exclamation*
1 said when you meet someone or start talking with someone: *Hullo, Sabine, how are things?*
2 used when you start speaking on the telephone: *Hullo, this is Alex.*

hum /hʌm/ *verb* (*present participle* **humming**, *past* **hummed**)
1 to sing without opening your mouth: *He was humming a tune.*
2 to make a continuous, low sound: *The computers were humming in the background.*
• **hum** *noun*
a low, continuous sound: *the hum of traffic*

human[1] /ˈhjuːmən/ *adj*
relating to people: *the human body* ○ *human behaviour*

human[2] /ˈhjuːmən/ (*also* ˌ**human ˈbeing**) *noun*
a man, woman, or child: *The disease affects both humans and animals.*

humankind /ˌhjuːmənˈkaɪnd/ *noun* **[no plural]**
all the people in the world

humble /ˈhʌmbl/ *adj*
not believing that you are important: *He's very humble about his success.*

humorous /ˈhjuːmᵊrəs/ *adj*
funny, or making you laugh: *a humorous book*

humour *UK* (*US* **humor**) /ˈhjuːməʳ/ *noun* **[no plural]**
1 the ability to laugh and know that something is funny: *He's got a great **sense of humour**.*
2 things that are funny: *His speech was full of humour.*

hump /hʌmp/ *noun*
a round, hard part on an animal's or person's back: *a camel's hump*

hundred /ˈhʌndrəd/
1 the number 100
2 hundreds *informal* a lot: ***Hundreds of** people wrote in to complain.*

hundredth /ˈhʌndrədθ/
100th written as a word

hung /hʌŋ/
past of hang

hunger /ˈhʌŋgəʳ/ *noun* **[no plural]**
1 the feeling that you want to eat
2 when you do not have enough

food: *Many of the refugees **died of hunger**.*

hungry /'hʌŋgri/ *adj*
wanting or needing food: *I'm hungry. What's for dinner?*
• **hungrily** *adv*

hunt /hʌnt/ *verb*
1 to chase and kill wild animals: *They are hunting rabbits.*
2 to search for something: *The children **hunted for** sea shells on the beach.*
• **hunter** /hʌntə[r]/ *noun*
a person who hunts wild animals

hurl /hɜːl/ *verb*
to throw something with a lot of force, usually in an angry way: *They **hurled** stones **at** the police.*

hurrah (*also* **hooray**) /hə'rɑː/ *exclamation*
something that you shout when you are happy because of something that has just happened: *Hurrah! Ian's won!*

hurricane /'hʌrɪkən/ *noun*
a violent storm with very strong winds

hurry[1] /'hʌri/ *verb* (*present participle* **hurrying**, *past* **hurried**)
to move or do things quickly: *Please hurry, the train is about to leave.*
hurry up *phrasal verb*
to start moving or doing something more quickly: *Hurry up! We're going to be late.*

hurry[2] /'hʌri/ *noun*
be in a hurry If you are in a hurry, you need to do something quickly: *I was in a hurry so I took a taxi.*

hurt[1] /hɜːt/ *verb* (*present participle* **hurting**, *past* **hurt**)
1 to cause someone pain or to injure them: *Simon hurt his knee playing football.*
2 If a part of your body hurts, it is painful: *My eyes really hurt.*
3 to upset someone: *I hope I didn't hurt him with my remarks.*

hurt[2] /hɜːt/ *adj*
1 injured or in pain: *Several people were seriously hurt in the accident.*
2 upset or unhappy: *She was deeply hurt by what he said.*

husband /'hʌzbənd/ *noun*
the man you are married to

hush /hʌʃ/ *noun* **[no plural]**
a period of silence: *A hush fell over the room.*

hut /hʌt/ *noun*
a small, simple building, often made of wood: *a mountain hut*

hydrogen /'haɪdrədʒən/ *noun* **[no plural]**
a gas that combines with oxygen to form water

hymn /hɪm/ *noun*
a song sung by Christians in church

hype /haɪp/ *noun* **[no plural]**
when people talk a lot about something, especially in newspapers, etc, and make it seem more important or exciting than it really is: *media hype* ○ *There's been a lot of **hype surrounding** his latest film.*

hyphen /'haɪfən/ *noun*
a mark (-) used to join two words together, or to show that a word continues on the next line

hysterical /hɪ'sterɪkəl/ *adj*
not able to control your behaviour because you are very frightened, angry, excited, etc: *hysterical laughter* ○ *As soon as Wendy saw the blood, she became hysterical.*

I, i /aɪ/
the ninth letter of the alphabet

I /aɪ/ *pronoun*
used when the person speaking or writing is the subject of the verb: *I've bought some chocolate.* ○ *I'll see you later.*

ice /aɪs/ *noun* **[no plural]**
water that is so cold it has become solid: *Would you like ice and lemon in your drink?*

iceberg /ˈaɪsbɜːg/ *noun*
a very large piece of ice that floats in the sea

ice cream /ˌaɪs ˈkriːm/ *noun* **[no plural]**
a sweet, cold food made from frozen milk: *vanilla ice cream*

ice cream

ice cube /ˈaɪs ˌkjuːb/ *noun*
a small piece of ice that you put into a drink to make it cold

ice skate /ˈaɪs skeɪt/ *noun*
a boot with a metal part on the bottom, used for moving across ice
● **ice skating** *noun* **[no plural]**

icicle /ˈaɪsɪkl/ *noun*
a long, thin piece of ice that hangs down from something

icicles

icing /ˈaɪsɪŋ/ *noun* **[no plural]**
a sweet mixture used to cover or fill cakes

icon /ˈaɪkɒn/ *noun*
a small picture on a computer screen that you choose in order to make the computer do something: *Click on the print icon.*

icy /ˈaɪsi/ *adj*
1 covered in ice: *icy roads*
2 very cold: *an icy wind*

I'd /aɪd/
1 *short for* I had: *Everyone thought I'd gone.*
2 *short for* I would: *I'd like to buy some stamps ,please.*

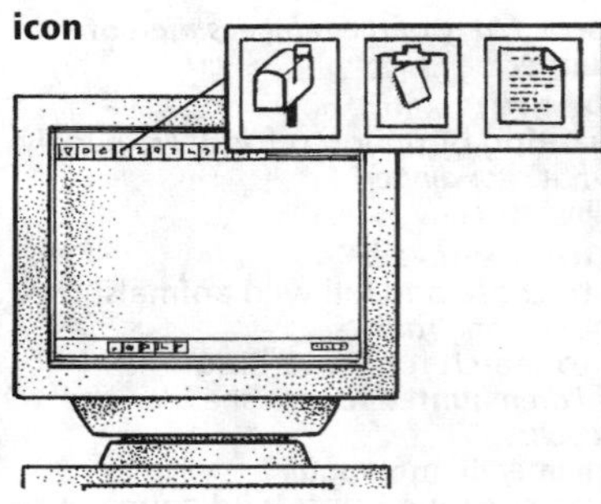

icon

idea /aɪˈdɪə/ *noun*
1 a suggestion or plan: *What a good idea!* ○ *It was Kate's idea to hire a car.*
2 an understanding, thought, or picture in your mind: *I think you've got the wrong idea about this.*

ideal /aɪˈdɪəl/ *adj*
perfect, or the best possible: *She is the ideal person for the job.*

identical /aɪˈdentɪkəl/ *adj*
exactly the same: *She found a dress* ***identical to*** *the one in the picture.*

identification /aɪˌdentɪfɪˈkeɪʃən/ *noun* **[no plural]**
an official document that shows who you are: *Do you have any identification on you?*

identify /aɪˈdentɪfaɪ/ *verb* (*present participle* **identifying,** *past* **identified)**
to say what someone's name is or what something's name is: *The victim has not yet been identified.*

identity /aɪˈdentəti/ *noun* (*plural* **identities)**
who someone is: *They kept her identity secret.*

idiom /ˈɪdiəm/ *noun*
a group of words used together with a meaning that you cannot guess

idiot /ˈɪdiət/ *noun*
a stupid person: *This idiot ran in front of my car.*
● **idiotic** /ˌɪdiˈɒtɪk/ *adj*
stupid: *an idiotic idea*

idol /ˈaɪdəl/ *noun*
1 someone that you admire and respect very much: *a pop idol*
2 a picture or object that people pray to as part of their religion

i.e. /ˌaɪˈiː/

used to explain exactly what you mean: *The price must be more realistic, i.e. lower.*

if /ɪf/ *conjunction*
1 used to say that something will happen only after something else happens or is true: *We'll have the party in the garden if the weather's good.*
2 used to talk about something that might happen or be true: *What will we do if this doesn't work?*
3 whether: *I wonder if he'll get the job.*
4 used to mean 'always' or 'every time': *If you mention his mother, he always cries.*

igloo /ˈɪgluː/ *noun*
a house made of pieces of hard snow

igloo

ignite /ɪgˈnaɪt/ *verb* (*present participle* **igniting**, *past* **ignited**) *formal*
to start to burn or make something start to burn: *The oil was accidentally ignited.*

ignorance /ˈɪgnᵊrᵊns/ *noun* **[no plural]**
when someone does not know enough about something: *I was shocked by her ignorance of the subject.*

ignorant /ˈɪgnᵊrᵊnt/ *adj*
not knowing enough about something: *She's completely* ***ignorant about*** *computers.*

ignore /ɪgˈnɔːʳ/ *verb* (*present participle* **ignoring**, *past* **ignored)**
to not give attention to something or someone: *I said hello but she ignored me.*

ill /ɪl/ *adj*
not feeling well, or suffering from a disease: *He was in bed, ill.*

I'll
short for I will: *I'll see you tomorrow.*

illegal /ɪˈliːgᵊl/ *adj*
not allowed by law: *illegal drugs* ○ *It is* ***illegal to*** *sell cigarettes to anyone under 16.* ➲Opposite **legal**
• **illegally** *adv*: *an illegally parked car*

illegible /ɪˈledʒəbl/ *adj*
Illegible writing is impossible to read. ➲Opposite **legible**

illiterate /ɪˈlɪtᵊrət/ *adj*
not able to read or write

illness /ˈɪlnəs/ *noun* (*plural* **illnesses)**
1 a disease: *He has a serious illness.*
2 [no plural] being ill: *Unfortunately I couldn't go because of illness.*

illusion /ɪˈluːʒᵊn/ *noun*
something that is not really what it seems to be: *There is a large mirror at one end to create the illusion of more space.*

illustrate /ˈɪləstreɪt/ *verb* (*present participle* **illustrating,** *past* **illustrated)**
to draw pictures for a book

illustration /ˌɪləˈstreɪʃᵊn/ *noun*
a picture in a book

I'm /aɪm/ *short for*
I am: *I'm Fiona* ○ *I'm too hot*

image /ˈɪmɪdʒ/ *noun*
1 the way that other people think someone or something is: *They want to improve the* ***public image of*** *the police.*
2 a picture, especially on film or television or in a mirror: *television images of starving children*
3 a picture in your mind: *I have an* ***image of*** *the way I want the garden to look.*

imaginary /ɪˈmædʒɪnᵊri/ *adj*
not real but imagined in your mind: *The story takes place in an imaginary world.*

imagination /ɪˌmædʒɪˈneɪʃᵊn/ *noun* **[no plural]**
the ability to have ideas or pictures in your mind: *The job needs someone with a bit of imagination.*

imagine /ɪˈmædʒɪn/ *verb* (*present participle* **imagining,** *past* **imagined)**
1 to make an idea or picture of something in your mind: *Imagine being able to do all your shopping from home.*
2 to believe that something is probably true: *I imagine he is quite difficult to live with.*

imitate /ˈɪmɪteɪt/ *verb* (*present participle* **imitating,** *past* **imitated)**
to copy someone: *He was imitating the president.*

imitation /ˌɪmɪˈteɪʃᵊn/ *noun*
a copy of something that looks like the real thing: *It wasn't a genuine*

a b c d e f g h **i** j k l m n o p q r s t u v w x y z

a b c d e f g h i j k l m n o p q r s t u v w x y z

Gucci handbag, just ***a cheap imitation****.*

immature /ˌɪmə'tjʊəʳ/ *adj* behaving like a younger person: *Some of the boys are quite immature for their age.*

immediate /ɪ'miːdiət/ *adj* happening now or very soon after something else: *The drugs had an immediate effect.*

immediately /ɪ'miːdiətli/ *adv* now, without waiting: *She asked him to come home immediately.*

immense /ɪ'mens/ *adj* very big: *He won an immense amount of money.*

immensely /ɪ'mensli/ *adv* very: *He was immensely popular.*

immigrant /'ɪmɪgrənt/ *noun* someone who comes to live in a different country

immigration /ˌɪmɪ'greɪʃᵊn/ *noun* **[no plural]** when someone comes to live in a different country: *immigration policy*
• **immigrate** /'ɪmɪgreɪt/ *verb* (*present participle* **immigrating,** *past* **immigrated)** to come to live in a different country

immune /ɪ'mjuːn/ *adj* If you are immune to a disease, you will not get it: *Once you've had the virus, you are* ***immune to*** *it.*

immunize /'ɪmjənaɪz/ *verb* (*present participle* **immunizing,** *past* **immunized)** to stop someone from getting a disease by giving them medicine: *He was* ***immunized against*** *the disease as a child.*

impatient /ɪm'peɪʃᵊnt/ *adj* If you are impatient you get angry with people who make mistakes or you hate waiting for things: *I get very* ***impatient with*** *the children when they won't do their homework.* ➲Opposite **patient**

imperative /ɪm'perətɪv/ *adj* An imperative form of a verb is used to say an order. In the sentence 'Stop the machine!', the verb 'stop' is an imperative verb.
• **imperative** *noun* the imperative form of a verb

the imperfect /ɪm'pɜːfɪkt/ (*also* **the imˌperfect 'tense)** *noun* The form of the verb that is used to show an action in the past which has not been completed. In the sentence 'We were crossing the road', 'were crossing' is in the imperfect.

imply /ɪm'plaɪ/ *verb* (*present participle* **implying,** *past* **implied)** to suggest or show something, without saying it directly: *She* ***implied that*** *she wasn't happy at work.*

impolite /ˌɪmpᵊl'aɪt/ *adj formal* rude

import /ɪm'pɔːt/ *verb*
1 to bring something into your country for people to buy: *We import about 20 percent of our food.*
2 to copy information from one computer or computer program to another: *to import data* ➲Compare **export**
• **import** *noun* something which one country gets from another country: *Japanese imports*

importance /ɪm'pɔːtᵊns/ *noun* **[no plural]** how important someone or something is: *I'm not sure you understand* ***the importance of*** *what I'm saying.*

important /ɪm'pɔːtᵊnt/ *adj*
1 valuable, useful, or necessary: *My family is very* ***important to*** *me.*
2 having a lot of power: *an important person*

impossible /ɪm'pɒsəbl/ *adj* not able to happen: *It is impossible to work with all this noise.* ➲Opposite **possible**

impress /ɪm'pres/ *verb* to make someone admire or respect you: *I was hoping to* ***impress*** *him* ***with*** *my knowledge.*

impression /ɪm'preʃᵊn/ *noun* an idea, feeling, or opinion about something or someone: *Monica* ***gives the impression*** *of being shy.* ○ *Remember that it* ***makes a*** *bad* ***impression*** *if you're late.*

impressive /ɪm'presɪv/ *adj* Someone or something that is impressive makes you admire and respect them: *an impressive performance*

imprison /ɪm'prɪzᵊn/ *verb* to put someone in prison: *Taylor was imprisoned in 1969 for burglary.*

improve /ɪm'pruːv/ *verb* (*present*

participle **improving**, *past* **improved**) to get better or to make something better: *Scott's behaviour has improved a lot lately.*

improvement /ɪmˈpruːvmənt/ *noun* when something gets better or when you make it better: *home improvements* ○ *There's been a big* ***improvement in*** *her work this term.*

impulse /ˈɪmpʌls/ *noun* a sudden feeling that you must do something: *Her first impulse was to run away.*

impulsive /ɪmˈpʌlsɪv/ *adj* doing things suddenly, without planning or thinking carefully: *It was an impulsive response*

in[1] /ɪn/ *preposition*
1 inside a container or place: *a shop in South London* ○ *He put his hand in his pocket.*
2 during a period of time: *We're going to Italy in April.*
3 involved in a particular type of job: *He wants a career in politics.*
4 connected with a particular subject: *advances in medical science*
5 wearing: *Do you know that man in the grey suit?*
6 arranged in a particular way: *Is this list in alphabetical order?*

in[2] /ɪn/ *adv*
1 into an area or space from the outside of it: *She took off her shoes and socks and jumped in.*
2 at the place where a person usually lives or works: *I phoned, but she wasn't in.*
3 If a train, plane, etc is in, it has arrived at the place it was going to: *My train gets in at 17.54.*

inaccurate /ɪnˈækjərət/ *adj* not correct or exact: *inaccurate information* ➲Opposite **accurate**

inadequate /ɪˈnædɪkwət/ *adj* not enough or not good enough: *Her skills were* ***inadequate for*** *the job.* ➲Opposite **adequate**

inappropriate /ˌɪnəˈprəupriət/ *adj* not suitable: *inappropriate behaviour* ➲Opposite **appropriate**

incapable *adj* not able to do something: *I think he is* ***incapable of*** *listening.* ➲Opposite **capable**

inch /ɪnʃ/ *noun* (*plural* **inches**) a unit for measuring length, equal to 2.54 centimetres

incident /ˈɪnsɪdənt/ *noun formal* something that happens, especially something bad: *Police are investigating the incident.*

incidentally /ɪnsɪˈdentəli/ *adv* used when you say something that is not as important as the main thing that you are talking about but is connected to it: *Incidentally, talking of Stephen, have you met his girlfriend?*

inclined /ɪnˈklaɪnd/ *adj* **inclined to do something** often behaving in a particular way: *Tom is inclined to be forgetful.*

include /ɪnˈkluːd/ *verb* (*present participle* **including**, *past* **included**)
1 to have something or someone as part of something larger: *The price includes flights and three nights' accommodation.*
2 to allow someone to take part in an activity: *Local residents were* ***included in*** *the planning discussions.* ➲Opposite **exclude**

including /ɪnˈkluːdɪŋ/ *preposition* used to show that someone or something is part of something larger: *It's £24.99, including postage and packing.* ➲Opposite **excluding**

income /ˈɪŋkʌm/ *noun* the money that you regularly get, for example from your job: *Many families are on low incomes.*

income tax /ˈiŋkʌm ˌtæks/ *noun* **[no plural]** money that the government take from the money that you earn

incomplete /ˌɪnkəmˈpliːt/ *adj* not finished, or with parts missing: *The building is still incomplete.* ➲Opposite **complete**

inconsiderate /ˌɪnkənˈsɪdərət/ *adj* not caring when you make problems for other people: *He shouldn't keep us waiting like this – it's very inconsiderate.* ➲Opposite **considerate**

inconvenience /ˌɪnkənˈviːniəns/ *noun* problems: *I apologize for any inconvenience caused.*

inconvenient /ˌɪnkənˈviːniənt/ *adj* causing problems: *It is very inconvenient living so far away from the shops.* ➲Opposite **convenient**

a b c d e f g h i j k l m n o p q r s t u v w x y z

incorrect /ˌɪnkəˈrekt/ *adj*
wrong: *His answers were incorrect.* ⊃Opposite **correct**
• **incorrectly** *adv*: *My name was spelled incorrectly.*

increase¹ /ɪnˈkriːs/ *verb* (*present participle* **increasing**, *past* **increased**)
to get bigger or to make something bigger: *Smoking increases the risk of serious illnesses.* ○ *Sales of computers have* ***increased by*** *15% since January.* ⊃Opposite **decrease**

increase² /ˈɪnkriːs/ *noun*
when the number or size of something gets bigger: *a price increase* ○ *We are seeing* ***an increase in*** *standards of living.* ⊃Opposite **decrease**

increasingly /ɪnˈkriːsɪŋli/ *adv*
more and more: *The sport is becoming increasingly popular.*

incredible /ɪnˈkredɪbl/ *adj*
1 *informal* very good and exciting: *The city itself is incredible.*
2 very large in amount or high in level: *She earned an incredible amount of money.* ○ *The planes make an incredible noise.*
3 If a fact is incredible, it is so strange that you cannot believe it: *It seems incredible that she didn't know what was happening.*
• **incredibly** *adv*
very: *The team played incredibly well.*

indeed /ɪnˈdiːd/ *adv*
1 used to make the word 'very' stronger: *Many people are very poor indeed.*
2 used when saying that something is correct: *"Is this your dog?." "It is indeed."*

indefinite /ɪnˈdefɪnət/ *adj*
with no definite end: *He will be staying here for an indefinite period.*

indefinite article /ɪnˌdefɪnət ˈɑːtɪkl/ *noun*
in grammar, a phrase used to mean the words 'a' or 'an'

independence /ˌɪndɪˈpendəns/ *noun* **[no plural]**
1 when someone looks after themselves and does not need help from other people: *Teenagers need a certain amount of independence.*
2 when a country has its own government and is not ruled by another country: *Mexico gained its independence from Spain in 1821.*

independent /ˌɪndɪˈpendənt/ *adj*
1 not controlled or ruled by anyone else: *an independent state*
2 not wanting or needing anyone else to help you: *She's a very independent four-year-old.* ⊃Opposite **dependent**

index /ˈɪndeks/ *noun* (*plural* **indexes**) a list of subjects or names at the end of a book, showing on what page in the book you can find them

indicate /ˈɪndɪkeɪt/ *verb* (*present participle* **indicating**, *past* **indicated**)
1 to show that something exists or is true: *Recent evidence* ***indicates that*** *the skeleton is about 3 million years old.*
2 to point to someone or something: *He indicated a man in a dark coat.*
3 *UK* to show that you are going to turn left or right when you are driving: *The driver turned right without indicating.*

indication /ˌɪndɪˈkeɪʃən/ *noun*
a sign showing that something exists or is true: *She* ***gave*** *no* ***indication that*** *she was unhappy.*

indicator /ˈɪndɪkeɪtər/ *noun UK*
a light that flashes on a car to show that the driver is turning right or left

indigestion /ˌɪndɪˈdʒestʃən/ *noun* **[no plural]**
when your stomach hurts after you have eaten something

indignant /ɪnˈdɪgnənt/ *adj*
angry because of something that is wrong or not fair: *He was very indignant when I suggested that he had made a mistake.*

indirect /ˌɪndɪˈrekt/ *adj*
connected with something, but not directly: *Her health problems are an indirect result of her job.* ⊃Opposite **direct**

individual¹ /ˌɪndɪˈvɪdʒuəl/ *adj*
1 considered separately from other things in a group: *Read out the individual letters of each word.*
2 relating to one particular person or thing: *He gets more individual attention from his teacher.*
• **individually** *adv*
separately and not as a group: *Ask the students to work individually.*

individual² /ˌɪndɪˈvɪdʒuəl/ *noun*
a person, especially when

considered separately and not as part of a group: *We try to treat our students as individuals.*

indoor /ˌɪnˈdɔːʳ/ *adj* in a building: *an indoor swimming pool* ➲Opposite **outdoor**

indoors /ˌɪnˈdɔːz/ *adv* into or inside a building: *If you're feeling cold, we can go indoors.* ➲Opposite **outdoors**

industrial /ɪnˈdʌstriəl/ *adj* connected with industry: *an industrial city*

industry /ˈɪndəstri/ *noun*
1 **[no plural]** the making of things in factories
2 (*plural* **industries**) all the companies involved in a particular type of business: *the entertainment industry*

inefficient /ˌɪnɪˈfɪʃᵊnt/ *adj* Inefficient people or things waste time, money, or effort, and do not do things as well as they should: *an inefficient heating system* ➲Opposite **efficient**

inevitable /ɪˈnevɪtəbl/ *adj* If something is inevitable, you cannot avoid or stop it: *It was **inevitable that** his crime would be discovered.*
• **inevitably** *adv*: *Inevitably, there was a certain amount of fighting between the groups.*

inexperienced /ˌɪnɪkˈspɪəriənst/ *adj* not having done something often: *Kennedy was young and inexperienced.* ➲Opposite **experienced**

infant /ˈɪnfənt/ *noun formal* a baby or very young child

infect /ɪnˈfekt/ *verb* to give someone a disease: *Thousands of people were infected with the virus.*

infection /ɪnˈfekʃᵊn/ *noun* a disease that is caused by bacteria or a virus: *a throat infection*
• **infectious** *adj* An infectious disease can be given by one person to another.

inferior /ɪnˈfɪəriəʳ/ *adj* not as good as someone or something else: *These are inferior products.* ➲Opposite **superior**

infinite /ˈɪnfɪnət/ *adj* very large or without limits: *God's power is infinite.*

infinitely /ˈɪnfɪnətli/ *adv* very or very much: *The book was infinitely better than the film.*

infinitive /ɪnˈfɪnətɪv/ *noun* the basic form of a verb that usually follows 'to'. In the sentence 'She decided to leave.', 'to leave' is an infinitive.

inflammable /ɪnˈflæməbl/ *adj* Something that is inflammable burns very easily.

inflate /ɪnˈfleɪt/ *verb* (*present participle* **inflating,** *past* **inflated)** to fill something with air or gas: *Inflate the tyres.*

inflation /ɪnˈfleɪʃᵊn/ *noun* **[no plural]** the rate at which prices increase, or an increase in prices: *rising inflation*

influence¹ /ˈɪnfluəns/ *noun*
1 the power to change people or things: *The drug companies have a lot of **influence on** doctors.*
2 someone or something that changes another person or thing: *Her father was a big **influence on** her.*

influence² /ˈɪnfluəns/ *verb* (*present participle* **influencing,** *past* **influenced)** to change the way that someone thinks or the way that something develops: *Were you influenced by anybody when you were starting your career?*

influential /ˌɪnfluˈenʃᵊl/ *adj* having the power to change people or things: *an influential figure in modern jazz*

inform /ɪnˈfɔːm/ *verb* to tell someone about something: *He **informed** us **that** we would have to leave.* ○ *Patients should be **informed about** the risks.*

informal /ɪnˈfɔːmᵊl/ *adj*
1 relaxed and friendly: *an informal meeting*
2 suitable for normal situations: *informal clothes* ○ *informal language* ➲Opposite **formal**
• **informally** *adv*: *We chatted informally* (= in a relaxed, friendly way) *before the interview.*

information /ˌɪnfəˈmeɪʃᵊn/ *noun* **[no plural]** facts about a situation, person, event, etc: *Do you have any **information about** local schools?* ○ *This was an important **piece of information**.*

informative /ɪnˈfɔːmətɪv/ *adj*
having a lot of useful facts: *a very informative book*

ingredient /ɪnˈɡriːdiənt/ *noun*
one of the different foods that a particular type of food is made from: *I don't have the ingredients for a cake.*

inhabit /ɪnˈhæbɪt/ *verb formal*
to live in a place: *The islands are inhabited by birds and small animals.*

inhabitant /ɪnˈhæbɪt^{ə}nt/ *noun*
someone who lives somewhere: *a city with 10 million inhabitants*

inherit /ɪnˈherɪt/ *verb*
to get money or things from someone after they die: *He inherited the house from his uncle.*
• **inheritance** *noun*
money or things that you get from someone after they die

initial /ɪˈnɪʃ^{ə}l/ *adj*
first, or happening at the start: *My initial reaction was one of anger.*
• **initially** *adv*
at the start: *Initially we thought it would cost six thousand euros.*

injection

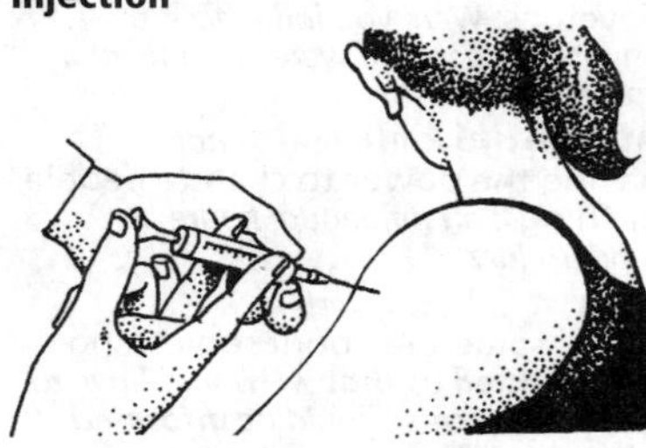

inject /ɪnˈdʒekt/ *verb*
to put a drug into someone's body using a needle
• **injection** *noun*
when a drug is put into someone's body using a needle *I **had** an **injection**.*

injure /ˈɪndʒə^{r}/ *verb* (*present participle* **injuring**, *past* **injured**)
to hurt a person or animal: *She injured her ankle when she fell.* ○ *No one was injured in the accident.*

injury /ˈɪndʒ^{ə}ri/ *noun* (*plural* **injuries**)
damage to someone's body: *head injuries* ○ *The passenger in the car escaped with minor injuries.*

injustice /ɪnˈdʒʌstɪs/ *noun*
a situation or action in which people are not treated fairly: *the fight against racial injustice*

ink /ɪŋk/ *noun* **[no plural]**
a coloured liquid that you use for writing, printing, or drawing

inland /ˈɪnlənd/ *adj, adv*
away from the sea: *The landscape changed as we drove further inland.*

inn /ɪn/ *noun*
a small hotel in the countryside

inner /ˈɪnə^{r}/ *adj*
on the inside, or near the middle of something: *Leading off the main hall is a series of inner rooms.* ➲Opposite **outer**

innocence /ˈɪnəs^{ə}ns/ *noun* **[no plural]**
when someone has not done a crime: *She fought to prove her innocence.* ➲Opposite **guilt**

innocent /ˈɪnəs^{ə}nt/ *adj*
If someone is innocent, they have not done a crime: *The jury decided he was innocent.* ➲Opposite **guilty**

inquire *formal* (*also UK* **enquire**) /ɪnˈkwaɪə^{r}/ *verb* (*present participle* **inquiring**, *past* **inquired**)
to ask someone for information about something: *I am **inquiring about** French classes in the area.*

inquiry (*also UK* **enquiry**) /ɪnˈkwaɪəri/ *noun* (*plural* **inquiries**)
1 *formal* a question that you ask to get information: *The company has received a lot of **inquiries about** its new Internet service.*
2 when people officially try to discover the facts about something bad that has happened: *There will be an official **inquiry into** the train crash.*

inquisitive /ɪnˈkwɪzətɪv/ *adj*
wanting to know as much as you can about things: *an inquisitive child*

insane /ɪnˈseɪn/ *adj*
crazy or very silly: *She must be insane going out in this weather!*

a b c d e f g h **i** j k l m n o p q r s t u v w x y z

insects

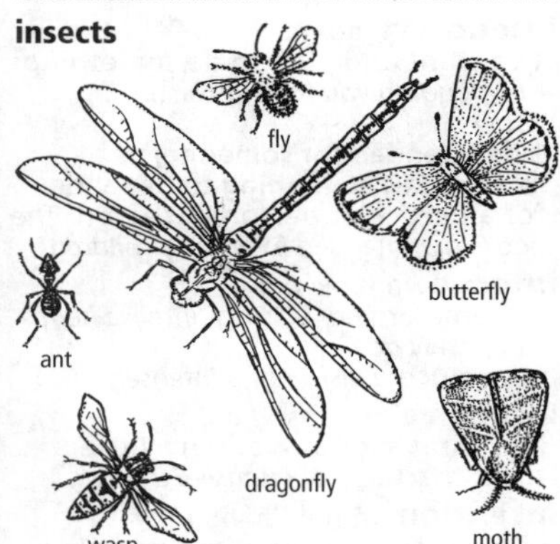

insect /ˈɪnsekt/ *noun*
a small creature with six legs, for example a bee or a fly

insensitive /ɪnˈsensətɪv/ *adj*
not noticing when other people are upset: *an insensitive remark*

insert /ɪnˈsɜːt/ *verb formal*
to put something into something else: *Insert the coin in the slot.*

inside¹ /ˌɪnˈsaɪd/ *noun*
1 the inside the part of something that is under its surface: *The inside of her house is nice.*
2 inside out If a piece of clothing is inside out, the part that is usually outside is on the inside: *You've got your sweater on inside out.*

inside² /ˌɪnˈsaɪd/ *adj*
in or on the part of something under its surface: *This jacket has an inside pocket.*

inside³ /ˌɪnˈsaɪd/ *adv, preposition*
in or into a room, building, or container: *There were some keys inside the box.* ○ *I'm cold – let's go back inside.*

insist /ɪnˈsɪst/ *verb*
1 to say that something is certainly true, especially when other people do not believe you: *Mia* ***insisted that*** *she and Carlo were just friends.*
2 to say that something must be done: *She* ***insisted on*** *seeing her lawyer.*

inspect /ɪnˈspekt/ *verb*
to look carefully at something to see if there is anything wrong: *Clara inspected her make-up in the mirror.*
• **inspection** *noun*

inspector /ɪnˈspektəʳ/ *noun*
1 someone whose job is to visit places and see if things are being done correctly: *a school inspector*
2 a police officer

inspiration /ˌɪnspərˈeɪʃən/ *noun* **[no plural]**
someone or something that gives you ideas for doing something: *Africa is a source of* ***inspiration for*** *his painting.*

inspire /ɪnˈspaɪəʳ/ *verb* (*present participle* **inspiring,** *past* **inspired)**
to make someone feel that they want to do something: *A teacher had inspired Sam to become an actor.*
• **inspiring** *adj*
giving you new ideas and making you feel you want to do something: *an inspiring book*

install /ɪnˈstɔːl/ *verb*
1 to put a piece of equipment somewhere and make it ready to use: *The school has installed a burglar alarm.*
2 to put software onto a computer

instalment /ɪnˈstɔːlmənt/ *noun*
1 a regular payment: *You can pay for your computer* ***in*** *six monthly* ***instalments.***
2 one part of a story that you can see every day or week in a magazine or on television

instance /ˈɪnstəns/ *noun*
for instance for example: *Many teenagers earn money, for instance by babysitting or cleaning cars.*

instant /ˈɪnstənt/ *adj*
1 happening immediately: *The book was an instant success in the US.*
2 Instant food or drink can be made quickly: *instant coffee*
• **instantly** *adv*
immediately: *A car hit them, killing them both instantly.*

instead /ɪnˈsted/ *adv*
in the place of someone or something else: *Why don't you help* ***instead of*** *complaining?*

instinct /ˈɪnstɪŋkt/ *noun*
the force that makes people and animals do things without first thinking: *It's the mother's instinct to protect her children.*

institute /ˈɪnstɪtjuːt/ *noun*
a place where people do scientific or

teaching work: *the Massachusetts Institute of Technology*

institution /ˌɪnstɪˈtjuːʃən/ *noun*
a large and important organization, such as a university or bank: *It is one of the country's top medical institutions.*

instruct /ɪnˈstrʌkt/ *verb*
1 to officially tell someone to do something: *Staff are instructed not to use the telephones for personal calls.*
2 *formal* to teach someone about something

instructions /ɪnˈstrʌkʃənz/ *plural noun*
information that explains how to do or use something: *I just* ***followed the instructions****.*

instructor /ɪnˈstrʌktəʳ/ *noun*
someone who teaches a particular sport or activity: *a driving instructor*

instrument /ˈɪnstrəmənt/ *noun*
1 a tool that is used for doing something: *scientific instruments*
2 an object that is used for playing music, for example a piano

insult /ɪnˈsʌlt/ *verb*
to say or do something rude to someone and upset them: *He annoyed me by insulting one of my friends.*
• **insulting** /ɪnˈsʌltɪŋ/ *adj*
rude: *an insulting remark*
• **insult** /ˈɪnsʌlt/ *noun*
something rude that you say or do to someone: *They were shouting insults at each other.*

insurance /ɪnˈʃʊərəns/ *noun* **[no plural]**
an agreement in which you pay a company money and they in the future give you money if you have an accident, are hurt, etc: *We need car insurance.*

insure /ɪnˈʃʊəʳ/ *verb* (*present participle* **insuring,** *past* **insured)**
to buy insurance from a company: *I need to get my car insured.*

intelligence /ɪnˈtelɪdʒəns/ *noun* **[no plural]**
the ability to learn and understand things: *a child of low intelligence*

intelligent /ɪnˈtelɪdʒənt/ *adj*
able to learn and understand things easily: *She is a highly intelligent young woman.*
• **intelligently** *adv*

intend /ɪnˈtend/ *verb*
1 to want and plan to do something: *How long do you* ***intend to*** *stay in Paris?*
2 be intended for someone; be intended as something to be made for a particular person or reason: *The books are intended for young children.*

intense /ɪnˈtens/ *adj*
extreme or very strong: *intense heat*
• **intensely** *adv*
very much: *I dislike him intensely.*

intensive /ɪnˈtensɪv/ *adj*
involving a lot of work in a little time: *ten weeks of intensive training*

intention /ɪnˈtenʃən/ *noun*
something that you want and plan to do: *I wanted to get here early – that was my intention.* ○ *I* ***have no intention*** *of seeing him again.*

intentional /ɪnˈtenʃənəl/ *adj*
planned: *If I upset you it wasn't intentional.*

interactive /ˌɪntərˈæktɪv/ *adj*
Interactive computer programs react to the person using them.

interest¹ /ˈɪntrəst/ *noun*
1 the feeling of wanting to know more about something: *I have always had an* ***interest in*** *science.* ○ *After a while he simply* ***lost interest in*** (= stopped being interested) *his studies.*
2 something you enjoy doing: *We share a lot of the same interests, particularly music and football.*
3 [no plural] the extra money that you must pay to a bank if you borrow money, or that you receive from the bank if you keep your money there: *low interest rates*

interest² /ˈɪntrəst/ *verb*
If someone or something interests you, you want to give them your attention and know more about them: *History doesn't really interest me.*

interested /ˈɪntrəstɪd/ *adj*
wanting to do something or know more about something: *Sarah's only* ***interested in*** *boys, CDs, and clothes.*

interesting /ˈɪntrəstɪŋ/ *adj*
keeping your attention: *an interesting person* ⇨Opposite **boring**

interfere /ˌɪntəˈfɪəʳ/ *verb* (*present participle* **interfering,** *past* **interfered)**
to try to become involved in a situation that you should not be

involved in: *You shouldn't **interfere in** other people's business.*
interfere with something *phrasal verb* to spoil something: *I try not to let my dancing classes interfere with my studies.*
• **interference** *noun*

interior /ɪn'tɪəriə^r/ *noun* **[no plural]** the inside part of something: *I have never seen the interior of the hotel.* ➲Opposite **exterior**

intermediate /ˌɪntə'miːdiət/ *adj* between the highest and lowest levels of knowledge or skill: *intermediate students*

internal /ɪn'tɜːnəl/ *adj* inside a place, or inside your body: *internal injuries* ➲Opposite **external**

international /ˌɪntə'næʃənəl/ *adj* relating to or involving two or more countries: *an international team of scientists* ○ *international politics*
• **internationally** *adv*

the Internet /'ɪntənet/ *noun* (*also* **the Net**) a system that connects computers around the world so you can share information with other people: *Check out this music website **on the Internet**.*

interpret /ɪn'tɜːprɪt/ *verb* to change what someone has said into another language: *We had to ask the guide to interpret for us.*

interpretation /ɪnˌtɜːprɪ'teɪʃən/ *noun* an explanation or opinion of what something means: *These are traditional **interpretations of** the Bible.*

interpreter /ɪn'tɜːprɪtə^r/ *noun* someone whose job is to change what someone else is saying into another language

interrupt /ˌɪntə'rʌpt/ *verb* to stop someone while they are talking or doing something, by saying or doing something yourself: *Sorry to interrupt, but what time is it?*

interruption /ˌɪntə'rʌpʃən/ *noun* when something stops someone while they are talking or doing something: *Due to constant interruptions, the meeting finished late.*

interval /'ɪntəvəl/ *noun* a period of time between two things: *After an interval of three days the peace talks started again.*

interview /'ɪntəvjuː/ *noun*
1 a meeting in which someone asks you questions to see if you are suitable for a job or course: *I **had an interview** last week for a job in London.*
2 a meeting in which someone asks a famous person questions for a newspaper, television, etc.
• **interview** *verb* to ask someone questions in an interview
• **interviewer** /'ɪntəvjuːə^r/ *noun*

into /'ɪntə, 'ɪntu/ *preposition*
1 towards the inside or middle of something: *Get into bed!* ○ *I went into the hotel.*
2 used to show when a person or thing changes into something else: *Chop the apple into small pieces.* ○ *We **turned** the smallest bedroom **into** an office.*
3 involving or about something: *There was an investigation into the cause of the fire.*
4 in the direction of something or someone: *She was looking into his eyes.*
5 used when dividing one number by another: *What's 5 into 125?*

intranet /'ɪntrənet/ *noun* a system that connects the computers in an organization so that people can share information

intransitive /ɪn'trænsətɪv/ *adj* An intransitive verb does not have an object. In the sentence 'John arrived first.', 'arrived' is an intransitive verb.

introduce /ˌɪntrə'djuːs/ *verb* (*present participle* **introducing**, *past* **introduced**)
1 to make something exist or happen for the first time: *We have introduced a new training scheme for employees.*
2 to tell someone another person's name the first time that they meet: *He took me round the room and **introduced** me **to** everyone.*

introduction /ˌɪntrə'dʌkʃən/ *noun*
1 [no plural] when you make something exist or happen for the first time: *the introduction of a new policy*
2 the first part of a book which tells you what the book is about

invade /ɪn'veɪd/ *verb* (*present*

a b c d e f g h i j k l m n o p q r s t u v w x y z

participle **invading,** *past* **invaded)**
to enter a country by force in order to take control of it: *Portugal was invaded by the French in 1807.*

invalid[1] /ˈɪnvəlɪd/ *noun*
someone who is so ill that they have to be looked after by other people

invalid[2] /ɪnˈvælɪd/ *adj*
An invalid document or ticket is not legally acceptable.

invasion /ɪnˈveɪʒᵊn/ *noun*
when an army enters a country by force in order to take control of it

invent /ɪnˈvent/ *verb*
to design or make something new: *Who invented the television?*

invention /ɪnˈvenʃᵊn/ *noun*
something that has been designed or made for the first time

inventor /ɪnˈventəʳ/ *noun*
someone who designs and makes new things

inverted commas /ɪnˌvɜːtɪdˈkɒməz/ *noun UK*
a pair of marks (" ") or (' ') used before and after a group of words to show that they are spoken or that someone else wrote them

invest /ɪnˈvest/ *verb*
to give money to a bank or business, or to buy something, because you hope to get a profit: *He's* ***invested*** *a million pounds* ***in*** *the project.*

investigate /ɪnˈvestɪgeɪt/ *verb* (*present participle* **investigating,** *past* **investigated)**
to try to get all the facts about something, especially a crime or accident: *Police are investigating the murder.*
• **investigation** /ɪnˌvestɪˈgeɪʃn/ *noun*
when police try to get all the facts about something, especially a crime or accident: *Police have begun an* ***investigation into*** *his death.*

invisible /ɪnˈvɪzəbl/ *adj*
Something that is invisible cannot be seen. ➲Opposite **visible**

invitation /ˌɪnvɪˈteɪʃᵊn/ *noun*
when someone asks you if you would like to do something: *I've had an* ***invitation to*** *Celia's party.*

invite /ɪnˈvaɪt/ *verb* (*present participle* **inviting,** *past* **invited)**
to ask someone to come to your house, to a party, etc: *They've* ***invited*** *us* ***to*** *the wedding.*

invoice /ˈɪnvɔɪs/ *noun*
a list that shows you how much you owe someone for work they have done or for things they have given you

involve /ɪnˈvɒlv/ *verb* (*present participle* **involving,** *past* **involved)**
1 If a situation or activity involves something, that thing is a part of it: *The trips often involve a lot of walking.* ○ *There are a lot of risks involved.*
2 to affect or include someone or something in an activity: *The event involves hundreds of people.*

involved /ɪnˈvɒlvd/ *adj*
be/get involved in something to do things and be part of an activity or event: *How did you get involved in acting?*

involvement /ɪnˈvɒlvmənt/ *noun*
when someone or something is part of an activity or event

inward[1] /ˈɪnwəd/ *adj*
towards the centre or the inside of something ➲Opposite **outward**

inward[2] /ˈɪnwəd/ (*also UK* **inwards)** *adv*
towards the inside or the centre: *The door slowly opened inward.* ➲Opposite **outwards**

IOU /ˌaɪəʊˈjuː/ *noun*
a piece of paper saying that you will pay back money you owe

IPA /ˌaɪpiːˈeɪ/ *noun* **[no plural]**
a system of symbols for showing how words are spoken

IQ /ˌaɪˈkjuː/ *noun*
a person's intelligence when measured by a special test: *a high/low IQ*

iron /aɪən/ *noun*
1 [no plural] a dark grey metal
2 a piece of electrical equipment that you use for making clothes smooth
• **iron** *verb*
to make clothes smooth using an iron

ironing /ˈaɪənɪŋ/ *noun* **[no plural]**
the activity of making clothes smooth using an iron (= a piece of electrical equipment): *John was* ***doing the ironing.***

ironing board /ˈaɪənɪŋ ˌbɔːd/ *noun*
a thin table that you use for ironing

irregular /ɪ'regjələ^{r}/ *adj*
1 Irregular actions or events happen with a different amount of time between each one: *an irregular heartbeat*
2 not following the general rules in grammar: *irregular verbs* ⊃Opposite **regular**

irrelevant /ɪ'reləv^{ə}nt/ *adj*
not important in a particular situation: *irrelevant information* ⊃Opposite **relevant**

irritate /'ɪrɪteɪt/ *verb* (*present participle* **irritating**, *past* **irritated**)
1 to make someone slightly angry: *His comments really irritated me.*
2 to make a part of your body hurt: *The smoke irritated her eyes.*

is *strong form* /ɪz/ *weak form* /z/
present simple of be *used with 'he', 'she', 'it'*

Islam /'ɪzlɑːm/ *noun* **[no plural]**
a religion based on the teachings of Mohammed

island /'aɪlənd/ *noun*
an area of land that has water around it: *the Hawaiian Islands*

isn't /'ɪz^{ə}nt/
short for is not: *Mike isn't coming with us.*

isolated /'aɪsəleɪtɪd/ *adj*
a long way from other places: *He lives in an isolated village in the mountains.*

issue[1] /'ɪʃuː/ *noun*
1 an important subject or problem that people are talking about: *environmental issues*
2 the newspaper, magazine, etc from a particular day

issue[2] /'ɪʃuː/ *verb* (*present participle* **issuing**, *past* **issued**)
to officially give something to someone: *All members will be* ***issued with*** *a membership card.*

IT /ˌaɪ'tiː/ *noun* **[no plural]**
the use of computers and other electronic equipment to keep and send information

it /ɪt/ *pronoun*
1 used to mean the thing, situation, or idea that has already been talked about: *"Have you seen my bag?" "It's in the hall."* ○ *It was a bad experience and I don't want to talk about it.*
2 used before some adjectives, nouns, or verbs to introduce an opinion or description of a situation: *It's unlikely that she'll arrive on time.* ○ *It's a pity you can't come with us.*
3 used with the verb 'be' in sentences giving the time, date, weather or distances: *It rained all day.* ○ *What time is it?*
4 used to say the name of a person or thing when the person you are speaking to does not know: *It's your Dad on the phone.*

itch /ɪtʃ/ *verb*
If a part of your body itches, you want to rub it with your nails: *Woollen sweaters make my arms itch.*
• **itch** *noun*: *I've* ***got an itch*** *in the middle of my back.*

itchy /'ɪtʃi/ *adj*
If a part of your body is itchy, you want to rub it: *an itchy nose*

it'd /'ɪtəd/
1 *short for* it would: *It'd be great if we could meet next week.*
2 *short for* it had: *It'd taken us an hour to find Bruce's house.*

item /'aɪtəm/ *noun*
a single thing in a set or on a list: *This is the last item on the list.* ○ *Various stolen items were found.*

it'll /'ɪt^{ə}l/
short for it will: *It'll take about twenty minutes to get there.*

it's /ɪts/
1 *short for* it is: *"What time is it?" "It's one o'clock."*
2 *short for* it has: *It's been hard work.*

its /ɪts/ *determiner*
belonging to or relating to the thing that has already been talked about: *The house has its own swimming pool.*

itself /ɪt'self/ *pronoun*
1 used to show that the thing or animal that does the action is also the thing or animal that is affected by it: *The cat licked itself clean.*
2 the thing that you are talking about: *The garden is enormous but the house itself is very small.*

I've /aɪv/
short for I have: *I've decided not to go.*

ivory /'aɪv^{ə}ri/ *noun* **[no plural]**
a hard, white substance from the long teeth of an elephant

ivy /'aɪvi/ *noun* **[no plural]**
a dark green plant that grows up walls

Jj

J, j /dʒeɪ/
the tenth letter of the alphabet

jab¹ /dʒæb/ *verb* (*present participle* **jabbing,** *past* **jabbed)**
to push something quickly into another thing or towards another thing: *He **jabbed** a finger **into** her back.*

jab² /dʒæb/ *noun UK informal*
an injection (= when a drug is put into your body using a needle): *a flu jab*

jacket

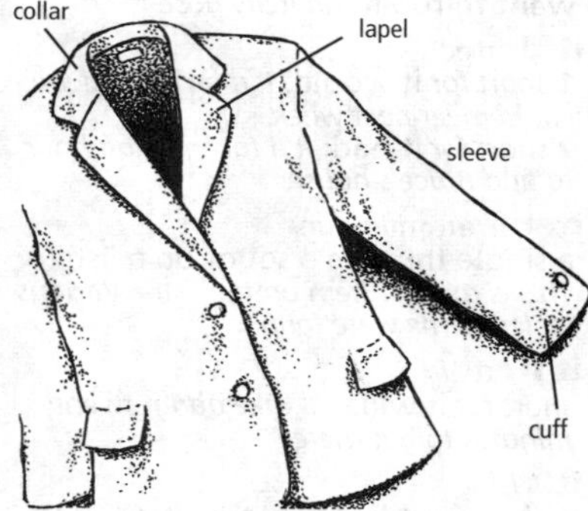

jacket /ˈdʒækɪt/ *noun*
a short coat: *a leather jacket*

jagged /ˈdʒægɪd/ *adj*
very rough and sharp: *jagged rocks*

jaguar /ˈdʒægjuəʳ/ *noun*
a large, wild cat that lives in Central and South America

jail /dʒeɪl/ *noun*
a place where criminals are kept as a punishment: *He is **in jail**.*

jam¹ /dʒæm/ *noun*
1 [no plural] a sweet food made from fruit that you put on bread: *a jar of strawberry jam*
2 (*also* **traffic jam)** a line of cars, trucks, etc that are moving slowly or not moving: *We were stuck **in a jam** for hours.*

jam² /dʒæm/ *verb* (*present participle* **jamming,** *past* **jammed)**
1 to push something somewhere firmly and tightly: *She jammed her hands into her pockets.*
2 If a machine or something that moves jams, or you jam it, it stops moving or working: *The machine keeps jamming.*
3 to fill a place completely: *The streets were **jammed with** cars.*

jangle /ˈdʒæŋgl/ *verb* (*present participle* **jangling,** *past* **jangled)**
If small, metal objects jangle, they hit together making a ringing noise: *I could hear coins jangling in his pocket.*

January /ˈdʒænjuəri/ *noun*
the first month of the year

jar /dʒɑːʳ/ *noun*
a glass container used for keeping food: *a jar of jam*

javelin /ˈdʒævəlɪn/ *noun*
a long, pointed stick that you throw as a sport ➲See colour picture **Sports 1** on page Centre 15

jaw /dʒɔː/ *noun*
1 either of the two bones in your mouth that contain your teeth
2 someone's jaw drops If someone's jaw drops, their mouth opens because they are very surprised.

jazz /dʒæz/ *noun* **[no plural]**
music with a strong beat that people often play without looking at written music: *a jazz band*

jealous /ˈdʒeləs/ *adj*
1 not happy because you want something that someone else has: *Dan's new bike was **making** his friends **jealous**.* ○ *I'm **jealous of** your new car.*
2 upset and angry because someone you love seems to like another person: *a jealous husband*

jealousy /ˈdʒeləsi/ *noun* **[no plural]**
jealous feelings

jeans /dʒiːnz/ *plural noun*
trousers made from denim (= a strong, usually blue, material): *a pair of jeans*

Jeep /dʒiːp/ *noun trademark*
a big, strong car with big wheels that is used for driving over rough ground

jeer /dʒɪəʳ/ *verb*
to laugh at someone and shout bad things: *The crowd outside his house jeered as he left.*

jelly /ˈdʒeli/ *noun UK* (*US* **Jell-O) [no plural]**
a soft, sweet food for children that

shakes when you move it: *jelly and ice cream*

jellyfish /ˈdʒelifɪʃ/ *noun* a sea creature with a clear body that can sting you (= put poison into your skin)

jellyfish

jerk¹ /dʒɜːk/ *verb* to move very quickly and suddenly, or to make something move like this: *The truck jerked forward.*

jerk² /dʒɜːk/ *noun* a quick, sudden movement: *a sudden jerk of the head*

Jesus Christ /ˌdʒiːzəsˈkraɪst/ *noun* the holy man that Christians believe is the Son of God

jet /dʒet/ *noun*
1 an aeroplane that flies very fast
2 water or gas that is forced out of something in a thin, strong line

Jew /dʒuː/ *noun* someone whose religion is Judaism, or who is related to the ancient people of Israel

jewel /ˈdʒuːəl/ *noun* a valuable stone that is used to make jewellery

jewellery *UK*, jewelry *US*
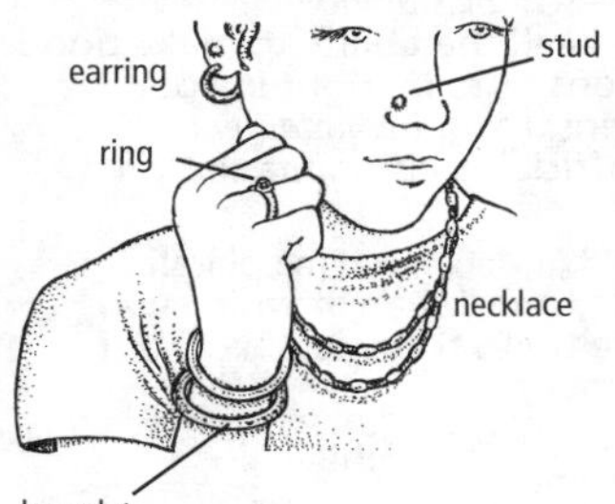

jewellery *UK* (*US* **jewelry**) /ˈdʒuːəlri/ *noun* **[no plural]** objects made from gold, silver, and valuable stones that you wear for decoration

Jewish /ˈdʒuːɪʃ/ *adj* relating or belonging to the Jews

jigsaw /ˈdʒɪgsɔː/ (*also* **ˈjigsaw ˌpuzzle**) *noun* a picture in many small pieces that you put together as a game

jigsaw

jingle /ˈdʒɪŋgl/ *verb* (*present participle* **jingling**, *past* **jingled**) to make the sound of small metal objects hitting against each other: *a pocket full of jingling coins*

job /dʒɒb/ *noun*
1 the work that you do in order to get money: *She **got** a **job** as a cleaner.*
2 a piece of work: *I **did** a few **jobs** around the house.*
3 something that you have to do: *It's my job to water the plants.*
4 make a bad/good job of something *UK* to do sth badly/well

jockey /ˈdʒɒki/ *noun* someone who rides horses in races

jog /dʒɒg/ *verb* (*present participle* **jogging**, *past* **jogged**) to run slowly for exercise: *I jog through the park every morning.*
• **jog** *noun* a slow run that you do for exercise *We could go for a jog.*

join /dʒɔɪn/ *verb*
1 to become a member of an organization: *He joined the army when he was eighteen.*
2 to do something or go somewhere with someone: *Would you like to join us for dinner?*
3 to fasten or connect things together: ***Join** the ends **together** with strong glue.*
4 to meet at a particular point: *This is the point where the two rivers join.*

join in (something) *phrasal verb* to do an activity with other people: *We're playing cards. Would you like to join in?*

joint¹ /dʒɔɪnt/ *adj* belonging to or done by two or more people: *The project was a joint effort by all the children in the class.*

joint
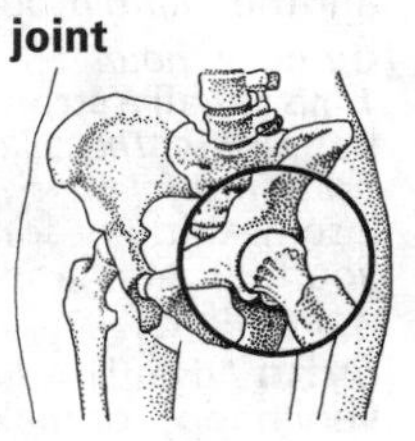

a b c d e f g h i **j** k l m n o p q r s t u v w x y z

joint² /dʒɔɪnt/
noun
1 a place in your body where two bones meet: *the knee joint*
2 *UK* a large piece of meat, usually cooked in the oven: *a joint of beef*
3 a place where parts of something are connected

joke¹ /dʒəʊk/ *noun*
a short, funny story which someone says to make people laugh: *Ben was* ***telling jokes*** *at the other end of the table.*

joke² /dʒəʊk/ *verb* (*present participle* **joking,** *past* **joked)**
1 to say funny things, or not be serious: *She always* ***jokes about*** *her husband's cooking.*
2 You must be joking! *informal* used to say that something is certainly not true: *"Does Jim do much cooking?" "You must be joking – he never cooks!"*

jolly /ˈdʒɒli/ *adj*
happy or enjoyable: *We had a very jolly evening.*

jolt¹ /dʒəʊlt/ *noun*
a sudden, violent movement: *With a sudden jolt the train started moving.*

jolt² /dʒəʊlt/ *verb*
to make someone or something suddenly move forward: *The bus stopped suddenly and the passengers were jolted forward.*

jot /dʒɒt/ *verb* (*present participle* **jotting,** *past* **jotted)**
jot something down *phrasal verb*
to write something quickly: *I jotted down some notes during his speech.*

journalism /ˈdʒɜːnəlɪzəm/ *noun* **[no plural]**
the work of writing for newspapers, magazines, television, or radio

journalist /ˈdʒɜːnəlɪst/ *noun*
someone whose job is journalism

journey /ˈdʒɜːni/ *noun*
when you travel from one place to another: *a train journey*

joy /dʒɔɪ/ *noun*
1 [no plural] a strong feeling of happiness: *The children have brought her so much joy.*
2 something or someone that makes you feel very happy: *She's a joy to work with.*

joyful /ˈdʒɔɪfəl/ *adj*
very happy, or making people feel very happy: *joyful news*

Judaism /ˈdʒuːdeɪɪzəm/ *noun* **[no plural]**
the religion of the Jewish people

judge¹ /dʒʌdʒ/ *noun*
1 someone who controls a court and decides how criminals should be punished: *The judge ruled that they had acted correctly.*
2 someone who decides which person or thing wins a competition: *the Olympic judges*

judge² /dʒʌdʒ/ *verb* (*present participle* **judging,** *past* **judged)**
1 to have or develop an opinion about something or someone, usually after thinking carefully: *The meeting was judged to be a great success.* ○ *You shouldn't* ***judge*** *people* ***on*** *their appearances.* ○ *He was judged guilty/insane.*
2 judging by/from used for saying the reasons why you have a particular opinion: *She must be popular judging by the number of letters that she receives.*
3 to decide the winner or results of a competition: *I've been asked to judge the art contest.*

judgment (*also* **judgement)** /ˈdʒʌdʒmənt/ *noun*
1 an opinion about someone or something after thinking carefully: *He has to* ***make*** *a* ***judgment*** *about how well the school is doing.*
2 [no plural] the ability to make good decisions or to be right in your opinions: *I trust her judgment.*
3 an official decision made by a judge

judo /ˈdʒuːdəʊ/ *noun* **[no plural]**
a sport from Japan in which two people try to throw each other to the ground

jug /dʒʌg/ *noun*
a container with a handle used for pouring out liquids: *a jug of water*

jug

juggle /ˈdʒʌgl/ *verb* (*present participle* **juggling,** *past* **juggled)**
1 to try to do

many things at the same time: *Many women have to juggle work and family.*
2 to throw two or more things, especially balls, from one hand to the other and keep doing this

juice /dʒuːs/ *noun* **[no plural]**
the liquid that comes from fruit or vegetables

juicy /ˈdʒuːsi/ *adj* **(juicier, juiciest)**
full of juice: *juicy apples*

jukebox /ˈdʒuːkbɒks/ *noun* (*plural* **jukeboxes)**
a machine which plays a song when you put money into it

July /dʒʊˈlaɪ/ *noun*
the seventh month of the year

jumble[1] /ˈdʒʌmbl/ *noun* **[no plural]**
a lot of things together in an untidy group: *He looked at the jumble of papers on his desk.*

jumble[2] /ˈdʒʌmbl/ (*also* **jumble up)** *verb* (*present participle* **jumbling,** *past* **jumbled)**
to mix things together in an untidy way: *Her clothes were all jumbled up in the suitcase.*

jump[1] /dʒʌmp/ *verb*
1 to push your body up and away from the ground using your feet and legs: *The children were jumping up and down with excitement.* ○ *They jumped into the water.*
2 to move somewhere suddenly and quickly: *She jumped into a taxi and rushed to the station.*
3 to make a sudden movement because you are frightened or surprised: *Her scream* ***made me jump****.*
jump at something *phrasal verb*
to be pleased to accept the chance to do something: *He jumped at the chance to travel.*

jump[2] /dʒʌmp/ *noun*
when you push your body up into the air using your feet and legs: *He won with a jump of 8.5 metres.*

jumper /ˈdʒʌmpəʳ/ *noun UK*
a warm piece of clothing which covers the top of your body and is pulled on over your head

junction /ˈdʒʌŋkʃᵊn/ *noun UK*
the place where two roads or railway lines meet

June /dʒuːn/ *noun*
the sixth month of the year

jungle /ˈdʒʌŋgl/ *noun*
an area of land in a hot country where trees and plants grow close together

junior /ˈdʒuːniəʳ/ *adj*
1 less important than other people doing the same job: *a junior minister*
➲Opposite **senior**
2 for or relating to young people: *a junior tennis tournament*

junior school /ˈdʒuːniəʳ ˌskuːl/ *noun*
a school in the UK for children who are 7 to 11 years old

junk /dʒʌŋk/ *noun* **[no plural]** *informal*
old things which no one wants

junk food /ˈdʒʌŋk ˌfuːd/ *noun* **[no plural]**
food which is bad for your body but quick to eat

jury /ˈdʒʊəri/ *noun* (*plural* **juries)**
a group of people in a court of law who decide if someone has done a crime

just[1] *strong form* /dʒʌst/ *weak form* /dʒəst/ *adv*
1 only: *I'll just have a small piece.* ○ *He just wants to win.* ○ *The film is not just about love.*
2 a very short time ago: *I've just seen him.* ○ *We've only just begun.*
3 used to make something you are saying strong: *I just hate it!*
4 *UK* almost not: *This dress* ***only just*** *fits.*
5 exactly: *Tim looks just like his father.*
6 now or very soon: *The film is just beginning.* ○ *I'm just coming!*
7 just about almost: *I think I've remembered just about everything.*
8 be just about to do something to be going to do something very soon: *I was just about to phone you.*
9 it's just as well used to say that it is lucky that something happened: *It's just as well we brought an umbrella.*

just[2] /dʒʌst/ *adj*
fair or morally right: *a just society*

justice /ˈdʒʌstɪs/ *noun* **[no plural]**
1 treatment of people that is fair: *She tried to bring about justice for all.*
➲Opposite **injustice**
2 the system of laws which judges or punishes people: *the criminal justice system*

Kk

K, k /keɪ/
the eleventh letter of the alphabet

kangaroo /ˌkæŋgᵊrˈuː/ *noun*
a large Australian animal that moves by jumping on its back legs

kangaroo

karate /kəˈrɑːti/ *noun* **[no plural]**
a sport from Japan in which people fight with the hands or feet

keen /kiːn/ *adj*
1 liking something very much: *a keen photographer* ○ *He's very **keen on** travelling.*
2 wanting to do something very much: *The shop is keen to attract new customers.*

keep /kiːp/ *verb* (*present participle* **keeping,** *past* **kept)**
1 to have something always, as your own: *You can keep that dress if you like it.* ○ *I've kept every letter he ever sent to me.*
2 keep something in/on, etc to always put something in a particular place: *I keep the keys in the drawer.*
3 keep doing something to continue to do something, or to often do something: *I keep telling her not to do it.* ○ *He keeps hitting me.*
4 keep (someone/something) awake/clean/safe, etc to make someone or something stay in a particular state: *This coat should keep you warm.* ○ *He keeps his car very clean.*
5 keep a secret to not tell anyone a secret
6 If food or drink keeps, it remains fresh.

keep at something *phrasal verb*
to continue working hard at something difficult: *Learning a language is hard but you've just got to keep at it.*

keep something down *phrasal verb*
to stop the number, level, or size of something from increasing: *I have to exercise to keep my weight down.*

keep on doing something *phrasal verb*
to continue to do something, or to do something again and again: *She kept on asking me questions the whole time.*

keep up *phrasal verb*
1 to stay with someone who is moving forward by moving as quickly as them: *She was walking so fast I couldn't **keep up with** her.*
2 to increase as quickly as something or someone else: *Prices have been rising very fast and wages haven't kept up.*

kennel /ˈkenᵊl/ *noun*
a small building for a dog to sleep in

kennel

kept /kept/
past of keep

kerb /kɜːb/ *noun*
the line of stones at the edge of a pavement (= path that people walk on) next to the road

ketchup /ˈketʃʌp/ *noun* **[no plural]**
a cold, red sauce made from tomatoes (= round, red fruit) that people add to food

kettle /ˈketl/ *noun*
a metal or plastic container with a lid, used for boiling water: *Charlotte **put the kettle on** to make some tea.*

key /kiː/ *noun*
1 a piece of metal that you use for locking doors or for starting engines: *I've lost my car keys.*
2 the key to something the thing that you must do in order to achieve something: *Hard work is the key to success.*
3 one of the parts you press with your fingers on a keyboard or musical instrument to produce letters, numbers, or to make a sound
4 a set of musical notes based on one particular note: *the key of D major*

key

keyboard /ˈkiːbɔːd/ *noun*
a set of keys on a computer, which you press to make it work, or the rows of keys on a piano

keyhole /ˈkiːhəʊl/ *noun*
a hole in a lock where you put a key

kg
written abbreviation for kilogram (= a unit for measuring weight)

khaki /ˈkɑːki/ *noun* **[no plural]**
a green-brown colour, often worn by soldiers
• **khaki** *adj* ➲See colour picture **Colours** on page Centre 6

kick¹ /kɪk/ *verb*
1 to hit or move something or someone with your foot: *The boys were kicking a ball around.*
2 to move your feet and legs forwards or backwards quickly: *The baby lay on the mat kicking.*
kick off *phrasal verb*
When a football match kicks off, it starts.
kick someone out *phrasal verb informal*
to make someone leave a place or organization: *His wife kicked him out.*

kick² /kɪk/ *noun*
1 when you hit something with your foot: *He **gave** her a **kick** in the ribs.*
2 *informal* a feeling of excitement and energy: *She **gets a kick out of** performing live.*

kid /kɪd/ *noun*
1 *informal* a child: *school kids*
2 a young goat

kidnap /ˈkɪdnæp/ *verb* (*present participle* **kidnapping**, *past* **kidnapped)**
to take someone away using force, saying that you will only bring them back if someone gives you money
• **kidnap** *noun*: *a kidnap attempt*
• **kidnapper** /ˈkɪdnæpəʳ/ *noun*

kidney /ˈkɪdni/ *noun*
one of the two parts in your body which remove bad things from the blood

kill /kɪl/ *verb*
1 to make someone or something die: *Their son was killed in a road accident.*
2 *informal* to hurt a lot: *My feet are killing me.*

killer /ˈkɪləʳ/ *noun*
someone who kills, or a disease or animal that kills: *Cancer and heart disease are the UK's biggest killers.*

kilo /ˈkiːləʊ/ *noun, short for* kilogram

kilobyte /ˈkɪləʊbaɪt/ *noun*
a unit for measuring the amount of information you can put on a computer

kilogram, kilogramme (*written abbreviation* **kg)** /ˈkɪləʊgræm/ *noun*
a unit for measuring weight, equal to 1000 grams

kilometre *UK* (*US* **kilometer)** /kɪˈlɒmɪtəʳ/ *noun*
a unit for measuring distance, equal to 1000 metres

kin /kɪn/ *noun formal* **[no plural]**
the people in your family

kind¹ /kaɪnd/ *noun*
1 a type of thing or person: *What **kind of** music do you like?* ○ ***All kinds of** people come to our church.*
2 some kind of used to talk about something when you are not sure of its exact type: *She has some kind of medical problem.*
3 kind of *informal* used when you are trying to explain or describe something, but you cannot be exact: *It's kind of unusual.*

kind² /kaɪnd/ *adj*
Kind people do things to help others and show that they care about them: *Your mother was very **kind to** us.* ○ *It was very **kind of** you to come and see me.* ➲Opposite **unkind**

kindly /ˈkaɪndli/ *adv*
in a kind way: *She very kindly offered to cook me lunch.*

kindness /ˈkaɪndnəs/ *noun* **[no plural]**
when someone is kind: *I wanted to thank her for her kindness.*

king /kɪŋ/ *noun*
a man who rules a country and is one of the royal family: *the kings and queens of England*

kingdom /ˈkɪŋdəm/ *noun*
1 a country with a king or queen: *the Kingdom of Belgium*
2 the animal kingdom all animals considered together

kiss

kiss¹ /kɪs/ *verb*
to put your lips against another person's lips or skin because you love or like them: *He kissed her cheek.* ○ *I*

kissed *her* ***goodbye****.*

kiss² /kɪs/ *noun* (*plural* **kisses**)
when you kiss someone: *She ran up and* ***gave*** *me* ***a*** *big* ***kiss****.*

kit /kɪt/ *noun*
1 things that you keep in a container ready for a particular use: *a tool kit*
2 *UK* the clothes that you wear for a particular sport: *a football kit*
3 a set of parts which you put together to make something: *He's making a model car from a kit.*

kitchen /ˈkɪtʃɪn/ *noun*
a room used to prepare and cook food in

kite /kaɪt/ *noun*
a toy made of paper or cloth which flies in the air on the end of a long string

kitten /ˈkɪtᵊn/ *noun*
a young cat

km
written abbreviation for kilometre (= a unit for measuring distance)

knead /niːd/ *verb*
to press the mixture for making bread with your hands before you cook it

knee

knee /niː/ *noun*
the middle part of your leg where it bends: *a knee injury*

kneel

kneel /niːl/ *verb* (*present participle* **kneeling**, *past* **knelt**)
to bend your legs and put one knee or both knees on the floor: *She knelt down beside the child.*

knew /njuː/
past tense of know

knickers /ˈnɪkəz/ *plural noun UK*
women's underwear that covers the bottom

knife /naɪf/ *noun* (*plural* **knives**)
a sharp metal thing used for cutting: *a knife and fork*

knit

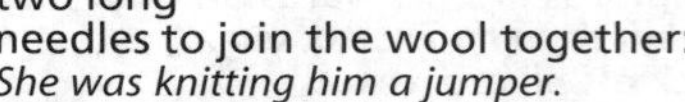

knit /nɪt/ *verb* (*present participle* **knitting**, *past tense* **knitted**, *past participle* **knitted**)
to make clothes using wool and two long needles to join the wool together: *She was knitting him a jumper.*

knob /nɒb/ *noun*
a round handle, or a round button on a machine: *a door knob* ○ ***Turn*** *the black* ***knob*** *to switch on the radio.*

knock¹ /nɒk/ *verb*
1 to hit a door with your closed hand so that people know you are there: *There's someone* ***knocking at*** *the door.*
2 to hit something or someone and make them move or fall down: *He accidentally knocked the plate off the table.* ○ *I knocked my glass over.*

knock someone down *phrasal verb UK*
to hit someone with a car and hurt or kill them: *She was knocked down by a bus.*

knock something down *phrasal verb*
to destroy a building or part of a building: *They knocked down the old factory and built a cinema.*

knock someone out *phrasal verb*
to make someone become unconscious, usually by hitting them on the head: *He was knocked out halfway through the fight.*

knock² /nɒk/ *noun*
a sudden short noise made when something or someone hits a surface: *There was a* ***knock at*** *the door.*

knot

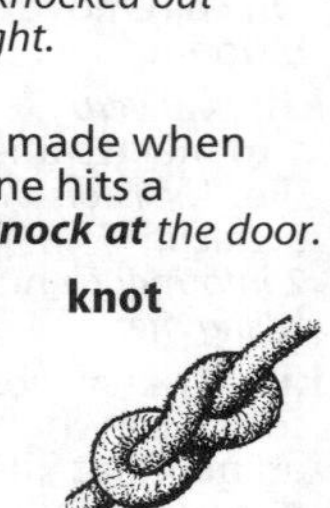

knot¹ /nɒt/ *noun*
a place where pieces of string, rope, etc have been tied together

knot² /nɒt/ *verb* (*present participle* **knotting**, *past* **knotted**) to tie knots in pieces of string, rope, etc

know /nəʊ/ *verb* (*present participle* **knowing,** *past tense* **knew,** *past participle* **known)**
1 to have information about something in your mind: *Andrew **knows** a lot **about** computers.* ○ *"How old is she?" "I don't know."* ○ *He **knew that** she was lying.*
2 to have spent time with someone or in a place so that they are not new to you: *I've known Al since we were children.* ○ *I grew up in Brussels so I know it well.*
3 to be able to do something: *Do you **know how to** ski?*
4 let someone know to tell someone something: *Let me know if you're going to the party.*
5 I know used when you agree with something someone has just said: *"It's a lovely day, isn't it?" "I know – let's hope it lasts."*
6 you know used to make sure someone understands which person or thing you are talking about: *I was talking about Rachel – you know, the tall woman with the blond hair.*

knowledge /ˈnɒlɪdʒ/ *noun* **[no plural]** information and understanding that you have in your mind: *His **knowledge of** history is amazing.*

knowledgeable /ˈnɒlɪdʒəbl/ *adj* knowing a lot: *He's very **knowledgeable about** art.*

known /nəʊn/ *past participle of* know

knuckle /ˈnʌkl/ *noun* one of the parts of your finger where it bends

koala

koala /kəʊˈɑːlə/ (*also* **koˈala ˌbear)** *noun* an Australian animal like a small bear with grey fur which lives in trees

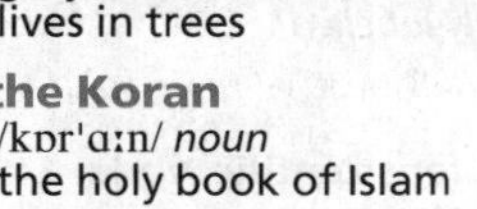

the Koran /kɒrˈɑːn/ *noun* the holy book of Islam

Ll

L, l /el/
the twelfth letter of the alphabet

l *written abbreviation for* litre (= a unit for measuring liquid)

lab /læb/ *noun*
short for laboratory (= a room used for scientific work)

label¹ /ˈleɪbᵊl/ *noun*
a piece of paper or material which is fixed to something and gives you information about it: *There are washing instructions on the label.*

label² /ˈleɪbᵊl/ *verb* (*present participle* **labelling,** *past* **labelled)**
to fix a small piece of paper or material to something which gives information about it: *Was the package clearly labelled?*

laboratory /ləˈbɒrətᵊri/ *noun* (*plural* **laboratories)**
a room used for scientific work: *research laboratories*

labour *UK* (*US* **labor)** /ˈleɪbəʳ/ *noun*
1 [no plural] work that you do with your hands and body: *Does that price include the cost of labour?*
2 [no plural] people who work: *cheap labour*
3 when a pregnant woman has pain in her stomach because the baby is coming out

labourer *UK* (*US* **laborer)** /ˈleɪbᵊrəʳ/ *noun*
a worker who does hard work with their hands and body: *a farm labourer*

lace /leɪs/ *noun*
1 [no plural] a thin white cloth with a pattern of holes in it: *a lace curtain*
2 a string used to tie shoes: *I'll just tie my laces.*

lack¹ /læk/ *noun* **[no plural]**
lack of something not having something, or not having enough of something: *My only problem is lack of money.*

lack² /læk/ *verb*
to not have something, or not have enough of something: *She really lacks confidence.*

ladder /ˈlædəʳ/ *noun*
a thing which you climb up when you want to reach a high place, which has two long pieces joined together by shorter pieces

ladder

the ladies /ˈleɪdiz/ *noun UK*
a toilet in a public place for women

lady /ˈleɪdi/ *noun* (*plural* **ladies)**
1 a polite way of saying 'woman': ***Ladies and gentlemen****, can I have your attention please?*
2 Lady a title used before the name of a woman of high social rank in the UK: *Lady Alison Weir*

lager /ˈlɑːgəʳ/ *noun* **[no plural]**
a light yellow beer: *A pint of lager, please.*

laid /leɪd/
past of lay

lain /leɪn/
past participle of lie¹

lake /leɪk/ *noun*
a large area of water which has land all around it: *Lake Windermere*

lamb /læm/ *noun*
1 a young sheep
2 [no plural] meat from a young sheep

lame /leɪm/ *adj*
A lame animal or person cannot walk because their foot or leg is hurt: *a lame horse*

lamp /læmp/ *noun*
an object that makes light: *I have a lamp next to my bed.*

lamppost /ˈlæmppəʊst/ *noun*
a tall post with a light at the top, which you see on roads where there are houses

lampshade /ˈlæmpʃeɪd/ *noun*
a cover for an electric light ➲See colour picture **The Living Room** on page Centre 11

land¹ /lænd/ *noun*
1 [no plural] an area of ground: *agricultural land*
2 [no plural] the surface of the Earth that is not sea: *We travelled over land and sea.*
3 a country: *a land of ice and snow*

land[2] /lænd/ *verb*
1 If an aeroplane lands, it arrives on the ground after flying: *We should **land in** Madrid at 7 a.m.*
2 If an object or person lands somewhere, they fall to the ground there: *She landed flat on her back.*

landing /ˈlændɪŋ/ *noun*
1 when an aeroplane arrives on the ground: *The plane had to make an emergency landing in Chicago.*
2 the area of floor at the top of a set of stairs

landlady /ˈlændˌleɪdi/ *noun* (*plural* **landladies)**
a woman who owns the house that you live in and who you give money to

landlord /ˈlændlɔːd/ *noun*
a man who owns the house that you live in and who you give money to

landscape /ˈlændskeɪp/ *noun* **[no plural]**
the appearance of an area of land, especially in the countryside: *The landscape is very beautiful.*

lane /leɪn/ *noun*
1 one of the parts of a big road that is shown by a painted line: *He was driving in the fast lane.*
2 a narrow road, usually in the countryside: *We drove down a winding country lane.*

language /ˈlæŋgwɪdʒ/ *noun*
1 [no plural] words that people use to speak or write: *The way that children's language develops is fascinating.*
2 the words used by the people of a country: *How many languages do you speak?*

lap /læp/ *noun*
1 the top part of your legs when you are sitting down: *His little daughter was sitting on his lap.*
2 one journey around a race track: *He's two laps behind the leaders.*

laptop /ˈlæptɒp/ *noun*
a small computer that you can carry around with you

laptop

large /lɑːdʒ/ *adj*
big: *a large number of people* ○ *He won a large amount of money.* ○ *She comes from quite a large family.* ➲Opposite **small**

laser /ˈleɪzə[r]/ *noun*
a very strong line of light that is used in machines and used for repairing parts of the body: *a laser beam* ○ *a laser printer*

lashes /ˈlæʃɪz/ *plural noun*
the small hairs on the edges of your eye: *She's got lovely long lashes.*

last[1] /lɑːst/ *adj, determiner*
1 the most recent: *What was the last film you saw?* ○ *It's rained for the last three days.*
2 Your last book, house, job, etc is the one before the one that you have now: *My last house was half this size.*
3 happening or coming at the end: *It's the last room on the left.* ○ *That's the last programme of the series.* ○ *I was the last person to arrive.* ➲Opposite **first**
4 only remaining: *Who wants the last piece of cake?*

last[2] /lɑːst/ *adv*
1 after everything or everyone else: *I came last in the running race.* ○ *We've still got to check the figures but we'll do that last.* ➲Opposite **first**
2 used to talk about the most recent time you did something: *When did you last see her?* ○ *I think it was July when I last spoke to him.*
3 last but not least something you say before you say the last person or thing on a list: *This is Jeremy, this is Olivia and, last but not least, this is Eva.*

last[3] /lɑːst/ *noun, pronoun*
1 the last a person or thing that comes after all the others: *We were the last to get there.*
2 the last of something the only part of something that remains: *We've just finished the last of the wine.*
3 at last finally: *At last, I've found a jacket I like.*

last[4] /lɑːst/ *verb*
1 to continue to happen or exist: *How long will the meeting last?* ○ *The batteries last about ten hours.* ○ *Enjoy the sun while it lasts!*
2 to be enough for a period of time: *We've got enough food to last another week.*

lasting /lɑːstɪŋ/ *adj*
continuing for a long time: *lasting peace*

a b c d e f g h i j k l m n o p q r s t u v w x y z

lastly /ˈlɑːstli/ *adv*
finally: *And lastly, I'd like to thank everyone who took part in the event.*

last name /ˈlɑːst ˌneɪm/ *noun*
the name that you and your family all have

late /leɪt/ *adj, adv*
1 after the usual time or the time that was arranged: *I was* ***late for*** *work this morning.* ○ *We got there too late and all the food had gone.* ○ *We had a late lunch.*
2 near the end of a period of time: *It was built in the late nineteenth century.* ○ *It was late at night.*
3 it's late something that you say when it is near the end of a day: *It's late – I really should be going.*

lately /ˈleɪtli/ *adv*
recently: *Lately, I've been walking to work.*

later /ˈleɪtəʳ/ *adj*
1 after some time: *I arranged it for a later date.*
2 more recent: *I'm not so familiar with his later work.*

later (on) /leɪtəʳ ɒn/ *adv*
after some time: *I'm off now – see you later.* ○ *He arrived later that night.*

latest[1] /ˈleɪtɪst/ *adj*
most recent: *She wears all the latest fashions.*

latest[2] /ˈleɪtɪst/ *noun*
at the latest If you tell someone to do something by a particular time at the latest, you mean they must do it before that time: *You need to be there by 8 o'clock at the latest.*

Latin /ˈlætɪn/ *noun* **[no plural]**
the language used by ancient Romans

latitude /ˈlætɪtjuːd/ *noun* **[no plural]**
the distance of a place north or south of the Equator (= imaginary line around the Earth's middle): *The latitude of Helsinki is approximately 60 degrees north.* ➲Compare **longitude**

the latter /ˈlætəʳ/ *noun*
the second of two people or things that you have just talked about: *She offered me more money or a car, and I chose the latter.*

laugh[1] /lɑːf/ *verb*
to smile and make sounds with your voice because something is funny: *You never* ***laugh at*** *my jokes.* ○ *She really* ***makes*** *me* ***laugh.***

laugh at someone/something *phrasal verb*
to show that you think someone or something is stupid: *The other children laughed at him because of his strange clothes.*

laugh[2] /lɑːf/ *noun*
1 when you smile and make sounds with your voice because something is funny: *He gave a nervous laugh.* ○ *At the time, I was embarrassed, but I* ***had a good laugh*** (= laughed a lot) *about it later.*
2 for a laugh *informal* If you do something for a laugh, you do it because it will be funny: *Just for a laugh, I pretended that I'd forgotten his birthday.*

laughter /ˈlɑːftəʳ/ *noun* **[no plural]**
the sound or act of laughing: *I heard the sound of laughter in the room next door.*

launch /lɔːnʃ/ *verb*
1 to send a spacecraft or bomb into the sky, or a ship into the water
2 to begin an important activity: *They have launched an inquiry into his death.*
3 to start selling a product: *The book was launched last February.*

launderette /ˌlɔːndəʳˈet/ *noun UK*
a place where you pay to wash and dry your clothes

laundry /ˈlɔːndri/ *noun* **[no plural]**
clothes, sheets, etc that need to be washed: *a laundry basket*

lava /ˈlɑːvə/ *noun* **[no plural]**
hot melted rock that comes out of a volcano

lavatory /ˈlævətəri/ *noun formal UK* (*plural* **lavatories**)
a toilet: *public lavatories*

law /lɔː/ *noun*
1 the law the system of official rules in a country: *You're* ***breaking the law.*** ○ *It's* ***against the law*** (= illegal) *not to wear seat belts.*
2 by law If you have to do something by law, it is illegal not to do it: *Children have to go to school by law.*
3 an official rule in a country: *There are* ***laws against*** *drinking in the street.*

lawn /lɔːn/ *noun*
an area of grass that is often cut

lawn mower /ˈlɔːn ˌməʊəʳ/ *noun*
a machine that you use to cut grass

lawyer /ˈlɔɪəʳ/ *noun*
someone whose job is to explain the law to people and give advice

lay[1] /leɪ/ *verb* (*present participle* **laying,** *past* **laid)**
1 to put something down somewhere: *She laid the baby on the bed.* ○ *He laid the plate on the table.*
2 lay eggs If an animal lays eggs, eggs come out of its body.
3 lay the table *UK* to put plates, knives, forks, etc on the table before a meal

lay[2] /leɪ/
past tense of lie[1]

layer /leɪəʳ/ *noun*
something that covers a surface, or something that is between two things: *The shelf was covered in a thick layer of dust.*

lazy /ˈleɪzi/ *adj* **(lazier, laziest)**
Someone who is lazy does not like working: *He's too lazy to make his bed in the morning.*
• **laziness** *noun* **[no plural]**

lb *written abbreviation for* pound (= a unit for measuring weight)

lead[1] /liːd/ *verb* (*present participle* **leading,** *past* **led)**
1 to show someone where to go, usually by taking them to a place: *You lead and we'll follow.* ○ *She led them down the hall.*
2 If a path or road leads somewhere, it goes there: *That path leads to the beach.*
3 to be winning a game: *They were* ***leading by*** *11 points at half-time.*
4 to be in control of a group, country, or situation: *Amy was leading the discussion.*
5 to live in a particular way: *He led a normal life despite his illness*
lead to something *phrasal verb*
to make something happen: *A bad diet can lead to health problems.*

lead[2] /liːd/ *noun*
1 when you are winning a competition: *She's* ***in the lead*** (= winning). ○ *France have a three-goal lead.*
2 the main person in a film or play: *She* ***plays the lead*** *in both films.*
3 *UK* (*US* **leash)** a rope, piece of leather, etc. that you fix to a dog's neck and hold in order to control the dog: *Dogs must be kept* ***on a lead.***

lead[3] /led/ *noun*
1 [no plural] a soft, heavy, grey metal
2 the black part inside a pencil

leader /ˈliːdəʳ/ *noun*
a person in control of a group, country, or situation: *a religious leader* ○ *He is the new* ***leader of*** *the Democratic Party.*

leadership /ˈliːdəʃɪp/ *noun* **[no plural]**
the job of being in control of a group, country, or situation: *She took over the leadership of the Republican party.* ○ *leadership skills*

leading /ˈliːdɪŋ/ *adj*
very important or most important: *He's a leading Hollywood producer.*

leaf /liːf/ *noun* (*plural* **leaves)**
a flat, green part of a plant that grows from a stem or branch: *an oak leaf* ○ *the falling leaves*

leaf

leaflet /ˈliːflət/ *noun*
a piece of folded paper which has information

league /liːg/ *noun*
a group of teams which compete against each other in a sport: *Which team are top of the league?*

leak[1] /liːk/ *verb*
1 If a container leaks, it allows liquid or gas to come out when it should not: *The bottle had leaked and the bag was all wet.*
2 to tell people information that is secret: *Details of the report had been* ***leaked to*** *the press.*

leak[2] /liːk/ *noun*
1 a hole in something that a liquid or gas comes out of: *There is a leak in the roof.*
2 when someone tells people information that is secret

leaky /ˈliːki/ *adj informal* **(leakier, leakiest)**
Something that is leaky has a hole in it and liquid or gas can get through: *a leaky roof*

lean[1] /liːn/ *verb* (*past* **leaned** or **leant)**
to move the top part of your body in a particular direction: *She leaned forward to speak to the child.* ○ *He was leaning out of the window.*

lean (something) against/on something *phrasal verb*
to sit or stand with part of your body against something: *He leaned against the wall.*

lean something against/on something *phrasal verb*
to put something against a wall or other surface: *Lean the ladder against the wall.*

lean² /liːn/ *adj*
1 thin and healthy: *lean and fit*
2 Lean meat has very little fat on it.

leant /lent/ *past of* lean

leap /liːp/ *verb* (*present participle* **leaping**, *past* **leapt**)
1 to suddenly move somewhere: *I leapt up to answer the phone.*
2 to jump somewhere: *She leapt over the wall.*

leapt /lept/ *past of* leap

leap year /ˈliːp jɪəʳ/ *noun*
a year that happens every four years, in which February has 29 days and not 28

learn /lɜːn/ *verb* (*past* **learned** or **learnt**)
1 to get knowledge or a new skill: *I **learned** a lot **about** computers. ◦ I'm **learning to** drive*
2 to make yourself remember some writing: *How do actors learn all those lines?*
3 to start to understand that you must change the way you behave: *She'll soon **learn that** she can't treat people so badly. ◦ You learn from your mistakes.*

learner /ˈlɜːnəʳ/ *noun*
someone who is getting knowledge or a new skill: *learners of English*

least¹ /liːst/ *adv*
1 less than anyone or anything else: *Which car costs least? ◦ I chose the least expensive restaurant.*
2 at least
a as much as, or more than, a number or amount: *You'll have to wait at least an hour.*
b something that you say when you are telling someone about a good thing in a bad situation: *It's a small house but at least there's a garden.*
3 not in the least not at all: *I don't mind staying at home, not in the least.*

least² /liːst/ *quantifier*
the smallest amount: *She earns the least money of all of us.*

leather /ˈleðəʳ/ *noun* **[no plural]**
the skin of animals that is used to make shoes and bags: *a leather jacket*

leave¹ /liːv/ *verb* (*present participle* **leaving**, *past* **left**)
1 to go away from a place: *I leave work at 5 o'clock. ◦ They **left for** Paris last night. ◦ She left school at 16.*
2 to not take something with you when you go away from a place: *I left my jacket in the car. ◦ She left a letter for me in the kitchen.*
3 to not use all of something: *They drank all the wine but they left some food.*
4 leave something open/on/off, etc to make something stay open/on/off, etc: *Who left the window open?*
5 to give something to something after you die: *His aunt left him a lot of money. ◦ He **left** the house **to** Julia.*
6 leave someone alone to stop speaking to someone: *Leave me alone! I'm trying to work.*

leave someone/something out *phrasal verb*
to not include someone or something: *Have I left anyone out of that list?*

be left out *phrasal verb*
to be sad because other people are doing something without you: *The older children had gone upstairs to play and she felt left out.*

leave² /liːv/ *noun* **[no plural]**
time when you do not go to work: *She's **on** sick **leave**.*

leaves /liːvz/
plural of leaf

lecture¹ /ˈlektʃəʳ/ *noun*
when someone speaks to a group of people about a subject: *We went to a **lecture on** Italian art.*

lecture² /ˈlektʃəʳ/ *verb* (*present participle* **lecturing**, *past* **lectured**)
to speak to a group of people about a subject, usually at a university: *For ten years she **lectured in** law.*

lecturer /ˈlektʃᵊrəʳ/ *noun UK*
someone who teaches at a university or college: *a lecturer in maths*

led /led/
past of lead

ledge /ledʒ/ *noun*
a long, flat surface that comes out under a window

leek /liːk/ *noun*
a long white and green vegetable that is similar to an onion

left[1] /left/ *adj, adv*
on or towards the side of your body where your heart is: *He had an earring in his left ear.* ○ ***Turn left*** *at the end of the corridor.* ➲Opposite **right**

left[2] /left/ *noun* **[no plural]**
the left side: *Ted was sitting* ***on*** *my* ***left****.* ➲Opposite **right**

left[3] /left/
past of leave

left-handed /ˌleftˈhændɪd/ *adj*
using your left hand to do most things ➲Opposite **right-handed**

leg

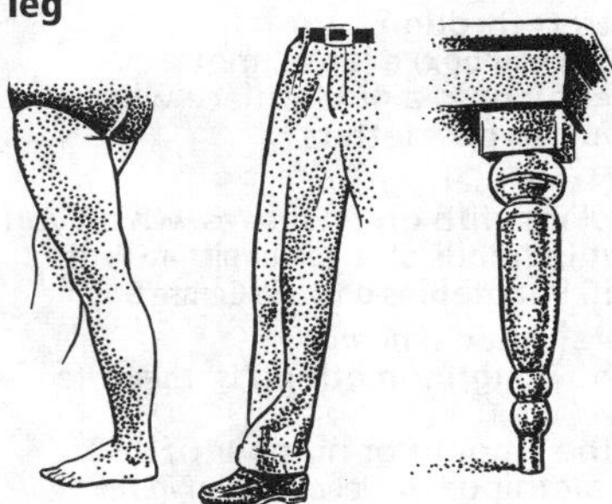

leg /leg/ *noun*
1 one of the parts of the body that is used for walking: *My legs are tired after so much walking.* ○ *He broke his leg in the accident.* ➲See colour picture **The Body** on page Centre 2
2 one of the parts of a chair, table, etc that it stands on: *a table leg*
3 be on its last legs *informal* If a machine is on its last legs, it is old and will stop working soon: *My computer is on its last legs.*

legal /ˈliːgəl/ *adj*
1 relating to the law: *legal advice*
2 allowed by law: *Is it legal to carry a gun?* ➲Opposite **illegal**
• **legally** *adv*: *Children under sixteen are not legally allowed to buy cigarettes.*

legend /ˈledʒənd/ *noun*
1 a story from a time in the past that was very long ago: *the legends of King Arthur*
2 a famous person: *Jazz legend, Ella Fitzgerald, once sang in this bar.*

legible /ˈledʒəbl/ *adj*
If writing is legible, you can read it. ➲Opposite **illegible**

leisure /ˈleʒər/ *noun* **[no plural]**
the time when you are not working: *Do you have much leisure time?*

lemon

lemon /ˈlemən/ *noun*
an oval, yellow fruit that has sour juice: *lemon juice* ➲See colour picture **Fruit and Vegetables** on page Centre 8

lemonade /ˌleməˈneɪd/ *noun* **[no plural]**
a cold drink that tastes of lemon

lend /lend/ *verb* (*present participle* **lending**, *past* **lent**)
1 to give something to someone for a period of time: *I* ***lent*** *my bike* ***to*** *Sara.* ○ *She lent me her car for the weekend.*
2 If a bank lends money, it gives money to someone who then pays the money back in small amounts over a period.

length /leŋθ/ *noun*
1 how long something is from one end to the other: *The room is over eight metres* ***in length****.* ○ *What length are the curtains?*
2 go to great lengths to do something to try very hard to do something: *He'll go to great lengths to get what he wants.*

lengthen /ˈleŋθən/ *verb*
to become longer or to make something longer: *They have lengthened the school day.*

lens /lenz/ *noun* (*plural* **lenses**)
a curved piece of glass in cameras, glasses, and scientific equipment used for looking at things

lent /lent/
past of lend

lentil /ˈlentəl/ *noun*
a very small dried bean which you cook and eat

a b c d e f g h i j k **l** m n o p q r s t u v w x y z

leopard

leopard /ˈlepəd/ *noun*
a large, wild animal of the cat family, with yellow fur and dark spots

less[1] /les/ *adv*
not as much: *You should eat less.*

less[2] /les/ *quantifier*
a smaller amount: *She gets about £50 a week or less.* ○ *I prefer my coffee with a little less sugar.*

lessen /ˈlesᵊn/ *verb*
to become less or to make something less: *Exercise lessens the chance of heart disease.*

lesson /ˈlesᵊn/ *noun*
1 a period of time when a teacher teaches people: *I am* ***taking*** *guitar* ***lessons****.* ○ *Lessons start at 9 a.m.*
2 teach someone a lesson to punish someone so that they will not behave badly again

let /let/ *verb* (*present participle* **letting,** *past* **let**)
1 to allow someone to do something or to allow someone to have something: *She let me use her camera.* ○ *I let her have some money.*
2 let's something that you say to ask someone if they want to do something with you: *Let's go shopping.*
3 If you let a building, you allow someone to live there and they give you money: *I* ***let*** *the top floor of my house* ***to*** *a student.*
4 let someone know to tell someone something: *I'll let you know where we are meeting nearer the time.*
5 let (something) go to stop holding something: *I* ***let go of*** *the rope.*

let someone down *phrasal verb*
to not do something that you promised to do: *I promised Sophie I would meet her and I can't let her down.*

let someone in *phrasal verb*
to allow someone to enter a room or building, often by opening the door: *Could you go down and let Rosa in?*

let someone off *phrasal verb*
to not punish someone who has done something wrong: *I'll let you off this time, but don't ever lie to me again.*

let someone/something out *phrasal verb*
to allow a person or animal to leave somewhere, especially by opening a door

lethal /ˈliːθᵊl/ *adj*
able to kill someone: *a lethal weapon*

letter /ˈletəʳ/ *noun*
1 some writing that you send to someone, usually by post: *I got a letter from Paul this morning.*
2 one of the symbols (for example, a, j, p) that we use to write words: *the letter K*

letterbox /ˈletəbɒks/ *noun UK* (*plural* **letterboxes)**
1 a small hole in a door that you put letters through
2 (*US* **mailbox**) a large, metal container in a public place where you can post letters

lettuce /ˈletɪs/ *noun*
a plant with green leaves, which you eat in salads ➲See colour picture **Fruit and Vegetables** on page Centre 8

level[1] /ˈlevᵊl/ *noun*
1 how high something is: *the water level*
2 the amount or number of something: *The level of iron in her blood was too low.*
3 how good someone is at doing something compared to other people: *Students at this level need a lot of help.*
4 a floor in a building: *The store had three levels.*

level[2] /ˈlevᵊl/ *adj*
1 at the same height: *I got down till my face was* ***level with*** *his.*
2 flat or horizontal: *Make sure the camera is level before you take the picture.*

lever /ˈliːvəʳ/ *noun*
1 a handle that you push or pull to make a machine work
2 a long bar that you use to lift or move something by pressing one end

liable /ˈlaɪəbl/ *adj*
be liable to do something to be likely to do something: *He is liable to get cross if you wake him.*

liar /ˈlaɪəʳ/ *noun*
someone who tells lies

liberal /ˈlɪbərəl/ *adj*
accepting beliefs and behaviour that are new or different from your own: *Her parents were very liberal.*

liberty /ˈlɪbəti/ *noun* **[no plural]**
the freedom to live, work and travel as you want to: *Many would fight to preserve their liberty.*

library /ˈlaɪbrəri/ *noun* (*plural* **libraries**)
a place with a lot of books that you can read or borrow

lice /laɪs/
plural of louse

licence *UK* (*US* **license**) /ˈlaɪsəns/ *noun*
a piece of paper that allows you to do or have something: *Can I see you driving licence, Sir?*

license /ˈlaɪsəns/ *verb* (*present participle* **licensing,** *past* **licensed**)
to allow someone officially to do or have something: *Are they licensed to carry guns?*

lick /lɪk/ *verb*
to move your tongue across something: *She licked her lips* ○ *We licked the chocolate off our fingers.*

lick

lid /lɪd/ *noun*
the top part of a container that you can take off: *Can you get the lid off this jar?*

lie¹ /laɪ/ *verb* (*present participle* **lying,** *past tense* **lay,** *past participle* **lain**)
1 lie in/on, etc to put your body flat on something or to be in this position: *He lay on the bed.* ○ *She was lying on her side.*
2 lie below/in/on/to, etc to be in a place: *The river lies 30 km to the south of the city.*

lie down *phrasal verb*
to move into a position in which your body is flat, usually in order to sleep or rest: *I'm not feeling well – I'm going to lie down.* ➲See colour picture **Phrasal Verbs** on page Centre 13

lie² /laɪ/ *verb* (*present participle* **lying,** *past* **lied**)
to say or write something that you know is not true: *Are you **lying to** me?* ○ *He **lied about** his qualifications for the job.*

lie³ /laɪ/ *noun*
something that you say or write which you know is not true: *I **told a lie** when I said I liked her haircut.*

lie-in /ˈlaɪˌɪn/ *noun UK*
when you stay in bed in the morning longer than usual: *I **had a** long **lie-in** this morning.*

lieutenant /lefˈtenənt/ *noun*
an officer of middle rank in the army, navy, or air force: *first/second lieutenant*

life /laɪf/ *noun*
1 [no plural] living things, such as animals and plants: *human life* ○ *Is there life in outer space?*
2 (*plural* **lives**) the time between a person's birth and their death: *He **had** a happy **life**.* ○ *Do you want to **spend** the rest of your **life** with him?*
3 (*plural* **lives**) a way of living: *You **lead** an exciting **life**.*
4 [no plural] energy and activity: *Like all small children, she was always so **full of life**.*
5 That's life. something you say which means bad things happen and you cannot stop them: *You don't get everything you want but that's life, isn't it?*
6 Get a life! *informal* something you say to a boring person when you want them to do more exciting things: *Surely you're not cleaning the house on Saturday night? Get a life!*

lifeboat /ˈlaɪfbəʊt/ *noun*
a small boat that is used to help people who are in danger at sea

lifestyle /ˈlaɪfstaɪl/ *noun*
the way that you live: *She has a very unhealthy lifestyle.*

lifetime /ˈlaɪftaɪm/ *noun*
the period of time that someone is alive: *She saw such huge changes in her lifetime.*

lift¹ /lɪft/ *verb*
to put something or someone in a higher position: *She **lifted** the baby **up** and put him in his chair.* ○ *He lifted his glass to his lips.*

lift² /lɪft/ *noun*
1 *UK* (*US* **elevator**) a machine that carries people up and down in tall

buildings: *Shall we use the stairs or take the lift?*
2 a free ride somewhere, usually in a car: *Can you **give** me **a lift** to the airport?*

lift-off /ˈlɪftɒf/ *noun*
the moment when a spacecraft leaves the ground

lights

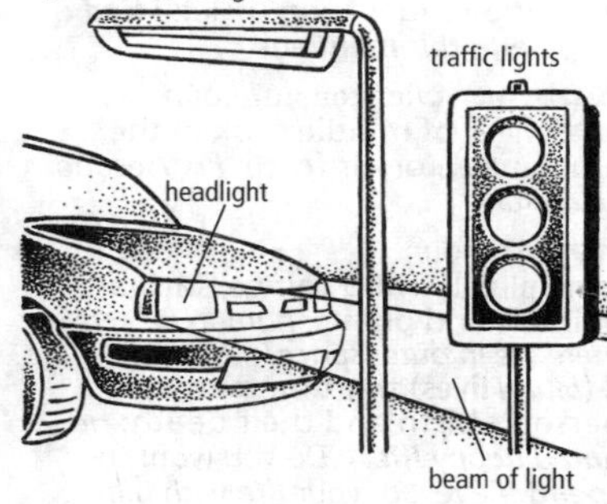

light[1] /laɪt/ *noun*
1 [no plural] the brightness that shines from the sun, from fire, or from an object, allowing you to see things: *bright light* ○ *This room gets a lot of light in the morning.*
2 an object that makes light: *car lights* ○ *Could you turn the kitchen light off?*

light[2] /laɪt/ *adj*
1 not heavy: *My bag is very light.*
2 small in amount: *light rain* ○ *I only had a light lunch.*
3 not strong or not forceful: *a light breeze*
4 Light colours are pale: *a light blue shirt* ➲Opposite **dark**
5 bright from the sun: *Let's go now while it's still light.*
• **lightness** *noun* **[no plural]**

light[3] /laɪt/ *verb* (*present participle* **lighting**, *past* **lit**)
1 to start to burn, or to make something start to burn: *She lit a cigarette.* ○ *The wood won't light.*
2 to make light somewhere so that you can see things: *The room was lit by a single light bulb.*

light bulb

light bulb /ˈlaɪt ˌbʌlb/ *noun*
a glass object containing a wire which makes light from electricity

lighten /ˈlaɪtᵊn/ *verb*
to become less dark, or to make something less dark: *The sun had lightened her hair.*
lighten up *phrasal verb informal*
to become happier and less serious: *I wish she'd lighten up.*

lighter /ˈlaɪtəʳ/ *noun*
a small object that makes fire and is used to make cigarettes start burning

lighthouse

lighthouse /ˈlaɪthaʊs/ *noun*
a tall building with a large light which shows ships that there are rocks

lighting /ˈlaɪtɪŋ/ *noun* **[no plural]**
the light that is used in a room or building

lightly /ˈlaɪtli/ *adv*
1 gently, without force: *He kissed her lightly on the cheek.*
2 not much: *I like lightly cooked vegetables.*

lightning /ˈlaɪtnɪŋ/ *noun* **[no plural]**
sudden bright light in the sky during a storm: *thunder and lightning*

like[1] /laɪk/ *preposition*
1 similar to someone or something: *He looks like his father.* ○ *They were acting like children.* ○ *It sounded like Harry.*
2 for example: *She looks best in bright colours, like red and pink.*
3 What is someone/something like? something you say when you want someone to describe someone or something: *I haven't met him – what's he like?* ○ *So what's your new dress like?*

like[2] /laɪk/ *verb* (*present participle* **liking**, *past* **liked**)
1 to enjoy something or think that someone or something is nice: *I like to paint in my spare time.* ○ *He really likes her.* ○ *What do you **like about** him?* ➲Opposite **dislike**
2 would like something to want something: *I'd **like to** meet him.* ○ *I'd like some bread, please.*
3 Would you like...? used to offer someone something: *Would you like a drink?* ○ *Would you like to eat now?*

like[3] /laɪk/ *conjunction informal*
in the same way as: *Do it exactly like I told you to.*

likeable /ˈlaɪkəbl/ *adj*
If you are likeable, you are nice and people like you.

likely /ˈlaɪkli/ *adj*
1 expected: *I'm* ***likely to*** *forget if you don't remind me.* ○ *It's* ***likely that*** *he'll say no.*
2 probably true: *This is the most likely explanation.* ➲Opposite **unlikely**

likewise /ˈlaɪkwaɪz/ *adv formal*
in the same way: *Water these plants twice a week and likewise the ones in the bedroom.*

liking /ˈlaɪkɪŋ/ *noun*
1 a feeling that you like someone or something: *He has* ***a liking for*** *young women.*
2 take a liking to someone to like someone when you meet them: *He obviously took a liking to her.*

lily /ˈlɪli/ *noun* (*plural* **lilies)**
a plant with big flowers that are often white

limb /lɪm/ *noun*
a leg or an arm of a person

lime /laɪm/ *noun*
a small, green fruit that is sour like a lemon

limit[1] /ˈlɪmɪt/ *noun*
the largest amount of something that is possible or allowed: *a time limit* ○ *There's a* ***limit to*** *how much time we can spend on this.*

limit[2] /ˈlɪmɪt/ *verb*
to control something so that it is less than a particular amount or number: *We'll have to limit the number of guests.*

limp[1] /lɪmp/ *adj*
soft and weak: *Her arms were limp, hanging by her side.*

limp[2] /lɪmp/ *verb*
to walk with difficulty because one of your legs or feet is hurt
• **limp** *noun*: *She walks with a limp.*

line[1] /laɪn/ *noun*
1 a long, thin mark: *Sign your name on the dotted line.* ○ *Draw a line around your hand.*
2 a row of people or things: *a line of trees* ○ *There was a long* ***line of*** *people outside the shop.*
3 a piece of rope or wire with a special purpose: *a fishing line*
4 a row of words on a page, for example in a song or poem: *The same line is repeated throughout the poem.*
5 lines the marks that older people have on their faces, when the skin is loose

line[2] /laɪn/ *verb* (*present participle* **lining**, *past* **lined)**
1 to form a row along the side of something: *Trees and cafés lined the street.*
2 be lined with something to cover the inside of a piece of clothing with a material: *a jacket lined with fur*

linen /ˈlɪnɪn/ *noun* **[no plural]**
1 an expensive cloth that is like rough cotton: *a linen jacket*
2 pieces of cloth that you use to cover tables and beds: *bed linen*

linger /ˈlɪŋgəʳ/ *verb*
to stay somewhere for a long time: *The smell of onions lingers.*

lining /ˈlaɪnɪŋ/ *noun*
a material that covers the inside of something: *a jacket lining*

link[1] /lɪŋk/ *noun*
1 a connection between two people, things, or ideas: *There's a direct* ***link between*** *smoking and cancer.* ○ *Their* ***links with*** *Britain are still strong.*
2 one ring of a chain
3 (*also* **hyperlink)** a connection between documents or areas on the Internet: *Click on this link to visit our online bookstore.*

link[2] /lɪŋk/ *verb*
to make a connection between two or more people, things, or ideas: *The drug has been* ***linked to*** *the deaths of several athletes.* ○ *The two offices will be linked by computer.*

lion

lion /ˈlaɪən/ *noun*
a large, wild animal of the cat family, with light brown fur

a b c d e f g h i j k **l** m n o p q r s t u v w x y z

a b c d e f g h i j k l m n o p q r s t u v w x y z

lip /lɪp/ *noun*
one of the two soft, red edges of the mouth: *He licked his lips.* ➲See colour picture **The Body** on page Centre 2

lipstick /ˈlɪpstɪk/ *noun* **[no plural]**
a colour that women put on their lips

lipstick

liquid /ˈlɪkwɪd/ *noun*
a substance, for example water, that is not solid and that you can pour easily
• **liquid** *adj*: *liquid fuel*

list[1] /lɪst/ *noun*
a lot of words that are written one under the other: *a shopping list* ○ *Is your name* ***on the list****?* ○ ***Make a list*** *of everything you need.*

list[2] /lɪst/ *verb*
to make a list, or to have something in a list: *All names are listed alphabetically.*

listen /ˈlɪsᵊn/ *verb*
to give attention to someone or something in order to hear them: *I* ***listen to*** *the radio while I have breakfast.* ○ *She does all the talking – I just sit and listen.* ○ *Listen, if you need money, I can give you some.*

lit /lɪt/
past of light

literature /ˈlɪtrətʃəʳ/ *noun* **[no plural]**
books, poems, etc that are considered to be art: *classical literature*

litre *UK* (*US* **liter**) /ˈliːtəʳ/ *noun*
a unit for measuring liquid

litter /ˈlɪtəʳ/ *noun* **[no plural]**
pieces of paper and other waste that are left in public places

little[1] /ˈlɪtl/ *adj*
1 small in size or amount: *I have a little bag.* ○ *She's so little.* ○ *I had* ***a little bit of*** *cake.*
2 short in time or distance: *Sit down* ***for a little while****.* ○ *Let's have a little break.*
3 not important: *It's only a little problem.*

little[2] /ˈlɪtl/ *quantifier*
not much or not enough: *There's so little choice.*

little[3] /ˈlɪtl/ *pronoun*
1 not much, or not enough: *We did* ***very little*** *on Sunday.*
2 a little a small amount: *"More wine?" "Just a little, please."*

live[1] /lɪv/ *verb* (*present participle* **living**, *past* **lived**)
1 to be alive: *I hope I live to see my grandchildren.*
2 to have your home somewhere: *They live in New York.* ○ *Where do you live?*
live up to something *phrasal verb*
to be as good as someone hopes: *Did the trip* ***live up to*** *your* ***expectations****?*

live[2] /laɪv/ *adj*
1 having life: *Millions of live animals are moved around the world each year.*
2 A live performance is done with people watching or listening: *a live concert* ○ *live music*

lively /ˈlaɪvli/ *adj*
full of energy and interest: *It was a lively debate.* ○ *a lively child*

liver /ˈlɪvəʳ/ *noun*
1 a part in your body that cleans your blood
2 [no plural] the liver of an animal that is eaten by people

lives /lɪvz/
plural of life

living /ˈlɪvɪŋ/ *noun* **[no plural]**
the money that you get from your job: *Like everyone else, I have to* ***make a living****.* ○ *What does he* ***do for a living*** (= how does he get money)*?*

living room /ˈlɪvɪŋ ˌruːm/ (*also UK* **sitting room**) *noun*
the room in a house where people sit to relax and watch television ➲See colour picture **The Living Room** on page Centre 11

lizard /ˈlɪzəd/ *noun*
a small animal with thick skin, a long tail, and four short legs

load[1] /ləʊd/ *noun*
1 things that are carried, often by a vehicle: *We were behind a truck carrying a load of coal.*
2 a load/loads *informal* a lot of something: *There were loads of people there.* ○ *Have some more food – there's loads.*

load[2] /ləʊd/ *verb*
1 to put a lot of things into a vehicle or machine: *I was just loading the washing machine.*
2 to put film in a camera or bullets in a gun

loaf /ləʊf/ *noun* (*plural* **loaves**)
bread that has been made in one large piece: *a loaf of bread*

loan[1] /ləʊn/ *noun*
money that someone borrows: *a bank loan* ○ *a student loan*

loan[2] /ləʊn/ *verb*
to give something to someone for a period of time: *My dad loaned me the money.*

loathe /ləʊð/ *verb* (*present participle* **loathing**, *past* **loathed**)
to hate someone or something: *I loathe housework*

loaves /ləʊvz/
plural of loaf

lobby /ˈlɒbi/ *noun* (*plural* **lobbies**)
a room at the main entrance of a building: *a hotel lobby*

lobster /ˈlɒbstəʳ/ *noun*
a sea animal that has two claws (= sharp, curved parts) and eight legs, or the meat of this animal

local /ˈləʊkᵊl/ *adj*
relating to an area near you: *She goes to the local school.*
• **locally** *adv*: *locally grown vegetables*

location /ləʊˈkeɪʃᵊn/ *noun*
a place or position: *Have they decided on* ***the location of*** *the factory?*

lock[1] /lɒk/ *verb*
1 to fasten something with a key: *Did you lock the door?* ➲Opposite **unlock**
2 to put something or someone in a place or container that is fastened with a key: *She locked herself in her bedroom.*

lock[2] /lɒk/ *noun*
1 the thing that you use to close a door, window, etc, and that needs a key to open it: *I heard someone turn a key in the lock.* ○ *safety locks*

locker /ˈlɒkəʳ/ *noun*
a small cupboard in a public area where you can keep things: *a luggage locker*

lodge /lɒdʒ/ *verb* (*present participle* **lodging**, *past* **lodged**)
1 to become stuck somewhere: *The bullet had lodged near his heart.*
2 to live in someone's home and give them money for it: *He* ***lodges with*** *a French family.*

lodger /ˈlɒdʒəʳ/ *UK* (*US* **boarder**) *noun*
someone who pays to live with someone in their home

loft /lɒft/ *noun*
the space under the roof of a house or other building

log[1] /lɒg/ *noun*
a thick piece of wood that has been cut from a tree: *We need more logs for the fire.*

log[2] /lɒg/ *verb* (*present participle* **logging**, *past* **logged**)
log in/on *phrasal verb*
to connect a computer to a system of computers by typing your name, usually to start working
log off/out *phrasal verb*
to stop a computer being connected to a computer system, usually to stop working

logo /ˈləʊgəʊ/ *noun*
a special design that a company uses to sell its products

lollipop /ˈlɒlipɒp/ *noun*
a large, hard sweet on a stick

lollipop

lonely /ˈləʊnli/ *adj*
sad because you are not with other people: *She gets lonely now that the kids have all left home.*

long[1] /lɒŋ/ *adj*
1 having a large distance from one end to the other: *long hair* ○ *long legs* ○ *a long dress* ➲Opposite **short**
2 continuing for a large amount of time: *a long film* ○ *I waited a long time.* ➲Opposite **short**
3 used when asking for or giving information about the distance or time of something: *It's about three metres long.* ○ *The concert was three hours long.* ○ *How long was the skirt?* ○ *How long is the film?*

long[2] /lɒŋ/ *adv*
1 for a long time: *Did you have to wait long for the train?*
2 as long as used when you are talking about something that must happen before something else can happen: *You can play football as long as you do your homework first.*

long[3] /lɒŋ/ *noun* **[no plural]**
a large amount of time: *She won't be away for long.*

long[4] /lɒŋ/ *verb formal*
to want something very much: *She*

longed to *see him again.* ○ *I'm* ***longing for*** *some sun.*

long-distance /ˌlɒŋˈdɪst^{ə}ns/ *adj*
travelling or speaking between two places that are a long way apart: *a long-distance race* ○ *a long-distance phone call*

long-haul /ˈlɒŋˌhɔːl/ *adj*
travelling a long distance: *a long-haul flight*

longing /ˈlɒŋɪŋ/ *noun* **[no plural]**
a feeling of wanting something or someone very much: *He gazed at her, his eyes full of longing.*

longitude /ˈlɒndʒɪtjuːd/ *noun* **[no plural]**
the distance of a place east or west of an imaginary line from the top to the bottom of the Earth ➲Compare **latitude**

look[1] /lʊk/ *verb*
1 to turn your eyes in the direction of something or someone so that you can see them: ***Look at*** *the picture on page two.* ○ *He was looking out of the window.*
2 to try to find someone or something: *I'm* ***looking for*** *my keys.* ○ *I've looked everywhere but I can't find my bag.*
3 look nice/strange, etc used to describe the appearance of a person or thing: *That food looks nice.* ○ *You look tired, my love.*
4 it looks like; it looks as if used to say that something will probably happen: *It looks as if he isn't coming.*
5 Look! something you say when you are annoyed and you want people to listen to you: *Look, I've had enough of your complaints.*

look after someone/something *phrasal verb*
to take care of someone or something: *Could you look after the children while I'm out?*

look forward to something *phrasal verb*
to feel happy and excited about something that is going to happen: *I'm really looking forward to seeing him.*

Look out! *phrasal verb*
something you say when someone is in danger: *Look out – there's a car coming!*

look something up *phrasal verb*
to look at a book or computer in order to find information: *I looked it up on the Internet.*

look[2] /lʊk/ *noun*
1 when you look at someone or something: ***Take a look*** *at these pictures.* ○ *You've got your photos back – can I* ***have a look****?*
2 an expression on someone's face: *She had a worried look on her face.*
3 someone's looks a person's appearance, especially how attractive they are: *I liked his looks.*

loop /luːp/ *noun*
a circle of something long and thin, such as a piece of string or wire

loose /luːs/ *adj*
1 not firmly fixed: *One of my buttons is loose.*
2 Loose clothes are large and not tight: *a loose dress*
3 An animal that is loose is free to move around: *Two lions escaped and are still loose.*

loosen /ˈluːs^{ə}n/ *verb*
to become loose or make something loose: *He loosened his tie.*

lord /lɔːd/ *noun*
1 (*also* **Lord**) in the UK, a title for a man of high social rank: *Lord Lichfield*
2 the Lord God or Christ

lorry /ˈlɒri/ *UK* (*US* **truck**) *noun* (*plural* **lorries**)
a large road vehicle for carrying things from place to place

lose /luːz/ *verb* (*present participle* **losing**, *past* **lost**)
1 to not be able to find someone or something: *I've lost my passport.* ○ *She's always losing her keys.*
2 to stop having someone or something that you had before: *She lost a leg in a car accident.* ○ *He lost his job.*
3 to have less of something than you had before: *She's lost a lot of weight.* ○ *He's losing his hair.*
4 If you lose a game, the team or person that you are playing against wins: *Chelsea lost by a goal.* ○ *They're losing 3-1.*

loser /ˈluːzə^{r}/ *noun*
1 someone who does not win a game or competition
2 *informal* someone who is not successful in anything they do

loss /lɒs/ *noun* (*plural* **losses**)

a b c d e f g h i j k **l** m n o p q r s t u v w x y z

THE BATHROOM

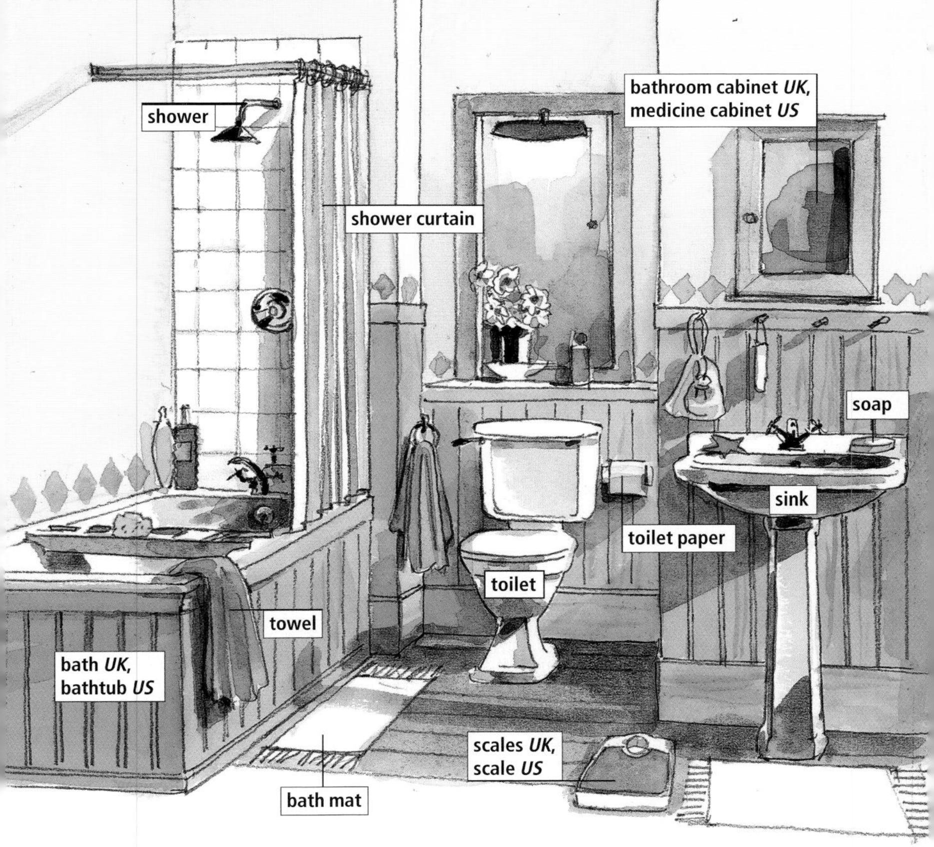

shower

bathroom cabinet *UK*,
medicine cabinet *US*

shower curtain

soap

sink

toilet paper

toilet

towel

bath *UK*,
bathtub *US*

scales *UK*,
scale *US*

bath mat

toothbrush

soap

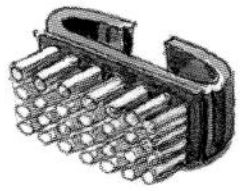

nail brush

toothpaste

cotton wool

razor

electric razor

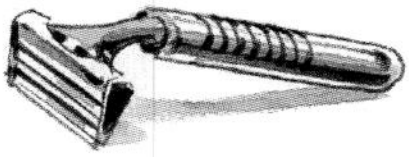

THE BODY

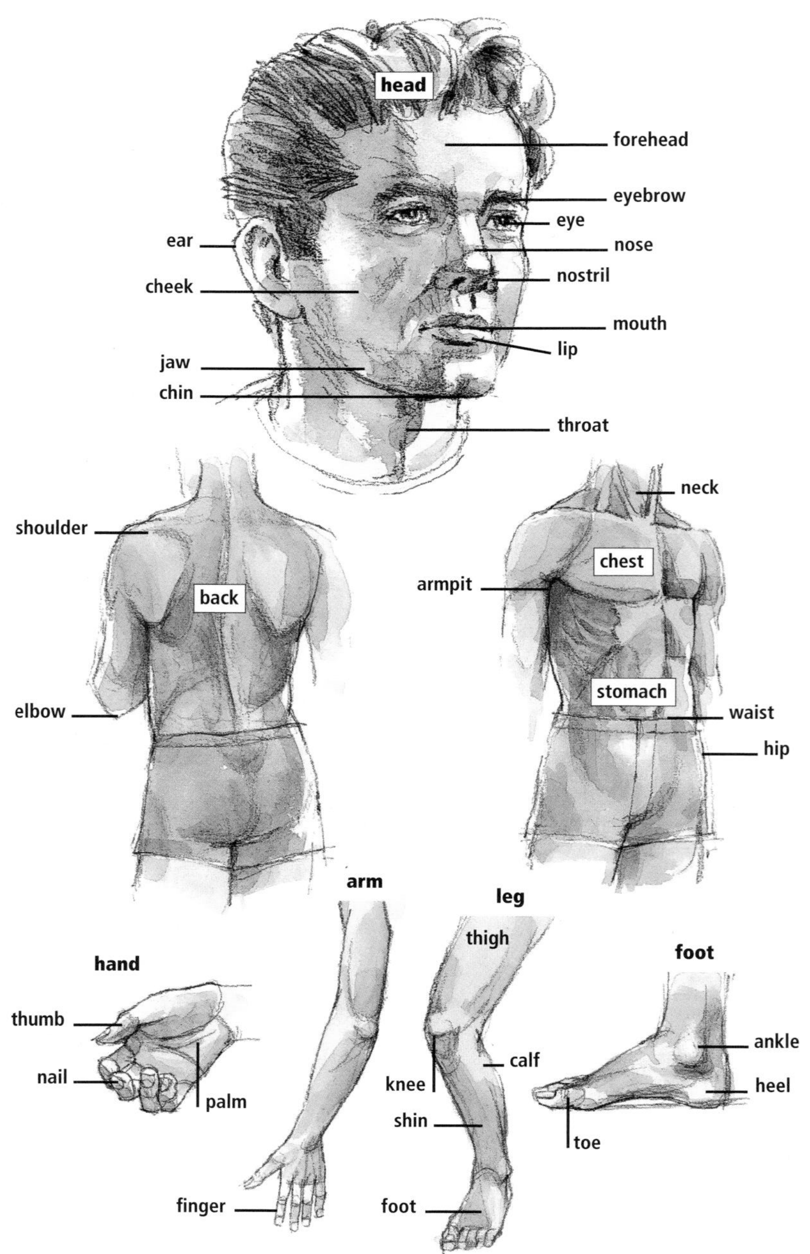
head
forehead
eyebrow
eye
ear
nose
cheek
nostril
mouth
lip
jaw
chin
throat
neck
shoulder
chest
armpit
back
stomach
elbow
waist
hip
arm
leg
thigh
hand
foot
thumb
ankle
calf
nail
palm
knee
heel
shin
toe
finger
foot

CAR

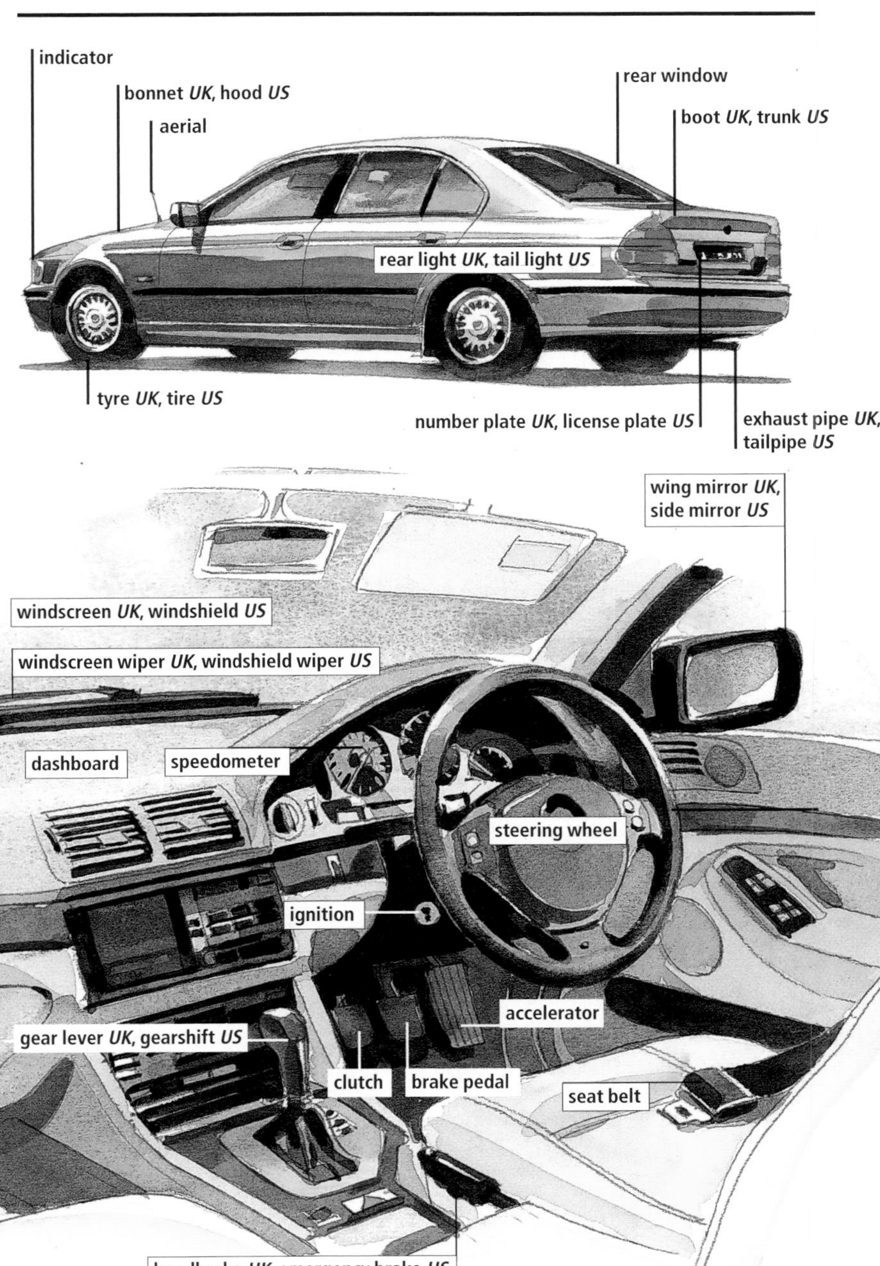
indicator
bonnet *UK*, hood *US*
aerial
rear window
boot *UK*, trunk *US*
rear light *UK*, tail light *US*
tyre *UK*, tire *US*
number plate *UK*, license plate *US*
exhaust pipe *UK*, tailpipe *US*
wing mirror *UK*, side mirror *US*
windscreen *UK*, windshield *US*
windscreen wiper *UK*, windshield wiper *US*
dashboard
speedometer
steering wheel
ignition
accelerator
gear lever *UK*, gearshift *US*
clutch
brake pedal
seat belt
handbrake *UK*, emergency brake *US*

THE CLASSROOM

CLOTHES

shirt
T-shirt
dress
evening dress
miniskirt
sweatshirt
jumper *UK*, sweater *US*
cardigan
skirt
jacket
waterproof jacket
coat
waistcoat
tie
scarf
scarf
belt
boots
sandals
buckle
shoes
trainers
trousers
jeans
shorts
cycling shorts
leggings
stockings
tights *UK*, pantyhose *US*
socks
bra
pants *UK*, panties *US*
boxer shorts
underpants
vest
bikini
sunglasses
trunks
hat
cap

COLOURS

red
blue
green
yellow
brown
black
grey
white
purple
pink
orange
navy blue
lime green
beige
maroon
khaki

FOOD

roll *UK*
sandwich
soup
salad
biscuits *UK*,
cookies *US*
cake
vegetables
pizza
rice
chips *UK*,
french fries *US*
cereal
pasta
peanuts
crisps *UK*,
chips *US*
honey
jam
fish
egg
butter
yoghurt
cheese
meat

FRUIT AND VEGETABLES

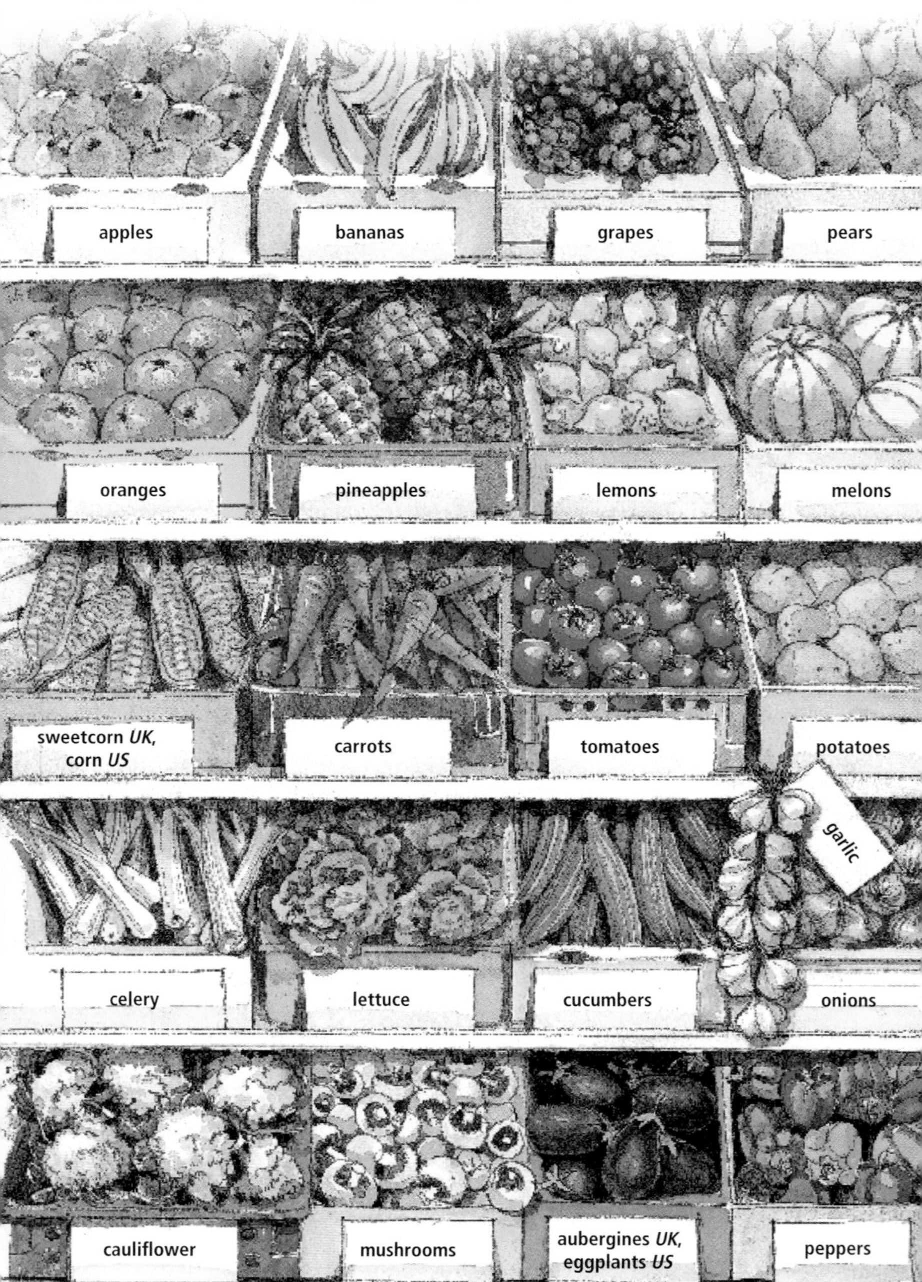

HAIR

blonde/fair
dark
red
grey
straight
curly
wavy
spiky
fringe *UK*,
bangs *US*
moustache
beard
stubble
plait *UK*,
braid *US*
ponytail
shoulder-length
long
short
bald

THE KITCHEN

chopping board

toaster

bread bin *UK*,
bread box *US*

tin opener *UK*,
can opener *US*

food processor

grater

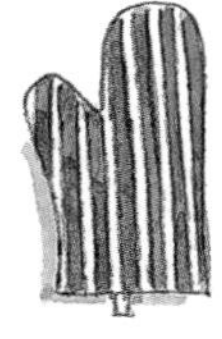
oven glove

kettle

blender

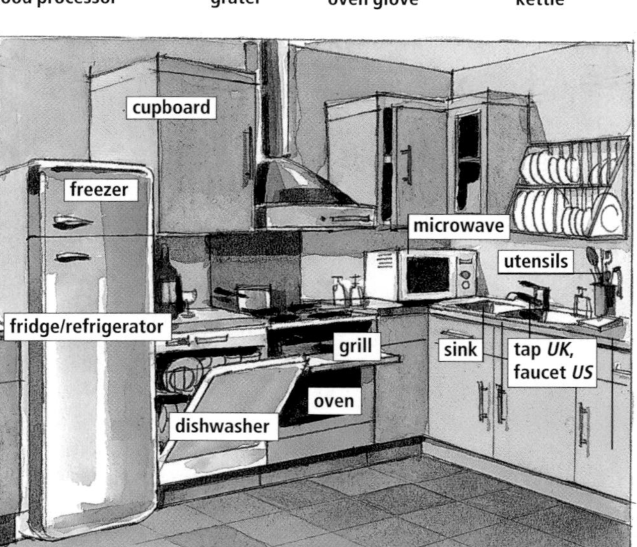

coffee maker

teapot

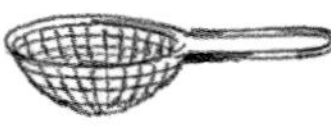
sieve

scales *UK*, scale *U*

cake tin *UK*,
cake pan *US*

rolling pin

saucepan

baking tray

frying pan

measuring spoons

THE LIVING ROOM

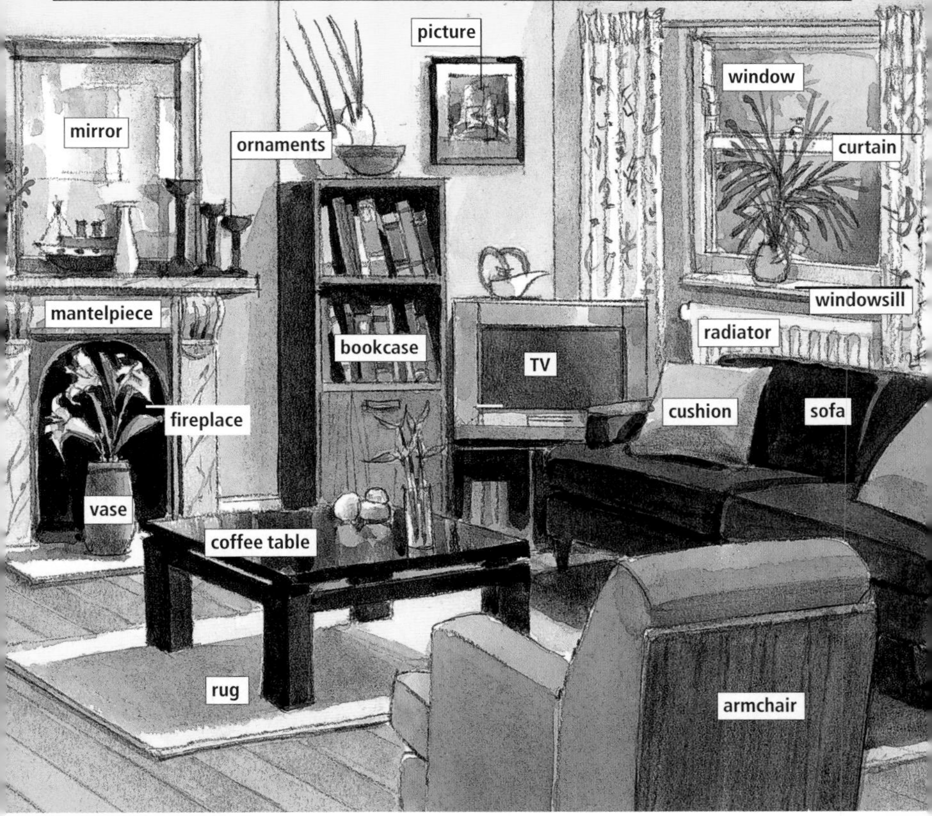

picture
window
mirror
ornaments
curtain
windowsill
mantelpiece
radiator
bookcase
TV
cushion
sofa
fireplace
vase
coffee table
rug
armchair

remote control

video *UK*, VCR *US*

candles

lampshade
lamp

speaker
stereo

clock

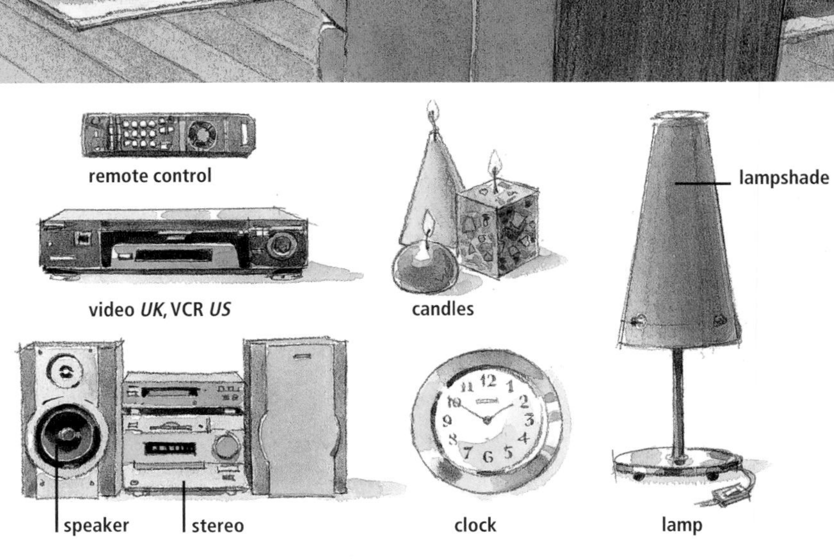

THE OFFICE

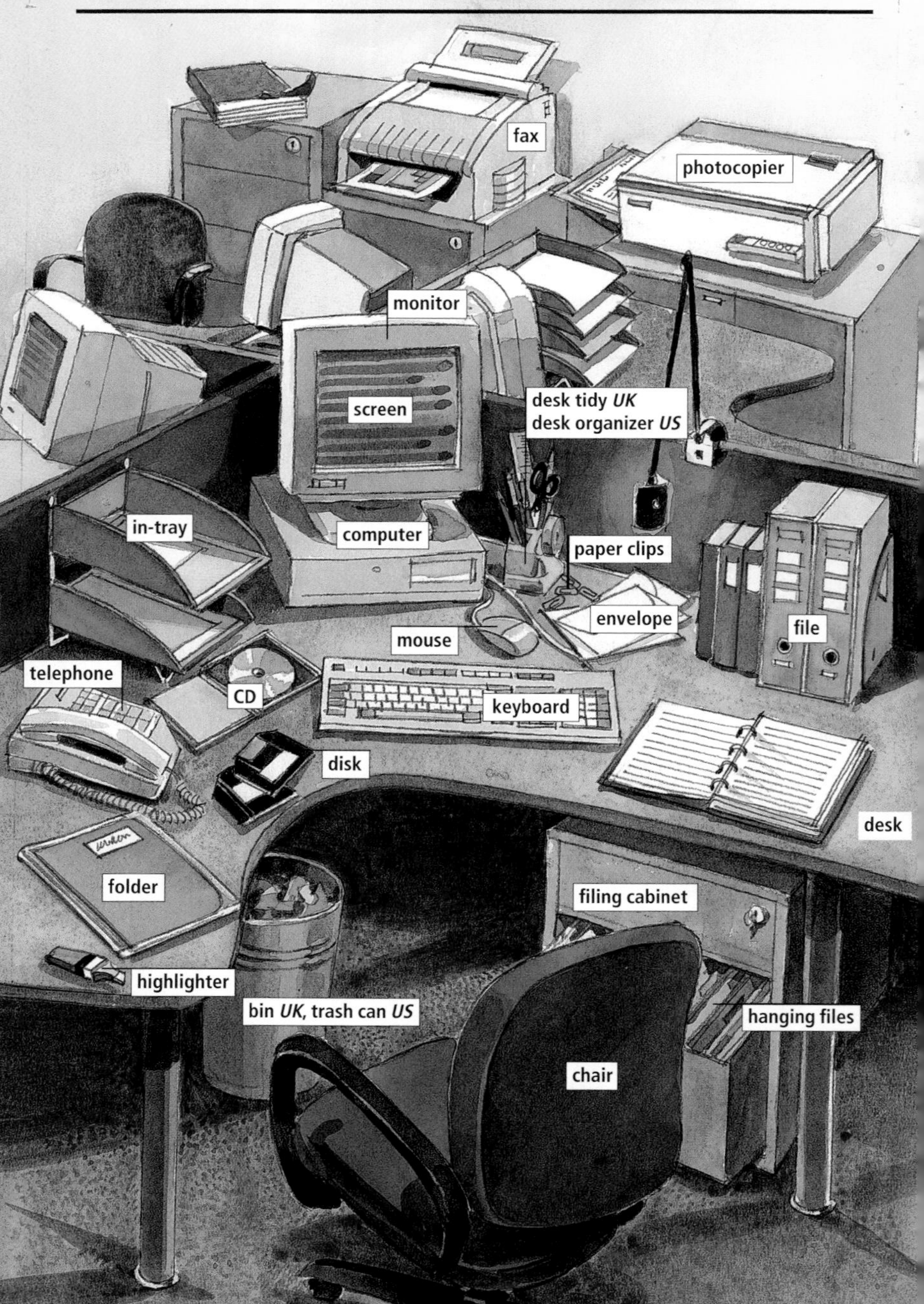
fax
photocopier
monitor
screen
desk tidy *UK*
desk organizer *US*
in-tray
computer
paper clips
envelope
file
mouse
telephone
CD
keyboard
disk
desk
folder
filing cabinet
highlighter
bin *UK*, trash can *US*
hanging files
chair

PHRASAL VERBS

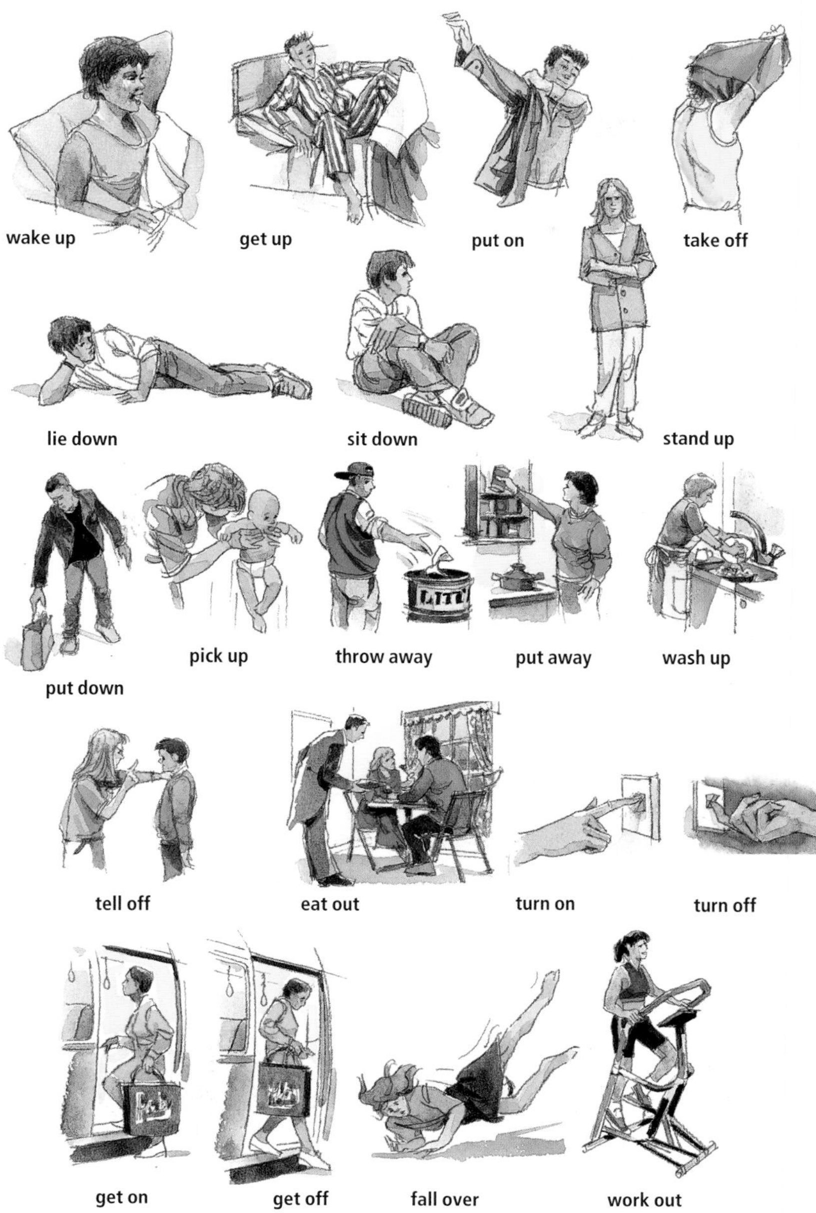

wake up

get up

put on

take off

lie down

sit down

stand up

put down

pick up

throw away

put away

wash up

tell off

eat out

turn on

turn off

get on

get off

fall over

work out

QUANTITIES

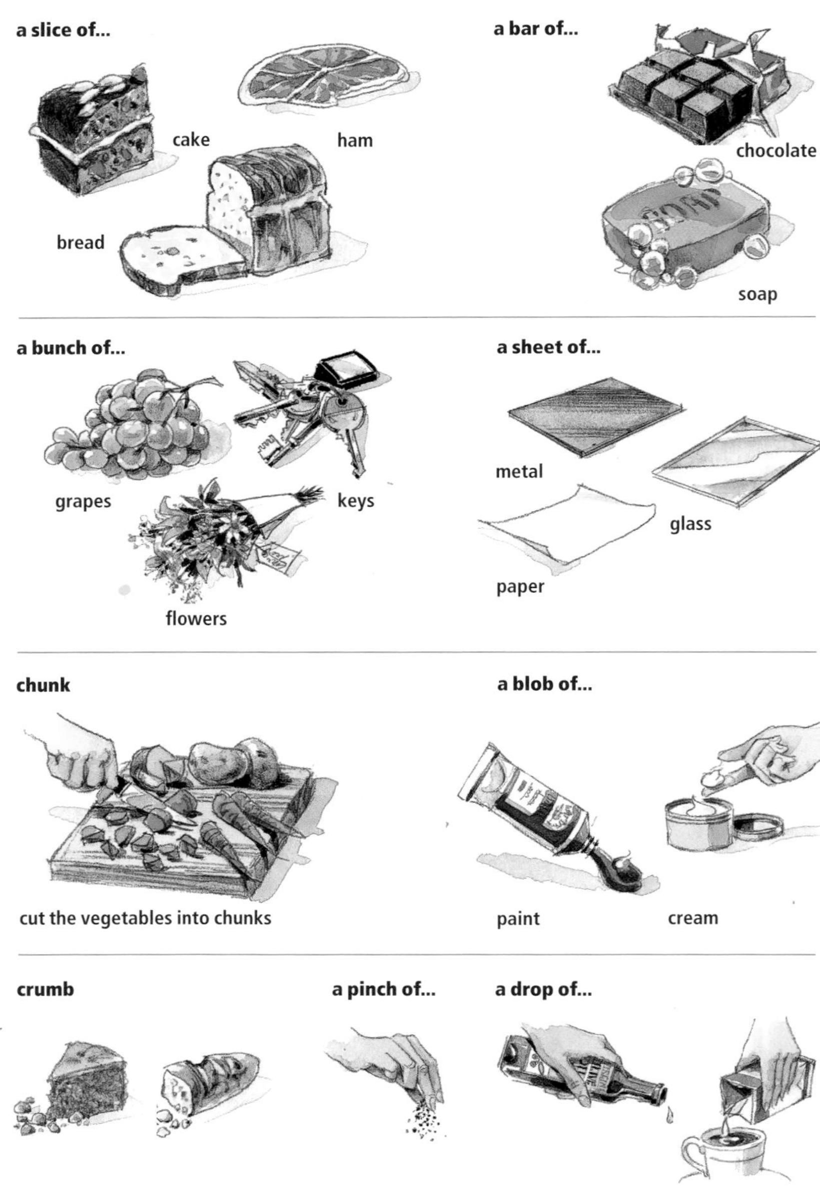
a slice of...
cake
ham
bread
a bar of...
chocolate
soap
a bunch of...
grapes
keys
flowers
a sheet of...
metal
glass
paper
chunk
cut the vegetables into chunks
a blob of...
paint
cream
crumb
cake crumbs
breadcrumbs
a pinch of...
salt
a drop of...
oil
milk

SPORTS (1)

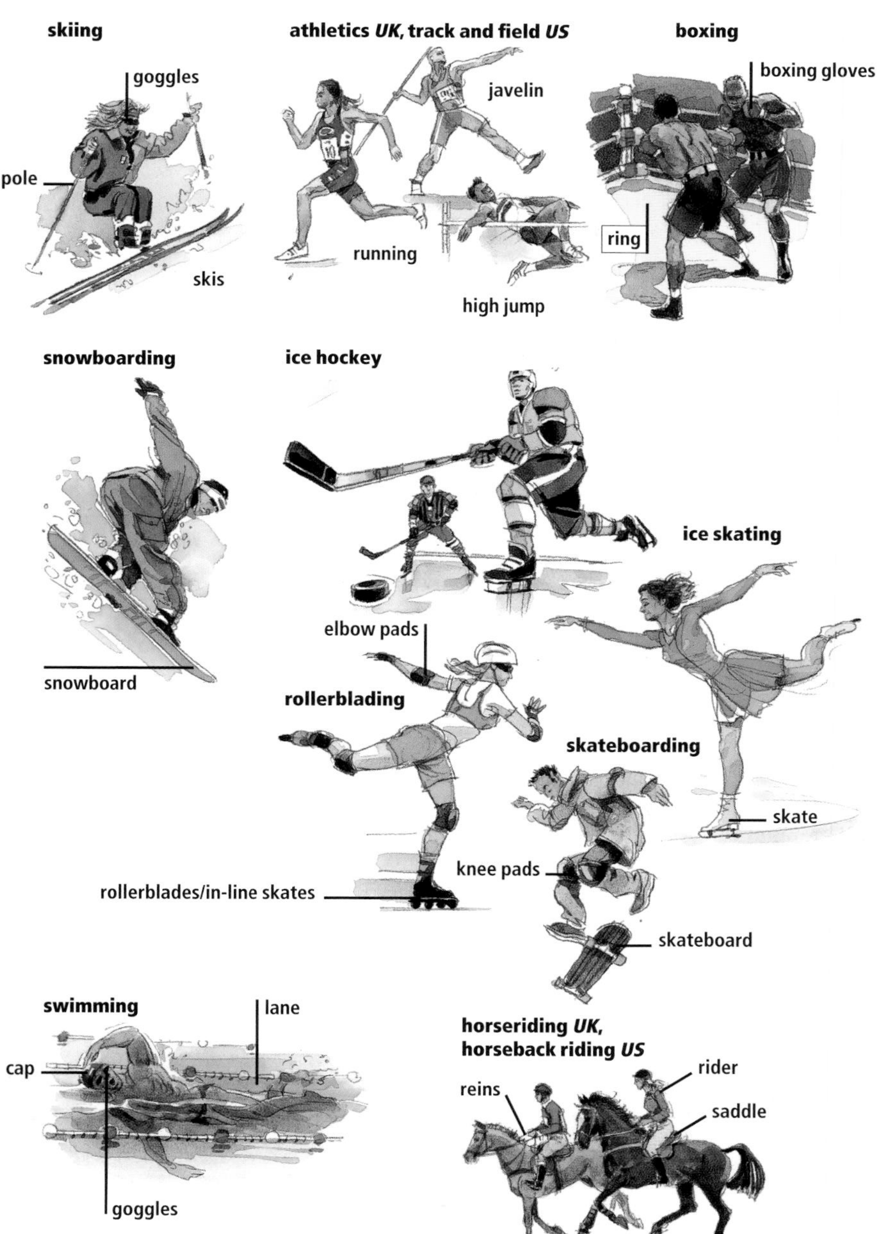
skiing
goggles
pole
skis
athletics UK, track and field US
javelin
running
high jump
boxing
boxing gloves
ring
snowboarding
snowboard
ice hockey
ice skating
elbow pads
rollerblading
skateboarding
skate
knee pads
rollerblades/in-line skates
skateboard
swimming
lane
cap
goggles
horseriding UK,
horseback riding US
rider
reins
saddle

SPORTS (2)

football UK, soccer US
goal
goalkeeper
referee
American football UK, football US
helmet
goal post
rugby
golf
cup
club
caddie
basketball
basket
cricket
bowler
stumps
batsman
baseball
cap
pitch
glove/mitt
batter
racket
tennis
net
cycling
helmet
bicycle
volleyball
net

Essential Phrasal Verbs

Phrasal verbs are verbs that have two or three words. For example 'look up' and 'carry on' are phrasal verbs. Over the next five pages you will find the most important phrasal verbs. Try to learn them.

account for something
to explain something
Could she account for the missing money?

add up something
to put two or more numbers together to get a total
Have you added up the figures?

base something **on** something
If you base something on facts or ideas, you use those facts or ideas to develop it.
Her latest book is based on a true story.

blow up something
1 to destroy something with a bomb
Terrorists blew up an office building in the city.
2 to fill something with air
I was blowing up balloons.

break down
If a car or machine breaks down, it stops working.
My car broke down on the way to work.

break into something
to get into a building or car using force, usually to steal something
Someone broke into the office and stole some computers.

bring up someone
to look after a child until he or she becomes an adult
Her grandparents brought her up.

call back or call someone **back**
to telephone someone a second time, or to telephone someone who telephoned you before
I'm a bit busy now – could I call you back later?

call off something
to decide that something that is planned will not happen
The game was called off because of bad weather.

carry on
to continue doing something
Carry on with your homework while I'm gone.

catch up
to reach someone or something that is in front of you by moving faster
We soon caught up with the car in front.

check in
1 to show your ticket at an airport
We have to check in two hours before the flight leaves.
2 to go to the desk at a hotel in order to say that you have arrived
I'll just check in and get my key.

check out
to leave a hotel after paying
Have you checked out yet?

cheer up
to stop feeling sad
Cheer up! It's not so bad!

close down
If a business closes down, it stops operating.
So many shops on this street are closing down.

come back
to return to a place
I've just come back from the office.

come in
to enter a room or building
Come in and have a drink.

Come on!
used to ask someone to come quickly or do something quickly
Come on! We're late already.

deal with something
to take action in order to do something
How do you deal with this problem?

depend on someone *or* something
1 to need the help of someone or something
Our economy depends on the car industry.
2 to be affected by someone or something
We might have the party in the garden but that depends on the weather.

drop someone/something **off**
to take someone or something to a place, usually by car
Could you drop me off at the station?

eat out
to eat at a restaurant
Let's eat out tonight.

end up
to finally be in a particular place or situation
He ended up in prison.

fall out
to argue with someone
Lucia and Marie have fallen out again.

fall over
to fall to the ground
She fell over and hurt her knee.

fill in/out something
to write all the information that is needed on a document
She filled in the form.

fill up *or* **fill** something **up**
to become full, or to make something become full
The restaurant soon filled up with people.

find something **out**
to get information about something
I must find out the train times.

finish off something
to do the last part of something
I have to finish off this report by Friday.

get away with something
to do something bad without being punished for it
If he is rude to you, don't let him get away with it.

get back
to return to a place
What time did you get back to the hotel?

get off *or* **get off** something
to leave a bus, train, aeroplane, or boat
We should get off at the next stop.

get on *or* **get on** something
1 to go onto a bus, train, aeroplane, or boat
I think we got on the wrong bus.
2 If two or more people get on, they like each other and are friends.
Karen and Sophie don't get on.

get out
to move out of a car
I'll get out at the traffic lights.

get over something
to feel better after being ill or sad
She's just getting over a cold.

get up
1 to wake up and get out of bed
It's time to get up, Molly.
2 to stand up
I got up to open the door.

give something **back**
to give something to the person who gave it to you
I must give you that book back.

give in
to finally agree to do something that someone wants
We will never give in to terrorists' demands.

give out
to give something to a lot of people
He gave out copies of the report.

give up something
1 If you give up something bad, such as smoking, you stop doing it or having it.
I gave up smoking two years ago.
2 to stop doing something because it is too difficult
I gave up trying to help her years ago.

go off
1 to leave a place and go somewhere else
She went off with Laurie.
2 If a bomb or gun goes off, it explodes or fires.
A bomb went off in a shopping centre.

go on
1 to last for a particular period of time
The film seemed to go on forever.
2 to continue doing something
We can't go on living like this.
3 to happen
What's going on?

go out
to leave a place in order to go somewhere else
Are you going out tonight?

grow up
to become older or an adult
She grew up in Madrid.

hand in something
to give a piece of writing to a teacher
Have you handed your history essay in yet?

hand out something
to give something to all the people in a group
A girl was handing out leaflets at the station.

hang around
to spend time somewhere, usually doing little
Teenagers hang around on street corners.

hang on
to wait for a short time
Hang on – I'm coming.

hang up
1 to finish a conversation on the telephone
She hung up before I'd finished.
2 to put something such as a coat somewhere where it can hang
You can hang up your jacket over there.

hold up someone *or* something
to make something or someone slow or late
I was held up by the traffic.

hurry up
to start moving or doing something more quickly
Hurry up! We're going to be late.

join in *or* **join in** something
to do an activity with other people
We're playing cards. Would you like to join in?

keep something **down**
to stop the number, level or size of something from increasing
I have to exercise to keep my weight down.

keep on doing something
to continue to do something, or to do something again and again
She kept on asking me questions the whole time.

keep up
1 to stay with someone who is moving forward by moving as quickly as them
She was walking so fast I couldn't keep up with her.
2 to increase as quickly as something or someone else
Prices have been rising very fast and wages haven't kept up.

knock someone **down**
to hit someone with a car, bus, etc and hurt or kill them
She was knocked down by a car and killed.

knock someone **out**
to make someone become unconscious, usually by hitting them on the head
He was knocked out halfway through the fight.

lead to something
to make something bad happen or exist
A bad diet can lead to health problems in later life.

leave something **out**
to not include someone or something
I've made a list of names – I hope I haven't left anyone out.

let someone **down**
to disappoint someone by not doing what you agreed to do
I promised to go to the party with Isabella and I can't let her down.

let someone **off**
to not punish someone who has done something wrong
I'll let you off this time, but don't ever lie to me again.

let out someone *or* something
to allow a person or animal to leave somewhere, especially by opening a door
I let the dogs out.

live up to something
to be as good as someone hopes
Did the trip live up to your expectations?

look after someone
to take care of someone or something by keeping them healthy or in a good condition
Could you look after the children while I'm out?

look for someone *or* something
to try to find someone or something
I'm looking for my keys.

look forward to something
to feel happy and excited about something that is going to happen
I'm really looking forward to the holidays.

look something **up**
to look at a book or computer in order to find information
I looked it up in the dictionary.

make out something *or* someone
to be able to see, hear, or understand something or someone
We could just make out a building through the trees.

make up something
to say or write something that is not true
I didn't want to go so I made up an excuse.

make up for something
to reduce the bad effect of something
I bought her some flowers to make up for forgetting her birthday.

meet up
to meet another person in order to do something together
Sylvie and I sometimes meet up and have dinner together.

move in
to begin living in a new home
We're moving in next week.

move out
to stop living in a particular home
He moved out when he was only sixteen.

pay off something
to pay all of the money that you owe
I'm planning to pay off my bank loan in five years.

phone up someone
to telephone someone
I phoned up an old friend of mine.

pick up someone *or* something
1 to lift something or someone by using your hands
He picked his coat up off the floor.
2 to collect someone who is waiting for you, or to collect something that you have left somewhere
Can you pick me up from the airport?

put something **away**
to put something in the place where you usually keep it
She put the plates away in the cupboard.

put down something *or* someone
to put something or someone that you are holding onto the floor or onto another surface
I'll just put my bag down for a minute – it's quite heavy.

put off something
to decide to do something at a later time
We could put off the meeting for a week.

put someone **off** someone *or* something
to make someone not like someone or something, or not want to do something
He was very rude to Helena and it put me off him.

put on something
to put clothes or shoes onto your body
I put on my warmest coat.

put out something
to make something that is burning stop burning
He put out the fire.

put up with something *or* someone
to accept something bad although you do not like it
He's so rude, I don't know how you put up with him.

read out something
to read something and say the words so that other people can hear
He read out the names of all the winners.

rely on someone *or* something
1 to need someone or something in order to be successful, work correctly, etc
I'm relying on Anthony to make all the food.
2 to trust someone or something
I know I can rely on you to help.

remind someone **of** something
to make someone think of something or someone else
Harry reminds me of my father.

ring back *or* **ring** someone **back**
to telephone someone a second time, or to telephone someone who rang you earlier
I'm a bit busy – can I ring you back later?

ring up someone
to telephone someone
Ring her up and ask her if she would like to come out.

rub something **out**
to remove writing from something by rubbing it with a piece of rubber or a cloth
Rub out any mistakes.

run out
to use all of something so that there is none left
We ran out of money.

save up
to keep money so that you can buy something with it in the future
I am saving up for a new car.

sell out
If a shop sells out of something, it sells all of that thing.
They had sold out of bread by the time I got there.

set off
to start a journey
What time are you setting off tomorrow morning?

set up something
to start a company or organization
He's setting up his own business.

settle down
to start living in a place where you will stay for a long time, usually with a person that you love
Do you think he'll ever settle down and have a family?

show off
to try to make people admire you in a way which is annoying
Stop showing off – we all know you've got a new car!

sort out something
to stop a problem
I had some trouble with my computer but Andy sorted it out.

take back something
to return something to the place you got or bought it from
I must take my books back to the library.

take off something
to remove something
I was hot so I took my jacket off

take off
If an aeroplane takes off, it begins to fly.
I like watching planes take off and land.

take over *or* **take** something **over**
to get control of or responsibility for something
Who will take over from Andrea when she leaves?

take something **up**
to start doing a particular job or activity
He has recently taken up golf.

tell someone **off**
to tell someone that they have done something wrong and that you are angry about it
The teacher told me off for being late.

throw away something
to get rid of something that you do not want
I threw away all those old papers.

try on something
to put on a piece of clothing to see if it fits you or if it looks good
I tried on every coat in the shop.

turn down something
to refuse an offer or request
We offered her the job but she turned it down.

wake up *or* **wake up** someone
to stop sleeping or to make someone else stop sleeping
I've only just woken up.
Could you wake me up before you go?

work out something
1 to calculate an amount
I'm trying to work out the total cost.
2 to understand something or decide something after thinking very carefully
I haven't worked out what to do yet.

write down something
to write something on a piece of paper so that you do not forget it
Did you write Aurora's number down?

1 when you do not have someone or something that you had before: *loss of memory ○ job losses*
2 when a company spends more money than it gets: *Both companies **suffered losses** this year.*
3 when a person dies: *They never got over the loss of their son.*

lost¹ /lɒst/ *adj*
1 not knowing where you are: *I **got lost** on the way.*
2 If something is lost, no one knows where it is: *The letter **got lost** in the post.*

lost² /lɒst/
past of lose

lost property /ˌlɒst ˈprɒpətɪ/ *noun* **[no plural]** *UK*
things that people have left in public places

lot /lɒt/ *noun*
1 **a lot; lots** a large number or amount of people or things: *There were **a lot of** people outside the building. ○ He earns **lots of** money. ○ I've got a lot to do this morning.*
2 **a lot better/older/quicker, etc** much better/older/quicker, etc: *It's a lot quicker by train.*

lotion /ˈləʊʃᵊn/ *noun*
a liquid that you put on your skin to make it soft or healthy: *suntan lotion*

lottery /ˈlɒtᵊri/ *noun* (*plural* **lotteries**)
a competition in which people buy tickets with numbers on them and then win money if their ticket has a particular number: *the national lottery*

loud /laʊd/ *adj*
making a lot of noise: *a loud noise ○ a loud voice*
• **loudly** *adv*

loudspeaker /ˌlaʊdˈspiːkəʳ/ *noun*
something that is used for making voices or sounds louder

lounge /laʊndʒ/ *noun UK*
a room with chairs where you can sit and relax

louse /laʊs/ *noun* (*plural* **lice**)
a small insect that lives on the bodies or in the hair of people or animals

lousy /ˈlaʊzi/ *adj informal*
very bad: *The food in the hotel was lousy.*

lovable (*also* **loveable**) /ˈlʌvəbl/ *adj*
very nice and easy to love: *a lovable child*

love¹ /lʌv/ *verb* (*present participle* **loving**, *past* **loved**)
1 to like someone very much and have sexual feelings for them: *Last night he told me he loved me.*
2 to like a friend or a person in your family very much: *I'm sure he loves his kids.*
3 to like something very much: *He loves his music. ○ She loves animals.*
4 **I'd love to** used to say that you would very much like to do something that someone is offering: *"I wondered if you'd like to meet up sometime?" "I'd love to."*

love² /lʌv/ *noun*
1 **[no plural]** when you like someone very much and have sexual feelings for them: *I'm **in love with** him* (= I love him). ○ *I was 20 when I first **fell in love*** (= started to love someone). ○ *a love song*
2 **make love** to have sex
3 **[no plural]** when you like a friend or person in your family very much: *Nothing is as strong as the **love** you have **for** your kids.*
4 something that interests you a lot: *his love of books*
5 **Love from; All my love** something you write at the end of a letter to a friend or someone in your family: *Love from Mum.*
6 *UK* You call someone 'love' to be friendly or to show that you like them: *"Anthony?" "Yes, love."*

love affair /ˈlʌv əˌfeəʳ/ *noun*
a romantic or sexual relationship

lovely /ˈlʌvli/ *adj*
1 very nice or enjoyable: *We had a lovely day together. ○ What lovely weather.*
2 very attractive: *a lovely dress ○ You look lovely!*

lover /ˈlʌvəʳ/ *noun*
1 If two people are lovers, they have a sexual relationship but they are not married.
2 someone who likes something very much: *She's a cat lover.*

loving /ˈlʌvɪŋ/ *adj*
showing that you love someone: *a loving father*

low /ləʊ/ *adj*
1 near the ground, not high: *low*

aircraft ○ *low ceilings*
2 under the usual level: *Their prices are very low.* ○ *a low number*
3 A low sound is deep or quiet: *a low voice* ○ *a low note*

lower[1] /ˈləʊə^{r}/ *adj*
being the bottom part of something: *I've got a pain in my lower back.*

lower[2] /ˈləʊə^{r}/ *verb*
to make something less in amount: *They have lowered the price.*

lower case /ˌləʊə^{r} ˈkeɪs/ *noun* **[no plural]**
letters of the alphabet which are not written as capital letters, for example a, b, c

loyal /lɔɪəl/ *adj*
always liking and supporting someone or something: *a loyal supporter* ○ *She's very* ***loyal to*** *her friends.*

loyalty /ˈlɔɪəlti/ *noun* **[no plural]**
when someone is loyal: *Your* ***loyalty to*** *the company is impressive.*

Ltd *written abbreviation for*
limited company (= used after the name of some companies): *Pinewood Supplies Ltd.*

luck /lʌk/ *noun* **[no plural]**
1 good and bad things caused by chance and not by your own actions: *It was just luck that we got on the same train.* ○ *He has had a lot of* ***bad luck*** *in his life.*
2 success: *He's been trying to find work but with no luck so far.*
3 Good luck! something you say to someone when you hope they will do well: *Good luck with your exam!*

lucky /ˈlʌki/ *adj* **(luckier, luckiest)**
having good things happen to you: *"I'm going on holiday." "Lucky you!"* ○ *And the lucky winner is ticket number 38!* ○ *You're* ***lucky to*** *live in such a beautiful city.* ➲Opposite **unlucky**

luggage /ˈlʌgɪdʒ/ *noun* **[no plural]**
bags that you carry with you when you travel

lukewarm /ˌluːkˈwɔːm/ *adj*
A liquid which is lukewarm is only slightly warm.

lump /lʌmp/ *noun*
a bit of something solid with no particular shape: *a lump of coal* ○ *She found a lump in her breast.*

luggage

backpack

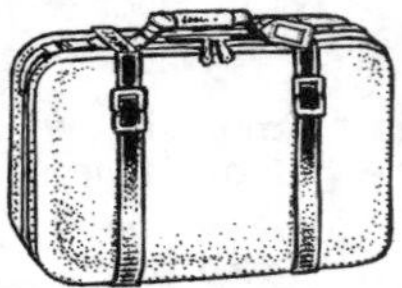
suitcase

holdall *UK*, carryall *US*

lumpy /ˈlʌmpi/ *adj*
covered with or containing lumps (= bits of something solid): *a lumpy sauce*

lunatic /ˈluːnətɪk/ *noun*
someone who behaves in a crazy way: *He drives like a lunatic.*

lunch /lʌnʃ/ *noun* (*plural* **lunches**)
the food that you eat in the middle of the day: *Shall we* ***have lunch****?*

lunchtime /ˈlʌnʃtaɪm/ *noun*
the time when you eat lunch

lung /lʌŋ/ *noun*
one of the two parts inside your chest that are used for breathing: *lung cancer*

lurk /lɜːk/ *verb*
to wait somewhere secretly, especially before doing something bad: *Someone was lurking in the shadows.*

luxurious /lʌgˈʒʊəriəs/ *adj*
very comfortable and expensive: *a luxurious hotel*

luxury /ˈlʌkʃ^{ə}ri/ *noun*
1 [no plural] very expensive and beautiful things: *They live* ***in luxury*** *in a fabulous apartment in Paris.*
2 (*plural* **luxuries**) something that you like having but do not need: *Having a car each is a luxury really.*

lying /ˈlaɪɪŋ/
present participle of lie[1,2]

lyrics /ˈlɪrɪks/ *plural noun*
the words of a song

a b c d e f g h i j k l m n o p q r s t u v w x y z

Mm

M, m /em/
the thirteenth letter of the alphabet

m *written abbreviation for*
metre (= a unit of length)

mac /mæk/ *noun UK*
a coat that you wear in the rain

machine /mə'ʃiːn/ *noun*
1 a piece of equipment with moving parts that uses power to do a particular job: *a fax machine* ○ *a coffee machine*
2 a computer

machine gun /mə'ʃiːn gʌn/ *noun*
a gun that fires a lot of bullets very quickly

machinery /mə'ʃiːnᵊri/ *noun* **[no plural]**
machines, often large machines: *farm machinery*

mad /mæd/ *adj*
1 *informal* stupid or crazy: *You are* ***mad to*** *walk home alone at night.*
2 *US* angry: *Were your parents* ***mad at*** *you when you came home late?*
3 go mad *UK informal* to become very angry: *Dad will go mad when he finds out you took the car.*
4 be mad about someone/something *informal* to love something or someone: *Jo is mad about skiing.*
5 like mad *informal* If you run, work, etc like mad, you do it very quickly.

madam /'mædəm/ *noun formal*
used to be polite when you speak or write to a woman who you do not know: *This way, madam.*

made /meɪd/
past of make

madly /mædli/ *adv*
1 with a lot of energy and enthusiasm: *We cheered madly as the team came out onto the field.*
2 be madly in love to love someone very much: *He's madly in love with Denise.*

madness /'mædnəs/ *noun* **[no plural]**
stupid or dangerous behaviour: *It is madness to drive that fast.*

magazine /ˌmægə'ziːn/ *noun*
a big, thin book that you can buy every week or month, that has pictures and writing: *a fashion magazine*

magazine

magic /'mædʒɪk/ *noun* **[no plural]**
1 special powers that can make things happen that seem impossible: *Do you believe in magic?*
2 clever things that a person does while other people watch, such as making things disappear

magical /'mædʒɪkᵊl/ *adj*
1 with special powers: *Diamonds were once thought to have* ***magical powers.***
2 special or exciting: *It was a magical night.*

magician /mə'dʒɪʃᵊn/ *noun*
someone who does clever things while other people watch, such as making things disappear

magnet /'mægnət/ *noun*
an iron object that makes other pieces of iron move towards it

magnet

magnetic /mæg'netɪk/ *adj*
with the power of a magnet: *a magnetic field*

magnificent /mæg'nɪfɪsᵊnt/ *adj*
very good or very beautiful: *The view from our room was magnificent.*

magnify /'mægnɪfaɪ/ *verb* (*present participle* **magnifying,** *past* **magnified)**
to make an object look bigger than it is: *The cells are first magnified under a microscope.*

magnifying glass /'mægnɪfaɪŋ ˌglɑːs/ *noun*
a piece of curved glass which makes objects look bigger than they are

maid /meɪd/ *noun*
a woman who cleans or cooks in a hotel or in someone's home

maiden name /'meɪdn ˌneɪm/ *noun*
the family name that a woman has before she gets married

mail¹ /meɪl/ *noun* **[no plural]**
letters and parcels that come by post: *We got loads of mail this morning.*

mail² /meɪl/ *verb US*
to send a letter or parcel or email something: *Could you* ***mail*** *it* ***to*** *me?*

mailbox /ˈmeɪlbɒks/ *noun US*
1 a small box outside your home where letters are put
2 (*UK* **post box**) a large, metal container in a public place where you can post letters

main /meɪn/ *adj*
most important or largest: *Our main problem is lack of money.* ○ *The main airport is 15 miles from the capital.*

mainly /ˈmeɪnli/ *adv*
mostly: *The people are mainly French.*

maintain /meɪnˈteɪn/ *verb*
1 to make a situation or activity continue in the same way: *The army has been brought in to maintain order in the region.*
2 to keep a building or area in good condition: *A large house is very expensive to maintain.*

maintenance /ˈmeɪntənəns/ *noun* **[no plural]**
the work that you do to keep something in good condition: *car maintenance*

maize /meɪz/ *UK* (*US* **corn**) *noun* **[no plural]**
a tall plant with yellow seeds that are eaten as food

majestic /məˈdʒestɪk/ *adj*
very beautiful and big: *majestic scenery*

majesty /ˈmædʒəsti/ *noun* (*plural* **majesties**)
His/Her/Your Majesty used when you are speaking to or about a king or queen: *His Majesty King Edward VII*

major¹ /ˈmeɪdʒəʳ/ *adj*
important or big: *a major problem* ○ *a major city* ⊃Opposite **minor**

major² /ˈmeɪdʒəʳ/ *noun*
an officer of middle rank in the army or air force

majority /məˈdʒɒrəti/ *noun* **[no plural]**
more than half of a group of people or things: ***The majority of*** *people in this country own their houses.* ⊃Opposite **minority**

make /meɪk/ *verb* (*present participle* **making**, *past* **made**)
1 to create something: *Shall I make some coffee?* ○ *They've made a film about her life.*
2 make someone do something to force someone to do something: *You can't make me go.*
3 make someone/something happy/sad/difficult, etc to cause someone or something to become happy, sad, difficult, etc: *You've made me very happy.*
4 If you make an amount of money, you earn it: *He makes £20,000 a year.*
5 If two or more numbers make a particular amount, that is the amount when they are added together: *That makes $40 altogether.*
6 make the bed to make the sheets and covers on a bed tidy
7 make it *informal*
a to arrive at a place at the right time: *Will we make it in time for the film?*
b to be successful: *Very few actors actually make it.*

make something/someone out *phrasal verb*
to be able to see, hear, or understand something or someone: *We could just make out a building through the trees.*

make something up *phrasal verb*
to say or write something that is not true: *I made up an excuse because I didn't want to go.*

make-up

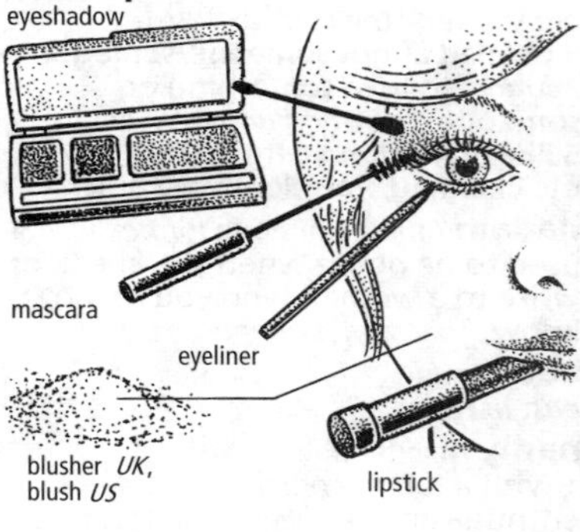

make-up, makeup /ˈmeɪkʌp/ *noun* **[no plural]**
coloured substances that a woman puts on her face in order to make herself more attractive: *She doesn't* ***wear*** *much* ***make-up***.

malaria /məˈleəriə/ *noun* **[no plural]**
a serious disease that you can get in hot countries if a mosquito (= small

insect) bites you

male[1] /meɪl/ *adj*
belonging to or relating to the sex that cannot have babies: *a male colleague* ➲Opposite **female**

male[2] /meɪl/ *noun*
a male person or animal

mall /mɔːl/ (*also* **shopping mall**) *noun*
a large, covered shopping area

mammal /ˈmæməl/ *noun*
an animal that drinks milk from its mother's body when it is young

man /mæn/ *noun* (*plural* **men**)
1 an adult male human: *a young man* ○ *men and women*
2 [no plural] used to refer to both men and women: *Man is still more intelligent than the cleverest robot.*

manage /ˈmænɪdʒ/ *verb* (*present participle* **managing,** *past* **managed)**
1 to do something that you have been trying to do: *I* ***managed to*** *persuade him to come.*
2 to be in control of an office, shop, team, etc: *He used to manage the bookshop on King Street.*

management /ˈmænɪdʒmənt/ *noun*
1 [no plural] being in control of an office, shop, team, etc: *management skills*
2 the people who are in control of an office, shop, team, etc: *Management have accepted the proposal.*

manager /ˈmænɪdʒəʳ/ *noun*
someone in control of an office, shop, team, etc: *She's the manager of the local sports club.*

mane /meɪn/ *noun*
the long hair on the necks of animals such as horses or lions

mango /ˈmæŋgəʊ/ *noun* (*plural* **mangoes)**
a sweet, orange fruit with a green skin and one big seed

manic /ˈmænɪk/ *adj*
behaving in an excited and uncontrolled way: *The kids were totally manic.*

manipulate /məˈnɪpjəleɪt/ *verb* (*present participle* **manipulating,** *past* **manipulated)**
to control someone or something in a clever way: *She knows how to manipulate the press.*

mankind /mænˈkaɪnd/ *noun* **[no plural]**
all people, considered as a group: *the history of mankind*

man-made /ˌmænˈmeɪd/ *adj*
not natural, but made by people: *man-made fibres*

manner /ˈmænəʳ/ *noun*
1 the way in which a person talks and behaves with other people: *She has a very friendly manner.*
2 the way something happens or something is done: *They dealt with the problem* ***in a*** *very efficient* ***manner***.

manners /ˈmænəz/ *plural noun*
ways of behaving with other people: *It is bad manners to be late.*

mansion /ˈmænʃən/ *noun*
a very large house

manual[1] /ˈmænjuəl/ *adj*
using your hands: *manual work*
● **manually** *adv*

manual[2] /ˈmænjuəl/ *noun*
a book that tells you how to use something or do something: *Where is the instructions manual for this washing machine?*

manufacture /ˌmænjəˈfæktʃəʳ/ *verb* (*present participle* **manufacturing,** *past* **manufactured)**
to make something, usually in large numbers in a factory: *He works for a company that manufactures plastic products.*
● **manufacture** *noun* **[no plural]** *the manufacture of computers*

manufacturer /ˌmænjəˈfæktʃərəʳ/ *noun*
a company that manufactures something: *a shoe manufacturer*

many /ˈmeni/ *pronoun, quantifier*
1 a large number of: *I don't have many clothes.* ○ *Were there many cars on the road?* ○ *I've got* ***so many*** *things to do this morning.*
2 how many? used in questions to ask about the number of something: *How many hours a week do you work?*

map /mæp/ *noun*
a picture that shows where countries, towns, roads, etc are: *a road map* ○ *a map of Europe*

map
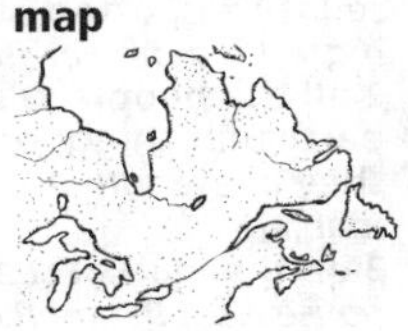

a b c d e f g h i j k l m n o p q r s t u v w x y z

marathon /ˈmærəθᵊn/ *noun*
a race in which people run for about 26 miles/42 km: *He ran the London marathon.*

marble /ˈmɑːbl/ *noun* **[no plural]**
hard, smooth stone which is often used for decoration

march¹ /mɑːtʃ/ *noun* (*plural* **marches**)
when people walk in a group to show that they disagree with something: *We* ***went on a march*** *to protest against the new law.*

march² /mɑːtʃ/ *verb*
1 to walk somewhere as a group to show that you disagree with something: *They marched to London to protest against the war.*
2 When soldiers march, they walk together with regular steps.
3 to walk somewhere fast: *She marched off angrily.*

March /mɑːtʃ/ *noun*
the third month of the year

margarine /ˌmɑːdʒəˈriːn/ *noun* **[no plural]**
a soft food which you put on bread and use in cooking

margin /ˈmɑːdʒɪn/ *noun*
an empty space down the side of a page of writing: *You can make notes* ***in the margin****.*

mark¹ /mɑːk/ *noun*
1 a dirty area on something: *He's left dirty marks all over the carpet.*
2 a number or letter that is written on a piece of work, saying how good the work is: *She always gets good marks in English.*

mark² /mɑːk/ *verb*
1 to show where something is by drawing or putting something somewhere: *I've marked my street on the map for you.*
2 to read a piece of written work and write on it how good or bad it is: *I marked essays last night.*

market¹ /ˈmɑːkɪt/ *noun*
1 a place where people go to buy or sell things, often outside: *a flower market* ○ *a market stall*
2 all the people who want to buy a particular thing, or the area where they live: *South America is our largest market.*
3 on the market ready to buy: *His house is on the market.*

market

market² /ˈmɑːkɪt/ *verb*
to try to sell things using advertising: *They market their products very cleverly.*
● **marketing** /ˈmɑːkɪtɪŋ/ *noun* **[no plural]** *a marketing campaign*

marriage /ˈmærɪdʒ/ *noun*
1 the legal relationship of a man and a woman being a husband and a wife: *It was a very happy marriage.* ○ *She's on her third marriage.*
2 the ceremony where a man and a woman become a husband and a wife

married /ˈmærid/ *adj*
1 A married man or woman has a wife or husband: *a married couple* ○ *She's been* ***married to*** *David for nearly ten years.* ○ *She's getting married in the spring.*
2 get married to begin a legal relationship with someone as their husband or wife: *We got married last year.* ○ *She's getting married in the spring.*

marry /ˈmæri/ *verb* (*present participle* **marrying**, *past* **married**)
to begin a legal relationship with someone as their husband or wife: *Will you marry me?* ○ *He never married.*

marsh /mɑːʃ/ *noun* (*plural* **marshes**)
an area of soft, wet land

marvellous *UK* (*US* **marvelous**) /ˈmɑːvᵊləs/ *adj*
very good: *What a marvellous idea!* ○ *We saw the most marvellous scenery.*

masculine /ˈmæskjəlɪn/ *adj*
having qualities that are like a man: *She had a rather masculine voice.*

mask

mask /mɑːsk/ *noun*
a cover for the face: *a surgeon's mask*

mass[1] /mæs/ *noun* (*plural* **masses**)
1 a lot of something together, with no clear shape: *Her hair was a mass of blond curls.*
2 masses *informal* a large amount or number of something: *There was **masses of** food.*

mass[2] /mæs/ *adj*
affecting a lot of people: *mass destruction* ○ *a mass murderer*

massacre /ˈmæsəkəʳ/ *noun*
the killing of a lot of people
● **massacre** *verb* (*present participle* **massacring**, *past* **massacred**)
to kill a lot of people

massage /ˈmæsɑːdʒ/ *noun*
when you press parts of someone's body in order to make them relax: *She gave me a foot massage.*
● **massage** *verb* (*present participle* **massaging**, *past* **massaged**)

massive /ˈmæsɪv/ *adj*
very big: *a massive building*

the mass media /ˌmæs ˈmiːdiə/ *noun*
newspapers, television, and radio

mast /mɑːst/ *noun*
1 a tall pole on a boat that supports its sails
2 a tall metal pole that sends out television and radio signals

master[1] /ˈmɑːstəʳ/ *noun*
1 In the past, a servant's master was the man that they worked for.
2 someone who does something very well: *He was a **master of** disguise.*

master[2] /ˈmɑːstəʳ/ *verb*
to learn how to do something well: *I lived in Italy for a year but didn't master the language.*

mat /mæt/ *noun*
a piece of material that you put on the floor, in order to protect it

match[1] /mætʃ/ *noun* (*plural* **matches**)
1 a sports competition in which two people or teams compete against each other: *a football match*
2 a thin, wooden stick which makes fire when you rub one end of it against a rough surface: *a box of matches*

match[2] /mætʃ/ *verb*
If two things match, they are the same colour or type: *I can't find anything to match my green shirt.* ○ *Your socks don't match.*

mate[1] /meɪt/ *noun*
1 *UK informal* a friend: *She's my best mate.*
2 *UK informal* You call a man 'mate' when you are speaking to him informally: *Thanks, mate.*
3 an animal's sexual partner

mate[2] /meɪt/ *verb* (*present participle* **mating**, *past* **mated**)
When animals mate, they have sex in order to produce babies.

material /məˈtɪəriəl/ *noun*
1 a solid substance from which things can be made: *building materials*
2 cloth for making clothes, curtains, etc: *Her dress was made of a soft, silky material.*

maternal /məˈtɜːnəl/ *adj*
1 like a mother
2 A maternal relation is part of your mother's family: *He's my maternal grandfather.* ➲Compare **paternal**

mathematical /ˌmæθəmˈætɪkəl/ *adj*
relating to mathematics

mathematics /mæθəmˈætɪks/ *noun* **[no plural]** *formal for* maths

maths /mæθs/ *noun* **[no plural]**
the study or science of numbers and shapes

matinée /ˈmætɪneɪ/ *noun*
an afternoon performance of a play or film

matter[1] /ˈmætəʳ/ *noun*
1 a subject or situation that you need to think about or do something about: *Could I talk to you about a personal matter?* ○ *This is a matter of some importance.*
2 **[no plural]** In science, matter is the physical substances that exist in the universe.

a b c d e f g h i j k l m n o p q r s t u v w x y z

3 what's the matter? used to ask about the reason for a problem: *What's the matter with your leg?*
4 no matter how/what/when, etc used to say that something cannot be changed: *I never manage to lose any weight, no matter how hard I try.*
5 as a matter of fact used to say that something is true, especially when it is surprising: *As a matter of fact, I used to live near him.*

matter² /'mætəʳ/ *verb*
to be important: *We were late, but it didn't seem to matter.* ○ *It doesn't **matter to** me whether he comes or not.*

mattress /'mætrəs/ *noun* (*plural* **mattresses)**
the soft part of a bed that you lie on

mature¹ /mə'tjʊəʳ/ *adj*
1 completely grown or developed: *mature trees*
2 behaving well, like an adult: *She seems very mature for thirteen.*
➲Opposite **immature**

mature² /mə'tjʊəʳ/ *verb* (*present participle* **maturing,** *past* **matured)**
1 to become completely grown or developed
2 to start to behave well, like an adult: *Girls mature sooner than boys.*

maximum¹ /'mæksɪməm/ *adj*
The maximum amount of something is the largest amount that is allowed or possible: *the maximum temperature*
➲Opposite **minimum**

maximum² /'mæksɪməm/ *noun* **[no plural]**
the largest amount that is allowed or possible: *The school has **a maximum of** 30 students per class.*

may /meɪ/ *verb*
1 used to talk about what is possibly true or will possibly happen: *There may be other problems that we don't know about.* ○ *I think I may have a cold.*
2 *formal* used when you ask if you can do something or say that someone can do something: *May I be excused, please?* ○ *You may begin.*

May /meɪ/ *noun*
the fifth month of the year

maybe /'meɪbi/ *adv*
possibly: *Maybe we're too early.* ○ *It could take a month, or maybe more, to complete.*

mayor /meəʳ/ *noun*
the leader of the group that is in charge of a town or city

me /miː/ *pronoun*
the person who is speaking or writing: *She gave me some money.* ○ *She never gave it to me.* ○ *Lydia is three years younger than me.*

meal /miːl/ *noun*
when you eat, or the food that you eat at that time: *a three-course meal* ○ *We **had** a nice **meal** together.*

mean¹ /miːn/ *verb* (*present participle* **meaning,** *past* **meant)**
1 to have a particular meaning: *What does this word mean?* ○ *The green light means go.*
2 mean to do something to want to do something: *I didn't mean to hurt her.*
3 to have a particular result: *These changes will mean better health care for everyone.*
4 I mean something that you say in order to correct yourself: *We went there in May – I mean June.*

mean² /miːn/ *adj*
1 not kind: *I thought my sister was being **mean to** me.*
2 *UK* A mean person does not like spending money, especially on other people: *He's too mean to buy her a ring.*

meaning /'miːnɪŋ/ *noun*
1 The meaning of words, signs, or actions is what they represent or show: *The word 'squash' has several meanings.*
2 [no plural] purpose: *She felt that her life had no meaning.*

means /miːnz/ *noun* (*plural* **means)**
1 a way of doing something: *We had no **means of** communication.*
2 money: *We don't have **the means to** buy the house.*
3 by no means not at all: *I am by no means an expert.*

meant /ment/
past of mean

meantime /'miːnˌtaɪm/ *noun* **[no plural]**
in the meantime in the time between two things happening, or while something else is happening: *Your computer will arive on Friday. In the meantime, you can use Julie's.*

meanwhile /'miːnˌwaɪl/ *adv*

in the time between two things happening, or while something else is happening: *The mother is ill. The child, meanwhile, is living with her grandparents.*

measles /ˈmiːzlz/ *noun* **[no plural]** a disease in which your skin is covered in small, red spots

measure[1] /ˈmeʒəʳ/ *verb* (*present participle* **measuring**, *past* **measured**)
1 to find the size, weight, amount, or speed of something: *I've measured all the windows.*
2 to be a certain size: *The whale measured around 60 feet in length.*

measure[2] /ˈmeʒəʳ/ *noun*
1 something that is done so that a bad situation is stopped: *We must* ***take measures*** *to stop the spread of the disease.* ○ *security measures*
2 [no plural] a way of measuring something: *The basic units of measure we use are distance, time, and mass.*

measurement /ˈmeʒəmənt/ *noun* the size and shape of something: *I've* ***taken measurements*** *of all the rooms.*

meat /miːt/ *noun* **[no plural]** the soft parts of animals, used as food: *I don't eat meat.* ○ *red/white meat*
➲See colour picture **Food** on page Centre 7

mechanic /mɪˈkænɪk/ *noun* someone whose job is to repair machines: *a car mechanic*

mechanical /mɪˈkænɪkəl/ *adj* relating to or operated by machines: *a mechanical engineer*
• **mechanically** *adv*

medal /ˈmedəl/ *noun* a piece of metal given as a prize in a competition or given to someone who has been very brave: *a bronze medal* ○ *an Olympic medal*

the media /ˈmiːdiə/ *noun* television, newspapers, magazines, and radio considered as a group: *The issue has been much discussed* ***in the media.***

medical /ˈmedɪkəl/ *adj* relating to medicine and different ways of curing illness: *medical treatment* ○ *a medical student*
• **medically** *adv*

medicine /ˈmedɪsən/ *noun*
1 something that you drink or eat when you are ill, to stop you being ill: *cough medicine* ○ *Have you* ***taken*** *your* ***medicine*** *today?*

medicine

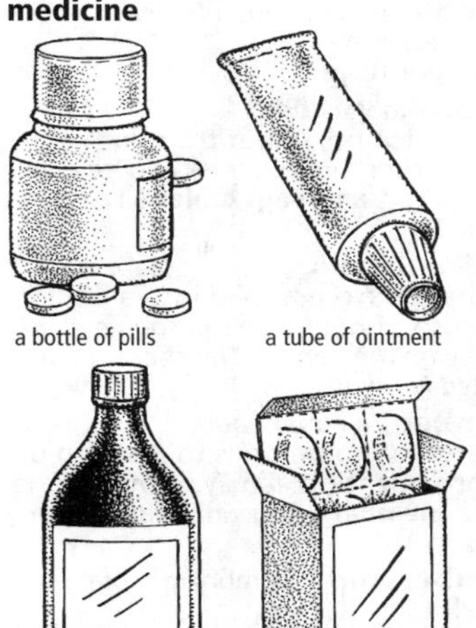
a bottle of pills
a tube of ointment
a bottle of medicine
a box of tablets

2 [no plural] the science of treating and preventing illness

medium /ˈmiːdiəm/ *adj* in the middle of a group of different amounts or sizes: *people of medium weight* ○ *The shirt comes in small, medium, and large.*

meet /miːt/ *verb* (*present participle* **meeting**, *past* **met**)
1 to come to the same place as someone else: *We met for coffee last Sunday.* ○ *I met an old friend at a party last Saturday.*
2 to see and speak to someone for the first time: *"This is Helen." "Pleased to meet you."*
3 to wait at a place for someone or something to arrive: *They met me at the airport.*
meet up *phrasal verb* to meet another person in order to do something together: *I* ***met up with*** *a few friends yesterday.*

meeting /ˈmiːtɪŋ/ *noun* when people come together for a reason, usually to talk about something: *We're having a meeting on Thursday to discuss the problem.* ○ *He's* ***in a meeting.***

a b c d e f g h i j k l **m** n o p q r s t u v w x y z

melody /ˈmelədi/ *noun* (*plural* **melodies**)
a song or tune

melon /ˈmelən/ *noun*
a large, round, sweet fruit with a thick, green or yellow skin ➲See colour picture **Fruit and Vegetables** on page Centre 8

melt /melt/ *verb*
to change from a solid into a liquid because of heat: *The sun soon melted the ice on the pond.* ○ *The chocolate had melted in my pocket.*

member /ˈmembəʳ/ *noun*
a person who belongs to a group or an organization: *family members* ○ *He was a* ***member of*** *the university rowing club.*

membership /ˈmembəʃɪp/ *noun* **[no plural]**
the state of belonging to a group or an organization: *I've applied for membership of the union.* ○ *a membership card*

memo /ˈmeməʊ/ *noun*
a written message that one person in an organization sends to another

memorize /ˈmemᵊraɪz/ *verb* (*present participle* **memorizing**, *past* **memorized**)
to learn something so that you remember it exactly: *I've memorized all my friends' birthdays.*

memory /ˈmemᵊri/ *noun* (*plural* **memories**)
1 your ability to remember things: *I have a good* ***memory for*** *names.*
2 something that you remember: *I have nice* ***memories of*** *my childhood.*

men /men/
plural of man

mend /mend/ *verb*
to repair something that is broken or not working correctly: *We need to get the TV mended.*

mental /ˈmentᵊl/ *adj*
relating to the mind: *mental illness*
• **mentally** *adv*: *a mentally ill person*

mention /ˈmenʃᵊn/ *verb*
to speak or write a few words about something or someone: *She didn't mention her daughter.* ○ *He* ***mentioned that*** *he liked skiing.*

menu /ˈmenjuː/ *noun*
1 a list of food and drinks that you can get in a restaurant: *a dinner menu*
2 a list of choices on a computer screen:

mercy /ˈmɜːsi/ *noun* **[no plural]**
kindness that makes you forgive someone and not punish them: *The prisoners pleaded for mercy.*

merely /ˈmɪəli/ *adv*
only: *I'm not arguing with you – I'm merely explaining the problem.*

merit /ˈmerɪt/ *verb formal*
to be important enough to get attention or punishment: *Her crimes were serious enough to merit a prison sentence.*

mermaid /ˈmɜːmeɪd/ *noun*
an imaginary creature in the sea that has the head and body of a woman and the tail of a fish

merry /ˈmeri/ *adj*
happy: *Merry Christmas!*

mess[1] /mes/ *noun*
1 an untidy or dirty place or thing: *The house is* ***in a mess.*** ○ *He* ***makes*** *such* ***a mess*** *in the kitchen.*
2 a situation in which there are a lot of problems: *She told me that her life was a mess.*

mess[2] /mes/ *verb*
mess about/around *phrasal verb informal*
to do silly things that are not important: *Stop messing around and do your homework!*

message /ˈmesɪdʒ/ *noun*
a piece of written or spoken information which one person gives to another: *Did you* ***get*** *my* ***message?*** ○ *I called her and left a message.*

messenger /ˈmesɪndʒəʳ/ *noun*
someone who takes a message between two people

messy /ˈmesi/ *adj* (**messier, messiest**)
untidy or dirty: *messy hair* ○ *a messy house/car*

met /met/
past of meet

metal /ˈmetᵊl/ *noun*
a hard, shiny material such as iron, gold, or silver

meter /ˈmiːtəʳ/ *noun*
1 a piece of equipment for measuring the amount of something such as electricity, time, or light: *a gas meter* ○ *a parking meter*
2 *US spelling of* metre

method /ˈmeθəd/ *noun*
a way of doing something, often one that involves a system or plan: *What's the best* ***method of*** *solving this problem?* ○ *traditional teaching methods*

metre *UK* (*US* **meter**) /ˈmiːtəʳ/ *noun*
a unit for measuring length, equal to 100 centimetres: *Our bedroom is five metres wide.*

metric /ˈmetrɪk/ *adj*
The metric system of measurement uses units based on the gram, metre, and litre.

metro /ˈmetrəʊ/ *noun*
an underground railway system in a large city: *the Paris metro*

miaow *UK* (*US* **meow**) /ˌmiːˈaʊ/ *noun*
the sound that a cat makes

mice /maɪs/
plural of mouse

microphone /ˈmaɪkrəfəʊn/ *noun*
a piece of electrical equipment for recording sounds, or for making sounds louder

microscope /ˈmaɪkrəskəʊp/ *noun*
a piece of scientific equipment which uses lenses (= pieces of curved glass) to make very small objects look bigger

microscope

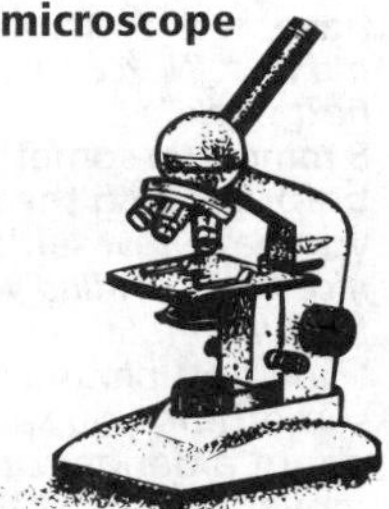

microwave /ˈmaɪkrəʊweɪv/ *noun*
an electric oven that uses waves of energy to quickly cook food or make it warmer ➲See colour picture **Kitchen** on page Centre 10

midday /ˌmɪdˈdeɪ/ *noun* **[no plural]**
12 o'clock in the middle of the day: *Beware the heat of the midday sun.*

middle¹ /ˈmɪdl/ *noun*
1 the centre of something: *We live right* ***in the middle*** *of the town.*
2 not the beginning or the end but the time in between: *The letter should arrive by* ***the middle of*** *next week.*
3 be in the middle of doing something to be busy: *I can't talk now – I'm in the middle of cooking a meal.*

middle² /ˈmɪdl/ *adj*
in a central position: *The middle layer is made of plastic.*

middle-aged /ˌmɪdlˈeɪdʒd/ *adj*
in the middle of your life before you are old: *a middle-aged couple*

midnight /ˈmɪdnaɪt/ *noun* **[no plural]**
12 o'clock at night

might /maɪt/ *verb*
1 used to talk about what will possibly happen: *I might come.* ○ *It might be finished by Thursday.*
2 used to talk about what is possibly true: *I think Isabel might be pregnant.*

mighty /ˈmaɪti/ *adj* **(mightier, mightiest)**
very powerful or successful: *In their next game they're playing the mighty Redskins.*

migrate /maɪˈgreɪt/ *verb* (*present participle* **migrating**, *past* **migrated)**
When birds or animals migrate, they travel from one place to another at the same time each year: *Many birds migrate from Europe to Africa for the winter.*

migration /maɪˈgreɪʃən/ *noun* **[no plural]**
when birds or animals travel from one place to another at the same time each year

mild /maɪld/ *adj*
1 When the weather in winter is mild, it is not cold.
2 Mild food does not have a strong taste: *a mild curry* ➲Opposite **hot**

mile /maɪl/ *noun*
a unit for measuring distance, equal to 1609 metres or 1760 yards: *The nearest station is two miles from here.*

military /ˈmɪlɪtri/ *adj*
relating to the army, navy, or air force: *military service*

milk¹ /mɪlk/ *noun* **[no plural]**
a white liquid that babies and baby animals drink that comes from their mothers' bodies: *a carton of milk* ○ *breast milk*

milk² /mɪlk/ *verb*
to take milk from a cow using your hands or a machine

mill /mɪl/ *noun*
1 a place where grain is pressed and made into flour: *a flour mill*
2 a factory where one material is made: *a cotton mill* ○ *a paper mill*

millennium /mɪˈleniəm/ *noun*

a period of 1000 years

millimetre *UK* (*US* **millimeter**) /ˈmɪlɪˌmiːtəʳ/ *noun*
a unit for measuring length, equal to 0.001 metres

million /ˈmɪljən/
1 (*plural* **million**) the number 1,000,000
2 millions *informal* a lot: *I've seen that film millions of times.*

millionaire /ˌmɪljəˈneəʳ/ *noun*
a very rich person

mime /maɪm/ *verb* (*present participle* **miming**, *past* **mimed**)
to act or tell a story without speaking, using movements of your hands, body and face
• **mime** *noun*: *a mime artist*

mimic[1] /ˈmɪmɪk/ *verb* (*present participle* **mimicking**, *past* **mimicked**)
to copy the way someone talks and behaves, usually to make people laugh: *He's always getting into trouble for mimicking his teachers.*

mimic[2] /ˈmɪmɪk/ *noun*
someone who is good at copying other people

mince[1] /mɪns/ *noun* **[no plural]** *UK*
meat, usually from a cow, which has been cut into very small pieces

mince[2] /mɪns/ *verb* (*present participle* **mincing**, *past* **minced**)
to cut food into small pieces in a machine: *Mince the garlic and add it to the onions.* ○ *minced beef/onions*

mind[1] /maɪnd/ *noun*
1 someone's memory or their ability to think, and feel emotions: *She has a very logical mind.*
2 have something on your mind to worry about something: *Jim has a lot on his mind at the moment.*
3 bear/keep someone/something in mind to remember someone or something that may be useful in the future: *I'll keep you in mind if another job comes up.*
4 make your mind up to make a decision: *I haven't made up my mind whether to go yet.*
5 change your mind to change a decision or opinion: *We've changed our minds about selling the house.*
6 be out of your mind *informal* to be crazy or very stupid: *You must be out of your mind going running in this weather.*
7 cross your mind If an idea crosses your mind, you think about it for a short time: *It crossed my mind that she might not want to go.*
8 put/set someone's mind at rest to say something to someone to stop them worrying: *Talking to the doctor put my mind at rest.*

mind[2] /maɪnd/ *verb*
1 to be angry or worried about something: *Would he mind if I borrowed his book?* ○ *I don't mind driving.*
2 do you mind?/would you mind? something you say when politely asking someone to do something: *Do you mind not smoking in here, please?*
3 something you say when telling someone to be careful with something dangerous: *Mind the iron – it's hot!*
4 never mind used to tell someone not to worry about something they have done: *"I forgot to bring any money." "Never mind, you can pay me next week."*
5 mind you something you say before saying the opposite of what you have just said: *We had a really nice holiday. Mind you, the weather was terrible.*
Mind out! *phrasal verb UK*
something you say to tell someone about a danger or to tell them to move: *Mind out – this plate's very hot!*

mine[1] /maɪn/ *pronoun*
the thing or things belonging to the person who is speaking or writing: *"Whose book is this?" "It's mine."* ○ *Can I use your pen? Mine's not working.*

mine[2] /maɪn/ *noun*
1 a hole in the ground where people dig out coal, gold, etc.
2 a bomb hidden in the ground or water which explodes when it is touched: *He was killed when he drove over a mine.*

miner /ˈmaɪnəʳ/ *noun*
someone who works in a hole in the ground, digging out coal, gold, etc: *a coal miner*

mineral /ˈmɪnᵊrᵊl/ *noun*
1 a valuable or useful substance that is dug out of the ground: *The region's*

a b c d e f g h i j k l **m** n o p q r s t u v w x y z

rich mineral deposits include oil, gold, and aluminium.
2 a chemical that your body needs to stay healthy

mineral water /ˈmɪnᵊrᵊl ˌwɔːtəʳ/ *noun* **[no plural]**
water which is taken from the ground

mingle /ˈmɪŋgl/ *verb* (*present participle* **mingling,** *past* **mingled)**
1 to mix, or be mixed: *The smell of fresh coffee mingled with cigarette smoke.*
2 to meet and talk to a lot of people: *I though I would* ***mingle with*** *the other students.*

miniature /ˈmɪnətʃəʳ/ *adj*
very small: *a miniature camera*

minibus /ˈmɪnibʌs/ *noun* (*plural* **minibuses)**
a small bus with seats for about ten people

minimum¹ /ˈmɪnɪməm/ *adj*
The minimum amount of something is the smallest amount that is allowed or possible: *There is a minimum charge of $5 for postage.*
➲Opposite **maximum**

minimum² /ˈmɪnɪməm/ *noun*
the smallest amount that is allowed or possible: *Please keep noise to an absolute minimum.* ➲Opposite **maximum**

miniskirt /ˈmɪnɪˌskɜːt/ *noun*
a very short skirt ➲See colour picture **Clothes** on page Centre 5

minister /ˈmɪnɪstəʳ/ *noun*
a politician who has an important position in the government: *a health minister*

ministry /ˈmɪnɪstri/ *noun* (*plural* **ministries)**
a government department which is responsible for a particular subject: *the Ministry of Defence*

minor /ˈmaɪnəʳ/ *adj*
not important or serious: *There are a few minor problems.* ○ *He suffered only minor injuries.* ➲Opposite **major**

minority /maɪˈnɒrəti/ *noun* (*plural* **minorities)**
less than half of a group of people or things: *The violence was caused by a* ***small minority*** *of football supporters.* ○ *I agreed to the suggestion, but I was* ***in the minority***. ➲Opposite **majority**

mint /mɪnt/ *noun*
1 a sweet with a fresh, strong taste
2 [no plural] a plant whose leaves are used to add flavour to food and drinks

minus¹ /ˈmaɪnəs/ *preposition*
1 used when the second of two numbers should be taken away from the first: *Five minus three is two.*
2 without something: *She arrived at the meeting minus her briefcase.*

minus² /ˈmaɪnəs/ *adj*
A minus number is less than zero: *The temperature last night was minus ten.*

minute¹ /ˈmɪnɪt/ *noun*
1 a period of time equal to 60 seconds: *It'll take you thirty minutes to get to the airport.* ○ *She was ten minutes late for her interview.*
2 (at) any minute very soon: *Her train will be arriving any minute.*
3 the last minute the latest time possible: *The concert was cancelled at the last minute.*
4 Wait/Just a minute. used when asking someone to wait for a short time: *Just a minute – I've left my coat in the restaurant.*

minute² /maɪˈnjuːt/ *adj*
very small: *Her hands are minute.*

miracle /ˈmɪrəkl/ *noun*
1 something that is very surprising or difficult to believe: *It's a* ***miracle that*** *he's still alive.*
2 something very strange which happens and which you cannot explain: *One of Christ's miracles was turning water into wine.*

miraculous /mɪˈrækjələs/ *adj*
very surprising or difficult to believe: *He made a miraculous recovery from his illness.*

mirror /ˈmɪrəʳ/ *noun*
a piece of special glass in which you can see yourself: *a bathroom mirror* ○ *He looked at himself* ***in the mirror***.
➲See colour picture **The Living Room** on page Centre 11

misbehave /ˌmɪsbɪˈheɪv/ *verb* (*present participle* **misbehaving,** *past* **misbehaved)**
to behave badly

mischief /ˈmɪstʃɪf/ *noun* **[no plural]**
behaviour, usually of a child, which is slightly bad

mischievous /ˈmɪstʃɪvəs/ *adj*

behaving in a way that is slightly bad but not serious: *a mischievous five-year-old*

miserable /ˈmɪzᵊrəbl/ *adj*
1 sad: *I just woke up feeling miserable.*
2 bad and making you sad: *People are living in miserable conditions.*

misery /ˈmɪzᵊri/ *noun* **[no plural]**
sadness and suffering: *The war brought misery to millions of people.*

misfortune /mɪsˈfɔːtʃuːn/ *noun*
something bad that happens to you: *He **had the misfortune** to fall in love with a married woman.*

miss /mɪs/ *verb*
1 to feel sad about someone or something that you have stopped seeing or having: *I'll miss you when you go.* ○ *He misses having a room of his own.*
2 to not go to something: *I missed my class this morning.*
3 to not see or hear something: *Sorry, I missed that, could you repeat it please?*
4 to not hit or catch a ball: *It should have been such an easy goal but he missed.*
5 to arrive too late to get on a bus, train, or aeroplane: *If I don't leave now, I'll miss my train.*
miss someone/something out *phrasal verb UK*
to not include someone or something

Miss /mɪs/ *noun* (*plural* **Misses**)
a title for a girl or woman who is not married: *Miss Olivia Allenby* ○ *Tell Miss Russell I'm here.*

missile /ˈmɪsaɪl/ *noun*
1 an explosive weapon which can travel long distances through the air: *nuclear missiles*
2 an object which someone throws through the air to hit someone

missing /ˈmɪsɪŋ/ *adj*
1 lost, not in the usual place: *Her daughter **went missing** a week ago.*
2 not included in something: *There are a couple of things **missing from** the list.*

mist /mɪst/ *noun* **[no plural]**
small drops of water in the air which makes it difficult to see objects which are not near: *Gradually the mist cleared and the sun began to shine.*

mistake[1] /mɪˈsteɪk/ *noun*
1 something that you do or think which is wrong: *a spelling mistake* ○ *He **made** a lot of **mistakes** in his written test.*
2 by mistake If you do something wrong by mistake, you do it without wanting to: *I picked up someone else's book by mistake.*

mistake[2] /mɪˈsteɪk/ *verb* (*present participle* **mistaking**, *past tense* **mistook**, *past participle* **mistaken**)
to not understand something correctly: *I think you mistook what I said.*
mistake someone for someone *phrasal verb*
to think that someone is a different person: *People sometimes mistake him for a girl.*

misty /ˈmɪsti/ *adj*
If the weather is misty, there is a cloud of small drops of water in the air: *a cold and misty morning*

mix /mɪks/ *verb*
1 to put different things together in order to make something new: ***Mix** the powder **with** water to form a paste.* ○ *Put the chocolate, butter, and egg in a bowl and **mix** them all **together**.*
2 to meet and talk to people: *She enjoys going to parties and **mixing with** people.*
mix something up *phrasal verb*
to make a group of things untidy: *The books were all mixed up in a box.*

mixture /ˈmɪkstʃəʳ/ *noun*
two or more different things or people that have been put together: *Add milk to the mixture and stir until smooth.* ○ *The class is an odd mixture of people.*

mm
written abbreviation for millimetre (= a unit for measuring length)

moan /məʊn/ *verb*
1 to say that something is wrong or that you are angry about something: *She's always **moaning about** work*
2 to make a low sound, especially because part of your body hurts: *He lay on the floor moaning.*
• **moan** *noun*

a b c d e f g h i j k l m n o p q r s t u v w x y z

mobile phone /ˌməʊbaɪl ˈfəʊn/ *noun*
a telephone that you can carry everywhere with you

mobile phone

mock /mɒk/ *verb*
to laugh at someone in a way that is not kind: *The other children mocked him whenever he spoke.*

model[1] /ˈmɒdəl/ *noun*
1 someone whose job is wearing clothes for photographs or fashion shows: *a top fashion model*
2 a smaller copy of a real object: *He makes models as a hobby.*

model[2] /ˈmɒdəl/ *verb* (*present participle* **modelling**, *past* **modelled**)
to wear clothes in fashion shows and photographs as a model: *She's been modelling for the same designer for years.*

modem /ˈməʊdem/ *noun*
a piece of equipment that is used to send information from a computer through a telephone system

moderate /ˈmɒdərət/ *adj*
average in size or amount and not too much: *Eating a moderate amount of fat is healthy.*
• **moderately** *adv*

modern /ˈmɒdən/ *adj*
1 relating to the present time and not to the past: *modern society* ○ *the stresses of modern life*
2 using the newest ideas, design, technology, etc and not traditional: *modern art/architecture*

modest /ˈmɒdɪst/ *adj*
A modest person does not talk about how good they are: *He's very modest about his achievements.*

moist /mɔɪst/ *adj*
slightly wet: *Keep the soil moist but not wet.*

moisture /ˈmɔɪstʃər/ *noun* **[no plural]**
very small drops of water in the air or on a surface

mole /məʊl/ *noun*
1 a small, dark mark on the skin
2 a small animal with black fur that lives under the ground

molecule /ˈmɒlɪkjuːl/ *noun*
the smallest unit of a substance, with one or more atoms

moment /ˈməʊmənt/ *noun*
1 a very short period of time: *I'll be back* ***in a moment***. ○ ***For a moment*** *I thought it was Anna.* ○ *Could you* ***wait a moment***?
2 a point in time: *Just* ***at that moment***, *the phone rang.*
3 at the moment now: *She's not here at the moment.*

monarch /ˈmɒnək/ *noun*
a king or queen

monarchy /ˈmɒnəki/ *noun* (*plural* **monarchies**)
when a country is ruled by a king or queen

monastery /ˈmɒnəstəri/ *noun* (*plural* **monasteries**)
a building where men live as a religious group

Monday /ˈmʌndeɪ/ *noun*
the day of the week after Sunday and before Tuesday

money /ˈmʌni/ *noun* **[no plural]**
the coins or pieces of paper that are used for buying things: *How much money have you got?* ○ *He* ***spends*** *all his* ***money*** *on clothes and CDs.* ○ *The company's not* ***making*** (= earning) *any money at the moment.*

monitor /ˈmɒnɪtər/ *noun*
a screen that shows information or pictures, usually connected to a computer: *a colour monitor* ➲See colour picture **The Office** on page Centre 12

monk /mʌŋk/ *noun*
a member of a group of religious men living away from other people

monkey /ˈmʌŋki/ *noun*
a hairy animal with a long tail that lives in hot countries and climbs trees

monotonous /məˈnɒtənəs/ *adj*
always the same and boring: *The work is very monotonous.*

monsoon /mɒnˈsuːn/ *noun*
the season when there is a lot of rain in Southern Asia

monster /ˈmɒnstər/ *noun*
an imaginary creature that is large, ugly, and frightening

month /mʌnθ/ *noun*
one of the twelve periods of time that a year is divided into: *Next month will be very busy.*

a b c d e f g h i j k l **m** n o p q r s t u v w x y z

monthly /ˈmʌnθli/ *adj, adv*
happening or made once a month: *a monthly magazine*

monument /ˈmɒnjəmənt/ *noun*
something that is built to make people remember a famous person or something important that happened: *a national monument*

moo /muː/ *noun*
the sound that a cow makes
•**moo** *verb*

mood /muːd/ *noun*
1 the way someone feels at a particular time: *You're* ***in a good mood****! ○ Ignore him – he's* ***in a bad mood****.*
2 be in the mood for something to want to do something: *I'm not really in the mood for shopping.*

moon /muːn/ *noun*
the round object that shines in the sky at night and moves around the Earth

moonlight /ˈmuːnlaɪt/ *noun* **[no plural]**
light that comes from the moon: *In the moonlight she looked even more beautiful.*

mop[1] /mɒp/ *noun*
a thing for cleaning floors that has a long handle and thick strings at one end

mop[2] /mɒp/ *verb* (*present participle* **mopping**, *past* **mopped**)
to use a mop: *I mopped the floor.*

moral[1] /ˈmɒr^{ə}l/ *adj*
relating to beliefs about what behaviour is good and what behaviour is bad: *He has very high moral standards.*
•**morally** *adv*

moral[2] /ˈmɒr^{ə}l/ *noun*
something which teaches you how to behave better: *The moral of the story is never lie.*

morals /ˈmɒrəlz/ *plural noun*
beliefs that you should behave well and treat other people well: *He doesn't care what he does, he has no morals at all.*

more[1] /mɔː^{r}/ *quantifier*
1 something extra to what you have now: *Is there any more soup? ○ Would anyone like some more food?*
2 a greater number or amount of people or things: *There are a lot more people here today than there were yesterday. ○ He knows more about computers than I do.*
3 more and more an increasing number: *More and more people are choosing not to get married.*

more[2] /mɔː^{r}/ *adv*
1 more beautiful/difficult/interesting, etc used to show that someone or something has a greater amount of a quality than someone or something else: *It's* ***more*** *expensive* ***than*** *the others. ○ She's far more intelligent than her sister.*
2 used to show that something happens a greater number of times than before: *We eat out a lot* ***more than*** *we used to.*
3 more or less almost: *We've more or less finished work on the house.*
4 more and more more as time passes: *It's becoming more and more difficult to pass the exam.*

morning /ˈmɔːnɪŋ/ *noun*
the first half of the day, from the time when the sun rises until the middle of the day: *Friday morning ○ tomorrow morning ○ I got up late this morning.*

mosaic

mosaic /məʊˈzeɪɪk/ *noun*
a picture or pattern that is made with small pieces of coloured stone, glass, etc

Moslem /ˈmɒzləm/ *another spelling of* Muslim (= someone who believes in Islam)
•**Moslem** *adj*

mosque /mɒsk/ *noun*
a building where Muslims say their prayers

mosquito /məˈskiː-/ *noun* (*plural* **mosquitoes**)
a small flying insect that drinks your blood, sometimes causing a disease

moss /mɒs/ *noun* **[no plural]**
a very small, green plant that grows

on the surface of rocks, trees, etc

most[1] /məʊst/ *adv*
1 the most important/popular, etc used to show that someone or something has the greatest amount of a quality: *She's the most beautiful girl I've ever seen.* ○ *There are various reasons but this is the most important.*
2 more than anyone or anything else: *Which subject do you like most?* ○ *I liked all the cities but I liked Venice **most of all**.*

most[2] /məʊst/ *quantifier*
1 almost all of a group of people or things: *Most people like her.* ○ *She wears jeans **most of** the time.*
2 a larger amount than anyone or anything else: *This one costs the most.* ○ *Which of you earns most?*
3 make the most of something to enjoy something as much as you can because it will end soon: *We should make the most of this good weather.*
4 at the most not more than a particular amount or number: *The journey will take an hour at the most.*

mostly /məʊstli/ *adv*
mainly or most of the time: *The students are mostly Spanish.* ○ *It's mostly quiet at nights.*

moth /mɒθ/ *noun*
an insect with large wings that often flies at night

mother /ˈmʌðəʳ/ *noun*
your female parent: *My mother and father are divorced.*

motherhood /ˈmʌðəhʊd/ *noun* **[no plural]**
being a mother

mother-in-law /ˈmʌðərɪnˌlɔː/ *noun* (*plural* **mothers-in-law**)
the mother of your husband or wife

motion /ˈməʊʃən/ *noun* **[no plural]**
when or how something moves: *The motion of the boat made him feel sick.*

motivate /ˈməʊtɪveɪt/ *verb* (*present participle* **motivating,** *past* **motivated)**
to make someone want to do something: *Teaching is all about **motivating** people **to** learn.*

motive /ˈməʊtɪv/ *noun*
a reason for doing something: *The police don't yet know the **motive for** the killing.*

motor /ˈməʊtəʳ/ *noun*
the part of a machine or car, etc that makes it work: *an electric motor*

motorcycle /ˈməʊtəˌsaɪkl/ (*also* **motorbike** /ˈməʊtəbaɪk/) *noun*
a vehicle with two wheels and an engine

motorist /ˈməʊtərɪst/ *noun*
someone who drives a car

motorway /ˈməʊtəweɪ/ *UK* (*US* **freeway**) *noun*
a long, wide road, usually used by traffic travelling fast

mould[1] /məʊld/ *noun*
1 [no plural] a green or black substance that grows in wet places or on old food
2 a container that is used to make something in a particular shape: *a chocolate mould*

mould[2] /məʊld/ *verb*
to make a soft substance a particular shape: *You mould the clay while it is wet.*

mouldy /ˈməʊldi/ *adj* **(mouldier, mouldiest)**
covered with mould: *mouldy cheese*

mound /maʊnd/ *noun*
1 a large pile of something: *There was a mound of clothes on the floor.*
2 a higher area of soil, like a small hill: *an ancient burial mound*

Mount /maʊnt/ *noun*
used in the names of mountains: *Mount Everest*

mount /maʊnt/ *verb*
to increase in amount or level: *Concern is mounting over fighting in the region.* ○ *mounting problems*
mount up *phrasal verb*
to become a large amount: *My homework is really mounting up this week.*

mountain /ˈmaʊntɪn/ *noun*
a very high hill: *to climb a mountain*

mountain

mourn /mɔːn/ *verb*
to feel very sad because someone has died: *He **mourned for** his dead son every day.*

mourning /ˈmɔːnɪŋ/ *noun* **[no plural]**
a feeling of sadness because

a b c d e f g h i j k l m n o p q r s t u v w x y z

someone has died: *The whole nation was* ***in mourning****.*

mouse /maʊs/ *noun* (*plural* **mice**)
1 a thing that is connected to a computer that you move with your hand to control what the computer does
2 a small animal with fur and a long, thin tail

mouse

moustache /mə'stɑːʃ/ *noun* a line of hair that some men grow above their mouths ➲See colour picture **Hair** on page Centre 9

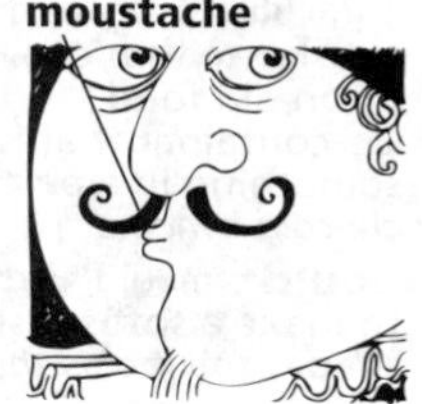
moustache

mouth /maʊθ/ *noun*
1 the part of the face that is used for eating and speaking ➲See colour picture **The Body** on page Centre 2
2 mouth of a cave/tunnel, etc the opening or entrance of a cave/tunnel, etc
3 mouth of a river where a river goes into the sea

mouthful /'maʊθfʊl/ *noun* the amount of food or drink that you can put into your mouth at one time

move /muːv/ *verb* (*present participle* **moving**, *past* **moved**)
1 to go to a different place: *Eventually, she* ***moved to*** *Germany.* ○ *She's* ***moving into*** *a new apartment.*
2 to change place or position, or to make something change place or position: *We* ***moved*** *the chairs* ***to*** *another room.* ○ *Someone was* ***moving around*** *upstairs.*
3 to make someone feel sad: *I was deeply moved by his speech.*
4 move house *UK* to leave your home in order to live in a new one

move in *phrasal verb* to begin living in a new home: *We're moving in next week.* ○ *She's just* ***moved in with*** *her boyfriend.* ○ *They want to* ***move in together*** *before they get married.*

move out *phrasal verb* to stop living in a particular home: *He moved out when he was only eighteen.*

movement /'muːvmənt/ *noun*
1 a group of people with the same beliefs who work together to do something: *the women's movement*
2 a change of position or place: *His movements were rather clumsy.*

movie /'muːvi/ *noun US* a film

mow /məʊ/ *verb* (*past participle* **mown**) to cut grass using a machine: *He was mowing the lawn.*

MP /ˌem'piː/ *noun abbreviation for* Member of Parliament: someone who has been elected to the government of the United Kingdom

mph *written abbreviation for* miles per hour: a unit for measuring speed: *a 30 mph speed limit*

Mr /'mɪstə^{r}/ *noun* a title for a man, used before his family name or full name: *Good morning, Mr Smith.*

Mrs /'mɪsɪz/ *noun* a title for a married woman, used before her family name or full name: *Hello, Mrs. Jones.*

Ms /mɪz/ *noun* a title for a woman, used before her family name or full name: *Ms Holly Fox*

much^{1} /mʌtʃ/ *quantifier*
1 In questions, 'much' is used to ask about the amount of something: *Was there much food there?* ○ ***How much*** *money will I need?*
2 In negative sentences, 'much' is used to say that there is not a large amount of something: *She doesn't earn much money.* ○ *Pete didn't say much at dinner.* ○ *"Is there any coffee left?" "****Not much****."*
3 too much/so much a large amount of something, often more than you want: *I'd love to come, but I've got too much work.* ○ *They have so much money.*

much^{2} /mʌtʃ/ *adv*
1 often or a lot: *Do you go to London much?* ○ *I don't like curry very much.*
2 much better/bigger/smaller, etc a lot better, bigger, smaller, etc: *Their old house was much bigger.*

mud /mʌd/ *noun* **[no plural]**
wet soil: *He'd been playing football and was covered in mud.*

muddle[1] /ˈmʌdl/ *noun*
when things are not organized and people do not understand what they should do: *There was a big muddle over who was buying the tickets.* ○ *I'm* ***in*** *such* ***a muddle*** *with these bills.*

muddle[2] /ˈmʌdl/ *verb* (*present participle* **muddling,** *past* **muddled)**
get someone/something muddled up
to think that a person or thing is someone or something else: *I often get Jonathan and his brother muddled up.*

muddy /ˈmʌdi/ *adj* **(muddier, muddiest)**
covered with soil: *muddy boots*

mug[1] /mʌg/ *noun*
a large cup with straight sides, used for hot drinks: *a coffee mug*

mug[2] /mʌg/ *verb* (*present participle* **mugging,** *past* **mugged)**
to attack someone and take something from them in a public place: *He was mugged as he walked across the park.*
• **mugger** *noun*
someone who mugs people

multiply /ˈmʌltɪplaɪ/ *verb* (*present participle* **multiplying,** *past* **multiplied)**
to add one number to itself a particular number of times: *Three* ***multiplied by*** *six equals eighteen.*

mum /mʌm/ *noun UK informal*
mother: *Can we go now, Mum?*

mumble /ˈmʌmbl/ *verb* (*present participle* **mumbling,** *past* **mumbled)**
to speak too quietly and not clearly: *He mumbled something about it being a waste of time.*

mummy /ˈmʌmi/ *noun UK informal* (*plural* **mummies)**
a word for 'mother', used especially by children: *Come here, Mummy!*

mumps /mʌmps/ *noun* **[no plural]**
an illness that children get which makes the neck swell

murder[1] /ˈmɜːdəʳ/ *noun*
the crime of killing someone

murder[2] /ˈmɜːdəʳ/ *verb*
to kill someone

murderer /ˈmɜːdᵊrəʳ/ *noun*
someone who has killed someone

murmur[1] /ˈmɜːməʳ/ *verb*
to speak very quietly: *"Go to sleep now," she murmured.*

murmur[2] /ˈmɜːməʳ/ *noun*
the sound of someone saying something very quietly: *I could hear the low* ***murmur of voices****.*

muscle /ˈmʌsl/ *noun*
one of many parts in the body that are connected to bones and which help you to move: *stomach muscles*

museum /mjuːˈziːəm/ *noun*
a building where you can look at important objects connected with art, history, or science: *a museum of modern art*

mushroom /ˈmʌʃruːm/ *noun*
a type of fungus (= organism like a plant) with a short stem and a round top, some types of which can be eaten

mushrooms

music /ˈmjuːzɪk/ *noun* **[no plural]**
1 a pattern of sounds that is made by playing instruments or singing, or a recording of this: *pop/dance music* ○ *classical music* ○ *He likes* ***listening to music****.* ○ *a music lesson/teacher*
2 written signs which represent sounds that can be sung or played with instruments: *I never learnt to* ***read music*** (= understand written music).

musical /ˈmjuːzɪkᵊl/ *adj*
1 relating to music: *a musical instrument*
2 good at playing music: *She comes from a very musical family.*

musician /mjuːˈzɪʃᵊn/ *noun*
someone who plays a musical instrument, often as a job: *a jazz musician*

Muslim (*also* **Moslem)** /ˈmʊzlɪm/ *noun*
someone who believes in Islam

must *strong form* /mʌst/ *weak forms* /məst, məs/ *verb*
1 used to say that it is necessary that something happens or is done: *The meat must be cooked thoroughly.* ○ *I must get some sleep.*
2 used to show that you are certain something is true: *You must be*

a b c d e f g h i j k l m n o p q r s t u v w x y z

exhausted! ○ *She must be very wealthy.*

mustard /ˈmʌstəd/ *noun* **[no plural]**
a spicy yellow or brown sauce often eaten in small amounts with meat

mustn't /ˈmʌsᵊnt/
short for must not: *You mustn't let her know I'm coming.*

mutter /ˈmʌtəʳ/ *verb*
to speak quietly, often when complaining about something: *She walked past me, muttering to herself.*

my /maɪ/ *determiner*
belonging to the person who is speaking or writing: *Tom's my older son.* ○ *It's not my fault.*

myself /maɪˈself/ *pronoun*
1 used to show that it is the person who is speaking who is affected by an action: *I've bought myself a new coat.* ○ *I looked at myself in the mirror.*
2 used to give more attention to the word 'I': *I'll tell her myself.* ○ *Jack always drinks red wine but I prefer white myself.*
3 (all) by myself alone or without anyone else's help: *I live by myself in a small flat.* ○ *Mummy, I got dressed all by myself!*

mysterious /mɪˈstɪəriəs/ *adj*
strange and not explained or understood: *the mysterious death of her son*

mystery /ˈmɪstᵊri/ *noun* (*plural* **mysteries**)
something strange that cannot be explained or understood: *They never did solve the mystery of his disappearance.*

a b c d e f g h i j k l m n o p q r s t u v w x y z

Nn

N, n /en/
the fourteenth letter of the alphabet

nag /næg/ *verb* (*present participle* **nagging**, *past* **nagged**)
to keep asking someone to do something: *She keeps nagging me to get my hair cut.*

nail /neɪl/ *noun*
1 a thin piece of metal with a sharp end, used to join pieces of wood together: *a hammer and nails*
2 the hard bit at the end of your fingers and toes: *She* ***bites*** *her* ***nails***.

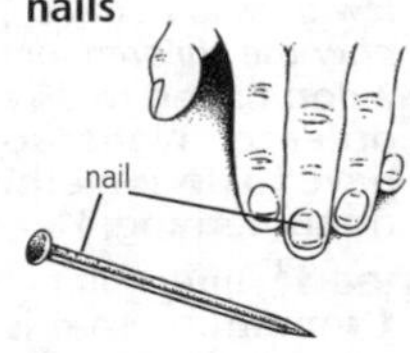

naked /ˈneɪkɪd/ *adj*
not wearing clothes: *naked bodies*

name[1] /neɪm/ *noun*
the word or group of words that is used to refer to a person, thing, or place: *What's your name?* ○ *My name's Alexis.* ○ *I can't remember the name of the street.*

name[2] /neɪm/ *verb* (*present participle* **naming**, *past* **named**)
to give someone or something a name: *We named our first son Edward.*

nanny /ˈnæni/ *noun* (*plural* **nannies**)
someone whose job is to look after a family's children

nap /næp/ *noun*
a short sleep: *He likes to* ***take a nap*** *after lunch.*

napkin /ˈnæpkɪn/ *noun*
a piece of cloth or paper that you use when you eat to keep your clothes clean

nappy /ˈnæpi/ *UK* (*US* **diaper**) *noun* (*plural* **nappies**)
a thick piece of paper or cloth worn by a baby on its bottom: *She had to* ***change*** *the baby's* ***nappy***.

narrow /ˈnærəʊ/ *adj*
not wide, being only a small distance from one side to the other: *a narrow street* ○ *narrow shoulders*

nasty /ˈnɑːsti/ *adj* (**nastier, nastiest**)
1 very bad: *He had a nasty cut above his eye.* ○ *There's a nasty smell in here.*
2 not kind: *She's always being* ***nasty to*** *her little brother.*

nation /ˈneɪʃᵊn/ *noun*
a country or the people living in a country: *African/Asian nations* ○ *The entire nation mourned her death.*

national /ˈnæʃᵊnᵊl/ *adj*
relating to the whole of a country: *a national newspaper*

national anthem /ˌnæʃᵊnᵊl ˈænθəm/ *noun*
the official song of a country

nationality /ˌnæʃᵊnˈæləti/ *noun* (*plural* **nationalities**)
If you have American/British/Swiss, etc nationality, you are legally a member of that country: *What nationality is she?*

native[1] /ˈneɪtɪv/ *adj*
1 Your native town or country is the place where you were born: *He returned to his native Algeria.*
2 Your native language is the first language you learn as a child: *native speakers of English*

native[2] /ˈneɪtɪv/ *noun*
someone who was born in a particular place: *He's* ***a native of*** *Texas.*

natural /ˈnætʃᵊrᵊl/ *adj*
1 made or caused by nature and not by people or machines: *natural gas* ○ *This product contains only natural ingredients.*
2 normal or expected: *It's natural to feel sad when you leave home.* ➲Opposite **unnatural**

naturally /ˈnætʃᵊrᵊli/ *adv*
1 as you would expect: *Naturally, he was disappointed to fail the exam.*
2 in a normal way: *Relax and try to behave naturally.*
3 existing or happening as part of nature and not made or done by people: *He died naturally in his sleep.*

nature /ˈneɪtʃəʳ/ *noun*
1 **[no plural]** all the plants, creatures and things that exist in the world, which are not made by people: *I like to get out and enjoy nature.*
2 someone's character: *It is not* ***in his nature*** *to be rude.*

a b c d e f g h i j k l m n o p q r s t u v w x y z

a b c d e f g h i j k l m n o p q r s t u v w x y z

naughty /ˈnɔːti/ *adj* (**naughtier, naughtiest**)
If a child is naughty, he or she behaves badly: *You are a naughty little girl!*

naval /ˈneɪvᵊl/ *adj*
relating to the ships that are used for fighting wars at sea: *a naval officer*

navigate /ˈnævɪgeɪt/ *verb* (*present participle* **navigating**, *past* **navigated**)
to find the right direction to travel by using maps or other equipment: *He navigated the ship back to Plymouth.*
• **navigation** /ˌnævɪˈgeɪʃᵊn/ *noun* **[no plural]**
when you find the right direction to travel by using maps or other equipment
• **navigator** /ˈnævɪgeɪtəʳ/ *noun*
a person who navigates

navy /ˈneɪvi/ *noun* (*plural* **navies**)
the Navy ships and soldiers used for fighting wars at sea: *He joined the navy.*

near¹ /nɪəʳ/ *adv, preposition*
1 not far away in distance: *Could you come a bit nearer, please?* ○ *I stood near the window.*
2 not far away in time: *We can decide nearer the time.*

near² /nɪəʳ/ *adj*
1 not far away in distance or time: *The school's very near.* ○ *The nearest garage is 10 miles away.*
2 in the near future at a time that is not far away: *Space travel may become very common in the near future.*

nearby /ˌnɪəˈbaɪ/ *adj, adv*
not far away: *a nearby town*

nearly /ˈnɪəli/ *adv*
almost: *I've nearly finished.* ○ *Nearly all the food had gone when I arrived.*

neat /niːt/ *adj*
1 tidy and clean: *He always looks very **neat and tidy**.*
2 *US informal* good: *What a neat idea!*

neatly /ˈniːtli/ *adv*
in a tidy way: *He was neatly dressed.*

necessary /ˈnesəsᵊri/ *adj*
needed in order to do something: *Is it really **necessary to** spend so much?* ○ *The police are prepared to use force, **if necessary**.* ➲Opposite **unnecessary**

necessity /nəˈsesəti/ *noun* (*plural* **necessities**)
something that you need: *We took food and clothing and other necessities.*

neck /nek/ *noun*
the part of the body between your head and your shoulders ➲See colour picture **The Body** on page Centre 2

necklace /ˈnekləs/ *noun*
a piece of jewellery that you wear around your neck: *a pearl necklace*

need¹ /niːd/ *verb*
1 If you need something, you must have it, and if you need to do something, you must do it: *I need some new shoes.* ○ *I **need to** ask you a few questions.* ○ *We need you to look after the children for us.*
2 don't need to do something used in order to say that someone does not have to do something or should not do something: *You didn't need to go.*

need² /niːd/ *noun*
1 something that is necessary to have or do: *There's an urgent **need for** more medical supplies.* ○ *Is there any **need to** change the current system?*
2 be in need of something to need something: *My car's in need of repair.*

needle /ˈniːdl/ *noun*
1 the thin metal part of a piece of medical equipment used to take blood out of the body, or to put drugs in
2 a thin, pointed metal object with a small hole at one end for thread, used in sewing: *a needle and thread*

needle

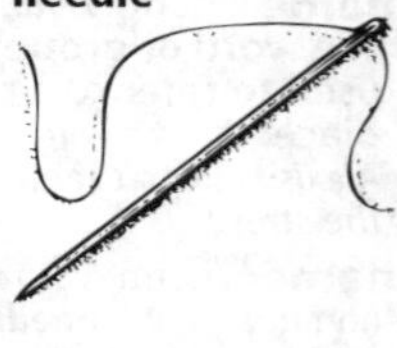

needless /ˈniːdləs/ *adj*
needless to say as you would expect: *Needless to say, I did all the work.*
• **needlessly** *adv*

needn't /ˈniːdᵊnt/
short for need not: *You needn't have come.*

negative¹ /ˈnegətɪv/ *adj*
1 not hopeful and not interested: *She seems very negative about her work.*
2 A negative number is less than zero.
3 with the meaning 'no' or 'not'

negative² /ˈnegətɪv/ *noun*
a piece of film from which a photograph is made

neglect¹ /nɪˈglekt/ *verb*
to not give enough attention to something or someone: *He neglects that poor dog.* ○ *I'm afraid I have neglected the garden.*

neglect² /nɪˈglekt/ *noun* **[no plural]**
when you do not give enough attention to something or someone: *The children had suffered years of neglect.*

negotiate /nɪˈgəʊʃieɪt/ *verb* (*present participle* **negotiating**, *past* **negotiated**)
to try to make or change an agreement by talking about it: *We are negotiating for a new contract.*

neighbour /ˈneɪbəʳ/ *noun*
someone who lives very near you, especially in the next house: *Our* ***next-door neighbours*** *are always arguing.*

neighbourhood /ˈneɪbəhʊd/ *noun*
an area of a town or city that people live in: *Are there any good restaurants* ***in the neighbourhood****?*

neighbouring /ˈneɪbᵊrɪŋ/ *adj*
near or next to somewhere: *neighbouring countries*

neither¹ /ˈnaɪðəʳ, ˈniːðəʳ/ *adv*
used to say that a negative fact is also true of someone or something else: *Jerry doesn't like it, and neither do I.* ○ *She's not very tall and neither is her husband.*

neither² /ˈnaɪðəʳ, ˈniːðəʳ/ *pronoun, determiner*
not either of two people or things: *Neither child was hurt in the accident.* ○ ***Neither of*** *us had ever been to London before.*

neither³ /ˈnaɪðəʳ, ˈniːðəʳ/ *conjunction*
neither ... nor used when a negative fact is true of two people or things: *Neither he nor his mother would talk to the police.*

nephew /ˈnefjuː/ *noun*
the son of your brother or sister
➲Compare **niece**

nerve /nɜːv/ *noun*
1 one of the very small parts in your body which carry messages between your brain and other parts of the body
2 the rudeness to do something that you know someone will not like: *I can't believe she* ***had the nerve*** *to talk to me after what happened!*

nerve-racking /ˈnɜːvˌrækɪŋ/ *adj*
making you very nervous: *It is nerve-racking speaking in front of a lot of people.*

nerves /nɜːvz/ *plural noun*
the state of being nervous: *I always suffer from nerves before a match.*
2 get on someone's nerves to annoy someone: *If we spend too much time together we get on each other's nerves.*

nervous /ˈnɜːvəs/ *adj*
1 worried and anxious: *She's very* ***nervous about*** *her driving test.*
2 relating to the nerves in the body: *the nervous system*

nest /nest/ *noun*
a home built by birds for their eggs

net /net/ *noun*
1 [no plural] material made of crossed threads with holes between them
2 something made with a piece of net, for example for catching fish, or for sports: *a fishing net* ○ *a basketball net*
3 the Net *short for* the Internet

netball /ˈnetbɔːl/ *noun* **[no plural]**
a game usually played by teams of women, where the players try to throw a ball through a high net

nettle /ˈnetl/ *noun*
a wild plant whose leaves hurt you if you touch them

network /ˈnetwɜːk/ *noun*
a system or group of connected parts: *a rail network* ○ *a network of tunnels*

neutral¹ /ˈnjuːtrᵊl/ *adj*
1 not supporting any side in an argument or fight: *He decided to remain neutral on the issue.*
2 Neutral colours are not strong or bright.

neutral² /ˈnjuːtrᵊl/ *noun* **[no plural]**
in driving, the position of the gears (= parts of a vehicle that control how fast the wheels turn) when they are not connected: *The car was* ***in neutral****.*

never /ˈnevəʳ/ *adv*
not ever, not one time: *"Have you ever been to Australia?" "No, never."* ○ *I've never even thought about that before.*

nevertheless /ˌnevəðəˈles/ *adv*
despite that: *I knew a lot about the subject already, but her talk was*

interesting nevertheless.

new /njuː/ *adj*
1 different from before: *I need some new shoes.* ○ *He starts his new job on Monday.*
2 recently made: *Their house is quite new.*
3 found or learned about a short time ago: *They have a new way of treating this illness.*

newcomer /ˈnjuːˌkʌməʳ/ *noun*
someone who has only recently arrived or started doing something: *He's a* ***newcomer to*** *the area.*

newly /ˈnjuːli/ *adv*
only a short time ago: *a newly married couple*

news /njuːz/ *noun* **[no plural]**
1 the news information about important things that have just happened on television, radio and in newspapers: *the local/national news*
2 new information: *Have you had any news about your job yet?*

newsagent's /ˈnjuːzˌeɪdʒᵊnts/ *noun UK*
a shop that sells newspapers and magazines

newspaper /ˈnjuːsˌpeɪpəʳ/ *noun*
large, folded sheets of paper which are printed with the news and sold every day or every week: *I read about his death* ***in the newspaper****.*

New Year's Day /ˌnjuː ˌjɪəz ˈdeɪ/ *noun*
1 January

next[1] /nekst/ *adj*
1 coming after this one: *I'm leaving next week.* ○ *She'll go to school next year.*
2 nearest to now: *What time's the next train to London?*
3 The next place is the one nearest to this place: *She only lives in the next village.*

next[2] /nekst/ *adv*
immediately after: *Where shall we go next?*

next[3] /nekst/ *preposition*
next to something/someone very close to something or someone, with nothing in between: *Come and sit next to me.*

next[4] /nekst/ *pronoun*
the person or thing that follows this person or thing: *Who's next to see the nurse?*

next-door /ˌnekst dɔːʳ/ *adj, adv*
in the next building: *What are your next-door neighbours like?*

nib /nɪb/ *noun*
the pointed end of a pen, where the ink comes out

nibble /ˈnɪbl/ *verb* (*present participle* **nibbling,** *past* **nibbled)**
to eat something by taking very small bites: *He was nibbling a biscuit.*

nice /naɪs/ *adj*
1 pleasant: *They have a very nice house.* ○ *We could go to the coast tomorrow, if the weather's nice.* ○ *It was* ***nice to*** *meet you.*
2 kind and friendly: *He's a really nice person.* ○ *She's always been very* ***nice to*** *me.*

nicely /ˈnaɪsli/ *adv*
1 well: *That table would fit nicely in the bedroom.*
2 in a pleasant way: *The room was nicely decorated.*

nickname /ˈnɪkneɪm/ *noun*
a name used informally instead of your real name: *His behaviour has earned him the nickname 'Mad Dog'.*
● **nickname** *verb* (*present participle* **nicknaming,** *past* **nicknamed)** *They nicknamed her 'The Iron Lady'.*

nicotine /ˈnɪkətiːn/ *noun* **[no plural]**
a poisonous chemical in tobacco

niece /niːs/ *noun*
the daughter of your brother or sister ➲Compare **nephew**

night /naɪt/ *noun*
1 the time in every 24 hours when it is dark and people sleep: *I slept really badly* ***last night****.* ○ *It can get quite cold* ***at night****.*
2 the period from the evening to the time when you go to sleep: *Are you doing anything* ***on*** *Friday* ***night****?*

nightclub /ˈnaɪtklʌb/ *noun*
a place where you can dance and drink at night

nightlife /ˈnaɪtlaɪf/ *noun* **[no plural]**
things to do at night, such as dancing and visiting bars: *Is the nightlife good around here?*

nightmare /ˈnaɪtmeəʳ/ *noun*
1 something very bad that happened to you: *The whole trip was a nightmare.*

a b c d e f g h i j k l m **n** o p q r s t u v w x y z

2 a frightening dream

nil /nɪl/ *noun* **[no plural]** *UK*
In sports results, nil means 'zero': *Germany beat England three nil* (= 3-0).

nine /naɪn/
the number 9

nineteen /ˌnaɪnˈtiːn/
the number 19
• **nineteenth**
19th written as a word

ninety /ˈnaɪnti/
the number 90
• **ninetieth**
90th written as a word

ninth¹ /naɪnθ/
9th written as a word

ninth² /naɪnθ/ *noun*
one of nine equal parts of something; ⅑

nip /nɪp/ *verb* (*present participle* **nipping,** *past* **nipped)**
1 *UK informal* to go somewhere quickly and for a short time: *I just nipped down the road to get a paper.*
2 to quickly bite someone

nipple /ˈnɪpl/ *noun*
the small, round area of darker skin in the centre of each breast in women, or on each side of the chest in men

no. *written abbreviation for* number

no¹ /nəʊ/ *exclamation*
something that you say in order to disagree, refuse something, or say that something is not true: *"Have you seen Louise?" "No, I haven't."* ○ *"Can I come too?" "No, I'm sorry."* ○ *"He's horrible." "No he isn't!"*

no² /nəʊ/ *determiner*
1 not any: *We have no money.*
2 a word used to say that something is not allowed: *No smoking.*

nobody /ˈnəʊbədi/ *pronoun*
no person: *There was nobody I could talk to.* ○ *Nobody was listening.*

nod /nɒd/ *verb* (*present participle* **nodding,** *past* **nodded)**
to move your head up and down as a way of agreeing: *I asked Barbara if she liked him and she nodded.*
• **nod** *noun*: *He **gave** a **nod** of approval.*

nod off *phrasal verb informal*
to start sleeping: *I nodded off after lunch.*

noise /nɔɪz/ *noun*
a sound, often a loud, bad sound: *Stop **making** so much **noise**!* ○ *I had to shout above the noise of the party.*

noisy /ˈnɔɪzi/ *adj* **(noisier, noisiest)**
Noisy people or things make a lot of noise: *We've had problems with noisy neighbours.* ➲Opposite **quiet**
• **noisily** *adv*

none /nʌn/ *quantifier*
not any: ***None of** my family smoke.* ○ *He wanted some food but there was none left.*

nonsense /ˈnɒnsᵊns/ *noun* **[no plural]**
1 something silly and not true that someone has said or written: *She talks such nonsense sometimes.* ○ *It's nonsense to suggest they could have cheated.*
2 silly behaviour: *Will you stop this childish nonsense!*

non-stop /ˌnɒnˈstɒp/ *adj, adv*
without stopping: *non-stop flights from Britain to the West Indies* ○ *We talked non-stop the whole journey.*

noodles /ˈnuːdlz/ *plural noun*
thin pieces of pasta (= food made from flour and water)

noon /nuːn/ *noun* **[no plural]**
12 o'clock in the middle of the day: *The service will be held at 12 noon.*

no one /ˈnəʊ wʌn/ *pronoun*
no person: *No one knows where he is.* ○ *There was no one there.*

nor /nɔːʳ/ *adv, conjunction*
1 neither...nor... used after 'neither' and before the second thing in a negative sentence: *Strangely, neither James nor Emma saw what happened.*
2 *UK* used after something negative to say that the same thing is true for someone or something else: *"I don't like cats." "Nor do I."* ○ *She couldn't speak a word of Italian and nor could I.*

normal /ˈnɔːmᵊl/ *adj*
usual and ordinary: *It's normal for couples to argue now and then.*

normally /ˈnɔːməli/ *adv*
1 usually: *Normally, I start work around nine o'clock.*
2 in the ordinary way that you expect: *The car is working normally now.*

north, North /nɔːθ/ *noun* **[no plural]**
1 the direction that is on your left when you face towards the rising

a b c d e f g h i j k l m n o p q r s t u v w x y z

north

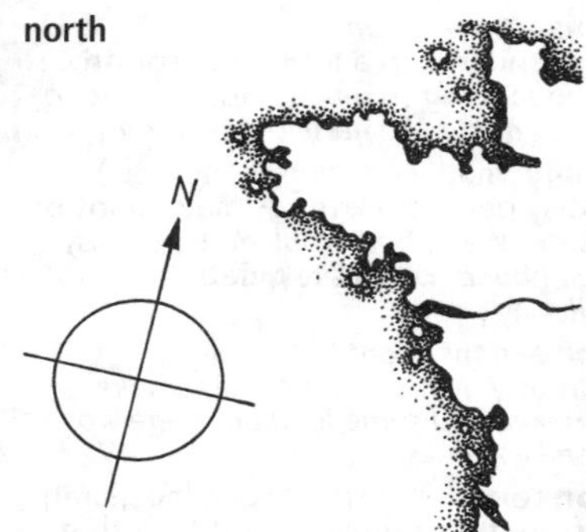

sun: *The stadium is to the north of the city.*
2 the north the part of an area that is further towards the north than the rest: *She's from the north of England.*
• **north** *adj*: *a north wind*
• **north** *adv*
towards the north: *I live north of the river.*

northeast, Northeast /ˌnɔːθ'iːst/ *noun* **[no plural]**
1 the direction between north and east
2 the northeast the northeast part of a country
• **northeast, Northeast** *adj, adv*

northeastern, Northeastern /ˌnɔːθ'iːstən/ *adj*
in or from the northeast

northern, Northern /'nɔːðᵊn/ *adj*
in or from the north part of an area: *Northern England*

the North Pole /ˌnɔθ 'pəʊl/ *noun*
a point on the Earth's surface which is furthest north

northwest, Northwest /ˌnɔːθ-'west/ *noun* **[no plural]**
1 the direction between north and west
2 the northwest the northwest part of a country
• **northwest, Northwest** *adj, adv*

northwestern, Northwestern /ˌnɔːθ'westən/ *adj*
in or from the northwest

nose /nəʊz/ *noun*
1 the part of your face that you breathe through and smell with ⊃See colour picture **The Body** on page Centre 2
2 get up someone's nose *UK informal* to annoy someone: *Paul gets right up my nose.*
3 turn your nose up at something *informal* to not accept something because it is not good enough: *He turned his nose up at my food.*

nostril /'nɒstrᵊl/ *noun*
one of the two holes at the end of your nose ⊃See colour picture **The Body** on page Centre 2

not /nɒt/ *adv*
used to give something the opposite meaning: *I'm not interested.* ○ *It's not mine.* ○ *It's for you, not Daniel.*

note[1] /nəʊt/ *noun*
1 a short letter: *He left a note on her desk.*
2 words that you write down to help you remember something: *She studied her notes before the exam.* ○ *Let me* ***make a note of*** (= write) *your phone number.*
3 a single musical sound
4 *UK* (*US* **bill**) a piece of paper money: *a ten-pound note*

note[2] /nəʊt/ *verb* (*present participle* **noting**, *past* **noted**)
to notice something: *I noted her absence.*
note down something *phrasal verb* to write something so that you do not forget it: *I noted down the telephone number for the police.*

notebook /'nəʊtbʊk/ *noun*
1 a book with empty pages that you can write in
2 a small computer that can be carried around and used anywhere

notepaper /'nəʊtˌpeɪpəʳ/ *noun* **[no plural]**
paper that you write letters on

nothing /'nʌθɪŋ/ *pronoun*
1 not anything: *I've had nothing to eat since breakfast.* ○ *He said he did nothing wrong.*
2 for nothing without a successful result: *I've come all this way for nothing.*

notice[1] /'nəʊtɪs/ *verb* (*present participle* **noticing**, *past* **noticed**)
to see something and be aware of it: *I* ***noticed that*** *he was alone.* ○ *No one noticed my new haircut.*

notice[2] /'nəʊtɪs/ *noun*
a sign giving information about something: *The notice said that the*

pool was closed for repairs.

noticeable /ˈnəʊtɪsəbl/ *adj*
easy to see or be aware of: *There has been a noticeable improvement in his work.*
• **noticeably** *adv*: *As summer approaches, the days get noticeably longer.*

noticeboard /ˈnəʊtɪsbɔːd/ *UK* (*US* **bulletin board**) *noun*
a board on a wall where you put pieces of paper telling people about things: *I saw the ad* ***on*** *the* ***noticeboard****.* ➲See colour picture **Classroom** on page Centre 4

notorious /nəʊˈtɔːriəs/ *adj*
famous for something bad: *a notorious criminal* ○ *She was* ***notorious for*** *her bad temper.*
• **notoriously** *adv*

nought /nɔːt/ *noun UK*
the number 0

noun /naʊn/ *noun*
a word that refers to a person, place, object, event, substance, idea, feeling, or quality. For example the words 'teacher', 'book' and 'beauty' are nouns.

novel[1] /ˈnɒvəl/ *noun*
a book that tells a story about people and things that are not real: *Have you read any good novels lately?*
• **novelist** *noun*
someone who writes novels

novel[2] /ˈnɒvəl/ *adj*
new or different from anything else: *That's a novel idea.*

November /nəʊˈvembəʳ/ *noun*
the eleventh month of the year

now /naʊ/ *adv*
1 at this time: *I'm going now.* ○ *What is Eva doing now?* ○ *I don't want to wait – I want it now!*
2 used when you start to tell someone something: *Now, I have been to Glasgow before.* ○ ***Now then****, would anyone else like to ask a question?*
3 now and then If something happens now and then, it happens sometimes but not often: *I love chocolate, but I only eat it now and then.*

nowhere /ˈnəʊweəʳ/ *adv*
not anywhere: *There was* ***nowhere to*** *sit.* ○ *We had* ***nowhere else*** *to go.*

nuclear /ˈnjuːkliəʳ/ *adj*
1 relating to the energy that is made when the nucleus (= central part) of an atom is divided: *nuclear weapons* ○ *a nuclear power plant*
2 relating to the nucleus (= central part) of an atom: *nuclear physics*

nucleus /ˈnjuːkliəs/ *noun* (*plural* **nuclei** /ˈnjuːkliaɪ/)
the central part of an atom or cell

nude /njuːd/ *adj*
not wearing any clothes: *Both children were* ***in the nude****.*

nudge /nʌdʒ/ *verb* (*present participle* **nudging**, *past* **nudged**)
to gently push someone or something: *She nudged me towards the door.*
• **nudge** *noun*: *I gave him a nudge.*

nuisance /ˈnjuːsəns/ *noun* **[no plural]**
a person, thing, or situation that annoys you or causes problems for you: *Not being able to use my computer is a real nuisance.*

numb /nʌm/ *adj*
If a part of your body is numb, you cannot feel it: *My fingers and toes were numb with cold.*

number[1] /ˈnʌmbəʳ/ *noun*
1 a symbol or word used in a counting system: *What's the number of his house?*
2 a group of numbers that represents something: *What's your phone number?*
3 a number of something many: *There have been a number of problems.*

number[2] /ˈnʌmbəʳ/ *verb*
to give something a number: *I have numbered the pages.*

number plate /ˈnʌmbəʳ ˌpleɪt/ *UK* (*US* **license plate**) *noun*
a sign with numbers and letters on the front and back of a car ➲See colour picture **Car** on page Centre 3

numerous /ˈnjuːmərəs/ *adj formal*
many: *He has written numerous articles.*

nun /nʌn/ *noun*
a member of a group of religious women living away from other people

nurse[1] /nɜːs/ *noun*
someone whose job is looking after people who are ill and hurt

nurse[2] /nɜːs/ *verb* (*present participle* **nursing**, *past* **nursed**)

a b c d e f g h i j k l m **n** o p q r s t u v w x y z

to look after a person or animal that is ill

nursery /ˈnɜːsəri/ *noun* (*plural* **nurseries)**
1 a place where babies and young children are looked after without their parents
2 a place where plants are grown and sold

nursery rhyme /ˈnɜːsəri ˌraɪm/ *noun*
a short poem or song for young children

nursery school /ˈnɜːsəri ˌskuːl/ *noun*
a school for very young children

nut /nʌt/ *noun*
1 the dry fruit of some trees which grows in a hard shell, and can often be eaten: *a brazil nut*
2 a piece of metal with a hole in it through which you put a bolt (= metal pin) to hold pieces of wood or metal together

nutritious /njuːˈtrɪʃəs/ *adj*
Nutritious food contains things that your body needs to stay healthy: *a nutritious meal*

nylon /ˈnaɪlɒn/ *noun* **[no plural]**
a strong material which is not natural and which is used to make clothes, ropes, etc: *nylon stockings*

Oo

O, o /əʊ/
the fifteenth letter of the alphabet

oak /əʊk/ *noun*
a large tree found in northern countries, or the wood of this tree

OAP /ˌəʊeɪ'piː/ *noun UK abbreviation for*
old-age pensioner: a person who gets money from the government because they are too old to work

oar /ɔːʳ/ *noun*
a long pole with a flat end that you use to move a boat through water

oasis /əʊ'eɪsɪs/ *noun* (*plural* **oases**)
a place in the desert where there is water and where plants grow

oath /əʊθ/ *noun*
a formal promise

oats /əʊts/ *plural noun*
grain which people eat or feed to animals

obedience /əʊ'biːdiəns/ *noun* **[no plural]**
when someone is willing to do what someone tells them to do: *He demanded complete obedience from his soldiers.*
• **obedient** /əʊ'biːdiənt/ *adj*
willing to do what people tell you to do: *an obedient child* ➲Opposite **disobedient**

obese /əʊ'biːs/ *adj*
very fat: *Obese people are more likely to suffer heart attacks.*

obey /əʊ'beɪ/ *verb*
to do what someone tells you to do: *If you do not obey the law, you will be arrested.* ➲Opposite **disobey**

object¹ /'ɒbdʒɪkt/ *noun*
1 a thing that you can see or touch but that is not alive: *I could see a bright, shiny object in the sky.*
2 the object of something the purpose of something: *The object of the game is to score more points than the opposing team.*
3 in grammar, the person or thing that is affected by the action of the verb

object² /əb'dʒekt/ *verb*
to say that you do not agree with a plan: *Carlos has **objected to** the proposal.*

objection /əb'dʒekʃᵊn/ *noun*
when someone says that they do not agree with a plan: *Our main **objection to** the new factory is that it's noisy.*

objective /əb'dʒektɪv/ *noun*
something that you are trying to do: *His main objective was to increase profits.*

obligation /ˌɒblɪ'geɪʃᵊn/ *noun*
something that you have to do because it is your duty: *Parents have an **obligation to** make sure their children receive a proper education.*

obligatory /ə'blɪgətᵊri/ *adj*
If something is obligatory, you must do it: *The wearing of seat belts in cars is obligatory.*

oblige /ə'blaɪdʒ/ *verb* (*present participle* **obliging,** *past* **obliged)**
be obliged to do something to have to do something: *It's my mother's party so I'm obliged to attend.*

obliged /ə'blaɪdʒd/ *adj*
feel obliged to do something to think that you must do something: *They helped us so I feel obliged to do the same for them.*

oblivious /ə'blɪviəs/ *adj*
not knowing anything about something that is happening: *She seemed completely **oblivious to** what was happening around her.*

obnoxious /əb'nɒkʃəs/ *adj*
very unpleasant or rude: *He was loud and obnoxious.*

observation /ˌɒbzə'veɪʃᵊn/ *noun*
[no plural] when someone watches someone or something carefully: *The doctor wants to keep him **under observation** for a week.*

observe /əb'zɜːv/ *verb* (*present participle* **observing,** *past* **observed)**
to watch someone or something carefully: *Children learn by observing adults.*

obstacle /'ɒbstəkl/ *noun*
something that makes it difficult for you to go somewhere or do something: *His refusal to talk is the main **obstacle to** peace.*

obstinate *adj*
not willing to change your ideas or

plans, although you are wrong

obstruct /əbˈstrʌkt/ *verb*
1 to be in a place that stops someone or something from moving: *The car had stopped and was obstructing the traffic.*
2 to try to stop something from happening: *He was accused of obstructing a police investigation.*
• **obstruction** /əbˈstrʌkʃən/ *noun* something that stops someone or something from moving: *Your car's causing an obstruction.*

obtain /əbˈteɪn/ *verb formal* to get something: *He obtained a law degree from the University of California.*

obvious /ˈɒbviəs/ *adj* easy to understand or see: ***It's obvious** that he doesn't like her.*

obviously /ˈɒbviəsli/ *adv* in a way that is easy to understand or see: *They're obviously in love.* ○ *Obviously we want to start as soon as possible.*

occasion /əˈkeɪʒən/ *noun*
1 a time when something happens: *We met on several occasions to discuss the issue.*
2 an important event: *a special occasion* ○ *She bought a new dress for the occasion.*
3 *UK* **on occasion(s)** sometimes, but not often: *I only drink alcohol on occasion.*

occasional /əˈkeɪʒənəl/ *adj* not happening often: *He still plays the occasional game of football.*
• **occasionally** *adv*: *They only meet occasionally.*

occupation /ˌɒkjəˈpeɪʃən/ *noun*
1 *formal* your job: *You have to give your occupation on the application form.*
2 something that you like doing in your free time: *Shopping is one of her favourite occupations.*

occupy /ˈɒkjəpaɪ/ *verb* (*present participle* **occupying**, *past* **occupied**)
1 to fill a place or period of time: *His book collection occupies most of the room.* ○ *The baby seems to occupy all our time.*
2 to live or work in a room or building: *They occupy the second floor of the building.*

occur /əˈkɜːʳ/ *verb* (*present participle* **occurring**, *past* **occurred**)
1 *formal* to happen, often without being planned: *According to the police, the shooting occurred at about 12.30 a.m.*
2 to exist or be present: *The disease mainly **occurs in** women over 40.*
occur to someone *phrasal verb* to suddenly think of something: ***It occurred to** me that he might be lying.*

ocean /ˈəʊʃən/ *noun* one of the five main areas of sea: *the Pacific Ocean*

o'clock /əˈklɒk/ *adv* **one/two/three, etc o'clock** used after the numbers one to twelve to mean exactly that hour when you tell the time: *It was ten o'clock when we got home.*

October /ɒkˈtəʊbəʳ/ *noun* the tenth month of the year

octopus /ˈɒktəpəs/ *noun* (*plural* **octopuses**) a sea creature with eight long arms

octopus

odd /ɒd/ *adj*
1 strange or unusual: *There is something odd about her.* ○ *It's a bit odd that he didn't come.*
2 being one of a pair when the other of the pair is missing: *an odd sock*

odd number /ˌɒd ˈnʌmbəʳ/ *noun* a number that does not produce a whole number when it is divided by two ⊃Opposite **even number**

odds /ɒdz/ *plural noun* the chance of something happening: *What are the odds of winning the top prize?*
2 odds and ends *informal* a group of different objects which are not important

of *strong form* /ɒv/ *weak form* /əv/ *preposition*
1 belonging or relating to someone or something: *A friend of mine told me.* ○ *I like the colour of her hair.*
2 used after words which show an amount: *a kilo of apples* ○ *both of us*
3 used with numbers, ages and dates: *a boy of six* ○ *the 14th of February 1995*
4 containing: *a glass of milk*
5 made or consisting of: *a bar of chocolate*

6 showing position or direction: *the front of the queue* ○ *a small town north of Edinburgh*

off[1] /ɒf/ *adv, preposition*
1 not touching or connected to something: *Keep off the grass!* ○ *A button came off my coat.*
2 away from a place or position: *He ran off to find his friend.*
3 not operating or being used: *Make sure you switch your computer off.*
4 **go off something/someone** *UK* to stop liking something or someone: *I've gone off meat.*
5 not at work: *I had 6 months off when my son was born.*

off[2] /ɒf/ *adj*
1 If food or drink is off, it is not now fresh and good to eat or drink: *This milk smells off.*
2 not at work: *He's off today – I think he's ill.*

offence /ə'fens/ *noun*
1 **[no plural]** when something rude makes someone upset or angry: *I hope my remark didn't cause offence.*
2 a crime: *He* ***committed*** *several serious* ***offences****.*

offend /ə'fend/ *verb*
to make someone upset or angry: *I was deeply offended by her comments.*

offensive /ə'fensɪv/ *adj*
likely to make people angry or upset: *an offensive remark*

offer[1] /'ɒfəʳ/ *verb*
1 to ask someone if they would like something: *They offered me a job.*
2 to say that you will do something for someone: *He* ***offered to*** *get me a cab.*

offer[2] /'ɒfəʳ/ *noun*
1 when you ask someone if they would like something: *an offer of help* ○ *a job offer*
2 an amount of money that you say you will pay for something: *They have* ***made*** *an* ***offer*** *on the house.*
3 **on offer** *UK* at a cheaper price than usual: *Are these jeans still on offer?*

office /'ɒfɪs/ *noun*
a room or building where people work: *an office worker* ○ *I never get to the office before nine.* ➲See colour picture **The Office** on page Centre 12

official[1] /ə'fɪʃəl/ *adj*
approved by the government or someone in power: *the official language of Singapore* ○ *an official document*
• **officially** *adv*

official[2] /ə'fɪʃəl/ *noun*
someone who has an important position in an organization such as the government: *a senior official*

often /'ɒfən, 'ɒftən/ *adv*
many times or regularly: *I often see her there.* ○ ***How often*** (= How many times) *do you go to the gym?*

oh /əʊ/ *exclamation*
1 used before you say something, often before replying to what someone has said: *"Ian's going." "Oh, I didn't realize."*
2 said when you are surprised, pleased, disappointed, etc: *Oh, no! I don't believe it!* ○ *"I don't think I can come." "Oh, that's a shame."*

oil /ɔɪl/ *noun* **[no plural]**
1 a thick liquid that comes from under the Earth's surface and that is used as a fuel: *an oil company* ○ *an oil well*
2 a thick liquid made from plants or animals that is used in cooking: *vegetable oil*

oil painting /'ɔɪl ˌpeɪntɪŋ/ *noun*
a picture made using paint which contains oil

ointment /'ɔɪntmənt/ *noun*
a smooth, thick substance that is put on painful skin

okay[1] (*also* **OK**) /əʊ'keɪ/ *adj, adv informal*
1 good enough: *Is your food okay?*
2 safe or healthy: *Is your grandmother okay now?*
3 allowed: *Is it okay if I leave early today?*

okay[2] (*also* **OK**) /əʊ'keɪ/ *exclamation informal*
used when agreeing to do something or when allowing someone to do something: *"Let's meet this afternoon." "Okay."* ○ *"Can I use the car?" "Okay."*

old /əʊld/ *adj*
1 having lived or existed for a long time: *an old man* ○ *an old house* ○ *We're all* ***getting older****.*
2 having been used or owned for a long time: *You might get dirty so wear some old clothes.*
3 used to describe or ask about

a b c d e f g h i j k l m n **o** p q r s t u v w x y z

a b c d e f g h i j k l m n **o** p q r s t u v w x y z

someone's age: *How old are you?* ○ *She'll be 4* ***years old*** *in March.*
4 used before or in the past: *I think the old system was better in many ways.*

old-fashioned /ˌəʊld'fæʃᵊnd/ *adj* not modern: *old-fashioned clothes*

olive /'ɒlɪv/ *noun* a small green or black fruit that is eaten or used to produce oil

olive oil /'ɒlɪv ˌɔɪl/ *noun* **[no plural]** oil made from olives, used for cooking or on salads

the Olympic Games /ðiːə'lɪmpɪkˌɡeɪmz/ (*also* **the Olympics**) *noun* an international sports competition that happens every four years

omelette /'ɒmlət/ *noun* a food made with eggs that have been mixed and fried: *a cheese omelette*

omit /əʊ'mɪt/ *verb* (*present participle* **omitting**, *past* **omitted**) to not include something: *He was* ***omitted from*** *the team because of his behaviour.*

on¹ /ɒn/ *preposition*
1 on a surface of something: *I put the book on that shelf.* ○ *He stood on my foot.*
2 in a particular place: *the diagram on page 22* ○ *I met her on a ship.*
3 being shown on television: *What's on television tonight?*
4 about: *a book on pregnancy*
5 next to or along the side of: *The post office is on Bateman Street.*
6 used to show the date or day when something happens: *He's due to arrive on 14 February.* ○ *I'm working on my birthday.*
7 using something: *I spoke to Mum on the phone.* ○ *I was working on my computer.*
8 used to show some methods of travelling: *Did you go over on the ferry?* ○ *Sam loves travelling on buses.*

on² /ɒn/ *adv*
1 used to show that an action or event continues: *The old tradition lives on.*
2 If you have something on, you are wearing it: *She's got a black coat on.* ○ *Why don't you* ***put*** *your new dress* ***on****?*
3 working or being used: *The heating has been on all day.*
4 into a bus, train, plane, etc: *Amy got on in Stamford.*
5 happening or planned: *I've got a lot on at the moment.* ○ *What's on at the cinema?*
6 on and off If something happens on and off during a period of time, it happens sometimes: *They've been seeing each other on and off since Christmas.*

once /wʌns/ *adv*
1 one time: *It's only snowed once or twice this year.* ○ *I go swimming* ***once a week*** (= one time every week).
2 in the past, but not now: *This house once belonged to my grandfather.*
3 at once
a immediately: *I knew at once that I would like it here.*
b at the same time: *They all started talking at once.*
4 once more one more time: *If you say that once more, I'm going to leave.*
5 for once used to mean that something is happening that does not usually happen: *For once, I think I have good news for him.*
6 once upon a time used at the beginning of a children's story to mean that something happened a long time ago

one¹ /wʌn/ the number 1

one² /wʌn/ *pronoun*
1 one person or thing in a group that has already been talked about: *I've just made some cakes, do you want one?* ○ *Chris is* ***the one*** *with glasses.*
2 *formal* any person in general: *One ought to respect one's parents.*

one³ /wʌn/ *determiner*
1 one person or thing in a group: ***One of*** *our daughters has just got married.*
2 used to refer to a time in the future which is not yet decided: *We must have a drink together one evening.*
3 at a particular time in the past: *I first met him one day in the park.*
4 one or two a few: *I'd like to make one or two suggestions.*

one-way /ˌwʌn'weɪ/ *adj* If a road is one-way, you can only drive on it in one direction: *a one-way street*

onion /'ʌnjən/ *noun* a round vegetable with layers that has a strong taste and smell ➲See colour picture **Fruit and Vegetables** on page Centre 8

online /ˌɒnˈlaɪn/ *adj, adv*
connected to a system of computers, especially the Internet: *Most newspapers are now available online.*

only[1] /ˈəʊnli/ *adv*
1 not more than a particular size or amount: *It'll only take a few minutes.* ○ *She's only fifteen.*
2 not anyone or anything else: *The offer is available to UK residents only.*
3 used to mean that something happened a very short time ago: *She's **only just** come.*

only[2] /ˈəʊnli/ *adj*
used to mean that there are no others: *This could be our only chance.* ○ *You're the only person here I know.*

only[3] /ˈəʊnli/ *conjunction*
but: *I would pay for it myself only I don't have the money.*

onto (*also* **on to**) /ˈɒntuː/ *preposition*
used to show movement into or on a particular place: *I stepped onto the platform.* ○ *Can you get back onto the path?*

onward /ˈɒnwəd/ (*also* **onwards**) *adv*
1 beginning at a time and continuing after it: *I'll be at home from 9 o'clock onwards.*
2 If you move onwards, you continue to go forwards.

oops /uːps/ *exclamation*
something you say when you do something slightly wrong: *Oops! I've spilled my coffee.*

ooze /uːz/ *verb* (*present participle* **oozing**, *past* **oozed**)
1 If a liquid oozes from something, it comes out slowly: *Blood was oozing out of the wound.*
2 *informal* to show a lot of a quality: *He oozes charm.*

open[1] /ˈəʊpᵊn/ *adj*
1 not closed or fastened: *an open door* ○ *Is there a bottle of wine open?*
2 A shop or business is open during the time it can do business: *Most shops are open on Sundays now.*
3 An open area of land has no buildings on it or near it: *large open spaces*

open

The window is open.

The book is open.

open[2] /ˈəʊpᵊn/ *verb*
1 If you open something, you make it change to a position that is not closed: *Could you open the window?* ○ *Open your eyes.*
2 If something opens, it changes to a position that is not closed: *The gate won't open.*
3 to remove part of a container or parcel so that you can see or use what it contains: *Come on, open your present!* ○ *I can't open this bottle.*
4 If a shop or office opens at a particular time of day, it starts to do business at that time: *What time does the bank open?*

opener /ˈəʊpənəʳ/ *noun*
bottle/can/tin, etc opener a piece of kitchen equipment used to open bottles/cans, etc

opening /ˈəʊpənɪŋ/ *noun*
a hole or space that something or someone can pass through: *We found an opening in the fence and climbed through.*

opera /ˈɒpᵊrə/ *noun*
a musical play in which most of the words are sung

operate /ˈɒpᵊreɪt/ *verb* (*present participle* **operating**, *past* **operated**)
1 If an organization or business operates, it works: *Our company is operating under very difficult conditions.*
2 If a machine operates, it works, and if you operate it, you make it work: *You have to be trained to operate the machinery.*

3 to cut someone's body and remove or repair part of it: *Did they have to* ***operate on*** *him?*

operation /ˌɒpərˈeɪʃən/ *noun*
1 when a doctor cuts someone's body to remove or repair part of it: *a heart operation* ○ *My son's got to* ***have an operation****.*
2 an organization or business: *a large commercial operation*

operator /ˈɒpəreɪtər/ *noun*
1 someone who helps to connect people on a telephone system
2 someone whose job is to control a machine or vehicle: *a computer operator*
3 a company that does a particular type of business: *a tour operator*

opinion /əˈpɪnjən/ *noun*
a thought or belief about something or someone: *What's your* ***opinion on*** *the matter?* ○ ***In my opinion*** (= I think) *he's the best football player we have in this country.*

opponent /əˈpəʊnənt/ *noun*
someone who you compete against in a game or competition: *He beat his opponent six games to two.*

opportunity /ˌɒpəˈtjuːnəti/ *noun* (*plural* **opportunities**)
a chance to do something good: *If you* ***get the opportunity*** *to go there, it is a wonderful city.*

oppose /əˈpəʊz/ *verb* (*present participle* **opposing,** *past* **opposed**)
to disagree with a plan or activity and to try to stop it: *The committee opposed a proposal to allow women to join the club.*

opposed /əˈpəʊzd/ *adj*
be opposed to something to disagree with a plan or activity: *We're not opposed to tax increases.*

opposite[1] /ˈɒpəzɪt/ *adj*
1 in a position facing someone or something but on the other side: *We live on opposite sides of the city.*
2 completely different: *My attempt to calm him down had the opposite effect.*

opposite[2] /ˈɒpəzɪt/ *adv, preposition*
in a position facing something or someone but on the other side: *The couple sat down opposite her.* ○ *Is there a bakery opposite your house?*

opposite[3] /ˈɒpəzɪt/ *noun*
someone or something that is completely different from another person or thing: *He's* ***the exact opposite of*** *my father.*

opt /ɒpt/ *verb*
opt for sth; opt to do something to choose something or to decide to do something: *Most people opt to have the operation.*

optician /ɒpˈtɪʃən/ *noun*
someone whose job is to make eye glasses

optimist /ˈɒptɪmɪst/ *noun*
someone who always thinks that good things will happen ➲Opposite **pessimist**

optimistic /ˌɒptɪˈmɪstɪk/ *adj*
always thinking that good things will happen: *We're* ***optimistic about*** *our chances of success.* ➲Opposite **pessimistic**

option /ˈɒpʃən/ *noun*
a choice: *We don't* ***have*** *many* ***options****.* ○ *You always have the* ***option of*** *not attending.*

optional /ˈɒpʃənəl/ *adj*
If something is optional, you can decide to have or do it but it is not necessary: *Two subjects are obligatory but one is optional.*

or *strong form* /ɔːr/ *weak form* /ər/ *conjunction*
used between possibilities, or before the last of many possibilities: *Is that a boy or a girl?* ○ *You can have beer or wine.*

oral /ˈɔːrəl/ *adj*
1 spoken: *an oral examination*
2 relating to the mouth: *oral medicine*

orange[1] /ˈɒrɪndʒ/ *adj*
being a colour that is a mixture of red and yellow: *a deep orange sunset* ➲See colour picture **Colours** on page Centre 6

orange[2] /ˈɒrɪndʒ/ *noun*
1 a round, sweet fruit with a thick skin and a centre that has many parts: *orange juice* ➲See colour picture **Fruit and Vegetables** on page Centre 8
2 a colour that is a mixture of red and yellow ➲See colour picture **Colours** on page Centre 6

orbit /ˈɔːbɪt/ *noun*
the circular journey that a spacecraft or planet makes around the sun, the

a b c d e f g h i j k l m n o p q r s t u v w x y z

moon, or another planet: *the Earth's orbit*
• **orbit** *verb*: *The moon orbits the Earth.*

orchard /ˈɔːtʃəd/ *noun*
a piece of land where there are fruit trees

orchestra /ˈɔːkɪstrə/ *noun*
a large group of musicians who play different instruments together

order[1] /ˈɔːdəʳ/ *noun*
1 the arrangement of a group of people or things in a list from first to last: *The names are* ***in alphabetical order****.* ○ *We put the tasks* ***in order of*** *importance.*
2 something that someone tells you that you must do: *You must* ***obey orders*** *at all times.*
3 when you ask for food or other things in return for money: *Has the waiter* ***taken your order****?*
4 [no plural] when everything is tidy and in its correct place: *I like order.*
5 out of order If a machine is out of order, it is not working: *The coffee machine's out of order.*
6 in order to do something so that you can do something: *She worked all summer in order to save enough money.*

order[2] /ˈɔːdəʳ/ *verb*
1 to tell someone they must do something: *He* ***ordered*** *them* ***to*** *leave.*
2 to ask for food or other things: *Have you ordered any drinks?* ○ *We ordered new lights for the kitchen.*
3 to arrange a group of people or things in a list from first to last: *Have you ordered the pages correctly?*

ordinary /ˈɔːdənəri/ *adj*
1 not special or different in any way: *an ordinary life* ○ *ordinary people* ○ *I had a very ordinary childhood.*
2 out of the ordinary different from usual: *Their relationship was a little out of the ordinary.*

ore /ɔːʳ/ *noun* **[no plural]**
rock or soil from which metal is made: *iron ore*

organ /ˈɔːgən/ *noun*
1 a part of an animal or plant that has a special purpose: *the internal organs*
2 a large musical instrument like a piano that is played in churches: *a church organ*

organic /ɔːˈgænɪk/ *adj*
not using chemicals when keeping animals or growing plants for food: *organic vegetables*

organism /ˈɔːgənɪzəm/ *noun*
a living thing, often a very small one

organization /ˌɔːgənaɪˈzeɪʃən/ *noun*
1 a group of people who work together for the same purpose: *a voluntary organization*
2 [no plural] the way that something is planned: *Who was responsible for the organization of the conference?*

organize /ˈɔːgənaɪz/ *verb* (*present participle* **organizing,** *past* **organized**)
to plan or arrange something: *She was busy organizing the wedding.*

organized /ˈɔːgənaɪzd/ *adj*
1 An organized person plans things well. ➲Opposite **disorganized**
2 involving a group of people who plan to do something together: *organized crime*

origin /ˈɒrɪdʒɪn/ *noun*
1 the cause of something, or where something comes from: *the origin of the universe*
2 the country, race, or social class of a person's family: *She's* ***of*** *Irish* ***origin****.*

original /əˈrɪdʒənəl/ *adj*
1 interesting and different from others: *Her essay was full of original ideas.*
2 being the first: *Do you still have the original document?*

originally /əˈrɪdʒənəli/ *adv*
at the beginning: *I originally planned to stay for a week but in the end stayed a month.*

ornament /ˈɔːnəmənt/ *noun*
an object that is used as a decoration in a home or garden ➲See colour picture **The Living Room** on page Centre 11

orphan /ˈɔːfən/ *noun*
a child whose parents are dead

orphanage /ˈɔːfənɪdʒ/ *noun*
a home for children whose parents are dead

ostrich /ˈɒstrɪtʃ/ *noun* (*plural* **ostriches**)
a very large bird from Africa which cannot fly but can run very fast

ostrich

other[1] /ˈʌðəʳ/

adj, determiner
1 more, not this or these: *I don't like chocolate – do you have* ***any other*** *desserts?* ○ *I don't think he's funny, but other people do.* ○ *Mario and Anna sat down to watch the other dancers.*
2 different from a thing or person which you have talked about: *Ask me some other time, when I'm not so busy.*
3 the other day/week, etc a day or week in the recent past: *I asked Carlos about it just the other day.*

other² /ˈʌðəʳ/ *pronoun*
1 a thing or person that is part of this set: *Some of the pieces were damaged, others were missing.*
2 others more things of the same type: *This is broken – do you have any others?*

others /ˈʌðəz/ *pronoun*
other people: *Don't expect others to do your work for you.*

otherwise¹ /ˈʌðəwaɪz/ *adv*
1 except for what you have just said: *She hurt her arm in the accident, but otherwise she was fine.*
2 different to what has just been said: *I'll meet you there at 6 o'clock unless I hear otherwise.*

otherwise² /ˈʌðəwaɪz/ *conjunction*
used when saying what will happen if someone does not do something: *You'd better phone home, otherwise your parents will start to worry.*

ouch /aʊtʃ/ *exclamation*
something you say when you suddenly hurt yourself slightly: *Ouch! That hurt!*

ought /ɔːt/ *verb*
ought to do something used to say or ask what someone should do: *You ought to see a doctor.* ○ *Ought I to phone her?*

ounce /aʊns/ *noun*
a unit for measuring weight, equal to 28.35 grams

our /aʊəʳ/ *determiner*
belonging to us: *Alice is our youngest daughter.*

ours /aʊəz/ *pronoun*
the thing or things that belong to us: *That's their problem – not ours.*

ourselves /ˌaʊəˈselvz/ *pronoun*
1 used to show that the person who is speaking and other people are affected by an action: *We've promised ourselves a holiday abroad this year.*
2 by ourselves alone or without anyone else's help: *We could invite some friends or we could go by ourselves.*

out /aʊt/ *adj, adv*
1 used to show movement away from the inside of somewhere: *He dropped the bag and all the apples fell out.*
2 outside a building or room: *It's cold out today.*
3 not in the place where you usually live or work: *I went round to see her but she was out.*
4 A fire or light that is out is not burning or shining: *Bring some more wood, the fire's gone out.*
5 ready to buy or see: *When's the new Spielberg film out?*

outdoor /ˌaʊtˈdɔːʳ/ *adj*
happening or used outside and not in a building: *an outdoor swimming pool* ○ *outdoor clothing* ➲Opposite **indoor**

outdoors /ˌaʊtˈdɔːz/ *adv*
not inside a building: *If it's warm this evening, we could eat outdoors.* ➲Opposite **indoors**

outer /ˈaʊtəʳ/ *adj*
on the edge or surface of something: *Remove the outer layers of the onion.* ➲Opposite **inner**

outfit /ˈaʊtfɪt/ *noun*
all the clothes that you wear at the same time, usually special clothes: *a cowboy outfit*

outgrow /ˌaʊtˈgrəʊ/ *verb* (*present participle* **outgrowing**, *past tense* **outgrew**, *past participle* **outgrown**)
to grow too big for something: *He's already outgrown these shoes.*

outing /ˈaʊtɪŋ/ *noun*
when a group of people go somewhere, usually to enjoy themselves

outline /ˈaʊtlaɪn/ *noun*
the shape made by the outside edge of something

out-of-date /ˌaʊtəvˈdeɪt/ *adj*
old and not useful or correct any more: *I do have a road map but I think it's out-of-date.* ➲Opposite **up-to-date**

outside¹ /ˌaʊtˈsaɪd/ *preposition*
1 near a building or room but not in it: *She waited outside his room for*

a b c d e f g h i j k l m n o p q r s t u v w x y z

nearly two hours. ➲Opposite **inside**
2 not in: *a flat just outside Oxford*

outside² /ˌaʊtˈsaɪd/ *adv*
not inside a building: *It's cold outside today.*

the outside /ˌaʊtˈsaɪd/ *noun*
the outer part or surface of something: *The outside of the house is very attractive.* ➲Opposite **the inside**

the outskirts /ˈaʊtskɜːts/ *plural noun*
the outer area of a city or town

outstanding /ˌaʊtˈstændɪŋ/ *adj*
excellent and much better than most: *He was an outstanding player.*

outward /ˈaʊtwəd/ *adj*
1 that you can see: *He was very ill but there were no outward signs of it.*
2 outward flight/journey, etc when you travel away from a place that you will return to ➲Opposite **inward**

oval /ˈəʊvəl/ *adj*
in the shape of an egg
• **oval** *noun*
an oval shape

oven /ˈʌvən/ *noun*
a piece of kitchen equipment which is used for cooking food: *an electric oven* ➲See colour picture **Kitchen** on page Centre 10

over¹ /ˈəʊvəʳ/ *adv, preposition*
1 above or higher than something: *A huge plane flew over.*
2 from one side of something to the other side: *I climbed over the wall.*
3 more than an amount, number, or age: *Suitable for children aged 5 and over.*
4 covering someone or something: *I put the blanket over her.*
5 down from a higher to a lower position: *The little boy fell over and started to cry.*

over² /ˈəʊvəʳ/ *adj*
finished: *The exams will be over next week.*

overhear /ˌəʊvəˈhɪəʳ/ *verb* (*present participle* **overhearing**, *past* **overheard**)
to hear what someone is saying to someone else: *I overheard him telling her he was leaving.*

overnight /ˌəʊvəˈnaɪt/ *adv*
1 during the night: *We stayed overnight at my grandmother's house.*
2 very quickly or suddenly: *Change does not happen overnight.*

overseas /ˌəʊvəˈsiːz/ *adj*
from another country: *an overseas student*
• **overseas** *adv*: *He worked overseas.*

oversleep /əʊvəˈsliːp/ *verb* (*present participle* **oversleeping**, *past* **overslept**)
to sleep longer than you wanted to: *Sorry I'm late, I overslept.*

overtake /ˌəʊvəˈteɪk/ *verb* (*present participle* **overtaking**, *past tense* **overtook**, *past participle* **overtaken**)
to go past a car or person that is going in the same direction: *Never overtake on a bend.*

overweight /ˌəʊvəˈweɪt/ *adj*
fat: *He's still a few pounds overweight.*

owe /əʊ/ *verb* (*present participle* **owing**, *past* **owed**)
to have to pay money back to someone who gave you money in the past: *You still owe me money.* ○ *He **owes** about £5000 **to** the bank.*

owing to /əʊɪŋ tuː/ *preposition*
because of: *The trip has been cancelled owing to the weather.*

owl /aʊl/ *noun*
a bird that has large eyes and hunts small animals at night

owl

own¹ /əʊn/ *adj, pronoun, determiner*
1 belonging to a particular person: *Each student has their own dictionary.* ○ *Petra makes all her own clothes.*
2 on your own alone: *Jessica lives on her own.*

own² /əʊn/ *verb*
to have something that belongs to you: *He owns a lot of land.*

owner /əʊnəʳ/ *noun*
someone who owns something: *car owners*

ox /ɒks/ *noun* (*plural* **oxen**)
a large, male cow

oxygen /ˈɒksɪdʒən/ *noun* **[no plural]**
a gas in the air that people and animals must breathe

oz *written abbreviation for*
ounce (= a unit for measuring weight)

ozone /ˈəʊzəʊn/ *noun* **[no plural]**

a form of oxygen that has a strong smell

the ozone layer /ˈəʊzəʊn ˌleɪəʳ/ *noun*

the layer of ozone high above the Earth's surface

Pp

P, p /piː/
the sixteenth letter of the alphabet

pace¹ /peɪs/ *noun* **[no plural]**
how fast someone walks or runs: *We started to walk at a much faster pace.*

pace² /peɪs/ *verb* (*present participle* **pacing**, *past* **paced**)
to walk around because you are worried about something: *She was pacing up and down, waiting for the phone to ring.*

pack¹ /pæk/ *verb*
1 to put your things into bags or boxes when you are going on holiday or leaving the place where you live: *I've got to go home and pack.* ○ *She was* ***packing her bags***. ➲Opposite **unpack**
2 If people pack a place, a lot of them go there: *Thousands of fans packed the club.*
pack something in *phrasal verb, informal*
to stop doing something: *He has packed in his job.*
pack (something) up *phrasal verb*
to put all your things together when you have finished doing something: *I'm about to pack my things up and go home.*

pack² /pæk/ *noun*
1 *US* a small box with a lot of the same thing in it: *a* ***pack of*** *cigarettes*
2 a bag that you carry on your back
3 a group of animals that live together, especially dogs: *a pack of dogs*
4 a set of playing cards

package /ˈpækɪdʒ/ *noun*
something that is covered in paper so that it can be sent by post: *He was carrying a package under his arm.*

packed /pækt/ *adj*
A packed place is full of people: *The hall was packed.*

packed lunch /ˌpækt ˈlʌntʃ/ *noun UK*
food that you put in a bag or box and take to eat at work, school, etc

packet /ˈpækɪt/ *UK noun*
a small box with a lot of the same thing in it: *a* ***packet of*** *cigarettes*

packing /ˈpækɪŋ/ *noun* **[no plural]**
when you put things into bags or boxes so that you can take them somewhere: *I've got to* ***do*** *my* ***packing*** *because I'm leaving tomorrow.*

pact /pækt/ *noun*
an agreement between two people or groups

pad /pæd/ *noun*
1 pieces of paper that have been fixed together at one edge: *There's a pad and pencil by the phone.*
2 a small piece of something soft that is used to protect something: *I wear knee pads when I go skating.*

padded /ˈpædɪd/ *adj*
Padded clothes are covered or filled with something soft, often so that they are warm: *a padded jacket*

paddle¹ /ˈpædl/ *noun*
1 a short pole with one flat end that you use to make a small boat move through the water
2 *UK* when you walk in water that is not deep: *The children* ***went for a paddle***.

paddle² /ˈpædl/ *verb* (*present participle* **paddling**, *past* **paddled**)
1 to move a small boat through water with a paddle
2 *UK* to walk in water that is not deep

padlock /ˈpædlɒk/ *noun*
a metal lock with a U-shaped part that you use for fastening bicycles, doors, etc
• **padlock** *verb*

page /peɪdʒ/ *noun*
1 a piece of paper in a book, magazine, etc, or one side of a piece of paper: *The article is on page 36.* ○ *I've only read 50 pages so far.*
2 (*also* **web page**) one part of a website (= area of information on the Internet) that you can see or print separately

paid /peɪd/
past of pay

pain /peɪn/ *noun*
1 a bad feeling in a part of your body when you are ill or hurt: *stomach pains* ○ *Are you* ***in pain***? ○ *I felt a sharp pain in my foot.*
2 **[no plural]** sadness: *I can't describe the pain I suffered when he died.*
3 **be a pain (in the neck)** *informal* to

be annoying: *My brother can be a real pain in the neck sometimes.*

painful /ˈpeɪnfəl/ *adj*
causing pain: *My hand is really painful where I hit it.*

painkiller /ˈpeɪnˌkɪləʳ/ *noun*
a drug which stops pain

paint[1] /peɪnt/ *noun*
a coloured liquid that you put on a surface to decorate it: *Have you chosen the paint for your bedroom?*

paint[2] /peɪnt/ *verb*
1 to cover a surface with paint: *We've painted the kitchen yellow.*
2 to make a picture of something or someone using paint: *These pictures were all painted by local artists.*

paintbrush /ˈpeɪntbrʌʃ/ *noun* (*plural* **paintbrushes)**
a brush that is used for painting

painter /ˈpeɪntəʳ/ *noun*
1 someone who paints pictures
2 someone whose job is to paint walls and doors, etc

painting /ˈpeɪntɪŋ/ *noun*
1 a picture that someone has painted
2 [no plural] the activity of painting pictures or painting surfaces

pair

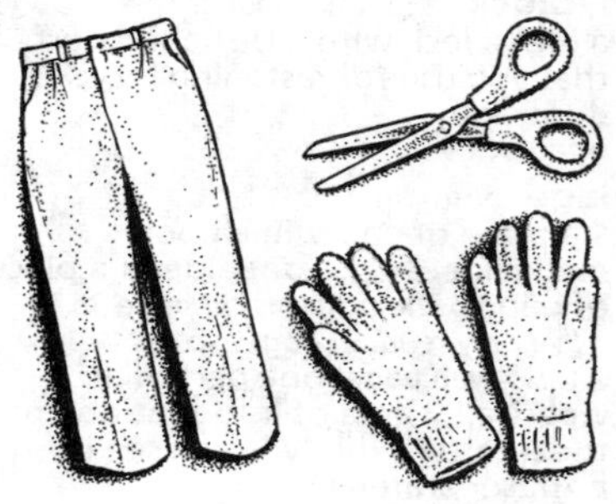

a pair of trousers
a pair of scissors
a pair of gloves

pair /peəʳ/ *noun*
1 two things that look the same and that are used together: *a pair of socks/shoes*
2 something that is made of two parts that are joined together: *a pair of scissors* ○ *a pair of jeans*
3 two people who are doing something together: *For the next exercise, you'll need to work* ***in pairs.***

pal /pæl/ *noun informal*
a friend: *He's an old pal of mine.*

palace /ˈpælɪs/ *noun*
a large house where a king or queen lives: *Buckingham Palace*

pale /peɪl/ *adj*
1 pale blue/green/red, etc light blue/green/red, etc: *a pale yellow dress*
2 If your face is pale, it has less colour than usual because you are ill: *You're looking a bit pale – are you all right?*

palm /pɑːm/ *noun*
1 the inside surface of your hand
➲See colour picture **The Body** on page Centre 2
2 a palm tree

palm tree /ˈpɑːm ˌtriː/ *noun*
a tall tree with long leaves at the top which grows in hot countries

pamphlet /ˈpæmflɪt/ *noun*
a very thin book with a paper cover that gives information about something

pan /pæn/ *noun*
a metal container with a handle that is used for cooking food in

pancake /ˈpænkeɪk/ *noun*
a thin, flat cake that you cook in a pan

panda /ˈpændə/ *noun*
a large, black and white animal that lives in forests in China

panda

pane /peɪn/ *noun*
a flat piece of glass in a window or door

panel /ˈpænəl/ *noun*
1 a flat, piece of wood, metal, etc that is the surface of a door, wall, etc
2 a group of people who are chosen to talk about something or make a decision about something: *a panel of experts*

pang /pæŋ/ *noun*
a sudden, strong feeling of a bad emotion: *Bernard felt a sharp pang of jealousy.*

panic[1] /ˈpænɪk/ *noun* **[no plural]**
a sudden, strong feeling of fear that makes you stop thinking clearly and

do silly things: *He was* ***in a panic*** *about his exams.*

panic² /ˈpænɪk/ *verb* (*present participle* **panicking,** *past* **panicked)**
to suddenly feel very afraid so that you stop thinking clearly and do silly things: *Don't panic, we've got plenty of time.*

panic-stricken /ˈpænɪkˌstrɪkən/ *adj*
very afraid so that you cannot think clearly

pant /pænt/ *verb*
to breathe quickly and loudly because you have been running

panties /ˈpæntiz/ *US* (*UK* **knickers)** *plural noun*
a piece of clothing for women that covers the bottom

pants /pænts/ *plural noun*
1 *US* (*UK* **trousers)** a piece of clothing that covers the legs and has a separate part for each leg
2 *UK* (*US* **underpants)** a piece of clothing for women that covers the bottom ➲See colour picture **Clothes** on page Centre 5

paper /ˈpeɪpəʳ/ *noun*
1 [no plural] thin, flat material used for writing on: *Have you got a piece of paper?*
2 a newspaper: *I buy a paper every morning.*
3 *UK* a part of an examination: *Candidates must answer two questions from each paper.*

paperback /ˈpeɪpəbæk/ *noun*
a book that has a soft paper cover

paper clip /ˈpeɪpəʳ ˌklɪp/ *noun*
a small piece of metal used to hold pieces of paper together ➲See colour picture **The Office** on page Centre 12

paper clip

parachute /ˈpærəʃuːt/ *noun*
a large piece of cloth which is fixed to your body by strings and helps you to drop safely from an aeroplane

parachute

parade /pəˈreɪd/ *noun*
when a line of people walk through a public place on a special day: *a victory parade*

paradise /ˈpærədaɪs/ *noun* **[no plural]**
1 in some religions, a place where good people go after they die
2 a perfect place or situation: *a tropical paradise*

paraffin /ˈpærəfɪn/ *UK* (*US* **kerosene**) *noun* **[no plural]**
oil used for heating and lights

paragraph /ˈpærəgrɑːf/ *noun*
a group of sentences that are together and start on a new line

parallel /ˈpærəlel/ *adj*
If two or more lines are parallel, the distance between them is the same along all their length: *The streets are parallel.*

paralyse /ˈpærəlaɪz/ *verb* (*present participle* **paralysing,** *past* **paralysed)**
to make someone unable to move all or part of their body: *He was paralysed from the waist down in the accident.*

paralysis /pəˈræləsɪs/ *noun* **[no plural]**
when someone cannot move all or part of their body because they are hurt or ill

parcel /ˈpɑːsəl/ *noun*
something that is covered in paper so that it can be sent by post

parcel

pardon /ˈpɑːdən/ *exclamation*
1 (*US* **pardon me)** a polite way of asking someone to say again what they have just said: *"You'll need an umbrella." "Pardon?" "I said you'll need an umbrella."*
2 Pardon me. used to say 'sorry' after you have done something rude, for example after burping (= letting air from your stomach out of your mouth)

parent /ˈpeərənt/ *noun*
your mother or father: *Her parents live in Oxford.*

parenthood /ˈpeərənthʊd/ *noun* **[no plural]**
being a parent: *I am not ready for parenthood.*

park¹ /pɑːk/ *noun*
a large area of grass, often in a town, where people can walk and

enjoy themselves: *We went for a walk in the park.*

park[2] /pɑːk/ *verb*
to leave a car in a place for a period of time: *You can park outside the school.*

parking /ˈpɑːkɪŋ/ *noun* **[no plural]**
leaving a car in a place for a period of time: *free parking*

parliament /ˈpɑːləmənt/ *noun*
in some countries, a group of people who make the laws for the country: *the Russian parliament*

parrot /ˈpærət/ *noun*
a bird with feathers of many, bright colours that can copy what people say

parsley /ˈpɑːsli/ *noun* **[no plural]**
a plant that you add to food to give it flavour

part[1] /pɑːt/ *noun*
1 one of the things that, with other things, makes the whole of something: ***Part of*** *this form seems to be missing.* ○ *That's only part of the problem.* ○ *You're part of the family.*
2 take part (in something) to do an activity with other people: *She doesn't usually take part in any of the class activities.*
3 a person in a film or play: *He* ***plays*** *the* ***part*** *of the father.*
4 a piece of a machine or vehicle: *aircraft parts*

part[2] /pɑːt/ *verb*
part with something *phrasal verb*
to give something to someone else, often when you do not want to: *It is so hard getting Simon to part with his money.*

partial /ˈpɑːʃ(ə)l/ *adj*
not complete: *He made a partial recovery.*

partially /ˈpɑːʃ(ə)li/ *adv*
not completely: *It was partially cooked.*

participant /pɑːˈtɪsɪp(ə)nt/ *noun*
someone who does an activity with other people: *All participants finishing the race will receive a medal.*

participate /pɑːˈtɪsɪpeɪt/ *verb*
(*present participle* **participating**, *past* **participated**)
to do an activity with other people: *She rarely* ***participates in*** *any of the discussions.*

• **participation** /pɑːˌtɪsɪˈpeɪʃ(ə)n/ *noun* **[no plural]**
when you do an activity with other people *Both shows encourage audience participation.*

participle /pɑːˈtɪsɪpl/ *noun*
the form of a verb that usually ends with '-ed' or '-ing' and is used in some verb tenses

particular /pəˈtɪkjələ(r)/ *adj*
1 used to talk about one thing or person and not others: *Is there any particular restaurant you'd like to go to?* ○ *"Why did you ask?" "No particular reason."*
2 special: *"Was anything important said at the meeting?" "Nothing of particular interest."*
3 in particular especially: *Are you looking for anything in particular?*

particularly /pəˈtɪkjələli/ *adv*
especially: *She didn't seem particularly interested.* ○ *"Was the food good?" "Not particularly."*

partly /ˈpɑːtli/ *adv*
to some degree but not completely: *The house is partly owned by her father.*

partner /ˈpɑːtnə(r)/ *noun*
1 someone that you are married to or having a sexual relationship with: *Are partners invited to the office dinner?*
2 someone that you are dancing or playing a sport or game with
3 someone who owns a business with another person: *He's a* ***partner in*** *a law firm.*

part-time /ˌpɑːtˈtaɪm/ *adj, adv*
working or studying only for part of the day or the week: *a part-time job*

party /ˈpɑːti/ *noun* (*plural* **parties**)
1 when people come together to enjoy themselves by talking, eating, drinking, and dancing: *a birthday party* ○ *We're* ***having*** *a* ***party*** *to celebrate the occasion.*
2 an organization that has the same political beliefs and tries to win elections: *a political party*
3 a group of people who are working or travelling together: *a party of tourists*

pass[1] /pɑːs/ *verb*
1 to go past something or someone: *She passed me this morning in the street.* ○ *Cars kept passing us on the motorway.*
2 to go in a particular direction:

Another plane ***passed over*** *our heads.* ○ *We* ***pass through*** *your village on the way home.*
3 to give something to someone: *Could you pass the salt, please?*
4 If a period of time passes, it happens: *Four years have passed since that day.*
5 pass (the) time to spend time doing something: *We played a few games to pass the time.*
6 to succeed at a test or an exam: *I passed my driving test the first time.*
7 in sports, to throw or kick a ball to someone else: *Edwards* ***passes to*** *Brinkworth.*
pass something on *phrasal verb*
to tell someone something that someone else has told you: *Did you pass on my message to him?*
pass out *phrasal verb*
to become unconscious: *I don't remember any more because I passed out at that point.*

pass² /pɑːs/ *noun* (*plural* **passes**)
1 a successful result in a test or a course: *A pass is above 60%.*
2 an official paper that allows you to do something: *You need a pass to get into the building.*
3 in sports, when you throw or kick a ball to someone else

passage /ˈpæsɪdʒ/ *noun*
1 a long, thin space that connects one place to another: *There's a passage to the side of the house, leading to the garden.*
2 a short part of a book or speech: *She read a passage from the novel.*

passenger /ˈpæsᵊndʒəʳ/ *noun*
someone who is travelling in a car, aeroplane, etc, but not controlling the car, aeroplane, etc: *a front-seat passenger* ○ *a passenger seat/train*

passer-by /ˌpɑːsəˈbaɪ/ *noun* (*plural* **passers-by**)
someone who is walking past something: *A passer-by saw the accident and told police.*

passion /ˈpæʃᵊn/ *noun* **[no plural]**
1 a strong, sexual feeling for someone: *She saw the passion in his eyes.*
2 when you have a very strong feeling about a subject: *She spoke with passion about the injustice.*

passionate /ˈpæʃᵊnət/ *adj*
1 having a strong, sexual feeling for someone: *They had a passionate love affair.*
2 showing a strong feeling about a subject: *She was a passionate speaker.*
• **passionately** *adv*

passive /ˈpæsɪv/ *adj*
A passive verb or sentence is one in which the subject does not do the action. For example 'It was written by a child.' is a passive sentence.

passport /ˈpɑːspɔːt/ *noun*
a small book with your photograph in that you need to enter a country: *a British passport*

password /ˈpɑːswɜːd/ *noun*
a secret word that allows you to do something, especially to use your computer: *Type in your password.*

past¹ /pɑːst/ *adj*
1 having happened or existed before now: *past relationships* ○ *I know this from past experience.*
2 past tense the form of the verb which is used to show what happened in the past

past² /pɑːst/ *noun*
1 the past
a the time before the present and all the things that happened then: ***In the past*** *people would bathe once a month.*
b the form of the verb which is used to show what happened in the past
2 someone's past all of the things that someone has done in their life: *I knew nothing about his past.*

past³ /pɑːst/ *adv, preposition*
1 further than: *I live on Station Road, just past the Post Office.*
2 up to and further than someone or something: *Three boys went past us on mountain bikes.* ○ *I've just seen the bus go past.*
3 *UK* used to say 'after' the hour when you are saying what time it is: *It's five past three.*

pasta /ˈpæstə/ *noun* **[no plural]**
a food that is made from flour and water and is made in many different shapes: *Spaghetti is my favourite pasta.*
➲See colour picture **Food** on page Centre 7

paste¹ /peɪst/ *noun* **[no plural]**
a wet sticky substance that is used to stick things together: *wallpaper paste*

paste² /peɪst/ *verb* (*present participle*

pasting, *past* **pasted)**
to stick a piece of paper to another piece of paper: *He had pasted the pictures into a book.*

pastime /ˈpɑːstaɪm/ *noun*
something that you like doing when you are not working: *Shopping is her favourite pastime.*

past participle /ˌpɑːst pɑːˈtɪsɪpl/ *noun*
the form of a verb that usually ends with '-ed'. For example 'walked' is the past participle of 'walk'.

pastry /ˈpeɪstri/ *noun*
1 [no plural] a food made of flour, fat, and water that you cook and use for covering or containing other food
2 (*plural* **pastries**) a small cake

past tense /ˌpɑːst ˈtens/ *noun*
a form of a verb that shows something in the past. For example, the past tense of 'work' is 'worked'.

pat¹ /pæt/ *verb* (*present participle* **patting,** *past* **patted)**
to touch a person or animal with a flat hand in a gentle, friendly way: *She stopped to pat the dog.*

pat² /pæt/ *noun*
1 when you touch a person or animal with a flat hand in a gentle, friendly way
2 a pat on the back when someone says how well you have done something and how pleased they are: *I got a pat on the back for all my hard work.*

patch /pætʃ/ *noun* (*plural* **patches)**
1 a small area that is different from the area around it: *There are icy patches on the road.*
2 a piece of material that you use to cover a hole in your clothes or in other material
3 a bad/rough patch a difficult time: *Their marriage is going through a bad patch.*

paternal /pəˈtɜːnəl/ *adj*
1 like a father: *paternal affection*
2 A paternal relation is part of your father's family: *He's my paternal grandfather.* ➲Compare **maternal**

path /pɑːθ/ *noun*
a long, thin area of ground for people to walk on: *There's a path through the forest.* ○ *a garden path*

pathetic /pəˈθetɪk/ *adj informal*
bad and showing that you have not tried or are not brave: *He made a rather pathetic attempt to apologize.*

patience /ˈpeɪʃəns/ *noun* **[no plural]**
when you are able to stay calm and not get angry, especially when something takes a long time: *You need patience when you are dealing with young children.* ○ *Finally, I* ***lost*** *my* ***patience*** *and shouted at her.*

patient¹ /ˈpeɪʃənt/ *adj*
able to stay calm and not get angry, especially when something takes a long time: *You need to be* ***patient with*** *children.* ➲Opposite **impatient**
• **patiently** *adv*

patient² /ˈpeɪʃənt/ *noun*
someone who is being treated by a doctor, nurse, etc: *a cancer patient*

patriotic /ˌpeɪtriˈɒtɪk/ *adj*
showing that you love your country and think it is very good: *a patriotic song*

patrol¹ /pəˈtrəʊl/ *noun*
the act of looking for trouble or danger around an area or building: *We passed a group of soldiers* ***on patrol.***

patrol² /pəˈtrəʊl/ *verb* (*present participle* **patrolling,** *past* **patrolled)**
to look for trouble or danger in an area or around a building: *Police patrol the streets night and day.*

pattern /ˈpætən/ *noun*
1 a particular way that something is often done or repeated: *behaviour patterns*
2 a design of lines, shapes, colours, etc: *The shirt has a pattern on it.*

pause /pɔːz/ *verb* (*present participle* **pausing,** *past* **paused)**
to stop doing something for a short time: *She* ***paused for*** *a moment and looked around her.*
• **pause** *noun*
when you stop doing something for a short time *There was a short pause before he spoke.*

pavement

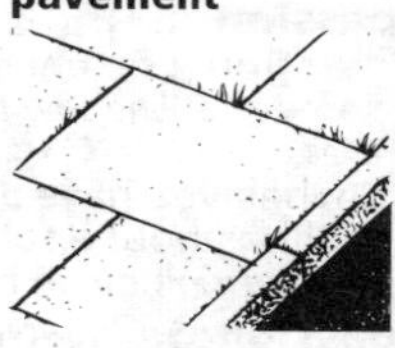

pavement /ˈpeɪvmənt/ *noun*
1 *UK* (*US* **sidewalk**) a path by the side of a road that people walk on
2 *US* the hard

surface of a road

paw /pɔː/ *noun*
the foot of an animal, such as a cat or a dog

paw

pay¹ /peɪ/ *verb* (*present participle* **paying**, *past* **paid**)
1 to give money to someone because you are buying something from them: *Helen* ***paid for*** *the tickets.*
2 to give someone money for the work that they do: *She* ***gets paid*** *twice a month.* ○ *We* ***paid*** *them £600* ***for*** *the work.*
3 pay attention to look at or listen to someone or something carefully: *I missed what she was saying because I wasn't paying attention.*
pay someone/something back *phrasal verb*
to pay someone the money that you owe them: *Has he paid you back the money he owes you?*
pay something off *phrasal verb*
to pay all of the money that you owe: *I'm planning to pay off my bank loan in five years.*

pay² /peɪ/ *noun* **[no plural]**
the money that you get for working: *a pay rise*

payment /ˈpeɪmənt/ *noun*
1 [no plural] the act of paying: *They will accept payment by credit card.*
2 the amount of money that is paid: *monthly payments*

PC /ˌpiːˈsiː/ *noun*
a personal computer (= a computer for one person to use)

pea /piː/ *noun*
a small, round, green seed that people eat as a vegetable

peace /piːs/ *noun* **[no plural]**
1 when there is no war, violence, or arguing: *There seems little hope for world peace.*
2 when there is quiet and calm: *After a busy day, all I want is* ***peace and quiet****.*

peaceful /ˈpiːsfəl/ *adj*
1 without violence: *a peaceful protest*
2 quiet and calm: *The church was empty and peaceful.*
• **peacefully** *adv*: *He died peacefully at home.*

peach /piːtʃ/ *noun* (*plural* **peaches**)
a soft, sweet, round fruit with red and yellow skin

peacock /ˈpiːkɒk/ *noun*
a large, male bird with long brightly coloured tail feathers

peacock

peak /piːk/ *noun*
1 the highest level or value of something: *House prices have probably* ***reached*** *their* ***peak****.* ○ *peak travel times*
2 the top of a mountain: *snow-covered peaks*

peak
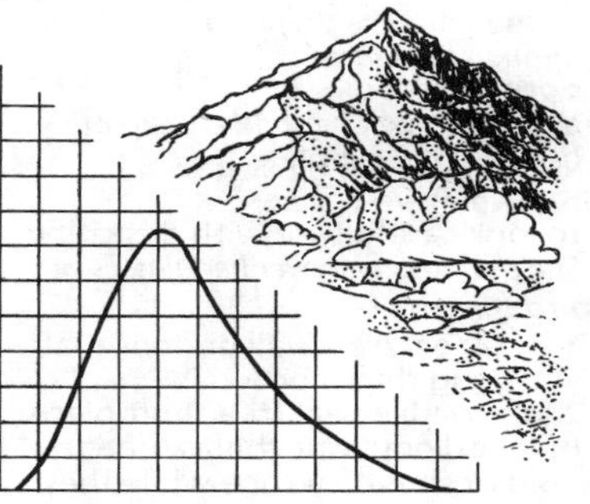

peanut /ˈpiːnʌt/ *noun*
an oval-shaped nut with a soft, brown shell ➲See colour picture **Food** on page Centre 7

pear /peəʳ/ *noun*
an oval-shaped, green or yellow fruit ➲See colour picture **Fruit and Vegetables** on page Centre 8

pear

pearl /pɜːl/ *noun*
a hard, white, round object that is made inside the shell of a sea creature and that is used to make jewellery: *a string of pearls*

peasant /ˈpezənt/ *noun*
a poor person who works on the land, usually in a poor country: *a peasant farmer*

pebble /ˈpebl/ *noun*
a small stone

peck /pek/ *verb*
If a bird pecks something, it quickly bites it: *chickens* ***pecking at*** *corn*

peculiar /pɪˈkjuːliəʳ/ *adj*

strange, often in a bad way: *The wine had a peculiar smell.*

pedal /ˈpedᵊl/ *noun*
a part of a machine that you press with your foot: *bicycle pedals*

pedestrian /pɪˈdestriən/ *noun*
a person who is walking

peel[1] /piːl/ *verb*
to take off the skin of fruit or vegetables: *Peel and chop the onions.*

peel[2] /piːl/ *noun* **[no plural]**
the skin of fruit or vegetables

peep /piːp/ *verb*
to quickly look at something, often when you do not want other people to see you: *She peeped at them through the fence.*
• **peep** *noun*
a quick look: *She **took a peep** at herself in the mirror.*

peer /pɪəʳ/ *verb*
to look carefully or with difficulty: *She peered at me over her glasses.*

peg /peg/ *noun*
1 an object on a wall or door that you hang things on
2 (*also* **clothes peg**) *UK* a short piece of wood or plastic that is used to hold clothes on a rope while they dry

pen /pen/ *noun*
a long, thin object that you use to write or draw in ink ➲See colour picture **Classroom** on page Centre 4

penalty /ˈpenᵊlti/ *noun* (*plural* **penalties**)
1 a punishment for doing something which is against a law or rule: *There's a £50 penalty for late cancellation of tickets.*
2 in sports, an advantage given to a team when the other team has broken a rule: *They won a penalty in the first five minutes of the game.*

pence /pens/ *noun*
plural of British penny; p

pencil /ˈpensᵊl/ *noun*
a long, thin wooden object with a black or coloured point that you write or draw with ➲See colour picture **Classroom** on page Centre 4

penetrate /ˈpenɪtreɪt/ *verb* (*present participle* **penetrating**, *past* **penetrated**)
If something penetrates an object, it moves into that object: *The bullet penetrated his skull.*

penguin /ˈpeŋgwɪn/ *noun*
a large, black and white sea bird that swims and cannot fly

penicillin /ˌpenɪˈsɪlɪn/ *noun* **[no plural]**
a type of medicine that kills bacteria and is used to treat illness

penis /ˈpiːnɪs/ *noun*
the part of a man's or male animal's body that is used for having sex

penny /ˈpeni/ *noun* (*plural* **pence** or **pennies**)
a coin with a value of 1⁄100 of a pound (= UK unit of money); p: *There are 100 pence in a pound.*

pension /ˈpenʃᵊn/ *noun*
money that is given to a person who has stopped working because they are old or ill
• **pensioner** *noun UK*
someone who gets a pension

people /ˈpiːpl/ *plural noun*
more than one person: *Our company employs over 400 people.*

pepper /ˈpepəʳ/ *noun*
1 [no plural] a powder that is made from seeds, used to give food a slightly spicy flavour: *salt and pepper*
2 a green, red, or yellow vegetable ➲See colour picture **Fruit and Vegetables** on page Centre 8

peppermint /ˈpepəmɪnt/ *noun* **[no plural]**
oil from a plant that is added to food to give it a strong, fresh taste

per *strong form* /pɜːʳ/ *weak form* /pəʳ/ *preposition*
for each: *The hotel room costs $60 per night.*

perceive /pəˈsiːv/ *verb* (*present participle* **perceiving,** *past* **perceived)** *formal*
to think of something or someone in a particular way: *The British are often perceived as being very formal.*

percent /pəˈsent/ *adj, adv*
out of every 100, shown by the symbol %: *a 40 percent increase in prices*

perch /pɜːtʃ/ *verb*
to sit near the edge of something: *The children **perched on** the edges of their seats.*

perfect[1] /ˈpɜːfɪkt/ *adj*
1 without fault, or as good as possible: *He was the perfect father.*
2 exactly right for someone or

something: *You'd be **perfect for** the job.*

perfect² /pəˈfekt/ *verb*
to make something as good as it can be: *I've spent hours perfecting my speech.*

the perfect /ˈpɜːfɪkt/ (*also* **the ˌperfect ˈtense)** *noun*
the form of the verb that is made with 'have' and a past participle. The sentence 'We have eaten,' is an example of the perfect tense.

perfection /pəˈfekʃᵊn/ *noun* **[no plural]**
when someone or something is perfect: *We ask the children to do their best but we don't expect perfection.*

perfectly /ˈpɜːfɪktli/ *adv*
1 very: *I made my feelings perfectly clear.*
2 in a perfect way: *The jacket fits perfectly.*

perform /pəˈfɔːm/ *verb*
1 to act, sing, dance or play music for other people to enjoy: *The orchestra will perform music by Mozart.*
2 *formal* to do a job or a piece of work: *Surgeons performed the operation in less than two hours.*
3 to succeed or not succeed: *Neither company has performed well this year.*

performance /pəˈfɔːməns/ *noun*
1 acting, singing, dancing, or playing music for other people to enjoy: *a performance of Shakespeare's Hamlet*
2 how successful someone or something is: *The company's performance was poor for the first two years.*

performer /pəˈfɔːməʳ/ *noun*
someone who acts, sings, dances or plays music for other people to enjoy

perfume /ˈpɜːfjuːm/ *noun*
a liquid with a nice smell that women put on their skin

perhaps /pəˈhæps/ *adv*
possibly: *Perhaps I'll go to the gym after work.* ○ *Perhaps Ben will come.*

period /ˈpɪəriəd/ *noun*
a length of time: *a 24-hour period* ○ *a period of four months*

perm /pɜːm/ *noun*
when chemicals are put on someone's hair to make it curly
• **perm** *verb*
to put chemicals on someone's hair to make it curly

permanent /ˈpɜːmᵊnənt/ *adj*
continuing always or for a long time: *She found a permanent job.*
• **permanently** *adv*

permission /pəˈmɪʃᵊn/ *noun* **[no plural]**
when you allow someone to do something: *I had to **get permission** to use the car.* ○ *He took the car **without permission**.*

permit¹ /pəˈmɪt/ *verb* (*present participle* **permitting,** *past* **permitted)**
formal to allow something: *Photography is not permitted inside the museum.*

permit² /ˈpɜːmɪt/ *noun*
a paper that allows you to do something: *a work permit*

person /ˈpɜːsᵊn/ *noun* (*plural* **people** or **persons**)
a human being: *You're the only person I know here.*

personal /ˈpɜːsᵊnᵊl/ *adj*
1 belonging to a particular person: *Please take all personal belongings with you when you leave the train.*
2 connected with relationships and feelings and the private parts of someone's life: *He's got a few personal problems at the moment.*

personality /ˌpɜːsᵊnˈæləti/ *noun* (*plural* **personalities)**
1 the qualities that make one person different from another: *She's got a lovely warm personality.*
2 a famous person: *He is a well-known TV personality.*

personally /ˈpɜːsənᵊli/ *adv*
1 done by you and not someone else: *I'd like to personally apologize for the delay.*
2 used when you are saying your opinion: *Personally, I don't like the man.*

persuade /pəˈsweɪd/ *verb* (*present participle* **persuading,** *past* **persuaded)**
to make someone agree to do something by talking to them a lot about it: *We managed to **persuade** him **to** come with us.*

persuasion /pəˈsweɪʒᵊn/ *noun* **[no plural]** when you persuade someone: *I'm sure she'll agree, she just*

a b c d e f g h i j k l m n o p q r s t u v w x y z

needs a little persuasion.

pessimist /ˈpesɪmɪst/ *noun* someone who always believes that bad things will happen: *Don't be such a pessimist!* ➲Opposite **optimist**

pessimistic /ˌpesɪˈmɪstɪk/ *adj* always believing that bad things will happen: *He was feeling **pessimistic about** the future.* ➲Opposite **optimistic**

pest /pest/ *noun*
1 an animal that causes damage to plants, food, etc: *Most farmers think foxes are pests.*
2 *informal* an annoying person

pester /ˈpestəʳ/ *verb* to annoy someone by asking them something again and again: *He's been **pestering** me **to** go out with him all week.*

pet /pet/ *noun* an animal that someone keeps in their home: *my pet rabbit*

petal /ˈpetᵊl/ *noun* one of the coloured parts on the outside of a flower: *rose petals*

petition /pəˈtɪʃᵊn/ *noun* a paper with a lot of people's names on it, which asks someone in authority to do something: *Will you sign this **petition against** experiments on animals?*

petrol /ˈpetrᵊl/ *UK* (*US* **gas**) *noun* **[no plural]** a liquid fuel used in cars

petrol station /ˈpetrᵊl ˌsteɪʃn/ *UK* (*US* **gas station**) *noun* a place where you can buy petrol

pharmacist /ˈfɑːməsɪst/ *noun* someone who prepares or sells medicines

pharmacy /ˈfɑːməsi/ *noun* (*plural* **pharmacies**) a shop that prepares and sells medicines

phase /feɪz/ *noun* a stage or period which is part of a longer period: *The first phase of the project has been completed.*

philosopher /fɪˈlɒsəfəʳ/ *noun* someone who studies or writes about the meaning of life

philosophy /fɪˈlɒsəfi/ *noun* **[no plural]** the study or writing of ideas about the meaning of life

phone¹ /fəʊn/ (*also* **telephone**) *noun*
1 a piece of equipment that is used to talk to someone who is in another place: *Would someone please **answer the phone**? ○ I could hear the **phone ringing**.*
2 on the phone using the phone: *She's been on the phone all night.*

phone² /fəʊn/ *verb* (*present participle* **phoning**, *past* **phoned**) to speak to someone by telephone: *I tried to phone her last night, but she was out.*

phone book /ˈfəʊn ˌbʊk/ *noun* a book that has the telephone numbers of people who live in an area

phone box /ˈfəʊn ˌbɒks/ *noun UK* (*plural* **phone boxes**) a small structure containing a public telephone

phone call /ˈfəʊn ˌkɔːl/ *noun* when you use the telephone: *I've got to **make a phone call**.*

phone number /ˈfəʊn ˌnʌmbəʳ/ *noun* the number of a particular telephone

phonetic /fəʊˈnetɪk/ *adj* relating to the sounds you make when you speak: *the international phonetic alphabet*

photo /ˈfəʊtəʊ/ *noun* a picture made with a camera: *I **took a photo of** Jack lying on the beach.*

photocopier /ˈfəʊtəʊˌkɒpiəʳ/ *noun* a machine which makes copies of papers with writing on them by photographing them ➲See colour picture **The Office** on page Centre 12

photocopy /ˈfəʊtəʊˌkɒpi/ *noun* (*plural* **photocopies**) a copy of a paper made with a photocopier: *I **made** a **photocopy** of my letter before sending it.*
• **photocopy** *verb* (*present participle* **photocopying**, *past* **photocopied**)

photograph¹ /ˈfəʊtəgrɑːf/ *noun* a picture made with a camera: *He **took a** lovely **photograph of** the children.*

photograph² /ˈfəʊtəgrɑːf/ *verb* to take a photograph of someone or something: *They were photographed leaving a nightclub together.*

photographer /fəˈtɒgrəfəʳ/ *noun*

someone whose job is to take photographs

photography /fəˈtɒɡrəfi/ *noun* **[no plural]**
the activity or job of taking photographs

phrasal verb /ˌfreɪzəlˈvɜːb/ *noun*
a verb that has two or three words. For example 'look up' and 'carry on' are phrasal verbs. ➲See colour picture **Phrasal Verbs** on page Centre 13

phrase /freɪz/ *noun*
a group of words which are often used together and have a particular meaning

physical /ˈfɪzɪkəl/ *adj*
1 relating to the body: *physical strength*
2 relating to real things that you can see and touch: *a physical object*

physically /ˈfɪzɪkəli/ *adv*
in a way that relates to the body: *He is physically fit.*

physicist /ˈfɪzɪsɪst/ *noun*
someone who studies physics

physics /ˈfɪzɪks/ *noun* **[no plural]**
the scientific study of natural forces, such as energy, heat, light, etc

pianist /ˈpiːənɪst/ *noun*
someone who plays the piano

piano /piˈænəʊ/ *noun*
a big, wooden musical instrument with black and white bars that make sounds when you press them

piano

pick¹ /pɪk/ *verb*
1 to choose something or someone: *He was picked for the school football team.*
2 If you pick flowers, fruit, etc, you take them off a tree or out of the ground: *I picked some apples this morning.*
3 pick a fight/argument to start a fight or argument with someone

pick on someone *phrasal verb*
to treat one person badly in a group of people: *He just started picking on me for no reason.*

pick something/someone up *phrasal verb*
1 to lift something or someone by using your hands: *He picked his coat up off the floor.* ➲See colour picture **Phrasal Verbs** on page Centre 13
2 to go somewhere in order to get someone or something: *Can you pick me up from the airport?*

pick² /pɪk/ *noun* **[no plural]**
take your pick to choose what you want: *We've got tea, coffee, or hot chocolate – take your pick.*

pickpocket /ˈpɪkˌpɒkɪt/ *noun*
someone who steals things from people's pockets

picnic /ˈpɪknɪk/ *noun*
food that you take from your home to eat outside: *We're going to* ***have a picnic*** *down by the lake.*

picture¹ /ˈpɪktʃəʳ/ *noun*
1 a drawing, painting, or photograph of something or someone: *She's got pictures of pop stars all over her bedroom.* ○ *Did you* ***take*** *many* ***pictures*** (= photograph many things) *while you were in Sydney?* ➲See colour picture **The Living Room** on page Centre 11

picture² /ˈpɪktʃəʳ/ *verb* (*present participle* **picturing**, *past* **pictured**)
to imagine something in a particular way: *The house was very different from how I'd pictured it.*

pie /paɪ/ *noun*
a type of food made with meat, vegetables, or fruit which is covered in pastry and baked: *an apple pie*

pie

piece /piːs/ *noun*
1 an amount of something, or a part of something: *a* ***piece of*** *paper* ○ *She cut the cake into eight pieces.* ○ *These shoes are* ***falling to pieces*** (= breaking into pieces).
2 one of a particular type of thing: *a piece of equipment* ○ *It's a beautiful piece of furniture.*

pierce /pɪəs/ *verb* (*present participle* **piercing**, *past* **pierced**)
to make a hole in something using a sharp point: *I had my ears pierced.*

piercing /ˈpɪəsɪŋ/ *adj*
A piercing noise, light, etc is very

strong and unpleasant: *I heard a loud, piercing scream.*

pig /pɪg/ *noun*
1 a large, pink farm animal that is kept for its meat
2 *informal* someone who is very unpleasant, or someone who eats a lot

pigeon /ˈpɪdʒən/ *noun*
a grey bird which often lives on buildings in towns

piglet /ˈpɪglət/ *noun*
a baby pig

pile

pile[1] /paɪl/ *noun*
a lot of something in the shape of a small hill, or a number of things on top of each other: *There was a big* ***pile of*** *sand in the garden.* ◦ *The clothes were arranged in piles on the floor.*

pile[2] /paɪl/ *verb* (*present participle* **piling**, *past* **piled**)
pile something up *phrasal verb*
to make a lot of things into a pile by putting them on top of each other: *Just pile those books up over there.*

pill /pɪl/ *noun*
a small, hard piece of medicine that you swallow: *a vitamin pill*

pillar /ˈpɪləʳ/ *noun*
a tall structure made of stone, wood, etc which supports something above it: *The new bridge will be supported by 100 concrete pillars.*

pillow /ˈpɪləʊ/ *noun*
a soft object which you put your head on in bed

pilot /ˈpaɪlət/ *noun*
someone who flies an aeroplane

pin[1] /pɪn/ *noun*
a thin piece of metal with a sharp point used to fasten pieces of cloth, etc together: *She pricked her finger on a pin.*

pin[2] /pɪn/ *verb* (*present participle* **pinning**, *past* **pinned**)
to fasten something with a pin: *She had a red ribbon* ***pinned to*** *her collar.*

pinch[1] /pɪnʃ/ *verb*
1 to press someone's skin between your thumb and finger, sometimes causing pain: *One of the other children had pinched her and she was crying.*
2 *UK informal* to steal something small: *Who's pinched my pen?*

pinch[2] /pɪnʃ/ *noun* (*plural* **pinches**)
a very small amount of something: *a pinch of salt* ➲See colour picture **Quantities** on page Centre 14

pine /paɪn/ *noun* (*also* ˈ**pine** ˌ**tree**)
a tall tree with long, thin leaves shaped like needles

pineapple

pineapple /ˈpaɪnæpl/ *noun*
a large fruit with leaves sticking out of the top which is sweet and yellow inside

pink /pɪŋk/ *adj*
being a pale red colour: *pretty, pink flowers*
• **pink** *noun* ➲See colour picture **Colours** on page Centre 6

pint /paɪnt/ *noun*
1 a unit for measuring liquid, equal to 0.568 litres in the UK and 0.473 litres in the US
2 *UK informal* a pint of beer

pioneer /ˌpaɪəˈnɪəʳ/ *noun*
someone who is one of the first people to do something: *He was one of the pioneers of modern science.*

pip /pɪp/ *noun UK*
a small seed inside fruit such as apples and oranges

pipe /paɪp/ *noun*
1 a long tube which liquid or gas can move through: *a water pipe*
2 a tube with a bowl-shaped part at one end, used to smoke tobacco: *He smokes a pipe.*

pirate /ˈpaɪərət/ *noun*
someone who attacks ships and steals from them

pistol /ˈpɪstᵊl/ *noun*
a small gun

pit /pɪt/ *noun*
1 a large hole which has been dug in the ground
2 *US* (*UK* **stone**) a large, hard seed that grows inside some types of fruit and vegetables
3 a place where coal is dug out from under the ground

pitch /pɪtʃ/ *noun* (*plural* **pitches**)
1 *UK* an area of ground where a sport is played: *a football pitch*
2 [no plural] how high or low a sound is

pity[1] /ˈpɪti/ *noun* **[no plural]**
1 It's a pity... used to say that something is disappointing: *It's a pity you're not staying longer.*
2 a feeling of sadness for someone who has problems: *She looked at me with such pity in her eyes.*

pity[2] /ˈpɪti/ *verb* (*present participle* **pitying**, *past* **pitied**)
to feel sorry for someone: *I pity her because she is lonely.*

pizza /ˈpiːtsə/ *noun*
a flat, round piece of bread covered with tomato, cheese, etc and cooked in an oven ➲See colour picture **Food** on page Centre 7

place[1] /pleɪs/ *noun*
1 a position, building, town, area, etc: *His leg's broken in two places.* ○ *Edinburgh would be a nice place to live.* ○ *What a stupid place to park!*
2 take place to happen: *The meeting will take place next week.*
3 all over the place in many different places: *There was blood all over the place.*
4 in place of something instead of something: *Try adding fruit to your breakfast cereal in place of sugar.*
5 *informal* someone's home: *They've just bought a place in Spain.*
6 in first/second/third, etc place If you are in first/second, etc place in a race or competition, that is your position: *He finished in fifth place.*

place[2] /pleɪs/ *verb* (*present participle* **placing**, *past* **placed**)
1 to put something somewhere carefully: *She placed a large dish in front of me.*
2 to cause someone to be in a situation: *One stupid action has placed us all at risk.*

plain[1] /pleɪn/ *adj*
1 simple and not complicated: *plain food*
2 not mixed with other colours: *a plain blue carpet*
3 obvious and clear: *It's* ***plain that*** *she is not happy here.*

plain[2] /pleɪn/ *noun*
a large area of flat land

plainly /ˈpleɪnli/ *adv*
1 in a simple way that is not complicated: *She was plainly dressed.*
2 in a clear and obvious way: *This is plainly wrong.*

plait /plæt/ *UK* (*US* **braid**) *verb*
to twist three pieces of hair, rope, etc together so that they form one long piece
• **plait** *UK* (*US* **braid**) *noun*: *She wore her hair in plaits.* ➲See colour picture **Hair** on page Centre 9

plan[1] /plæn/ *noun*
1 something that you are going to do: *What are your* ***plans for*** *the weekend?* ○ *The plan is that we'll buy a car once we're there.*
2 a drawing that shows how something appears from above: *a street plan.*

plan[2] /plæn/ *verb* (*present participle* **planning**, *past* **planned**)
to decide what you are going to do or how you are going to do something: *We're just planning our holidays.* ○ *I'd* ***planned*** *the meeting* ***for*** *Friday.*

plane /pleɪn/ *noun*
a vehicle that flies and has an engine and wings: *What time does her plane get in* (= arrive)*?*

planet /ˈplænɪt/ *noun*
a large, round object in space that moves around the sun or another star

plank /plæŋk/ *noun*
a long, flat piece of wood: *wooden planks*

plant[1] /plɑːnt/ *noun*
a living thing that grows in the soil or water and has leaves and roots: *Have you* ***watered the plants****?* ○ *tomato plants*

plant[2] /plɑːnt/ *verb*
to put seeds or plants in the ground

a b c d e f g h i j k l m n o p q r s t u v w x y z

so that they will grow: *We planted some trees in the garden.*

plaster[1] /ˈplɑːstəʳ/ *noun*
1 [no plural] a substance that is spread on walls in order to make them smooth
2 *UK* a small piece of sticky material that you put on cuts on your body

plaster[2] /ˈplɑːstəʳ/ *verb*
to cover most of a surface with something: *My boots were **plastered with** mud.*

plastic /ˈplæstɪk/ *noun* **[no plural]**
a light substance that can be made into different shapes when it is soft and has many uses: *Most children's toys are made of plastic.*
• **plastic** *noun*: *plastic bags*

plate /pleɪt/ *noun*
a flat, round object which is used for putting food on: *a dinner plate* ○ *a **plate of** biscuits*

platform /ˈplætfɔːm/ *noun*
1 a high part of the floor for a person to stand on: *The speakers all stood on a platform.*
2 the area in a railway station where you get on and off the train: *The train for London, Paddington, will depart from platform 12.*

play[1] /pleɪ/ *verb*
1 When you play a sport or game, you do it: *You play tennis, don't you, Sam?* ○ *We often used to play cards.*
2 When children play, they enjoy themselves with toys and games: *She likes playing with her dolls.*
3 to make music with a musical instrument: *Tim was playing the piano.*
4 to be a character in a film or play: *Morgan played the father in the film version.*

play[2] /pleɪ/ *noun*
1 a story that is written for actors to perform, usually in a theatre: *We saw a play at the National Theatre.*
2 [no plural] when children enjoy themselves with toys and games: *a play area*

player /ˈpleɪəʳ/ *noun*
someone who plays a sport or game: *tennis players*

playful /ˈpleɪfəl/ *adj*
funny and not serious: *a playful remark*

playground /ˈpleɪgraʊnd/ *noun*
an area of land where children can play, especially at a school

playing card /ˈpleɪ-ɪŋ ˌkɑːd/ *noun*
one of a set of 52 small pieces of stiff paper with numbers and pictures on, used for playing games

playing field /ˈpleɪ-ɪŋ ˌfiːld/ *noun*
an area of land used for sports such as football

plea /pliː/ *noun*
when someone asks for something that they really want: *a **plea for** help*

plead /pliːd/ *verb*
1 to say in a court of law if you have done a crime or not done a crime: *He **pleaded** not guilty **to** the crime.*
2 to ask for something in a strong and emotional way: *He **pleaded with** her to come back.*

pleasant /ˈplezənt/ *adj*
good or enjoyable: *pleasant weather* ○ *We had a very pleasant evening.*
• **pleasantly** *adv*: *I was pleasantly surprised.*

please[1] /pliːz/ *exclamation*
1 something that you say to be polite when you are asking for something: *Could I have a coffee, please?* ○ *Please may I use your telephone?*
2 Yes, please. used to accept something politely: *"Would you like a drink?" "Oh yes, please."*

please[2] /pliːz/ *verb* (*present participle* **pleasing**, *past* **pleased**)
to make someone happy: *I only got married to please my parents.*

pleased /pliːzd/ *adj*
1 happy about something: *I'm **pleased to** be back home.* ○ *I'm really **pleased with** her work.* ○ *I wasn't very **pleased about** having to pay.*
2 Pleased to meet you. a polite thing to say to someone you are meeting for the first time

pleasure /ˈpleʒəʳ/ *noun*
1 [no plural] a feeling of happiness or enjoyment: *The children **give** her a lot of **pleasure**.*
2 an enjoyable activity: *Food is one of life's great pleasures.*

plenty /ˈplenti/ *quantifier*
a lot of something, more than you need: *Don't bring any food – we've got plenty.* ○ *There's **plenty of** room here.*

plot[1] /plɒt/ *noun*

1 the things that happen in a story: *I don't like movies with complicated plots.*
2 a plan to do something bad: *There was a **plot to** blow up the embassy.*
3 a piece of land: *a building plot*

plot² /plɒt/ *verb* (*present participle* **plotting**, *past* **plotted**)
to plan to do something bad: *They plotted to bring down the government.*

plough *UK* (*US* **plow**) /plaʊ/ *noun*
a large tool used by farmers to turn over the soil before planting crops

pluck /plʌk/ *verb*
1 to quickly pull something or someone from the place where they are: *He plucked a £50 note out of his wallet.*
2 If you pluck the strings of a musical instrument, you pull them with your fingers to make a sound.
3 **pluck your eyebrows** to pull hairs out of your eyebrows (= lines of hair above your eyes) to make them look tidy

plug

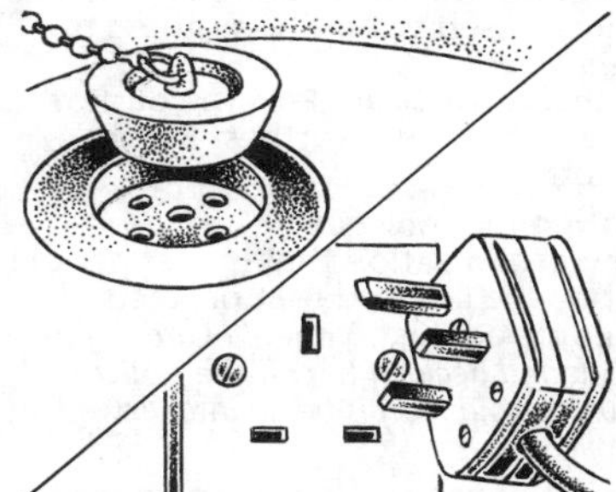

plug¹ /plʌg/ *noun*
1 an object with metal parts, used to connect electrical equipment to an electricity supply: *I need to change the plug on my hairdryer.*
2 something you put in a hole to block it: *a bath plug*

plug² /plʌg/ *verb* (*present participle* **plugging**, *past* **plugged**)
to block a hole
plug something in *phrasal verb*
to connect a piece of electrical equipment to an electricity supply: *Could you plug the iron in for me?*

plum /plʌm/ *noun*
a soft, round fruit with red or yellow skin and a stone in the middle

plumber /ˈplʌməʳ/ *noun*
someone whose job is to repair or connect water pipes and toilets and baths

plumbing /ˈplʌmɪŋ/ *noun* **[no plural]**
the water pipes in a building

plump /plʌmp/ *adj*
quite fat: *a plump child*

plunge /plʌndʒ/ *verb* (*present participle* **plunging**, *past* **plunged**)
to fall or move down very quickly and with force: *He plunged into the water.*

plural /ˈplʊərᵊl/ *noun*
a word or part of a word which shows that you are talking about more than one person or thing. For example 'babies' is the plural of 'baby'.
• **plural** *adj*: *'Cattle' and 'trousers' are plural nouns.*

plus /plʌs/ *preposition*
1 added to: *Five plus three is eight.*
2 and also: *You've won their latest CD plus two tickets for their concert.*

p.m. /ˌpiːˈem/
in the afternoon or evening: *Opening hours: 9 a.m. – 6 p.m.* ➲Compare **a.m.**

pocket /ˈpɒkɪt/ *noun*
a part of a piece of clothing that you can put things in: *My wallet was in my coat pocket.*

pocket

pocket money
/ˈpɒkɪt ˌmʌni/ *noun* **[no plural]**
an amount of money that parents give to a child each week

pod /pɒd/ *noun*
the long, flat part of some plants that has seeds in it: *a pea pod*

poem /ˈpəʊɪm/ *noun*
a piece of writing, especially one that has short lines and uses words that sound the same: *love poems*

poet /ˈpəʊɪt/ *noun*
someone who writes poems

poetry /ˈpəʊɪtri/ *noun* **[no plural]**
poems in general

point¹ /pɔɪnt/ *noun*
1 an opinion, idea, or fact which someone says or writes: *He **made** some interesting **points** about the father-son relationship.* ○ *He explained his point by drawing a diagram.*

a b c d e f g h i j k l m n o **p** q r s t u v w x y z

2 an opinion or fact that should be considered seriously: *"She's always complaining that the office is cold." "Well, she's* ***got a point****."* (= that is true) ○ *"How are we going to get there if there are no trains?" "That's a point."*
3 the point the most important part of what has been said or written: *Come on,* ***get to the point****!* ○ ***The point is****, if you don't claim the money now you might never get it.*
4 the thin, sharp end of something: *the point of a needle*
5 a particular place: *This is the point where the pipes enter the building.*
6 a particular time in an event or process: *At this point in the day, I'm too tired to think.*
7 the reason for or purpose of something: *What's the* ***point of*** *studying if you can't get a job afterwards?*
8 make a point of doing something to be certain that you always do a particular thing: *He made a point of learning all the names of his staff.*
9 up to a point partly: *What he says is true up to a point.*
10 a unit used for showing who is winning in a game: *With 3 games still to play, Manchester United are 5 points ahead.*
11 a quality which someone has: *I know she's bossy, but she has lots of* ***good points*** *too.*
12 (*also* **decimal point**) the mark (.) that is used to separate the two parts of a decimal: *One mile equals one point six* (= 1.6) *kilometres.*

point² /pɔɪnt/ *verb*
to show where someone or something is by holding your finger or a thin object towards it: *She* ***pointed to*** *a bird in the tree.*
point something out *phrasal verb*
to tell someone a fact: *If he makes a mistake I point it out immediately.*

pointless /ˈpɔɪntləs/ *adj*
Something that is pointless has no purpose: *It would be* ***pointless to*** *argue with him.*
• **pointlessly** *adv*

point of view /ˌpɔɪnt əv ˈvjuː/ *noun* (*plural* **points of view**)
an opinion: *I can see* (= understand) *his point of view.*

poison¹ /ˈpɔɪzᵊn/ *noun*
a substance that makes you ill or kills you if you eat or drink it

poison² /ˈpɔɪzᵊn/ *verb*
to try to kill someone by giving them a dangerous substance to drink or eat: *He tried to poison his wife.*

poisonous /ˈpɔɪzᵊnəs/ *adj*
containing poison: *poisonous gas*

poke /pəʊk/ *verb* (*present participle* **poking**, *past* **poked**)
to quickly push your finger or other pointed object into someone or something: *Nell kept poking me in the arm.*

poker /ˈpəʊkəʳ/ *noun* **[no plural]**
a game played with cards in which people try to win money from each other

polar /ˈpəʊləʳ/ *adj*
relating to the North or South Pole

polar bear /ˌpəʊləʳ ˈbeəʳ/ *noun*
a large, white bear that lives in the North Pole (= most northern part of the Earth)

pole /pəʊl/ *noun*
1 a long, thin stick made of wood or metal, used to hold something up: *tent poles*
2 the North/South Pole the part of the Earth that is furthest North/South

police /pəˈliːs/ *noun*
the organization that makes people obey the law and that protects people against crime: *I heard a gun shot and decided to* ***call the police****.* ○ *A 30-year-old man is being interviewed by police.*

policeman, policewoman /pəˈliːsmən, pəˈliːsˌwʊmən/ *noun* (*plural* **policemen, policewomen**)
a man/woman who is a member of the police

police officer /pəˈliːs ˌɒfɪsəʳ/ *noun* *UK*
someone who is a member of the police

police station /pəˈliːs ˌsteɪʃn/ *noun*
the office of the police

policy /ˈpɒləsi/ *noun* (*plural* **policies**)
a set of ideas or a plan that has been agreed by a government, business, etc: *economic policy* ○ *It is company policy to help staff progress in their careers.*

polish¹ /ˈpɒlɪʃ/ *noun* **[no plural]**

a substance that you rub on something in order to make it shine

polish[2] /ˈpɒlɪʃ/ *verb*
to rub something with a cloth in order to make it shine: *I polished my shoes.*

polite /pəˈlaɪt/ *adj*
behaving in a way that is not rude and shows that you think about other people: *She was too polite to point out my mistake.*
• **politely** *adv*: *He thanked them politely.*

political /pəˈlɪtɪkᵊl/ *adj*
relating to or involved in politics: *There are two main political parties in my country.*

politician /ˌpɒlɪˈtɪʃᵊn/ *noun*
someone who works in politics, especially a member of the government: *Churchill was a distinguished politician.*

politics /ˈpɒlətɪks/ *noun* **[no plural]**
1 ideas and activities relating to how a country or area is governed: *He has little interest in politics.*
2 a job in politics: *She's planning to retire from politics next year.*

poll /pəʊl/ *noun*
when people are asked questions to discover what they think about a subject: *A recent poll indicated that 77 percent of Americans supported the president.*

pollen /ˈpɒlən/ *noun* **[no plural]**
a powder made by flowers, which is carried by insects and makes other flowers produce seeds

pollute /pəˈluːt/ *verb* (*present participle* **polluting**, *past* **polluted**)
to make water, air, soil, etc dirty or harmful: *We need a fuel that won't pollute the environment.*

pollution /pəˈluːʃᵊn/ *noun* **[no plural]**
damage caused to water, air, etc by bad substances or waste

pond /pɒnd/ *noun*
a small area of water

pony /ˈpəʊni/ *noun* (*plural* **ponies**)
a small horse

ponytail /ˈpəʊniteɪl/ *noun*
hair tied at the back of your head ➲See colour picture **Hair** on page Centre 9

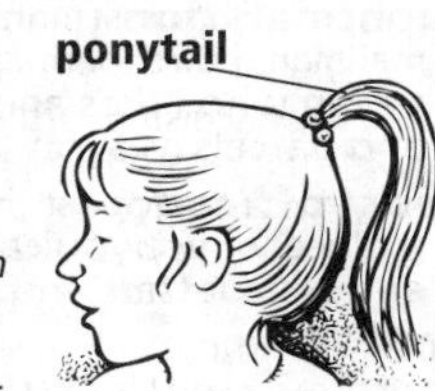

pool[1] /puːl/ *noun*
1 an area of water that has been made for people to swim in: *The hotel has two outdoor pools.*
2 a small area of water or other liquid on a surface: *a pool of blood*

pool[2] /puːl/ *verb*
to collect something together so that it can be shared or used for a particular purpose: *Several villages pooled their resources to set up a building project.*

poor /pɔːr/ *adj*
1 having little money: *He comes from a very poor family.* ➲Opposite **rich**
2 of bad quality: *It was a poor performance.*
3 used to show that you are sad for someone: *That cold sounds terrible, you poor thing!*

poorly /ˈpɔːli/ *adv*
badly: *They were poorly educated.*

pop[1] /pɒp/ *verb* (*present participle* **popping**, *past* **popped**)
1 to make a short sound like a small explosion: *The music played and champagne corks popped.*
2 *informal* to go to a particular place: *I'll pop into the supermarket on my way home.*

pop[2] /pɒp/ *noun*
1 [no plural] (*also* **ˈpop ˌmusic**) modern music with a strong beat which is popular with young people
2 a short sound like a small explosion

popcorn /ˈpɒpkɔːn/ *noun* **[no plural]**
yellow seeds of grain that break open and get bigger when you cook them

Pope /pəʊp/ *noun*
the leader of the Roman Catholic Church

popular /ˈpɒpjələʳ/ *adj*
liked by many people: *'Jack' was the most popular boy's name.* ➲Opposite **unpopular**

popularity /ˌpɒpjəˈlærəti/ *noun* **[no plural]**
the quality of being liked by many people

population /ˌpɒpjəˈleɪʃᵊn/ *noun*
the number of people living in a particular area: *What's the* ***population of*** *Brazil?*

a b c d e f g h i j k l m n o **p** q r s t u v w x y z

pork /pɔːk/ *noun* **[no plural]**
meat from a pig

port /pɔːt/ *noun*
a town or an area of a town next to water where ships arrive and leave from: *the Belgian port of Zeebrugge*

portable /ˈpɔːtəbl/ *adj*
able to be carried: *a portable computer*

portion /ˈpɔːʃᵊn/ *noun*
1 a part of something: *A* ***portion of*** *their profits go to charity.*
2 the amount of food given to one person in a restaurant: *The portions in the restaurant were very small.*

portrait /ˈpɔːtrɪt/ *noun*
a painting, drawing, or photograph of someone: *a portrait of the princess*

posh /pɒʃ/ *adj*
1 expensive and for rich people: *a posh hotel*
2 *UK* from a high social class: *She has a posh voice.*

position /pəˈzɪʃᵊn/ *noun*
1 the way someone is sitting, standing, or lying: *What position do you sleep in?*
2 the situation that someone is in: *She's* ***in*** *a very difficult* ***position.***
3 the place where someone or something is: *I'm trying to find our position on the map.*
4 in first/second/third, etc position in first/second/third, etc place in a race or other competition: *She finished the race in third position.*
5 a job: *He has applied for a senior position.*

positive /ˈpɒzətɪv/ *adj*
1 feeling happy about your life and your future: *She has a very positive attitude.*
2 certain that something is true: *"Are you sure you saw him?" "Absolutely positive."*

possess /pəˈzes/ *verb formal*
to have or own something: *Certainly, he possesses the skills for the job.*

possession /pəˈzeʃᵊn/ *noun*
a thing that you own: *personal possessions*

possibility /ˌpɒsəˈbɪləti/ *noun* (*plural* **possibilities)**
1 a chance that something may happen or be true: *Is there any* ***possibility of*** *changing this ticket?* ○ *There's a* ***possibility that*** *Harvey might come.*
2 something that you can choose to do: *Have you considered the* ***possibility of*** *flying?*

possible /ˈpɒsəbl/ *adj*
If something is possible, it can happen or be done: *Is it* ***possible to*** *speak to the manager please?* ○ *I'll send it today,* ***if possible.*** ⊃Opposite **impossible**

possibly /ˈpɒsəbli/ *adv*
used when something is not certain: *Someone, possibly Tom, had left the window open.*

post[1] /pəʊst/ *noun*
1 [no plural] *UK* (*US* **mail)** letters, parcels, etc that you send or get: *Has the post arrived yet?*
2 *formal* a job: *a teaching post*
3 a long piece of wood or metal fixed into the ground at one end: *I found the dog tied to a post.*

post[2] /pəʊst/ *verb UK* (*US* **mail)**
to send a letter or parcel by post: *Did you post my letter?*

postage /ˈpəʊstɪdʒ/ *noun* **[no plural]**
money that you pay to send a letter or parcel: *first-class postage*

post box /ˈpəʊst ˌbɒks/ *UK* (*US* **mailbox)** *noun* (*plural* **post boxes)**
a large, metal container in a public place where you can post letters

postcard /ˈpəʊstkɑːd/ *noun*
a card with a picture on one side that you send without an envelope

postcode /ˈpəʊstkəʊd/ *noun UK*
a group of letters and numbers that comes at the end of someone's address in the UK

poster /ˈpəʊstəʳ/ *noun*
a large, printed picture or notice that you put on a wall

postgraduate /ˌpəʊstˈgrædʒuət/ *noun UK*
a student who has one degree

postman /ˈpəʊstmən/ *UK* (*US* **mailman)** *noun* (*plural* **postmen)**
a man who takes and brings letters and parcels as a job

post office /ˈpəʊst ˌɒfɪs/ *noun*
a place where you can buy stamps and send letters and parcels

pot /pɒt/ *noun*
a round container, usually used for

keeping things or cooking: *a flower pot* ○ *a pot of coffee*

potato /pəˈteɪtəʊ/ *noun* (*plural* **potatoes**)
a round, white vegetable that grows in the ground ➲See colour picture **Fruit and Vegetables** on page Centre 8

potato chip /pəˈteɪtəʊ ˌtʃɪp/ *US* (*UK* **crisp**) *noun*
a very thin, dry, fried slice of potato

pottery /ˈpɒtᵊri/ *noun* **[no plural]**
1 plates, bowls, etc that are made from clay
2 the activity of making plates, bowls, etc from clay

poultry /ˈpəʊltri/ *noun* **[no plural]**
chickens and other birds that people keep for meat and eggs

pounce /paʊns/ *verb* (*present participle* **pouncing**, *past* **pounced**)
to suddenly move towards a person or animal that you want to catch

pound /paʊnd/ *noun*
1 the unit of money used in the UK and Ireland; £: *a hundred pounds/£100*
2 a unit for measuring weight, equal to 453.6 grams or 16 ounces: *a pound of potatoes* ○ *The baby weighed just four pounds when she was born.*

pour /pɔːʳ/ *verb*
1 to make a liquid flow from or into a container: *I* ***poured*** *the milk* ***into*** *a jug.*
2 to rain a lot: *We can't go out in this weather – it's pouring!*

pour

poverty /ˈpɒvəti/ *noun* **[no plural]**
when you are very poor: *They live* ***in poverty****.*

powder /ˈpaʊdəʳ/ *noun* **[no plural]**
a dry substance made of many small, loose grains: *curry powder*
• **powdered** *adj*
in the form of a powder: *powdered milk/sugar*

power /paʊəʳ/ *noun*
1 [no plural] control over people and things that happen: *He likes to have* ***power over*** *people.*
2 [no plural] political control in a country: *This government have been* ***in power*** *too long.*
3 [no plural] energy, usually electricity, that is used to make light, heat, etc: *nuclear power*
4 the legal right to do something: *It's not* ***in my power*** *to stop him publishing this book.*

powerful /ˈpaʊəfᵊl/ *adj*
1 A powerful person is able to control people and things that happen.
2 very strong: *a powerful weapon*

powerless /ˈpaʊələs/ *adj*
not able to control things that happen: *The police were* ***powerless to*** *stop the fighting.*

practical /ˈpræktɪkᵊl/ *adj*
1 relating to real situations: *They can offer practical help.*
2 able to be done successfully: *The plan is simply not practical.*
3 Someone who is practical is good at planning things: *She has a lot of interesting ideas but she's not very practical.*
4 good at repairing and making things

practically /ˈpræktɪkᵊli/ *adv*
almost: *We see her practically every day.*

practice /ˈpræktɪs/ *noun*
1 [no plural] when you do an activity again and again to get better at it: *We need a bit more practice before the concert.*
2 what people do or how they do it: *business practices* ○ *the illegal practice of copying CDs*
3 be out of practice to not do something well because you have not done it recently: *I didn't play very well today – I'm out of practice.*

practise /ˈpræktɪs/ *verb* (*present participle* **practising**, *past* **practised**)
to do something again and again in order to get better at it: *They're* ***practising for*** *tomorrow's concert.*

praise¹ /preɪz/ *verb* (*present participle* **praising**, *past* **praised**)
to say that someone or something is very good: *He praised the team's performance.*

praise² /preɪz/ *noun* **[no plural]**
words that you say to show that you think someone or something is very good: *They deserve* ***praise for*** *their achievements.*

a b c d e f g h i j k l m n o p q r s t u v w x y z

prawn /prɔːn/ *noun*
a small, pink sea animal which you can eat

pray /preɪ/ *verb*
to speak to a god in order to show your feelings or to ask for something: *Let us **pray for** all the sick children.*

prayer /preəʳ/ *noun*
1 the words you say to a god: *Shall we **say a prayer for** him?*
2 [no plural] when you say words to a god

preach /priːtʃ/ *verb*
to talk to a group of people about a religious subject, usually in a church

preacher /ˈpriːtʃəʳ/ *noun*
someone who speaks in public about a religious subject

precaution /prɪˈkɔːʃᵊn/ *noun*
something that you do to stop bad things happening in the future: *They called the doctor **as a precaution**.* ○ *He **took** the **precaution** of locking the door.*

precious /ˈpreʃəs/ *adj*
1 very important to you: *His books are his most precious possessions.*
2 very valuable: *a precious metal*

precise /prɪˈsaɪs/ *adj*
exact and accurate: *Her instructions were very precise.*

precisely /prɪˈsaɪsli/ *adv*
exactly: *At 6 o' clock precisely he arrived.*

predict /prɪˈdɪkt/ *verb*
to say what you think will happen in the future: *Companies are predicting massive profits.*

prediction /prɪˈdɪkʃᵊn/ *noun*
when you say what you think will happen in the future: *I wouldn't like to **make** any **predictions about** the result of this match.*

prefer /prɪˈfɜːʳ/ *verb* (*present participle* **preferring**, *past* **preferred**)
to like someone or something more than another person or thing: *I **prefer** dogs **to** cats.* ○ *She prefers watching tennis to playing.*

preferably /ˈprefᵊrəbli/ *adv*
if possible: *Serve the pudding with ice cream, preferably vanilla.*

preference /ˈprefᵊrᵊns/ *noun*
when you like something or someone more than another person or thing: *personal preferences* ○ *We have white and brown bread. Do you **have a preference**?*

prefix /ˈpriːfɪks/ *noun* (*plural* **prefixes**)
a group of letters that you add to the beginning of a word to make another word. In the word 'unimportant', 'un-' is a prefix.

pregnancy /ˈpregnənsi/ *noun* (*plural* **pregnancies**)
when a woman is pregnant: *a healthy pregnancy*

pregnant /ˈpregnənt/ *adj*
A pregnant woman has a baby developing inside her body: *She's five months pregnant.*

prejudice /ˈpredʒədɪs/ *noun*
when someone does not like a group of people or treats them badly because they are a different race, sex, religion, etc: *racial prejudice*

prejudiced /ˈpredʒədɪst/ *adj*
not liking a group of people or treating them badly because they are a different race, sex, religion, etc: *Are the police **prejudiced against** black people?*

preparation /ˌprepᵊrˈeɪʃᵊn/ *noun* **[no plural]**
the things that you do to prepare for something: *Did you **do** much **preparation for** your interview?*

prepare /prɪˈpeəʳ/ *verb* (*present participle* **preparing**, *past* **prepared**)
1 to get someone or something ready for something in the future: *I haven't prepared my speech yet.* ○ *We're preparing the students for their end-of-year exam.*
2 to make food ready to be eaten: *I was preparing lunch.*

prepared /prɪˈpeəd/ *adj*
1 ready for a situation: *I wasn't **prepared for** the cold.*
2 be prepared to do something to be willing to do something: *You must be prepared to work hard.*

preposition /ˌprepəˈzɪʃᵊn/ *noun*
a word or group of words that is used before a noun or pronoun to show place, direction, time, etc. For example 'on' in 'Your keys are on the table.' is a preposition.

prescribe /prɪˈskraɪb/ *verb* (*present participle* **prescribing**, *past* **prescribed**) to say what medicine an ill person needs

prescription /prɪˈskrɪpʃ^{ə}n/ *noun* a piece of paper saying what medicine an ill person needs: *a doctor's prescription*

presence /ˈprez^{ə}ns/ *noun* **[no plural]** when someone or something is in a place: *Your presence at the meeting would be appreciated.* ○ *She signed the document* ***in the presence of*** *two witnesses.*

present[1] /ˈprez^{ə}nt/ *adj*
1 be present to be in a particular place: *The whole family was present.*
2 happening or existing now: *What is your present occupation?*
3 present tense the form of the verb which is used to show what happens or exists now

present[2] /ˈprez^{ə}nt/ *noun*
1 the present
a the period of time that is happening now: *Let's talk about the present.*
b the form of the verb which is used to show what happens or exists now
2 something that you give to someone, usually on a special day: *a birthday present*
3 at present now: *At present she's working abroad.*

present[3] /prɪˈzent/ *verb* to give something to someone, often at a formal ceremony: *They* ***presented*** *her* ***with*** *a prize.*

present

presentation /ˌprez^{ə}nˈteɪʃ^{ə}n/ *noun*
1 [no plural] the way you show something to people: *Presentation is important if you want people to buy your products.*
2 a formal ceremony at which you give someone something: *a presentation ceremony*

present participle /ˌprez^{ə}nt ˈpɑːtɪsɪpl/ *noun* the form of a verb that ends with '-ing'

the present perfect /ˌprez^{ə}nt ˈpɜːfɪkt/ *noun* the form of the verb that is used to show things that have happened in a period of time up to now. The sentence 'I have never been to Australia.' is in the present perfect.

preservation /ˌprezəˈveɪʃ^{ə}n/ *noun* **[no plural]** when you keep something the same or stop it from being destroyed: *the preservation of wildlife*

preserve /prɪˈzɜːv/ *verb* (*present participle* **preserving**, *past* **preserved**) to keep something the same or stop it from being destroyed: *to preserve the environment*

president /ˈprezɪd^{ə}nt/ *noun*
1 the highest political position in some countries, usually the leader of the government: *the president of the United States*
2 the person in charge of a company or organization

press[1] /pres/ *verb* to push something firmly: *Press the button to start the machine.* ○ *He pressed his face against the window.*

press[2] /pres/ *noun* **[no plural]** **the press** newspapers and magazines, or the people who write them: *the national press*

pressure /ˈpreʃə^{r}/ *noun*
1 [no plural] when someone tries to make someone else do something by arguing, persuading, etc: *public/political pressure* ○ *Teachers are* ***under pressure*** *to work longer hours.*
2 difficult situations that make you feel worried or unhappy: *the pressures of work*
3 [no plural] the force that you produce when you push something

pretend /prɪˈtend/ *verb* to behave as if something is true when it is not: *I can't* ***pretend that*** *I like him.* ○ *Were you just* ***pretending to*** *be interested?*

pretty[1] /ˈprɪti/ *adv informal* quite, but not very: *The traffic was pretty bad.* ○ *I'm pretty sure they'll accept.*

pretty[2] /ˈprɪti/ *adj* (**prettier, prettiest**) nice to look at, attractive: *Your daughter is very pretty.* ○ *a pretty little village*

prevent /prɪˈvent/ *verb* to stop something happening or to stop someone doing something: *to* *prevent crime ○ Members of the public were* ***prevented from*** *entering the building.*

prevention /prɪˈvenʃᵊn/ *noun* **[no plural]**
when you stop something happening or stop someone doing something: *crime prevention ○ the prevention of diseases*

previous /ˈpriːviəs/ *adj*
existing or happening before this one: *the previous day/year ○ his previous marriage*
• **previously** *adv*
before: *He previously worked as a teacher.*

prey /preɪ/ *noun* **[no plural]**
an animal that is hunted and killed by another animal

price /praɪs/ *noun*
the amount of money that you pay to buy something: *high/low prices ○ The* ***price of*** *fuel has gone up again.*

priceless /ˈpraɪsləs/ *adj*
very valuable: *a priceless antique/painting*

prick /prɪk/ *verb*
to make a very small hole in something with a sharp object: *I pricked my finger on a pin.*
• **prick** *noun*: *The injection won't hurt – you'll just feel a slight prick.*

pride /praɪd/ *noun* **[no plural]**
a feeling of satisfaction at your achievements or the achievements of your family or friends: *She felt a great sense of pride as she watched him accept the award.*

priest /priːst/ *noun*
someone who performs religious duties and ceremonies

primary /ˈpraɪmᵊri/ *adj*
most important: *Her primary responsibility is to train new employees.*

primary school /ˈpraɪmᵊri ˌskuːl/ (*also US* **elementary school**) *noun*
a school for children aged 5 to 11

prime minister /ˌpraɪm ˈmɪnɪstəʳ/ *noun*
the leader of an elected government in some countries

primitive /ˈprɪmɪtɪv/ *adj*
relating to a time long ago when people lived in a simple way without machines or a writing system: *primitive man*

prince /prɪns/ *noun*
1 the son of a king or queen, or one of their close male relatives: *Prince Edward*
2 the male ruler of a small country

princess /prɪnˈses/ *noun* (*plural* **princesses**)
1 the daughter of a king or queen, or one of their close female relatives
2 the wife of a prince

principal[1] /ˈprɪnsəpᵊl/ *adj*
main, or most important: *Her principal reason for moving is to be nearer her mother.*

principal[2] /ˈprɪnsəpᵊl/ *noun*
the person in charge of a school or college

principle /ˈprɪnsəpl/ *noun*
1 a belief about how you should behave: *He must be punished – it's a matter of principle.*
2 on principle If you refuse to do something on principle, you refuse to do it because you think it is morally wrong: *She doesn't wear fur on principle.*

print[1] /prɪnt/ *verb*
1 to make writing or images on paper or other material with a machine: *The instructions are printed on the side of the box.*
2 to make books, newspapers, magazines, etc, usually in large quantities, using machines: *Fifty thousand leaflets have been printed for the exhibition.*

print[2] /prɪnt/ *noun*
1 [no plural] words, letters, or numbers that are made on paper by a machine: *The print's so small in this book that I can hardly read it.*
2 a mark that is left on a surface where someone has walked: *The dog left prints all over the kitchen floor.*

printer /ˈprɪntəʳ/ *noun*
1 a machine which is connected to a computer and which makes writing or images on paper: *a laser printer*
2 a person or company that prints books, newspapers, magazines, etc

prison /ˈprɪzᵊn/ *noun*
a place where criminals are kept as a punishment: *He's spent most of his life* ***in prison.***

prisoner /ˈprɪzᵊnəʳ/ *noun*
someone who is being kept in prison

as a punishment

private /'praɪvɪt/ *adj*
1 only for one person or group and not for everyone: *You can't park here – this is private property.*
2 controlled by or paid for by a person or company and not by the government: *Charles went to a private school.*
3 If information or an emotion is private, you do not want other people to know about it: *This is a private matter – it doesn't concern you.*
4 in private If you do something in private, you do it where other people cannot see or hear you: *I need to talk to you in private.*

privilege /'prɪvəlɪdʒ/ *noun*
an advantage that only one person or group has, usually because of their position or because they are rich

prize /praɪz/ *noun*
something valuable that is given to someone who wins a competition: *to win a prize ○ first/second prize*

probable /'prɒbəbl/ *adj*
likely to be true or to happen: *The probable cause of death was heart failure.*

probably /'prɒbəbli/ *adv*
used to mean that something is very likely: *I'll probably be home by midnight.*

problem /'prɒbləm/ *noun*
1 a situation that causes difficulties: *health problems ○ I'm **having problems with** my computer. ○ Drugs have become a serious problem in the area.*
2 No problem. *informal*
a something that you say to mean you can or will do what someone has asked you to do: *"Can you get me to the airport by 11.30?" "No problem."*
b something that you say when someone has thanked you for something: *"Thanks for taking me home." "No problem."*
3 have a problem with something/someone to not like something or someone: *She can smoke in here – I don't have a problem with that.*

proceed /prəʊ'siːd/ *verb formal*
1 to continue as planned: *His lawyers have decided not to **proceed with** the case.*
2 proceed to do something to do something after you have done something else: *She sat down and proceeded to tell me about her skiing trip.*

process /'prəʊses/ *noun (plural* **processes)**
1 a series of actions that you take in order to do something: *Buying a house can be a long and complicated process.*
2 a series of changes that happen naturally: *the process of growing old*

procession /prə'seʃən/ *noun*
a line of people or cars that moves forward slowly as part of a ceremony or public event: *a funeral procession*

produce[1] /prə'djuːs/ *verb (present participle* **producing**, *past* **produced)**
1 to make or grow something: *The factory produces about 900 cars a year.*
2 to cause a particular result: *Nuts produce an allergic reaction in some people.*
3 to control how a film, play, programme, or musical recording is made: *He's produced some of the top Broadway shows.*

produce[2] /'prɒdjuːs/ *noun* **[no plural]**
food that is grown or made in large quantities to be sold: *dairy produce*

producer /prə'djuːsər/ *noun*
1 a company, country, or person that makes things or grows food: *Australia is one of the world's main producers of wool.*
2 someone who controls how a film, play, programme, or musical recording is made: *a film/record producer*

product /'prɒdʌkt/ *noun*
something that someone makes or grows so that they can sell it: *We have a new range of skincare products.*

production /prə'dʌkʃən/ *noun*
1 [no plural] when you make or grow something: *Sand is used in the production of glass.*
2 [no plural] the amount of something that is made or grown: *We need to increase production by 20%.*
3 a performance or series of performances of a play or show: *a school production of 'Romeo and Juliet'*
4 [no plural] when someone controls how a film, play, programme, or musical recording is made: *She wants*

a career in TV production.

productive /prəˈdʌktɪv/ *adj* having a good or useful result: *We had a very productive meeting and sorted out a lot of problems.*

profession /prəˈfeʃən/ *noun* a type of work that needs special training or education: *He's working in a restaurant, but he's a teacher* ***by profession*** (= he trained to be a teacher).

professional /prəˈfeʃənəl/ *adj*
1 relating to a job that needs special training or education: *You should get some professional advice about your finances.*
2 Someone is professional if they get money for a sport or activity which most people do as a hobby: *a professional athlete/musician* ➲Opposite **amateur**
3 showing skill and careful attention: *a professional attitude*

professor /prəˈfesər/ *noun* the highest rank of teacher in a British university, or a teacher in an American university or college: *a professor of history at Oxford*

profit /ˈprɒfɪt/ *noun* money that you get from selling something for more than it cost you to buy: *a profit of $4.5 million* ○ *It's very hard for a new business to* ***make a profit*** *in its first year.*

profitable /ˈprɒfɪtəbl/ *adj* making a profit: *a profitable business*

program[1] /ˈprəʊɡræm/ *noun*
1 a set of instructions that you put into a computer to make it do something: *to write a computer program*
2 *US spelling of* programme

program[2] /ˈprəʊɡræm/ *verb* (*present participle* **programming,** *past* **programmed)**
If you program a computer, you give it a set of instructions to do something.

programme *UK* (*US* **program)** /ˈprəʊɡræm/ *noun*
1 a show on television or radio: *a TV programme*
2 a thin book that you buy at a theatre, sports event, etc

programmer /ˈprəʊɡræmər/ *noun* someone who writes computer programs as a job

progress[1] /ˈprəʊɡres/ *noun* **[no plural]**
1 development and improvement of skills, knowledge, etc: *technological progress* ○ *He has* ***made*** *good* ***progress*** *in French this year.*
2 movement towards a place

progress[2] /prəʊˈɡres/ *verb*
1 to improve: *Technology has progressed rapidly in the last 100 years.*
2 to continue gradually: *I began to feel more relaxed as the evening progressed.*

prohibit /prəʊˈhɪbɪt/ *verb formal* to say by law that you must not do something: *Smoking is prohibited on most international flights.*

project /ˈprɒdʒekt/ *noun*
1 a planned piece of work that has a particular purpose: *The new building project will cost $45 million.*
2 a piece of school work in which children study a particular subject: *We're* ***doing*** *a class* ***project on*** *the environment.*

prominent /ˈprɒmɪnənt/ *adj*
1 important or famous: *a prominent businessman*
2 very easy to see or notice: *prominent eyes*
• **prominently** *adv*

promise[1] /ˈprɒmɪs/ *verb* (*present participle* **promising,** *past* **promised)**
to say that you will certainly do something or that something will certainly happen: *She* ***promised to*** *write to me every week.* ○ *Paul* ***promised*** *me* ***that*** *he'd cook dinner tonight.*

promise[2] /ˈprɒmɪs/ *noun* when you say that you will certainly do something: *I'm not sure I can do it so I won't* ***make*** *any* ***promises.*** ○ *I've said I'll take her swimming and I don't want to* ***break*** *my* ***promise*** (= not do what I said I would).

promote /prəˈməʊt/ *verb* (*present participle* **promoting,** *past* **promoted)**
1 to advertise something: *The band is promoting their new album.*
2 to give someone a more important job in the same organization: *She's just been* ***promoted to*** *manager.*

promotion /prəˈməʊʃən/ *noun*
1 activities to advertise something: *a sales promotion*
2 when someone is given a more

important job in the same organization: *She was **given** a **promotion** in her first month with the company.*

prompt /prɒmpt/ *adj*
done or acting quickly and without waiting: *a prompt reply*
• **promptly** *adv*

pronoun /ˈprəʊnaʊn/ *noun*
a word that is used instead of a noun which has usually already been talked about. For example the words 'she', 'it', and 'mine' are pronouns.

pronounce /prəˈnaʊns/ *verb* (*present participle* **pronouncing**, *past* **pronounced**)
to make the sound of a letter or word: *How do you pronounce his name?*

pronunciation /prəˌnʌnsiˈeɪʃᵊn/ *noun*
how words are pronounced: *There are two different pronunciations of this word.*

proof /pruːf/ *noun* **[no plural]**
a fact or a piece of information that shows something exists or is true: *She showed us her passport as **proof of** her identity.* ○ *My landlord has asked for **proof that** I'm employed.*

propeller /prəˈpeləʳ/ *noun*
a piece of equipment that turns around and makes a ship or aeroplane move

propeller

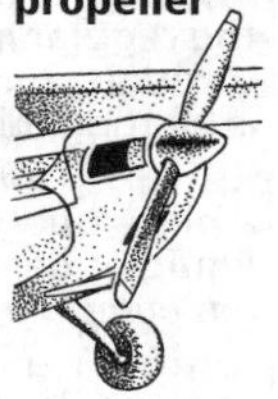

proper /ˈprɒpəʳ/ *adj*
1 correct or suitable: *Please put those books back in the proper place.*
2 *UK* real and satisfactory: *You should eat some proper food instead of just sweets.*

properly /ˈprɒpᵊli/ *adv*
correctly, or in a satisfactory way: *She doesn't eat properly.*

property /ˈprɒpəti/ *noun*
1 (*plural* **properties**) a building or area of land: *Private property – no parking.*
2 **[no plural]** objects that belong to someone: *The police recovered a large amount of stolen property.*

prophet /ˈprɒfɪt/ *noun*
someone sent by God to tell people what to do, or to say what will happen in the future

proportion /prəˈpɔːʃᵊn/ *noun*
a part of a total number or amount: *Children make up a large **proportion of** the world's population.*

proposal /prəˈpəʊzᵊl/ *noun*
1 a suggestion for a plan: *a **proposal to** raise taxes*
2 when someone asks someone to marry them

propose /prəˈpəʊz/ *verb* (*present participle* **proposing**, *past* **proposed**)
1 to suggest a plan or action: *I **propose that** we delay our decision until we have more information.*
2 to ask someone to marry you: *He **proposed to** me on my birthday.*

prosperous /ˈprɒspᵊrəs/ *adj*
successful, getting a lot of money

protect /prəˈtekt/ *verb*
to keep someone or something safe from something dangerous or bad: *It's important to **protect** your skin **from** the harmful effects of the sun.*
• **protection** /prəˈtekʃᵊn/ *noun* **[no plural]** when you keep someone or something safe from something dangerous or bad: *This coat doesn't provide any **protection against** the rain.*

protest[1] /ˈprəʊtest/ *noun*
when people show that they disagree with something by standing somewhere, shouting, carrying signs, etc: *There was a **protest against** the war.*

protest[2] /prəʊˈtest/ *verb*
to show that you disagree with something by standing somewhere, shouting, carrying signs, etc: *They're on strike to **protest against** job losses.*

Protestant /ˈprɒtɪstᵊnt/ *adj*
belonging or relating to part of the Christian religion
• **Protestant** *noun*

proud /praʊd/ *adj*
1 feeling very pleased about something of yours or something you have done: *She was so **proud of** her son.* ○ *I'm very **proud to** be involved in this project.*
2 feeling that you are more important than you really are
• **proudly** *adv*

prove /pruːv/ *verb* (*present participle*

a b c d e f g h i j k l m n o p q r s t u v w x y z

proving, *past* **proved)**
to show that something is true: *Can you **prove that** you weren't there? ○ He's desperately trying to prove his innocence.*

proverb /'prɒvɜːb/ *noun*
a famous phrase or sentence which gives you advice: *an ancient Chinese proverb*

provide /prəʊ'vaɪd/ *verb* (*present participle* **providing,** *past* **provided)**
to give something to someone: *It's a new scheme to **provide** schools **with** free computers.*

provided (that) /prəʊ'vaɪdɪd ðæt/ (*also* **providing (that))** *conjunction*
only if: *He's welcome to come, provided that he behaves himself.*

province /'prɒvɪns/ *noun*
one of the large areas which some countries are divided into: *the Canadian province of Alberta*

provision /prə'vɪʒ^{ə}n/ *noun* **[no plural]**
when something is given to someone: *We need to increase the **provision of** health care for the elderly.*

provoke /prə'vəʊk/ *verb* (*present participle* **provoking,** *past* **provoked)**
to cause a strong and usually angry reaction: *Her statement provoked an angry response.*

prowl /praʊl/ *verb*
to walk around somewhere slowly as if hunting: *to prowl the streets*

pub /pʌb/ *noun*
a place where you can get drinks such as beer and usually food

public[1] /'pʌblɪk/ *adj*
1 public awareness/health/support, etc the awareness/health/support, etc of all ordinary people: *Public opinion has turned against him.*
2 public parks/toilets/transport, etc parks/toilets/transport, etc that are for everyone to use: *Smoking should be banned in public places.*

public[2] /'pʌblɪk/ *noun* **[no plural]**
1 the (general) public all ordinary people: *a member of the public ○ The public has a right to know about this.*
2 in public where everyone can see you: *He shouldn't behave like that in public.*

publish /'pʌblɪʃ/ *verb*
1 to prepare and print a book, newspaper, magazine, article, etc so that people can buy it: *This book is published by Cambridge University Press.*
2 to make information available to the public

publisher /'pʌblɪʃə^{r}/ *noun*
a company or person who prepares and prints books, newspapers, magazines, etc

pudding /'pʊdɪŋ/ *noun*
in the UK, sweet food that is usually eaten as the last part of a meal: *We've got apple pie for pudding.*

puddle /'pʌdl/ *noun*
a pool of liquid on the ground, usually from rain

puff[1] /pʌf/ *verb*
to breathe fast and with difficulty, usually because you have been running

puff[2] /pʌf/ *noun*
a small amount of smoke, gas, powder, etc: *a puff of smoke*

pull /pʊl/ *verb*
to take hold of something and move it somewhere: *He **pulled off** his boots. ○ She bent down and **pulled up** her socks.*

pullover /'pʊləʊvə^{r}/ *noun*
a warm piece of clothing which covers the top of your body and is pulled on over your head

pulse /pʌls/ *noun*
the regular movement of blood through your body when your heart is beating: *My **pulse rate** is 70.*

pump[1] /pʌmp/ *noun*
a piece of equipment which forces liquid or gas to move somewhere: *a gas pump ○ a water pump*

pump[2] /pʌmp/ *verb*
to force liquid or gas to move somewhere: *Your heart pumps blood around your body.*

pump something up *phrasal verb*
to fill something with air using a pump: *You should pump your tyres up.*

pumpkin /'pʌmpkɪn/ *noun*
a large, round vegetable with thick, orange skin

pumpkin

punch[1] /pʌnʃ/ *verb*
1 to hit someone or something with your fist (= closed hand): *He punched me twice in the stomach.*

2 punch a hole in something to make a hole in something with a special piece of equipment

punch² /pʌnʃ/ *noun* (*plural* **punches**) when you hit someone or something with your fist (= closed hand): *a punch on the nose*

punctual /ˈpʌŋktʃuəl/ *adj* arriving at the right time and not too late
• **punctually** *adv*

punctuate /ˈpʌŋktʃueɪt/ *verb* (*present participle* **punctuating**, *past* **punctuated**) to add punctuation marks to written words

punctuation /ˌpʌŋktʃuˈeɪʃᵊn/ *noun* **[no plural]** the use of punctuation marks in writing so that people can see when a sentence begins and finishes, that something is a question, etc

punctuation mark /pʌŋktʃʊˈeɪʃᵊn ˌmɑːk/ *noun* a symbol used in punctuation

puncture¹ /ˈpʌŋktʃəʳ/ *noun*
1 a small hole made by a sharp object
2 *UK* a hole in a tyre that makes the air come out

puncture² /ˈpʌŋktʃəʳ/ *verb* (*present participle* **puncturing**, *past* **punctured**) to make a hole in something: *The knife went through his ribs and punctured his lung.*

punish /ˈpʌnɪʃ/ *verb* to make someone suffer because they have done something bad: *They must be severely* ***punished for*** *these crimes.*

punishment /ˈpʌnɪʃmənt/ *noun* when someone is punished: *He had to stay in his bedroom as a punishment for fighting.*

pupil /ˈpjuːpᵊl/ *noun*
1 a student at school: *The school has 1,100 pupils aged 11 to 18.*
2 the black, round part in the centre of your eye

puppet

puppet /ˈpʌpɪt/ *noun* a toy in the shape of a person or animal that you can move with strings or by putting your hand inside: *a glove puppet*

puppy /ˈpʌpi/ *noun* (*plural* **puppies**) a young dog

purchase¹ /ˈpɜːtʃəs/ *verb* (*present participle* **purchasing**, *past* **purchased**) *formal* to buy something: *Tickets must be purchased two weeks in advance.*

purchase² /ˈpɜːtʃəs/ *noun formal*
1 when you buy something: *the illegal purchase of guns*
2 something that you buy

pure /pjʊəʳ/ *adj*
1 A pure substance is not mixed with anything else: *pure gold*
2 clean and healthy: *pure air/water*

purely /pjʊəli/ *adv* only: *She married him purely for his money.*

purple /ˈpɜːpl/ *adj* being a colour that is a mixture of red and blue
• **purple** *noun* ➲See colour picture **Colours** on page Centre 6

purpose /ˈpɜːpəs/ *noun*
1 why you do something or why something exists: *The main* ***purpose of*** *the meeting is to discuss the future of the company.*
2 on purpose If you do something bad on purpose, you wanted or planned to do it: *I didn't do it on purpose, it was an accident.*

purposely /ˈpɜːpəsli/ *adv* wanting to do something: *I wasn't purposely trying to hurt you.*

purr /pɜːʳ/ *verb* If a cat purrs, it makes a soft sound in its throat to show pleasure.

purse /pɜːs/ *noun*
1 *UK* a small container for money, usually used by a woman: *a leather purse*
2 *US* (*UK* **handbag**) a bag, usually carried by a woman

pursue /pəˈsjuː/ *verb* (*present participle* **pursuing**, *past* **pursued**) to try to do something over a period of time: *She decided to pursue a career in television.*

push¹ /pʊʃ/ *verb*
1 to move someone or something by pressing them with your hands or body: *He* ***pushed*** *me* ***out*** *of the door.* ○ *Someone* ***pushed*** *him* ***into*** *the river.*

2 to press something: *If you push this button, your seat goes back.*

push² /pʊʃ/ *noun* (*plural* **pushes**)
when you move someone or something by pressing them with your hands or body: *She **gave** him a little **push** towards the door.*

pushchair /ˈpʊʃtʃeəʳ/ *UK* (*US* **stroller**) *noun*
a chair on wheels which is used to move small children

put /pʊt/ *verb* (*present participle* **putting**, *past* **put**)
to move something to a place or position: *Where have you put the keys?* ○ *She put her bag on the floor.* ○ *He put his arm around her.*

put something away *phrasal verb*
to put something in the place where you usually keep it: *She folded the towels and put them away in the cupboard.* ➲See colour picture **Phrasal Verbs** on page Centre 13

put something down *phrasal verb*
to put something that you are holding onto the floor or onto another surface: *I'll just put my bag down for a minute, it's rather heavy.* ➲See colour picture **Phrasal Verbs** on page Centre 13

put something off *phrasal verb*
to decide or arrange to do something at a later time: *I must talk to her about this, I can't put it off any longer.*

put someone off (something) *phrasal verb*
to make someone not like someone or something, or not want to do something: *Jan was talking about her operation and it put me off my food.*

put something on *phrasal verb*
to put clothes or shoes onto your body: *You'd better put your coat on, it's cold outside.* ➲See colour picture **Phrasal Verbs** on page Centre 13

put something out *phrasal verb*
to make something that is burning stop burning: *to put out a fire*

put up with someone/something *phrasal verb*
to accept something that is bad although you do not like it: *He's so rude, I don't know how you put up with him.*

puzzle /ˈpʌzl/ *noun*
1 a game or activity in which you have to put pieces together or answer questions using skill: *a jigsaw puzzle*
2 a situation which is very difficult to understand: *Scientists have been trying to **solve** this **puzzle** for years.*

puzzled /ˈpʌzld/ *adj*
confused because you do not understand something: *He had a puzzled look on his face.*

pyjamas /pɪˈdʒɑːməz/ *plural noun*
shirt and trousers that you wear in bed

pyjamas

pyramid /ˈpɪrəmɪd/ *noun*
a shape with a square base and four triangular sides that meet to form a point at the top

Qq

Q, q /kjuː/
the seventeenth letter of the alphabet

quack /kwæk/ *noun*
the sound made by a duck (= water bird)
• **quack** *verb*

quaint /kweɪnt/ *adj*
attractive and different in an old-fashioned way: *a quaint little village*

qualification /ˌkwɒlɪfɪˈkeɪʃᵊn/ *noun*
UK what you get when you pass an exam or a course: *medical qualifications* ○ *What qualifications do you need to be a nanny?*

qualified /ˈkwɒlɪfaɪd/ *adj*
having passed exams or courses: *a newly qualified teacher*

qualify /ˈkwɒlɪfaɪ/ *verb* (*present participle* **qualifying**, *past* **qualified**)
1 If you qualify for something, you are allowed to do it: *To* ***qualify for*** *the competition, you must be over 18.*
2 to succeed in getting into a competition: *Nigeria were the first team to* ***qualify for*** *the World Cup.*

quality /ˈkwɒləti/ *noun*
1 [no plural] how good or bad something is: *good/high quality* ○ *The air quality in this area is terrible.*
2 (*plural* **qualities**) part of the character of someone or something: *Anthony has leadership qualities.*

quantity /ˈkwɒntəti/ *noun* (*plural* **quantities**)
the amount or number of something: *A vast quantity of information is available on the Internet.*

quarrel¹ /ˈkwɒrᵊl/ *noun*
an argument: *She walked out after* ***having a quarrel*** *with her boss.*

quarrel² /ˈkwɒrᵊl/ *verb* (*present participle* **quarrelling**, *past* **quarrelled**)
to have an argument with someone: *She'd been* ***quarrelling with*** *her mother all morning.*

quarry /ˈkwɒri/ *noun* (*plural* **quarries**)
a place where stone is dug out of a large hole in the ground: *a marble quarry*

quarter /ˈkwɔːtəʳ/ *noun*
1 (*also US* **fourth**) one of four equal parts of something; ¼: *I waited a quarter of an hour for her.*
2 a period of 15 minutes before or after the hour: *It's* ***quarter to*** *three* (= 2.45). ○ *We're leaving at* ***quarter past*** *six* (= 6.15).

quarter

quay /kiː/ *noun*
a structure built next to water where ships stop and things are taken on and off

queen /kwiːn/ *noun*
1 a female ruler in some countries: *Queen Elizabeth II*
2 the wife of a king

quench /kwenʃ/ *verb*
quench your thirst to drink liquid so that you stop being thirsty

query /ˈkwɪəri/ *noun* (*plural* **queries**)
a question: *I have a query about the last exercise.*

question¹ /ˈkwestʃən/ *noun*
1 a sentence or phrase that asks you for information: *Is it OK if I* ***ask*** *you a few* ***questions****?* ○ *He refused to* ***answer*** *my* ***question****.*
2 [no plural] doubt: *There is* ***no question*** *that this was an accidental fire.*

question² /ˈkwestʃən/ *verb*
1 to ask someone questions: *Detectives were* ***questioning*** *a boy* ***about*** *the murder.*
2 to show or feel doubt about something: *I'm just* ***questioning whether*** *we need the extra staff.*

question mark /ˈkwestʃən ˌmɑːk/ *noun*
a mark (?) used at the end of a question

queue /kjuː/ *UK* (*US* **line**) *noun*
a row of people waiting for something, one behind the other: *Are you* ***in the queue****?*
• **queue (up)** *UK* (*US* **line up**) *verb*
to stand in a row in order to wait for something: *They're queueing up to get tickets.*

queue

a b c d e f g h i j k l m n o p **q** r s t u v w x y z

quick /kwɪk/ *adj*
doing something fast or taking only a short time: *I tried to catch him but he was too quick for me.*

quickly /ˈkwɪkli/ *adv*
fast or in a short time: *I quickly shut the door.*

quiet[1] /kwaɪət/ *adj*
1 making little or no noise: *Can you* ***be quiet****, please? We're trying to work.*
2 without much noise or activity: *I fancy a quiet night in tonight.*
• **quietly** *adv*

quiet[2] /kwaɪət/ *noun* **[no plural]**
when there is little or no noise: *She needs a bit of* ***peace and quiet****.*

quit /kwɪt/ *verb* (*present participle* **quitting,** *past* **quit)**
1 to leave your job: *She recently quit her job to spend more time with her family.*
2 to stop doing something: *I quit smoking and put on weight.*

quite /kwaɪt/ *adv*
1 *UK* a little or a lot but not completely: *I'm quite tired, but I'm happy to walk a little further.*
2 completely: *The two situations are quite different.*
3 quite a bit/a few/a lot, etc a large amount or number: *There are quite a few letters for you here.*

quiver /ˈkwɪvəʳ/ *verb*
to shake slightly

quiz /kwɪz/ *noun* (*plural* **quizzes)**
1 a game in which you answer questions: *a television quiz show*
2 *US* a short test on a subject in school

quota /ˈkwəʊtə/ *noun*
a limited amount of something that is officially allowed: *an import quota*

quotation /kwəʊˈteɪʃᵊn/ *noun*
a sentence or phrase that is taken out of a book, poem, or play: *a quotation from Shakespeare*

quote /kwəʊt/ *verb* (*present participle* **quoting,** *past* **quoted)**
1 to repeat what someone has said or written: *I was* ***quoting from*** *Marx.* ○ *Witnesses were* ***quoted as saying*** *there were two gunmen.*
2 to say how much a piece of work will cost before you do it

the Qur'an /kɒrˈɑːn/ *noun another spelling of*
the Koran (= the holy book of Islam)

Rr

R, r /ɑːʳ/
the eighteenth letter of the alphabet

rabbit /ˈræbɪt/ *noun*
a small animal with fur and long ears that lives in a hole in the ground

race[1] /reɪs/ *noun*
1 a competition in which people run, ride, drive, etc against each other in order to see who is the fastest: *a horse race*
2 one of the groups that people are divided into, having the same colour of skin or hair and other things that are the same: *people of many different races*

race[2] /reɪs/ *verb* (*present participle* **racing**, *past* **raced**)
1 to compete in a race: *I'll race you to the end of the road!*
2 to move somewhere very quickly: *I raced over to see what was the matter.*
3 to take someone somewhere very quickly: *Ambulances raced the injured to a nearby hospital.*

racial /ˈreɪʃᵊl/ *adj*
relating to people's race: *a racial minority*

racism /ˈreɪsɪzᵊm/ *noun* **[no plural]**
the belief that other races of people are not as good as your own

racist /ˈreɪsɪst/ *noun*
someone who believes that other races of people are not as good as their own
• **racist** *adj*: *a racist attack*

rack /ræk/ *noun*
a type of shelf that you can put things on or hang things from: *a luggage rack*

racket /ˈrækɪt/ *noun*
1 a piece of equipment that you use to hit a ball in sports such as tennis ➲See colour picture **Sports 2** on page Centre 16
2 *informal* a loud noise: *The neighbours were* ***making*** *such* ***a racket.***

racket

radar /ˈreɪdɑːʳ/ *noun* **[no plural]**
a system that uses radio waves to find out the position of something you cannot see

radiator /ˈreɪdieɪtəʳ/ *noun*
1 a metal piece of equipment that is filled with hot water and is used to heat a room ➲See colour picture **The Living Room** on page Centre 11
2 a part of a car that makes the engine cool

radio /ˈreɪdiəʊ/ *noun*
1 a piece of equipment used for listening to radio broadcasts: *a car radio*
2 the radio the programmes that you hear when you listen to the radio: *We heard him speaking* ***on the radio*** *this morning.*
3 [no plural] a system of sending and getting sound through the air: *local radio*

radius /ˈreɪdiəs/ *noun* (*plural* **radii**)
the distance from the centre of a circle to its edge

rag /ræg/ *noun*
a piece of old cloth that you use to clean things

rage /reɪdʒ/ *noun*
strong anger that you cannot control: *a jealous rage*

raid[1] /reɪd/ *noun*
a sudden attack on a place by soldiers: *an air raid*

raid[2] /reɪd/ *verb*
If soldiers raid a place, they suddenly attack it.

rail /reɪl/ *noun*
1 *UK* a bar on the wall that you hang things on: *a curtain rail*
2 [no plural] trains as a method of transport: *rail travel*

railing /ˈreɪlɪŋ/ *noun*
a fence made from posts and bars: *an iron railing*

railway /ˈreɪlweɪ/ *noun*
1 the metal tracks that trains travel on: *Repairs are being carried out on the railway.*
2 the railway(s) the organizations connected with trains: *He worked on the railways all his life.*

railway station /ˈreɪlweɪ ˌsteɪʃᵊn/ *noun*
a place where trains stop so that you can get on or off them

rain[1] /reɪn/ *noun* **[no plural]**
water that falls from the sky in small drops: *heavy rain*

rain[2] /reɪn/ *verb*
it rains If it rains, water falls from the sky in small drops: *It was raining all weekend.*

rainbow /ˈreɪnbəʊ/ *noun*
a half circle with seven colours that is sometimes in the sky when the sun shines through rain

rainbow

raincoat /ˈreɪnkəʊt/ *noun*
a coat that you wear when it is raining

raindrop /ˈreɪndrɒp/ *noun*
a single drop of rain

rainforest /ˈreɪnˌfɒrɪst/ *noun*
a forest with a lot of tall trees where it rains a lot: *a tropical rainforest*

rainy /ˈreɪni/ *adj*
raining a lot: *a rainy afternoon*

raise /reɪz/ *verb* (*present participle* **raising,** *past* **raised)**
1 to lift something to a higher position: *She raised her hand.*
2 to make an amount or level go up: *They have raised taxes.*
3 to look after a child until he or she has become an adult

raisin /ˈreɪz(ə)n/ *noun*
a dried grape (= small round fruit)

rally /ˈræli/ *noun* (*plural* **rallies)**
1 a large public meeting in support of something: *an election/campaign rally*
2 a car or motorcycle race: *a rally driver*

ram /ræm/ *noun*
a male sheep

RAM /ræm/ *noun* **[no plural]**
a computer's ability to immediately store information

ran /ræn/
past tense of run

ranch /rɑːnʃ/ *noun* (*plural* **ranches)**
a large farm where animals are kept: *a cattle ranch*

random /ˈrændəm/ *adj*
by chance: *Winners will be chosen* ***at random.***

rang /ræŋ/
past tense of ring[2]

range /reɪndʒ/ *noun*
1 a group of different things of the same general type: *We discussed a wide range of subjects.*
2 the amount or number between a particular set of limits: *The product is aimed at young people in the 18-25 age range.*
3 [no plural] the distance from which things can be seen, heard, or reached: *He was shot at close range* (= from very near).
4 a line of hills or mountains

rank /ræŋk/ *noun*
a position in society or in an organization, for example the army: *He holds the rank of colonel.*

ransom /ˈræns(ə)m/ *noun*
the money that is demanded for the return of someone who is being kept as a prisoner

rap /ræp/ *noun* **[no plural]**
a type of music in which the words are spoken and there is a strong beat: *a rap artist*

rapid /ˈræpɪd/ *adj*
happening or moving very quickly: *rapid change*
• **rapidly** *adv*

rare /reə(r)/ *adj* **(rarer, rarest)**
very unusual: *a rare disease* ○ *It's very* ***rare to*** *see these birds in England.*

rarely /ˈreəli/ *adv*
not often: *I rarely see her these days.*

rash[1] /ræʃ/ *noun* (*plural* **rashes)**
a group of small, red spots on the skin: *an itchy rash*

rash[2] /ræʃ/ *adj*
done suddenly and without thinking carefully: *It was a rash decision.*

rat /ræt/ *noun*
an animal that looks like a large mouse and has a long tail: *Rats carry disease.*

rat

rate /reɪt/ *noun*
1 how often something happens, or how many people something happens to: *the birth rate* ○ *the rate of unemployment*
2 a fixed amount of money given for

something: *rates of pay*
3 the speed at which something happens: *the rate of progress*

rather /ˈrɑːðəʳ/ *adv*
1 slightly: *I find her books rather dull.*
2 rather than instead of: *He saw his music as a hobby rather than a career.*
3 would rather If you would rather do something, you would prefer to do that thing: *I'd much rather go out for a meal than stay at home and watch TV.*

ration[1] /ˈræʃᵊn/ *noun*
the amount of something that you are allowed to have when there is little of it: *a food/petrol ration*

ration[2] /ˈræʃᵊn/ *verb*
to give people only a small amount of something because there is little of it: *They might have to start rationing water.*

rational /ˈræʃᵊnᵊl/ *adj*
based on facts and not affected by someone's emotions or imagination: *a rational decision*

rattle[1] /ˈrætl/ *verb* (*present participle* **rattling**, *past* **rattled**)
to keep making a noise by knocking against something: *The wind blew hard, rattling the doors and windows.*

rattle[2] /ˈrætl/ *noun*
a toy that a baby shakes to make a noise

raw /rɔː/ *adj*
not cooked: *raw meat/vegetables*

ray /reɪ/ *noun*
a narrow beam of light, heat, or energy: *the rays of the sun*

razor /ˈreɪzəʳ/ *noun*
a piece of equipment with a sharp blade used for removing hair from the face, legs, etc ↄSee colour picture **The Bathroom** on page Centre 1

razor

razor blade /ˈreɪzə ˌbleɪd/ *noun*
a very thin, sharp blade that you put in a razor

Rd *written abbreviation for* road: *17, Lynton Rd*

reach[1] /riːtʃ/ *verb*
1 to arrive somewhere: *We won't reach Miami till five or six o'clock.*
2 to stretch your arm and hand to touch or take something: *She* ***reached for*** *a cigarette.* ○ *He* ***reached out*** *and grabbed her arm.*
3 can reach (something) to be able to touch or take something with your hand: *Could you get that book down for me – I can't reach.*

reach[2] /riːtʃ/ *noun* **[no plural]**
1 out of reach too far away for someone to take hold of: *I keep the medicines up here, out of the childrens' reach.*
2 be within reach to be close enough for someone to take hold of: *The gun lay within reach.*

react /riˈækt/ *verb*
to say, do, or feel something because of something else that has been said or done: *He* ***reacted*** *angrily* ***to*** *her comments.*

reaction /riˈækʃᵊn/ *noun*
1 something you say, feel, or do because of something that has happened: *What was his* ***reaction to*** *the news?*
2 reactions *UK* the ability to move quickly when something suddenly happens: *Drivers need to have quick reactions.*

read /riːd/ *verb* (*present participle* **reading**, *past* **read**)
to look at words and understand what they mean: *What was the last book you read?* ○ *I've been* ***reading about*** *John F Kennedy.*

read something out *phrasal verb*
to read something and say the words so that other people can hear: *He read out the names of all the winners.*

reader /ˈriːdəʳ/ *noun*
someone who reads: *She's a slow reader.*

readily /ˈredɪli/ *adv*
quickly and easily: *Information is readily available on the Internet.*

ready /ˈredi/ *adj*
1 prepared for doing something: *Are you* ***ready to*** *go yet?* ○ *We're going at eight, so you've got an hour to* ***get ready****.*
2 prepared and available to be eaten, drunk, used, etc: *Is dinner ready?*

real /rɪəl/ *adj*
1 existing and not imagined: *He's not*

real you know, he's just a character in a book. ○ Romance is never like that ***in real life***.
2 not false: *real fur/leather*

realistic /ˌrɪə'lɪstɪk/ *adj*
accepting the true facts of a situation: *Let's be realistic – we're not going to finish this by Friday.*

reality /ri'æləti/ *noun* **[no plural]**
the way things or situations really are and not the way you would like them to be: *Listening to music is my escape from reality. ○ He may seem charming but **in reality** he's actually quite unpleasant.*

realize /'rɪəlaɪz/ *verb*
to notice or understand something that you did not notice or understand before: *I suddenly realized I'd met him before*

really /'rɪəli/ *adv*
1 very or very much: *She's really nice. ○ I really don't want to go. ○ "Did you like it then?" "**Not really**"* (= no).
2 used when you are saying what is the truth of a situation: *She tried to hide what she was really thinking.*
3 Really? used when you are surprised at what someone has just said: *"Apparently, he's leaving." "Really?"*

rear[1] /rɪə^r/ *noun*
the rear the back part of something: *the rear of the train*
• **rear** *adj*: *a rear window*

rear[2] /rɪə^r/ *verb*
If you rear children or young animals, you look after them until they are adults.

reason /'riːz^ən/ *noun*
1 the facts about why something happens or why someone does something: *Is there any particular **reason why** he doesn't want to come? ○ He left without **giving a reason**. ○ That was the **reason for** telling her.*
2 something that makes it right for you to do something: *I think we have **reason to** be concerned.*

reasonable /'riːz^ənəbl/ *adj*
1 fair and showing good judgment: *It's not reasonable to expect people to work those hours.*
2 big enough or large enough in number, although not very big or not many: *There were a reasonable number of people there.*
3 not expensive: *reasonable prices*

reasonably /'riːz^ənəbli/ *adv*
1 in a fair way, showing good judgment: *Why can't we discuss this reasonably, like adults?*
2 reasonably good/successful/well, etc good/successful/well, etc enough but not very good or very well: *I did reasonably well at school but not as well as my sister.*

reassure /ˌriːə'ʃʊə^r/ *verb*
to say something which stops someone from worrying: *He reassured me that I would be paid soon.*

rebel[1] /'reb^əl/ *noun*
someone who does not like authority and refuses to obey rules

rebel[2] /rɪ'bel/ *verb* (*present participle* **rebelling**, *past* **rebelled**)
to refuse to obey rules: *She **rebelled against** her family.*

rebellion /rɪ'beliən/ *noun*
when people fight against the government in their country

receipt /rɪ'siːt/ *noun*
a piece of paper that proves that you have received goods or money: *Could I have a receipt?*

receive /rɪ'siːv/ *verb* (*present participle* **receiving**, *past* **received**)
to get something that someone has given or sent to you: *Occasionally, he **receives** letters **from** fans.*

receiver /rɪ'siːvə^r/ *noun*
the part of a telephone that you hold in your hand and use for listening and speaking

recent /'riːs^ənt/ *adj*
happening or starting from a short time ago: *a recent photo ○ In recent years, sales have decreased.*

recently /'riːsəntli/ *adv*
not long ago: *Have you seen any good films recently?*

reception /rɪ'sepʃ^ən/ *noun*
1 the place in a hotel or office building where people go when they arrive: *Ask for me at reception.*
2 a formal party to celebrate a special event or to welcome someone: *a wedding reception*

recipe /'resɪpi/ *noun*
a list of foods and a set of instructions telling you how to cook something: *a recipe for carrot cake*

reckless /'rekləs/ *adj*
doing something dangerous and not

caring about what might happen: *reckless driving*
• **recklessly** *adv*

reckon /ˈrekᵊn/ *verb*
1 to think that something is probably true: *I reckon he likes her.*
2 to guess that a particular number is correct: *His fortune is* ***reckoned at*** *$5 million.*

recognition /ˌrekəgˈnɪʃᵊn/ *noun*
1 when you accept that something is true or real: *There is a growing* ***recognition of*** *the size of the problem.*
2 **[no plural]** when you know something or someone because you have seen them before: *I waved at her, but she showed no sign of recognition.*

recognize /ˈrekəgnaɪz/ *verb* (*present participle* **recognizing**, *past* **recognized**)
1 to know someone or something because you have seen them before: *I recognized her from her picture.*
2 to accept that something is true or real: *Smoking is* ***recognized as*** *a leading cause of lung cancer.*

recommend /ˌrekəˈmend/ *verb*
to say that someone or something is good or suitable for a particular purpose: *Can you recommend a good wine to go with this dish?*

recommendation /ˌrekəmen-ˈdeɪʃᵊn/ *noun*
a suggestion that someone or something is good or suitable for a particular purpose: *I bought this book* ***on*** *Andy's* ***recommendation***.

record[1] /ˈrekɔːd/ *noun*
1 information that is written on paper or stored on computer so that it can be used in the future: *medical records* ○ *My teacher* ***keeps*** *a* ***record of*** *my absences.*
2 A person's or company's record is their behaviour or achievements: *Of all airlines they have the best safety record.*
3 the best, biggest, longest, tallest, etc: *He* ***holds the*** *world* ***record*** *for 100 metres.*
4 a flat, round, plastic disc that music is stored on, used especially in the past: *to play a record*

record[2] /rɪˈkɔːd/ *verb*
1 to write down information or store it on a computer so that it can be used in the future: *He recorded details of their conversation in his diary.*
2 to store sounds or pictures using electronic equipment, a camera, etc so that you can listen to them or see them again: *They have just recorded a new album.* ○ *I recorded that programme for you.*

record-breaking /ˈrekɔːdˌbreɪkɪŋ/ *adj*
better, bigger, longer, etc than anything else before: *record-breaking sales of the new video*

recorder /rɪˈkɔːdəʳ/ *noun*
1 a machine for storing sounds or pictures: *a video recorder*
2 a long, thin instrument that you play by blowing into it

recording /rɪˈkɔːdɪŋ/ *noun*
sounds or moving pictures that have been recorded, or the process of recording: *a new system of digital recording*

recover /rɪˈkʌvəʳ/ *verb*
to become healthy again after being ill or hurt: *It takes a long time to* ***recover from*** *surgery.*

recovery /rɪˈkʌvᵊri/ *noun* **[no plural]**
when you feel better again after being ill or hurt: *She only had the operation last month but she's* ***made a*** *good* ***recovery***.

recreation /ˌrekriˈeɪʃᵊn/ *noun*
activities that you do for enjoyment when you are not working: *Shopping seems to be her only form of recreation.*
• **recreational** *adj*

recruit[1] /rɪˈkruːt/ *verb*
to try to persuade someone to join an organization
• **recruitment** *noun* **[no plural]**
when you recruit people: *graduate recruitment*

recruit[2] /rɪˈkruːt/ *noun*
someone who has recently joined an organization: *a new recruit*

rectangle /ˈrektæŋgl/ *noun*
a shape with four 90° angles and four sides, with opposite sides of equal length and two sides longer than the other two
• **rectangular** /rekˈtæŋgjələʳ/ *adj*
shaped like a rectangle: *a rectangular room*

recycle /ˌriːˈsaɪkl/ *verb* (*present participle* **recycling**, *past* **recycled**)
to use paper, glass, plastic, etc again

a b c d e f g h i j k l m n o p q **r** s t u v w x y z

and not throw it away: *We recycle all our newspapers and bottles.*

recycled /ˌriːˈsaɪkld/ *adj*
Recycled paper, glass, plastic, etc has been used before.

red[1] /red/ *adj*
being the same colour as blood: *a red shirt* ➲See colour picture **Colours** on page Centre 6

red[2] /red/ *noun*
the colour of blood ➲See colour picture **Colours** on page Centre 6

reduce /rɪˈdjuːs/ *verb* (*present participle* **reducing,** *past* **reduced)**
to make something less: *Prices have been reduced by almost 50 percent.*

reduction /rɪˈdʌkʃ(ə)n/ *noun*
when something is made less: *price reductions*

reel /riːl/ *noun*
an object shaped like a wheel that you can put film, thread, etc around

refer /rɪˈfɜː(r)/ *verb* (*present participle* **referring,** *past* **referred)**
refer to someone/something *phrasal verb*
1 to talk or write about someone or something: *She didn't once refer to her son.*
2 If writing or information refers to someone or something, it relates to that person or thing: *The sales figures refer to UK sales only.*

referee /ˌref(ə)rˈiː/ *noun*
someone who makes sure that players follow the rules during a sports game ➲See colour picture **Sports 2** on page Centre 16

reference /ˈref(ə)r(ə)ns/ *noun*
1 when you say or write a few words about someone or something: *In his book, he* ***makes*** *several* ***references to*** *his time in France.*
2 [no plural] when you look at information: *Please keep this handout for* ***future reference*** (= to look at in the future).
3 a letter that is written by someone who knows you, to say if you are suitable for a job or course

reflect /rɪˈflekt/ *verb*
1 to show or be a sign of something: *The statistics reflect a change in people's spending habits.*
2 If a surface such as a mirror or water reflects something, you can see the image of that thing in the mirror, water, etc: *He saw himself* ***reflected in*** *the shop window.*

reflection

reflection /rɪˈflekʃ(ə)n/ *noun*
1 the image of something in a mirror, on a shiny surface, etc: *I saw my reflection in the window.*
2 a reflection of something
something that is a sign or result of a particular situation: *His poor job performance is a reflection of his lack of training.*

reform[1] /rɪˈfɔːm/ *noun*
when changes are made to improve a system, organization, or law: *political reform*

reform[2] /rɪˈfɔːm/ *verb*
to change a system, organization, or law in order to improve it: *Efforts have been made to reform the education system.*

refreshed /rɪˈfreʃt/ *adj*
feeling less tired: *I felt refreshed after a good night's sleep.*

refreshing /rɪˈfreʃɪŋ/ *adj*
1 different and interesting: *It's refreshing to see a film that's so original.*
2 making you feel less hot or tired: *a refreshing shower*

refreshments /rɪˈfreʃmənts/ *plural noun*
food and drinks that are given at a meeting, on a journey, etc

refrigerator /rɪˈfrɪdʒ(ə)reɪtə(r)/ *noun*
a large container that uses electricity to keep food cold ➲See colour picture **Kitchen** on page Centre 10

refuge /ˈrefjuːdʒ/ *noun*
a place where you are protected from danger: *a refuge for homeless people*

refugee /ˌrefjʊ'dʒiː/ *noun*
someone who has been forced to leave their country, especially because of a war: *a refugee camp*

refusal /rɪ'fjuːzᵊl/ *noun*
when someone says they will not do or accept something: *I was surprised by his* ***refusal to*** *admit his mistake.*

refuse[1] /rɪ'fjuːz/ *verb (present participle* **refusing,** *past* **refused)**
to say that you will not do or accept something: *I asked him to leave but he refused.* ○ *Cathy* ***refuses to*** *admit that she was wrong.*

refuse[2] /'refjuːs/ *noun* **[no plural]** *formal*
things that no one needs that have been thrown away: *a pile of refuse*

regard[1] /rɪ'gɑːd/ *verb*
to think of someone or something in a particular way: *She is generally* ***regarded as*** *one of the greatest singers this century.*

regard[2] /rɪ'gɑːd/ *noun* **[no plural]**
respect or admiration for someone or something: *I* ***have*** *the greatest* ***regard for*** *her.*

regarding /rɪ'gɑːdɪŋ/ *preposition formal*
about or relating to: *I am writing to you regarding your application dated 29 April.*

regardless /rɪ'gɑːdləs/ *adv*
regardless of something despite something: *She'll make a decision regardless of what we think.*

regards /rɪ'gɑːdz/ *plural noun*
friendly greetings: ***Give my regards*** *to your mother when you see her.*

reggae /'regeɪ/ *noun* **[no plural]**
a type of popular music from Jamaica with a strong beat

regiment /'redʒɪmənt/ *noun*
a large group of soldiers

region /'riːdʒᵊn/ *noun*
a particular area in a country or the world: *China's coastal region*

register[1] /'redʒɪstəʳ/ *noun*
an official list of names: *the class register*

register[2] /'redʒɪstəʳ/ *verb*
1 to put information about someone or something, especially a name, on an official list: *Students need to* ***register for*** *the course by the end of April.*
2 to show an amount on an instrument that measures something: *The earthquake registered 7.3 on the Richter scale.*

registration /ˌredʒɪ'streɪʃᵊn/ *noun* **[no plural]** when a name or information is recorded on an official list

regret[1] /rɪ'gret/ *verb (present participle* **regretting,** *past* **regretted)**
to feel sorry about a situation, especially something that you wish you had not done: *If you don't tell her the truth you'll regret it later.* ○ *I really regret leaving school so young.*

regret[2] /rɪ'gret/ *noun*
a feeling of sadness about a situation, especially something that you wish you had not done: *We married very young but we've been really happy and I've* ***no regrets****.*

regular /'regjələʳ/ *adj*
1 repeated with the same amount of time or space between one thing and the next: *a regular pulse* ○ *Plant the trees at regular intervals.*
2 happening or doing something often, especially at the same time every week, year, etc: *a regular visitor to Brussels*
3 *US* usual or normal: *I couldn't see my regular dentist.*
4 *informal* being a standard size: *a burger and regular fries*
5 following the usual rules or patterns in grammar: *'Talk' is a regular verb but 'go' is not.* ⊃Opposite **irregular**
• **regularity** /ˌregjə'lærəti/ *noun* **[no plural]**
when something is regular

regularly /'regjələli/ *adv*
1 often: *Accidents occur regularly on this stretch of the road.*
2 at the same time each day, week, month, etc: *They meet regularly – usually once a week.*

regulation /ˌregjə'leɪʃᵊn/ *noun*
an official rule that controls how something is done: *building regulations*

rehearsal /rɪ'hɜːsᵊl/ *noun*
a time when people practise a play, dance, etc. in order to prepare for a performance

a b c d e f g h i j k l m n o p q r s t u v w x y z

rehearse /rɪˈhɜːs/ *verb* (*present participle* **rehearsing**, *past* **rehearsed**)
to practise a play, dance, etc in order to prepare for a performance

reign[1] /reɪn/ *noun*
a period of time when a king or queen rules a country: *the reign of Henry VIII*

reign[2] /reɪn/ *verb*
to be the king or queen of a country: *Queen Victoria reigned for 64 years.*

rein /reɪn/ *noun*
a long, thin piece of leather that helps you to control a horse: *Hold the reins in your left hand.* ➲See colour picture **Sports 1** on page Centre 15

reindeer /ˈreɪndɪəʳ/ *noun* (*plural* **reindeer**)
a type of deer with large horns that lives in northern parts of Europe, Asia, and America

reject /rɪˈdʒekt/ *verb*
1 to refuse to accept or agree with something: *The United States government rejected the proposal.*
2 to refuse to accept someone for a job, course, etc

rejection /rɪˈdʒekʃᵊn/ *noun*
1 when you refuse to accept or agree with something: *Their **rejection of** the peace plan is very disappointing for the government.*
2 a letter that says you have not been successful in getting a job, a place at college, etc: *I've sent off ten applications but I've only had rejections so far.*

relate /rɪˈleɪt/ *verb* (*present participle* **relating**, *past* **related**)
to be connected, or to find or show the connection between two or more things: *How do the two proposals relate?*
relate to someone/something *phrasal verb*
to be connected to someone or something: *Please provide all information relating to the claim.*

related /rɪˈleɪtɪd/ *adj*
If two or more people are related, they belong to the same family: *Did you know that I'm **related to** Jackie?*

relation /rɪˈleɪʃᵊn/ *noun*
someone who belongs to the same family as you

relationship /rɪˈleɪʃᵊnʃɪp/ *noun*
1 the way two people feel and behave towards each other: *He has a very good **relationship with** his older sister.*
2 a sexual or romantic friendship: *I don't feel ready for a relationship at the moment.*

relative /ˈrelətɪv/ *noun*
someone in your family: *a party for friends and relatives*

relatively /ˈrelətɪvli/ *adv*
quite, when compared with other things or people: *Students will find the course relatively easy.*

relax /rɪˈlæks/ *verb*
to become happy and comfortable because nothing is worrying you, or to make someone do this: *I find it difficult to relax.*
• **relaxation** /ˌriːlækˈseɪʃᵊn/ *noun* **[no plural]**

relaxed /rɪˈlækst/ *adj*
feeling happy and comfortable because nothing is worrying you: *She seemed relaxed and in control of the situation.*

relaxing /rɪˈlæksɪŋ/ *adj*
making you feel relaxed: *a relaxing bath*

release[1] /rɪˈliːs/ *verb* (*present participle* **releasing**, *past* **released**)
1 to allow a prisoner to be free: *Six hostages were released shortly before midday.*
2 to make a record or film ready for people to buy or see: *The album is due to be released in time for Christmas.*

release[2] /rɪˈliːs/ *noun*
when someone is allowed to leave prison: *After his release from jail, Jackson found it difficult to find work.*

reliable /rɪˈlaɪəbl/ *adj*
able to be trusted or believed: *a reliable car ○ reliable information*
➲Opposite **unreliable**

relief /rɪˈliːf/ *noun* **[no plural]**
the good feeling that you have when something bad stops or does not happen: *It was such a relief when the exams were over.*

relieve /rɪˈliːv/ *verb* (*present participle* **relieving**, *past* **relieved**)
to make pain or a bad feeling less bad: *Breathing exercises can help to relieve stress.*

relieved /rɪˈliːvd/ *adj*
feeling happy because something bad did not happen: *I'm just* ***relieved that*** *she's safe and well.*

religion /rɪˈlɪdʒᵊn/ *noun*
the belief in a god or gods, or a particular system of belief in a god or gods: *the Christian religion*

religious /rɪˈlɪdʒəs/ *adj*
1 relating to religion: *religious paintings*
2 having a strong belief in a religion: *He's a very religious man.*

reluctant /rɪˈlʌktᵊnt/ *adj*
not wanting to do something: *I'm* ***reluctant to*** *spend all that money.*
• **reluctance** /rɪˈlʌktᵊns/ *noun* **[no plural]** when someone does not want to do something
• **reluctantly** *adv*

rely /rɪˈlaɪ/ *verb* (*present participle* **relying,** *past* **relied)**
rely on someone/something
to need someone or something: *Families rely more on wives' earnings than before.*

remain /rɪˈmeɪn/ *verb*
1 to continue to exist when everything or everyone else has gone: *Only a few hundred of these animals remain today.*
2 to continue to be in the same state: *Despite the chaos around him, he remained calm.*

remaining /rɪˈmeɪnɪŋ/ *adj*
continuing to exist when everything or everyone else has gone or been done: *Mix in half the butter and keep the remaining 50g for later.*

remains /rɪˈmeɪnz/ *plural noun*
the parts of something that exist when other parts of it have gone: *the remains of a Buddhist temple*

remark¹ /rɪˈmɑːk/ *noun*
something that you say: *He* ***made a remark*** *about her clothes.*

remark² /rɪˈmɑːk/ *verb*
to say something: *He* ***remarked that*** *she was looking thin.*

remarkable /rɪˈmɑːkəbl/ *adj*
very unusual in a way that you admire: *He has a remarkable memory.*

remarkably /rɪˈmɑːkəbli/ *adv*
in a way that makes you feel surprised: *She is remarkably young-looking for 50.*

remedy /ˈremədi/ *noun* (*plural* **remedies)**
1 something that makes you better when you are ill: *a flu remedy*
2 something that stops a problem: *So what is the* ***remedy for*** *the traffic problem?*

remember /rɪˈmembəʳ/ *verb*
to keep something in your mind, or bring it back into your mind: *I can't remember his name.* ○ *I don't remember signing a contract.* ○ *I suddenly* ***remembered that*** *it was her birthday.*

remind /rɪˈmaɪnd/ *verb*
to make someone remember something, or remember to do something: *Every time we meet he* ***reminds*** *me* ***about*** *the money he lent me.* ○ *Will you* ***remind*** *me* ***to*** *buy some eggs?*
remind someone of something/someone *phrasal verb*
to make someone think of something or someone else: *This song reminds me of our trip to Spain.*

remote /rɪˈməʊt/ *adj*
far away: *a remote mountain village*

remote control /rɪˈməʊt kənˈtrəʊl/ *noun*

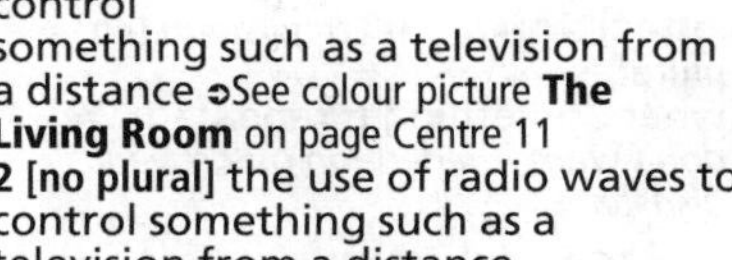
remote control

1 (*also* **remote)** a piece of equipment that is used to control something such as a television from a distance ➲See colour picture **The Living Room** on page Centre 11
2 [no plural] the use of radio waves to control something such as a television from a distance

remotely /rɪˈməʊtli/ *adv*
not remotely interested/surprised, etc not at all interested, surprised, etc: *I'm not remotely interested in football.*

removal /rɪˈmuːvᵊl/ *noun* **[no plural]**
when you remove something: *stain removal*

remove /rɪˈmuːv/ *verb* (*present participle* **removing,** *past* **removed)**
1 to take something away: *An operation was needed to* ***remove*** *the bullets* ***from*** *his chest.*
2 to take something off: *She removed her jacket and hung it on a chair.*

a b c d e f g h i j k l m n o p q r s t u v w x y z

rent[1] /rent/ *verb*
1 to pay money to live in a building that someone else owns: *He rents an apartment.*
2 *US* (*UK* **hire**) to pay money to use something for a short time: *We could rent a car for the weekend.*

rent[2] /rent/ *noun*
the amount of money that you pay to live in a building that someone else owns

repaid /ˌriːˈpeɪd/
past of repay

repair[1] /rɪˈpeəʳ/ *verb*
to fix something that is broken or damaged: *I must **get** my bike **repaired**.*

repair[2] /rɪˈpeəʳ/ *noun*
something that you do to fix something that is broken or damaged: *The repairs cost me £150.*

repay /ˌriːˈpeɪ/ *verb* (*present participle* **repaying,** *past* **repaid**)
to pay back money that you have borrowed: *to repay a loan*

repeat /rɪˈpiːt/ *verb*
to say or do something more than once: *He repeated the number.* ○ *The test must be repeated several times.*

repeated /rɪˈpiːtɪd/ *adj*
done or happening more than once: *He has refused repeated requests to be interviewed.*
• **repeatedly** *adv*: *The victim was stabbed repeatedly with a knife.*

repetition /ˌrepɪˈtɪʃᵊn/ *noun* **[no plural]**
when something is repeated: *We don't want a repetition of last year's disaster.*

replace /rɪˈpleɪs/ *verb* (*present participle* **replacing,** *past* **replaced**)
to get a new thing in place of something older: *We'll have to replace this carpet soon.*

replacement /rɪˈpleɪsmənt/ *noun*
a new thing or person in place of something or someone that was there before: *It's not going to be easy to find a replacement for you.*

replay /ˈriːpleɪ/ *noun UK*
a game of sport that is played again

reply[1] /rɪˈplaɪ/ *verb* (*present participle* **replying,** *past* **replied**)
to answer: *"I don't understand," she replied.* ○ *He didn't **reply to** my email.*

reply[2] /rɪˈplaɪ/ *noun* (*plural* **replies**)
an answer: *Have you had a **reply to** your letter?*

report[1] /rɪˈpɔːt/ *noun*
1 a description of something that happened: *a police report*
2 *UK* when teachers write about a child's progress at school for their parents

report[2] /rɪˈpɔːt/ *verb*
1 to describe something that has just happened, especially on television, radio, or in a newspaper: *She **reported that** the situation had changed dramatically.*
2 to tell someone in authority that something has happened, especially an accident or crime: *He should have reported the accident immediately.*

reporter /rɪˈpɔːtəʳ/ *noun*
someone whose job is to discover information about news events and describe them on television, radio, or in a newspaper

represent /ˌreprɪˈzent/ *verb*
1 to officially speak for someone else because they have asked you to: *The union represents over 200 employees.*
2 to be a sign or symbol of something: *The crosses on the map represent churches.*

representative /ˌreprɪˈzentətɪv/ *noun*
someone who speaks or does something officially for another person

reproduce /ˌriːprəˈdjuːs/ *verb* (*present participle* **reproducing,** *past* **reproduced**)
1 to make a copy of something
2 *formal* If people, animals, or plants reproduce, they produce babies or young animals or plants.

reproduction /ˌriːprəˈdʌkʃᵊn/ *noun*
1 [no plural] the process of producing babies or young animals and plants
2 a copy of something, especially a painting

reptile /ˈreptaɪl/ *noun*
an animal whose body is covered with scales (= pieces of hard skin), and whose blood changes temperature, for example a snake

republic /rɪˈpʌblɪk/ *noun*
a country with no king or queen but

with an elected government: *France is a republic.*

reputation /ˌrepjəˈteɪʃᵊn/ *noun* the opinion that people have about someone or something: *Both hotels have a good reputation.*

request /rɪˈkwest/ *noun* when you ask for something: *His doctor **made** an urgent **request for** a copy of the report.*

request /rɪˈkwest/ *verb* to ask for something: *We have requested two more computers.*

require /rɪˈkwaɪəʳ/ *verb* (*present participle* **requiring**, *past* **required**) to need something: *The job requires a high level of concentration.*

requirement /rɪˈkwaɪəmənt/ *noun* something that is needed: *college entrance requirements*

rescue[1] /ˈreskjuː/ *verb* (*present participle* **rescuing**, *past* **rescued**) to save someone from a dangerous situation: *Fifty passengers had to be rescued from a sinking ship.*

rescue[2] /ˈreskjuː/ *noun* when someone is saved from a dangerous situation: *a rescue attempt*

research[1] /rɪˈsɜːtʃ/ *noun* **[no plural]** when someone studies a subject in order to discover new information: *She does research into language development.*

research[2] /rɪˈsɜːtʃ/ *verb* to study a subject in order to discover new information about it
• **researcher** *noun*

resemblance /rɪˈzembləns/ *noun* the way in which two people or things appear similar: *There's a striking **resemblance between** Diane and her mother.*

resemble /rɪˈzembl/ *verb* (*present participle* **resembling**, *past* **resembled**) to look like or be like someone or something: *She resembles her father.*

resent /rɪˈzent/ *verb* to feel angry and upset about an unfair situation: *I resent having to work late.*

resentment /rɪˈzentmənt/ *noun* **[no plural]** a feeling of anger about an unfair situation

reservation /ˌrezəˈveɪʃᵊn/ *noun* an arrangement that you make to have a seat on an aeroplane, a room in a hotel, etc: *I'd like to **make a reservation** for Friday evening.*

reserve[1] /rɪˈzɜːv/ *verb* (*present participle* **reserving**, *past* **reserved**) to arrange to have a seat on an aeroplane, a room in a hotel, etc: *I'd like to reserve two seats on the 9:15 to Birmingham.*

reserve[2] /rɪˈzɜːv/ *noun*
1 an amount of something that you keep until it is needed: *emergency cash reserves*
2 in reserve ready to be used if needed: *I always keep a little money in reserve.*

reservoir /ˈrezəvwɑːʳ/ *noun* a place where water is kept before it goes to people's houses

residence /ˈrezɪdᵊns/ *noun formal* a building where someone lives: *the Queen's official residence*

resident /ˈrezɪdᵊnt/ *noun* someone who lives in a particular place: *We have had complaints from local residents.*

residential /ˌrezɪˈdenʃᵊl/ *adj* A residential area has only houses and not offices or factories.

resign /rɪˈzaɪn/ *verb* to officially tell your employer that you are leaving your job: *Mr Aitken has **resigned from** the company.*
resign yourself to something *phrasal verb* to make yourself accept something bad because you cannot change it: *He resigned himself to living alone.*

resignation /ˌrezɪɡˈneɪʃᵊn/ *noun*
1 when someone tells their employer that they are leaving their job: *a letter of resignation* ○ *I **handed in my resignation** yesterday.*
2 [no plural] when you accept something bad because you cannot change it

resist /rɪˈzɪst/ *verb*
1 to stop yourself from doing something that you want to do: *I can't resist chocolate.*
2 to refuse to accept something and try to stop it from happening: *The President is resisting calls for him to resign.*
3 to fight against someone or

a b c d e f g h i j k l m n o p q r s t u v w x y z

something that is attacking you: *British troops resisted the attack for two days.*

resistance /rɪˈzɪstᵊns/ *noun* **[no plural]**
when people disagree with a change, idea, etc and refuse to accept it: *resistance to political change*

resolution /ˌrezᵊlˈuːʃᵊn/ *noun*
a promise to yourself to do something: *My **New Year's resolution** is to do more exercise.*

resolve /rɪˈzɒlv/ *verb* (*present participle* **resolving**, *past* **resolved**)
formal to decide that you will certainly do something: *I have **resolved to** lose some weight.*

resort /rɪˈzɔːt/ *noun*
a place where many people go for a holiday: *a ski resort*

resource /rɪˈzɔːs/ *noun*
something that a country, person, or organization has which they can use: *financial/natural resources*

respect¹ /rɪˈspekt/ *noun*
1 [no plural] when you are polite to someone, especially because they are older or more important than you: *You should show more **respect for** your parents.*
2 in this respect/many respects in a particular way, or in many ways: *The school has changed in many respects.*

respect² /rɪˈspekt/ *verb*
to admire someone because they know a lot or have done good things: *I **respect** him **for** his honesty.*

respectable /rɪˈspektəbl/ *adj*
behaving well, in a way that most people think is right: *a respectable family*

respond /rɪˈspɒnd/ *verb*
to answer someone or react to something: *How quickly did the police **respond to** the call?*

response /rɪˈspɒns/ *noun*
an answer or reaction to something that has been said or done: *I'm writing **in response to** your letter of 14 February.*

responsibility /rɪˌspɒnsəˈbɪləti/ *noun* (*plural* **responsibilities**)
something that it is your job or duty to do: *It is your **responsibility to** make sure that your homework is done on time.*

responsible /rɪˈspɒnsəbl/ *adj*
1 having to do something as your duty: *I'm **responsible for** organizing the conferences.*
2 having caused something to happen, especially something bad: *Who was **responsible for** the accident?*

rest¹ /rest/ *noun*
1 the rest the part of something that remains: *Do you want to spend **the rest of** your life with him?*
2 a period of time when you relax or sleep: *Why don't you **have a rest**?*

rest² /rest/ *verb*
1 to relax or sleep because you are tired: *Pete's resting after his long drive.*
2 to put something on or against a surface: *She rested her head on his shoulder.*

restaurant /ˈrestərɒnt/ *noun*
a place where you can buy and eat a meal: *an Italian restaurant*

restful /ˈrestfᵊl/ *adj*
making you calm and relaxed: *restful music*

restless /ˈrestləs/ *adj*
not able to be still or relax because you are bored or nervous: *The audience was getting restless.*

restore /rɪˈstɔːʳ/ *verb* (*present participle* **restoring**, *past* **restored**)
1 to make something good exist again: *We hope to restore peace in the region.*
2 to repair something old: *to restore antiques*

restrain /rɪˈstreɪn/ *verb*
to stop someone doing something, sometimes by using force: *He became violent and had to be physically restrained.*

restrict /rɪˈstrɪkt/ *verb*
to limit something: *They've brought in new laws to restrict the sale of cigarettes.* ○ *I **restrict** myself **to** two glasses of wine most evenings.*

restriction /rɪˈstrɪkʃᵊn/ *noun*
a rule or law that limits what people can do: *parking restrictions*

restroom /ˈrestruːm/ *noun US*
a room with toilets that is in a public place

result¹ /rɪˈzʌlt/ *noun*
something that happens or exists because something else has happened: *Most accidents are **the***

result of *human error.*

result² /rɪ'zʌlt/ *verb*

result in something *phrasal verb*
to be the reason something happens: *The improvements in training resulted in better performance.*

retire /rɪ'taɪəʳ/ *verb* (*present participle* **retiring**, *past* **retired**)
to leave your job and stop working because you are old: *She* ***retired from*** *the company in 1990.*

retirement /rɪ'taɪəmənt/ *noun* **[no plural]**
the period of your life after you have stopped working: *We wish you a long and happy retirement.*

retreat /rɪ'triːt/ *verb*
When soldiers retreat, they move away from the enemy, especially to avoid fighting: *The army was forced to retreat.*

return¹ /rɪ'tɜːn/ *verb*
1 to go or come back to a place where you were before: *She* ***returned to*** *America in 1954.*
2 to give, send, or put something back where it came from: *I have to return the book by Friday.*

return² /rɪ'tɜːn/ *noun*
1 when someone goes or comes back to a place where they were before: ***On*** *his* ***return*** *to Sydney, he started up a business.*
2 *UK* a ticket that lets you travel to a place and back again
3 **[no plural]** a key on a computer keyboard that is used to make the computer accept information: *Type in the password and* ***press return***.

reveal /rɪ'viːl/ *verb*
to tell someone a piece of secret information: *It was revealed in this morning's papers that the couple intend to marry.*

revenge /rɪ'vendʒ/ *noun* **[no plural]**
something that you do to punish someone who has done something bad to you: *He was shot* ***in revenge*** *for the murder.*

Reverend /'revᵊrᵊnd/ *adj*
used as a title before the name of some Christian officials: *the Reverend Clive Jones*

reverse /rɪ'vɜːs/ *verb* (*present participle* **reversing**, *past* **reversed**)
1 to drive backwards: *I reversed into a parking space.*
2 to change a situation or change the order of things so that it becomes the opposite: *It is unlikely that the judge will reverse his decision.*

review /rɪ'vjuː/ *noun*
a piece of writing in a newspaper that gives an opinion about a new book, film, etc: *a book review*

revise /rɪ'vaɪz/ *verb* (*present participle* **revising**, *past* **revised**)
1 to change something so that it is more accurate: *a revised edition of the book*
2 *UK* (*US* **review**) to study a subject before you take a test

revision /rɪ'vɪʒᵊn/ *noun* **[no plural]**
UK when you study a subject before taking a test

revive /rɪ'vaɪv/ *verb* (*present participle* **reviving**, *past* **revived**)
to become conscious again or make someone conscious again: *A police officer tried to revive her.*

revolt /rɪ'vəʊlt/ *noun*
when people try to change a government, often using violence

revolting /rɪ'vəʊltɪŋ/ *adj*
very unpleasant: *The food was revolting.*

revolution /ˌrevᵊl'uːʃᵊn/ *noun*
a change in the way a country is governed, usually to a different political system and often using violence: *the French Revolution*

revolutionary /ˌrevᵊl'uːʃᵊnᵊri/ *adj*
1 completely different from what was done before: *a revolutionary new medical treatment*
2 relating to a political revolution: *a revolutionary movement*

revolve /rɪ'vɒlv/ *verb* (*present participle* **revolving**, *past* **revolved**)
to move in a circle around a central point: *A fan was revolving slowly.*

revolver /rɪ'vɒlvəʳ/ *noun*
a small gun

reward¹ /rɪ'wɔːd/ *noun*
something good that you get because you have done something good: *There'll be a* ***reward for*** *whoever finishes first.*

reward² /rɪ'wɔːd/ *verb*
to give a reward to someone: *She was* ***rewarded for*** *her bravery.*

a b c d e f g h i j k l m n o p q r s t u v w x y z

rewind /ˈriːwaɪnd/ *verb* (*present participle* **rewinding**, *past* **rewound**)
to make a sound or television recording go back to the beginning

rheumatism /ˈruːmətɪzᵊm/ *noun* **[no plural]**
a disease in which there is pain in the joints (= parts of the body where bones connect)

rhino /ˈraɪnəʊ/ *noun short for* rhinoceros

rhinoceros /raɪˈnɒsᵊrəs/ *noun* (*plural* **rhinoceroses**)
a large animal from Africa or Asia that has thick skin and one or two horns on its nose

rhyme¹ /raɪm/ *verb* (*present participle* **rhyming**, *past* **rhymed**)
If a word rhymes with another word, the end part of the words sound the same: *'Moon' rhymes with 'June.'*

rhyme² /raɪm/ *noun*
1 a short poem that has words that rhyme at the end of each line
2 a word that rhymes with another word

rhythm /ˈrɪðᵊm/ *noun*
a regular, repeating pattern of sound: *You need a sense of rhythm to be a good dancer.*
• **rhythmically** *adv*

rib /rɪb/ *noun*
one of the curved bones in the chest

ribbon /ˈrɪbᵊn/ *noun*
a long, thin piece of cloth that is used for decoration

rice /raɪs/ *noun* **[no plural]**
small grains from a plant that are cooked and eaten ➲See colour picture **Food** on page Centre 7

rich /rɪtʃ/ *adj*
1 A rich person has a lot of money. ➲Opposite **poor**
2 Rich food has a lot of butter, cream, or eggs in it: *a rich sauce*

rid /rɪd/ *adj* **get rid of something**
to throw something away: *We must get rid of some of those old books.*

ridden /ˈrɪdᵊn/
past participle of ride

riddle /ˈrɪdl/ *noun*
a strange and difficult question that has a clever and often funny answer

ride¹ /raɪd/ *verb* (*present participle* **riding**, *past tense* **rode**, *past participle* **ridden**)
to travel by sitting on a horse, bicycle, or motorcycle and controlling it: *I ride my bike to work.*

ride² /raɪd/ *noun*
a journey in a car or train: *Can I give you a ride to the station?*

rider /ˈraɪdəʳ/ *noun*
someone who rides a horse, bicycle, or motorcycle

ridiculous /rɪˈdɪkjələs/ *adj*
very silly: *It was a ridiculous suggestion.*

rifle /ˈraɪfl/ *noun*
a long gun that you hold against your shoulder when you shoot

right¹ /raɪt/ *adj*
1 correct or true: *He only got half the answers right.* ○ *You're* ***right about*** *Alison – she's incredible!* ○ *"You came here in 1979, didn't you?"* ***"That's right."***
2 on or towards the side of your body that is to the east when you are facing north: *your right hand*

right² /raɪt/ *adv*
1 exactly in a place or time: *He's right here with me.*
2 correctly: *Nothing was going right.*
3 to the right side: *Turn right after the bridge.*
4 right away/now immediately: *Do you want to start right away?*
5 all the way: *Did you read it right through to the end?*

right³ /raɪt/ *noun*
1 something that the law allows you to do: *the* ***right to*** *vote*
2 [no plural] the right side of your body, or the direction towards this side: *You'll find her in the second room* ***on the right.***
3 [no plural] morally good behaviour: *She knows the difference between right and wrong.*

right angle /ˈraɪt æŋgl/ *noun*
an angle of the type that is in a square

right-handed /ˌraɪtˈhændɪd/ *adj*
using your right hand to do most things

rigid /ˈrɪdʒɪd/ *adj*
1 not able to change or be changed easily: *I found the rules a little too rigid.*
2 not able to bend or move easily: *a rigid structure*

rim /rɪm/ *noun*

the edge of something round: *the rim of a cup*

rind /raɪnd/ *noun*
the thick skin of fruits such as oranges and lemons and other foods, for example cheese

ring[1] /rɪŋ/ *noun*
1 a round piece of jewellery that you wear on your finger: *a wedding ring*
2 something that is the shape of a circle: *The children sat in a ring around the teacher.*
3 the sound a bell makes: *The ring of the doorbell woke him up.*
4 give someone a ring to telephone someone

ring[2] /rɪŋ/ *verb* (*present participle* **ringing**, *past tense* **rang**, *past participle* **rung**)
1 If something rings, it makes the sound of a bell, and if you ring a bell, you cause it to make a sound: *The phone's ringing.*
2 *UK* to telephone someone: *Have you rung your mother?*
ring (someone) back *phrasal verb UK* to telephone someone a second time, or to telephone someone who rang you earlier: *I'm a bit busy – can I ring you back later?*

ringtone /rɪŋtəʊn/ *noun*
the sound that a mobile phone makes

rinse /rɪns/ *verb* (*present participle* **rinsing**, *past* **rinsed**)
to wash something in clean water in order to remove dirt or soap: *Rinse the beans with cold water.*

riot /raɪət/ *noun*
angry, violent behaviour by a crowd of people: *a race riot*

rip /rɪp/ *verb* (*present participle* **ripping**, *past* **ripped**)
to tear quickly and suddenly: *She ripped her dress getting off her bike.* ○ *He ripped open the parcel.*

ripe /raɪp/ *adj*
developed enough and ready to be eaten: *ripe bananas*

rip-off /ˈrɪpɒf/ *noun informal*
something that costs far too much money: *The drinks here are a complete rip-off.*

ripple /ˈrɪpl/ *noun*
a small wave or series of small waves on the surface of water: *She dived in, sending ripples across the pool.*

rise[1] /raɪz/ *verb* (*present participle* **rising**, *past tense* **rose**, *past participle* **risen**)
1 to get bigger in level: *Prices **rose by** 10 percent.*
2 to move up: *The balloon rose slowly into the air.*
3 to stand, especially after sitting: *He rose from his seat.*
4 When the sun or moon rises, it appears in the sky: *The sun rises in the East.*

rise[2] /raɪz/ *noun*
when the level of something goes up: *a tax rise*

risk[1] /rɪsk/ *noun*
1 the possibility of something bad happening: *the risk of heart disease*
2 take a risk to do something although something bad might happen because of it

risk[2] /rɪsk/ *verb*
If you risk something bad, you do something although that bad thing might happen: *I'd like to help you, but I can't risk losing my job.*

rival /ˈraɪvəl/ *noun*
someone or something that is competing against another person or thing: *political rivals*
• **rivalry** *noun* (*plural* **rivalries**)
when two people or things are rivals: *There is intense **rivalry between** the two teams.*

river /ˈrɪvər/ *noun*
a long, natural area of water that flows across the land: *the River Thames*

road /rəʊd/ *noun*
a long, hard surface built for cars to drive on: *Be careful when you cross the road.* ○ *The journey takes about three hours **by road*** (= in a car, bus, etc).

roar[1] /rɔːr/ *verb*
to make a loud, deep sound: *She **roared with laughter**.*

roar[2] /rɔːr/ *noun*
a loud, deep sound: *a lion's roar*

roast /rəʊst/ *verb*
If you roast food, you cook it in an oven or over a fire: *Roast the lamb in a hot oven for 35 minutes.*
• **roast** *adj*: *roast beef*

rob /rɒb/ *verb* (*present participle*

robbing, *past* **robbed)**
to steal from someone or somewhere, often using violence: *to rob a bank*

robber /ˈrɒbər/ *noun*
someone who steals: *a bank robber*

robbery /ˈrɒbəri/ *noun* (*plural* **robberies)**
the crime of stealing from someone or somewhere: *a bank robbery*

robe /rəʊb/ *noun*
a long, loose piece of clothing, covering most of the body

robot /ˈrəʊbɒt/ *noun*
a machine controlled by a computer, which can move and do other things that people can do

rock[1] /rɒk/ *noun*
1 [no plural] the hard, natural substance which forms part of the Earth's surface
2 a large piece of rock or stone: *Huge waves were crashing against the rocks.*
3 [no plural] loud, modern music with a strong beat, often played with electric guitars and drums: *a rock band*

rock[2] /rɒk/ *verb*
to move backwards and forwards or from side to side, or to make someone or something do this: *She rocked back and forth on her chair.* ○ *He gently rocked the baby to sleep.*

rocket /ˈrɒkɪt/ *noun*
a tube-shaped vehicle for travelling in space

rocky /ˈrɒki/ *adj*
with lots of rocks: *a rocky beach*

rod /rɒd/ *noun*
a thin, straight pole: *a fishing rod*

rode /rəʊd/ *past tense of* ride

rodent /ˈrəʊdənt/ *noun*
an animal with long, sharp teeth, such as a mouse

role /rəʊl/ *noun*
a part in a play or film: *In his latest film, he* ***plays the role of*** *a violent gangster.*

roll[1] /rəʊl/ *verb*
1 to move somewhere by turning in a circular direction, or to make something move this way: *The ball rolled through the goalkeeper's legs.* ○ *She rolled over onto her side.*
2 to turn something around itself to make the shape of a ball or tube: *to roll a cigarette*

roll

roll of film

roll

roll[2] /rəʊl/ *noun*
1 something that has been turned around itself into a round shape like a tube: *a roll of toilet paper*
2 a small loaf of bread for one person

Rollerblades /ˈrəʊləbleɪdz/ *plural noun, trademark*
boots with a single line of wheels on the bottom, used for moving across the ground
• **rollerblading** *noun* **[no plural]** *Lots of people* ***go rollerblading*** *in Central Park.*
➲See colour picture **Sports 1** on page Centre 15

roller skate /ˈrəʊlə skeɪt/ *noun*
a boot with wheels on the bottom, used for moving across the ground
• **roller skating** *noun* **[no plural]**

Roman Catholic /ˌrəʊmən ˈkæθəlɪk/ *adj*
related to the part of the Christian religion that has the Pope (= a very important priest) as its leader
• **Roman Catholic** *noun*

romance /rəʊˈmæns/ *noun*
1 an exciting relationship of love between two people, often a short one: *They had a brief romance.*
2 a story about love

romantic /rəʊˈmæntɪk/ *adj*
relating to exciting feelings of love: *a romantic dinner for two*

roof /ruːf/ *noun*
the surface that covers the top of a building or vehicle: *He climbed onto the roof.*

roof

room /ruːm, rʊm/ *noun*

1 a part of the inside of a building, which is separated from other parts by walls, floors, and ceilings: *a hotel room*
2 **[no plural]** space for things to fit into: *Is there enough* ***room for*** *all of us in your car?*

root /ruːt/ *noun*
the part of a plant that grows under the ground

rope /rəʊp/ *noun*
very thick, strong string

rose[1] /rəʊz/ *noun*
a flower with a pleasant smell and thorns (= sharp points on the stem)

rose[2] /rəʊz/
past tense of rise

rosy /ˈrəʊzi/ *adj*
Rosy faces are a healthy pink colour.

rot /rɒt/ *verb* (*present participle* **rotting,** *past* **rotted)**
to become bad and soft because of being dead or old: *The fruit had been left to rot on the trees.* ○ *Sugar rots your teeth.*

rotate /rəʊˈteɪt/ *verb* (*present participle* **rotating,** *past* **rotated)**
to turn in a circular direction, or to make something turn in a circular direction: *The television rotates for viewing at any angle.*
• **rotation** /rəʊˈteɪʃən/ *noun*: *the rotation of the Earth* ○ *crop rotation*

rotten /ˈrɒtən/ *adj*
1 old and bad: *rotten eggs*
2 *informal* very bad: *rotten weather*

rough /rʌf/ *adj*
1 A rough surface is not smooth: *rough hands*
2 not completely accurate but close: *Can you give me a rough idea of the cost?*
3 dangerous or violent: *Hockey can be quite a rough game.*

roughly /ˈrʌfli/ *adv*
1 close to a particular number, although not exactly that number: *There's been an increase of roughly 30% since last year.*
2 with force or violence: *He pushed us roughly out of the door.*

round[1] /raʊnd/ *adj*
in the shape of a circle or ball: *a round table* ○ *round eyes*

round[2] /raʊnd/ (*also* **around**) *adv, preposition*
1 on all sides of something: *We sat round the table.*
2 to the opposite direction: *She looked round.*
3 to or in different parts of a place: *He showed me round the flat.*
4 near an area: *Do you live round here?*

roundabout /ˈraʊndəˌbaʊt/ *noun*
UK (*US* **traffic circle)** a circular place where roads meet and where cars drive around until they arrive at the road that they want to turn into

route /ruːt/ *noun*
the roads you follow to get from one place to another place

routine /ruːˈtiːn/ *noun*
the things that you do every day at the same time: *a daily routine*

row[1] /rəʊ/ *noun*
a straight line of people or things: *a* ***row of*** *chairs*

row[2] /rəʊ/ *verb*
to move a boat or move someone in a boat through the water using oars (= poles with flat ends)
• **rowing** *noun* **[no plural]**

row[3] /raʊ/ *noun UK*
a loud, angry argument: *The couple next door are always* ***having rows****.*

royal /ˈrɔɪəl/ *adj*
relating to a queen or king and their family: *the British royal family*

royalty /ˈrɔɪəlti/ *noun* **[no plural]**
the people in the royal family

rub /rʌb/ *verb* (*present participle* **rubbing,** *past* **rubbed)**
to press your hand or a cloth on a surface and move it backwards and forwards: *He rubbed himself dry with a towel.* ○ *Rub the stain with a damp cloth.*
rub something out *phrasal verb UK*
to remove writing from something by rubbing it with a piece of rubber or a cloth

rubber /ˈrʌbər/ *noun*
1 **[no plural]** a strong material that bends easily, and is used to make tyres, boots, etc
2 *UK* (*US* **eraser)** a small object which is used to remove pencil marks from paper ➲See colour picture **Classroom** on page Centre 4

rubber band /ˌrʌbər ˈbænd/ (*also UK* **elastic band)** *noun*
a thin circle of rubber used to hold

a b c d e f g h i j k l m n o p q r s t u v w x y z

things together

rubbish /ˈrʌbɪʃ/ *noun* **[no plural]** *UK*
1 things that you throw away because you do not want them: *Our rubbish gets collected on Thursdays.*
2 *informal* something that is of bad quality: *There's so much rubbish on TV.*

ruby /ˈruːbi/ *noun* (*plural* **rubies**)
a valuable red stone which is used in jewellery

rucksack /ˈrʌksæk/ *noun UK*
a bag that you carry on your back

rude /ruːd/ *adj*
1 behaving in a way which is not polite and upsets other people: *a rude remark* ○ *He was very* ***rude to*** *me.* ○ *It would be rude to leave without saying goodbye.* ⊃Opposite **polite**
2 Rude words or jokes relate to sex or going to the toilet.
• **rudely** *adv*
• **rudeness** *noun* **[no plural]**

rug /rʌg/ *noun*
a soft piece of material used to cover the floor: *The dog was lying on the rug in front of the fire.* ⊃See colour picture **The Living Room** on page Centre 11

rug

rugby /ˈrʌgbi/ *noun* **[no plural]**
a sport played by two teams with an oval ball and H-shaped goals ⊃See colour picture **Sports 2** on page Centre 16

rugged /ˈrʌgɪd/ *adj*
If an area of land is rugged, it looks rough and has lots of rocks: *a rugged coastline*

ruin¹ /ˈruːɪn/ *verb*
to spoil or destroy something: *They were late and the dinner was ruined.*

ruin² /ˈruːɪn/ *noun*
the broken parts that are left from an old building or town: *Thousand of tourists wander around these ancient ruins every year.*

rule¹ /ruːl/ *noun*
an official instruction about what you must or must not do: *You can't smoke at school, it's* ***against the rules*** (= not allowed).

rule² /ruːl/ *verb* (*present participle* **ruling**, *past* **ruled**)
to be in control of somewhere, usually a country: *They were ruled for many years by a dictator.*

ruler /ˈruːləʳ/ *noun*
1 the leader of a country
2 a flat, straight stick which is used to measure things ⊃See colour picture **Classroom** on page Centre 4

rum /rʌm/ *noun* **[no plural]**
a strong, alcoholic drink made from sugar

rumble /ˈrʌmbl/ *verb* (*present participle* **rumbling**, *past* **rumbled**)
to make a deep, long sound: *The smell of cooking made his stomach rumble.*

rumour *UK* (*US* **rumor**) /ˈruːməʳ/ *noun*
a fact that a lot of people are talking about although they do not know if it is true: *I* ***heard a rumour*** *that you were leaving.*

run¹ /rʌn/ *verb* (*present participle* **running**, *past tense* **ran**, *past participle* **run**)
1 to move on your feet at a faster speed than walking: *He can run very fast.* ○ *I run about three miles every morning.*
2 to organize or control something: *She ran her own restaurant for five years.*
3 If a piece of equipment is running, it is switched on and working: *The engine is running more smoothly now.*
4 If trains or buses are running, they are available to travel on: *The buses only run until 11 p.m.*
5 If liquid runs somewhere, it flows: *Tears ran down her face.*

run away *phrasal verb*
to secretly leave a place because you are unhappy there: *He ran away from home as a child.*

run out *phrasal verb*
to use all of something so that there is none left: *I've nearly* ***run out of*** *money.*

run someone/something over *phrasal verb*
to hit someone or something with a car, bus, etc and hurt or kill them: *He was run over by a bus as he crossed the road.*

run² /rʌn/ *noun*
1 when you move on your feet at a speed faster than walking as a sport: *to go for a run*
2 in cricket or baseball, a single

a b c d e f g h i j k l m n o p q r s t u v w x y z

point: *to score a run*

rung /rʌŋ/
past participle of ring[2]

runner /ˈrʌnəʳ/ *noun*
someone who runs: *a long-distance runner*

running /ˈrʌnɪŋ/ *noun* **[no plural]**
the sport of moving on your feet at a speed faster than walking: *I* ***go running*** *three times a week.* ➲See colour picture **Sports 1** on page Centre 15

runny /ˈrʌni/ *adj*
1 A runny substance is more liquid than usual: *runny egg*
2 runny nose If you have a runny nose, liquid is coming out of your nose.

rural /ˈrʊərᵊl/ *adj*
relating to the countryside and not to towns: *a rural area*

rush[1] /rʌʃ/ *verb*
to hurry or move quickly somewhere: *We had to rush to catch the bus.*

rush[2] /rʌʃ/ *noun* **[no plural]**
when you have to hurry or move somewhere quickly: *I'm sorry I can't talk now, I'm* ***in a rush****.*

rust /rʌst/ *noun* **[no plural]**
a dark orange substance that you get on metal when it is wet
• **rust** *verb*

rustle /ˈrʌsl/ *verb* (*present participle* **rustling**, *past* **rustled)**
If things such as paper or leaves rustle, they move about and make a soft, dry sound: *Outside, the trees rustled in the wind.*

rusty /ˈrʌsti/ *adj*
Rusty metal has rust (= an orange substance) on its surface: *rusty nails*

rut /rʌt/ *noun*
in a rut in a bad situation where you do the same things all the time: *He seems to be stuck in a rut at the moment.*

Ss

S, s /es/
the nineteenth letter of the alphabet

sack¹ /sæk/ *noun*
1 a large, strong bag used to carry or keep things
2 get the sack *UK* When someone gets the sack, they are told to leave their job: *He got the sack from his last job.*

sack

sack² /sæk/ *verb UK*
to tell someone to leave their job: *He was sacked for being late.*

sacred /ˈseɪkrɪd/ *adj*
relating to a religion or considered to be holy: *sacred music*

sacrifice¹ /ˈsækrɪfaɪs/ *noun*
1 something good that you must stop having in order to achieve something: *Sometimes you have to **make sacrifices** to succeed.*
2 an animal that is killed and offered to a god in a religious ceremony

sacrifice² /ˈsækrɪfaɪs/ *verb* (*present participle* **sacrificing,** *past* **sacrificed)**
1 to stop having something good in order to achieve something: *There are thousands of men ready to **sacrifice** their lives **for** their country.*
2 to kill an animal and offer it to a god in a religious ceremony

sad /sæd/ *adj* **(sadder, saddest)**
1 unhappy: *I was very sad when our cat died. ○ a sad book*
2 *UK informal* boring or not fashionable: *I cleaned the house on Saturday night, which is a bit sad.*
• **sadness** *noun* **[no plural]**

saddle /ˈsædl/ *noun*
1 a leather seat that you put on a horse so that you can ride it
⊃See colour picture **Sports 1** on page Centre 15
2 a seat on a bicycle or motorcycle

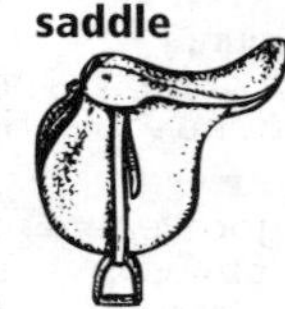
saddle

sadly /ˈsædli/ *adv*
1 in a sad way: *She shook her head sadly.*
2 used to say that you are sorry something is true: *Sadly, the marriage ended.*

safari /səˈfɑːri/ *noun*
a journey, usually to Africa, to see wild animals

safe¹ /seɪf/ *adj*
1 not dangerous: *a safe driver ○ Air travel is generally quite safe.*
2 not hurt or in danger: *She said that all the hostages were safe.*
• **safely** *adv*: *Drive safely!*

safe² /seɪf/ *noun*
a strong metal box with locks where you keep money, jewellery, etc

safety /ˈseɪfti/ *noun* **[no plural]**
when you are safe: *road safety*

safety belt /ˈseɪfti ˌbelt/ *noun*
a strap that you fasten across your body when travelling in a car or aeroplane: *Please fasten your safety belt for take-off.*

sag /sæg/ *verb* (*present participle* **sagging,** *past* **sagged)**
to sink or bend down: *Our mattress sags in the middle.*

said /sed/
past of say

sail¹ /seɪl/ *verb*
to travel in a boat or a ship: *We sailed to Malta.*

sail² /seɪl/ *noun*
a large piece of material that is fixed to a pole on a boat to catch the wind and make the boat move

sailor /ˈseɪləʳ/ *noun*
someone who sails ships or boats as their job or as a sport

saint /seɪnt/ *noun*
a dead person who lived their life in a holy way

sake /seɪk/ *noun*
1 for the sake of someone in order to help or please someone: *He asked her to stay for the sake of the children.*
2 For goodness sake! something you say when you are angry about something: *For goodness sake, will you come here!*

salad /ˈsæləd/ *noun*
a cold mixture of vegetables that have not been cooked ➲See colour picture **Food** on page Centre 7

salad

salary /ˈsælᵊri/ *noun* (*plural* **salaries**)
the money that you get, usually every month, for working

sale /seɪl/ *noun*
1 the act of selling something: *The sale of alcohol is now banned.*
2 a time when a shop sells things for less money than usual: *I bought this dress **in the sale**.*

salesman, saleswoman /ˈseɪlzmən, ˈseɪlzˌwʊmən/ *noun* (*plural* **salesmen, saleswomen**)
someone whose job is selling things

salmon /ˈsæmən/ *noun* (*plural* **salmon**)
a large, silver fish, or the pink meat of this fish

salt /sɔːlt, sɒlt/ *noun* **[no plural]**
a white substance used to add flavour to food: *salt and pepper*

salute¹ /səˈluːt/ *noun*
a sign of respect to someone of a higher rank in a military organization, often made by putting the right hand at the side of the head

salute² /səˈluːt/ *verb* (*present participle* **saluting**, *past* **saluted**)
to give a salute to someone of a higher rank in a military organization

same¹ /seɪm/ *adj, pronoun*
the same
a exactly alike: *He's **the same** age **as** me.* ○ *We work at the same speed.*
b not changed: *He looks exactly **the same as** he did ten years ago.*

same² /seɪm/ *adv*
the same in the same way: *We treat all our children the same.*

sample /ˈsɑːmpl/ *noun*
a small amount of something that shows you what it is like: *She brought in some samples of her work.* ○ *The doctor took a blood sample.*

sand /sænd/ *noun* **[no plural]**
a substance that is found on beaches, which is made from very small grains of rock

sandal /ˈsændᵊl/ *noun*
a light shoe with straps that you wear in warm weather ➲See colour picture **Clothes** on page Centre 5

sandwich /ˈsænwɪdʒ/ *noun* (*plural* **sandwiches**)
two slices of bread with meat, cheese, etc between them: *a cheese sandwich* ➲See colour picture **Food** on page Centre 7

sandwich

sandy /ˈsændi/ *adj* **(sandier, sandiest)**
covered with sand: *a sandy beach*

sane /seɪn/ *adj*
having a healthy mind ➲Opposite **insane**

sang /sæŋ/
past tense of sing

sank /sæŋk/
past tense of sink

sap /sæp/ *noun* **[no plural]**
the liquid inside plants and trees

sapphire /ˈsæfaɪəʳ/ *noun*
a bright blue stone

sarcasm /ˈsɑːkæzᵊm/ *noun* **[no plural]**
when you say the opposite of what you mean to be unpleasant to someone or show them that you are angry

sarcastic /sɑːˈkæstɪk/ *adj*
using sarcasm: *Are you being sarcastic?*

sardine /sɑːˈdiːn/ *noun*
a small sea fish that you can eat

sat /sæt/
past of sit

satellite /ˈsætᵊlaɪt/ *noun*
a piece of equipment that is sent into space around the Earth to get and send signals: *a weather satellite*

satin /ˈsætɪn/ *noun* **[no plural]**
a smooth, shiny cloth

satisfaction /ˌsætɪsˈfækʃᵊn/ *noun* **[no plural]**
a good feeling because you have done something well: *job satisfaction*

satisfactory /ˌsætɪsˈfæktᵊri/ *adj*
good enough: *We hope to find a satisfactory solution to the problem.* ➲Opposite **unsatisfactory**

satisfied /ˈsætɪsfaɪd/ *adj*
pleased because you have got what you wanted: *Are you* ***satisfied with*** *the new arrangement?* ➲Opposite **dissatisfied**

satisfy /ˈsætɪsfaɪ/ *verb* (*present participle* **satisfying**, *past* **satisfied**)
to please someone by giving them what they want: *They sell 31 flavours of ice cream – enough to satisfy everyone!*

Saturday /ˈsætədeɪ/ *noun*
the day of the week after Friday and before Sunday

sauce /sɔːs/ *noun*
a liquid that you put on food to add flavour: *pasta with tomato sauce*

saucepan /ˈsɔːspən/ *noun*
a metal pan with a long handle and a lid, that is used to cook food in ➲See colour picture **Kitchen** on page Centre 10

saucer /ˈsɔːsə^{r}/ *noun*
a small plate that you put under a cup

sauna /ˈsɔːnə/ *noun*
a room that is hot and filled with steam where people sit to relax or feel healthy

sausage /ˈsɒsɪdʒ/ *noun*
a mixture of meat and spices pressed into a long tube

sausage

save /seɪv/ *verb* (*present participle* **saving**, *past* **saved**)
1 to stop someone or something from being killed or destroyed: *He was badly injured, but the doctors saved his life.*
2 (*also* **save up**) to keep money so that you can buy something with it in the future: *We've* ***saved*** *almost $900* ***for*** *our wedding.*
3 save money/space/time, etc to reduce the amount of money/space/time, etc that you have to use: *You'll save time by doing it yourself.*
4 save files/work, etc to store work or information electronically on a computer
5 save a goal to stop a player from scoring a goal

savings /ˈseɪvɪŋz/ *plural noun*
money that you have saved, usually in a bank: *a savings account*

saw^{1} /sɔː/ *noun*
a tool with a sharp edge that you use to cut wood or other hard material

saw^{2} /sɔː/
past tense of see

saxophone /ˈsæksəfəʊn/ *noun*
a metal musical instrument that you play by blowing into it and pressing keys

say /seɪ/ *verb* (*present participle* **saying**, *past* **said**)
1 to speak words: *"I'd like to go home," she said.* ○ *How do you say this word?*
2 to tell someone about a fact or opinion: *He* ***said that*** *he was leaving.*
3 to give information in writing, numbers, or signs: *My watch says one o'clock.*

saying /ˈseɪɪŋ/ *noun*
a famous phrase that people use to give advice about life

scab /skæb/ *noun*
a layer of dried blood that covers a cut in the skin

scaffolding /ˈskæf^{ə}ldɪŋ/ *noun* **[no plural]**
a temporary structure made of flat boards and metal poles used to work on a tall building

scale /skeɪl/ *noun*
1 [no plural] the size or level of something: *We don't yet know the scale of the problem.*
2 the set of numbers, amounts, etc used to measure or compare the level of something: *How would you rate her work* ***on a scale of*** *1-10?*
3 *US* (*UK* **scales**) a piece of equipment for measuring weight: *a bathroom scale* ➲See colour picture **Kitchen** on page Centre 10, **The Bathroom** ➲on page Centre 1
4 how the size of things on a map, model, etc relates to the same things in real life: *a map with a scale of one centimetre per ten kilometres*
5 a series of musical notes that is always played in order and that goes up from the first note
6 one of the flat pieces of hard material that covers the skin of fish and snakes

scales /skeɪlz/ *plural noun UK* (*US* **scale**)
a piece of equipment for measuring weight: *kitchen scales* ⊃See colour picture **Kitchen** on page Centre 10, **The Bathroom** ⊃on page Centre 1

scalp /skælp/ *noun*
the skin on the top of your head under your hair

scandal /ˈskændᵊl/ *noun*
something that shocks people because they think it is very bad: *a sex scandal*

scanner /ˈskænəʳ/ *noun*
a piece of equipment that copies words or pictures from paper into a computer

scar /skɑːʳ/ *noun*
a permanent mark left on the body from a cut or other injury
• scar *verb* (*present participle* **scarring**, *past* **scarred**)
to cause a scar: *He was* ***scarred for life*** *by the accident.*

scarce /skeəs/ *adj*
rare, existing only in small amounts: *scarce resources*

scarcely /ˈskeəsli/ *adv*
only just: *They had scarcely finished eating when the doorbell rang.*

scare[1] /skeəʳ/ *verb* (*present participle* **scaring**, *past* **scared**)
to frighten a person or animal: *Sudden, loud noises scare me.*

scare[2] /skeəʳ/ *noun*
1 a sudden feeling of fear or worry: *The earthquake* ***gave*** *us a* ***scare****.*
2 a situation that worries or frightens people: *a health scare*

scarecrow /ˈskeəkrəʊ/ *noun*
a model of a person that is put in a field to frighten birds and stop them from eating the plants

scared /skeəd/ *adj*
frightened or worried: *Robert's* ***scared of*** *heights.*

scarf /skɑːf/ *noun* (*plural* **scarves**)
a piece of cloth that you wear around your neck or head to keep warm or for decoration ⊃See colour picture **Clothes** on page Centre 5

scatter /ˈskætəʳ/ *verb*
1 to throw a lot of small objects over an area: *He scattered some flower seeds in the garden.*
2 to suddenly move away in different directions: *The crowd scattered at the sound of gunshots.*

scene /siːn/ *noun*
1 a short part of a film, play, or book in which things happen in one place: *a love scene*
2 a view or picture of a place, event, or activity: *scenes of horror*
3 a place where a bad thing has happened: *the scene of the crime*

scenery /ˈsiːnᵊri/ *noun* **[no plural]**
1 the attractive, natural things that you see in the countryside
2 the large pictures of buildings, countryside, etc used on a theatre stage

scent /sent/ *noun*
1 a nice smell: *the sweet scent of orange blossoms*
2 a nice smelling liquid that people put on their skin

schedule /ˈskedʒuːl/ *noun*
a plan that tells you when things will happen: *Will the work be completed* ***on schedule*** (= at the expected time)*?*

scheme[1] /skiːm/ *noun UK*
an official plan or system: *a savings scheme*

scheme[2] /skiːm/ *verb* (*present participle* **scheming**, *past* **schemed**)
to make a secret plan

scholar /ˈskɒləʳ/ *noun*
someone who has studied a subject and knows a lot about it: *a legal scholar*

scholarship /ˈskɒləʃɪp/ *noun*
an amount of money given to a person by an organization to pay for their education

school /skuːl/ *noun*
1 a place where children go to learn things: *I ride my bike to school.*
2 **[no plural]** the time that you spend at school: *I like school.* ○ *I started school when I was five.*
3 *US informal* in the US, any college or university, or the time you spend there

science /saɪəns/ *noun*
1 **[no plural]** the study of the structure of natural things and the way that they behave
2 a particular type of science: *Chemistry, physics, and biology are all sciences.*

a b c d e f g h i j k l m n o p q r s t u v w x y z

science fiction /ˌsaɪəns ˈfɪkʃən/ *noun* **[no plural]**
stories about life in the future or in other parts of the universe

scientific /ˌsaɪənˈtɪfɪk/ *adj*
relating to science: *scientific experiments*

scientist /ˈsaɪəntɪst/ *noun*
someone who studies science or works in science

scissors /ˈsɪzəz/ *plural noun*
a tool for cutting paper, hair, etc that you hold in your hand and that has two blades: *a pair of scissors*

scissors

scoop /skuːp/ *verb*
to remove something from a container using a spoon, your curved hands, etc: *She scooped the ice cream into the dishes.*

scooter /ˈskuːtə^r/ *noun*
1 a small motorcycle
2 a child's vehicle that has two wheels fixed to the ends of a long board and a long handle

score[1] /skɔː^r/ *noun*
the number of points someone gets in a game or test: *a high/low score* ○ *What's the score?*

score[2] /skɔː^r/ *verb* (*present participle* **scoring**, *past* **scored**)
to get points in a game or test: *He scored just before half-time to put Liverpool 2-1 ahead.*

scorn /skɔːn/ *noun* **[no plural]** *formal*
the belief that something is stupid

scorpion /ˈskɔːpiən/ *noun*
a small, insect-like creature with a curved, poisonous tail

scowl /skaʊl/ *verb*
to look at someone angrily: *He* ***scowled at*** *me from behind his paper.*
● **scowl** *noun*

scramble /ˈskræmbl/ *verb* (*present participle* **scrambling**, *past* **scrambled**)
to move or climb quickly but with difficulty, often using your hands: *We scrambled up the hill.*

scrap /skræp/ *noun*
a small piece or amount of something: *He wrote his phone number on* ***a scrap of*** *paper.*

scrape /skreɪp/ *verb* (*present participle* **scraping**, *past* **scraped**)
1 to damage the surface of something by rubbing it against something rough: *Jamie fell over and scraped his knee.*
2 to remove something from a surface using a sharp edge: *I had to scrape the ice off the car.*

scratch[1] /skrætʃ/ *verb*
1 to rub your skin with your nails: *My skin was so itchy, I was scratching all night.*
2 to make a slight cut or long, thin mark with a sharp object: *The car was scratched.*

scratch[2] /skrætʃ/ *noun* (*plural* **scratches**)
1 a slight cut or a long, thin mark made with a sharp object: *I've got all these scratches on my arm from the cat.*
2 from scratch from the beginning: *We didn't have any furniture of our own so we had to start from scratch.*

scream[1] /skriːm/ *verb*
to make a loud, high noise with your voice because you are afraid or hurt: *Someone was screaming in the street.*

scream[2] /skriːm/ *noun*
when someone screams: *We heard screams coming from their apartment.*

screech /skriːtʃ/ *verb*
to make an unpleasant, high, loud sound: *A car came screeching around the corner.*

screen /skriːn/ *noun*
1 the part of a television or computer which shows images or writing: *I spend most of my day working in front of a computer screen.*
2 on screen using a computer: *Do you work on screen?*
3 a large, flat surface where a film or an image is shown
4 cinema films: *She first appeared on screen in 1965.*

screw[1] /skruː/ *noun*
a small, pointed piece of metal that you turn round and round to fix things together

screw[2] /skruː/ *verb*
1 to fasten something with a screw: *You need to screw the cabinet to the wall.*
2 to fasten something by turning it round until it is tight

screwdriver /ˈskruːˌdraɪvəʳ/ *noun*
a tool for turning screws

scribble /ˈskrɪbl/ *verb* (*present participle* **scribbling**, *past* **scribbled**)
to write or draw something quickly and without care: *She scribbled some notes in her book.*

scripture /ˈskrɪptʃəʳ/ *noun* **[no plural]**
the holy books of a religion

scroll /skrəʊl/ *verb*
to move text or an image on a computer screen so that you can look at the part that you want

scrub /skrʌb/ *verb* (*present participle* **scrubbing**, *past* **scrubbed**)
to clean something by rubbing it hard with a brush: *She scrubbed the floor.*

sculptor /ˈskʌlptəʳ/ *noun*
someone who makes sculpture

sculpture /ˈskʌlptʃəʳ/ *noun*
a piece of art that is made from stone, wood, clay, etc: *a wooden sculpture*

sea /siː/ *noun*
1 a large area of salt water: *I'd like to live by the sea.* ○ *We went swimming in the sea.*
2 Sea a particular area of salt water: *the Black Sea*

seafood /ˈsiːfuːd/ *noun* **[no plural]**
animals from the sea that are eaten as food

seagull /ˈsiːgʌl/ *noun*
a grey and white bird that lives near the sea

seagull

seal¹ /siːl/ *noun*
an animal with smooth fur that eats fish and lives near the sea

seal² /siːl/ *verb*
to close an entrance or container so that air or liquid cannot enter or leave it: *She sealed the bottle.*

seam /siːm/ *noun*
a line of sewing where two pieces of cloth have been joined together

search¹ /sɜːtʃ/ *verb*
to try to find someone or something: *He searched in his pockets for some change.* ○ *Police are still* ***searching*** *the woods* ***for*** *the missing girl.*

search² /sɜːtʃ/ *noun* (*plural* **searches**)
1 when you try to find someone or something: *Police are continuing their* ***search for*** *the missing girl.*
2 when you try to find an answer to a problem: *the search for happiness*

sea shell /ˈsiː ˌʃel/ *noun*
the empty shell of some types of sea animals

the seashore /ˈsiːʃɔːʳ/ *noun*
the area of land along the edge of the sea

seasick /ˈsiːsɪk/ *adj*
feeling ill because of the way a boat is moving

the seaside /ˈsiːsaɪd/ *noun*
an area or town next to the sea: *We had a picnic* ***at the seaside***.

season /ˈsiːzᵊn/ *noun*
1 one of the four periods of the year; winter, spring, summer, or autumn
2 a period of the year when a particular thing happens: *the holiday season*

seat /siːt/ *noun*
something that you sit on: *Please,* ***have/take a seat*** (= sit down).

seat belt /ˈsiːt ˌbelt/ *noun*
a strap that you fasten across your body when travelling in a car or aeroplane ➲See colour picture **Car** on page Centre 3

second¹ /ˈsekᵊnd/ *adj, pronoun*
being the one after the first: *You're second on the list.* ○ *This is my second piece of chocolate cake.*

second² /ˈsekᵊnd/ *noun*
1 one of the 60 parts a minute is divided into
2 *informal* a very short period of time: *I'll be back in just a second.*

secondary school /ˈsekəndrɪ ˌskuːl/ *noun UK*
a school for students aged between 11 and 18

second-class /ˌsekənd'klɑːs/ *adj*
relating to the less expensive way of travelling that most people use: *a second-class ticket*

second-hand /ˌsekᵊnd'hænd/ *adj, adv*
If something is second-hand, someone else had it or used it

a b c d e f g h i j k l m n o p q r **s** t u v w x y z

before you: *second-hand books*

secret¹ /ˈsiːkrət/ *adj*
If something is secret, other people are not allowed to know about it: *a secret meeting* ○ *I'll tell you but you must* ***keep it secret***.
• **secretly** *adv*: *He secretly taped their conversation.*

secret² /ˈsiːkrət/ *noun*
something that you tell no one about or only a few people: *I'm having a party for him but it's a secret.* ○ *Can you* ***keep a secret****?*

secretary /ˈsekrətᵊri/ *noun* (*plural* **secretaries**)
1 someone who works in an office, typing letters, answering the telephone, etc
2 an official who is in charge of a large department of the government: *the Secretary of State*

section /ˈsekʃᵊn/ *noun*
one of the parts that something is divided into: *a non-smoking section in a restaurant* ○ *the business section of a newspaper*

secure /sɪˈkjʊəʳ/ *adj*
1 not likely to fail or be lost: *a secure job*
2 safe from danger: *I don't feel that the house is secure.*
3 firmly fastened and not likely to fall: *Check that all windows and doors are secure.*

security /sɪˈkjʊərəti/ *noun* **[no plural]**
1 the things that are done to keep someone or something safe: *airport security*
2 when something is not likely to fail or be lost: *job security*

see /siː/ *verb* (*present participle* **seeing**, *past tense* **saw**, *past participle* **seen**)
1 to notice people and things with your eyes: *Have you seen Jo?* ○ *Turn the light on so I can see.*
2 to understand something: *I see what you mean.* ○ *I don't see why I should go.*
3 to meet or visit someone: *I'm seeing Peter tonight.*
4 to watch a film, television programme, etc: *Did you see that film last night?*
5 to find out information: *I'll just see what time the train gets in.*
6 I'll/we'll see used to say that you will make a decision about something later: *"Dad, can I have a guitar?" "We'll see."*
7 See you! *informal* used for saying goodbye

seed /siːd/ *noun*
a small round thing that a new plant can grow from

seek /siːk/ *verb* (*present participle* **seeking**, *past* **sought**)
to try to find or get something: *I am seeking advice on the matter.*

seem /siːm/ *verb*
to appear to be: *She seemed happy.* ○ *It* ***seemed like*** *a good idea at the time.* ○ *There doesn't* ***seem to be*** *any real solution.*

seen /siːn/
past participle of see

seesaw

seesaw /ˈsiːsɔː/ *noun*
a long board that children play on by sitting at each end and going up and down

seize /siːz/ *verb* (*present participle* **seizing**, *past* **seized**)
to take hold of something quickly and firmly: *She seized my arm and pulled me towards her.*

select /sɪˈlekt/ *verb*
to choose someone or something: *We've selected three candidates.*

selection /sɪˈlekʃᵊn/ *noun*
a group of people or things that has been chosen: *We have a wide selection of furniture.*

self /self/ *noun* (*plural* **selves**)
your character: *Lucy didn't seem her usual cheerful self today.*

self-confident /ˌselfˈkɒnfidᵊnt/ *adj*
feeling sure about yourself and your abilities
• **self-confidence** *noun* **[no plural]** being self-confident

self-control /ˌselfkənˈtrəʊl/ *noun* **[no plural]**
the ability to control your emotions, especially when you are angry or upset

selfish /ˈselfɪʃ/ *adj*
caring only about yourself and not other people
• **selfishly** *adv*
• **selfishness** *noun* **[no plural]**

self-service /ˌselfˈsɜːvɪs/ *adj*
A self-service restaurant or shop is one in which you get food or things yourself.

sell /sel/ *verb* (*present participle* **selling,** *past* **sold)**
1 to give something to someone who gives you money for it: *He **sold** his guitar **for** £50. ○ I **sold** my bike **to** Claire.*
2 to offer something for people to buy: *Excuse me, do you sell newspapers?*
sell out *phrasal verb*
to sell all of one thing in a shop: *They'd **sold out of** bread when I got there.*

Sellotape /ˈseləʊteɪp/ *UK trademark noun* **[no plural]**
clear, thin material with glue on it, used to stick things together, especially paper ➲See colour picture **Classroom** on page Centre 4

semester /sɪˈmestəʳ/ *noun US*
one of the two time periods that a school or college year is divided into

semicircle /ˈsemɪˌsɜːkl/ *noun*
half a circle

semicolon /ˌsemɪˈkəʊlən/ *noun*
a mark (;) used to separate parts of a sentence

semifinal /ˌsemɪˈfaɪnᵊl/ *noun*
one of the two games in a sports competition that are played to decide who will play in the final game

the Senate /ˈsenɪt/ *noun*
a part of a government in some countries

senator /ˈsenətəʳ/ *noun*
someone who has been elected to the Senate

send /send/ *verb* (*present participle* **sending,** *past* **sent)**
1 to arrange for something to go or be taken somewhere, especially by post: *I sent him a letter last week.*
2 to make someone go somewhere: *I sent him into the house to fetch some glasses.*

senior /ˈsiːniəʳ/ *adj*
1 having a more important job or position than someone else: *a senior executive* ➲Opposite **junior**
2 older: *senior students* ➲Opposite **junior**

sensation /senˈseɪʃᵊn/ *noun*
1 a physical feeling, or the ability to physically feel things: *a burning sensation ○ Three months after the accident she still has no sensation in her right foot.*
2 **[no plural]** a lot of excitement and interest: *Their affair **caused a sensation**.*

sense[1] /sens/ *noun*
1 **[no plural]** the ability to make good decisions and do things which will not make problems: *He had the **good sense** to book a seat in advance.*
2 the ability to do something: *a **sense of** direction ○ good business sense*
3 one of the five natural abilities of sight, hearing, touch, smell, and taste: *I have a very poor **sense of** smell.*
4 **a sense of humour** *UK* the ability to understand funny things and to be funny yourself
5 the meaning of a word, phrase, or sentence
6 **make sense**
a to have a meaning or reason that you can understand: *He's written me this note but it doesn't make any sense.*
b to be a good thing to do: *It makes sense to buy now while prices are low.*

sense[2] /sens/ *verb* (*present participle* **sensing,** *past* **sensed)**
to understand what someone is thinking or feeling without being told about it: *I **sensed that** you weren't happy.*

sensible /ˈsensɪbl/ *adj*
showing the ability to make good decisions and do things which will not make problems: *That seems a sensible decision. ○ Wouldn't it be more **sensible to** leave before the traffic gets bad?*
• **sensibly** *adv*: *She eats sensibly.*

sensitive /ˈsensɪtɪv/ *adj*
1 able to understand what people are feeling and behave in a way that does not upset them: *I want a man*

a b c d e f g h i j k l m n o p q r s t u v w x y z

who's kind and sensitive.
2 often upset by the things people say or do: *She's very **sensitive about** her weight.*

sent /sent/
past of send

sentence /ˈsentəns/ *noun*
a group of words, usually containing a verb, that expresses a complete idea

separate[1] /ˈsepᵊrət/ *adj*
1 not joined or touching anything else: *I try to keep meat **separate from** other food.*
2 different: *Use a separate sheet of paper for the next exercise.*
• separately *adv*

separate[2] /ˈsepᵊreɪt/ *verb* (*present participle* **separating,** *past* **separated**)
1 to divide into parts, or to make something divide into parts: *I **separated** the class **into** three groups.*
2 to move apart, or to make people move apart: *I shall separate you two if you don't stop talking!*

September /sepˈtembəʳ/ *noun*
the ninth month of the year

sequence /ˈsiːkwəns/ *noun*
a group of related events or things that have a particular order: *We still don't know the sequence of events that led to his death.*

sergeant /ˈsɑːdʒᵊnt/ *noun*
1 an officer of low rank in the police
2 a soldier of middle rank in the army or air force

serial /ˈsɪəriəl/ *noun*
a story that is told in separate parts over a period of time

series /ˈsɪəriːz/ *noun* (*plural* **series**)
many things or events of the same type that come one after the other: *a series of lectures*

serious /ˈsɪəriəs/ *adj*
1 A serious problem or situation is bad and makes people worry: *a serious accident/illness* ○ *This is a serious matter.*
2 thinking or speaking honestly about something and not joking: *Are you **serious about** changing your job?*
3 A serious person is quiet and does not laugh often: *a serious child*

seriously /ˈsɪəriəsli/ *adv*
1 in a serious way: *Smoking can seriously damage your health.*
2 take someone/something seriously to believe that someone or something is important and that you should give attention to them: *The police have to take any terrorist threat seriously.*

servant /ˈsɜːvᵊnt/ *noun*
someone who works and lives in someone else's house, especially in the past

serve /sɜːv/ *verb* (*present participle* **serving,** *past* **served**)
1 to give someone food or drink, especially in a restaurant or bar: *Are you still serving?*
2 to help customers and sell things to them in a shop: *Are you being served?*
3 to do work that helps society: *to serve in the army*
4 to be useful as something: *The spare bedroom also **serves as** a study.*
5 to be in prison for a period of time

service /ˈsɜːvɪs/ *noun*
1 [no plural] when people help you and bring you things in a place such as a shop, restaurant, or hotel: *The food was nice, but the service wasn't very good.*
2 a system that supplies something that people need: *financial services* ○ *They **provide** a free bus **service** from the station.*
3 [no plural] the time you spend working for an organization: *He retired last week after 25 years' service.*
4 a religious ceremony: *They **held a** memorial **service** for the victims of the bombing.*

session /ˈseʃᵊn/ *noun*
a period during which you do one activity: *We're having a training session this afternoon.*

set[1] /set/ *verb* (*present participle* **setting,** *past* **set**)
1 to arrange a time when something will happen: *The next meeting is **set for** 6 February.*
2 set fire to something to make something start burning
3 set someone free to allow someone to leave prison
4 set the table to put plates, knives, forks, etc on the table before you have a meal
5 When the sun sets, it moves down in the sky so that it cannot be seen.

6 If a liquid substance sets, it becomes solid.
7 *UK* If you set work or an exam at a school or college, you ask the students to do it: *Mr Harley forgot to set us any maths homework.*
8 If a book, play, or film is set in a place or period of time, the story happens there or at that time: *It's a historical adventure set in India in the 1940s.*
set off *phrasal verb*
to start a journey: *What time are you setting off tomorrow morning?*
set something up *phrasal verb*
to start a company or organization: *He has just set up his own company.*

set² /set/ *noun*
1 a group of things which belong together: *a set of instructions* ○ *a set of keys*
2 a television or radio: *a TV set*

settle /ˈsetl/ *verb* (*present participle* **settling**, *past* **settled**)
1 If you settle an argument, you stop the problem and stop arguing.
2 to start living somewhere that you are going to live for a long time: *Finally he settled in Vienna.*
3 to decide or arrange something: *Right, that's settled. We're going to Spain.*
4 to relax into a comfortable position: *She settled herself into the chair opposite.*
5 settle a bill to pay the money that you owe: *I've got some bills to settle.*
settle down *phrasal verb*
to start living in a place where you will stay for a long time, usually with a person you love: *Do you think he'll ever settle down and have a family?*
settle in *phrasal verb*
to begin to feel relaxed and happy in a new home or job: *Are you settling in OK?*

seven /ˈsevᵊn/
the number 7

seventeen /ˌsevᵊnˈtiːn/
the number 17
• **seventeenth**
17th written as a word

seventh¹ /ˈsevᵊnθ/
7th written as a word

seventh² /ˈsevᵊnθ/ *noun*
one of seven equal parts of something; ⅐

seventy /ˈsevᵊnti/
the number 70
• **seventieth**
70th written as a word

several /ˈsevᵊrᵊl/ *pronoun, determiner*
some, but not a lot: *Several people have complained about the scheme.*

severe /sɪˈvɪəʳ/ *adj*
1 very bad: *a severe headache* ○ *severe weather conditions*
2 not kind or gentle: *a severe punishment*
• **severely** *adv*: *He was severely injured.*

sew /səʊ/ *verb* (*past participle* **sewn**)
to join things together with a needle and thread: *I need to sew a button on my shirt.*

sewing /ˈsəʊɪŋ/ *noun* **[no plural]**
the activity of joining pieces of cloth together with a needle and thread

sex /seks/ *noun*
1 [no plural] sexual activity between people
2 (*plural* **sexes**) whether a person or animal is male or female: *Do you know what sex the baby is?*

sexual /ˈsekʃʊəl/ *adj*
relating to sex: *sexual organs* ○ *sexual equality*
• **sexually** *adv*

shabby /ˈʃæbi/ *adj*
not tidy and in bad condition: *shabby clothes*

shade¹ /ʃeɪd/ *noun*
1 [no plural] an area where there is no light from the sun and it is darker: *I'd prefer to sit **in the shade**.*
2 a colour, especially when saying how dark or light it is: *a pale/dark **shade of** grey*

shade² /ʃeɪd/ *verb* (*present participle* **shading**, *past* **shaded**)
to cover something in order to protect it from the sun: *He shaded his eyes with his hand.*

shadow /ˈʃædəʊ/ *noun*
a dark area made by something that is stopping the light: *Our dog chases his own shadow.*

shady /ˈʃeɪdi/ *adj* (**shadier, shadiest**)
A shady place is protected from the sun and is darker and cooler: *We found a shady spot to sit in.*

shake /ʃeɪk/ *verb* (*present participle* **shaking,** *past tense* **shook,** *past participle* **shaken)**
1 to make quick, short movements from side to side or up and down, or to make something or someone do this: *He was shaking with nerves.* ○ *Shake the bottle.*
2 shake hands to hold someone's hand and move it up and down when you meet them for the first time: *The two leaders smiled and shook hands for the photographers.*
3 shake your head to move your head from side to side to mean 'no'

shaken /ˈʃeɪkən/ *past participle of* **shake**

shall *strong form* /ʃæl/ *weak form* /ʃəl/ *verb*
shall I/we...?
a used to make an offer or suggestion: *Shall I cook dinner tonight?*
b used to ask someone what to do: *Who shall I ask?*

shallow /ˈʃæləʊ/ *adj*
1 not deep: *shallow water* ⊃Opposite **deep**
2 not showing any interest in serious ideas

shame /ʃeɪm/ *noun*
1 what a shame something you say about something that disappoints you: *What a shame that Joe couldn't come.*
2 [no plural] when you feel bad about something wrong that you have done

shampoo /ʃæmˈpuː/ *noun*
a liquid substance that you use to wash your hair
• **shampoo** *verb*

shape /ʃeɪp/ *noun*
the physical form of something made by the line around its outer edge: *a circular shape* ○ *I like the shape of the jacket.*
• **-shaped** /ʃeipt/ *suffix*: *a heart-shaped cake*

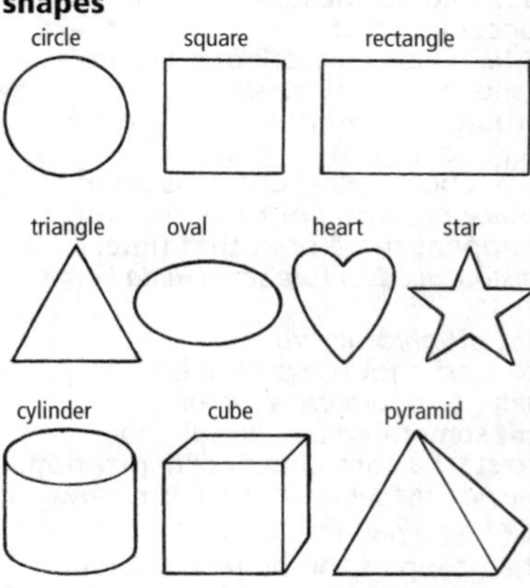

share¹ /ʃeəʳ/ *verb* (*present participle* **sharing,** *past* **shared)**
1 to have or use something at the same time as someone else: *She* ***shares*** *a house* ***with*** *Paul.*
2 to divide something between two or more people: *We shared a pizza and a bottle of wine.*
share something out *phrasal verb* to divide something and give one amount to each person in a group: *We shared out the profits between us.*

share² /ʃeəʳ/ *noun*
1 one of the equal parts that the value of a company is divided into when it is owned by a group of people: *We own shares in a number of companies.*
2 a part of something that has been divided: *When am I going to get my share of the money?*

shark /ʃɑːk/ *noun*
a large fish with very sharp teeth

shark

sharp /ʃɑːp/ *adj*
1 having a very thin edge or point that can cut things: *a sharp knife* ○ *sharp teeth*
2 sudden and very large: *a sharp rise in house prices*
3 quick to notice and understand things: *a sharp mind*

sharpen /ˈʃɑːpən/ *verb*
to make something sharper: *to sharpen a knife*

shatter /ˈʃætəʳ/ *verb*
to break into very small pieces: *The*

windscreen shattered.

shave¹ /ʃeɪv/ *verb (present participle* **shaving,** *past* **shaved)** to cut hair off your face or body: *He shaves every day.*

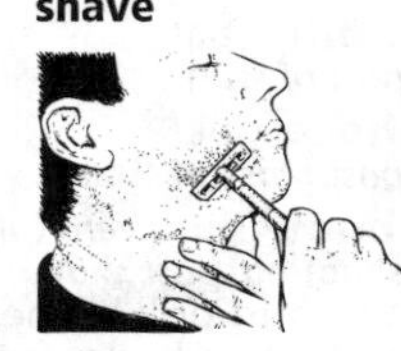
shave

shave² /ʃeɪv/ *noun* when a man shaves the hair growing on his face

shaver /ˈʃeɪvəʳ/ *noun* a piece of electrical equipment used to cut hair off the head or body

she *strong form* /ʃiː/ *weak form* /ʃi/ *pronoun* used when talking about a woman who has already been talked about: *"When is Ruth coming?" "She'll be here soon."*

shears /ʃɪəz/ *plural noun* a cutting tool with two large blades

she'd /ʃiːd/
1 *short for* she had: *By the time I got there, she'd fallen asleep.*
2 *short for* she would: *She knew that she'd be late.*

shed¹ /ʃed/ *noun* a small building used to keep things in such as tools: *a garden shed*

shed² /ʃed/ *verb (present participle* **shedding,** *past* **shed)**
shed leaves/skin/hair, etc to lose something because it falls off: *A lot of trees shed their leaves in the autumn.*

sheep /ʃiːp/ *noun (plural* **sheep)** a farm animal whose skin is covered with wool: *a flock of sheep*

sheep

sheer /ʃɪəʳ/ *adj*
1 used to say that a feeling or quality is very strong: *a look of sheer delight ○ sheer determination*
2 very steep: *a sheer cliff face*

sheet /ʃiːt/ *noun*
1 a large piece of cloth on a bed that you lie on or under
2 a sheet of paper/glass/metal, etc a flat piece of paper/glass, etc

shelf /ʃelf/ *noun (plural* **shelves)** a board used to put things on, often fixed to a wall: *a book shelf*

she'll /ʃiːl/
short for she will: *She'll be away until Tuesday.*

shell

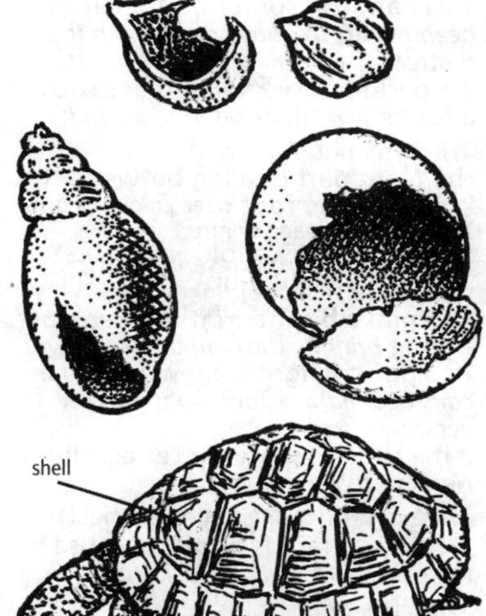

shell /ʃel/ *noun* the hard outer covering of some creatures and of eggs, nuts, or seeds: *a snail's shell ○ an egg shell*

shelter¹ /ˈʃeltəʳ/ *noun*
1 a place that protects you from bad weather or danger: *a bomb shelter*
2 [no plural] protection from bad weather or danger: *We* ***took shelter*** *from the rain in a doorway.*

shelter² /ˈʃeltəʳ/ *verb* to go under a cover or inside a building to be protected from bad weather or danger: *We sheltered from the rain under a tree.*

shepherd /ˈʃepəd/ *noun* someone whose job is to look after sheep

she's /ʃiːz/
1 *short for* she is: *She's very nice.*
2 *short for* she has: *She's been working very hard.*

shield¹ /ʃiːld/ *noun* a large, flat object that soldiers hold in front of their bodies to protect themselves

a b c d e f g h i j k l m n o p q r **s** t u v w x y z

shield² /ʃiːld/ *verb*
to protect someone or something from something bad: *She* ***shielded*** *her eyes* ***from*** *the sun.*

shift /ʃɪft/ *noun*
1 a change in something: *There has been a* ***shift in*** *public opinion on this matter.*
2 a period of work in a place such as a factory or hospital: *a night shift*

shin /ʃɪn/ *noun*
the front part of a leg between the knee and the foot ➲See colour picture **The Body** on page Centre 2

shine /ʃaɪn/ *verb* (*present participle* **shining**, *past* **shone**)
1 to make bright light: *The sun was shining brightly through the window.*
2 to point a light somewhere: *The car's headlights shone right into my eyes.*
3 If a surface shines, it reflects light: *Her hair really shines.*

shiny /ˈʃaɪni/ *adj* (**shinier, shiniest**)
A shiny surface is bright because it reflects light: *shiny, black shoes*

ship /ʃɪp/ *noun*
a large boat that carries people or things by sea

shirt /ʃɜːt/ *noun*
a piece of clothing worn on the top part of the body, fastened with buttons down the front ➲See colour picture **Clothes** on page Centre 5

shiver /ˈʃɪvəʳ/ *verb*
to shake because you are cold or frightened: *She* ***shivered with*** *cold.*
• **shiver** *noun*

shock¹ /ʃɒk/ *noun*
1 a big, unpleasant surprise: *Her death* ***came as a*** *terrible* ***shock*** *to him.*
2 (*also* **electric shock**) a sudden, painful feeling that you get when electricity flows through your body

shock² /ʃɒk/ *verb*
to surprise and upset someone: *Many people were shocked by the violent scenes in the film.*

shocking /ˈʃɒkɪŋ/ *adj*
very bad and making you feel upset: *shocking news*

shoe /ʃuː/ *noun*
a strong covering for the foot, often made of leather: *a pair of shoes* ➲See colour picture **Clothes** on page Centre 5

shoelace /ˈʃuːleɪs/ *noun*
a long, thin piece of material used to fasten shoes

shone /ʃɒn/
past of shine

shook /ʃʊk/
past tense of shake

shoot¹ /ʃuːt/ *verb* (*present participle* **shooting**, *past* **shot**)
1 to hurt or kill a person or animal by firing a bullet from a gun: *He was* ***shot dead*** *in the incident.*
2 to fire a bullet from a gun: *Don't shoot!*
3 to move somewhere very quickly: *She shot out of the room.*

shoot² /ʃuːt/ *noun*
a new branch or stem growing on a plant: *bamboo shoots*

shop¹ /ʃɒp/ (*US* **store**) *noun*
a building or part of a building where you can buy things: *a book shop*

shop² /ʃɒp/ *verb* (*present participle* **shopping**, *past* **shopped**)
to buy things in shops: *I'm* ***shopping for*** *baby clothes.*

shop assistant /ˈʃɒp əˌsɪstənt/ *UK* (*US* **sales clerk**) *noun*
someone whose job is selling things in a shop

shopping /ˈʃɒpɪŋ/ *noun* **[no plural]**
1 when you buy things from shops: *I love shopping.* ○ *I usually go shopping on Saturday.*
2 the things that you buy from a shop or shops: *Can you help me unpack the shopping?*

shore /ʃɔːʳ/ *noun*
the area of land along the edge of the sea or a lake

short /ʃɔːt/ *adj*
1 having a small distance from one end to the other: *short, brown hair* ○ *short legs* ➲Opposite **long**
2 continuing for a small amount of time: *a short visit* ➲Opposite **long**
3 A short person is not as tall as most people. ➲Opposite **tall**
4 not having enough of something: *I'm a bit* ***short of*** *money at the moment.*

shortage /ˈʃɔːtɪdʒ/ *noun*
when there is not enough of something: *food shortages*

shortcut /ˈʃɔːtkʌt/ *noun*
1 a quicker way of getting

somewhere or doing something: *I **took a shortcut** through the car park.*
2 in computing, a quick way to start or use a computer program

shorten /ˈʃɔːtᵊn/ *verb*
to become shorter or to make something shorter: *Smoking shortens your life.*

shortly /ˈʃɔːtli/ *adv*
soon: *Our plans for the next year will be announced shortly.*

shorts /ʃɔːts/ *plural noun*
1 a very short pair of trousers that stop above the knees: *cycling shorts*
2 *US* men's underwear to wear under trousers ➲See colour picture **Clothes** on page Centre 5

shot¹ /ʃɒt/ *noun*
1 when a bullet is fired from a gun: *Three **shots** were **fired**.*
2 when someone tries to score points in sports such as football: *Good shot!*

shot² /ʃɒt/
past of shoot

should *strong form* /ʃʊd/ *weak form* /ʃəd/ *verb*
1 used to say or ask what is the correct or best thing to do: *He should go to the doctor.* ○ *Should I apologize to her?*
2 used to say that you think something is true or that you think something will happen: *She should be feeling better by now.* ○ *The letter should arrive by Friday.*

shoulder /ˈʃəʊldəʳ/ *noun*
where your arm joins your body next to your neck: *He put his arm around my shoulder.*

shoulder

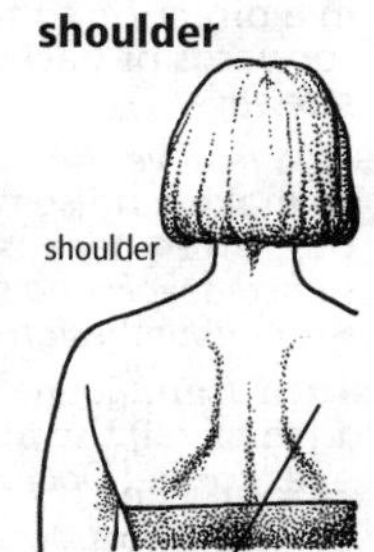

shouldn't /ˈʃʊdᵊnt/ *short for* should not: *I shouldn't have said that.*

should've /ˈʃʊdəv/ *short for* should have: *She should've finished by now.*

shout¹ /ʃaʊt/ *verb*
to say something very loudly: *"Look out!" she shouted.* ○ *I was angry and I **shouted at** him.*

shout² /ʃaʊt/ *noun*
when you say something very loudly: *He was woken by a loud shout.*

show¹ /ʃəʊ/ *verb (past participle* **shown)**
1 to prove that something is true: *Sales figures showed a significant increase last month.*
2 to let someone look at something: *Show me your photos.*
3 to teach someone how to do something by explaining it or by doing it yourself: *She **showed** me **how** to use the new computer system.* ○ *Have you **shown** him **what to do**?*
4 to express a feeling so that other people are able to notice it: *If she was upset, she certainly didn't show it.*
5 to take someone to or round a place: *She showed me round the factory.*

show off *phrasal verb*
to try to make people think you are clever or rich: *Stop showing off!*

show² /ʃəʊ/ *noun*
1 a television or radio programme or a theatre performance: *He's got his own show on Channel 5.*
2 a time at which a group of similar things are brought together for the public to see: *a fashion show* ○ *a flower show*

shower /ʃaʊəʳ/ *noun*
1 when you wash your whole body while standing under a flow of water: *I **had a shower** and got dressed.*
2 a piece of bathroom equipment that you stand under to wash your whole body: *He's **in the shower**.* ➲See colour picture **The Bathroom** on page Centre 1
3 a short period of rain

shown /ʃəʊn/
past participle of show

shrank /ʃræŋk/
past tense of shrink

shred /ʃred/ *noun*
a very small piece that has been torn from something: *She tore the letter **to shreds**.*

shrewd /ʃruːd/ *adj*
clever at making decisions which give you an advantage: *a shrewd businessman*

a b c d e f g h i j k l m n o p q r s t u v w x y z

shrine /ʃraɪn/ *noun*
a holy place where people go to pray

shrink /ʃrɪŋk/ *verb* (*present participle* **shrinking,** *past tense* **shrank,** *past participle* **shrunk)**
to become smaller, or to make something smaller: *My shirt shrank in the wash.*

shrub /ʃrʌb/ *noun*
a large plant that is smaller than a tree

shrug /ʃrʌg/ *verb* (*present participle* **shrugging,** *past* **shrugged)**
to move your shoulders up and down to show that you do not care about something or that you do not know something: *I told him we weren't happy with it but he just shrugged his shoulders.*
• **shrug** *noun*

shrunk /ʃrʌŋk/
past participle of shrink

shudder /ˈʃʌdəʳ/ *verb*
to shake, usually because you are thinking of something bad: *She* ***shuddered with*** *horror.*
• **shudder** *noun*

shut /ʃʌt/ *verb* (*present participle* **shutting,** *past* **shut)**
1 to close something, or to become closed: *Shut the door.* ○ *He lay back and shut his eyes.* ○ *The door shut with a bang.*
2 When a shop, restaurant, etc shuts, it stops serving customers and does not allow people to enter: *The museum shuts at 4 o'clock on a Friday.*
shut up *phrasal verb, informal*
to stop talking: *Just shut up and get on with your work!*

shy /ʃaɪ/ *adj*
not confident, especially about meeting new people: *He was too shy to say anything to her.*

sick /sɪk/ *adj*
1 ill: *He was off work sick for most of last week.*
2 be sick If you are sick, food and drink comes up from your stomach and out of your mouth: *The baby was sick all down his shirt.*
3 feel sick to feel that the food or drink in your stomach will soon come up through your mouth
4 be sick of something *informal* to be bored with or angry about something: *I'm sick of people telling me how to run my life!*

sickness /ˈsɪknəs/ *noun* **[no plural]**
1 when you are ill
2 when the food or drink in your stomach come up through your mouth: *travel sickness*

side /saɪd/ *noun*
1 one of the two parts that something would divide into if you drew a line down the middle: *Which side of the bed do you sleep on?*
2 a flat, outer surface of an object, especially one that is not its top, bottom, front, or back: *The side of the car was badly scratched.*
3 one edge of something: *A square has four sides.*
4 the area next to something: *There were trees growing by the side of the road.*
5 either of the two surfaces of a thin, flat object such as a piece of paper or a coin: *Write on both sides of the paper.*
6 one of the people or groups who are arguing, fighting, or competing: *Whose* ***side*** *is he* ***on****?*
7 *UK* the players in a sports team: *He's been selected for the national side.*
8 one of the two areas of your body from under your arms to the tops of your legs: *She lay on her side.*

sidewalk /ˈsaɪdwɔːk/ *US* (*UK* **pavement)** *noun*
a path with a hard surface by the side of a road that people walk on

sideways /ˈsaɪdweɪz/ *adv*
in a direction to the left or right, not forwards or backwards: *He glanced sideways.*

sigh /saɪ/ *verb*
to make a noise when you breathe out, often because you are sad: *He sighed deeply and sat down.*
• **sigh** *noun*: *a sigh of relief*

sight /saɪt/ *noun*
1 [no plural] the ability to use your eyes to see: *Doctors managed to save his sight.*
2 when you see someone or something: *The sight of so much blood had shocked him.*
3 something which you see, especially something interesting: *the sights and sounds of the market*
4 the sights the beautiful or

interesting places in a city or country: *He took me around New York and showed me the sights.*

sightseeing /ˈsaɪtsiːɪŋ/ *noun* **[no plural]**
the activity of visiting interesting or beautiful places: *a sightseeing tour of London*
● **sightseer** /ˈsaɪtˌsiːəʳ/ *noun*
a person who goes sightseeing

sign¹ /saɪn/ *noun*
1 something which shows that something is happening: *Flowers are the first* ***sign of*** *Spring.* ○ *It's a* ***sign that*** *things are improving.*
2 a symbol or message in a public place which gives information or instructions: *a road sign* ○ *a 'no-smoking' sign*
3 a symbol which has a particular meaning: *a pound sign*
4 a movement you make to give someone information or tell them what to do

sign² /saɪn/ *verb*
to write your name on something to show that you wrote or painted, etc it or to show that you agree to it: *He signs his letters 'Prof. James D. Nelson'.*

signal¹ /ˈsɪgnəl/ *noun*
a movement, light, or sound which gives information, or tells people what to do: *Don't move until I give the signal.*

signal² /ˈsɪgnəl/ *verb* (*present participle* **signalling,** *past* **signalled)**
1 to make a movement which gives information or tells people what to do: *He* ***signalled for*** *them to be quiet.*
2 to show that you are ready to do something: *The US signalled that they were ready to enter talks.*

signature /ˈsɪgnətʃəʳ/ *noun*
your name written in your own way which is difficult for someone else to copy

significance /sɪgˈnɪfɪkəns/ *noun* **[no plural]**
the importance or meaning of something: *I still don't understand* ***the significance of*** *his remark.*

significant /sɪgˈnɪfɪkənt/ *adj*
important: *These measures will save a significant amount of money.*

signpost /ˈsaɪnpəʊst/ *noun*
a sign by the side of the road that gives information

silence /ˈsaɪləns/ *noun* **[no plural]**
when there is no sound: *The three men ate* ***in silence****.*

silent /ˈsaɪlənt/ *adj*
without any sound: *The building was dark and silent.*
● **silently** *adv*: *The snow fell silently all around them.*

silk /sɪlk/ *noun* **[no plural]**
a type of cloth which is light and smooth: *a silk dress*

silky /ˈsɪlki/ *adj*
soft and smooth, like silk: *a cat with silky, grey fur*

silly /ˈsɪli/ *adj* **(sillier, silliest)**
stupid: *Do I look silly in this hat?* ○ *It's silly to spend money on something you don't need.*

silver¹ /ˈsɪlvəʳ/ *noun* **[no plural]**
a valuable, shiny, grey-white metal used to make jewellery: *silver and gold*

silver² /ˈsɪlvəʳ/ *adj*
1 made of silver: *a silver necklace*
2 being the colour of silver: *a silver sports car*

similar /ˈsɪmɪləʳ/ *adj*
Something which is similar to something else has many things the same, although it is not exactly the same: *The two houses are remarkably similar.*

similarity /ˌsɪmɪˈlærəti/ *noun* (*plural* **similarities)**
when two things or people are similar, or a way in which they are similar: *There are a number of* ***similarities between*** *the two systems.*
➲Opposite **difference**

simple /ˈsɪmpl/ *adj* **(simpler, simplest)**
1 not difficult to do or to understand: *It's very simple to use.*
2 not complicated: *a simple life* ○ *a simple black dress* (= dress without decoration)

simplify /ˈsɪmplɪfaɪ/ *verb* (*present participle* **simplifying,** *past* **simplified)**
to make something easier to do or understand: *We need to simplify the instructions.*

simply /ˈsɪmpli/ *adv*
in a way which is not complicated or difficult to understand: *simply prepared food* ○ *He explained it as simply as he could.*

sin /sɪn/ *noun*
something which is against the rules of a religion: *the sin of pride*

since[1] /sɪns/ *adv, preposition*
from a time in the past until a later time or until now: *They've been waiting since March.* ○ *The factory had been closed since the explosion.*

since[2] /sɪns/ *conjunction*
from a time in the past until a later time or until now: *I've known Tim since he was seven.*

sincere /sɪn'sɪəʳ/ *adj*
honest and saying what you really feel or believe: *He seems to be sincere.*

sincerely /sɪn'sɪəli/ *adv*
1 in a sincere way: *I sincerely hope that this never happens again.*
2 Yours sincerely *formal* used at the end of formal letters where you know the name of the person you are writing to

sing /sɪŋ/ *verb* (*present participle* **singing,** *past tense* **sang,** *past participle* **sung)**
to make musical sounds with your voice: *They all sang 'Happy Birthday' to him.*

singer /'sɪŋəʳ/ *noun*
someone who sings: *a jazz singer*

single[1] /'sɪŋgl/ *adj*
1 only one: *There was a single light in the corner of the room.*
2 used to make the word 'every' stronger: *I call him* ***every single*** *day.* ○ *He could hear every single word we said.*
3 not married: *He's young and single.*
4 looking after your children alone: *a single mother*
5 for only one person: *a single bed*

single[2] /'sɪŋgl/ *noun UK*
a ticket for a journey that is from one place to another but not back again: *Could I have a single to London, please?*

the singular /'sɪŋgjələʳ/ *noun*
the form of a word for one person or thing and no more

sink[1] /sɪŋk/ *verb* (*present participle* **sinking,** *past tense* **sank,** *past participle* **sunk)**
1 to go down or make something go down under the surface of water and not come back up: *The Titanic sank after hitting an iceberg.*
2 to go down, or make something go down, into something soft: *My feet keep sinking into the sand.*

sink[2] /sɪŋk/ *noun*
a bowl that is fixed to the wall in a kitchen or bathroom that you wash dishes or your hands, etc in ➲See colour picture **The Bathroom** on page Centre 1

sip /sɪp/ *verb* (*present participle* **sipping,** *past* **sipped)**
to drink, taking only a small amount at a time: *She sipped her champagne.*
●**sip** *noun*: *He* ***took a sip of*** *his coffee and then continued.*

sir /sɜːʳ/ *noun*
1 (*also* **Sir)** You call a man 'sir' when you are speaking to him politely: *Excuse me, sir, is this seat taken?*
2 You write 'Sir' at the beginning of a formal letter to a man when you do not know his name: *Dear Sir, I am writing to...*
3 Sir a title used in the UK before the name of a man who has been officially respected or who has a high social rank: *Sir Cliff Richard*

siren /'saɪərən/ *noun*
a piece of equipment that makes a loud sound as a warning: *a police siren*

sister /'sɪstəʳ/ *noun*
a girl or woman who has the same parents as you: *an older/younger sister*

sister-in-law /'sɪstᵊrɪnlɔː/ *noun* (*plural* **sisters-in-law)**
the woman married to your brother, or the sister of your husband or wife

sit /sɪt/ *verb* (*present participle* **sitting,** *past* **sat)**
1 to be in a position with the weight of your body on your bottom and the top part of your body up, for example, on a chair: *Emma was* ***sitting on*** *a stool.* ○ *The children* ***sat at*** *the table by the window.*
2 (*also* **sit down)** to move your body into a sitting position after you have been standing: *She sat down on the grass.* ➲See colour picture **Phrasal Verbs** on page Centre 13

sit up *phrasal verb*
to move your body to a sitting position after you have been lying down: *I sat up and opened my eyes.*

site /saɪt/ *noun*
1 the place where something

important happened in the past: *the site of a battle*
2 an area that is used for something or where something happens: *a building site*
3 *short for* website (= an area on the Internet where information about a particular subject, organization, etc can be found)

sitting room /'sɪtɪŋ ruːm/ *noun UK*
the room in a house where people sit to relax and, for example, watch television

situated /'sɪtjueɪtɪd/ *adj formal*
be situated in/on/by, etc to be in a particular place: *a hotel situated by Lake Garda*

situation /ˌsɪtju'eɪʃᵊn/ *noun*
the set of things that are happening at a particular time and place: *the current political situation* ○ *He's* ***in a*** *difficult* ***situation****.*

six /sɪks/
the number 6

sixteen /ˌsɪk'stiːn/
the number 16
● **sixteenth**
16th written as a word

sixth[1] /sɪksθ/
6th written as a word

sixth[2] /sɪksθ/ *noun*
one of six equal parts of something; ⅙

sixth form /'sɪksθ ˌfɔːm/ *noun*
in Britain, the part of a school for students between the ages of 16 and 18

sixty /'sɪksti/
the number 60
● **sixtieth**
60th written as a word

size /saɪz/ *noun*
how big or small something is: *It's an area about the size of Oxford.* ○ *The size of some of those trees is incredible.* ○ *What* ***size*** *shoes do you* ***take****?*

skate[1] /skeɪt/ *noun*
1 (*also* **roller skate**) a boot with wheels on the bottom, used for moving across the ground: *a pair of skates*
2 (*also* **ice skate**) a boot with a metal part on the bottom, used for moving across ice ➲See colour picture **Sports 1** on page Centre 15

skate[2] /skeɪt/ *verb* (*present participle* **skating**, *past* **skated**)
to move using skates
● **skater** *noun*
● **skating** *noun* **[no plural]**

skateboard /'skeɪtbɔːd/ *noun*
a board with wheels on the bottom, that you stand on and move forward by pushing one foot on the ground ➲See colour picture **Sports 1** on page Centre 15

skeleton /'skelɪtᵊn/ *noun*
the structure made of all the bones in the body of a person or animal: *the skeleton of a dog*

sketch[1] /sketʃ/ *noun* (*plural* **sketches**)
a simple picture that you draw quickly: *He did a quick* ***sketch of*** *the cat.*

sketch[2] /sketʃ/ *verb*
to draw a sketch: *I sketched a map for him on a scrap of paper.*

ski[1] /skiː/ *noun*
one of a pair of long, thin pieces of wood or plastic that you wear on the bottom of boots to move over snow ➲See colour picture **Sports 1** on page Centre 15

ski[2] /skiː/ *verb* (*present participle* **skiing**, *past* **skied**)
to move over snow wearing skis
● **skiing** *noun* **[no plural]** *I'd like to* ***go skiing*** *in Switzerland.*

skid /skɪd/ *verb* (*present participle* **skidding**, *past* **skidded**)
If a car etc skids, it slides along a surface and you cannot control it: *The car skidded on ice and hit a tree.*

skilful /'skɪlfᵊl/ *adj*
good at doing something: *a skilful artist*
● **skilfully** *adv*

skill /skɪl/ *noun*
the ability to do an activity or job well, especially because you have done it many times: *You need good communication skills to be a teacher.*

skilled /skɪld/ *adj*
having the abilities needed to do an activity or job well: *a highly skilled* (= very skilled) *photographer* ○ *He has become* ***skilled in*** *dealing with the media.*

skin /skɪn/ *noun*
1 the outer layer of a person or animal's body: *dark skin*
2 the outer layer of a fruit or

a b c d e f g h i j k l m n o p q r **s** t u v w x y z

vegetable: *a banana skin*

skinny /ˈskɪni/ *adj* **(skinnier, skinniest)**
too thin

skip /skɪp/ *verb* (*present participle* **skipping,** *past* **skipped)**
1 to move forward, jumping quickly from one foot to the other: *She watched her daughter skipping down the street.*
2 to jump over a rope while you or two other people move it over and then under your body again and again: *I skip for ten minutes every day to keep fit.*
3 to not do something that you usually do: *I think I'll skip lunch today.*

skirt /skɜːt/ *noun*
a piece of women's clothing that hangs from the waist and has no legs ➲See colour picture **Clothes** on page Centre 5

skull /skʌl/ *noun*
the bones in your head

sky /skaɪ/ *noun* (*plural* **skies)**
the area above the Earth where you can see clouds, the sun, the moon, etc: *a beautiful, blue sky*

skyscraper /ˈskaɪˌskreɪpəʳ/ *noun*
a very tall building

slab /slæb/ *noun*
a thick, flat piece of something, especially stone: *a slab of concrete*

slack /slæk/ *adj*
1 loose or not tight: *Suddenly the rope became slack.* ➲Opposite **tight**
2 not trying hard enough in your work: *slack management*

slam /slæm/ *verb* (*present participle* **slamming,** *past* **slammed)**
to close with great force, or to make something close with great force: *Kate heard the front door slam.*

slang /slæŋ/ *noun* **[no plural]**
informal language

slant¹ /slɑːnt/ *verb*
to slope in a particular direction: *Pale sunlight **slanted through** the curtain.*

slant² /slɑːnt/ *noun*
1 a position that is sloping: *The road is **on a slant**.*
2 a way of writing about something that shows who or what you support: *a political slant*

slap¹ /slæp/ *verb* (*present participle* **slapping,** *past* **slapped)**
to hit someone with the flat, inside part of your hand: *She slapped him across the face.*

slap² /slæp/ *noun*
a hit with the flat, inside part of your hand

slaughter¹ /ˈslɔːtəʳ/ *verb*
1 to kill an animal for meat
2 to kill a lot of people in a very cruel way

slaughter² /ˈslɔːtəʳ/ *noun* **[no plural]**
when a lot of people or animals are killed in a cruel way

slave¹ /sleɪv/ *noun*
someone who is owned by someone else and has to work for them: *He treats his mother like a slave.*

slave² /sleɪv/ *verb* (*present participle* **slaving,** *past* **slaved)** *informal*
to work very hard: *Giorgio was **slaving away at** his homework.*

slavery /ˈsleɪvəri/ *noun* **[no plural]**
when people keep slaves

sledge /sledʒ/ *UK noun*
a vehicle that is used for travelling on snow

sleek /sliːk/ *adj*
Sleek hair is smooth and very shiny.

sleep¹ /sliːp/ *verb* (*present participle* **sleeping,** *past* **slept)**
1 to be in the state of rest when your eyes are closed, your body is not active, and your mind is unconscious: *We had to sleep in the car that night.* ○ *Did you sleep well?*
sleep in *phrasal verb*
to sleep longer in the morning than you usually do

sleep² /sliːp/ *noun* **[no plural]**
1 the state you are in when you are sleeping, or a period of time when you are sleeping: *You need to go home and **get some sleep**.* ○ *It took me ages to **get to sleep*** (= to succeed in sleeping).
2 go to sleep to begin to sleep: *Babies often go to sleep after a feed.*

sleeping bag /ˈsliːpɪŋ ˌbæg/ *noun*
a long bag made of thick material that you sleep inside

sleepless /ˈsliːpləs/ *adj*
sleepless night a night when you are not able to sleep

sleepy /ˈsliːpi/ *adj* **(sleepier, sleepiest)**

feeling tired and wanting to go to sleep: *The heat had made me sleepy.*

sleet /sliːt/ *noun* **[no plural]**
a mixture of snow and rain
● **sleet** *verb* ***It was sleeting*** *when I looked outside.*

sleeve /sliːv/ *noun*
the part of a jacket, shirt, etc that covers your arm: *He rolled up his sleeves to do the dishes.*
2 have something up your sleeve *informal* to have a secret plan

slender /ˈslendəʳ/ *adj*
thin in an attractive way

slept /slept/
past of sleep

slice¹ /slaɪs/ *noun*
a flat piece of food that has been cut from a larger piece: *a slice of bread/cake* ➲See colour picture **Quantities** on page Centre 14

slice² /slaɪs/ *verb* (*present participle* **slicing,** *past* **sliced)**
(*also* **slice up**) to cut food into flat pieces: *Could you slice the tomatoes?*

slide¹ /slaɪd/ *verb* (*present participle* **sliding,** *past* **slid)**
to move smoothly over a surface: *He likes sliding on the ice.*

slide² /slaɪd/ *noun*
1 a small piece of film that you shine light through in order to see a photograph
2 a large object that children climb and slide down as a game

slight /slaɪt/ *adj*
1 small and not important: *slight differences in colour*
2 Someone who is slight is thin.

slightly /ˈslaɪtli/ *adv*
a little: *I find it slightly worrying.*

slim¹ /slɪm/ *adj*
Someone who is slim is thin in an attractive way.

slim² /slɪm/ *verb* (*present participle* **slimming,** *past* **slimmed)** *UK*
to eat less in order to become thinner

slime /slaɪm/ *noun* **[no plural]**
a thick, sticky liquid that is unpleasant to touch

slimy /ˈslaɪmi/ *adj*
covered in slime

sling /slɪŋ/ *noun*
a piece of cloth that you wear around your neck and put your arm into when it is hurt

slip¹ /slɪp/ *verb* (*present participle* **slipping,** *past* **slipped)**
1 to slide by accident and fall or almost fall: *She slipped on the ice and broke her ankle.*
2 to slide out of the correct position: *The photo had slipped from the frame.*
3 to go somewhere quietly or quickly: *I'll slip out of the room if I get bored.*
slip up *phrasal verb*
to make a mistake

slip² /slɪp/ *noun*
1 a small piece of paper: *He wrote the number on a slip of paper.*
2 a small mistake
3 a slip of the tongue a mistake made by using the wrong word

slipper /ˈslɪpəʳ/ *noun*
a soft, comfortable shoe that you wear in the house

slippery /ˈslɪpᵊri/ *adj*
smooth and wet and difficult to hold or walk on: *Be careful - the floor's slippery.*

slit¹ /slɪt/ *noun*
a long, thin cut or hole in something

slit² /slɪt/ *verb* (*present participle* **slitting,** *past* **slit)**
to make a long, thin cut in something: *She slit her wrists.*

slob /slɒb/ *noun informal*
a lazy or dirty person

slogan /ˈsləʊgən/ *noun*
a short phrase that is easy to remember and is used to make people notice something: *an advertising slogan*

slope¹ /sləʊp/ *noun*
a surface or piece of land that is high at one end and low at the other: *There's a* ***steep slope*** *to climb before we're at the top.*

slope² /sləʊp/ *verb* (*present participle* **sloping,** *past* **sloped)**
to be high at one end and low at the other: *The field* ***slopes down*** *to the river.*

sloppy /ˈslɒpi/ *adj* **(sloppier, sloppiest)**
not done carefully: *His work was sloppy and full of spelling mistakes.*

slot /slɒt/ *noun*
a long, thin hole that you put something into, especially money

slot machine /ˈslɒt məˌʃiːn/ *noun*
a machine that you put money into in order to try to win money

slow[1] /sləʊ/ *adj*
1 moving, happening, or doing something without much speed: *He's a very slow reader.* ➲Opposite **fast**
2 If a clock is slow, it shows a time that is earlier than the correct time. ➲Opposite **fast**

slow[2] /sləʊ/ *verb*
slow (something) down *phrasal verb* to become slower or to make something become slower: *Slow down, Claire, you're walking too fast!*

slowly /ˈsləʊli/ *adv*
at a slow speed: *Could you speak more slowly, please?*

slug /slʌg/ *noun*
a small, soft creature with no legs that moves slowly and eats plants

slum /slʌm/ *noun*
a poor and crowded area of a city: *He grew up in the slums of Mexico City.*

slump /slʌmp/ *verb*
1 If a price, value, or amount slumps, it goes down suddenly: *Sales have slumped by 50%.*
2 to fall or sit down suddenly because you feel tired or weak: *She slumped back in her chair, exhausted.*

smack /smæk/ *verb*
to hit someone with the flat, inside part of your hand

small /smɔːl/ *adj*
1 little in size or amount: *We teach the children in small groups.* ➲Opposite **big** or **large**
2 A small child is very young: *a woman with three small children*
3 not important or serious: *a small mistake*

smart /smɑːt/ *adj*
1 clever: *Rachel's one of the smartest kids in the class.*
2 If you look smart or your clothes are smart, you look clean and tidy: *I need to look a bit smarter for my interview.*
3 fashionable and expensive: *a smart, new restaurant*

smash /smæʃ/ *verb*
to break into a lot of pieces with a loud noise, or to make something break into a lot of pieces with a loud noise: *Someone had smashed the shop window.*

smash

smear[1] /smɪəʳ/ *verb*
to spread a thick liquid or sticky substance over something: *His shirt was **smeared with** paint.*

smear[2] /smɪəʳ/ *noun*
a dirty mark: *There was a smear of oil on his cheek.*

smell[1] /smel/ *verb* (*past* **smelt**)
1 to have a particular quality that people notice by using their nose: *That soup smells delicious – what's in it?*
2 to notice something by using your nose: *I think I can smell something burning.*
3 to have a bad smell: *Your running shoes really smell!*

smell[2] /smel/ *noun*
1 the quality that something has which you notice by using your nose: *The **smell of** roses filled the room.*
2 a bad smell: *I wish I could get rid of that smell in the bathroom.*
3 **[no plural]** the ability to notice smells: *Smoking can affect your **sense of smell**.*

smelly /ˈsmeli/ *adj* **(smellier, smelliest)**
having a bad smell: *smelly feet*

smelt /smelt/
past of smell

smile[1] /smaɪl/ *verb* (*present participle* **smiling**, *past* **smiled**)
to make the corners of your mouth go up so that you look happy or friendly: *She **smiled at** me.*

smile[2] /smaɪl/ *noun*
when the corners of your mouth go up so that you look happy or friendly: *He gave me a big smile and wished me good luck.*

smoke[1] /sməʊk/ *noun* **[no plural]**
the grey or black gas that is made when something burns

smoke[2] /sməʊk/ *verb* (*present participle* **smoking**, *past* **smoked**)
1 to breathe smoke into your mouth from a cigarette: *Do you mind if I smoke?*
2 to make or send out smoke: *smoking chimneys*

smoker /ˈsməʊkəʳ/ *noun*
someone who often smokes cigarettes

smoking /ˈsməʊkɪŋ/ *noun* **[no plural]**
when someone smokes a cigarette

smoky /ˈsməʊki/ *adj* **(smokier, smokiest)**

filled with smoke: *a smoky bar*

smooth /smuːð/ *adj*
1 having a regular surface that has no holes or lumps in it: *soft, smooth skin* ⊃Opposite **rough**
2 A substance that is smooth has no lumps in it: *Mix the butter and sugar together until smooth.* ⊃Opposite **lumpy**
3 happening without any sudden movements: *The plane made a smooth landing.*

smoothly /ˈsmuːðli/ *adv*
go smoothly to happen without any problems: *Everything was going smoothly until Darren arrived.*

smother /ˈsmʌðəʳ/ *verb*
to kill someone by covering their face with something so that they cannot breathe
smother something with something *phrasal verb*
to cover something completely with a substance: *She smothered the cake with cream.*

smoulder /ˈsməʊldəʳ/ *verb*
to burn slowly, producing smoke but no flames: *The fire was still smouldering the next morning.*

smudge[1] /smʌdʒ/ *noun*
a dirty mark: *a smudge of ink*

smudge[2] /smʌdʒ/ *verb* (*present participle* **smudging,** *past* **smudged)**
If ink, paint, etc smudges, or if it is smudged, it becomes dirty or not clear because someone has touched it: *Be careful you don't smudge the drawing.*

smuggle /ˈsmʌgl/ *verb* (*present participle* **smuggling,** *past* **smuggled)**
to take something into or out of a place in an illegal or secret way: *He was arrested for smuggling drugs into Britain.*
• **smuggler** *noun*: *drug smugglers*

snack /snæk/ *noun*
a small amount of food

snag /snæg/ *noun informal*
a problem

snail /sneɪl/ *noun*
a small creature with a long, soft body and a round shell

snail

snake /sneɪk/ *noun*
a long, thin creature with no legs that slides along the ground

snap[1] /snæp/ *verb* (*present participle* **snapping,** *past* **snapped)**
1 If something long and thin snaps, it breaks making a short, loud sound, and if you snap it, you break it, making a short, loud sound: *The twigs snapped as we walked on them.*
2 to say something suddenly in an angry way: *I was **snapping at** the children because I was tired.*
3 If an animal snaps, it tries to bite someone.
snap something up *phrasal verb, informal*
to buy or get something quickly: *The dress was perfect, so I snapped it up.*

snap[2] /snæp/ *noun*
1 a sudden, short, loud sound like something breaking: *I heard a snap as I sat on the pencil.*
2 *UK informal* a photograph: *holiday snaps*

snarl /snɑːl/ *verb*
1 to speak angrily: *"Go away!" he snarled.*
2 If an animal snarls, it shows its teeth and makes an angry sound.

snatch /snætʃ/ *verb*
to take something or someone quickly and suddenly: *Bill snatched the telephone from my hand.*

sneak /sniːk/ *verb*
to go somewhere quietly because you do not want anyone to hear you: *I sneaked into his bedroom while he was asleep.*

sneeze /sniːz/ *verb* (*present participle* **sneezing,** *past* **sneezed)**
When you sneeze, air suddenly comes out through your nose and mouth: *He had a cold and was sneezing a lot.*
• **sneeze** *noun*

sniff /snɪf/ *verb*
1 to breathe air in through your nose in a way that makes a noise: *Sam had a cold and she kept sniffing.*
2 to breathe air in through your nose in order to smell something: *She sniffed the flowers.*
• **sniff** *noun*

snob /snɒb/ *noun*
someone who thinks they are better than other people

snooker /ˈsnuːkəʳ/ *noun* **[no plural]**

a b c d e f g h i j k l m n o p q r s t u v w x y z

a game in which two people use long sticks to hit balls into holes at the edge of a table

snooze /snuːz/ *verb* (*present participle* **snoozing,** *past* **snoozed**) *informal*
to sleep for a short time, especially during the day: *Granddad was snoozing in his chair.*
•**snooze** *noun, informal*: *Why don't you* ***have a snooze****?*

snore /snɔː^r/ *verb* (*present participle* **snoring,** *past* **snored**)
to breathe in a very noisy way while you are sleeping
•**snore** *noun*

snow[1] /snəʊ/ *noun* **[no plural]**
soft white pieces of frozen water that fall from the sky when the weather is cold: *Children were playing in the snow.*

snow[2] /snəʊ/ *verb*
it snows If it snows, snow falls from the sky: *It snowed all day yesterday.*

snowball /ˈsnəʊbɔːl/ *noun*
a ball made from snow that children throw at each other

snowboarding /ˈsnəʊbɔːdɪŋ/ *noun* **[no plural]**
a sport in which you stand on a large board and move over snow

snowflake /ˈsnəʊfleɪk/ *noun*
a small piece of snow that falls from the sky

snowman /ˈsnəʊmæn/ *noun* (*plural* **snowmen**)
something that looks like a person and is made from snow

snowy /ˈsnəʊi/ *adj* (**snowier, snowiest**)
snowing or covered with snow: *a cold, snowy day*

so[1] /səʊ/ *adv*
1 used before an adjective or adverb to make that adjective or adverb stronger: *I was so tired when I got home.* ○ *I love her so much.* ○ *I was so upset that I couldn't speak.*
2 used to give a short answer to a question to avoid repeating a phrase: *"Is Ben coming to the party?" "I hope so."*
3 or so used after a number or amount to show that it is not exact: *"How many people were at the party?" "Fifty or so, I guess."*
4 So (what)? used to say that you do not think something is important, especially in a rude way: *"She might tell Emily." "So what?"*
5 and so on used after a list of things to show that you could add other similar things: *She plays a lot of tennis and squash and so on.*

so[2] /səʊ/ *conjunction*
1 used to say that something is the reason why something else happens: *I was tired so I went to bed.* ○ *Greg had some money so he bought a bike.*
2 so (that) in order to make something happen or be possible: *He put his glasses on so that he could see the television better.*

soak /səʊk/ *verb*
1 to put something in a liquid for a period of time: *Soak the bread in the milk.*
2 to make something very wet: *The rain soaked my clothes.*

soaking /ˈsəʊkɪŋ/ *adj*
completely wet: *The dog was* ***soaking wet****.*

soap /səʊp/ *noun*
1 [no plural] a substance that you use for washing: *a bar of soap* ➲See colour picture **The Bathroom** on page Centre 1
2 (*also* ˈ**soap** ˌ**opera**) a television programme about the lives of a group of people that is shown every week

soar /sɔː^r/ *verb*
1 to go up to a high level very quickly: *House prices have soared.*
2 to move quickly and smoothly in the sky: *The birds were soaring high above.*

sob /sɒb/ *verb* (*present participle* **sobbing,** *past* **sobbed**)
to cry in a noisy way
•**sob** *noun*

sober /ˈsəʊbə^r/ *adj*
Someone who is sober is not drunk.

soccer /ˈsɒkə^r/ (*also UK* **football**) *noun* **[no plural]**
a game in which two teams of eleven people kick a ball and try to score goals

sociable /ˈsəʊʃəbl/ *adj*
Someone who is sociable likes being with people and meeting new people.

social /ˈsəʊʃ^{ə}l/ *adj*
1 relating to society and the way people live: *social problems*

a b c d e f g h i j k l m n o p q r s t u v w x y z

2 relating to the things you do with other people for enjoyment when you are not working: *I have a very good* ***social life****.*

socialize /ˈsəʊʃəlaɪz/ *verb* (*present participle* **socializing**, *past* **socialized**) to spend time enjoying yourself with other people: *The cafe is a place where students can* ***socialize with*** *teachers.*

society /səˈsaɪəti/ *noun*
1 **[no plural]** a large group of people who live in the same country or area and have the same laws, traditions, etc: *Unemployment is a problem for society.*
2 (*plural* **societies**) an organization for people who have the same interest: *the London Zoological Society*

sock /sɒk/ *noun* something that you wear on your foot inside your shoe: *a pair of black socks* ➲See colour picture **Clothes** on page Centre 5

socket /ˈsɒkɪt/ *noun* the place on a wall where you connect electrical equipment to the electricity supply

sofa /ˈsəʊfə/ *noun* a large, comfortable seat for more than one person ➲See colour picture **The Living Room** on page Centre 11

sofa

soft /sɒft/ *adj*
1 not hard, and easy to press: *a soft cushion* ○ *Cook the onion until it's soft.* ➲Opposite **hard**
2 smooth and pleasant to touch: *soft hair/skin* ➲Opposite **rough**
3 A soft sound is very quiet: *He spoke in a soft voice.*
4 A soft colour or light is not bright: *soft lilac paint* ➲Opposite **bright**
5 too kind: *You're too soft to be a teacher.*

soft drink /ˌsɒft ˈdrɪŋk/ *noun UK* a cold, sweet drink that does not have alcohol in it

soften /ˈsɒfən/ *verb* to become softer or to make something become softer: *Heat the butter until it softens.*

softly /ˈsɒftli/ *adv* in a quiet or gentle way: *"Are you OK?" she said softly.*

software /ˈsɒftweəʳ/ *noun* **[no plural]** programs that you use to make a computer do different things: *educational software* ➲Compare **hardware**

soggy /ˈsɒgi/ *adj* **(soggier, soggiest)** very wet and soft: *soggy ground*

soil /sɔɪl/ *noun* **[no plural]** the top layer of earth that plants grow in

solar /ˈsəʊləʳ/ *adj* relating to the sun: *solar energy*

sold /səʊld/ *past of* sell

soldier /ˈsəʊldʒəʳ/ *noun* a person in an army

sole[1] /səʊl/ *adj* only: *the sole survivor*

sole[2] /səʊl/ *noun* the bottom part of your foot that you walk on

solely /ˈsəʊlli/ *adv* only, and not involving anyone or anything else: *I bought it solely for that purpose.*

solemn /ˈsɒləm/ *adj* serious or sad: *solemn music*

solicitor /səˈlɪsɪtəʳ/ *noun* in Britain, a lawyer who gives legal advice and help

solid[1] /ˈsɒlɪd/ *adj*
1 hard and firm without holes or spaces, and not liquid or gas: *solid ground* ○ *solid food*
2 strong and not easily broken or damaged: *solid furniture*

solid[2] /ˈsɒlɪd/ *noun* a substance or object that is not a liquid or a gas

solution /səˈluːʃən/ *noun* the way to stop a problem: *There's no easy* ***solution to*** *this problem.*

solve /sɒlv/ *verb* (*present participle* **solving**, *past* **solved**) to find the answer to something or to stop a problem: *We have solved the problem.* ○ *Police are still no nearer to solving the crime.*

some *strong form* /sʌm/ *weak form* /səm/ *pronoun, quantifier*
1 used to mean an amount of something without saying exactly

how much or how many: *You'll need a pair of scissors and some glue.* ○ *I can't eat all this chocolate, would you like some?* ○ *Could I have some more paper, please?*
2 used to mean a part of a larger amount or number of something and not all of it: *Some people don't like this.* ○ ***Some of*** *the children were frightened.*

somebody /ˈsʌmbədi/ *pronoun*
another word for someone

somehow /ˈsʌmhaʊ/ *adv*
in a way which you do not know or do not understand: *Don't worry, we'll fix it somehow.* ○ *Somehow they managed to get in.*

someone /ˈsʌmwʌn/ (*also* **somebody**) *pronoun*
1 used to mean a person when you do not know who they are or when it is not important who they are: *There's someone at the door.* ○ *Will someone please answer the phone?*
2 someone else a different person: *Sorry, I thought you were talking to someone else.*

somersault /ˈsʌməsɔːlt/ *noun*
when you roll your body forwards or backwards so that your feet go over your head and come back down to the ground again

something /ˈsʌmθɪŋ/ *pronoun*
used to mean a thing when you do not know what it is or when it is not important what it is: *As soon as I walked in, I noticed that something was missing.* ○ *We know about the problem and we're trying to do something about it.* ○ *There's* ***something else*** (= another thing) *I wanted to tell you.*

sometime /ˈsʌmtaɪm/ *adv*
used to mean a time when you do not know exactly what it is or when it is not important what it is: *We'll arrange it for sometime before June.* ○ *You must come over and visit sometime.*

sometimes /ˈsʌmtaɪmz/ *adv*
on some occasions but not always or often: *He does cook sometimes, but not very often.* ○ *Sometimes I feel so lonely.*

somewhere /ˈsʌmweəʳ/ *adv*
used to mean a place when you do not know exactly where it is or when it is not important exactly where it is: *They had difficulties finding somewhere to live.* ○ *He comes from somewhere near London.* ○ *Can you think of* ***somewhere else*** (= a different place) *we could go?*

son /sʌn/ *noun*
your male child

song /sɒŋ/ *noun*
words that go with a short piece of music: *a love song* ○ *to sing a song*

son-in-law /ˈsʌnɪnlɔː/ *noun* (*plural* **sons-in-law**)
your daughter's husband

soon /suːn/ *adv*
1 after a short period of time: *I've got to leave quite soon.* ○ *It's too soon to make a decision.*
2 as soon as at the same time or a very short time after: *They want it as soon as possible.*
3 sooner or later used to say that you do not know exactly when something will happen, but you are sure that it will happen: *Sooner or later they'll realize that it's not going to work.*

soot /sʊt/ *noun* **[no plural]**
a black powder made when coal, wood, etc is burnt

soothe /suːð/ *verb* (*present participle* **soothing**, *past* **soothed**)
1 to make something feel less painful: *I had a long, hot bath to soothe my aching muscles.*
2 to make someone feel calm or less worried: *to soothe a crying baby*
●**soothing** *adj*
making you feel calm or in less pain: *soothing music*

sore /sɔːʳ/ *adj*
painful, especially when touched: *a sore throat* ○ *Her eyes were red and sore.*

sorry /ˈsɒri/ *adj*
1 (I'm) sorry something that you say to be polite when you have done something wrong: *Sorry I'm late.* ○ *Oh, I'm sorry. I didn't see you there.*
2 used to show that you are sad about a person or situation: *I was* ***sorry to hear*** *about your brother's accident.*
3 Sorry? *UK* used as a polite way to say that you did not hear what someone has just said: *Sorry? What was that?*
4 used to say that you wish something in the past had been different: *I'm sorry that I ever met him.*

sort¹ /sɔːt/ *noun*
1 a type of something: *We both like the same **sort of** music.* ○ *What sort of shoes does she wear?*
2 all sorts of many different types of something

sort² /sɔːt/ *verb*
to put things into different groups or types or into an order: *The names are sorted alphabetically.*
sort something out *phrasal verb*
to do something which stops a problem: *Have you sorted out your schedule yet?*

sought /sɔːt/
past of seek

soul /səʊl/ *noun*
the part of a person which is not their body, which some people believe continues to exist after they die

sound¹ /saʊnd/ *noun*
something that you hear: *I could **hear** the **sounds** of the city through the open window.* ○ *She stood completely still, not **making a sound**.*

sound² /saʊnd/ *verb*
1 sound good/interesting/strange, etc to seem good/interesting/strange, etc, from what you have heard or read: *Your job sounds really interesting.*
2 sound angry/happy/rude, etc to seem angry/happy/rude, etc when you speak: *You don't sound too sure about it.*

sound³ /saʊnd/ *adj*
good or safe and able to be trusted: *sound advice*

sound⁴ /saʊnd/ *adv*
sound asleep in a deep sleep

soundly /ˈsaʊndli/ *adv*
sleep soundly to sleep well

soup /suːp/ *noun* **[no plural]**
a hot, liquid food, made from vegetables, meat, or fish: *chicken soup* ➲See colour picture **Food** on page Centre 7

sour /saʊəʳ/ *adj*
having a sharp taste like a lemon, and not sweet: *These plums are a bit sour.*

source /sɔːs/ *noun*
where something comes from: *Oranges are a good **source of** vitamin C.*

south, South /saʊθ/ *noun* **[no plural]**
1 the direction that is on your right when you face towards the rising sun
2 the south the part of an area that is further towards the south than the rest
• **south** *adj*: *the south side of the house*
• **south** *adv*
towards the south

southeast, Southeast /ˌsaʊθˈiːst/ *noun* **[no plural]**
1 the direction between south and east
2 the southeast the southeast part of a country

southeastern, Southeastern /ˌsaʊθˈiːstən/ *adj*
in or from the southeast

southern, Southern /ˈsʌðən/ *adj*
in or from the south part of an area: *the southern half of the country*

the South Pole /ˌsaʊθ ˈpəʊl/ *noun*
a point on the Earth's surface which is furthest south

southwest, Southwest /ˌsaʊθˈwest/ *noun* **[no plural]**
the direction between south and west

souvenir /ˌsuːvᵊnˈɪəʳ/ *noun*
something which you buy or keep to remember a special time or holiday: *I kept the ticket as a **souvenir of** my trip.*

sow /səʊ/ *verb* (*past participle* **sown**)
to put seeds into the ground

space /speɪs/ *noun*
1 an empty area which is free to be used: *a parking space* ○ *We need more open spaces for children to play in.* ○ *There wasn't enough **space for** everyone.*
2 [no plural] the area outside the Earth: *space travel*

spacecraft /ˈspeɪskrɑːft/ *noun*
a vehicle which can travel outside the Earth and into space

spade /speɪd/ *noun*
a tool with a long handle and a flat, metal part at one end used for digging

spade

spaghetti /spəˈgeti/ *noun* **[no plural]**

long, thin pieces of pasta

spam /spæm/ *noun* **[no plural]**
emails that you do not want, usually advertisements

span /spæn/ *noun*
the period of time that something exists or happens: *an average life span of seventy years*
• **span** *verb* (*present participle* **spanning**, *past* **spanned**)
to continue for a particular amount of time: *Her acting career spanned almost forty years.*

spaniel /ˈspænjəl/ *noun*
a dog with long hair and long ears

spanner /ˈspænəʳ/ *noun UK*
a tool with a round end that is used to turn nuts and bolts (= metal objects used to fasten things together)

spare[1] /speəʳ/ *adj*
1 If something is spare, it is extra and not being used: *a spare bedroom* ○ *spare cash*
2 spare time time when you are not working: *I enjoy gardening **in my spare time**.*

spare[2] /speəʳ/ *verb* (*present participle* **sparing**, *past* **spared**)
to give time or money to someone: *I have to go soon, but I can spare a few minutes.*

spark /spɑːk/ *noun*
a very small, bright piece of burning material: *The fire was caused by a spark from a cigarette.*

sparkle /ˈspɑːkl/ *verb* (*present participle* **sparkling**, *past* **sparkled**)
to shine brightly because of reflected light: *The water sparkled in the sun.*

sparrow /ˈspærəʊ/ *noun*
a small, brown bird

spat /spæt/
past of spit

speak /spiːk/ *verb* (*present participle* **speaking**, *past tense* **spoke**, *past participle* **spoken**)
1 to say something using your voice: *She speaks very quietly.* ○ *There was complete silence – nobody spoke.*
2 speak to someone *UK* (*US* **speak with someone**) to talk to someone: *Could I speak to Mr Davis, please?*
3 speak English/French/German, etc to be able to say things in English/French/German, etc: *Do you speak English?*
speak up *phrasal verb*
to say something in a louder voice so that people can hear you: *Could you speak up a bit? I can't hear you.*

speaker /ˈspiːkəʳ/ *noun*
1 the part of a radio, CD player, etc which the sound comes out of ↄSee colour picture **The Living Room** on page Centre 11
2 someone who makes a speech to a group of people: *a guest speaker*

spear /spɪəʳ/ *noun*
a long weapon with a sharp point at one end used for hunting

special /ˈspeʃəl/ *adj*
1 better or more important than usual things: *I'm cooking something special for her birthday.*
2 special attention/treatment treatment that is better than usual
3 different from normal things, or used for one purpose only: *You need to use a special kind of paint.*

specialist /ˈspeʃəlɪst/ *noun*
someone who has a lot of knowledge or skill in one subject: *a software specialist* ○ *He's **a specialist in** childhood illnesses.*

specialize /ˈspeʃəlaɪz/ *verb* (*present participle* **specializing**, *past* **specialized**)
to spend most of your time studying one subject or doing one type of business: *She works for a company **specializing in** business law.*

specially /ˈspeʃəli/ *adv*
for one purpose: *I made this **specially for** you.*

species /ˈspiːʃiːz/ *noun* (*plural* **species**)
a group of plants or animals which are the same in some way: *a rare species of bird*

specific /spəˈsɪfɪk/ *adj*
1 particular and not general: *I asked you for a specific reason.* ○ *Could we arrange a specific time to meet?*
2 exact or containing details: *Could you **be** more **specific about** the problem?*

specifically /spəˈsɪfɪkəli/ *adv*
1 for one reason, purpose, etc: *They're designed **specifically for** children.*
2 exactly or in detail: *I specifically told them that she doesn't eat meat.*

specify /ˈspesɪfaɪ/ *verb* (*present participle* **specifying**, *past* **specified**)
to say or describe something in an exact way: *They didn't specify what colour they wanted.*

specimen /ˈspesəmɪn/ *noun*
an animal, plant, etc used as an example of its type, especially for scientific study: *This is one of the museum's finest specimens.*

speck /spek/ *noun*
a very small amount of something: *a* ***speck of*** *dirt*

spectacular /spekˈtækjələʳ/ *adj*
very good or exciting: *a spectacular view*
• **spectacularly** *adv*: *a spectacularly beautiful country*

spectator /spekˈteɪtəʳ/ *noun*
someone who watches an event, sport, etc: *They won 4-0 in front of 40,000 cheering spectators.*

sped /sped/
past of speed

speech /spiːtʃ/ *noun*
1 [no plural] someone's ability to talk, or an example of someone talking: *His speech was very slow and difficult to understand.*
2 (*plural* **speeches**) a formal talk that someone gives to a group of people: *I had to* ***make a speech*** *at my brother's wedding.*

speed¹ /spiːd/ *noun*
how fast something moves or happens: *He was travelling* ***at a speed of*** *90 mph.*

speed² /spiːd/ *verb* (*present participle* **speeding**, *past* **sped**)
1 to move somewhere or happen very fast: *The three men jumped into a car and sped away.*
2 be speeding to be driving faster than you are allowed to
speed up *phrasal verb*
to move or happen faster: *Can you try to speed up a bit please?*

speed limit /ˈspiːd ˌlɪmɪt/ *noun*
the fastest speed that a car is allowed to travel on a particular road: *I never break the speed limit.*

spell¹ /spel/ *verb* (*past* **spelled** or **spelt**)
1 to write or tell someone the letters which are used to make a word: *How do you spell that?*
2 If you can spell, you know how to write the words of a language correctly: *My grammar's all right, but I can't spell.*

spell² /spel/ *noun*
1 a period of time: *a short spell in Australia*
2 a magic instruction: *The witch* ***cast a spell*** *over him and he turned into a frog.*

spelling /ˈspelɪŋ/ *noun*
1 the letters that are used to write a word: *There are two possible spellings of this word.* ○ *spelling mistakes*
2 [no plural] someone's ability to spell words: *My spelling is terrible.*

spend /spend/ *verb* (*present participle* **spending**, *past* **spent**)
1 to use money to buy or pay for something: *She* ***spends*** *a lot* ***on*** *clothes.* ○ *How much did you spend?*
2 to use time doing something or being somewhere: *He spent 18 months working on the project.* ○ *He's planning to* ***spend*** *some* ***time*** *at home with his family.*

sphere /sfɪəʳ/ *noun*
a round object shaped like a ball

spice /spaɪs/ *noun*
a substance made from a plant, which is used to give a special taste to food: *herbs and spices*

spicy /ˈspaɪsi/ *adj* (**spicier, spiciest**)
containing strong flavours from spice: *spicy food*

spider /ˈspaɪdəʳ/ *noun*
a creature with eight long legs which catches insects in a web (= structure like a net)

spike /spaɪk/ *noun*
a long, thin piece of metal, wood, etc with a sharp point at one end
• **spiky** *adj*
covered with spikes or having that appearance: *spiky hair* ➲See colour picture **Hair** on page Centre 9

spill /spɪl/ *verb* (*past* **spilled** or **spilt**)
to pour liquid somewhere where you do not want it, by accident: *I spilt wine all over the carpet.*

spin /spɪn/ *verb* (*present participle* **spinning**, *past* **spun**)
1 If something spins or you spin something, it turns around and around quickly: *The car* ***spun across*** *the road.*
2 to make thread by twisting

together cotton, wool, etc

spinach /ˈspɪnɪtʃ/ *noun* **[no plural]**
a vegetable with large, dark green leaves

spine /spaɪn/ *noun*
the long line of bones in a person or animal's back

spiral /ˈspaɪərəl/ *noun*
a shape made by a curve turning around and around a central point: *a spiral staircase*

spiral

spire /spaɪəʳ/ *noun*
a tall, pointed tower on the top of a building such as a church

spirit /ˈspɪrɪt/ *noun*
1 the way people think and feel about something: *a* ***spirit of*** *optimism*
2 the part of a person which is not their body, which some people believe continues to exist after they die
3 a strong alcoholic drink, such as whisky

spiritual /ˈspɪrɪtʃuəl/ *adj*
relating to deep feelings and beliefs, especially religious beliefs: *a spiritual leader*

spit /spɪt/ *verb* (*present participle* **spitting**, *past* **spat**)
to force out the liquid in your mouth: *He took a mouthful of coffee and then* ***spat*** *it* ***out****.*

spite /spaɪt/ *noun*
1 in spite of something although something exists or happens: *In spite of a bad storm, the plane landed safely.*
2 [no plural] a feeling of anger towards someone which makes you want to upset them: *He hid my new jacket* ***out of spite****.*

spiteful /ˈspaɪtfəl/ *adj*
said or done to upset someone: *That was a very spiteful thing to do.*

splash[1] /splæʃ/ *verb*
1 If a liquid splashes or you splash a liquid, drops of it fall on something: *She splashed some cold water on her face.*
2 to move in water so that drops of it go in all directions: *The children splashed about in the puddles.*

splash[2] /splæʃ/ *noun* (*plural* **spashes**)
1 a drop of liquid which has fallen on something, or the mark made by it: *There were several small splashes of paint on the carpet.*
2 the sound of something falling into water

splendid /ˈsplendɪd/ *adj*
very good or very beautiful: *a splendid idea ○ a splendid view*

splinter /ˈsplɪntəʳ/ *noun*
a small, sharp piece of wood, glass, etc which has broken from a large piece: *I've got a splinter in my finger.*

split /splɪt/ *verb* (*present participle* **splitting**, *past* **split**)
1 If something splits or if you split it, it tears so that there is a long, thin hole in it: *He split his trousers when he bent over.*
2 to share something by dividing it into smaller parts: *The cost of the wedding will be* ***split between*** *the two families.*

split up *phrasal verb*
If two people split up, they end their relationship: *She* ***split up with*** *her boyfriend.*

spoil /spɔɪl/ *verb* (*past* **spoiled** or **spoilt**)
1 to stop something from being enjoyable or successful: *The picnic was spoiled by the bad weather.*
2 If you spoil a child, you let them have anything they want, usually making them badly behaved.

spoilt /spɔɪlt/ *adj UK*
badly behaved because you are always given what you want or allowed to do what you want: *He was behaving like a* ***spoilt child****.*

spoke /spəʊk/
past tense of speak

spoken /ˈspəʊkən/
past participle of speak

sponge /spʌndʒ/ *noun*
a soft substance full of small holes, which is used for washing things
• **spongy** *adj*
soft, like a sponge

sponge

spoon /spuːn/ *noun*
an object with a handle and a round, curved part at one end, used for eating and serving food: *knives,*

forks, and spoons

spoonful /ˈspuːnfʊl/ *noun*
the amount of something which can be held on a spoon: *Add a* ***spoonful of*** *yoghurt.*

sport /spɔːt/ *noun*
a game or activity which people do to keep healthy or for enjoyment, often competing against each other: *winter sports* ○ *team sports* ○ *a sports centre* ➲See colour picture **Sports 1 & 2** on page Centre 15 & 16

sports car /ˈspɔːts kɑːʳ/ *noun*
a fast car, often with only two seats and an open roof

sporty /ˈspɔːti/ *adj*
good at sports

spot[1] /spɒt/ *noun*
1 a small, round mark which is a different colour to the surface it is on: *a blue shirt with white spots*
2 *UK* a small, red mark on your skin: *He suffered badly with spots as a teenager.*
3 a place: *We found a good spot to sit and have our picnic.*

spot[2] /spɒt/ *verb* (*present participle* **spotting,** *past* **spotted)**
to see or notice something or someone: *She soon spotted the mistake.*

spotless /ˈspɒtləs/ *adj*
very clean: *Her house is spotless.*

spotty /ˈspɒti/ *adj UK*
1 having a lot of small, red marks on your skin: *a spotty young man with greasy hair*
2 with a pattern of round marks: *a spotty dress*

spout /spaʊt/ *noun*
an opening of a container, in the shape of a tube: *the spout of a teapot*

sprain /spreɪn/ *verb*
to hurt part of your body by twisting it: *I slipped on the ice and sprained my ankle.*

sprang /spræŋ/
past tense of spring

spray[1] /spreɪ/ *noun*
liquid in a container which forces it out in small drops: *hair spray*

spray[2] /spreɪ/ *verb*
to force liquid out of a container in many small drops: *She sprayed a little perfume on her wrists.*

spread /spred/ *verb* (*present participle* **spreading,** *past* **spread)**
1 to arrange something so that it covers a large area: *He* ***spread*** *the cards* ***out*** *on the table.*
2 to affect a larger number of people: *The virus is spread by rats.*
3 to move a soft substance across a surface so that it covers it: *He* ***spread*** *a thin layer of glue* ***on*** *the paper.*
4 to tell information to a lot of people: *News of his death spread quickly.*

spring[1] /sprɪŋ/ *noun*
1 the season of the year between winter and summer, when the weather becomes warmer and plants start to grow again
2 a piece of metal which curves round and round: *bed springs*
3 a place where water comes out of the ground: *hot springs*

spring[2] /sprɪŋ/ *verb* (*present participle* **springing,** *past tense* **sprang,** *past participle* **sprung)**
to jump or move somewhere suddenly: *The cat sprang onto the sofa.*

sprinkle /ˈsprɪŋkl/ *verb* (*present participle* **sprinkling,** *past* **sprinkled)**
to gently drop small pieces of something over a surface: *Sprinkle the cake with sugar before serving.*

sprinkle

sprout[1] /spraʊt/ *verb*
If a plant sprouts, or if it sprouts something, it begins to make leaves, flowers, etc: *The seeds I planted are just beginning to sprout.*

sprout[2] /spraʊt/ *noun*
a small, green vegetable which is round and made of leaves

sprung /sprʌŋ/
past participle of spring

spun /spʌn/
past tense of spin

spy[1] /spaɪ/ *noun* (*plural* **spies)**
someone who secretly tries to find information about a person, country, etc

spy[2] /spaɪ/ *verb* (*present participle* **spying,** *past* **spied)**

to see someone or something, often from a long way away: *I spied him on the dance floor.*

spy on **someone** *phrasal verb*
to secretly watch someone: *He spied on her through the keyhole.*

squabble /ˈskwɒbl/ *verb* (*present participle* **squabbling**, *past* **squabbled**)
to argue about something that is not important: *They're always squabbling over money.*
• squabble *noun*

square¹ /skweəʳ/ *noun*
1 a shape with four equal sides and four 90°angles
2 an open area with buildings around it, often in the centre of a town: *Trafalgar Square*

square² /skweəʳ/ *adj*
having the shape of a square: *a square room*

squash¹ /skwɒʃ/ *noun* **[no plural]**
a sport in which two people hit a small rubber ball against the four walls of a room

squash² /skwɒʃ/ *verb*
to press something into a flat shape: *I stepped on a spider and squashed it.*

squeak /skwiːk/ *verb*
to make a short, high sound: *His shoes squeaked loudly as he walked.*
• squeak *noun*

squeal /skwiːl/ *verb*
to make a loud, high sound, often because of fear or excitement: *She* ***squealed with*** *delight.*
• squeal *noun*: *squeals of laughter*

squeeze /skwiːz/ *verb* (*present participle* **squeezing**, *past* **squeezed**)
to press something firmly: *She squeezed his hand and said goodbye.*

squid /skwɪd/ *noun*
a sea creature with a long body and ten long arms

squirrel /ˈskwɪrᵊl/ *noun*
a small animal with a big, fur tail that climbs trees and eats nuts

squirrel

St *written abbreviation for*
1 street: *42 Oxford St*
2 saint: *St Patrick*

stab /stæb/ *verb* (*present participle* **stabbing**, *past* **stabbed**)
to push a knife into someone: *He was stabbed several times in the chest.*

stable¹ /ˈsteɪbl/ *adj*
1 not likely to change or end suddenly: *a stable relationship*
2 fixed or safe and not likely to move: *Be careful! That chair isn't very stable.*

stable² /ˈsteɪbl/ *noun*
a building where horses are kept

stack¹ /stæk/ *noun*
a tidy pile of things: *a* ***stack of*** *books/CDs*

stack² /stæk/ *verb*
to put things in a tidy pile: *Can you help me stack these chairs?*

stadium /ˈsteɪdiəm/ *noun* (*plural* **stadiums** or **stadia**)
a large, open area with seats around it, used for playing and watching sports: *a football stadium*

staff /stɑːf/ *noun* **[no plural]**
the people who work for an organization: *The company has a staff of over 500 employees.*

stage /steɪdʒ/ *noun*
1 a period of development, or a particular time in a process: *an early stage in his career ○ Our project is in its final stages.*
2 the raised area in a theatre where actors perform: *He's* ***on stage*** *for most of the play.*

stagger /ˈstægəʳ/ *verb*
to walk as if you might fall

stain¹ /steɪn/ *noun*
a dirty mark on something that is difficult to remove: *a blood stain ○ a stain on the carpet*

stain² /steɪn/ *verb*
to leave a dirty mark on something which is difficult to remove: *That wine I spilt has stained my shirt.*

staircase /ˈsteəkeɪs/ *noun*
a set of stairs and the structure around them: *a spiral staircase*

stairs /steəz/ *plural noun*
a set of steps from one level in a building to another: *to go up/down the stairs*

stale /steɪl/ *adj*
old and not fresh: *stale bread*

stalk /stɔːk/ *noun*
the main stem of a plant

stall /stɔːl/ *noun* *UK*
a small shop with an open front or a table from which things are sold: *a market stall*

stall

stamp[1] /stæmp/ *noun*
1 a small piece of paper that you buy and stick onto a letter before you post it
2 a tool for putting a special ink mark on something, or the mark made by it: *a stamp in a passport*

stamp[2] /stæmp/ *verb*
1 to make a mark on something with a tool that you put ink on and press down: *She stamped the date on the invoice.*
2 to put your foot down on the ground hard and quickly, often to show anger: *"No!" she shouted, stamping her foot.*

stand[1] /stænd/ *verb* (*present participle* **standing,** *past* **stood)**
1 to be in a vertical position on your feet: *We'd been standing for hours.* ○ *He's standing over there, next to Karen.*
2 (*also* **stand up**) to rise to a vertical position on your feet from sitting or lying down: *I get dizzy if I stand up too quickly.* ○ *Please stand when the bride arrives.* ➲See colour picture **Phrasal Verbs** on page Centre 13
3 can't stand someone/something *informal* to hate someone or something: *I can't stand him.* ○ *She can't stand doing housework.*

stand for something *phrasal verb*
If a letter stands for a word, it is used to mean it: *UFO stands for 'unidentified flying object'.*

stand out *phrasal verb*
to be very easy to see or notice: *The bright blue letters really stand out on the page.*

stand[2] /stænd/ *noun*
1 a small shop with an open front or a table from which things are sold: *Visit our stand at the trade fair.*
2 *UK* a structure in a sports ground where people can stand or sit to watch an event

standard[1] /ˈstændəd/ *noun*
1 a level of quality, especially a level that is good enough: *a high standard of service* ○ *low safety standards* ○ *His work was below standard* (= not good enough).
2 a level of behaviour, especially a level that is good enough: *high moral standards*

standard[2] /ˈstændəd/ *adj*
usual and not special: *standard practice*

stank /stæŋk/
past tense of stink

star

star[1] /stɑːʳ/ *noun*
1 a ball of burning gases that you see as a small point of light in the sky at night
2 a famous singer, actor, sports person, etc: *a pop star*
3 a shape that has five or more points

star[2] /stɑːʳ/ *verb* (*present participle* **starring,** *past* **starred)**
to be the main person in a film, play, etc: *a film starring Meg Ryan*

stare /steəʳ/ *verb* (*present participle* **staring,** *past* **stared)**
to look at someone or something for a long time and not move your eyes: *Sean was* ***staring at*** *me.*
● **stare** *noun*

start[1] /stɑːt/ *verb*
1 to begin doing something: *Maria started to laugh.* ○ *We start work at nine o'clock.*
2 to begin to happen or to make something begin to happen: *The fire started in the kitchen.*

start[2] /stɑːt/ *noun*
the beginning of something: *Our teacher checks who is in class at the start of each day.* ○ *Ivan has been*

a b c d e f g h i j k l m n o p q r **s** t u v w x y z

involved in the project ***from the start***.

startle /ˈstɑːtl/ *verb* (*present participle* **startling**, *past* **startled**)
to suddenly surprise or frighten someone: *The sound startled me.*

starve /stɑːv/ *verb* (*present participle* **starving**, *past* **starved**)
to become ill or die because you do not have enough food,: *Many people have* ***starved to death*** *in parts of Africa.*
• **starvation** /stɑːˈveɪʃᵊn/ *noun* **[no plural]** *Children were dying of starvation.*

starving /ˈstɑːvɪŋ/ *adj*
1 dying because there is not enough food: *starving people*
2 *informal* very hungry: *I'm absolutely starving.*

state¹ /steɪt/ *noun*
1 the condition that something or someone is in: *the state of the economy* ○ *The building is in a terrible state.*
2 in a state *informal* very upset or nervous: *Ben was in a real state before the exam.*
3 (*also* **State**) one of the parts that some countries such as the US are divided into: *Alaska is the largest state in the US.*
4 the state the government of a country: *financial help from the state*

state² /steɪt/ *verb* (*present participle* **stating**, *past* **stated**)
to officially say or write something: *Two medical reports stated that he was mentally ill.*

statement /ˈsteɪtmənt/ *noun*
something that someone says or writes officially: *The government is expected to* ***make a statement*** *later today.*

station /ˈsteɪʃᵊn/ *noun*
1 a place where trains stop so that you can get on or off them: *Dad met me at the station.*
2 a company that shows or sends out television or radio programmes: *a classical music station*

stationary /ˈsteɪʃᵊnᵊri/ *adj*
not moving: *stationary cars*

stationery /ˈsteɪʃᵊnᵊri/ *noun* **[no plural]**
things that you use for writing, such as pens and paper

statistics /stəˈtɪstɪks/ *noun* **[no plural]**
the subject that involves collecting and studying numbers to show information

statue /ˈstætʃuː/ *noun*
a model that looks like a person or animal, usually made from stone or metal

stay /steɪ/ *verb*
1 to continue to be in a place, job, etc and not leave: *The weather was bad so we stayed at home.*
2 to continue to be in a particular state: *The supermarket stays open late.*
3 to spend a short period of time in a place: *We* ***stayed in*** *a hotel.*

steady /ˈstedi/ *adj* **(steadier, steadiest)**
1 happening at a gradual, regular rate: *a steady improvement*
2 still and not shaking: *You need steady hands to be a dentist.*
3 not changing: *She drove at a steady speed.*
• **steadily** *adv*

steak /steɪk/ *noun*
a thick, flat piece of meat or fish

steal /stiːl/ *verb* (*present participle* **stealing**, *past tense* **stole**, *past participle* **stolen**)
to secretly take something that belongs to someone else: *Burglars broke into the house and stole a computer.*

steam /stiːm/ *noun* **[no plural]**
the gas that water makes when you heat it

steam

steel /stiːl/ *noun* **[no plural]**
a very strong metal made from iron, used for making knives, machines, etc

steep /stiːp/ *adj*
A steep slope, hill, etc goes up or down very quickly: *The hill was too steep to cycle up.*
• **steeply** *adv*

steer /stɪəʳ/ *verb*
to control the direction of a car, boat, etc: *I tried to steer the boat away from the bank.*

steering wheel /ˈstɪərɪŋ ˌwiːl/ *noun*
a wheel that you turn to control the direction of a vehicle

stem /stem/ *noun*
the long, thin part of a plant that

the leaves and flowers grow on

step[1] /step/ *noun*
1 one of the movements you make with your feet when you walk: *She **took** a few **steps** forward.*
2 one of the things that you do to achieve something: *This meeting is the first step towards a peace agreement.*
3 one of the surfaces that you walk on when you go up or down stairs

step[2] /step/ *verb* (*present participle* **stepping**, *past* **stepped**)
1 to move somewhere by lifting your foot and putting it down in a different place: *She stepped carefully over the dog.*
2 to put your foot on or in something: *I accidentally stepped on her foot.*

stepfather /ˈstepˌfɑːðəʳ/ *noun*
the man who has married your mother but is not your father

stepmother /ˈstepˌmʌðəʳ/ *noun*
the woman who has married your father but is not your mother

stereo /ˈsteriəʊ/ *noun*
a piece of equipment for playing CDs, listening to the radio, etc that has two speakers (= parts where sound comes out): *a car stereo* ➲See colour picture **The Living Room** on page Centre 11

sterling /ˈstɜːlɪŋ/ *noun* **[no plural]**
British money

stern /stɜːn/ *adj*
very serious and not friendly or funny: *a stern face*

stew /stjuː/ *noun*
food made of vegetables and meat cooked together in liquid: *beef stew*

steward /ˈstjuːəd/ *noun*
a man who looks after people on an aeroplane, boat, or train: *an air steward*

stewardess /ˈstjuːədɪs/ *noun* (*plural* stewardesses)
a woman who looks after people on an aeroplane, boat, or train: *air stewardess*

stick

The boy stuck his tongue out.

stick[1] /stɪk/ *verb* (*present participle* **sticking**, *past* **stuck**)
1 to become joined to something else or to make something become joined to something else, usually with a substance like glue: *Annie stuck a picture of her boyfriend on the wall.*
2 *informal* to put something somewhere: *Just stick your bag under the table.*
3 If you stick something sharp somewhere, you push it into something: *She stuck the needle into his arm.*
4 to become fixed in one position and not be able to move: *This drawer has stuck – I can't open it.*

stick something out *phrasal verb*
to make part of your body come forward from the rest of your body: *The little boy stuck his tongue out.*

stick up *phrasal verb*
to point up above a surface and not lie flat: *I can't go out with my hair sticking up like this.*

stick[2] /stɪk/ *noun*
1 a long, thin piece of wood
2 walking/hockey, etc stick a long, thin piece of wood that you use when you are walking/playing hockey, etc

sticky /ˈstɪki/ *adj* **(stickier, stickiest)**
made of or covered with a substance that can stick to other things: *sticky fingers ○ sticky tape*

stiff /stɪf/ *adj*
1 hard and difficult to bend: *stiff material*
2 A door, drawer, etc that is stiff does not move as easily as it should.

still[1] /stɪl/ *adv*
1 used to say that something is continuing to happen now: *He's still here if you want to speak to him. ○ Do you still play basketball?*
2 used to say that something continues to be possible: *We could still catch the train if we leave now.*
3 used to show that you did not expect something to happen: *He didn't do much work but still came top of the class.*

still[2] /stɪl/ *adj*
stand/stay/sit, etc still to stand, stay, sit, etc without moving: *Sit still so I can brush your hair.*

sting[1] /stɪŋ/ *verb* (*present participle* **stinging**, *past* **stung**)
If an insect, plant, etc stings you, it causes pain by putting poison into your skin: *He was stung by a wasp.*

sting[2] /stɪŋ/ *noun*

painful skin that you get when an insect, plant, etc puts poison into your skin: *a wasp/bee sting*

stink¹ /stɪŋk/ *verb* (*present participle* **stinking**, *past tense* **stank**, *past participle* **stunk**)
to smell very bad: *The kitchen* ***stinks of*** *fish.*

stink² /stɪŋk/ *noun*
a very bad smell

stir /stɜːʳ/ *verb* (*present participle* **stirring**, *past* **stirred**)
1 to mix food or liquid by moving a spoon round and round in it: *Stir the mixture until it is smooth.*
2 to move slightly: *The baby stirred in its sleep.*

stitch¹ /stɪtʃ/ *noun* (*plural* **stitches**)
a short line of thread that is sewn through a piece of material

stitch² /stɪtʃ/ *verb*
to sew two things together or to repair something by sewing: *I need to get my shoes stitched.*

stock¹ /stɒk/ *noun*
1 **[no plural]** all the things that you can buy in a shop: *We're expecting some new stock in this afternoon.*
2 be in stock/out of stock to be available/not available in a shop
3 an amount of something that is ready to be used: *stocks of weapons*
4 the value of a company, or a share in its value: *to buy/sell stock*

stock² /stɒk/ *verb*
to have something for people to buy: *They stock a wide range of books and magazines.*

stocking /ˈstɒkɪŋ/ *noun*
a very thin piece of clothing that covers a woman's foot and leg: *a pair of stockings* ➲See colour picture **Clothes** on page Centre 5

stole /stəʊl/
past tense of steal

stolen /ˈstəʊlᵊn/
past participle of steal

stomach /ˈstʌmək/ *noun*
1 the part of your body where food is digested
2 the front part of your body just below your chest ➲See colour picture **The Body** on page Centre 2

stomach ache /ˈstʌmək ˌeɪk/ *noun*
pain in your stomach

stone /stəʊn/ *noun*
1 **[no plural]** a hard, natural substance that is found in the ground: *a stone wall*
2 a small rock or piece of rock
3 a hard, valuable substance that is often used in jewellery: *precious stones*
4 (*plural* **stone**) *UK* a unit for measuring weight, equal to 6.35 kilograms or 14 pounds
5 the hard seed that is at the centre of some fruits: *a cherry stone*

stood /stʊd/
past of stand

stool /stuːl/ *noun*
a seat that does not have a back or arms

stoop /stuːp/ *verb*
to bend the top half of your body forward and down: *He stooped to pick up the letter.*

stop¹ /stɒp/ *verb* (*present participle* **stopping**, *past* **stopped**)
1 to finish doing something: *Stop laughing – it's not funny.* ○ *He started to say something and then stopped.*
2 to not move any more, or make someone or something not move any more: *A car stopped outside the house.*
3 to make something end: *We must find a way to stop the war.*
4 to prevent something from happening or someone from doing something: *Health workers are trying to stop the disease from spreading.*

stop² /stɒp/ *noun*
1 a place where a bus or train stops so that people can get on or off: *We need to get off at the next stop.*
2 put a stop to something to end something bad: *We must put a stop to the violence.*

store¹ /stɔːʳ/ *noun*
1 *US* a shop: *a book store* ○ *She works at a men's clothing store.*
2 an amount of something that you are keeping to use later: *a store of grain*

store² /stɔːʳ/ *verb* (*present participle* **storing**, *past* **stored**)
1 to put something somewhere and not use it until you need it: *We have a lot of old clothes stored in the attic.*

2 to keep information on a computer: *All the data is stored on diskettes.*

storey /ˈstɔːri/ *noun*
a level of a building: *a three-storey house*

storm /stɔːm/ *noun*
very bad weather with a lot of rain, snow, wind, etc: *a snow/thunder storm*

stormy /ˈstɔːmi/ *adj* **(stormier, stormiest)**
If it is stormy, the weather is bad with a lot of wind and rain: *a stormy night*

story /ˈstɔːri/ *noun* (*plural* **stories)**
a description of a series of real or imaginary events which people read for enjoyment: *a horror story* ○ *She* ***reads stories*** *to the children every night.*

straight[1] /streɪt/ *adj*
1 not curved or bent: *a straight road* ○ *straight hair* ➲See colour picture **Hair** on page Centre 9
2 in a position that is level or vertical: *That shelf's not straight.*
3 honest: *a straight answer*

straight[2] /streɪt/ *adv*
1 in a straight line: *It's straight ahead.*
2 now: *I went straight back to sleep.*
3 sit up/stand up straight to sit or stand with your body vertical
4 straight away now: *Go there straight away.*

straighten /ˈstreɪtᵊn/ *verb*
to become straight or to make something straight

strain[1] /streɪn/ *noun*
when you feel worried and nervous about something: *The strain of looking after four children was too much for her.*

strain[2] /streɪn/ *verb*
1 to try hard to do something, usually to see or hear something: *I had to strain to hear the music.*
2 to hurt part of your body by using it too much: *I think I've strained a muscle.*

strait /streɪt/ *noun*
a narrow area of sea that connects two large areas of sea: *the straits of Florida*

strand /strænd/ *noun*
a thin piece of hair, thread, rope, etc: *She tucked a strand of hair behind her ear.*

stranded /ˈstrændɪd/ *adj*
not able to leave a place: *We were stranded at the airport for ten hours.*

strange /streɪndʒ/ *adj*
unusual or not expected: *It's strange that she hasn't called.* ○ *What a strange-looking man.*
● **strangely** *adv*: *She's been behaving very strangely* (= in an unusual way) *recently.*

stranger /ˈstreɪndʒəʳ/ *noun*
someone you have never met before

strangle /ˈstræŋgl/ *verb* (*present participle* **strangling,** *past* **strangled)**
to kill someone by pressing their throat

strap /stræp/ *noun*
a thin piece of material used to fasten two things together or to carry something: *a watch strap* ○ *I want a bag with a shoulder strap.*
● **strap** *verb* (*present participle* **strapping,** *past* **strapped)**
to fasten something using a strap

strategy /ˈstrætedʒi/ *noun* (*plural* **strategies)**
a plan that you use to do something: *a sales strategy*

straw /strɔː/ *noun*
1 [no plural] the long, dried stems of plants such as wheat (= plant for grain), often given to animals: *a straw hat*
2 a thin plastic or paper tube that you use for drinking through

strawberry /ˈstrɔːbᵊri/ *noun* (*plural* **strawberries)**
a small, red fruit with small, brown seeds on its surface

stray /streɪ/ *adj*
A stray animal is lost or has no home: *a stray dog*

streak /striːk/ *noun*
a thin line or mark: *She has a streak of white hair.*

stream /striːm/ *noun*
1 a small river
2 a stream of something a line of people or cars moving in the same direction: *a constant stream of traffic*

street /striːt/ *noun*
a road in a town or city that has houses or other buildings: *We live on the same street.*

street light /ˈstriːt ˌlaɪt/ *noun*
a light on a tall post next to a street

strength /streŋθ/ *noun*
1 **[no plural]** when someone or something is strong: *A good boxer needs skill as well as strength.*
2 **[no plural]** the power that an organization, country, etc has: *economic strength*
3 a good quality or ability: *We all have our strengths and weaknesses.*

strengthen /ˈstreŋθᵊn/ *verb*
to become stronger or make something become stronger: *These exercises strengthen the leg muscles.*

stress[1] /stres/ *noun* **[no plural]**
1 feelings of worry caused by difficult situations such as problems at work: *work-related stress* ○ *She's been* ***under*** *a lot of* ***stress*** *recently.*
2 (*plural* **stresses)** **[no plural]** when you say one part of a word more strongly: *In the word 'blanket', the* ***stress*** *is* ***on*** *the first syllable.*

stress[2] /stres/ *verb*
to show that something is important: *I stressed that this was our policy.*

stressful /ˈstresfᵊl/ *adj*
making someone worry a lot: *a stressful job*

stretch /stretʃ/ *verb*
1 to become longer or wider, or to pull something so that it becomes longer or wider: *Don't pull my sweater – you'll stretch it.*
2 to make your body or part of your body straighter and longer: *Stretch your arms above your head.*
3 to cover a large area: *The fields stretched away into the distance.*

stretcher /ˈstretʃəʳ/ *noun*
a flat structure covered with cloth which is used to carry someone who is hurt

stretcher

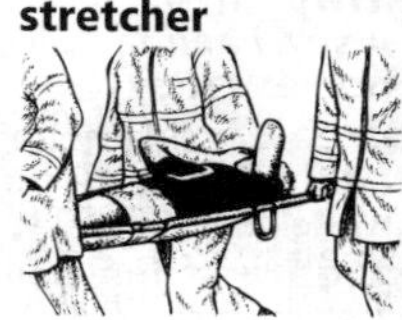

strict /strɪkt/ *adj*
A strict person makes sure that children or people working for them behave well and does not allow them to break any rules: *a strict teacher* ○ *My parents were very* ***strict with*** *us.*

strictly /ˈstrɪktli/ *adv*
1 exactly or correctly: *That's not strictly true.*
2 done for a particular person or purpose: *Her visit is strictly business.*

strike[1] /straɪk/ *verb* (*present participle* **striking**, *past* **struck**)
1 to hit someone or something: *Two climbers were struck by falling rocks.* ○ *His car went out of control and struck a tree.*
2 If a thought or idea strikes you, you suddenly think of it: ***It struck me that*** *I'd forgotten to order the champagne.*
3 to stop working for a period of time because you want more money, etc: *Bus drivers are threatening to strike.*
4 If a clock strikes, a bell rings to show what the time is.

strike[2] /straɪk/ *noun*
a period of time when people are not working because they want more money, etc: *Teachers are planning to* ***go on strike*** *next month.*

string /strɪŋ/ *noun*
1 **[no plural]** very thin rope used for tying things: *a ball of string*
2 a piece of wire that is part of a musical instrument: *guitar strings*

strip[1] /strɪp/ *verb* (*present participle* **stripping**, *past* **stripped)**
to remove all your clothes, or to remove all someone else's clothes: *She was stripped and searched by the guards.*

strip[2] /strɪp/ *noun*
a long, thin piece of something: *a strip of paper*

stripe /straɪp/ *noun*
a long, straight area of colour: *white with blue stripes*

striped /straɪpt/ *adj*
with a pattern of stripes: *a striped shirt*

stroke[1] /strəʊk/ *noun*
1 a sudden problem in your brain that makes you unable to move part of your body
2 a movement that you make against something with your hand, a pen, brush, etc: *a brush stroke*
3 a style of swimming
4 a stroke of luck something good that happens to you by chance

stroke² /strəʊk/ *verb* (*present participle* **stroking**, *past* **stroked**)
to gently move your hand over a surface: *She stroked the dog.*

stroll /strəʊl/ *verb*
to walk somewhere in a slow and relaxed way: *They strolled along the beach.*
●**stroll** *noun*: *Shall we* ***go for a stroll*** *around the garden?*

strong /strɒŋ/ *adj*
1 A strong person or animal is physically powerful: *Are you strong enough to lift this table on your own?* ➲Opposite **weak**
2 A strong object does not break easily or can support heavy things: *a strong box*
3 of a good quality or level and likely to be successful: *a strong team* ○ *a strong economy*
4 A strong feeling, belief, or opinion is felt in a very deep and serious way: *a strong sense of pride*
5 If a taste, smell, etc is strong, it is very easy to notice: *There's a strong smell of burning.*

strongly /ˈstrɒŋli/ *adv*
very much or in a very serious way: *He is strongly opposed to violence of any sort.*

struck /strʌk/
past of strike

structure /ˈstrʌktʃəʳ/ *noun*
1 the way that parts of something are arranged or put together: *cell structure* ○ *grammatical structure*
2 a building or something that has been built

struggle¹ /ˈstrʌgl/ *verb* (*present participle* **struggling**, *past* **struggled**)
1 to try very hard to do something difficult: *He's* ***struggling to*** *pay off his debts.*
2 to fight someone when they are holding you: *She struggled but couldn't break free.*

struggle² /ˈstrʌgl/ *noun*
1 when you try very hard to do something difficult: *It was a real* ***struggle to*** *stay awake during the film.*
2 a fight between people

stubborn /ˈstʌbən/ *adj*
never changing your ideas, plans, etc, even when you should
●**stubbornly** *adv*

stuck¹ /stʌk/ *adj*
1 not able to move anywhere: *We were stuck at the airport for twelve hours.*
2 not able to continue reading, answering questions, etc because something is too difficult: *I keep getting stuck on difficult words.*

stuck² /stʌk/
past of stick

student /ˈstjuːdᵊnt/ *noun*
someone who is studying at a school or university: *a law student*

studio /ˈstjuːdiəʊ/ *noun*
1 a room where an artist or photographer works
2 a room where television/radio programmes or musical recordings are made

study¹ /ˈstʌdi/ *verb* (*present participle* **studying**, *past* **studied**)
1 to learn about a subject, usually at school or university: *I studied biology before going into medicine.*
2 to look at something very carefully: *He studied his face in the mirror.*

study² /ˈstʌdi/ *noun* (*plural* **studies**)
1 when someone studies a subject in detail in order to find new information: *For years, studies have shown the link between smoking and cancer.*
2 **[no plural]** when you learn about a subject, usually at school or university: *the study of English literature*
3 a room in a house where you can read, write, etc

stuff¹ /stʌf/ *noun* **[no plural]** *informal*
used to mean a substance or a group of things or ideas, etc without saying exactly what they are: *There's some sticky stuff on the carpet.* ○ *Can I leave my stuff at your house?*

stuff² /stʌf/ *verb*
1 to quickly push something into a small space: *He stuffed the papers into his briefcase and left.*
2 to completely fill a container with something: *an envelope stuffed with money*

stuffy /ˈstʌfi/ *adj* (**stuffier, stuffiest**)
hot, with no clean air: *a stuffy room*

stumble /ˈstʌmbl/ *verb* (*present participle* **stumbling**, *past* **stumbled**)

a b c d e f g h i j k l m n o p q r **s** t u v w x y z

to step badly and almost fall over: *Rachel stumbled on the rocks.*

stump /stʌmp/ *noun*
the short part of something that is left after most of it has been removed: *a tree stump*

stung /stʌŋ/
past of sting

stunk /stʌŋk/
past participle of stink

stupid /'stjuːpɪd/ *adj*
very silly or not clever: *That's a stupid thing to say.* ○ *Don't be stupid!*

stupidity /stjuː'pɪdəti/ *noun* **[no plural]**
when someone is very silly or says or does something that is not clever: *I can't believe the stupidity of these people!*

sturdy /'stɜːdi/ *adj* **(sturdier, sturdiest)**
very strong and solid: *sturdy walking boots*

stutter /'stʌtəʳ/ *verb*
to repeat the first sound of a word many times when you talk, usually because you have a speech problem: *"C-c-can we g-go now?" she stuttered.*
● **stutter** *noun*

style /staɪl/ *noun*
1 a way of doing something that is typical of a particular person, group, place, or period: *a **style of** painting*
2 a way of designing hair, clothes, furniture, etc: *She's had her hair cut in a really nice style.*

stylish /'staɪlɪʃ/ *adj*
fashionable and attractive

subject /'sʌbdʒɪkt/ *noun*
1 what someone is writing or talking about: *The subject of the programme was mental health.*
2 an area of knowledge studied in school or university: *Chemistry is my favourite subject.*
3 the person or thing which does the action described by the verb. In the sentence 'Bob phoned me yesterday.', 'Bob' is the subject.
4 someone who is from a particular country: *a British subject*

submarine /ˌsʌbmᵊr'iːn/ *noun*
a boat that travels under water

substance /'sʌbstᵊns/ *noun*
a solid, liquid, or gas: *a dangerous substance*

subtle /'sʌtl/ *adj*
not obvious or easy to notice: *a subtle change*

subtract /səb'trækt/ *verb*
to take one number away from another number: *You need to **subtract** 25% **from** the final figure.*
● **subtraction** /səb'trækʃᵊn/ *noun*

suburb /'sʌbɜːb/ *noun*
an area where people live outside the centre of a city: *a suburb of New York*
● **suburban** /sə'bɜːbᵊn/ *adj*
relating to a suburb: *a suburban area*

succeed /sək'siːd/ *verb*
to do something good that you have been trying to do: *He finally **succeeded in** passing his exams.*
➲Opposite **fail**

success /sək'ses/ *noun*
1 [no plural] when you do something good that you have been trying to do: *Her success is due to hard work and determination.* ➲Opposite **failure**
2 (*plural* **successes**) something that has a good result or that is very popular: *His first film was a great success.* ➲Opposite **failure**

successful /sək'sesfᵊl/ *adj*
1 having a good result: *The operation was successful.*
2 very popular: *a successful book*
● **successfully** *adv*

such /sʌtʃ/ *pronoun, determiner*
1 like the person or thing you were just talking about: *It's difficult to know how to treat such cases.*
2 used to make an opinion stronger: *She's such a nice person.* ○ *It's such a shame that he's leaving.*
3 such as for example: *She can't eat dairy products, such as milk and cheese.*

suck /sʌk/ *verb*
to have something in your mouth and use your tongue, lips, etc to pull on it: *I was sucking a sweet.* ○ *Martha still sucks her thumb.*

sudden /'sʌdᵊn/ *adj*
1 done or happening quickly and not expected: *a sudden change* ○ *His sudden death was a great shock to us all.*
2 all of a sudden quickly and in a way that was not expected: *All of a sudden she got up and walked out.*

suddenly /'sʌdᵊnli/ *adv*

a b c d e f g h i j k l m n o p q r s t u v w x y z

quickly and when not expected: *I suddenly realized who she was.*

sue /suː/ *verb* (*present participle* **suing**, *past* **sued**)
to take legal action against someone and try to get money from them because they have harmed you: *He's threatening to **sue** the newspaper **for** slander.*

suede /sweɪd/ *noun* **[no plural]**
leather that has a slightly rough surface

suffer /ˈsʌfəʳ/ *verb*
1 to feel pain or sadness and worry: *I can't bear to see animals suffering.*
2 suffer from something to have an illness: *She suffers from depression.*

suffering /ˈsʌfərɪŋ/ *noun* **[no plural]**
when someone feels pain or feels sadness and worry: *human suffering*

sufficient /səˈfɪʃᵊnt/ *adj*
enough: *She didn't have sufficient time to answer all the questions.*

suffix /ˈsʌfɪks/ *noun* (*plural* **suffixes**)
a group of letters that you add to the end of a word to make another word. In the word 'slowly', '-ly' is a suffix.

sugar /ˈʃʊgəʳ/ *noun* **[no plural]**
a very sweet substance used to give flavour to food and drinks: *coffee with milk and sugar*

suggest /səˈdʒest/ *verb*
to say an idea or plan for someone else to consider: *I **suggest that** we park the car here.* ○ *He suggested having the meeting at his house.*

suggestion /səˈdʒestʃᵊn/ *noun*
an idea or plan that someone suggests: *Phillip **made** a few **suggestions**.*

suit[1] /suːt/ *noun*
a jacket and trousers or a jacket and skirt that are made from the same material: *She wore a dark blue suit.*

suit[2] /suːt/ *verb*
1 to make someone look more attractive: *Green really suits you.*
2 to be acceptable or right for someone: *It would suit me better if we left a bit earlier.*

suitable /ˈsuːtəbl/ *adj*
acceptable or right for someone or something: *What is a suitable time to call?* ○ *This film is **suitable for** children.* ➲Opposite **unsuitable**
•**suitably** *adv*: *He was suitably dressed for an interview.*

suitcase /ˈsuːtkeɪs/ *noun*
a rectangular case with a handle that you use for carrying clothes when you are travelling

sulk /sʌlk/ *verb*
to look unhappy and not speak to anyone because you are angry about something: *He's upstairs sulking in his bedroom.*
•**sulky** *adj* (**sulkier, sulkiest**)
often sulking: *a sulky teenager*

sum /sʌm/ *noun*
1 an amount of money: *a large **sum of** money*
2 *UK* a simple mathematical calculation such as adding two numbers together: *Kids these days can't **do sums** without a calculator.*

summer /ˈsʌməʳ/ *noun*
the warmest season of the year, between spring and autumn: *We usually go away **in the summer**.*

summit /ˈsʌmɪt/ *noun*
the top of a mountain: *We hope to **reach the summit** before night.*

summon /ˈsʌmən/ *verb, formal*
to officially order someone to come to a place: *He was summoned to a meeting.*

sun /sʌn/ *noun*
1 the sun the large, bright star that shines in the sky during the day and gives light and heat to the Earth
2 the light and heat that comes from the sun: *I can't sit **in the sun** for too long.*

sunbathe /ˈsʌnbeɪð/ *verb* (*present participle* **sunbathing**, *past* **sunbathed**)
to sit or lie in the sun so that your skin becomes brown
•**sunbathing** *noun* **[no plural]**

sunburn /ˈsʌnbɜːn/ *noun* **[no plural]**
when your skin becomes painful and red from being in the sun too long

Sunday /ˈsʌndeɪ/ *noun*
the day of the week after Saturday and before Monday

sung /sʌŋ/
past participle of sing

sunglasses /ˈsʌnˌglɑːsɪz/ *plural noun*
dark glasses that you wear to protect your eyes from the sun ➲See colour picture **Clothes** on page Centre 5

a b c d e f g h i j k l m n o p q r s t u v w x y z

sunk /sʌŋk/
past participle of sink

sunlight /ˈsʌnlaɪt/ *noun* **[no plural]**
the light from the sun

sunny /ˈsʌni/ *adj* **(sunnier, sunniest)**
bright because of light from the sun: *a lovely sunny day*

sunrise /ˈsʌnraɪz/ *noun*
when the sun appears in the morning and the sky becomes light

sunset /ˈsʌnset/ *noun*
when the sun disappears in the evening and the sky becomes dark

sunshine /ˈsʌnʃaɪn/ *noun* **[no plural]**
the light from the sun: *Let's sit over there in the sunshine.*

suntan /ˈsʌntæn/ (*also* **tan**) *noun*
when your skin is brown from being in the sun: *suntan oil*
• **suntanned** (*also* **tanned**) *adj*

super /ˈsuːpəʳ/ *adj, adv informal*
very good: *We had a super time.*

superb /suːˈpɜːb/ *adj*
excellent: *a superb restaurant*

superior /suːˈpɪəriəʳ/ *adj*
better than other things: *This car is far* ***superior to*** *the others.* ➲Opposite **inferior**

superlative /suːˈpɜːlətɪv/ *noun*
the form of an adjective or adverb that is used to show that someone or something has more of a particular quality than anyone or anything else. For example 'best' is the superlative of 'good' and 'slowest' is the superlative of 'slow'.

supermarket /ˈsuːpəˌmɑːkɪt/ *noun*
a large shop that sells food, drink, things for the home, etc

superstition /ˌsuːpəˈstɪʃᵊn/ *noun*
when someone believes that particular actions or objects are lucky or unlucky

supervise /ˈsuːpəvaɪz/ *verb* (*present participle* **supervising,** *past* **supervised)**
to watch a person or activity and make certain that everything is done correctly, safely, etc: *Students must be supervised by a teacher at all times.*
• **supervisor** *noun*
someone who supervises

supervision /ˌsuːpəˈvɪʒᵊn/ *noun* **[no plural]**
when you supervise someone or something: *He needs constant supervision.*

supper /ˈsʌpəʳ/ *noun*
a meal that you eat in the evening: *What are we having for supper?*

supply[1] /səˈplaɪ/ *verb* (*present participle* **supplying,** *past* **supplied)**
to give things that people want or need, often over a long period of time: *This lake* ***supplies*** *the whole town* ***with*** *water.*

supply[2] /səˈplaɪ/ *noun* (*plural* **supplies)**
an amount of something that is ready to be used: *a supply of water* ○ *food supplies*

support[1] /səˈpɔːt/ *verb*
1 to agree with an idea, group, or person: *Do you support their views on nuclear weapons?*
2 to hold the weight of someone or something: *Is this ladder strong enough to support me?*
3 *UK* to like a particular sports team and want them to win: *Who do you support?*

support[2] /səˈpɔːt/ *noun*
1 [no plural] agreement with an idea, group or person: *Is there much public* ***support for*** *the death penalty?*
2 [no plural] help: *She gets a lot of financial support from her parents.*
3 an object that can hold the weight of something

supporter /səˈpɔːtəʳ/ *noun UK*
someone who likes a particular sports team and wants them to win: *English football supporters*

suppose /səˈpəʊz/ *verb* (*present participle* **supposing,** *past* **supposed)**
1 to think that something is probably true: *I suppose he feels angry with her.*
2 be supposed to do something to be expected to do something, especially when this does not happen: *He was supposed to be here by nine.*

supreme /suːˈpriːm/ *adj*
1 of the greatest importance: *the supreme ruler*
2 very great: *a supreme effort*
• **supremely** *adv*
very: *He is supremely confident.*

sure /ʃɔːʳ/ *adj*
1 certain: *I'm* ***sure that*** *he won't mind.* ○ *I'm quite* ***sure about*** *the second*

answer. ➲Opposite **unsure**
2 make sure (that) to take action so that you are certain that something happens, is true, etc: *Make sure that you close all the windows before you leave.*
3 for sure without any doubts: *I think he's from Korea but don't know for sure.*

surely /ˈʃɔːli/ *adv*
used to show surprise that something has happened or is going to happen: *You surely didn't tell him, did you?*

surf /sɜːf/ *verb*
1 to ride on a wave in the sea using a special board
2 surf the Internet/Net/Web to look at information on the Internet by moving from one page to another using electronic links (= connections)
• **surfer** *noun*
someone who surfs
• **surfing** *noun* **[no plural]**

surface /ˈsɜːfɪs/ *noun*
the top or outside part of something: *the Earth's surface* ○ *The sun was reflected on the surface of the water.*

surfboard /ˈsɜːfbɔːd/ *noun*
a long piece of wood or plastic that you use to ride on waves in the sea

surgeon /ˈsɜːdʒᵊn/ *noun*
a doctor who cuts people's bodies and removes or repairs part of them

surgeon

surgery /ˈsɜːdʒᵊri/ *noun* **[no plural]**
when a doctor cuts your body open and repairs or removes something: *She has had surgery for the problem.* ○ *heart surgery*

surname /ˈsɜːneɪm/ *noun*
the name that you and other people in your family all have: *His surname is Walker.*

surprise¹ /səˈpraɪz/ *noun*
1 something that you did not expect to happen: *I didn't know that my parents were coming – it was a lovely surprise.* ○ *a surprise party*
2 [no plural] the feeling that you get when something happens that you did not expect: *He agreed to everything, much **to** my **surprise**.*

surprise² /səˈpraɪz/ *verb* (*present participle* **surprising,** *past* **surprised)**
to make someone feel surprise: *I didn't tell her I was coming home early – I thought I'd surprise her.*

surprised /səˈpraɪzd/ *adj*
feeling surprise because something has happened that you did not expect: *I'm **surprised to** see you here.* ○ *She wasn't **surprised at** his decision.*

surprising /səˈpraɪzɪŋ/ *adj*
not expected and making someone feel surprised: *That was a surprising decision.*

surrender /sᵊrˈendəʳ/ *verb*
to stop fighting because you know the other side will win: *Rebel troops are refusing to surrender.*
• **surrender** *noun*

surround /səˈraʊnd/ *verb*
to be or go everywhere around something or someone: *The house is surrounded by a large garden.* ○ *The police have surrounded the building.*

surroundings /səˈraʊndɪŋz/ *plural noun*
the place where someone or something is and the things that are in it: *Have you got used to your new surroundings?*

survival /səˈvaɪvᵊl/ *noun* **[no plural]**
when someone continues to live, especially after a dangerous situation: *Flood victims had to fight for survival.*

survive /səˈvaɪv/ *verb* (*present participle* **surviving,** *past* **survived)**
to continue to live after almost dying because of an accident, illness, etc: *No one survived the plane crash.*

survivor /səˈvaɪvəʳ/ *noun*
someone who continues to live after almost dying because of an accident, illness, etc: *Rescuers have given up hope of finding any more survivors.*

suspect¹ /ˈsʌspekt/ *noun*
someone who may have done a crime: *He's a suspect in the murder case.*

suspect² /səˈspekt/ *verb*
1 to think that someone may have done a crime or done something

else bad: *He was* ***suspected of*** *drug dealing.*
2 to think that something is probably true: *They* ***suspected that*** *he was lying.*

suspend /sə'spend/ *verb*
1 to stop something happening for a short time: *The match was suspended because of bad weather.*
2 to hang something from somewhere: *A light bulb was* ***suspended from*** *the ceiling.*

suspense /sə'spens/ *noun* **[no plural]**
the feeling of excitement that you have when you are waiting for something to happen: *What's your answer then? Don't* ***keep*** *me* ***in suspense***.

suspicion /sə'spɪʃᵊn/ *noun*
1 a belief that someone has done something wrong: *They were arrested* ***on suspicion of*** *drug dealing.*
2 an idea that something may be true: *I had a* ***suspicion that*** *he might like her.*

suspicious /sə'spɪʃəs/ *adj*
1 making you feel that something is wrong or that something bad is happening: *suspicious behaviour* ○ *I called police after noticing a suspicious-looking package.*
2 not trusting someone: *Many of them remain* ***suspicious of*** *journalists.*

swallow[1] /'swɒləʊ/ *verb*
to move your throat in order to make food or drink go down: *These tablets are too big to swallow.*

swallow[2] /'swɒləʊ/ *noun*
a small bird with a tail with two points

swam /swæm/
past tense of swim

swamp /swɒmp/ *noun*
an area of very wet, soft land

swan /swɒn/ *noun*
a large, white bird with a long neck which lives on lakes and rivers

swap /swɒp/ *verb* (*present participle* **swapping,** *past* **swapped)**
to give something to someone and get something from them in return: *Would you mind if Dave* ***swapped*** *places* ***with*** *you for a bit?*
● swap *noun*: *We'll* ***do a swap***.

sway /sweɪ/ *verb*
to move slowly from one side to the other: *The trees swayed gently in the wind.*

swear /sweəʳ/ *verb* (*present participle* **swearing,** *past tense* **swore,** *past participle* **sworn)**
1 to use rude language about sex, the body, etc: *He was sent home because he* ***swore at*** *the teacher.*
2 to promise: *I swear I won't tell anyone.*

swear word /'sweəʳ ˌwɜːd/ *noun*
a rude word about sex, the body, etc

sweat /swet/ *verb*
to make liquid through your skin because you are hot: *I'd been running and I was sweating.*
● sweat *noun* **[no plural]**
the liquid that is on your skin when you are hot *The sweat was running down his face.*

sweater /'swetəʳ/ (*also UK* **jumper)** *noun*
a warm piece of clothing which covers the top of your body and is pulled on over your head ➲See colour picture **Clothes** on page Centre 5

sweatshirt /'swetʃɜːt/ *noun*
a piece of clothing made of soft cotton which covers the top of your body ➲See colour picture **Clothes** on page Centre 5

sweaty /'sweti/ *adj* **(sweatier, sweatiest)**
covered in sweat: *He was hot and sweaty from working in the garden.*

sweep /swiːp/ *verb* (*present participle* **sweeping,** *past* **swept)**
1 to clean the floor using a brush: *She's just swept the floor.*
2 to push or carry something with force: *Many trees were swept away in the flood.*

sweet[1] /swiːt/ *adj*
1 with a taste like sugar: *The sauce was too sweet.*
2 attractive, often because of being small: *Look at that sweet little puppy!*
3 kind: *It was really sweet of you to come.*

sweet[2] /swiːt/ *UK* (*US* **candy)** *noun*
a small piece of sweet food, often made of sugar or chocolate: *Sweets are bad for your teeth.*

sweetcorn /'swiːtkɔːn/ *noun* **[no plural]** *UK*
the sweet, yellow seeds of maize (=

a plant) which are eaten as a vegetable ➲See colour picture **Fruit and Vegetables** on page Centre 8

sweetheart /ˈswiːthɑːt/ *noun*
You call someone 'sweetheart' to show that you like them: *Come here, sweetheart.*

swell /swel/ *verb* (*past participle* **swollen**)
to get bigger: *One side of his face had swollen up where he'd been stung.*

swelling /ˈswelɪŋ/ *noun*
a part of your body which has become bigger because of illness or injury: *The doctor gave me drugs to reduce the swelling in my ankle.*

swept /swept/
past of sweep

swerve /swɜːv/ *verb* (*present participle* **swerving**, *past* **swerved**)
to change direction suddenly, especially when you are driving a car: *He swerved to avoid a cyclist and hit another car.*

swift /swɪft/ *adj*
happening or moving quickly: *a swift response*
• **swiftly** *adv*

swim¹ /swɪm/ *verb* (*present participle* **swimming**, *past tense* **swam**, *past participle* **swum**)
to move through water by moving your body: *I learnt to swim when I was about 5 years old.* ➲See colour picture **Sports 1** on page Centre 15
• **swimming** *noun* **[no plural]** *I usually **go swimming** about twice a week.*
• **swimmer** *noun*: *I'm not a very strong swimmer.*

swim² /swɪm/ *noun*
a time when you swim: *I **went for a swim** before breakfast.*

swimming pool /ˈswɪmɪŋ ˌpuːl/ *noun*
an area of water that has been made for people to swim in

swimsuit /ˈswɪmsuːt/ *noun*
a piece of clothing that girls and women wear to go swimming

swing¹ /swɪŋ/ *verb* (*present participle* **swinging**, *past* **swung**)
to move smoothly backwards and forwards, or to make something do this: *She swings her arms when she walks.*

swing² /swɪŋ/ *noun*
a chair hanging on two ropes that children sit on and swing backwards and forwards

switch¹ /swɪtʃ/ *verb*
to change from one thing to another: *He's just switched jobs.*
switch (something) off *phrasal verb*
to turn off a light, television, etc by using a switch: *Have you switched the computer off?*
switch (something) on *phrasal verb*
to turn on a light, television, etc by using a switch: *Could you switch on the light?*

switch² /swɪtʃ/ *noun* (*plural* **switches**)
1 a small object that you push up or down with your finger to turn something electrical on or off
2 a change: *There has been a switch in policy.*

swollen¹ /ˈswəʊlən/ *adj*
bigger than usual: *a swollen wrist* ○ *swollen rivers*

swollen² /ˈswəʊlən/
past participle of swell

sword /sɔːd/ *noun*
a weapon with a long, metal blade and a handle, used especially in the past

swore /swɔːʳ/
past tense of swear

sworn /swɔːn/
past participle of swear

swum /swʌm/
past participle of swim

swung /swʌŋ/
past of swing

syllable /ˈsɪləbl/ *noun*
a word or part of a word that has one vowel sound: *'But' has one syllable and 'apple' has two syllables.*

syllabus /ˈsɪləbəs/ *noun* (*plural* **syllabuses** or **syllabi**)
a list of the subjects that are included in a course of study

symbol /ˈsɪmbᵊl/ *noun*
a sign or object that is used to mean something: *A heart shape is the symbol of love.*

sympathetic /ˌsɪmpəˈθetɪk/ *adj*
showing that you understand and care about someone's problems: *My boss is very **sympathetic about** my situation.*

sympathy /ˈsɪmpəθi/ *noun* **[no plural]**

a b c d e f g h i j k l m n o p q r s t u v w x y z

when you show that you understand and care about someone's problems: *You have my sympathy – it's horrible having a bad cold.*

symptom /ˈsɪmptəm/ *noun*
a physical feeling or problem which shows that you have a particular illness: *A sleeping problem is often a* ***symptom of*** *some other illness.*

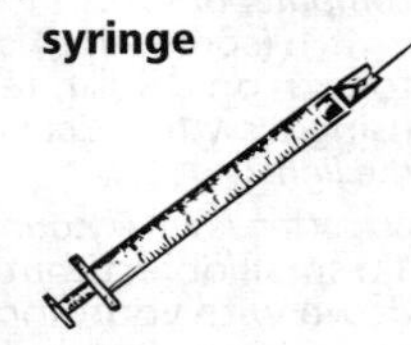

synagogue /ˈsɪnəɡɒɡ/ *noun*
a building in which Jewish people pray

synonym /ˈsɪnənɪm/ *noun*
a word that means the same as another word

syringe /sɪˈrɪndʒ/ *noun*
a piece of medical equipment used to push liquid into or take liquid out of someone's body

syrup /ˈsɪrəp/ *noun* **[no plural]**
a very sweet liquid made from sugar and water

system /ˈsɪstəm/ *noun*
1 a way or method of doing things: *the American legal system* ◦ *the public transport system*
2 a set of connected pieces of equipment that work together: *We have an alarm system at home.*

a b c d e f g h i j k l m n o p q r s t u v w x y z

Tt

T, t /tiː/
the twentieth letter of the alphabet

table /ˈteɪbl/ *noun*
a piece of furniture with four legs, used for eating off, putting things on, etc: *the kitchen table*

table

tablecloth /ˈteɪblklɒθ/ *noun*
a piece of material that covers a table

tablet /ˈtæblət/ *noun*
a small, round thing containing medicine that you swallow

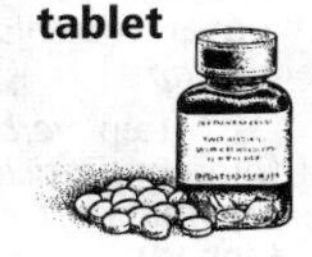
tablet

table tennis /ˈteɪbl ˌtenɪs/ *noun* **[no plural]**
a game in which two or four people hit a small ball over a low net on a large table

tabloid /ˈtæblɔɪd/ *noun*
a small newspaper with a lot of pictures and short, simple news stories

tackle[1] /ˈtækl/ *verb* (*present participle* **tackling**, *past* **tackled**)
1 to try to stop a problem: *We must find new ways to tackle crime.*
2 to try to get the ball from someone in a game like football

tackle[2] /ˈtækl/ *noun*
when you try to get the ball from someone in a game like football

tacky /ˈtæki/ *adj* **(tackier, tackiest)** *informal*
cheap and of bad quality: *tacky holiday souvenirs*

tact /tækt/ *noun* **[no plural]**
the ability to talk to people about difficult subjects without upsetting them

tactful /ˈtæktfəl/ *adj*
careful not to say or do anything that could upset someone

tactless /ˈtæktləs/ *adj*
not being careful about saying or doing something that could upset someone

tag /tæg/ *noun*
a small piece of paper or plastic with information on it that is fixed to something: *a price tag*

tail /teɪl/ *noun*
the long, narrow part that sticks out at the back of an animal's body: *The dog's pleased to see you – he's* ***wagging*** *his* ***tail****.*

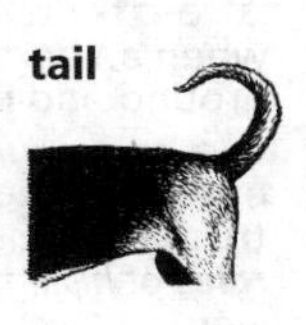
tail

take /teɪk/ *verb* (*present participle* **taking**, *past tense* **took**, *past participle* **taken**)
1 to get and carry something with you when you go somewhere: *I always* ***take*** *my umbrella* ***with*** *me.*
2 to go somewhere with someone, often paying for them: *I'm* ***taking*** *my wife* ***to*** *Florence for the weekend.*
3 to remove something without asking someone: *Someone's taken my coat.*
4 to get hold of something and move it: *He reached across and took the glass from her.*
5 to accept something: *So, are you going to take the job?*
6 If something takes a particular amount of time, or a particular quality, you need that amount of time or that quality in order to be able to do it: *It's taken me three days to get here.*
7 to swallow or use medicine: *Take two tablets, three times a day.*

take after someone *phrasal verb*
to be similar to an older person in your family: *Peter's very tall – he takes after his father.*

take something back *phrasal verb*
to return something to the place where you got it

take something off *phrasal verb*
to remove something: *If you're hot, take your jacket off.* ➲See colour picture **Phrasal Verbs** on page Centre 13

take off *phrasal verb*
If an aeroplane takes off, it begins to fly.

take (something) over *phrasal verb*
to get control of something: *They've recently been taken over by a larger company.*

take something up *phrasal verb*
to start doing a particular job or activity: *I've taken up cycling.*

takeaway /ˈteɪkəweɪ/ *UK* (*US* **takeout** /ˈteɪkaʊt/) *noun* a meal that you buy in a restaurant but eat at home

take-off /ˈteɪkɒf/ *noun*
when an aeroplane leaves the ground and begins to fly

tale /teɪl/ *noun*
a story, especially one which is not true: *My grandfather used to* ***tell*** *us* ***tales*** *of his time as a pilot during the war.*

talent /ˈtælənt/ *noun*
a natural ability to do something: *She showed an early* ***talent for*** *drawing.*
• **talented** *adj*
showing natural ability in a particular area: *a talented young musician*

talk[1] /tɔːk/ *verb*
to say things to someone: *We were just* ***talking about*** *Simon's new girlfriend.* ○ *I was just* ***talking to*** *Adam.*

talk[2] /tɔːk/ *noun*
1 when two people speak, often about a particular subject: *I* ***had a*** *long* ***talk with*** *Chris at the weekend about going to university.*
2 when someone speaks to a group of people about a particular subject: *She* ***gave a talk about*** *road safety at the school.*

tall /tɔːl/ *adj*
1 being higher than most other people or things: *He's tall and thin.* ○ *It's one of the tallest buildings in the city.* ⊃Opposite **short**
2 used to describe or ask how high someone or something is: *How tall is she?* ○ *He's almost 2 metres tall.*

tame[1] /teɪm/ *adj*
If an animal is tame, it is not wild and not frightened of people.

tame[2] /teɪm/ *verb* (*present participle* **taming,** *past* **tamed)**
to make a wild animal tame

tan /tæn/ (*also* **suntan)** *noun*
when your skin is brown from being in the sun
• **tan** *verb* (*present participle* **tanning,** *past* **tanned)** *I tan quite easily.*

tangerine /ˌtændʒərˈiːn/ *noun*
a fruit like a small orange

tangle /ˈtæŋgl/ *noun*
many things which have become twisted together in an untidy way: *a tangle of hair*

tangled /ˈtæŋgld/ *adj* (*also* **tangled up)**
twisted together in an untidy way: *The wires are all tangled.*

tank /tæŋk/ *noun*
1 a large container for keeping liquid or gas: *a hot-water tank*
2 a large, strong military vehicle with a gun on it

tanker /ˈtæŋkər/ *noun*
a ship or truck used to carry large amounts of liquid or gas: *an oil tanker*

tap[1] /tæp/ *noun*
UK (*also US* **faucet)**
the part at the end of a pipe which controls the flow of water: *the cold/hot tap*

tap ***UK*****, faucet** ***US***

tap[2] /tæp/ *verb*
(*present participle* **tapping,** *past* **tapped)**
to knock or touch something gently: *I* ***tapped*** *her* ***on*** *the back to get her attention.*

tape[1] /teɪp/ *noun*
1 a long, thin piece of plastic which is used to store sound, pictures, or information, or a plastic box containing it: *I've got the match* ***on tape****.*
2 [no plural] a thin piece of plastic which has glue on one side and is used for sticking things together: *sticky tape*

tape[2] /teɪp/ *verb* (*present participle* **taping,** *past* **taped)**
1 to record something onto tape: *Their conversations were taped by the police.*
2 to stick something somewhere using tape

tape measure /ˈteɪp ˌmeʒər/ *noun*
a long, thin piece of cloth or metal used to measure lengths

tape recorder /ˈteɪp rɪˈkɔːdər/ *noun*
a machine used to record sound onto tape

tar /tɑːr/ *noun* **[no plural]**
a thick, black substance that is sticky when hot and is used to cover roads

target /ˈtɑːgɪt/ *noun*
1 something or someone that you attack, shoot at, try to hit, etc: *It's*

a b c d e f g h i j k l m n o p q r s **t** u v w x y z

very difficult to hit a moving target.
2 something that you are trying to do: *I'm hoping to save £3,000 by June – that's my target.*

tart /tɑːt/ *noun*
an open pastry case with a sweet filling, often of fruit: *an apple tart*

tart

tartan /ˈtɑːtᵊn/ *noun* **[no plural]**
cloth with a pattern of different coloured squares and crossing lines

task /tɑːsk/ *noun*
a piece of work, especially something unpleasant: *I was given the task of tidying the shelves.*

taste¹ /teɪst/ *noun*
1 the flavour of a particular food in your mouth: *a bitter taste* ○ *It's got quite a strong taste.*
2 [no plural] the ability to feel different flavours in your mouth: *When you've got a cold you often lose your sense of taste.*
3 the particular things you like, such as styles of music, clothes, decoration, etc: *I don't like his* ***taste in*** *music.*

taste² /teɪst/ *verb* (*present participle* **tasting**, *past* **tasted**)
1 taste funny/nice/sweet, etc If food tastes a particular way, it has that flavour: *This sauce tastes strange.*
2 to put food or drink in your mouth to find out what its flavour is like: *I always taste food while I'm cooking it.*

tasty /ˈteɪsti/ *adj* **(tastier, tastiest)**
Food which is tasty has a good flavour and is nice to eat.

tattoo /tætˈuː/ *noun*
a picture on someone's skin that is put on using ink and a needle

tattoo

taught /tɔːt/
past of teach

tax¹ /tæks/ *noun* (*plural* **taxes**)
money that you have to pay to the government from what you earn or from when you buy things: *They're putting up the* ***tax on*** *cigarettes.*

tax² /tæks/ *verb*
to make someone pay a tax

taxi /ˈtæksi/ *noun*
a car with a driver who you pay to take you somewhere: *I'll take a taxi to the airport.*

tea /tiː/ *noun*
1 [no plural] a hot drink that you make by pouring water onto dried leaves: *Would you like* ***a cup of tea*** *or coffee?*
2 *UK* a small afternoon meal of cakes, biscuits, etc and tea to drink: *They invited us for* ***afternoon tea****.*
3 *UK* the meal that you eat in the evening

teach /tiːtʃ/ *verb* (*present participle* **teaching**, *past* **taught**)
1 to give classes in a particular subject at a school, university, etc: *He teaches history.*
2 to show or explain to someone how to do something: *My dad* ***taught*** *me* ***to*** *drive.*

teacher /ˈtiːtʃəʳ/ *noun*
someone whose job is to teach in a school, college, etc: *a science teacher* ➲See colour picture **Classroom** on page Centre 4

team /tiːm/ *noun*
1 a group of people who play a sport or game together: *a football team*
2 a group of people who work together to do something: *a management team*

teapot /ˈtiːpɒt/ *noun*
a container used for making and serving tea ➲See colour picture **Kitchen** on page Centre 10

teapot

tear¹ /teəʳ/ *verb* (*present participle* **tearing**, *past tense* **tore**, *past participle* **torn**)
1 to pull paper, cloth, etc into pieces, or to make a hole in it by accident: *The nail had* ***torn a hole in*** *my skirt.*
2 be torn between something and something to be unable to decide between two choices: *I'm torn between the apple pie and the chocolate tart.*

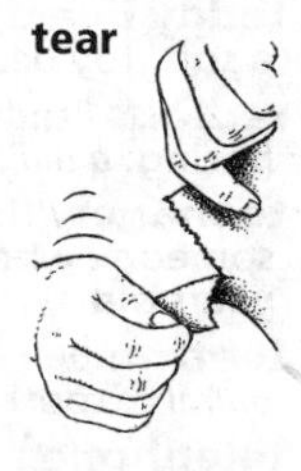
tear

a b c d e f g h i j k l m n o p q r s t u v w x y z

tear something up *phrasal verb*
to tear paper into a lot of small pieces: *He tore up her photograph.*

tear[2] /teəʳ/ *noun*
a hole in a piece of cloth, paper, etc where it has been torn

tear[3] /tɪəʳ/ *noun*
a drop of water that comes from your eye when you cry: *I was* ***in tears*** (= crying) *by the end of the film.*

tease /tiːz/ *verb* (*present participle* **teasing,** *past* **teased)**
to laugh at someone or say bad things to them: *They were* ***teasing*** *Dara* ***about*** *her new haircut.*

teaspoon /ˈtiːspuːn/ *noun*
a small spoon that is used for mixing drinks and measuring small amounts of food

technical /ˈteknɪkᵊl/ *adj*
relating to the knowledge, machines, or methods used in science and industry: *We're having a few technical problems.*

technician /tekˈnɪʃᵊn/ *noun*
someone whose job involves practical work with scientific or electrical equipment: *a computer technician*

technique /tekˈniːk/ *noun*
a particular way of doing something: *It's a new technique for taking blood samples.*

technology /tekˈnɒlədʒi/ *noun* **[no plural]**
knowledge, equipment, and methods that are used in science and industry: *computer technology*
• **technological** /ˌteknəˈlɒdʒɪkᵊl/ *adj*
relating to, or involving technology: *technological developments*

teddy bear /ˈtediˌbeə/ *noun*
a soft, toy bear

tedious /ˈtiːdiəs/ *adj*
boring: *a tedious job*

teenager /ˈtiːnˌeɪdʒəʳ/ *noun*
someone who is between 13 and 19 years old

teeth

teeth /tiːθ/
plural of tooth

telephone[1] /ˈtelɪfəʊn/ (*also* **phone)** *noun*
a piece of equipment that is used to talk to someone who is in another place: *The* ***telephone rang*** *and she hurried to pick it up.* ◦ *Could you* ***answer*** *the* ***telephone****?*

telephone

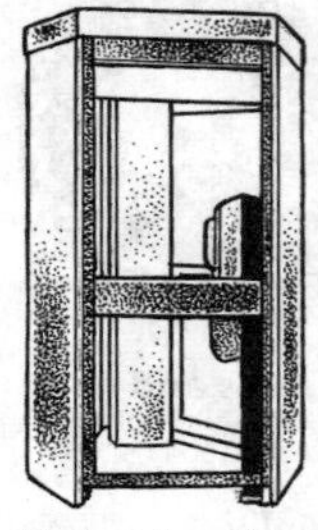

telephone box *UK*, telephone booth *US*

telephone

mobile phone

telephone[2] /ˈtelɪfəʊn/ (*also* **phone)** *verb* (*present participle* **telephoning,** *past* **telephoned)** *formal*
to speak to someone by telephone

telephone number /ˈtelɪfəʊn ˌnʌmbəʳ/ (*also* **phone number)** *noun*
the number of a particular telephone

telescope

telescope /ˈtelɪskəʊp/ *noun*
a piece of equipment, in the shape of a tube, that makes things which are far away look bigger

television

television /ˈtelɪvɪʒᵊn/ *noun*
1 a piece of equipment in the shape of a box, with a screen on the front, used for watching programmes: *Richard switched the television on.*
2 [no plural] the programmes that are shown on a television: *I mostly* ***watch television*** *in the evening.*

tell /tel/ *verb* (*present participle* **telling,** *past* **told)**
1 to say something to someone, usually giving them information: *He* ***told*** *me* ***about*** *his new school.*
2 tell someone to do something to order someone to do something: *I told you to stay here.*

3 can tell to know something from what you hear, see, etc: *You could tell that he was tired.*
tell someone off *phrasal verb*
to tell someone that they have done something wrong and that you are angry about it: *Darren* ***got told off*** *for talking in class.* ➲See colour picture **Phrasal Verbs** on page Centre 13

telly /ˈteli/ *noun UK informal short for* television

temper /ˈtempəʳ/ *noun*
1 when someone becomes angry very easily: *He's got a really* ***bad temper****.*
2 lose your temper (with someone) to suddenly become very angry: *I lost my temper with the children this morning.*

temperature /ˈtemprətʃəʳ/ *noun*
1 how hot or cold something is: *Last night the temperature dropped to below freezing.*
2 have a temperature to be hotter than usual because you are ill

temple /ˈtempl/ *noun*
a building where people in some religions go to pray: *a Buddhist temple*

temporary /ˈtempᵊrᵊri/ *adj*
existing or happening for only a short time: *a temporary job*
• **temporarily** *adv*

tempt /tempt/ *verb*
to make someone want to have or do something that they should not: *Can I tempt you to go shopping?*

temptation /tempˈteɪʃᵊn/ *noun*
a feeling that you want to do or have something, although you know you should not

ten /ten/
the number 10

tenant /ˈtenənt/ *noun*
someone who pays money to live in a room, house, etc

tend /tend/ *verb*
tend to do something to often do a particular thing: *I tend to wear dark colours.*

tendency /ˈtendənsi/ *noun* (*plural* **tendencies**)
something that someone often does, or something that often happens: *She* ***has a tendency*** *to talk for too long.*

tender /ˈtendəʳ/ *adj*
1 kind and gentle: *a tender kiss*
2 Tender meat or vegetables are soft and easy to cut.
• **tenderness** *noun* **[no plural]**

tennis /ˈtenɪs/ *noun* **[no plural]**
a sport in which two or four people hit a small ball to each other over a net ➲See colour picture **Sports 2** on page Centre 16

tense¹ /tens/ *adj*
1 nervous and not able to relax: *The students looked tense as they waited for their exam results.*
2 A tense situation makes you feel nervous.

tense² /tens/ *noun*
the form of a verb which shows the time at which an action happened. For example 'I sing' is in the present tense and 'I will sing' is in the future tense.

tent /tent/ *noun*
a structure for sleeping in made of cloth fixed to metal poles: *It only took twenty minutes to* ***put the tent up*** (= make it ready to use).

tenth¹ /tenθ/
10th written as a word

tenth² /tenθ/ *noun*
one of ten equal parts of something; 1/10; 0.1

term /tɜːm/ *noun*
1 a word or phrase that is used to mean a particular thing: *a legal term*
2 a fixed period of time: *a prison term*
3 one of the periods of time that the school or university year is divided into: *We've got a test at the end of term.*

terminal /ˈtɜːmɪnᵊl/ *noun*
a building where you can get onto an aeroplane, bus, or ship

terms /tɜːmz/ *plural noun*
1 the rules of an agreement
2 in ... terms used to explain which part of a situation you mean: *In financial terms, the project was not a success.*
3 come to terms with something to accept a sad situation: *He still hasn't*

| j yes | k cat | ŋ ring | ʃ she | θ thin | ð this | ʒ decision | dʒ jar | tʃ chip | æ cat | e bed | ə ago | ɪ sit | i cosy | ɒ hot | ʌ run | ʊ put |

a b c d e f g h i j k l m n o p q r s t u v w x y z

come to terms with his brother's death.

terrace /ˈterɪs/ *noun*
1 a flat area outside a house, restaurant, etc where you can sit
2 *UK* a row of houses that are joined together

terraced house /ˌterɪst ˈhaʊz/ *UK* (*US* **row house**) *noun*
one of a row of houses that are joined together

terrible /ˈterəbl/ *adj*
very bad: *a terrible accident* ○ *The weather was terrible.*

terribly /ˈterəbli/ *adv*
1 very: *She was terribly upset.*
2 very badly: *I slept terribly last night.*

terrific /təˈrɪfɪk/ *adj*
excellent: *I thought she looked terrific.*

terrified /ˈterəfaɪd/ *adj*
very frightened: *I'm* ***terrified of*** *flying.*

terror /ˈterə^{r}/ *noun* **[no plural]**
a feeling of being very frightened

terrorism /ˈter^{ə}rɪz^{ə}m/ *noun* **[no plural]**
the use of violence for political purposes, for example putting bombs in public places: *an act of terrorism*

terrorist /ˈterərɪst/ *noun*
someone who is involved in terrorism: *a terrorist attack*

test[1] /test/ *noun*
a set of questions to find out how much someone knows or how well they can do something: *a driving test* ○ *You have to* ***take a test****.*

test[2] /test/ *verb*
1 to do a medical examination of part of someone's body: *I'm going to get my hearing tested.*
2 to give someone a set of questions, in order to find out how much they know or how well they can do something: *You'll be* ***tested on*** *all the subjects we've studied this term.*

test tube /ˈtest ˌtjuːb/ *noun*
a glass tube that is open at one end and used in scientific experiments

text[1] /tekst/ *noun*
the written words in a book, magazine, etc, not the pictures: *a page of text*

text[2] /tekst/ *verb*
to send a text message (= written message from a mobile phone)

textbook /ˈtekstbʊk/ *noun*
a book about a particular subject, written for students: *a chemistry textbook* ➲See colour picture **Classroom** on page Centre 4

text message /ˈtekst ˌmesɪdʒ/ *noun* **[no plural]**
a message in writing sent from one mobile phone to another

texture /ˈtekstʃə^{r}/ *noun*
the way that something feels when you touch it: *wood with a rough texture*

than *strong form* /ðæn/ *weak form* /ð^{ə}n/ *preposition, conjunction*
used to compare two different things or amounts: *Susannah's car is bigger than mine.* ○ *It cost less than I expected.*

thank /θæŋk/ *verb*
to tell someone that you are pleased about something they have given you or done for you: *I must* ***thank*** *her* ***for*** *her present.*

thanks /θæŋks/ *exclamation informal*
1 used to tell someone that you are pleased about something they have given you or done for you: *Can you pass me the book? Thanks very much.* ○ ***Thanks for*** *all your help.*
2 no, thanks used to refuse someone's offer: *"Would you like a cup of coffee?" "No, thanks."*

thank you! /ˈθæŋk ˌjuː/ *exclamation*
1 used to tell someone that you are pleased about something they have given you or done for you: ***Thank you*** *very much* ***for*** *the birthday card.* ○ *"Here's the money I promised you." "Thank you."*
2 no, thank you used to refuse someone's offer: *"Would you like something to eat?" "No, thank you."*

that[1] /ðæt/ *determiner* (*plural* **those**)
1 used to mean something or someone that has already been talked about or seen: *Did you see that woman in the post office?* ○ *How much are those shoes?*
2 used to mean something or someone that is not near you: *Have you seen that man over there?*

that[2] /ðæt/ *pronoun* (*plural* **those**)
1 used to mean something that has already been talked about or seen: *That looks heavy.*
2 used to mean something that is

not near you: *What's that in the corner?*
3 that's it used to say that something is correct: *You need to push the two pieces together. That's it.*

that[3] *strong form* /ðæt/ *weak form* /ðət/ *conjunction*
1 used after some verbs, nouns, and adjectives to start a new part of a sentence: *He said that he'd collect it later.*
2 used instead of 'who' or 'which' in the middle of a sentence: *Have you eaten all the cake that I made yesterday?*

thaw /θɔː/ *verb*
to become warmer and softer or change to liquid: *Allow the meat to thaw before cooking it.*

the *strong form* /ðiː/ *weak forms* /ði, ðə/ *determiner*
1 used before nouns to mean things or people that have already been talked about or are already known: *Can you pass the salt?* ○ *I'll pick you up at the station.*
2 used before nouns when only one of something exists: *the Eiffel Tower* ○ *the world*
3 used before some adjectives to make them into nouns: *a home for the elderly*
4 used before numbers which refer to dates: *Thursday the 29th of April*

theatre /ˈθɪətəʳ/ *noun*
a building with a stage where people go to watch plays: *the Arts Theatre*

theft /θeft/ *noun*
the action or crime of stealing something: *car theft*

their /ðeəʳ/ *determiner*
belonging to or relating to them: *It was their problem, not mine.*

theirs /ðeəz/ *pronoun*
the things that belong or relate to them: *I think she's a friend of theirs.*

them *strong form* /ðem/ *weak form* /ðəm/ *pronoun*
the group of people, animals, or things that have already been talked about: *I'm looking for my keys – have you seen them?*

theme /θiːm/ *noun*
the subject of a book, film, speech, etc: *The theme of loss runs through most of his novels.*

themselves /ðəmˈselvz/ *pronoun*
1 used to show that the people who do the action are also the people who are affected by it: *They're both 16 – they're old enough to look after themselves.*
2 used to give more attention to the word 'them': *They've decided to run the club themselves.*
3 (all) by themselves alone or without anyone else's help: *The children arranged the party all by themselves.*

then /ðen/ *adv*
1 at that time: *Call me tomorrow – I'll have time to speak then.*
2 next, or after something has happened: *Let me finish my drink, then we'll go.*
3 so or because of that: *Have a rest now, then you won't be tired this evening.*

theory /ˈθɪəri/ *noun* (*plural* **theories**)
an idea or set of ideas that explains something: *Darwin's theory of evolution*

there[1] *strong form* /ðeəʳ/ *weak form* /ðəʳ/ *pronoun*
There is/are/was, etc used to show that something exists or happens: *There are three pubs in the village.* ○ *Is there any milk?*

there[2] /ðeəʳ/ *adv*
1 in or at a particular place: *We live in York because my wife works there.*
2 used when you are pointing at something in order to make someone look somewhere: *Put them in that box there.*

therefore /ˈðeəfɔːʳ/ *adv*
for that reason: *There has been an accident on the road and people are therefore asked to avoid it.*

thermometer /θəˈmɒmɪtəʳ/ *noun*
a piece of equipment that shows how hot or cold someone or something is

thermometer

these /ðiːz/ *pronoun, determiner*
plural of this

they /ðeɪ/ *pronoun*
used as the subject of the verb when meaning a group of people,

a b c d e f g h i j k l m n o p q r s t u v w x y z

animals, or things that have already been talked about: *I saw Kate and Nigel yesterday – they came over for dinner.*

they'd /ðeɪd/ *short for*
1 they had: *They'd just left when I arrived.*
2 they would: *They'd like to take us out to dinner.*

they'll /ðeɪl/ *short for*
they will: *They'll be in Scotland next week.*

they're /ðeəʳ/ *short for*
they are: *They're both from Washington.*

they've /ðeɪv/ *short for*
they have: *They've got three children – two girls and a boy.*

thick /θɪk/ *adj*
1 Something that is thick is larger than usual between its opposite sides: *a thick layer of snow* ➲Opposite **thin**
2 **10cm/2m, etc thick** being 10cm/2m, etc thick: *a piece of wood 2cm thick*
3 growing very close together and in large amounts: *thick, dark hair*
4 Thick smoke, cloud, or fog is difficult to see through: *Thick, black smoke was pouring out of the chimney.*
5 *UK informal* not intelligent

thief /θiːf/ *noun* (*plural* **thieves**)
someone who steals things: *a car thief*

thigh /θaɪ/ *noun*
the top part of your leg above your knee ➲See colour picture **The Body** on page Centre 2

thin /θɪn/ *adj*
1 Something that is thin is smaller than usual between its opposite sides: *a thin slice of meat* ➲Opposite **thick**
2 A thin person or animal has very little fat on their body.
3 A thin substance or liquid has a lot of water in it: *thin soup*

thing /θɪŋ/ *noun*
1 used to mean an object without saying its name: *I need to get a few things in town.*
2 one part of a situation, problem, or subject: *The best thing about the holiday was the food.*
3 **thing to do/say** something that is done or said: *What a silly thing to do.*

things /θɪŋz/ *plural noun*
the objects that you own: *I'll just get my things and then I'll be ready.*

think /θɪŋk/ *verb* (*present participle* **thinking**, *past* **thought**)
1 to have an opinion about something or someone: *Do you think it's going to rain?* ○ *What did you* ***think of*** *the film?*
2 to consider an idea or a problem: *He thought for a few seconds before answering.*
3 **think about/of** to consider doing something: *I'm thinking of moving to Sydney.*

third[1] /θɜːd/
3rd written as a word

third[2] /θɜːd/ *noun*
one of three equal parts of something; ⅓

thirst /θɜːst/ *noun* **[no plural]**
the feeling that you want to drink something

thirsty /ˈθɜːsti/ *adj* **(thirstier, thirstiest)**
wanting or needing a drink: *I felt really hot and thirsty after my run.*

thirteen /θɜːˈtiːn/
the number 13
● **thirteenth**
13th written as a word

thirty /ˈθɜːti/
the number 30
● **thirtieth**
30th written as a word

this[1] /ðɪs/ *determiner*
1 used to mean something that you have already talked about: *Most people don't agree with this decision.*
2 used to mean something or someone that is near you or that you are pointing to: *How much does this CD cost?*
3 used to mean the present week, month, year, etc or the one that comes next: *I'll see you this evening.*

this[2] /ðɪs/ *pronoun*
1 used to mean something that you have already talked about: *When did this happen?*
2 used to mean something or someone that is near you or that you are pointing to: *This is my girlfriend, Beth.*

thorn /θɔːn/ *noun*
a small, sharp point on the stem of a plant

thorough /ˈθʌrə/ *adj*
careful and covering every detail: *She wrote a very thorough report on the matter.*

thoroughly /θʌrəli/ *adv*
1 very carefully: *Wash the fruit thoroughly*
2 very, or very much: *We thoroughly enjoyed ourselves.*

those /ðəʊz/ *pronoun, determiner plural of*
that: *These apples look much nicer than those.* ○ *I want those shoes.*

though /ðəʊ/ *conjunction*
1 used before a fact or opinion that makes the other part of the sentence surprising: *And though she's quite small, she's very strong.* ○ *Nina didn't phone,* ***even though*** *she said she would.*
2 but: *They're coming next week, though I don't know when.*

thought[1] /θɔːt/ *noun*
1 an idea or opinion: *The thought of seeing her again filled him with happiness.*
2 **[no plural]** the activity of thinking: *You'll need to* ***give*** *the matter some* ***thought***.

thought[2] /θɔːt/
past of think

thousand /ˈθaʊzənd/
the number 1000

thousandth[1] /ˈθaʊzəndθ/
1000th written as a word

thousandth[2] /ˈθaʊzəndθ/ *noun*
one of a thousand equal parts of something; 1/1000; .001: *a thousandth of a second*

thread /θred/ *noun*
a long, thin piece of cotton, wool, etc that is used for sewing: *a needle and thread*

threat /θret/ *noun*
when someone says they will do something bad to you if you do not do what they want: *a death threat*

threaten /ˈθretən/ *verb*
to tell someone that you will do something bad to them if they do not do what you want: *He* ***threatened to*** *report her to the police.*

three /θriː/
the number 3

threw /θruː/
past tense of throw

thrill /θrɪl/ *noun*
a strong feeling of excitement and pleasure: *It was a big thrill meeting the stars of the show.*

throat /θrəʊt/ *noun*
1 the back part of your mouth and the part inside your neck: *a sore throat*
2 the front of your neck: *He grabbed her round the throat.* ➲See colour picture **The Body** on page Centre 2

throne /θrəʊn/ *noun*
the special chair that a king or queen sits on

through /θruː/ *preposition*
1 from one end or side of something to the other: *The River Seine flows through Paris.*
2 from the start to the end of something: *He worked through the night.*
3 *US* (*UK* **to**) from one time until another time: *The store is open Monday through Friday.*

throughout /θruˈaʊt/ *adv, preposition*
1 in every part of a place: *The same laws apply throughout much of Europe.*
2 during the whole of a period of time: *He yawned throughout the performance.*

throw

throw /θrəʊ/ *verb*
(*present participle* **throwing,** *past tense* **threw,** *past participle* **thrown)**
to make something move through the air by pushing it out of your hand: *Amy* ***threw*** *the ball* ***to*** *the dog.*

throw something away *phrasal verb*
to get rid of something that you do not want any more: *He read the magazine and then threw it away.* ➲See colour picture **Phrasal Verbs** on page Centre 13

thud /θʌd/ *noun*
the sound that is made when something heavy falls: *There was a thud as he fell on the floor.*

thug /θʌg/ *noun*
a bad person who behaves violently

thumb /θʌm/ *noun*
the short, thick finger on the side of

a b c d e f g h i j k l m n o p q r s t u v w x y z

your hand ➲See colour picture **The Body** on page Centre 2

thump /θʌmp/ *verb UK*
to hit someone with your fist (= closed hand)

thunder /ˈθʌndər/ *noun* **[no plural]**
the loud noise in the sky that you hear during a storm: *thunder and lightning*

thunderstorm /ˈθʌndəstɔːm/ *noun*
a storm that has thunder (= loud noise) and lightning (= sudden flashes of light in the sky)

Thursday /ˈθɜːzdeɪ/ *noun*
the day of the week after Wednesday and before Friday

tick[1] /tɪk/ *noun*
1 the sound that a clock or watch makes every second
2 *UK* (*US* **check**) a mark (✓) that shows something is correct or has been done

tick[2] /tɪk/ *verb*
1 If a clock or watch ticks, it makes a sound every second.
2 *UK* to mark something with a tick

ticket /ˈtɪkɪt/ *noun*
a small piece of paper that shows you have paid to do something, for example travel on a bus, watch a film, etc: *a lottery ticket* ◦ *plane tickets*

tickets

tickle /ˈtɪkl/ *verb* (*present participle* **tickling,** *past* **tickled)**
to touch someone lightly with your fingers, in order to make them laugh

tide /taɪd/ *noun*
the regular rise and fall in the level of the sea: *high/low tide*

tidy[1] /ˈtaɪdi/ *adj* **(tidier, tidiest)**
having everything in the right place and arranged in a good order: *Her room was clean and tidy.*

tidy[2] /ˈtaɪdi/ (*also* **tidy up**) *verb* (*present participle* **tidying,** *past* **tidied)** *UK*
to make a place tidy: *I'm tidying up before our guests arrive.*

tie /taɪ/ *verb* (*present participle* **tying,** *past* **tied)**
1 to fasten something with string, rope, etc: *The dog was tied to a tree.*
2 to make a knot in a piece of string, rope, etc: *She tied the scarf.* ➲Opposite **untie**

tie

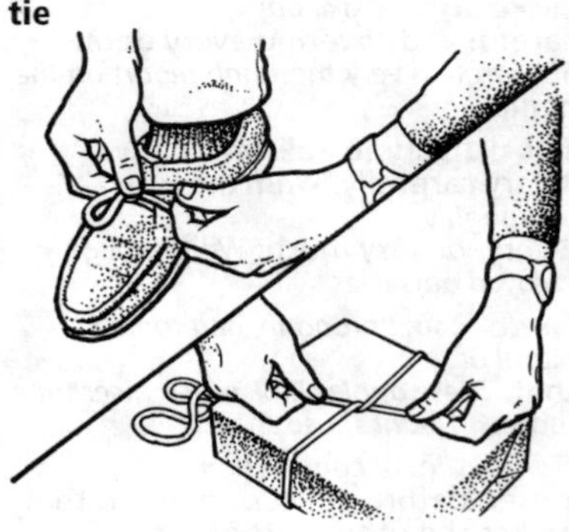

tie something up *phrasal verb*
to fasten something together using string, rope, etc

tiger /ˈtaɪgər/ *noun*
a large wild cat that has yellow fur with black lines on it

tight /taɪt/ *adj*
1 firm and difficult to move: *Make sure the knot is tight.*
2 fitting your body very closely: *a tight skirt* ➲Opposite **loose**
● **tightly** *adv*

tighten /ˈtaɪtən/ *verb*
to become tighter or to make something become tighter: *His hand tightened around her arm.*

tights /taɪts/ *plural noun UK*
a piece of women's clothing made of very thin material that covers the legs and bottom ➲See colour picture **Clothes** on page Centre 5

tile /taɪl/ *noun*
one of the flat, square pieces that are used for covering roofs, floors, or walls
● **tile** *verb* (*present participle* **tiling,** *past* **tiled)** *a tiled kitchen*

till[1] /tɪl/ *preposition, conjunction*
until: *The supermarket is open till midnight.*

till[2] /tɪl/ *noun UK*
a machine that holds the money in a shop

tilt /tɪlt/ *verb*
to move into a position where one end or side is higher than the other:

a b c d e f g h i j k l m n o p q r s t u v w x y z

He tilted backwards on his chair.

timber /ˈtɪmbəʳ/ *noun* **[no plural]** *UK* (*US* **lumber**)
wood that is used for building

time¹ /taɪm/ *noun*
1 [no plural] Time is what we measure in minutes, hours, days, etc: *He wants to **spend** more **time** with his family.*
2 a particular point in the day or night: *What time is it? ○ What time do you leave for school in the mornings?*
3 it's time for/to do something used to say that something should happen or be done now: *It's time to get up.*
4 on time not early or late: *I got to school on time.*
5 can tell the time to be able to know what time it is by looking at a clock or watch
6 a period of minutes, hours, years, etc: *I lived in Switzerland for a long time.*
7 have time to have enough time to do something: *I never have time to eat breakfast.*
8 in no time very soon: *We'll be home in no time.*
9 an occasion when something happens: *How many times have you been to Germany?*
10 at the same time If two things happen at the same time, they happen together: *We arrived at the same time.*
11 all the time very often: *"She's been late twice this week." "It happens all the time."*
12 three/eight/nine, etc times used to say how much bigger, better, worse, etc one thing is than another thing: *Ben earns three times more than me.*
13 in a day's/two months', etc time a week, two months, etc from now: *I have to go to the doctor again in a month's time.*
14 at times sometimes: *At times, I wish I didn't have to go to school.*
15 a period of time in the past: *Did you enjoy your time in Japan?*
16 from time to time sometimes, but not often: *I still see my ex-boyfriend from time to time.*
17 take your time to do something without hurrying

time² /taɪm/ *verb* (*present participle* **timing**, *past* **timed**)
to measure how long it takes for something to happen: *It's a good idea to time yourself while you do the exercises.*

timetable /ˈtaɪmˌteɪbl/ *noun*
a list of times when buses, trains, etc arrive and leave

tin /tɪn/ *noun*
1 *UK* (*US* **can**) a metal container in which food is sold: *a tin of soup*
2 *UK* a metal container with a lid that you keep food or other substances in: *a biscuit tin*

tinned /tɪnd/ *UK* (*US* **canned**) *adj*
Tinned food is sold in metal containers.

tin opener /ˈtɪn ˈəʊpənəʳ/ *UK* (*US* **can opener**) *noun*
a piece of kitchen equipment for opening metal food containers ↄSee colour picture **Kitchen** on page Centre 10

tiny /ˈtaɪni/ *adj* **(tinier, tiniest)**
very small: *a tiny baby*

tip¹ /tɪp/ *noun*
1 the end of something long and narrow: *the tips of your fingers*
2 a piece of useful advice: *gardening tips*
3 an extra amount of money that you give to a driver, etc to thank them: *We left a tip because the waiter was so friendly.*

tip² /tɪp/ *verb* (*present participle* **tipping**, *past* **tipped**)
1 to move so that one side is higher than the other side: *The table tipped and all the drinks fell on the floor.*
2 to make the contents of a container fall out by turning the container over: *She tipped the contents of her purse onto the table.*
3 to give an extra amount of money to a driver, etc to thank them

tiptoe¹ /ˈtɪptəʊ/ *noun*
on tiptoe standing on your toes

tiptoe² /ˈtɪptəʊ/ *verb* (*present participle* **tiptoeing**, *past* **tiptoed**)
to walk quietly on your toes

tired /taɪəd/ *adj*
1 feeling that you want to rest or sleep: *I'm too tired to go out tonight.* ○ *He was **tired out** (= very tired) by the end of the day.*
2 tired of doing something bored or angry about something that has

happened too often: *I'm tired of listening to her problems.*

tissue /ˈtɪʃuː/ *noun*
1 the material that animals and plants are made of: *human brain tissue*
2 a soft piece of paper that you use for cleaning your nose

title /ˈtaɪtl/ *noun*
1 the name of a book, film, etc
2 a word such as 'Lord', 'Dr', etc that is used before someone's name

to[1] /tə/
1 used with a verb to make the infinitive: *I want to learn Spanish.*
2 used to give the reason for doing something: *I'm just going out to get some milk.*

to[2] *strong form* /tuː/ *weak forms* /tʊ, tə/ *preposition*
1 in the direction of somewhere: *I ran to the door.*
2 used to show who gets something: *Could you give these keys to Pete?*
3 from ... to ... used to give information about periods of time and distances: *The museum is open from Monday to Saturday.* ○ *The bus goes from London to Cambridge.*
4 *UK* used to say 'before' the hour when you are saying what time it is: *It's five to three.*

toad /təʊd/ *noun*
a small, brown animal with long back legs for swimming and jumping

toast /təʊst/ *noun* **[no plural]**
bread that has been heated to make it brown: *a slice of toast*

toaster /ˈtəʊstəʳ/ *noun*
a machine that heats bread so that it becomes brown ➲See colour picture **Kitchen** on page Centre 10

tobacco /təˈbækəʊ/ *noun* **[no plural]**
dried leaves that are inside cigarettes

today /təˈdeɪ/ *noun, adv* **[no plural]**
1 this day, or on this day: *It's Johann's birthday today.* ○ *Today is Friday.*
2 the period of time that is happening now or in this period of time: *More young people smoke today than in the past.*

toddler /ˈtɒdləʳ/ *noun*
a child who has just learned to walk

toe /təʊ/ *noun*
one of the five separate parts at the end of your foot ➲See colour picture **The Body** on page Centre 2

toffee /ˈtɒfi/ *noun*
a sticky brown sweet

together /təˈgeðəʳ/ *adv*
1 with each other: *They live together.*
2 in the same place or close to each other: *We all sat together.*
3 at the same time: *We can deal with both problems together.*

toilet /ˈtɔɪlɪt/ *noun*
1 a bowl that you sit on or stand near when you get rid of waste substances from your body ➲See colour picture **The Bathroom** on page Centre 1
2 *UK* (*US* **bathroom**) a room with a toilet in it

toilet paper /ˈtɔɪlɪt ˌpeɪpəʳ/ *noun* **[no plural]**
paper used for cleaning your body after you have used the toilet

told /təʊld/
past of tell

tomato /təˈmɑːtəʊ/ *noun* (*plural* **tomatoes**)
a soft, round, red fruit eaten in salads or as a vegetable ➲See colour picture **Fruit and Vegetables** on page Centre 8

tomb /tuːm/ *noun*
a place where a dead person is buried

tombstone /ˈtuːmstəʊn/ *noun*
a stone that shows the name of a dead person who is buried under it

tomorrow /təˈmɒrəʊ/ *noun, adv* **[no plural]**
1 the day after today or on the day after today: *It's my birthday tomorrow.*
2 the future, or in the future: *the children of tomorrow*

ton /tʌn/ *noun*
a unit for measuring weight, equal to 1016 kilograms in the UK and 907 kilograms in the US

tone /təʊn/ *noun*
the quality of a sound, especially of someone's voice: *I knew by her* ***tone of voice*** *that she was serious.*

tongue /tʌŋ/ *noun*
the soft thing inside your mouth that you use for tasting and speaking

tonight /tə'naɪt/ *noun, adv* **[no plural]** the night of this day, or during the night of this day: *What are you doing tonight?*

tonne /tʌn/ *noun UK* a metric ton (= unit for measuring weight, equal to 1000 kilograms)

too /tuː/ *adv*
1 too small/heavy/much, etc used before adjectives and adverbs to mean 'more than is allowed, necessary, possible, etc': *It's too late.* ○ *The film was too long.*
2 also: *Do you know Jason too?*

took /tʊk/ *past tense of* take

tool /tuːl/ *noun* a piece of equipment that you use with your hands in order to help you do something

tooth /tuːθ/ *noun* (*plural* **teeth**) one of the hard, white things in your mouth that you use for biting: *You should* ***brush*** *your* ***teeth*** *twice a day.*

toothache /'tuːθeɪk/ *noun* **[no plural]** a pain in one of your teeth

toothbrush /'tuːθbrʌʃ/ *noun* (*plural* **toothbrushes**) a small brush that you use to clean your teeth

toothbrush

toothpaste /'tuːθpeɪst/ *noun* **[no plural]** a substance that you use to clean your teeth ↄSee colour picture **The Bathroom** on page Centre 1

top¹ /tɒp/ *noun*
1 the highest part of something: *They were waiting for him* ***at the top of*** *the stairs.*
2 the lid or cover of a container, pen, etc: *Put the top back on the bottle.*
3 a piece of women's clothing worn on the upper part of the body

top² /tɒp/ *adj*
1 the best, most important, or most successful: *He's one of the country's top athletes.*
2 at the highest part of something: *I can't reach the top shelf.*

topic /'tɒpɪk/ *noun* a subject that you talk or write about

torch /tɔːtʃ/ *noun* (*plural* **torches**)
1 *UK* (*US* **flashlight**) a small electric light that you hold in your hand
2 a long stick with material that burns tied to the top of it

tore /tɔːʳ/ *past tense of* tear

torn /tɔːn/ *past participle of* tear

tornado /tɔː'neɪdəʊ/ (*also US* **twister**) *noun* (*plural* **tornadoes** or **tornados**) an extremely strong wind that blows in a circle

torpedo /tɔː'piːdəʊ/ *noun* (*plural* **torpedoes**) a long, thin bomb that moves under water

torrent /'tɒrᵊnt/ *noun* **a torrent of something** a lot of something bad: *a torrent of abuse*

torrential /tə'renʃᵊl/ *adj* Torrential rain is very heavy rain.

tortoise /'tɔːtəs/ *noun* a slow animal with a thick, hard shell

tortoise

torture¹ /'tɔːtʃəʳ/ *verb* (*present participle* **torturing**, *past* **tortured**) to cause someone pain, often in order to make them tell you something

torture² /'tɔːtʃəʳ/ *noun* **[no plural]**
1 when someone is tortured
2 a very unpleasant experience: *I had to sit there listening to her for two whole hours – it was torture!*

toss /tɒs/ *verb* to throw something somewhere carelessly: *He read the letter quickly, then tossed it into the bin.*

total /'təʊtᵊl/ *adj*
1 including everything: *The total cost of the work was $800.*
2 extreme or complete: *The whole evening was a total disaster.*

totally /'təʊtᵊli/ *adv* completely: *They look totally different.*

touch¹ /tʌtʃ/ *verb*
1 to put your hand on something: *You can look at them but please don't touch them.*
2 If two things touch, they are so

close to each other that there is no space between them: *These two wires must not touch.*
3 to feel pleased because someone has been kind to you: *I was deeply touched by her letter.*

touch² /tʌtʃ/ *noun*
1 (*plural* **touches**) when you put your hand on something: *I felt the touch of his hand on my face.*
2 [no plural] the ability to feel things by putting your hand on them: *It was cold* ***to the touch*** (= when I touched it).
3 keep in touch to often speak to someone or write to them
4 lose touch to stop speaking with someone or writing to them: *We've lost touch over the years.*

tough /tʌf/ *adj*
1 difficult: *Starting a new job can be tough.*
2 not easily damaged, cut, etc: *Children's shoes have to be tough.*
3 strong and not afraid of violence: *a tough guy*

tour¹ /tʊəʳ/ *noun*
a visit to and around a place, area, or country: *a tour of Europe*

tour² /tʊəʳ/ *verb*
to travel around a place for pleasure: *to tour the States*

tourism /ˈtʊərɪzᵊm/ *noun* **[no plural]**
the business of providing services for tourists

tourist /ˈtʊərɪst/ *noun*
someone who visits a place for pleasure and does not live there

tournament /ˈtʊənəmənt/ *noun*
a competition: *a tennis tournament*

tow /təʊ/ *verb*
to pull a car, boat, etc: *His car was* ***towed away*** *by the police.*

towards /təˈwɔːdz/ *UK* (*US* **toward**) *preposition*
1 in the direction of someone or something: *She stood up and walked towards him.*
2 near to a time or place: *Your seats are towards the back of the theatre.*

towel /taʊəl/ *noun*
a soft piece of cloth or paper that you use for drying yourself: *a bath towel* ➲See colour picture **The Bathroom** on page Centre 1

tower /taʊəʳ/ *noun*
a very tall, narrow building, or part of a building: *a church tower*

town /taʊn/ *noun*
a place where people live and work which is larger than a village: *It's a small town in the north of England.*

toxic /ˈtɒksɪk/ *adj*
poisonous: *toxic chemicals*

toy /tɔɪ/ *noun*
an object for children to play with: *a toy car*

trace¹ /treɪs/ *verb* (*present participle* **tracing**, *past* **traced**)
to find someone or something that was lost: *Police are trying to trace the missing woman.*

trace² /treɪs/ *noun*
proof that someone or something was in a place: *There was no trace of her anywhere.*

track¹ /træk/ *noun*
1 a narrow path or road: *We followed a dirt track off the main road.*
2 the long metal lines which a train travels along
3 a path, often circular, used for races: *a race track*
4 one song or piece of music on a CD, record, etc
5 lose track to not know what is happening to someone or something any more: *I've lost track of how much we've spent.*

track² /træk/ *verb*
to follow a person or animal: *The wolves are tracked by using radio collars.*

tractor /ˈtræktəʳ/ *noun*
a strong vehicle with large back wheels used on farms for pulling things

trade¹ /treɪd/ *noun*
1 [no plural] the buying and selling of large numbers of things, especially between countries: *a trade agreement*
2 a type of business: *the tourist trade*
3 someone's job: *He's a builder* ***by trade***.

trade² /treɪd/ *verb* (*present participle* **trading**, *past* **traded**)
to buy and sell things, especially between countries: *Do you* ***trade with*** *Asia?*

tradition /trəˈdɪʃᵊn/ *noun*
a custom or way of behaving that has continued for a long time in a

group of people: *There is a great tradition of dance in St Petersburg.*

traditional /trəˈdɪʃᵊnᵊl/ *adj* following the customs or ways of behaving that have continued in a group of people for a long time: *traditional farming methods*
• **traditionally** *adv*

traffic /ˈtræfɪk/ *noun* **[no plural]** the cars, trucks, etc using a road: *Sorry we're late – we got stuck in traffic.*

traffic jam /ˈtræfɪk ˌdʒæm/ *noun* a line of cars, trucks, etc that are moving slowly

traffic light /ˈtræfɪk ˌlaɪt/ *noun* a set of red, green, and yellow lights that is used to stop and start traffic

tragedy /ˈtrædʒədi/ *noun* (*plural* **tragedies**) something very sad which happens, usually involving death: *the tragedy of their daughter's death*

tragic /ˈtrædʒɪk/ *adj* very sad, often involving death: *a tragic accident*
• **tragically** *adv*

trail /treɪl/ *noun*
1 a line of marks that someone or something leaves behind as they move: *a trail of muddy footprints*
2 a path through the countryside: *a nature trail*

trailer /ˈtreɪləʳ/ *noun* a container with wheels that can be pulled by a car or a truck

train¹ /treɪn/ *noun* a long, thin vehicle which travels along metal tracks and carries people or goods: *We could go **by train**.*

train² /treɪn/ *verb*
1 to learn the skills you need to do a job: *He **trained as** a lawyer in Vienna.*
2 to practise a sport or exercise in order to prepare for a sporting event

trainer /ˈtreɪnəʳ/ *noun*
1 someone who trains people: *a fitness trainer*
2 *UK* a soft sports shoe: *a pair of trainers* ➲See colour picture **Clothes** on page Centre 5

training /ˈtreɪnɪŋ/ *noun* **[no plural]**
1 when you learn a skill: *computer training*
2 when you prepare for a sport or competition: *weight training*

traitor /ˈtreɪtəʳ/ *noun* someone who does something that harms their country, especially by helping its enemies

tramp /træmp/ *noun* someone who has no home, job, or money and who lives outside

trample /ˈtræmpl/ *verb* (*present participle* **trampling**, *past* **trampled**) to walk on something, usually damaging it: *She shouted at the boys for trampling on her flowers.*

transfer /trænsˈfɜːʳ/ *verb* (*present participle* **transferring**, *past* **transferred**) to move someone or something from one place to another: *She was **transferred to** a different hospital.*
• **transfer** /ˈtrænsfɜːʳ/ *noun*: *I'm hoping for a **transfer to** the Brussels office.*

transform /trænsˈfɔːm/ *verb* to change something completely, usually to improve it: *You have transformed this house!*
• **transformation** /ˌtrænsfəˈmeɪʃᵊn/ *noun* a complete change

transitive /ˈtrænsətɪv/ *adj* A transitive verb always has an object. In the sentence 'I'll make a drink.', 'make' is a transitive verb.

translate /trænzˈleɪt/ *verb* (*present participle* **translating**, *past* **translated**) to change words from one language to another: *We were asked to translate a list of sentences.*

translation /trænzˈleɪʃᵊn/ *noun* something which has been changed from one language to another

transparent /trænˈspærᵊnt/ *adj* If a substance or material is transparent, you can see through it: *transparent plastic*

transport¹ /ˈtrænspɔːt/ *noun* **[no plural]**
1 a vehicle or system of vehicles, such as buses, trains, aeroplanes, etc for getting from one place to another: *I rely on **public transport**.*
2 when people or things are moved from one place to another: *the transport of live animals*

transport² /trænˈspɔːt/ *verb* to move people or things from one place to another

trap¹ /træp/ *noun*

a piece of equipment for catching animals: *a mouse trap*

trap² /træp/ *verb* (*present participle* **trapping**, *past* **trapped**)
1 If someone or something is trapped, they cannot escape from a place or situation: *The car turned over, trapping the driver underneath.*
2 to catch an animal using a trap

travel /ˈtrævᵊl/ *verb* (*present participle* **travelling**, *past* **travelled**)
1 to make a journey: *I spent a year travelling around Asia.*
2 If light, sound, or news travels, it moves from one place to another: *News of the accident travelled fast.*

travel agency /ˈtrævᵊl ˌeɪdʒᵊnsi (*also* ˈ**travel ˌagent's**) *noun* (*plural* **travel agencies**)
a shop that makes travel arrangements for people

traveller /ˈtrævᵊləʳ/ *noun*
someone who is travelling

traveller's cheque /ˈtrævᵊləz ˌtʃek/ *noun UK*
a special piece of paper which you exchange for the money of another country

trawler /ˈtrɔːləʳ/ *noun*
a large ship which is used for catching fish

tray /treɪ/ *noun*
a flat object with higher edges, used for carrying food and drinks

tread /tred/ *verb* (*present participle* **treading**, *past tense* **trod**, *past participle* **trodden**) *UK*
to put your foot on something: *I **trod on** a piece of broken glass.*

treason /ˈtriːzᵊn/ *noun* **[no plural]**
the crime of doing something that harms your country, especially by helping its enemies

treasure /ˈtreʒəʳ/ *noun* **[no plural]**
a collection of gold, silver, jewellery and valuable objects: *buried treasure*

treat¹ /triːt/ *verb*
1 to behave towards someone in a particular way: *He treats her really badly.* ○ *They **treat** her **like** one of their own children.*
2 to give medical care to someone who is ill or hurt: *He's being **treated for** cancer at a hospital in Manchester.*
3 to do or buy something special for someone: *I **treated** her **to** dinner at an Italian restaurant.*

treat² /triːt/ *noun*
something special which you buy or do for someone else: *a birthday treat* ○ *As a special treat I'm taking him out for dinner.*

treatment /ˈtriːtmənt/ *noun*
1 something which you do to try to cure an illness or injury: *She's receiving treatment for a lung infection.*
2 **[no plural]** the way you behave towards someone: *There have been complaints about the treatment of prisoners.*

treaty /ˈtriːti/ *noun* (*plural* **treaties**)
a written agreement between two or more countries: *a peace treaty*

tree /triː/ *noun*
a tall plant with a thick stem which has branches coming from it and leaves

tremble /ˈtrembl/ *verb* (*present participle* **trembling**, *past* **trembled**)
to shake slightly, especially because you are frightened or cold

tremendous /trɪˈmendəs/ *adj*
1 very good: *I think she's doing a tremendous job.*
2 very large, great, strong, etc: *a tremendous amount of money*
● **tremendously** *adv*
very much

trench /trenʃ/ *noun* (*plural* **trenches**)
a long, narrow hole dug into the ground

trend /trend/ *noun*
a general development or change in a situation: *I'm not familiar with the latest **trends in** teaching.*

trendy /ˈtrendi/ *adj informal* (**trendier, trendiest**)
fashionable at the moment: *She has some trendy new glasses.*

trespass /ˈtrespəs/ *verb*
to go on someone's land when they do not allow it
● **trespasser** *noun*

trial /traɪəl/ *noun*
1 a legal process to decide if someone has done a crime: *The two men are now **on trial for** attempted murder.*
2 a test of something new to find out if it is safe, works correctly, etc: *The drug is currently undergoing clinical trials.*

triangle /ˈtraɪæŋgl/ *noun*
a flat shape with three sides
• **triangular** /traɪˈæŋgjələʳ/ *adj*
shaped like a triangle

tribe /traɪb/ *noun*
a group of people who live together, usually in areas far away from cities, and who still have a traditional way of life: *Native American tribes*
• **tribal** *adj*
relating to a tribe

tribute /ˈtrɪbjuːt/ *noun*
something which you do or say to show that you respect and admire someone: *The concert was organized as* ***a tribute to*** *the singer who died last year.*

trick[1] /trɪk/ *noun*
1 something you do to deceive someone, or to make someone look stupid: *I wasn't really ill – it was just a trick.*
2 something that is done to entertain people and that seems to be magic: *a card trick*

trick[2] /trɪk/ *verb*
to deceive someone: *They tricked him into signing the papers.*

trickle /ˈtrɪkl/ *verb* (*present participle* **trickling**, *past* **trickled**)
If liquid trickles somewhere, it flows slowly and in a thin line: *The sweat trickled down her back.*
• **trickle** *noun*: *a trickle of blood*

tricky /ˈtrɪki/ *adj* (**trickier, trickiest**)
difficult: *a tricky question*

tried /traɪd/ *past of*
try

trigger /ˈtrɪgəʳ/ *noun*
the part of a gun that you pull when you shoot

trim /trɪm/ *verb* (*present participle* **trimming**, *past* **trimmed**)
to cut a small amount from something: *I've had my hair trimmed.*

trip[1] /trɪp/ *noun*
a journey in which you visit a place for a short time and come back again: *a business trip*

trip[2] /trɪp/ *verb* (*present participle* **tripping**, *past* **tripped**)
to fall because you hit your foot on something when you are moving: *She* ***tripped over*** *the cat.*

triumph /ˈtraɪəmf/ *noun*
an important success: *Barcelona's 2-0 triumph over Manchester United*

trivial /ˈtrɪviəl/ *adj*
small and not important: *a trivial problem*

trod /trɒd/
past tense of tread

trodden /ˈtrɒdᵊn/
past participle of tread

trolley

trolley /ˈtrɒli/ *noun UK* (*plural* **trolleys**)
a metal structure on wheels that is used for carrying things: *a luggage trolley*

troops /truːps/ *noun*
soldiers: *UN troops*

trophy

trophy /ˈtrəʊfi/ *noun* (*plural* **trophies**)
a prize, such as a silver cup, that you get for winning a competition

tropical /ˈtrɒpɪkᵊl/ *adj*
from or in the hottest parts of the world: *a tropical climate*

the tropics /ˈtrɒpɪks/ *noun*
the hottest parts of the world,

trot /trɒt/ *verb* (*present participle* **trotting**, *past* **trotted**)
to walk with quick, short steps: *The little boy trotted along behind his father.*

trouble[1] /ˈtrʌbl/ *noun*
1 problems: *We had trouble finding somewhere to park.*
2 the trouble with someone/something used to say what is wrong with someone or something: *The trouble with a white floor is that it gets dirty so quickly.*
3 [no plural] a problem with a machine or part of your body: *back trouble* ○ *car trouble*
4 [no plural] when you have done something wrong and will be

a b c d e f g h i j k l m n o p q r s t u v w x y z

punished: *They* ***got into trouble*** *with the police.*

trouble² /ˈtrʌbl/ *verb* (*present participle* **troubling,** *past* **troubled)**
1 to make someone worry: *The situation has been troubling me for a while.*
2 *formal* used to ask someone politely to help you: *I'm sorry to trouble you, but could you tell me how to get to the station?*

trough /trɒf/ *noun*
a long, narrow container that animals eat or drink from

trousers

trousers /ˈtraʊzəz/ (*also US* **pants)** *plural noun*
a piece of clothing that covers the legs and has a separate part for each leg: *a pair of trousers* ➲See colour picture **Clothes** on page Centre 5

truant /ˈtruːənt/ *noun*
a child who stays away from school without permission

truck /trʌk/ (*also UK* **lorry)** *noun*
a large road vehicle for carrying things from place to place

true /truː/ *adj*
1 based on facts and not imagined: *a true story* ○ *Is it true that Martin and Sue are getting married?*
2 real: *true love*
3 come true If a dream or hope comes true, it really happens.

truly /ˈtruːli/ *adv*
used to say that something is sincere or honest: *I truly believe that he is innocent.*

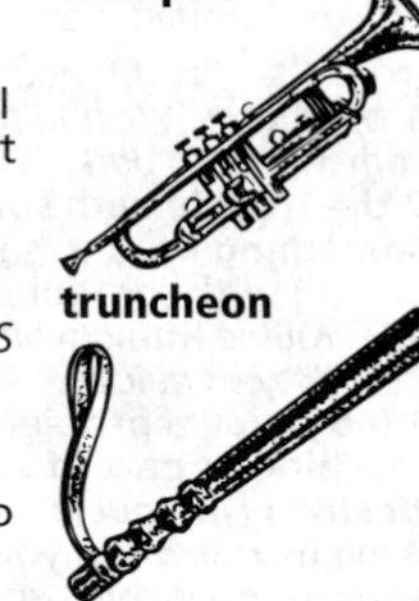

trumpet /ˈtrʌmpɪt/ *noun*
a metal musical instrument that you play by blowing into it

truncheon /ˈtrʌnʃᵊn/ *UK* (*US* **nightstick)** *noun*
a short stick that police officers carry to use as a weapon

trunk /trʌŋk/ *noun*
1 the thick stem of a tree that the branches grow from
2 the long nose of an elephant

trunks /trʌŋks/ (*also* **swimming trunks)** *plural noun*
a piece of clothing that boys and men wear when they swim ➲See colour picture **Clothes** on page Centre 5

trust¹ /trʌst/ *verb*
1 to believe that someone is good and honest and will not harm you: *My sister warned me not to trust him.*
2 trust someone to do something to be sure that someone will do the right thing: *I trust them to make the right decision.*

trust² /trʌst/ *noun*
[no plural] the belief that you can trust someone or something: *a marriage based on love and trust*

truth /truːθ/ *noun* **[no plural]**
the truth the real facts about a situation: *Do you think he was* ***telling the truth****?*

truthful /ˈtruːθfᵊl/ *adj*
honest and not containing or telling any lies: *a truthful answer*
• **truthfully** *adv*
• **truthfulness** *noun* **[no plural]**

try¹ /traɪ/ *verb* (*present participle* **trying,** *past* **tried)**
1 to attempt to do something: *I tried to open the window but couldn't.*
2 to do, test, taste, etc something to discover if it works or if you like it: *I tried that recipe you gave me last night.*
try something on *phrasal verb*
to put on a piece of clothing to see if it fits you: *Could I try this dress on, please?*

try² /traɪ/ *noun* (*plural* **tries)**
an attempt to do something

T-shirt

T-shirt (*also* **tee shirt)** /ˈtiːʃɜːt/ *noun*
a piece of cotton clothing for the top part of the body with short sleeves and no collar ➲See colour picture **Clothes** on page Centre 5

tub /tʌb/ *noun*
a small, plastic container with a lid, used for keeping food: *a tub of ice cream*

tube /tjuːb/ *noun*

1 a pipe made of glass, plastic, metal, etc, especially for liquids or gases to flow through
2 a long, thin container for a soft substance, that you press to get the substance out: *a tube of toothpaste*
3 the Tube the system of railways under the ground in London

tuck /tʌk/ *verb*
to push a loose piece of clothing or material somewhere to make it tidy: *Tuck your shirt in.*

Tuesday /ˈtjuːzdeɪ/ *noun*
the day of the week after Monday and before Wednesday

tuft /tʌft/ *noun*
a small group of hairs, grass, etc

tug /tʌg/ *verb* (*present participle* **tugging**, *past* **tugged**)
to pull something suddenly and strongly: *Tom* ***tugged at*** *his mother's arm.*

tumble /ˈtʌmbl/ *verb* (*present participle* **tumbling,** *past* **tumbled)**
to suddenly fall: *He* ***tumbled down*** *the stairs.*

tummy /ˈtʌmi/ *noun informal* (*plural* **tummies)**
stomach

tune /tjuːn/ *noun*
a series of musical notes that are nice to listen to: *He was humming a tune.*

tunnel /ˈtʌnəl/ *noun*
a long passage under the ground or through a mountain: *The train went into the tunnel.*

tunnel

turkey /ˈtɜːki/ *noun*
a bird that looks like a large chicken

turn¹ /tɜːn/ *verb*
1 to move your body so that you are looking in a different direction: *Ricky turned and saw Sue standing in the doorway.*
2 to change direction when you are moving, or to make a car do this: *Turn left at the traffic lights.* ○ *I turned the car into the drive.*
3 to move around a central point in a circle, or to make something do this: *Turn the steering wheel as quickly as you can.*
4 turn blue/cold/sour, etc to become blue, cold, etc: *The sky turned black and it started to rain.*
5 turn a page to move a page in a book or magazine in order to see the next one

turn something down *phrasal verb*
to refuse an offer or request: *They did offer me the job, but I turned it down.*

turn something down *phrasal verb*
to reduce the level of sound or heat that a machine produces: *Could you turn the radio down, please?*

turn something off *phrasal verb*
to move the switch on a machine, light, etc so that it stops working: *How do you turn the computer off?* ➲See colour picture **Phrasal Verbs** on page Centre 13

turn something on *phrasal verb*
to move the switch on a machine, light, etc so that it starts working: *Ben turned the TV on.* ➲See colour picture **Phrasal Verbs** on page Centre 13

turn up *phrasal verb, informal*
to arrive: *Fred turned up late again.*

turn something up *phrasal verb*
to increase the level of sound or heat that a machine produces: *Could you turn the heating up please?*

turn² /tɜːn/ *noun*
1 the time when you can or must do something, usually before or after someone else: *You'll have to be patient and* ***wait*** *your* ***turn****.*
2 take turns (*also UK* **take it in turns)** If two or more people take turns, one person does something, then another person does something, etc: *The children took it in turns to hold the baby.*
3 in turn one after another: *He spoke to the three boys in turn.*
4 a change in the direction in which you are moving or facing: *a right/left turn*
5 a bend or corner in a road, river, etc: *Take the next turn on the right.*

turning /ˈtɜːnɪŋ/ *noun UK*
a corner where one road meets another: *Take the second turning on the left.*

turtle /ˈtɜːtl/ *noun*
an animal with four legs and a hard shell that lives mainly in water

a b c d e f g h i j k l m n o p q r s t u v w x y z

a b c d e f g h i j k l m n o p q r s t u v w x y z

tusk /tʌsk/ *noun*
one of the two long, pointed teeth that come out of the mouth of some animals

tutor /ˈtjuːtəʳ/ *noun*
someone who teaches one person or a very small group of people: *a private tutor*
• **tutor** *verb*

TV /ˌtiːˈviː/ *noun*
television: *What's **on TV** tonight?* ➲See colour picture **The Living Room** on page Centre 11

tweezers /ˈtwiːzəz/ *plural noun*
a small tool with two narrow pieces of metal joined at one end, used for picking up very small things

tweezers

twelfth[1] /twelfθ/
12th written as a word

twelfth[2] /twelfθ/ *noun*
one of twelve equal parts of something; 1⁄12

twelve /twelv/
the number 12

twenty /ˈtwenti/
the number 20
• **twentieth**
20th written as a word

twice /twaɪs/ *adv*
two times: *I've been there twice.*

twig /twɪg/ *noun*
a small, thin branch on a tree

twin /twɪn/ *noun*
one of two children who are born to the same mother at the same time

twinkle /ˈtwɪŋkl/ *verb* (*present participle* **twinkling**, *past* **twinkled**)
If light twinkles, it shines and seems to be quickly flashing on and off: *The lights of the town twinkled in the distance.*

twist[1] /twɪst/ *verb*
1 to turn something using your hand: *She twisted the ring around on her finger.*
2 to bend and turn something many times and change its shape: *The wheels of the bike had been twisted in the accident.*
3 If a road, river, etc twists, it has a lot of bends in it.

twist[2] /twɪst/ *noun*
1 a sudden change in a story or situation that you do not expect: *The story has an unusual twist at the end.*
2 when you twist something
3 a bend in a river, road, etc

twitch /twɪtʃ/ *verb*
If a part of your body twitches, it suddenly makes a slight movement: *His face twitched nervously.*
• **twitch** *noun*

two /tuː/
the number 2

tying /ˈtaɪɪŋ/
present participle of tie

type[1] /taɪp/ *noun*
a group of people or things that have similar qualities: *They sell over 20 different types of cheese.* ○ *Illnesses of this type are very common in children.*

type[2] /taɪp/ *verb* (*present participle* **typing**, *past* **typed**)
to write something using a keyboard
• **typing** *noun* **[no plural]**

typical /ˈtɪpɪkəl/ *adj*
having all the qualities you expect a particular person, object, place, etc to have: *typical German food* ○ *This style of painting is **typical of** Monet.*

typist /ˈtaɪpɪst/ *noun*
someone who types (= writes using a machine), especially as their job

tyrant /ˈtaɪərənt/ *noun*
someone who has too much power and uses it in a cruel way

tyre *UK* (*US* **tire**) /taɪəʳ/ *noun*
a thick, round piece of rubber filled with air, that fits around a wheel: *My bike's got a **flat tyre*** (= tyre with no air in it). ➲See colour picture **Car** on page Centre 3

Uu

U, u /juː/
the twenty-first letter of the alphabet

ugly /ˈʌgli/ *adj* **(uglier, ugliest)**
bad to look at: *an ugly city*

ulcer /ˈʌlsəʳ/ *noun*
a painful, infected area on your skin or inside your body: *a mouth ulcer*

ultimate /ˈʌltɪmət/ *adj*
better, worse, or greater than all similar things: *Climbing Mount Everest is the ultimate challenge.*

umbrella /ʌmˈbrelə/ *noun*
a thing that you hold above your head to keep yourself dry when it is raining

umbrella

umpire /ˈʌmpaɪəʳ/ *noun*
someone whose job is to watch a sports game and make sure that the players obey the rules: *a tennis umpire*
• **umpire** *verb* (*present participle* **umpiring**, *past* **umpired**)

the UN /ˌjuːˈen/ *noun abbreviation for* the United Nations

unable /ʌnˈeɪbl/ *adj*
be unable to do something to not be able to do something: *Some days he is unable to get out of bed.*

unanimous /juːˈnænɪməs/ *adj*
agreed by everyone: *The jury was unanimous in finding him guilty.*

unattractive /ˌʌnəˈtræktɪv/ *adj*
bad to look at: *I felt old and unattractive.*

unaware /ˌʌnəˈweəʳ/ *adj*
not knowing about something: *He seems totally* ***unaware of*** *the problem.*

unbearable /ʌnˈbeərəbl/ *adj*
very painful or unpleasant: *The heat was almost unbearable.*
• **unbearably** *adv*

unbelievable /ˌʌnbɪˈliːvəbl/ *adj*
extremely bad or good and making you feel surprised: *It's unbelievable how lucky she's been.*

uncertain /ʌnˈsɜːtᵊn/ *adj*
not sure or not able to decide about something: *We're a bit* ***uncertain about*** *what we're doing this weekend.*

uncle /ˈʌŋkl/ *noun*
the brother of your mother or father, or the husband of your aunt

uncomfortable /ʌnˈkʌmftəbl/ *adj*
1 not making you feel comfortable and pleasant: *These shoes are really uncomfortable.*
2 slightly embarrassed, or making you feel slightly embarrassed: *an uncomfortable silence*

unconscious /ʌnˈkɒnʃəs/ *adj*
in a state as though you are sleeping, for example because you have been hit on the head: *She was* ***knocked unconscious***.

uncontrollable /ˌʌnkənˈtrəʊləbl/ *adj*
unable to be controlled: *uncontrollable anger*

uncover /ʌnˈkʌvəʳ/ *verb*
to discover something that had been secret or hidden: *The inspectors uncovered evidence of corruption.*

undeniable /ˌʌndɪˈnaɪəbl/ *adj*
certainly true: *an undeniable fact*

under /ˈʌndəʳ/ *preposition*
1 below something: *She pushed her bag under the table.*
2 less than a number, amount, or age: *You can buy the whole system for just under $2000.*

under-age /ˌʌndərˈeɪdʒ/ *adj*
younger than the legal age when you are allowed to do something: *under-age drinking*

undergo /ˌʌndəˈgəʊ/ *verb* (*present participle* **undergoing,** *past tense* **underwent**, *past participle* **undergone**)
to experience something, especially a change or medical treatment: *He is undergoing surgery for a heart problem.*

undergraduate /ˌʌndəˈgrædʒuət/ *noun*
a student who is studying for their first university degree (= qualification)

underground[1] /ˈʌndəgraʊnd/ *adj, adv*
under the surface of the ground: *an animal that lives underground*

underground[2] /ˈʌndəgraʊnd/ *noun UK*
a system of trains that is built under

a city: *the London Underground*

undergrowth /ˈʌndəɡrəʊθ/ *noun* **[no plural]**
short plants and bushes that grow around trees

underneath /ˌʌndəˈniːθ/ *adv, preposition*
under something: *I found her shoes underneath the bed.*

underpants /ˈʌndəpænts/ *plural noun*
a piece of clothing for men that covers the bottom ➲See colour picture **Clothes** on page Centre 5

understand /ˌʌndəˈstænd/ *verb* (*present participle* **understanding**, *past* **understood**)
1 to know the meaning of something that someone says: *She didn't understand so I explained it again.*
2 to know why or how something happens or works: *We still don't fully understand how the brain works.*
3 to know how someone feels or why they behave in a particular way: *I don't understand James sometimes.*

understanding[1] /ˌʌndəˈstændɪŋ/ *noun* **[no plural]**
knowledge about a subject, situation, etc: *We now have a better understanding of this disease.*

understanding[2] /ˌʌndəˈstændɪŋ/ *adj*
showing sympathy for someone's problems: *Fortunately, my girlfriend is very understanding.*

understood /ˌʌndəˈstʊd/
past of understand

underwater /ˌʌndəˈwɔːtəʳ/ *adj, adv*
under the surface of water: *an underwater camera*

underwear /ˈʌndəweəʳ/ *noun* **[no plural]**
the clothes that you wear next to your skin, under your other clothes

underwent /ˌʌndəˈwent/
past tense of undergo

undid /ʌnˈdɪd/
past tense of undo

undo /ʌnˈduː/ *verb* (*present participle* **undoing**, *past tense* **undid**, *past participle* **undone**)
to open something that is fastened: *I undid my coat.*

undone /ʌnˈdʌn/ *adj*
not fastened or tied: *Her coat was undone.*

undoubtedly /ʌnˈdaʊtɪdli/ *adv*
used to say that something is true: *She is undoubtedly good at her job.*

undress /ʌnˈdres/ *verb*
to remove your clothes or someone else's clothes
• **undressed** *adj*: *I* ***got undressed*** *and went to bed.*

uneasy /ʌnˈiːzi/ *adj*
worried because you think something bad might happen: *I feel a bit* ***uneasy about*** *her travelling alone.*

unemployed /ˌʌnɪmˈplɔɪd/ *adj*
not having a job: *I've been unemployed for six months.*

unemployment /ˌʌnɪmˈplɔɪmənt/ *noun* **[no plural]**
the number of people who are unemployed: *a rise in unemployment*

uneven /ʌnˈiːvᵊn/ *adj*
not level or smooth: *an uneven floor*
• **unevenly** *adv*

unexpected /ˌʌnɪkˈspektɪd/ *adj*
Something that is unexpected surprises you because you did not know it was going to happen: *His death was completely unexpected.*
• **unexpectedly** *adv*

unfair /ʌnˈfeəʳ/ *adj*
not treating people in an equal way: *an unfair system*
• **unfairly** *adv*

unfashionable /ʌnˈfæʃᵊnəbl/ *adj*
not fashionable at a particular time

unfasten /ʌnˈfɑːsᵊn/ *verb*
to open something that is closed or fixed together: *to unfasten a seat belt*

unfit /ʌnˈfɪt/ *adj*
1 not suitable or good enough: *The food was judged* ***unfit for*** *human consumption.*
2 *UK* not healthy because you do too little exercise

unfortunate /ʌnˈfɔːtʃᵊnət/ *adj*
bad and causing problems: *an unfortunate mistake*

unfortunately /ʌnˈfɔːtʃənətli/ *adv*
used to say that you wish something was not true or that something had not happened: *I'd love to come, but unfortunately I have to work.*

unfriendly /ʌnˈfrendli/ *adj*
not friendly

ungrateful /ʌnˈɡreɪtfᵊl/ *adj*
not thanking someone who has

done something good for you

unhappy /ʌn'hæpi/ *adj*
1 sad: *an unhappy childhood*
2 not satisfied: *Giorgio was **unhappy with** his test results.*
• **unhappiness** *noun* **[no plural]**

unhealthy /ʌn'helθi/ *adj* **(unhealthier, unhealthiest)**
1 likely to damage your health: *Eating too much is unhealthy.*
2 looking ill: *She looks pale and unhealthy.*

unhelpful /ʌn'helpfʊl/ *adj*
not wanting to help someone: *The taxi driver was rude and unhelpful.*

uniform /'juːnɪfɔːm/ *noun*
a special set of clothes that are worn by people who do a particular job or children at school: *a school uniform* ○ *a nurse's uniform*

unimportant /ˌʌnɪm'pɔːtᵊnt/ *adj*
not important

uninhabited /ˌʌnɪn'hæbɪtɪd/ *adj*
If a place is uninhabited, no one lives there: *an uninhabited island*

union /'juːnjən/ *noun*
1 (*also* **trade union**) an organization that represents people who do a particular job: *a teachers' union*
2 when two or more countries, groups, etc join together to make one country, group, etc

unique /juː'niːk/ *adj*
1 different from everyone and everything else: *Everyone's fingerprints are unique.*
2 unusual and special: *a unique opportunity*

unit /'juːnɪt/ *noun*
1 a measure used to express an amount or quantity: *The kilogram is a **unit of** weight.*
2 a single, complete thing that is part of a larger thing: *a French course book with ten units*

unite /juː'naɪt/ *verb* (*present participle* **uniting**, *past* **united)**
to join together as a group, or to make people join together as a group: *We need a leader who can unite the party.*

the United Nations /juːnˌaɪtɪd 'neɪʃᵊnz/ *noun*
an international organization that tries to stop world problems in a peaceful way

universal /ˌjuːnɪ'vɜːsᵊl/ *adj*
relating to everyone in the world, or to everyone in a particular group: *Kittens and puppies have an almost universal appeal.*
• **universally** *adv*: *It's a style of music that is universally popular.*

the universe /'juːnɪvɜːs/ *noun*
everything that exists, including stars, space, etc

university /ˌjuːnɪ'vɜːsəti/ *noun* (*plural* **universities)**
a place where students study at a high level to get a degree (= type of qualification): *Cambridge University*

unkind /ʌn'kaɪnd/ *adj*
slightly cruel: *an unkind remark*

unknown /ʌn'nəʊn/ *adj*
1 not known: *The cause of his death is still unknown.*
2 not famous: *an unknown actor*

unleaded /ʌn'ledɪd/ *adj*
Unleaded fuel does not contain lead (= a metal).

unless /ən'les/ *conjunction*
except if: *I won't call you unless there are any problems.*

unlike /ʌn'laɪk/ *preposition*
different from someone or something

unlikely /ʌn'laɪkli/ *adj*
not expected to happen: *It's **unlikely that** I'll be able to come to the party.*

unlock /ʌn'lɒk/ *verb*
to open something which is locked using a key

unlucky /ʌn'lʌki/ *adj*
having or causing bad luck: *Some people think it's unlucky to walk under ladders.*

unmarried /ʌn'mærɪd/ *adj*
not married

unmistakable /ˌʌnmɪ'steɪkəbl/ *adj*
Something that is unmistakable is very obvious and cannot be confused with anything else: *an unmistakable look of disappointment*

unnatural /ʌn'nætʃᵊrᵊl/ *adj*
not normal or right: *an unnatural interest in death*

unnecessary /ʌn'nesəsᵊri/ *adj*
not needed: *Don't make any unnecessary car journeys in this weather.*

a b c d e f g h i j k l m n o p q r s t u v w x y z

unpack /ʌn'pæk/ *verb* to take things out of a bag, box, etc: *Bella unpacked her suitcase.*

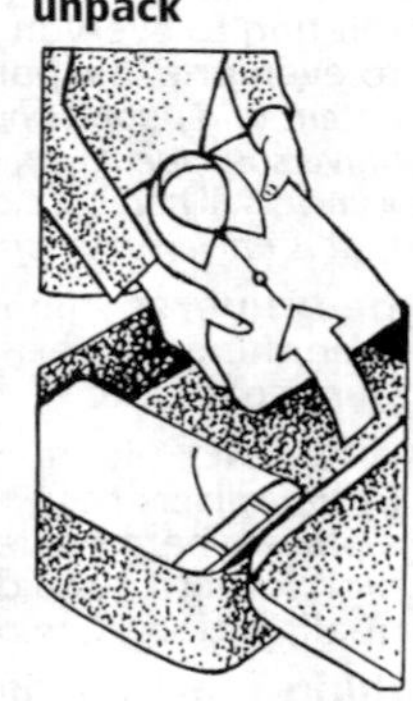

unpleasant /ʌn'plezᵊnt/ *adj* not enjoyable or pleasant: *an unpleasant experience*

unpopular /ʌn'pɒpjələʳ/ *adj* disliked by most people: *an unpopular idea*

unpredictable /ˌʌnprɪ'dɪktəbl/ *adj* changing so much that you do not know what will happen next: *unpredictable weather conditions*

unreasonable /ʌn'riːzᵊnəbl/ *adj* not fair: *unreasonable demands*

unreliable /ˌʌnrɪ'laɪəbl/ *adj* not able to be trusted or depended on: *The trains were noisy, dirty, and unreliable.*

unruly /ʌn'ruːli/ *adj* behaving badly and difficult to control: *unruly children*

unsafe /ʌn'seɪf/ *adj* dangerous: *The building is unsafe.*

unsatisfactory /ʌnˌsætɪs'fæktᵊri/ *adj* not good enough to be acceptable: *Many school buildings are in an unsatisfactory condition.*

unsuccessful /ˌʌnsək'sesfᵊl/ *adj* not achieving what was wanted or planned: *an unsuccessful attempt*
• **unsuccessfully** *adv*

unsuitable /ʌn'suːtəbl/ *adj* not acceptable or right for someone or something: *My parents considered the programme unsuitable for children.*

unsure /ʌn'ʃʊəʳ/ *adj* not certain or having doubts: *I'm a bit* ***unsure about*** *what to do.*

unsympathetic /ˌʌnsɪmpə'θetɪk/ *adj* showing that you do not understand or care about someone's problems: *I told him I'd got a cold but he was completely unsympathetic.*

untidy /ʌn'taɪdi/ *adj* not tidy: *an untidy room* ○ *She's really untidy at home.*

untie /ʌn'taɪ/ *verb* (*present participle* **untying**, *past* **untied**) to open a knot or something that has been tied with a knot: *I untied my shoelaces and kicked off my shoes.*

until /ᵊn'tɪl/ (*also* **till**) *preposition, conjunction* continuing to happen before a particular time and then stopping: *The show will be on until the end of the month.* ○ *We walked until it got dark.*

untrue /ʌn'truː/ *adj* false

unusual /ʌn'juːʒuəl/ *adj* different and not ordinary, often in a way that is interesting: *an unusual name*

unwilling /ʌn'wɪlɪŋ/ *adj* not wanting to do something: *A lot of people are unwilling to accept change.*

unwind /ʌn'waɪnd/ *verb* (*present participle* **unwinding**, *past* **unwound**) *informal* to relax, especially after working: *Music helps me to unwind.*

unwise /ʌn'waɪz/ *adj* stupid and likely to cause problems: *an unwise decision*
• **unwisely** *adv*

unwrap /ʌn'ræp/ *verb* to remove the paper, cloth, etc that is covering something: *She carefully unwrapped the present.*

up[1] /ʌp/ *adv, preposition*
1 towards or in a higher place: *He ran up the stairs.* ○ *She looked up and smiled at me.*
2 vertical or as straight as possible: *He stood up.* ○ *She sat up.*
3 to a greater degree, amount, volume, etc: *Can you turn up the heat?*
4 used to say that someone completes an action or uses all of something: *I used up all my money.* ○ *Eat up the rest of your dinner.*
5 up to 10, 20, etc any amount under 10, 20, etc: *We can invite up to 65 people.*
6 be up to something *informal* to be doing or planning something bad: *What are you two up to?*

up[2] /ʌp/ *adj* not in bed: *Is she up yet?*

update /ʌp'deɪt/ *verb* (*present*

participle **updating,** *past* **updated)**
to add new information: *We've just updated our website.*

upgrade /ʌp'greɪd/ *verb* (*present participle* **upgrading,** *past* **upgraded)**
to get something that is newer and better: *We have upgraded our computer.*
• **upgrade** /'ʌpgreɪd/ *noun*

uphill /ʌp'hɪl/ *adv*
towards the top of a hill: *We'd walked half a mile uphill.*

upon /ə'pɒn/ *preposition formal*
on

upper /'ʌpəʳ/ *adj*
at a higher position: *an upper floor* ○ *the upper lip*

upper case /ˌʌpəʳ 'keɪs/ *noun* **[no plural]**
letters written as capitals, such as A, B, C, D

upright /'ʌpraɪt/ *adj*
straight up or vertical: *Please return your seat to an upright position.*

upset¹ /ʌp'set/ *adj*
sad or worried because something bad has happened: *They'd had an argument and she was still* ***upset about*** *it.*

upset² /ʌp'set/ *verb* (*present participle* **upsetting,** *past* **upset)**
1 to make someone feel sad or worried: *The phone call had clearly upset her.*
2 to cause problems for something: *If I arrived later would that upset your plans?*

upsetting /ʌp'setɪŋ/ *adj*
making you sad or worried: *I found the programme very upsetting.*

upside down

upside down /ˌʌpsaɪd 'daʊn/ *adv, adj*
turned so that the part that is usually at the top is now at the bottom: ***Turn*** *the jar* ***upside down*** *and shake it.*

upstairs /ʌp'steəz/ *adv*
on or to a higher level of a building: *He ran upstairs to answer the phone.*
• **upstairs** *adj*: *an upstairs bedroom*

up-to-date /ˌʌptə'deɪt/ *adj*
modern, and using the most recent technology or knowledge

upwards /'ʌpwədz/ *adv UK*
towards a higher place or level: *House prices have started moving upwards again.*

urban /'ɜːbᵊn/ *adj*
belonging or relating to a town: *urban areas*

urge¹ /ɜːdʒ/ *verb* (*present participle* **urging,** *past* **urged)**
urge someone to do something to try to persuade someone to do something: *His parents urged him to go to university.*

urge² /ɜːdʒ/ *noun*
a strong wish or need: *I felt a powerful urge to slap him.*

urgent /'ɜːdʒᵊnt/ *adj*
very important and needing you to take action immediately: *an urgent message*
• **urgently** *adv*: *I need to speak to you urgently.*

us *strong form* /ʌs/ *weak forms* /əs, s/ *pronoun*
used after a verb or preposition to mean the person who is speaking or writing and one or more other people: *She gave us all a present.*

use¹ /juːz/ *verb* (*present participle* **using,** *past* **used)**
If you use something, you do something with it for a particular purpose: *Can I use your pen?* ○ *She* ***uses*** *her car* ***for*** *work.*
use something up *phrasal verb*
to finish an amount of something: *Someone's used up all the milk.*

use² /juːs/ *noun*
1 [no plural] when you use something, or when something is being used: *Guests have free use of the hotel swimming pool.*
2 a purpose for which something is used: *Can you* ***find a use for*** *this box?*
3 be no use used to say that trying to do something has no effect: *It was no use talking to him – he wouldn't listen.*

used /juːst/ *adj*
used to something/doing something If you are used to something, you

a b c d e f g h i j k l m n o p q r s t **u** v w x y z

have done it or had it many times before: *He's used to working long hours.*

used to /ˈjuːsttuː/ *verb*
used to do/be something If something used to happen, it happened often or existed in the past but it does not happen now: *I used to go out every night when I was a student.* ○ *Monica used to live in Glasgow.*

useful /ˈjuːsfᵊl/ *adj*
helping you to do or get something: *useful information*

useless /ˈjuːsləs/ *adj*
If something is useless, it does not work well or it has no effect: *This umbrella's useless – there's a big hole in it.*

user /ˈjuːzəʳ/ *noun*
someone who uses a product, machine, or service: *a new service for Internet users*

user-friendly /juːzə ˈfrendli/ *adj*
easy to use or understand: *user-friendly software*

usual /ˈjuːʒuəl/ *adj*
1 normal and happening most often: *I went to bed at my usual time.* ○ *This winter has been much colder than usual.* ➲Opposite **unusual**
2 as usual in the way that happens most of the time: *As usual, Nick was the last to arrive.*

usually /ˈjuːʒəli/ *adv*
in the way that most often happens: *I usually get home at about six o'clock.*

utensil /juːˈtensᵊl/ *noun*
a tool that you use for doing jobs in the house, especially cooking: *wooden cooking utensils* ➲See colour picture **Kitchen** on page Centre 10

utter /ˈʌtəʳ/ *adj*
complete: *She said the article was utter nonsense.*

utterly /ˈʌtəli/ *adv*
completely: *It's utterly ridiculous.*

Vv

V, v /viː/
the twenty-second letter of the alphabet

v *UK* (*US* **vs**) /viː/ *preposition*
abbreviation for versus (= used to say that one team or person is competing against another): *Germany v France*

vacancy /ˈveɪkənsi/ *noun* (*plural* **vacancies**)
1 a room that is not being used in a hotel: *Do you have any vacancies?*
2 a job that is free for someone to do: *Tell me if you hear of any vacancies for secretaries.*

vacant /ˈveɪkənt/ *adj*
1 Somewhere that is vacant is not being used: *a vacant building*
2 A vacant job is free for someone to do.

vacation /vəˈkeɪʃən/ *noun US* (*UK* **holiday**)
a period of time when you are not at home but are staying somewhere else for enjoyment: *We're **taking a vacation** in Florida.*

vaccinate /ˈvæksɪneɪt/ *verb* (*present participle* **vaccinating**, *past* **vaccinated**)
to give someone a substance to stop them from getting a disease: *Have you been **vaccinated against** the disease?*
• **vaccination** /ˌvæksɪˈneɪʃən/ *noun*

vacuum /ˈvækjuːm/ *verb*
to clean somewhere using a vacuum cleaner

vacuum cleaner /ˈvækjuːm ˌkliːnər/ *noun*
an electric machine that cleans floors by sucking up dirt

vagina /vəˈdʒaɪnə/ *noun*
the part of a woman's body that connects her outer sex organs to the place where a baby grows

vague /veɪg/ *adj*
not clear or certain: *I have a vague idea of where the hotel is.*
• **vaguely** *adv*: *I vaguely* (= slightly) *remember meeting her.*
• **vagueness** *noun* **[no plural]**

vain /veɪn/ *adj*
too interested in your own appearance and thinking you are very attractive

valid /ˈvælɪd/ *adj*
A valid ticket or document is legally acceptable: *The ticket is valid for three months.* ➲Opposite **invalid**

valley /ˈvæli/ *noun*
an area of low land between hills or mountains

valuable /ˈvæljuəbl/ *adj*
1 Valuable objects could be sold for a lot of money: *valuable paintings*
2 Valuable information, help, advice, etc is very helpful.

value[1] /ˈvæljuː/ *noun*
1 how much money something could be sold for: *Cars quickly go down in value.*
2 **[no plural]** how useful or important something is: *a document of great historical value*

value[2] /ˈvæljuː/ *verb* (*present participle* **valuing**, *past* **valued**)
1 If you value something or someone, they are very important to you: *I always value his opinion.*
2 to judge how much money something could be sold for: *The ring was **valued at** $1000.*

valve /vælv/ *noun*
something that opens and closes to control the flow of liquid or gas

van /væn/ *noun*
a vehicle that is used for carrying things but which is smaller than a truck

van

vandal /ˈvændəl/ *noun*
someone who damages things in public places: *Vandals had smashed the shop window.*

vandalism /ˈvændəlɪzəm/ *noun* **[no plural]**
the crime of damaging things in public places

vandalize /ˈvændəlaɪz/ *verb* (*present participle* **vandalizing**, *past* **vandalized**)
to damage things in public places

vanilla /vəˈnɪlə/ *noun* **[no plural]**
a substance that is used to give flavour to some sweet foods: *vanilla ice cream*

vanish /ˈvænɪʃ/ *verb*
to disappear suddenly: *The sun vanished behind the trees.*

vanity /ˈvænəti/ *noun* **[no plural]**
when someone thinks they are very attractive

vapour /ˈveɪpəʳ/ *noun* **[no plural]**
many small drops of liquid in the air which look like a cloud

varied /ˈveərɪd/ *adj*
having many different types of things: *a long and varied career*

variety /vəˈraɪəti/ *noun*
1 a variety of something/someone many different types of things or people: *Dan has done a variety of jobs.* **2** (*plural* **varieties)** a different type of something: *a new variety of potato* **3 [no plural]** a lot of different activities, situations, people, etc: *I need more variety in my life.*

various /ˈveəriəs/ *adj*
many different: *They have offices in various parts of the country.*

varnish¹ /ˈvɑːnɪʃ/ *noun* (*plural* **varnishes)**
a clear liquid that you paint onto wood to protect it

varnish² /ˈvɑːnɪʃ/ *verb*
to put varnish on a surface

vary /ˈveəri/ *verb* (*present participle* **varying,** *past* **varied)**
If things of the same type vary, they are different from each other: *Car prices vary greatly across Europe.*

vase /vɑːz/ *noun*
a container that you put flowers in

vase

vast /vɑːst/ *adj*
very big: *a vast amount of money*

've /v/ *short for*
have: *I've already eaten.*

vegetable /ˈvedʒtəbl/ *noun*
a plant that you eat, for example a potato, onion, etc
➲See colour picture **Fruit and Vegetables** on page Centre 8

vegetarian¹ /ˌvedʒɪˈteəriən/ *noun*
someone who does not eat meat or fish

vegetarian² /ˌvedʒɪˈteəriən/ *adj*
not eating or containing meat or fish: *a vegetarian restaurant*

vehicles

vehicle /ˈviːɪkl/ *noun formal*
something such as a car or bus that takes people from one place to another

veil /veɪl/ *noun*
a thin piece of material that covers a woman's face

vein /veɪn/ *noun*
one of the tubes in your body that carries blood to your heart
2 in the same vein in the same style of speaking or writing

Velcro /ˈvelkrəʊ/ *noun* **[no plural]** *trademark*
material that consists of two pieces of cloth that stick together, used to fasten clothes

velvet /ˈvelvɪt/ *noun* **[no plural]**
cloth that has a thick, soft surface on one side: *a black velvet jacket*

ventilate /ˈventɪleɪt/ *verb* (*present participle* **ventilating,** *past* **ventilated)**
to let air come into and go out of a room or building
• **ventilation** /ˌventɪˈleɪʃᵊn/ *noun* **[no plural]** *a ventilation system*

verb /vɜːb/ *noun*
a word or group of words that refers to an action, state, or experience. For example the words 'arrive', 'make', 'be', and 'feel' are verbs.

verdict /ˈvɜːdɪkt/ *noun*
a decision in a court of law saying if someone has done a crime: *a guilty verdict*

verse /vɜːs/ *noun*
1 one of the parts that a song or poem is divided into: *I only know the first verse.*
2 [no plural] words that are in the

form of poetry: *The story was told in verse.*

version /ˈvɜːʃᵊn/ *noun*
one form of something that has many forms: *I saw the original version of the film.*

versus /ˈvɜːsəs/ *preposition*
used to say that one team or person is competing against another: *Tomorrow's game is Newcastle versus Arsenal.*

vertical /ˈvɜːtɪkᵊl/ *adj*
pointing straight up from a surface: *a vertical line*

very /ˈveri/ *adv*
1 used to make an adjective or adverb stronger: *She was very pleased.* ○ *Thank you very much.*
2 not very good/tall/happy, etc not good, happy, etc: *The film wasn't very good.*

vest /vest/ *noun UK*
a piece of underwear that you wear under a shirt ➲See colour picture **Clothes** on page Centre 5

vet /vet/ *noun*
someone whose job is to give medical care to animals that are ill

via /vaɪə/ *preposition*
going through or stopping at a place on the way to another place: *The train to Utrecht goes via Amsterdam.*

vibrate /vaɪˈbreɪt/ *verb* (*present participle* **vibrating,** *past* **vibrated**)
to shake with small, quick movements: *The music was so loud that the floor was vibrating.*
• **vibration** /vaɪˈbreɪʃᵊn/ *noun*

vicar /ˈvɪkəʳ/ *noun*
a priest in some Christian churches

vice /vaɪs/ *noun*
something bad that someone often does: *Smoking is his only vice.*

vice president /ˌvaɪs ˈprezɪdᵊnt/ *noun*
the person who is a rank lower than the president of a country

vicinity /vɪˈsɪnəti/ *noun* **[no plural]**
in the vicinity (of something) *formal* in the area near a place: *A number of buildings in the vicinity of the fire were damaged.*

vicious /ˈvɪʃəs/ *adj*
violent and dangerous: *a vicious attack on a child*

victim /ˈvɪktɪm/ *noun*
someone who has been hurt or killed: *victims of crime* ○ *flood victims*

victorious /vɪkˈtɔːriəs/ *adj*
having won a fight or competition: *a victorious army*

victory /ˈvɪktᵊri/ *noun* (*plural* **victories**)
when you win a fight or competition: *Phoenix managed a 135-114* ***victory over*** *Denver.*

video /ˈvɪdiəʊ/ *noun*
1 a plastic box that you put into a machine in order to record a television programme or watch a programme that is already recorded: *You can get the film* ***on video.***
2 *UK* (*also* **video recorder**) a machine that you use for recording a television programme or watching a video ➲See colour picture **The Living Room** on page Centre 11

video game /ˈvɪdiəʊ ˌgeɪm/ *noun*
a game in which you make pictures move on a screen

video recorder /ˈvɪdiəʊ rɪˈkɔːdəʳ/ *noun*
a video machine

view /vjuː/ *noun*
1 your opinion: *We have different* ***views on*** *education.* ○ ***In*** *her* ***view*** *this is wrong.*
2 the things that you can see from a place: *There was a lovely view of the lake from the bedroom window.*
3 how well you can see something from a place: *We had a great view of the procession.*

viewer /ˈvjuːəʳ/ *noun*
someone who watches a television programme

vigorous /ˈvɪgᵊrəs/ *adj*
showing or needing a lot of physical energy: *vigorous exercise*

villa /ˈvɪlə/ *noun*
a large house, especially one used for holidays in a warm country

village /ˈvɪlɪdʒ/ *noun*
a place where people live in the countryside which is smaller than a town: *She lives in a small village outside Oxford.*

villain /ˈvɪlən/ *noun*
a bad person in a film, book, etc

vine /vaɪn/ *noun*
a plant that grapes (= small, green

or purple fruit used for making wine) grow on

vinegar /ˈvɪnɪgəʳ/ *noun* **[no plural]**
a sour liquid that is used in cooking, often made from wine

vineyard /ˈvɪnjəd/ *noun*
an area of land where someone grows grapes (= small, green or purple fruit) for making wine

violence /ˈvaɪələns/ *noun* **[no plural]**
when someone hurts or kills someone else: *A number of people were killed in the violence.*

violent /ˈvaɪələnt/ *adj*
1 involving violence: *I don't like violent films* (= films that show violence).
2 likely to hurt or kill someone else: *a violent criminal*
3 sudden and causing damage: *a violent storm*
• **violently** *adv*

violin /ˌvaɪəˈlɪn/ *noun*
a wooden musical instrument that you hold against your neck and play by moving a stick across strings

violin

VIP /ˌviːaɪˈpiː/ *noun abbreviation for* very important person: someone who is famous or powerful and is treated in a special way

virtue /ˈvɜːtjuː/ *noun*
1 a useful quality: *The great* ***virtue of*** *having a small car is that you can park it easily.*
2 a good quality that someone has: *Patience is not among his virtues.*

virus /ˈvaɪərəs/ *noun* (*plural* **viruses**)
1 a very small thing that causes illnesses, or an illness that it causes
2 a program that is secretly put onto a computer in order to destroy the information that is stored on it

visa /ˈviːzə/ *noun*
an official mark in your passport (= book showing where you come from) that allows you to enter or leave a particular country

visible /ˈvɪzəbl/ *adj*
able to be seen: *The fire was visible from five kilometres away.* ➲Opposite **invisible**

vision /ˈvɪʒən/ *noun*
1 an idea or image in your mind of what something could be like in the future: *a vision of a better society*
2 **[no plural]** the ability to see: *He has poor vision in his left eye.*

visit[1] /ˈvɪzɪt/ *verb*
to go somewhere to see someone or a place: *Did you visit St Petersburg while you were in Russia?* ○ *We have friends coming to visit this weekend.*

visit[2] /ˈvɪzɪt/ *noun*
when you visit a place or a person: *the President's visit to Hong Kong*

visitor /ˈvɪzɪtəʳ/ *noun*
someone who visits a person or place: *The museum attracts large numbers of visitors.*

vital /ˈvaɪtəl/ *adj*
necessary: *Tourism is* ***vital to*** *the country's economy.*

vitamin /ˈvɪtəmɪn/ *noun*
one of a group of natural substances in food that you need to be healthy: *Oranges are full of vitamin C.*

vivid /ˈvɪvɪd/ *adj*
1 Vivid descriptions or memories produce strong, clear images in your mind: *He gave a very vivid description of life in Caracas.*
2 A vivid colour is very bright.

vocabulary /vəʊˈkæbjələri/ *noun* (*plural* **vocabularies**)
words: *Reading helps to widen your vocabulary.* ○ *Computing has its own specialist vocabulary.*

voice /vɔɪs/ *noun*
the sounds that you make when you speak or sing: *I could hear voices in the next room.* ○ *Jessie has a beautiful singing voice.*

voice mail /ˈvɔɪs ˌmeɪl/ *noun* **[no plural]**
an electronic telephone answering system

volcano

volcano /vɒlˈkeɪnəʊ/ *noun* (*plural* **volcanoes**)
a mountain with a large hole at the top which sometimes explodes
• **volcanic** /vɒlˈkænɪk/ *adj*
relating to a volcano: *volcanic ash*

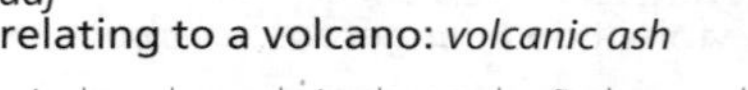

volleyball /ˈvɒlibɔːl/ *noun* **[no plural]** a game in which two teams use their hands to hit a ball over a net ➲See colour picture **Sports 2** on page Centre 16

volt /vɒlt/ *noun* a unit for measuring the force of an electric current

volume /ˈvɒljuːm/ *noun*
1 [no plural] the level of sound made by a television, radio, etc: *Could you turn the volume down?*
2 [no plural] the amount of space inside an object
3 a book, especially one of a set: *a new dictionary in two volumes*

voluntary /ˈvɒləntᵊri/ *adj* Voluntary work is done without being paid and usually involves helping people: *She does voluntary work for the Red Cross.*
• **voluntarily** /ˌvɒlənˈteərᵊli/ *adv*: *She left voluntarily.*

volunteer¹ /ˌvɒlənˈtɪəʳ/ *verb* to offer to do something without being asked to do it: *Rob volunteered to look after the kids.*

volunteer² /ˌvɒlənˈtɪəʳ/ *noun* someone who works without being paid, especially work that involves helping people: *a Red Cross volunteer*

vomit¹ /ˈvɒmɪt/ *verb* If someone vomits, the food or liquid that was in their stomach comes up and out of their mouth.

vomit² /ˈvɒmɪt/ *noun* **[no plural]** the food or liquid that comes from your mouth when you vomit

vote¹ /vəʊt/ *verb* (*present participle* **voting**, *past* **voted**) to choose someone or something in an election or meeting by writing a cross on an official piece of paper or putting your hand up: *Who did you **vote for**?* ○ *Staff have voted to accept the pay offer.*

vote² /vəʊt/ *noun* when someone chooses someone or something in an election or meeting by writing a cross on an official piece of paper or putting their hand up: *He lost the election by twenty votes.*

vowel /vaʊəl/ *noun* a speech sound that you make with your lips and teeth open, shown in English by the letters 'a', 'e', 'i', 'o' or 'u'

vulnerable /ˈvʌlnᵊrəbl/ *adj* easy to hurt or attack: *The troops are in a vulnerable position.*

vulture /ˈvʌltʃəʳ/ *noun* a large bird with no feathers on its head or neck that eats dead animals

Ww

W, w /ˈdʌbljuː/
the twenty-third letter of the alphabet

wade /weɪd/ *verb* (*present participle* **wading,** *past* **waded)**
to walk through water: *He waded across the river.*

wag /wæg/ *verb* (*present participle* **wagging,** *past* **wagged)**
If a dog wags its tail, it moves it from side to side.

wage /weɪdʒ/ *noun* (*also* **wages)**
the amount of money a person regularly gets for their job: *weekly wages*

wail /weɪl/ *verb*
to cry loudly because you are very sad: *"I've lost my mummy," she wailed.*

waist /weɪst/ *noun*
the part around the middle of your body where you wear a belt ➲See colour picture **The Body** on page Centre 2

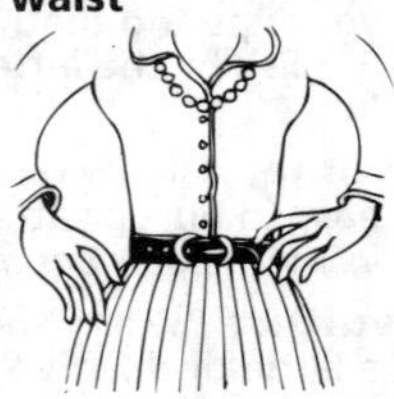

waistcoat /ˈweɪstkəʊt/ *noun UK*
a piece of clothing with buttons at the front and no sleeves, that you wear over a shirt ➲See colour picture **Clothes** on page Centre 5

wait¹ /weɪt/ *verb*
1 to stay in a place until someone or something arrives: *I'm* ***waiting for*** *Guy.* ○ *How long did you wait for a taxi?*
2 can't wait *informal* used to say how excited you are about something that you are going to do: *I can't wait to see him.*

wait² /weɪt/ *noun*
when you stay in a place until someone or something arrives or someone or something is ready for you: *We had a long wait at the airport.*

waiter /ˈweɪtəʳ/ *noun*
a man who works in a restaurant, bringing food to customers

waiting room /ˈweɪtɪŋ ˌruːm/ *noun*
a room in which people wait for something, for example to see a doctor

waitress /ˈweɪtrəs/ *noun* (*plural* **waitresses)**
a woman who works in a restaurant, bringing food to customers

wake /weɪk/ (*also* **wake up)** *verb* (*present participle* **waking,** *past tense* **woke,** *past participle* **woken)**
to stop sleeping or to make someone else stop sleeping: *I've only just woken up.* ○ *Could you wake me up before you go?* ➲See colour picture **Phrasal Verbs** on page Centre 13

wake-up call /ˈweɪkʌp ˌkɔːl/ *noun*
something bad that happens and shows you that you need to do something to change a situation

walk¹ /wɔːk/ *verb*
to move forward by putting one foot in front of the other and then repeating the action: *She walks to school.* ○ *We walked twenty miles in all.*

walk² /wɔːk/ *noun*
a journey that you make by walking, often for enjoyment: *He took the dog for a walk.*

wall /wɔːl/ *noun*
1 one of the sides of a room or building: *There were several large paintings on the wall.*
2 a structure made of brick or stone that divides areas that are owned by different people: *a garden wall*

wallet /ˈwɒlɪt/ (*also US* **billfold)** *noun*
a small, flat container for paper money and credit cards (= plastic cards used for paying with), usually used by a man

wallpaper /ˈwɔːlˌpeɪpəʳ/ *noun* **[no plural]**
paper, usually with a pattern, that you decorate walls with
● **wallpaper** *verb*

walnut /ˈwɔːlnʌt/ *noun*
a nut that is in two halves inside a brown shell

wander /ˈwɒndəʳ/ *verb*
to walk slowly about a place without any purpose: *They wandered around the town.*

want /wɒnt/ *verb*
1 to hope to have or do something:

He wants a new car. ○ *I don't* ***want to*** *talk about it.*
2 to need something: *This soup wants more salt.*
3 want to do something *UK informal* used to give advice to someone: *You want to go to bed earlier if you are tired.*

war /wɔːʳ/ *noun*
fighting, using soldiers and weapons, between two or more countries, or two or more groups inside a country: *They've been* ***at war*** *for the past five years.*

ward /wɔːd/ *noun*
a room in a hospital: *the cancer ward*

warden /ˈwɔːdᵊn/ *noun UK*
someone who looks after a building or the people in it

wardrobe /ˈwɔːdrəʊb/ *noun UK* (*US* **closet**)
a large cupboard for keeping clothes in

warehouse /ˈweəhaʊs/ *noun*
a large building for keeping things that are going to be sold

warfare /ˈwɔːfeəʳ/ *noun* **[no plural]**
fighting in a war, especially using a particular type of weapon: *chemical warfare*

warm¹ /wɔːm/ *adj*
1 having a temperature between cool and hot: *It's nice and warm in here.* ○ *Are you warm enough?*
2 Warm clothes or covers keep your body warm: *a warm sweater*
3 friendly: *a warm welcome*

warm² /wɔːm/ *verb*
to become warm or to make something become warm: *I'll warm the soup.*
warm up *phrasal verb*
to do gentle exercises before a sport: *They were warming up before the match.*
warm (someone/something) up *phrasal verb*
to become warmer or to make someone or something warmer: *A hot drink will warm you up.*

warmly /ˈwɔːmli/ *adv*
in a friendly way

warmth /wɔːmθ/ *noun* **[no plural]**
1 the heat that is made by something: *the warmth of the fire*
2 when someone is friendly: *There was no warmth in his eyes.*

warn /wɔːn/ *verb*
to tell someone that something bad may happen in the future: *I* ***warned*** *you* ***that*** *it would be cold but you still wouldn't wear a coat.*

warning /ˈwɔːnɪŋ/ *noun*
something that tells or shows you that something bad may happen: *All cigarette packets carry a warning.*

was
past tense of be, used with 'I', 'he', 'she' and 'it': *He was young.*

wash¹ /wɒʃ/ *verb*
1 to make something clean using water and soap: *Dad was washing the dishes.*
2 to clean part of your body with water and soap: *Have you washed your hands?*
wash (something) up *phrasal verb UK*
to wash the dishes, pans, and other things you have used for cooking and eating a meal ➲See colour picture **Phrasal Verbs** on page Centre 13
wash up *phrasal verb US*
to wash your hands, especially before a meal

wash² /wɒʃ/ *noun*
1 a wash
a when you wash a part of your body: *Have you* ***had a wash****?*
b *UK* when you wash something: *Could you* ***give*** *the car* ***a wash****?*
2 clothes, sheets, etc that are being washed together: *Your jeans are* ***in the wash****.*

washbasin /ˈwɒʃˌbeɪsᵊn/ *noun UK*
a bowl in a bathroom, used for washing your face or hands

washing /ˈwɒʃɪŋ/ *noun* **[no plural]**
clothes, sheets, etc that are being washed, or when you wash these: *I'm* ***doing*** *the* ***washing*** *this morning.*

washing machine /ˈwɒʃɪŋ məˌʃiːn/ *noun*
a machine that washes clothes

wasn't /ˈwɒzᵊnt/ *short for*
was not: *I wasn't hungry this morning.*

wasp /wɒsp/ *noun*
a flying insect with a thin, black and yellow body

wasp

waste¹ /weɪst/ *noun* **[no plural]**
1 a bad use of something useful,

such as time or money: *Meetings are* ***a waste of*** *time.* ○ *They throw away loads of food – it's such a waste.*
2 things that are not wanted: *household waste*

waste^{2} /weɪst/ *verb* (*present participle* **wasting**, *past* **wasted**)
to use too much of something or use something badly: *Why waste your money on things you don't need?*

watch^{1} /wɒtʃ/ *verb*
1 to look at something for a period of time: *The kids are watching TV.* ○ *I watched him as he arrived.*
2 to be careful about something: *She has to watch what she eats.*
watch out *phrasal verb*
used to tell someone to be careful: *Watch out! There's a car coming!*

watch

watch^{2} /wɒtʃ/ *noun* (*plural* **watches**)
1 a small clock on a strap that you fasten round your arm
2 when you watch or give attention to something or someone: *We're* ***keeping a*** *close* ***watch*** *on the situation.*

water^{1} /ˈwɔːtə^{r}/ *noun* **[no plural]**
the clear liquid that falls from the sky as rain and that is in seas, lakes, and rivers: *hot/cold water* ○ *a drink of water*

water^{2} /ˈwɔːtə^{r}/ *verb*
to pour water over plants

waterfall /ˈwɔːtəfɔːl/ *noun*
a stream of water that falls from a high place, often to a pool below

waterproof /ˈwɔːtəpruːf/ *adj*
Waterproof material or clothing does not let water through: *a waterproof sleeping bag*

watt /wɒt/ *noun*
a unit for measuring electrical power: *a 60 watt light bulb*

wave^{1} /weɪv/ *verb* (*present participle* **waving**, *past* **waved**)
1 to put your hand up and move it from side to side in order to attract someone's attention or to say goodbye: ***Wave goodbye*** *to Grandma.* ○ *She* ***waved at*** *him.*
2 to move from side to side in the air or make something move this way: *The long grass waved in the breeze.*

wave

a wave — She's waving.

wave^{2} /weɪv/ *noun*
1 a line of higher water that moves across the surface of the sea or a lake: *I could hear the waves crashing against the rocks.*
2 when you put your hand up and move it from side to side in order to attract someone's attention or say goodbye: *She* ***gave a*** *little* ***wave*** *as the train left.*

wax /wæks/ *noun* **[no plural]**
a solid substance that becomes soft when warm and melts easily, often used to make candles

way /weɪ/ *noun*
1 how you do something: *I must* ***find a way*** *to help him.* ○ *We looked at various* ***ways of*** *solving the problem.*
2 the route you take to get from one place to another: *Is there another way out of here?* ○ *I must buy a paper* ***on the way*** *home.*
3 make your way to move somewhere, often with difficulty: *We made our way through the shop to the main entrance.*
4 be on her/my/its, etc way to be arriving soon: *Apparently she's on her way.*
5 get in the way to stop someone from doing or continuing with something: *Don't let your new friends get in the way of your studies.*
6 be under way to be already happening: *Building work is already under way.*
7 give way If something gives way, it falls because it is not strong enough to support the weight on top of it: *Suddenly the ground gave way under me.*
8 a direction something faces or travels in: *This bus is going the wrong way.*

a b c d e f g h i j k l m n o p q r s t u v w x y z

9 an amount of space or time: *We're **a long way** from home. ○ The exams are still **a long way away/off**.*
10 in a way/in many ways used to say that you think something is partly true: *In a way his behaviour is understandable.*
11 No way! *informal* certainly not: *"Would you invite him to a party?" "No way!"*
12 get/have your own way to get what you want, although it upsets other people: *She always gets her own way in the end.*

WC /ˌdʌbljuːˈsiː/ *noun UK*
a toilet, especially in a public place

we *strong form* /wiː/ *weak form* /wi/ *pronoun*
used as the subject of the verb when the person speaking or writing means themselves and one or more other people: *My wife and I both play golf and we love it.*

weak /wiːk/ *adj*
1 not physically strong: *He felt too weak to sit up.*
2 likely to break and not able to support things: *a weak bridge*
3 A weak drink has little taste or contains little alcohol: *weak coffee/beer* ⊃Opposite **(1, 2, 3) strong**
● **weakly** *adv*

weaken /ˈwiːkᵊn/ *verb*
to become less strong or powerful, or to make someone or something less strong or powerful: *Another war would weaken the economy.*

weakness /ˈwiːknəs/ *noun*
1 [no plural] when someone or something is not strong or powerful: *Asking for help is not a sign of weakness.*
2 (*plural* **weaknesses**) a part or quality of something or someone that is not good: *What do you think are your weaknesses as a manager?*

wealth /welθ/ *noun* **[no plural]**
when someone has a lot of money

wealthy /ˈwelθi/ *adj* **(wealthier, wealthiest)**
rich: *a wealthy businessman*

weapon /ˈwepən/ *noun*
a gun, knife, or other object used to kill or hurt someone: *nuclear weapons*

wear /weəʳ/ *verb* (*present participle* **wearing,** *past tense* **wore,** *past participle* **worn)**
1 to have a piece of clothing, jewellery, etc on your body: *I wear jeans a lot of the time. ○ She wears glasses.*
2 to become thin and damaged after being used a lot, or to make this happen: *The carpet is already starting to wear in places.*
wear off *phrasal verb*
If a feeling or the effect of something wears off, it gradually stops: *The anaesthetic is starting to wear off.*
wear someone out *phrasal verb*
to make someone very tired: *All this walking is wearing me out.*
wear something out *phrasal verb*
to use something so much that it is damaged and cannot be used any more: *He's already worn out two pairs of shoes this year.*

weary /ˈwɪəri/ *adj* **(wearier, weariest)**
tired: *You look weary, my love.*
● **wearily** *adv*

weather /ˈweðəʳ/ *noun* **[no plural]**
the temperature or conditions outside, for example if it is hot, cold, sunny, etc: *bad/good weather*

weave /wiːv/ *verb* (*present participle* **weaving,** *past tense* **wove,** *past participle* **woven)**
to make cloth on a machine by crossing threads under and over each other

web /web/ *noun*
1 a type of net made by a spider (= creature with eight legs) to catch insects: *a spider's web*
2 the Web part of the Internet that consists of all the connected websites (= pages of text and pictures)

webcam /ˈwebkæm/ *noun*
a camera which records moving pictures and sounds and allows these to be shown on the Internet as they happen

web page /ˈweb ˌpeɪdʒ/ *noun*
a part of a website that can be read on a computer screen

website /ˈwebsaɪt/ *noun*
an area on the Web (= computer information system) where information about a particular

a b c d e f g h i j k l m n o p q r s t u v w x y z

subject, organization, etc can be found

we'd /wiːd/ *short for*
1 we had: *By the time she arrived we'd eaten.*
2 we would: *We'd like two tickets, please.*

wedding /ˈwedɪŋ/ *noun*
an official ceremony at which a man and woman get married: *We're going to a wedding on Saturday.*

Wednesday /ˈwenzdeɪ/ *noun*
the day of the week after Tuesday and before Thursday

weed[1] /wiːd/ *noun*
a wild plant that you do not want in your garden

weed[2] /wiːd/ *verb*
to remove wild plants from a garden where they are not wanted

week /wiːk/ *noun*
a period of seven days: *last week* ○ *I've got three exams this week.*

weekday /ˈwiːkdeɪ/ *noun*
one of the five days from Monday to Friday, when people usually go to work or school

weekend /ˌwiːkˈend/ *noun*
Saturday and Sunday, the two days in the week when many people do not work: *Are you doing anything this weekend?*

weekly /ˈwiːkli/ *adj, adv*
happening once a week or every week: *a weekly newspaper*

weep /wiːp/ *verb* (*present participle* **weeping,** *past* **wept)**
to cry, usually because you are sad

weigh /weɪ/ *verb*
1 weigh 200g/75 kg/10 stone, etc to have a weight of 200g/75 kg/10 stone, etc: *How much do you weigh?*
2 to measure how heavy someone or something is: *Can you weigh that piece of cheese for me?*

weight /weɪt/ *noun* **[no plural]**
how heavy someone or something is: *He's about average height and weight.*

weird /wɪəd/ *adj*
very strange: *I had a really weird dream last night.*

welcome[1] /ˈwelkəm/ *exclamation*
said to someone who has just arrived somewhere: *Welcome home!* ○ ***Welcome to*** *the UK.*

welcome[2] /ˈwelkəm/ *verb* (*present participle* **welcoming,** *past* **welcomed)**
1 to say hello to someone who has arrived in a place: *Both families were there to welcome us.*
2 to be pleased about something and want it to happen: *The decision was welcomed by everybody.*

welcome[3] /ˈwelkəm/ *noun*
when someone says hello to someone who arrives somewhere: *He was* ***given*** *a warm* ***welcome*** *by his fans.*

welfare /ˈwelfeəʳ/ *noun* **[no plural]**
Someone's welfare is their health and happiness: *He is concerned about the welfare of young men in prison.*

we'll /wiːl/ *short for*
we will: *We'll be home on Friday.*

well[1] /wel/ *adj*
healthy: *You look well!* ○ *I'm not very well.*

well[2] /wel/ *adv*
1 in a good way: *I thought they played well.* ○ *He's* ***doing well*** *at school.*
2 in a complete way or as much as possible: *I know him quite well.*
3 as well also: *Are you going to invite Steve as well?*
4 as well as something in addition to something: *They have lived in the United States as well as Britain.*
5 Well done! used to tell someone how pleased you are about their success: *"I passed my exams." "Well done!"*

well[3] /wel/ *exclamation*
something you say before you start speaking: *"You'll go, won't you?" "Well, I'm not sure."*

well[4] /wel/ *noun*
a deep hole in the ground from which you can get water, oil, or gas

well-known /ˌwelˈnəʊn/ *adj*
famous: *a well-known actor*

went /went/
past tense of go

wept /wept/
past of weep

we're /wɪəʳ/ *short for*
we are: *Hurry! We're late!*

weren't /wɜːnt/ *short for*
were not: *They weren't there.*

west, West /west/ *noun* **[no plural]**

1 the direction that you face to see the sun go down
2 the west the part of an area that is further towards the west than the rest
3 the West the countries of North America and western Europe
• **west** *adj*: *the west coast of Ireland*
• **west** *adv*
towards the west

western, Western /ˈwestən/ *adj*
1 in or from the west part of an area: *western France*
2 related to the countries of North America and western Europe: *a Western diplomat*

wet /wet/ *adj* **(wetter, wettest)**
1 covered in water or another liquid: *a wet towel*
2 raining: *a wet and windy day*
3 not dry yet: *wet paint*

we've /wiːv/ *short for*
we have: *We've bought a house.*

whale /weɪl/ *noun*
a very large animal that looks like a large fish and lives in the sea

whale

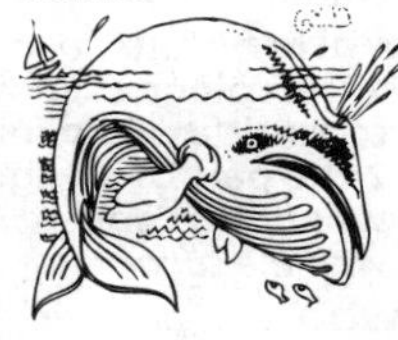

what /wɒt/ *pronoun, determiner*
1 used to ask for information about something: *What's this?* ○ *What time is it?*
2 used to mean something without giving it a name: *I heard what he said.* ○ *Do you know what I mean?*
3 *informal* used when you have not heard what someone has said and you want them to repeat it. Some people think this use is not polite: *"Do you want a drink Tom?" "What?"*
4 *informal* used to ask what someone wants when they call you: *"Jenny?" "Yes, what?"*
5 what a/an ... used to give your opinion: *What an awful day!*
6 what about...? used to suggest something: *What about asking Martin to help?*

whatever /wɒtˈevəʳ/ *adv,pronoun, determiner*
1 anything or everything: *He eats whatever I put in front of him.*
2 used to say that what happens is not important because it does not change a situation: *Whatever happens I'll still love you.*

wheat /wiːt/ *noun* **[no plural]**
a plant whose grain is used for making flour, or the grain itself

wheel /wiːl/ *noun*
a circular object fixed under a vehicle so that it moves smoothly over the ground: *My bike needs a new front wheel.*

wheelbarrow /ˈwiːlˌbærəʊ/ *noun*
a big, open container with a wheel at the front and handles that is used to move things

wheelchair /ˈwiːltʃeəʳ/ *noun*
a chair with wheels used by someone who cannot walk

when[1] /wen/ *adv*
used to ask at what time something happened or will happen: *When's your birthday?* ○ *When did he leave?*

when[2] /wen/ *conjunction*
used to say at what time something happened or will happen: *I found it when I was cleaning out the cupboards.* ○ *We'll go when you're ready.*

whenever /wenˈevəʳ/ *conjunction*
every time or at any time: *You can go whenever you want.*

where[1] /weəʳ/ *adv*
used to ask about the place or position of someone or something: *Where does she live?* ○ *Where are my car keys?*

where[2] /weəʳ/ *conjunction*
at, in, or to a place or position: *I know where to go.*

wherever /weəˈrevəʳ/ *conjunction*
1 in or to any place or every place: *You can sit wherever you like.*
2 wherever possible every time it is possible: *We try to use natural fabrics wherever possible.*

whether /ˈweðəʳ/ *conjunction*
1 used to talk about a choice between two or more possibilities: *I didn't know **whether or not** to go.*
2 if: *I wasn't sure whether you'd like it.*

which /wɪtʃ/ *pronoun, determiner*
1 used to ask or talk about a choice between two or more things: *Which of these do you like best?* ○ *Which way is it to the station?*
2 used to show what thing is being talked about or written about: *These*

are principles which we all believe in.
3 used to give more information about something: *The book, which includes a map, gives you all the information you need about Venice.*

while[1] /ˈwaɪl/ *conjunction*
during the time that: *I can't talk to anyone while I'm driving.*

while[2] /ˈwaɪl/ *noun*
a while a period of time: *I'm going out for a while.*

whimper /ˈwɪmpəʳ/ *verb*
to make quiet crying sounds because of fear or pain: *The dog was whimpering with pain.*

whine /waɪn/ *verb* (*present participle* **whining**, *past* **whined**)
to complain in an annoying way: *She's always whining about something.*

whinge /wɪndʒ/ *verb* (*present participle* **whingeing**, *past* **whinged**) *UK informal*
to complain in an annoying way: *Oh, stop whingeing!*
• **whinge** *noun UK informal*

whip[1] /wɪp/ *noun*
a long piece of leather fixed to a handle and used to hit an animal or person

whip[2] /wɪp/ *verb* (*present participle* **whipping**, *past* **whipped**)
1 to hit a person or animal with a whip
2 to make a food such as cream more solid by mixing it hard with a kitchen tool

whirl /wɜːl/ *verb*
to move or make something move quickly round and round

whisker /ˈwɪskəʳ/ *noun*
one of the long, stiff hairs that grows around the mouths of animals such as cats

whisky /ˈwɪski/ *noun* **[no plural]**
a strong, alcoholic drink made from grain

whisper /ˈwɪspəʳ/ *verb*
to speak very quietly so that other people cannot hear: *She whispered something to the girl sitting next to her.*

whisper

• **whisper** *noun*

whistle[1] /ˈwɪsl/ *verb* (*present participle* **whistling**, *past* **whistled**)
to make a sound by breathing air out through a small hole made with your lips: *Someone whistled at her as she walked past.*

whistle[2] /ˈwɪsl/ *noun*
1 a small, simple instrument that makes a high sound when you blow through it: *The referee* ***blew the whistle*** *to end the game.*
2 the sound made by someone or something whistling

white[1] /waɪt/ *adj*
1 being the colour of snow or milk: *a white T-shirt ○ white walls* ➲See colour picture **Colours** on page Centre 6
2 Someone who is white has skin that is pale in colour.
3 *UK* White coffee has milk or cream added to it: *Two coffees please, one black and one white.*
4 White wine is a light yellow colour.

white[2] /waɪt/ *noun*
1 the colour of snow or milk ➲See colour picture **Colours** on page Centre 6
2 the part of an egg that is white when it is cooked: *Mix the egg whites with the sugar.*

who /huː/ *pronoun*
1 used to ask about someone's name or which person or group someone is talking about: *Who told you? ○ Who's that?*
2 used to show which person or group of people you are talking about: *That's the man who I saw in the bank.*
3 used to give more information about someone: *My brother, who's only just seventeen, has already passed his driving test.*

who'd /huːd/ *short for*
1 who had: *I read about a man who'd sailed around the world.*
2 who would: *Who'd like to go?*

whoever /huːˈevəʳ/ *pronoun*
1 the person who: *Whoever broke the window will have to pay for it.*
2 used to ask who a person is when you are surprised: *Whoever could that be phoning at this time?*

whole[1] /həʊl/ *adj*
complete, including every part: *She spent the whole afternoon studying.*

whole[2] /həʊl/ *noun* **[no plural]**
1 the whole of something all of something: *His behaviour affects the whole of the class.*
2 as a whole when considered as a group and not in parts: *The population as a whole is getting healthier.*
3 on the whole generally: *On the whole we're very happy.*

who'll /huːl/ *short for*
who will: *Who'll be at your party?*

wholly /ˈhəʊlli/ *adv*
completely: *The news was wholly unexpected.*

whom /huːm/ *pronoun formal*
used instead of 'who' as the object of a verb or preposition: *I met a man with whom I used to work.*

who's /huːz/ *short for*
1 who is: *Who's your new friend?*
2 who has: *Who's been using my computer?*

whose /huːz/ *pronoun, determiner*
used to ask who something belongs to or who someone or something is connected with: *Whose gloves are these?* ○ *Whose car shall we use?*

why /waɪ/ *adv*
1 used to ask or talk about the reasons for something: *Why didn't you call me?* ○ *I wonder why he didn't come.*
2 Why don't you? used to make a suggestion: *Why don't you come with us?* ○ *Why not give it a try?*

wicked /ˈwɪkɪd/ *adj*
1 very bad and morally wrong: *a wicked man*
2 *informal* very good: *They sell some wicked clothes.*

wide[1] /waɪd/ *adj* **(wider, widest)**
1 measuring a long distance or longer than usual from one side to the other: *a wide road* ○ *I have very wide feet.*
2 5 miles/3 inches/6 metres, etc wide having a distance of 5 miles/3 inches/6 metres, etc from one side to the other: *The swimming pool is five metres wide.*
3 a wide range/selection, etc a lot of different types of thing: *They have a wide range of goods.*

wide[2] /waɪd/ *adv*
wide apart/open as far apart/open as possible: *The window was wide open.*

widely /waɪdli/ *adv*
including a lot of different places, people, subjects, etc: *He has travelled widely in Europe.*

widen /ˈwaɪdᵊn/ *verb*
to become wider or make something become wider: *The road is being widened to two lanes.*

widow /ˈwɪdəʊ/ *noun*
a woman whose husband has died

widower /ˈwɪdəʊəʳ/ *noun*
a man whose wife has died (*plural* **wives)**

width /wɪtθ/ *noun*
the distance from one side of something to the other side: *a width of 2 metres*

wife /waɪf/ *noun* (*plural* **wives)**
the woman that a man is married to

wig /wɪg/ *noun*
a covering of hair that you wear on your head

wild /waɪld/ *adj*
1 A wild animal or plant lives or grows in its natural place and not where people live: *a wild dog* ○ *wild flowers*
2 not controlled: *a wild party* ○ *wild dancing*
3 be wild about something *informal* to like something very much: *I'm not wild about jazz.*

wildlife /ˈwaɪldlaɪf/ *noun* **[no plural]**
animals, birds and plants in the place where they live

will[1] *strong form* /wɪl/ *weak forms* /wᵊl, ᵊl/ *verb*
1 used to talk about what is going to happen in the future, especially things that you are certain about: *Claire will be five next month.* ○ *I'll see him on Saturday.* ○ *She'll have a great time.*
2 used to talk about what someone or something is willing or able to do: *Ask Susie if she will take them.* ○ *The car won't start.*

will[2] /wɪl/ *noun*
1 the power to control your thoughts and actions: *She has a very strong will.* ○ *He lacks the will to win.*
2 [no plural] what someone wants: *She was forced to marry him* ***against*** *her* ***will***.
3 a piece of paper that says who will

a b c d e f g h i j k l m n o p q r s t u v **w** x y z

get your money, house and things when you die: *She left me some money **in** her **will**.*

willing /ˈwɪlɪŋ/ *adj*
1 be willing to do something to be happy to do something: *He's willing to lend us some money.*
2 wanting to do something: *He is a very willing assistant.* ➲Opposite **unwilling**

win¹ /wɪn/ *verb* (*present participle* **winning**, *past* **won**)
1 to get the most points or succeed in a competition, fight or war: *Barcelona won the game 6-0.* ○ *Who do you think will win the election?*
2 to get a prize in a game or competition: *He won $500.* ○ *She won a gold medal at the Olympics.*

win² /wɪn/ *noun*
when someone wins a game or competition: *The Jets have only had three wins this season.*

wind¹ /wɪnd/ *noun*
a natural, fast movement of air: *The wind blew her hat off.*

wind² /waɪnd/ *verb* (*present participle* **winding**, *past* **wound**)
1 to turn or twist something long and thin around something else several times: *She **wound** the rope **around** the tree.*
2 If a river, road, etc winds somewhere, it bends a lot and is not straight: *The path winds along the edge of the bay.*

wind someone up
phrasal verb UK informal
to annoy someone: *He keeps complaining and it really winds me up.*

windmill

windmill /ˈwɪndmɪl/ *noun*
a building with long parts at the top that turn in the wind, used for producing power

window

window /ˈwɪndəʊ/ *noun*
1 a space in the wall of a building or car that has glass in it, used for letting light and air inside and for looking through: *Open the window if you're too hot.* ➲See

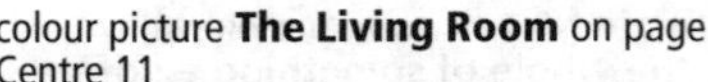
colour picture **The Living Room** on page Centre 11
2 a separate area on a computer screen showing information and which you can move around

windscreen /ˈwɪndskriːn/ *noun UK*
the window at the front end of a car, bus, etc ➲See colour picture **Car** on page Centre 3

windy /ˈwɪndi/ *adj* **(windier, windiest)**
with a lot of wind: *a windy day*

wine /waɪn/ *noun* **[no plural]**
an alcoholic drink that is made from the juice of grapes (= small, green or purple fruit): *a glass of wine*

wing

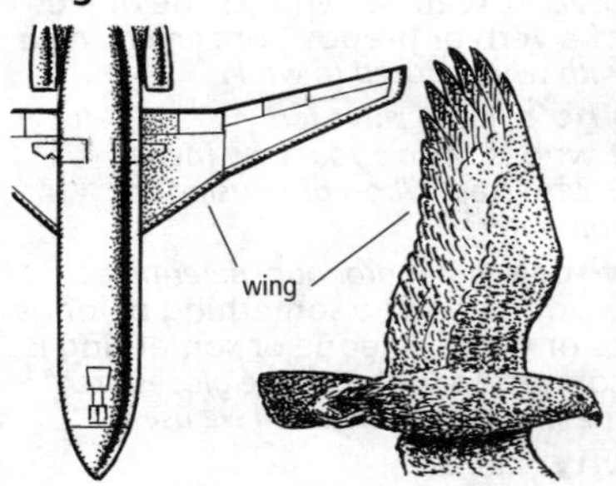

wing /wɪŋ/ *noun*
1 one of the two parts that a bird or insect uses to fly
2 one of the two long, flat parts at the sides of an aeroplane that make it stay in the sky

wink

wink¹ /wɪŋk/ *verb*
to quickly close and then open one eye, in order to be friendly or to show that something is a joke: *She smiled and **winked at** me.*

wink² /wɪŋk/ *noun*
when you wink at someone: *He gave me a friendly wink.*

winner /ˈwɪnəʳ/ *noun*
someone who wins a game, competition, or election: *the winners of the World Cup*

winter /ˈwɪntəʳ/ *noun*

the coldest season of the year, between autumn and spring: *We went skiing last winter.*

wipe[1] /waɪp/ *verb* (*present participle* **wiping**, *past* **wiped**) to clean or dry something by moving a cloth across it: *She wiped her hands on the towel.*

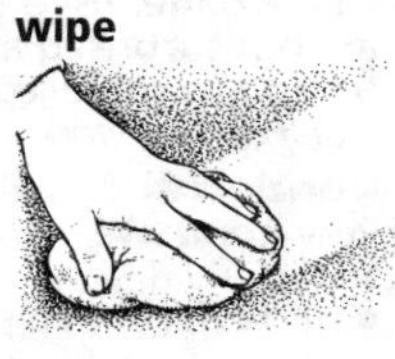
wipe

wipe[2] /waɪp/ *noun*
1 when you clean or dry something with a cloth: *I'll **give** the table **a wipe**.*
2 a thin cloth or piece of paper used for cleaning: *baby wipes*

wire /waɪəʳ/ *noun*
1 [no plural] thin, metal thread, used to fasten things or to make fences, cages, etc
2 a long, thin piece of metal thread, usually covered in plastic, that carries electricity: *electrical wires*

wisdom /ˈwɪzdəm/ *noun* **[no plural]** the ability to use your knowledge and experience to make good decisions

wise /waɪz/ *adj* A wise decision or action shows good judgment and is the right thing to do: *I think we've made a wise choice.* ➲Opposite **unwise**
•**wisely** *adv*

wish[1] /wɪʃ/ *verb*
1 wish (that) to want a situation that is different from the one that exists: *I wish that I didn't have to go to work.* ○ *I **wish** he **would** leave.*
2 wish to do something *formal* to want to do something: *I wish to speak to the manager.*
3 wish someone luck/success, etc to say that you hope someone will be lucky, successful, etc: *I wished him luck for his test.*

wish[2] /wɪʃ/ *noun* (*plural* **wishes**)
1 what you want to do or what you want to happen: *I **have no wish to** leave.*
2 best wishes something you write at the end of a letter: *Best wishes, Pete*

wit /wɪt/ *noun* **[no plural]** the ability to say things that are funny and clever

witch /wɪtʃ/ *noun* (*plural* **witches**) in stories, a woman who has magical powers

witch

with /wɪð/ *preposition*
1 used to say that people or things are in a place together or are doing something together: *Emma lives with her boyfriend.* ○ *Hang your coat with the others.*
2 having or including something: *a house with a swimming pool* ○ *a woman with brown eyes*
3 using something: *She hit him over the head with a tennis racket.*
4 used to describe the way someone does something: *He plays with great enthusiasm.*
5 used to say what fills, covers, etc something: *a bucket filled with water* ○ *shoes covered with mud*
6 because of something: *She was trembling with fear.*
7 relating to something or someone: *There's something wrong with the car.*

withdraw /wɪðˈdrɔː/ *verb* (*present participle* **withdrawing**, *past tense* **withdrew**, *past participle* **withdrawn**)
1 to take money out of a bank account: *She withdrew $50.*
2 to remove something, especially because of an official decision: *He has threatened to withdraw his support.*
3 If an army withdraws, or if someone withdraws it, it leaves the place where it is fighting: *The President has ordered troops to be **withdrawn from** the area.*

wither /ˈwɪðəʳ/ *verb* If a plant withers, it becomes dry and starts to die.

within /wɪˈðɪn/ *preposition*
1 before a particular period of time has finished: *The ambulance arrived within 10 minutes.*
2 less than a particular distance from something: *She was born within 20 miles of New York.*
3 inside an area, group or system: *There's a pharmacy within the hospital building.*

without /wɪˈðaʊt/ *preposition*

1 not having, using, or doing something: *I did the test without any problems.* ○ *I can't see without my glasses.*
2 when someone is not with someone else: *You can start the meeting without me.*

witness[1] /ˈwɪtnəs/ *noun* (*plural* **witnesses**)
someone who sees an accident or crime: *Police are appealing for witnesses to the shooting.*

witness[2] /ˈwɪtnəs/ *verb*
to see something happen, especially an accident or crime: *Did anyone witness the attack?*

witty /ˈwɪti/ *adj* **(wittier, wittiest)**
using words in a funny and clever way: *He was witty and charming.*

wives /waɪvz/
plural of wife

wizard /ˈwɪzəd/ *noun*
in stories, a man who has magical powers

wobble /ˈwɒbl/ *verb* (*present participle* **wobbling,** *past* **wobbled)**
If something wobbles, it moves from side to side, often because it is not on a flat surface: *The ladder started to wobble.*
● **wobbly** *adj*
likely to wobble: *a wobbly chair*

woke /wəʊk/
past tense of wake

woken /ˈwəʊk^{ə}n/
past participle of wake

woman /ˈwʊmən/ *noun* (*plural* **women)**
an adult female person: *a 30-year-old woman*

womb /wuːm/ *noun*
the part inside a woman's body where a baby grows

won /wɒn/
past of win

wonder[1] /ˈwʌndə^{r}/ *verb*
1 to want to know something or to try to understand the reason for something: *I wonder what he's making for dinner.*
2 **I/we wonder if ...** used to politely ask someone for something or to suggest something: *I wonder if you could help me?*

wonder[2] /ˈwʌndə^{r}/ *noun*
1 **[no plural]** surprise and admiration: *The boys gazed* ***in wonder*** *at the shiny, red Ferrari.*
2 **no wonder** used to say that you are not surprised about something: *No wonder she failed the test if she didn't do any work.*

wonderful /ˈwʌndəf^{ə}l/ *adj*
very good: *We had a wonderful time in Spain.*
● **wonderfully** *adv*

won't /wəʊnt/ *short for*
will not: *I won't be home before midnight.*

wood /wʊd/ *noun*
1 **[no plural]** the hard material that trees are made of: *a piece of wood*
2 (*also* **woods)** a large area of trees growing near each other: *We went for a walk in the woods.*

wooden /ˈwʊd^{ə}n/ *adj*
made of wood: *a wooden chair*

wool /wʊl/ *noun* **[no plural]**
1 the soft, thick hair on a sheep
2 thick thread or material that is made from the hair of a sheep: *a wool suit*

woollen *UK* (*US* **woolen)** /ˈwʊlən/ *adj*
made of wool: *woollen gloves*

word /wɜːd/ *noun*
1 a group of letters or sounds that mean something: *'Hund' is the German word for 'dog'.*
2 **have a word with someone** to talk to someone for a short time: *I'll have a word with Ted and see if he wants to come.*
3 **in other words** used to explain what something means in a different way: *He said he's too busy, in other words, he isn't interested.*
4 **word for word** using the exact words that were originally used: *She repeated word for word what he had told her.*

wore /wɔː^{r}/
past tense of wear

work[1] /wɜːk/ *verb*
1 to do a job that you get money for: *Helen* ***works for*** *a computer company.* ○ *He* ***works as*** *a waiter in an Italian restaurant.*
2 If a machine or piece of equipment works, it is not broken: *The washing machine isn't working.*
3 If something works, it is successful:

a b c d e f g h i j k l m n o p q r s t u v **w** x y z

Her plan to get rid of me didn't work.
work something out *phrasal verb*
to calculate an amount: *I'm trying to work out the total cost.*
work out *phrasal verb*
1 If a problem or difficult situation works out, it gradually becomes better: *Don't worry – everything will work out in the end.*
2 to do exercises to make your body stronger ➲See colour picture **Phrasal Verbs** on page Centre 13

work[2] /wɜːk/ *noun* **[no plural]**
1 when you use effort to do something: *Decorating that room was hard work.*
2 the place where you go to do your job: *He had an accident* ***at work****.*
3 something you do to get money: *Has she got any work yet?*
4 the activities that you do at school, for your job, etc: *Have you got a lot of work to do?*
5 get/set to work to start doing something

worker /ˈwɜːkəʳ/ *noun*
someone who works for a company or organization but does not have a powerful position: *an office worker*

worksheet /ˈwɜːkˌʃiːt/ *noun*
a piece of paper with questions and exercises for students

world /wɜːld/ *noun*
1 the world the Earth and all the people, places, and things on it: *Everest is the highest mountain in the world.* ○ *She's travelled all over the world.*
2 the people and things that are involved in a particular activity or subject: *the world of politics*
3 be out of this world *informal* to be very good: *Their chocolate cake is just out of this world!*

the World Wide Web /ˌwɜːld waɪd ˈweb/ *noun*
part of the Internet that consists of all the connected websites (= pages of text and pictures)

worm /wɜːm/ *noun*
a small creature with a long, thin, soft body and no legs

worn /wɔːn/ *past participle of* wear

worn-out /ˌwɔːnˈaʊt/ *adj*
1 very tired: *I was worn-out after all that dancing.*
2 damaged after being used too much: *a worn-out carpet*

worried /ˈwʌrid/ *adj*
unhappy because you are thinking about bad things that might happen: *She's really* ***worried about*** *her son.* ○ *I'm* ***worried that*** *she'll tell Maria.*

worry[1] /ˈwʌri/ *verb* (*present participle* **worrying,** *past* **worried)**
to think about problems or bad things that might happen: ***Don't worry*** *– she'll be all right.* ○ *She's always* ***worrying about*** *something.*

worry[2] /ˈwʌri/ *noun* (*plural* **worries)**
a problem that makes you feel unhappy: *health worries*

worse[1] /wɜːs/ *adj (comparative of* bad*)*
1 more unpleasant or difficult than something else that is also bad: *The exam was* ***worse than*** *I expected.* ○ *We'll have to stop the game if the rain* ***gets*** *any* ***worse****.*
2 more ill: *The drugs aren't working, he just seems to be* ***getting worse****.*

worship /ˈwɜːʃɪp/ *verb* (*present participle* **worshipping,** *past* **worshipped)**
1 to show respect for a god by saying prayers
2 to love and respect someone very much: *She worshipped her mother.*
• **worship** *noun* **[no plural]** *a place of worship* (= a religious building)

worst[1] /wɜːst/ *adj* (*superlative of* bad)
the worst the most unpleasant or difficult: *What's the worst job you've ever had?*

worst[2] /wɜːst/ *noun*
the worst the most unpleasant or difficult thing, person, or situation: *I've made some mistakes in the past, but this is definitely the worst.*

worth[1] /wɜːθ/ *adj*
1 be worth something to have a particular value, especially in money: *Our house is worth about £600,000.*
2 be worth doing/seeing/trying, etc to be useful or enjoyable to do/see/try, etc: *It's not as good as his last book but it's definitely worth reading.*
3 be worth it to be useful or enjoyable despite needing a lot of effort: *It was a long climb up the mountain but the view was worth it.*

a b c d e f g h i j k l m n o p q r s t u v **w** x y z

worth² /wɜːθ/ *noun* **[no plural]**
1 £20/$100, etc worth of something the amount of something that you can buy for £20/$100, etc: *I've put £2 worth of stamps on the letter.*
2 a month's/year's, etc worth of something the amount of something that can be done or used in a month/year, etc: *an hour's worth of free phone calls*

worthless /ˈwɜːθləs/ *adj* having no value in money

worthwhile /ˌwɜːθˈwaɪl/ *adj* useful and enjoyable, despite needing a lot of effort: *It's a difficult course but it's very worthwhile.*

worthy /ˈwɜːði/ *adj* **(worthier, worthiest)** deserving respect or support: *a worthy cause*

would *strong form* /wʊd/ *weak form* /wəd/ *verb*
1 used to say what might happen if something else happens: *What would you do if you lost your job?*
2 used as the past form of 'will': *Lottie promised that she would help.* ○ *The car wouldn't start this morning.*
3 would like/love something used to say politely that you want something: *I'd* (= I would) *like a cup of coffee, please.*
4 would you? used to politely ask someone something: *Would you like a drink?*

wouldn't /ˈwʊdᵊnt/ *short for* would not: *She wouldn't let us watch TV.*

wound¹ /wuːnd/ *noun* an injury

wound² /wuːnd/ *verb* to hurt someone, especially with a knife or gun: *He was badly wounded in the attack.*

wound³ /waʊnd/ *past of* wind²

wove /wəʊv/ *past tense of* weave

woven /wəʊvᵊn/ *past participle of* weave

wrap /ræp/ *verb* (*present participle* **wrapping,** *past* **wrapped)** (*also* **wrap up**) to cover something or someone with paper, cloth, etc: *to wrap a present* ○ *They wrapped him in a blanket.* ➲Opposite **unwrap**

wreath /riːθ/ *noun* a large ring of leaves and flowers used to show respect for someone who has died

wreck /rek/ *verb* to destroy something completely: *The explosion wrecked several cars.*

wreckage /ˈrekɪdʒ/ *noun* **[no plural]** the parts that remain of a car, ship, or aeroplane that has been destroyed: *Two survivors were pulled from the wreckage.*

wrench /renʃ/ *verb* to pull something violently away from a fixed position: *The phone had been wrenched off the wall.*

wrestle /ˈresl/ *verb* (*present participle* **wrestling,** *past* **wrestled)** to fight with someone by holding them and trying to push them to the ground

wrestling /ˈreslɪŋ/ *noun* **[no plural]** a sport in which two people fight and try to push each other to the ground
• **wrestler** *noun*

wriggle /ˈrɪgl/ *verb* (*present participle* **wriggling,** *past* **wriggled)** to twist your body or move part of your body with short, quick movements: *She wriggled her toes in the warm sand.*

wring /rɪŋ/ (*also* **wring out**) *verb* (*present participle* **wringing,** *past* **wrung)** to twist a cloth or piece of clothing with your hands to remove water from it: *He wrung out his socks and hung them up to dry.*

wrinkle /ˈrɪŋkl/ *noun* a small line on your face that you get when you grow old

wrist /rɪst/ *noun* the part of your body between your hand and your arm

write /raɪt/ *verb* (*present participle* **writing,** *past tense* **wrote,** *past participle* **written)**
1 to make words, letters, or numbers on a surface using a pen or pencil: *Write your name at the top of the page.*
2 to create a book, story, article, etc or a piece of music: *He's writing a book on Russian literature.*
3 to send someone a letter: *I wrote her a letter last week.*

write something down *phrasal verb*
to write something on a piece of paper so that you do not forget it: *Did you write Jo's phone number down?*

writer /ˈraɪtəʳ/ *noun*
someone whose job is writing books, stories, articles, etc

writing /ˈraɪtɪŋ/ *noun* **[no plural]**
1 words that have been written or printed: *The writing was too small to read.*
2 the way that someone writes: *You've got very neat writing.*
3 the activity or job of creating books, stories, or articles

written /ˈrɪtᵊn/
past participle of write

wrong¹ /rɒŋ/ *adj*
1 not correct: *the wrong answer* ○ *We're going the wrong way.*
2 be wrong to think or say something that is not correct: *You were **wrong about** the party – it's today, not tomorrow.*
3 morally bad: *It's wrong to tell lies.*
4 not suitable: *I think she's **wrong for** this job.*

wrong² /rɒŋ/ *adv*
1 in a way that is not correct: *He always says my name wrong.*
2 go wrong to develop problems: *Something's gone wrong with my computer.*

wrong³ /rɒŋ/ *noun* **[no plural]**
when something is not morally right: *She's old enough to know the difference between right and wrong.*

wrongly /ˈrɒŋli/ *adv*
in a way that is not correct: *The letter was wrongly addressed.*

wrote /rəʊt/
past tense of write

wrung /rʌŋ/
past of wring

www /ˌdʌbljuːˌdʌbljuːˈdʌbljuː/ *noun*
abbreviation for
World Wide Web (= part of the Internet that consists of all the connected websites)

a b c d e f g h i j k l m n o p q r s t u v w x y z

Xx

X, x /eks/
1 the twenty-fourth letter of the alphabet
2 used to show that an answer is wrong
3 used to mean a kiss at the end of a letter
4 used to mean an unknown person or thing

Xmas /ˈkrɪstməs/ *noun* **[no plural]**
informal used as a short way of writing 'Christmas' (= a Christian holiday), mainly on signs or cards: *Happy Xmas!*

X-ray /ˈeksreɪ/ *noun*
a photograph that shows the inside of your body: *They **took an X-ray** of his leg.*
• **X-ray** *verb*
to take a photograph that shows the inside of something

Yy

Y, y /waɪ/
the twenty-fifth letter of the alphabet

yacht /jɒt/ *noun*
a large boat with sails used for pleasure or in races: *a luxury yacht*

yacht

yard /jɑːd/ *noun*
1 a unit for measuring length, equal to 0.9144 metres or 3 feet
2 *US* (*UK* **garden**) an area of land in front of or behind a house

yawn /jɔːn/ *verb*
to take a deep breath with your mouth wide open, because you are tired or bored: *She yawned and looked at her watch.*
• **yawn** *noun*

yd *written abbreviation for* yard (= a unit for measuring length)

yeah /jeə/ *exclamation informal spoken*
yes: *Yeah, I agree.*

year /jɪəʳ/ *noun*
1 a period of 12 months, or 365 or 366 days, especially from 1 January to 31 December: *He joined the company a year ago.*
2 years a long time: *I haven't seen Linda for years.*

yearly /jɪəli/ *adj, adv*
happening once a year or every year: *a yearly fee*

yeast /jiːst/ *noun* **[no plural]**
a substance used to make bread rise and to make beer and wine

yell /jel/ *verb*
to shout something very loudly: *The policeman* ***yelled at*** *them to stop.*
• **yell** *noun*

yellow /ˈjeləʊ/ *adj*
being the same colour as a lemon or the sun: *a bright yellow tablecloth*
• **yellow** *noun*
the colour yellow ➲See colour picture **Colours** on page Centre 6

yes /jes/ *exclamation*
1 used to agree with something, or to give a positive answer to something: *"Can I borrow your pencil?" "Yes, of course."* ○ *"Coffee?" " Yes, please."*
2 used as an answer when someone calls you: *"Jack!" "Yes?"*

yesterday /ˈjestədeɪ/ *noun, adv* **[no plural]**
the day before today: *I went to see the doctor yesterday.*

yet /jet/ *adv*
1 before now or before that time: *Have you read his book yet?* ○ *"Has he called?" "No, not yet."*
2 now or as early as this time: *I don't want to go home yet.*
3 the best/worst, etc yet the best or worst, etc until now: *That was my worst exam yet.*

yield /jiːld/ *verb*
1 to make or provide something: *to yield a profit*
2 yield to demands/pressure, etc to be forced to do something

yo /jəʊ/ *exclamation US informal*
used as a way of saying hello

yob /jɒb/ *noun UK informal*
a rude or violent young man

yoga /ˈjəʊgə/ *noun* **[no plural]**
a set of exercises for the mind and body, based on the Hindu religion: *She does yoga three times a week.*

yoghurt /ˈjɒgət/ *noun*
a thick, liquid food with a slightly sour taste which is made from milk ➲See colour picture **Food** on page Centre 7

yolk /jəʊk/ *noun*
the round, yellow part in the middle of an egg

you *strong form* /juː/ *weak form* /ju, jə/ *pronoun*
1 used to mean the person or people you are talking to: *I love you.* ○ *You said I could go with you.*
2 people generally: *You learn to accept these things as you get older.*

you'd /juːd/ *short for*
1 you had: *You'd better go home now.*
2 you would: *I expect you'd like some lunch.*

you'll /juːl/ *short for*
you will: *I hope you'll come again.*

young[1] /jʌŋ/ *adj*
having lived or existed for only a short time and not old: *young people*

young² /jʌŋ/ *noun* **[no plural]**
1 the young young people generally: *It's the sort of music that appeals mainly to the young.*
2 something's young an animal's babies

your *strong form* /jɔːʳ/ *weak form* /jəʳ/ *determiner*
1 belonging or relating to the person or people you are talking to: *Can I borrow your pen?* ○ *It's not your fault.*
2 belonging or relating to people in general: *You never stop loving your children.*

you're /jɔːʳ/ *short for* you are: *You're my best friend.*

yours /jɔːz/ *pronoun*
1 the things that belong or relate to the person or people you are talking to: *Is this pen yours?*
2 Yours faithfully/sincerely, etc used just before your name at the end of a polite or formal letter

yourself /jɔːˈself/ *pronoun*
1 used to show that it is you who is affected by an action: *Don't cut yourself with that sharp knife.*
2 used to give more attention to the word 'you': *Did you make the dress yourself?*
3 by yourself/yourselves alone or without anyone else's help: *I'm amazed you managed to move those boxes all by yourself.*

youth /juːθ/ *noun formal*
1 a young man: *gangs of youths*
2 [no plural] young people generally: *the youth of today*
3 [no plural] someone's youth the period of time when someone is young: *I was very shy* ***in*** *my* ***youth****.*
4 [no plural] the quality of being young

youth hostel /ˈjuːθ ˌhɒstəl/ *noun* a cheap, simple hotel, especially for young people who are travelling around

you've /juːv/ *short for* you have: *If you've finished your work, you can go.*

yuck /jʌk/ *exclamation informal* used to say that something looks or tastes very bad

yummy /ˈjʌmi/ *adj informal* **(yummier, yummiest)** If food or drink is yummy, it tastes very good.

Zz

Z, z /zed/
the twenty-sixth and last letter of the alphabet

zebra /'zebrə/ *noun*
an animal like a horse with black and white lines

zebra crossing /ˌzebrə 'krɒsɪŋ/ *noun UK*
a part of the road painted with black and white lines where people can cross over safely

zero /'zɪərəʊ/
the number 0

zigzag /'zɪgzæg/ *noun*
a line that changes direction from left to right and back again at sharp angles

zinc /zɪŋk/ *noun* **[no plural]**
a blue-white metal

zip[1] /zɪp/ *UK* (*US* **zipper**) *noun*
a thing for fastening clothes, bags, etc consisting of two rows of very small parts that connect together: *Your zip's undone.*

zip[2] /zɪp/ *verb* (*present participle* **zipping,** *past* **zipped)**
(*also* **zip up**) to fasten something with a zip: *He zipped up his jacket.*

zipper /'zɪpəʳ/ *noun US*
a zip

zoo /zuː/ *noun*
a place where wild animals are kept and people come to look at them

Irregular Verbs

This list gives the infinitive form of the verb, its past tense, and then the past participle.

Infinitive	Past Tense	Past Participle
arise	arose	arisen
awake	awoke	awoken
be	was/were	been
bear	bore	borne
beat	beat	beaten, (*also US*) beat
become	became	become
begin	began	begun
bend	bent	bent
bet	bet, betted	bet, betted
bid	bid, bade	bid, bidden
bind	bound	bound
bite	bit	bitten
bleed	bled	bled
blow	blew	blown
break	broke	broken
breed	bred	bred
bring	brought	brought
broadcast	broadcast	broadcast
build	built	built
burn	burnt, burned	burnt, burned
burst	burst	burst
buy	bought	bought
cast	cast	cast
catch	caught	caught
choose	chose	chosen
cling	clung	clung
come	came	come
cost	cost	cost
creep	crept	crept
cut	cut	cut
deal	dealt	dealt
dig	dug	dug
dive	dived, (*also US*) dove	dived
draw	drew	drawn
dream	dreamed, dreamt	dreamed, dreamt
drink	drank	drunk
drive	drove	driven
eat	ate	eaten
feed	fed	fed
fall	fell	fallen
feel	felt	felt
fight	fought	fought
find	found	found
flee	fled	fled
fling	flung	flung
fly	flew	flown
forbid	forbade	forbidden
forecast	forecast, forecasted	forecast, forecasted
foresee	foresaw	foreseen
forget	forgot	forgotten
forgive	forgave	forgiven
freeze	froze	frozen
get	got	got, (*also US*) gotten
give	gave	given
go	went	gone
grind	ground	ground
grow	grew	grown
hang	hung, hanged	hung, hanged
have	had	had
hear	heard	heard
hide	hid	hidden
hit	hit	hit
hold	held	held
hurt	hurt	hurt
keep	kept	kept
kneel	knelt, kneeled	knelt, kneeled
know	knew	known

Infinitive	Past Tense	Past Participle
lay	laid	laid
lead	led	led
lean	leaned, (*also UK*) leant	leaned, (*also UK*) leant
leap	leapt, leaped	leapt, leaped
learn	learned, (*also UK*) learnt	learned, (*also UK*) learnt
leave	left	left
lend	lent	lent
let	let	let
lie	lay, lied	lain, lied
light	lit, lighted	lit, lighted
lose	lost	lost
make	made	made
mean	meant	meant
meet	met	met
mistake	mistook	mistaken
misunderstand	misunderstood	misunderstood
mow	mowed	mown, mowed
outgrow	outgrew	outgrown
overhear	overheard	overheard
oversleep	overslept	overslept
overtake	overtook	overtaken
pay	paid	paid
plead	pleaded, (*also US*) pled	pleaded, (*also US*) pled
prove	proved	proved, (*also US*) proven
put	put	put
quit	quit	quit
read	read	read
rebuild	rebuilt	rebuilt
repay	repaid	repaid
rewind	rewound	rewound
ride	rode	ridden
ring	rang	rung
rise	rose	risen
run	ran	run
saw	sawed	sawn, (*also US*) sawed
say	said	said
see	saw	seen

Infinitive	Past Tense	Past Participle
seek	sought	sought
sell	sold	sold
send	sent	sent
set	set	set
sew	sewed	sewn, sewed
shake	shook	shaken
shed	shed	shed
shine	shone	shone
shoot	shot	shot
show	showed	shown, showed
shrink	shrank	shrunk
shut	shut	shut
sing	sang	sung
sink	sank	sunk
sit	sat	sat
sleep	slept	slept
slide	slid	slid
slit	slit	slit
smell	smelled, (*also UK*) smelt	smelled, (*also UK*) smelt
sow	sowed	sown, sowed
speak	spoke	spoken
speed	sped, speeded	sped, speeded
spell	spelled, (*also UK*) spelt	spelled, (*also UK*) spelt
spend	spent	spent
spill	spilled, (*also UK*) spilt	spilled, (*also UK*) spilt
spin	spun	spun
spit	spat, (*also US*) spit	spat, (*also US*) spit
split	split	split
spoil	spoiled, spoilt	spoiled, spoilt
spread	spread	spread
spring	sprang	sprung
stand	stood	stood
steal	stole	stolen
stick	stuck	stuck
sting	stung	stung
stink	stank, (*also US*) stunk	stunk
stride	strode	strode

Infinitive	Past Tense	Past Participle	Infinitive	Past Tense	Past Participle
strike	struck	struck	undergo	underwent	undergone
string	strung	strung	understand	understood	understood
swear	swore	sworn	undo	undid	undone
sweep	swept	swept	unwind	unwound	unwound
swell	swelled	swollen, swelled	upset	upset	upset
swim	swam	swum	wake	woke	woken
swing	swung	swung	wear	wore	worn
take	took	taken	weave	wove, weaved	woven, weaved
teach	taught	taught	weep	wept	wept
tear	tore	torn	win	won	won
tell	told	told	wind	wound	wound
think	thought	thought	withdraw	withdrew	withdrawn
throw	threw	thrown	wring	wrung	wrung
tread	trod	trodden	write	wrote	written

Describing your day and describing your family

Maria's day

In this paragraph, Maria describes a typical day. There are 14 mistakes in it. Try to find and correct them. For answers, see key on page 10.

I am getting up early every day because my son wake me at 6:00. He is five and he go to a school. I make breakfast for my family. Usually we have some breads and juice. After we get dressed and wash our teeth and then we walk in school. After I leave my son in school, I go to work. I work in a restaurant like a waitress. I am working three hours every day Monday to Friday. I finish at half-past two and then I collect my son from the school. My husband comes to home late most days. If he is home he prepare the meal but most days I prepare the meal for the whole family. In the evening, we look at the TV or sometime we see some friends.

Maria's family

In this paragraph, Maria describes her family. There are 14 mistakes in it. Try to find and correct them. For answers, see key on page 10.

My family is come from Mexico. I live in this country for more than one year now. My husband come over before me and then I join him with our son. My son his name is Daniel and my husband is Enrique. Enrique has thirty-six years and Daniel has four. Enrique is doctor at the nearby hospital. He is working there two years. He work very hard and many hours. My son speak Spanish with me and my husband but English with his friends and his teacher. When I come to this country I was sad and missed my family and friends but now I used to living here.

Regular verb tenses: The simple tenses

Present simple

I/we/you/they	arrive (**do not** arrive)
he/she/it	arrive**s** (**does not** arrive)

You use this tense:

1. for things that are happening now

e.g. *He teaches older children.*

2. for things that are always true or that often happen

e.g. *It is very cold in the winter.*

e.g. *She eats too much.*

3. for saying what you believe or feel

e.g. *He is very kind.*

e.g. *I love him.*

Past simple

I/we/you/they	arrive**d** (**did not** arrive)
he/she/it	arrive**d** (**did not** arrive)

You use this tense for things that happened in the past. When you use this tense you sometimes say when that thing happened and sometimes do not.

e.g. *We walked to the shops.*

e.g. *I arrived at work at 9:00.*

Future simple

I/we/you/they	**will** arrive (**will not** arrive)
he/she/it	**will** arrive (**will not** arrive)

You use this tense:

1. for making plans with someone

e.g. *So I will see you at the train station at 9:00.*

2. for saying what you think will happen

e.g. *He will be very angry.*

Present perfect

I/we/you/they	**have** arrive**d** (**have not** arrive**d**)
he/she/it	**has** arrive**d** (**has not** arrive**d**)

This tense is used for things that happened in the past. When you use this tense you do not say when something happened.

e.g. *I have been to Italy.*